A VISITOR & PHOTO-LOCATION GUIDEBOOK

PHOTOGRAPHING
CORNWALL AND DEVON
INCLUDING DARTMOOR AND EXMOOR

ADAM BURTON

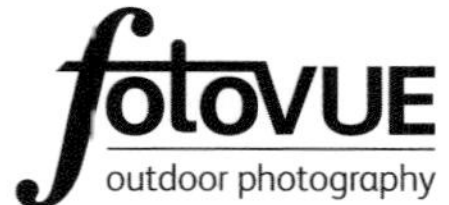

PHOTOGRAPHING **CORNWALL AND DEVON**

by Adam Burton

First published in the United Kingdom in 2016 by fotoVUE.
First reprinted March 2020. This reprint January 2023.
www.fotovue.com

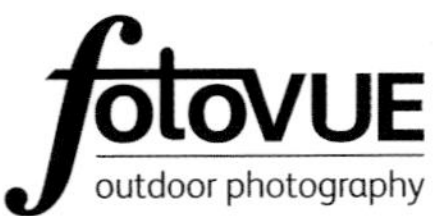

Editors: Mick Ryan and Stuart Holmes, fotoVUE Ltd.
Layout: Stuart Holmes and Vicky Barlow.
Photo Editor: Stuart Holmes
Book Managing Editor: Mick Ryan.
Book design by fotoVUE and Mountain Creative
Cover design by Nathan Ryder – Vertebrate Publishing.

All maps within this publication were produced by Don Williams of Bute Cartographics.
Map location overlay by Mick Ryan.
Maps contain Ordnance Survey data © Crown copyright and database right 2016.

A CIP catalogue record for this book is available from the British Library.

ISBN 978-0-9929051-3-2
10 9 8 7 6 5 4 3

Front cover: Dramatic sunset over Hartland Quay's rocky ledges.
Nikon D800E, 17-35mm at 28mm, ISO 50, 4 sec at f/13. April.
Inside rear flap photo: Adam Burton self portrait.
Rear cover left: A glorious misty dawn at Littaford Tors.
Rear cover right: Sea thrift flowering on the Rumps in Cornwall.
Photo opposite: Pink sunset over the dramatic sea stacks of Land's End.

Printed and bound in Europe by Latitude Press Ltd.

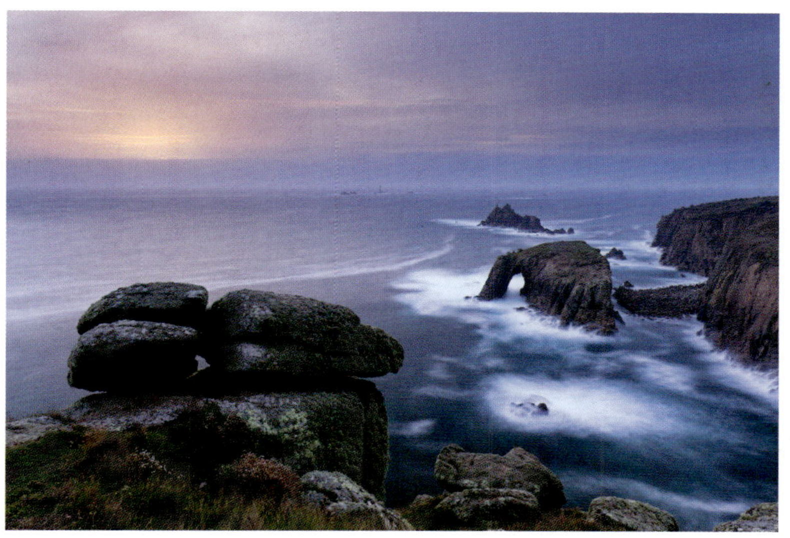

"Cornwall is very primeval: great, black, jutting cliffs and rocks, like the original darkness, and a pale sea breaking in, like dawn. It is like the beginning of the world, wonderful…"

D H Lawrence, Letter, 1916

CONTENTS

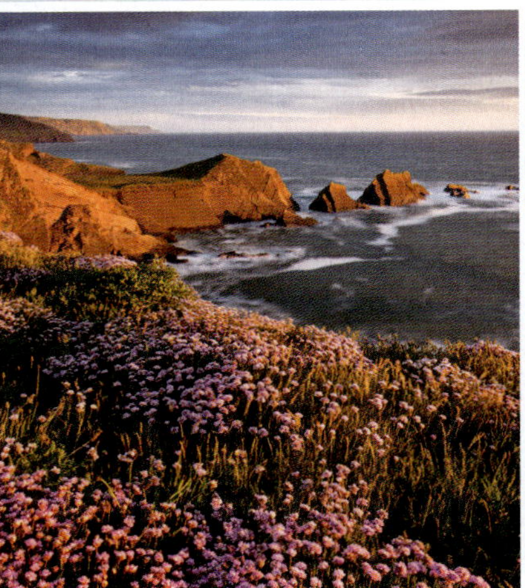
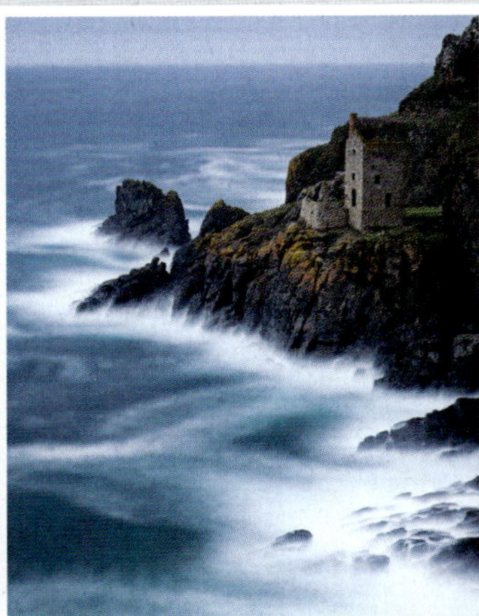
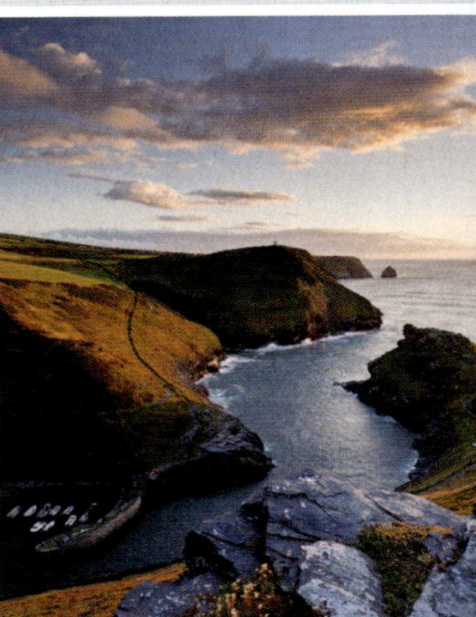

West and South Cornwall

North Cornwall

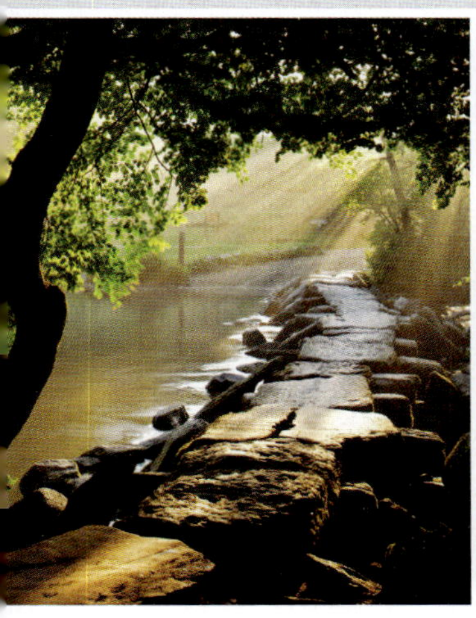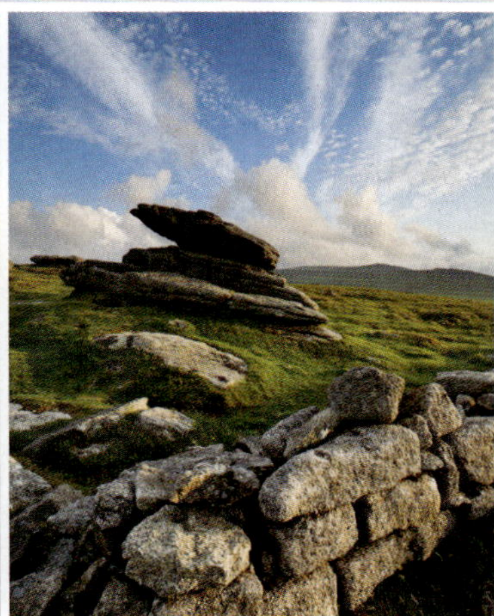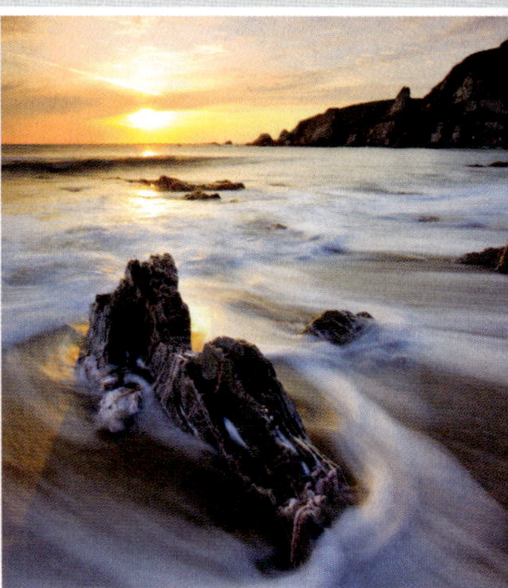

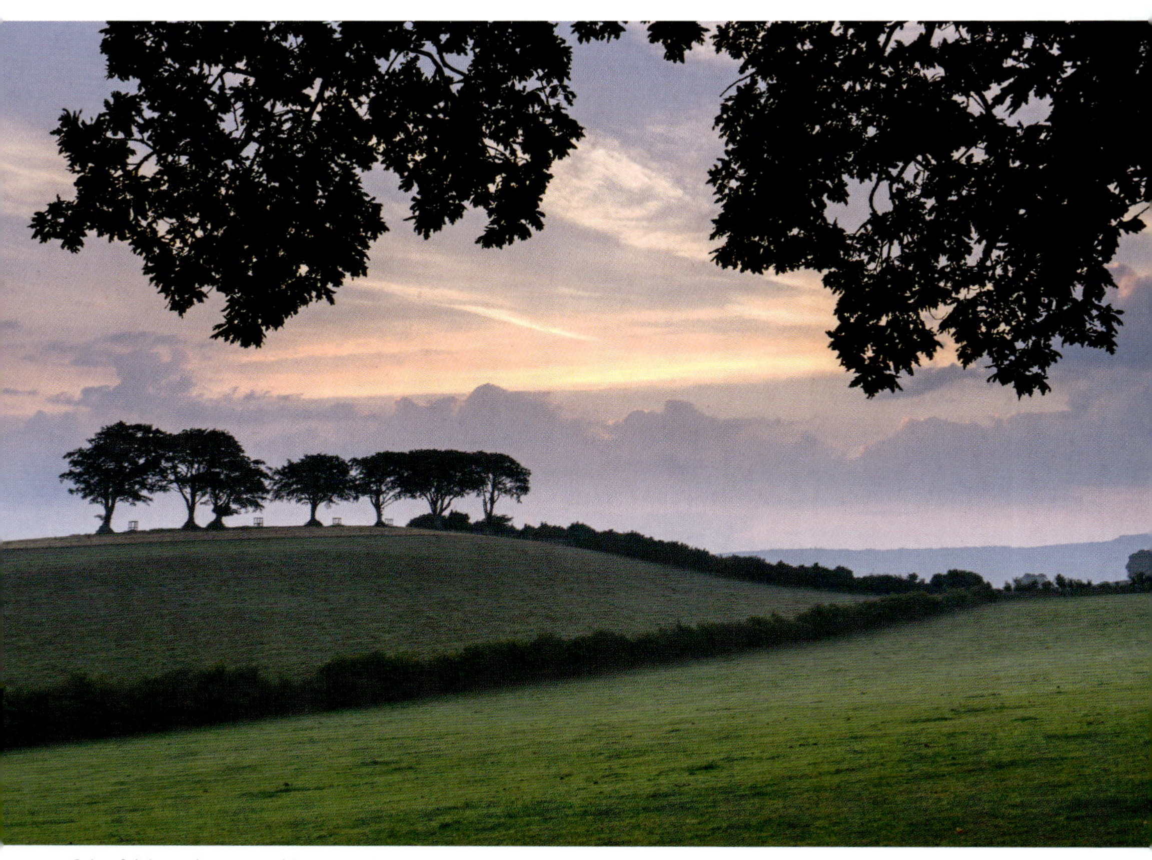

Colourful dawn sky over rural Exmoor, Nikon D800E, 24-70mm at 34mm, ISO 100, 0.3 sec at f/11. August

Acknowledgements

All book projects are challenging for photographers, involving considerable time and effort both to write and capture images for. This project was to be no exception, and has been a continuous presence in my life over the past year. Fortunately, from the moment I met with Mick Ryan and Stuart Holmes from fotoVue to discuss the project, I immediately knew they were going to be great guys to work with.

Over the course of the project both Mick and Stuart have been very supportive and encouraging, giving me the freedom to work at my own pace and to follow my own style throughout. As photographers themselves, they appreciate how precious us artistic types can be and have encouraged my input in all stages of the design process and picture selection. For all these things, not to mention the initial opportunity to write this book they have my sincere gratitude. Thanks so much, guys!

Above all, my thanks have to go to my long-suffering family! Landscape photography can be a particularly unsociable pursuit, involving many ridiculously early starts and especially late finishes. The images included in this book haven't just been captured over the past year, but over a decade or so. Throughout all this time, my wife Beth has been a continuous support, always encouraging and incredibly positive. Today is a typical example; yet another bank holiday where I am confined to my office finishing off the book while Beth entertains our young children Tom, Ellen and Ted in the spring sunshine.

Adam Burton
June 2016

Cornwall and Devon

Foreword by Mark Owen

I have long admired Adam's photography, having first come across his work when he won our annual South West Coast Path photo competition, which he has since helped judge.

Being lucky enough to live on Dartmoor and having worked on the Coast Path for nearly twenty years, I know many of the places featured in this book well. Adam's photography reveals these familiar and favourite spots in a new light, making me feel inspired to go and visit them all over again, to explore new places and also rediscover some forgotten corners.

As a decidedly amateur photographer, I've often been disappointed with my photos, but the tips and advice in this book will I'm sure help me raise my game. I hope you are equally inspired by this book and use it as your guide to explore, create beautiful pictures, and form lasting memories of the stunning landscapes found across the coast and countryside of Devon and Cornwall.

Mark Owen
South West Coast Path National Trail Officer
June 2016

Sea thrift and kidney vetch wildflowers flowering on the cliffs above a stormy Bedruthan Steps in North Cornwall, Nikon D800E, 17-35mm at 26mm, ISO 320, 6 sec at f/13. May

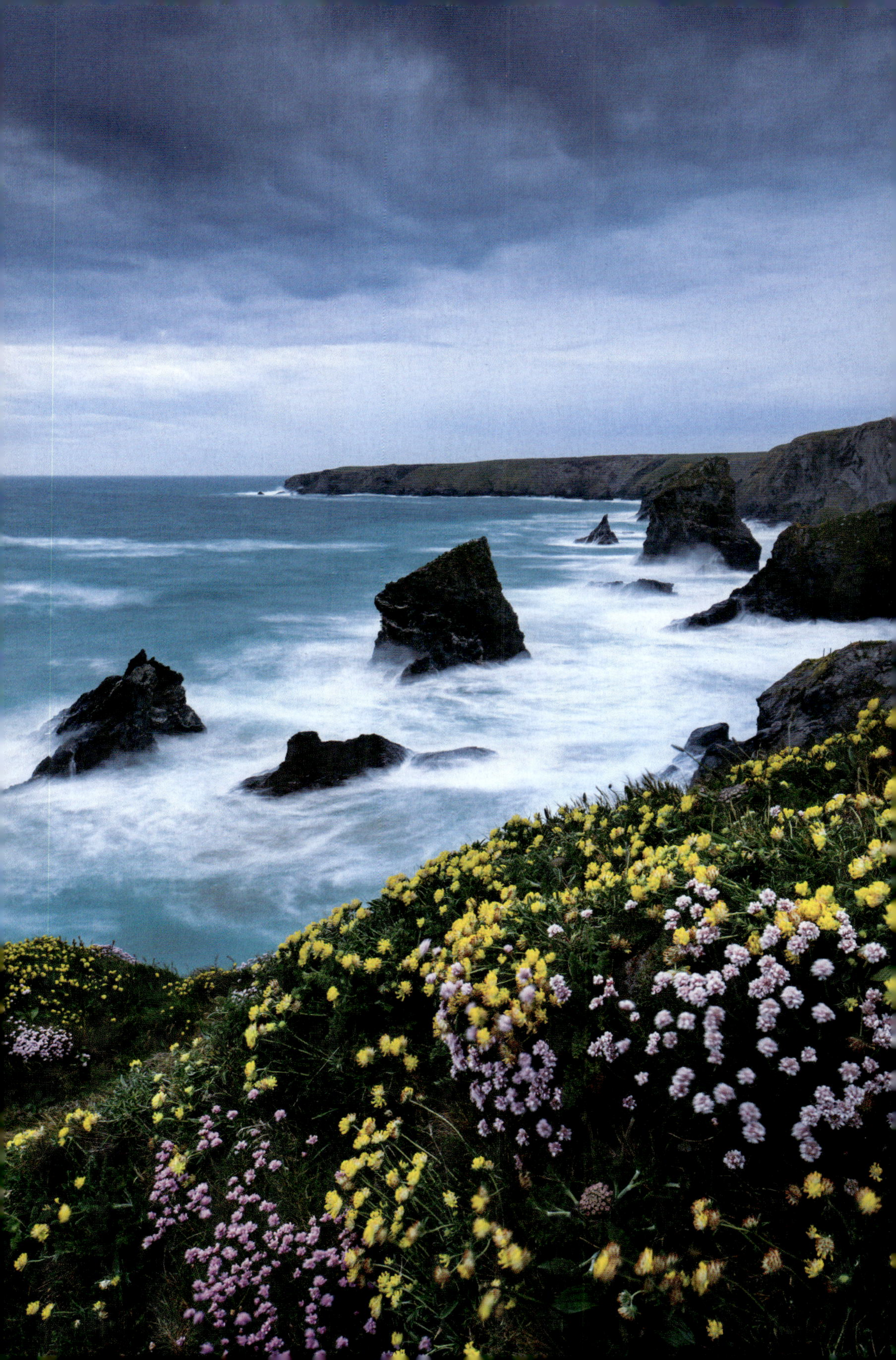

Introduction

With much of the UK's spectacular coastline, together with endless rolling hills of patchwork countryside and the high moorland of Exmoor and Dartmoor, Cornwall and Devon are renowned for their beautiful landscapes and are rich with photographic potential.

Given so much choice of location, a decision was made early on to concentrate on specific highlights within each county, namely the superb coastlines and the national parks. Yet this guidebook covers a broader geographical area than the title might suggest with most of the Exmoor locations being in Somerset.

Each location was selected purely through personal appeal; some are popular areas for photographers whilst others are less well known. Many iconic spots have been written about, others left to be covered at a later stage. If I have missed out a favourite of yours I apologise, but at the same time hope that through this book I can introduce you to a few new special places.

Whether you are looking for beach or cliff top views, moorland, river or forest, the end result is a book that contains a tremendous variety of landscapes to help, guide and inspire you when visiting the South West with your camera, regardless of the season.

Each and every location covered in these pages has motivated and inspired me over the years and I hope they can engender similar feelings in you. Landscape photography is such a wonderful hobby, one that provides us with plentiful opportunity to get outside of our homes and explore the beautiful natural areas that are so abundant throughout the UK.

Adam Burton
Devon, June 2016

Dramatic evening light at Hartland Quay on North Devon's rugged coast, Nikon D800E, 17-35mm at 17mm, ISO 100, 6 sec at f/16. May

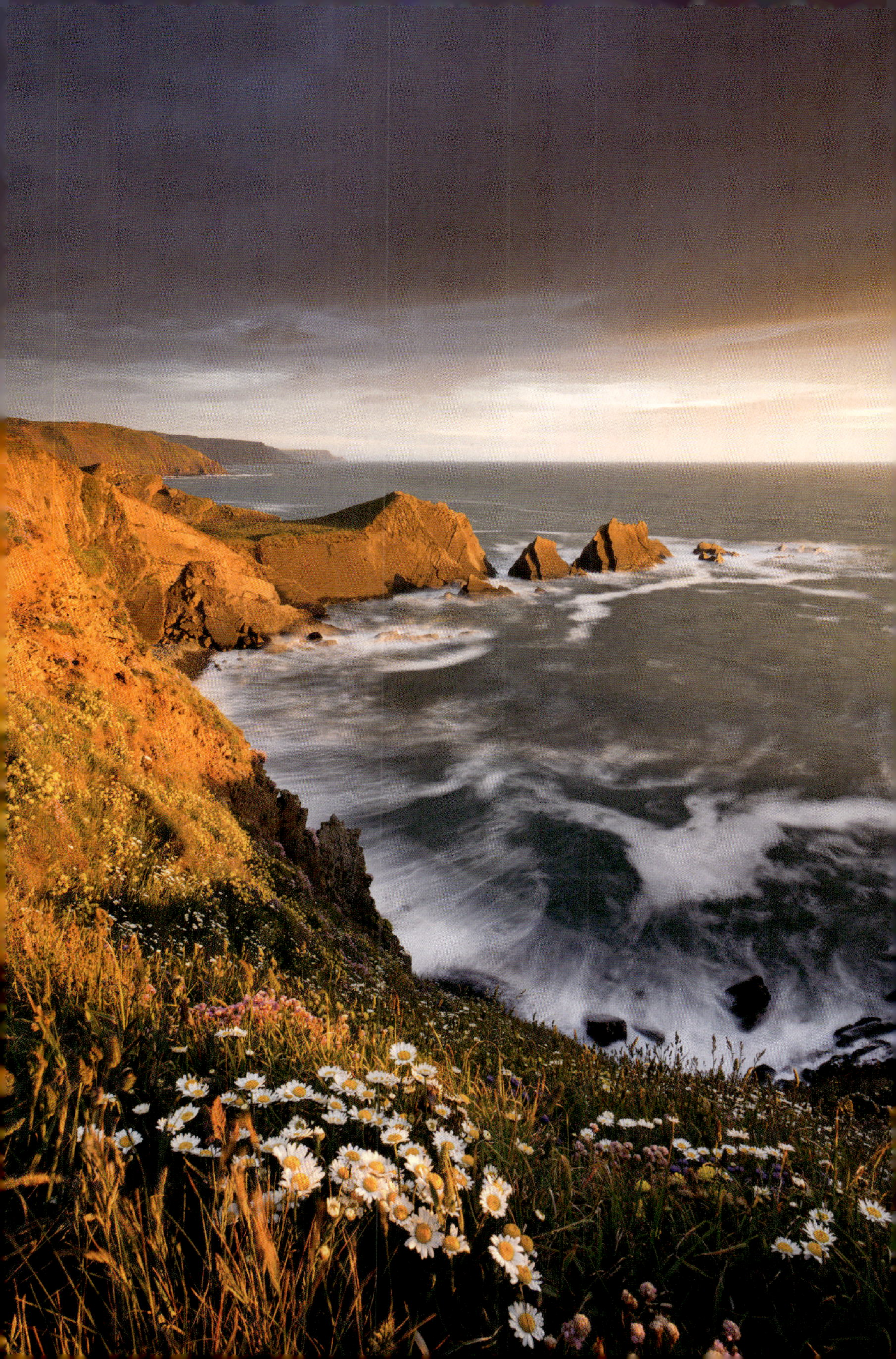

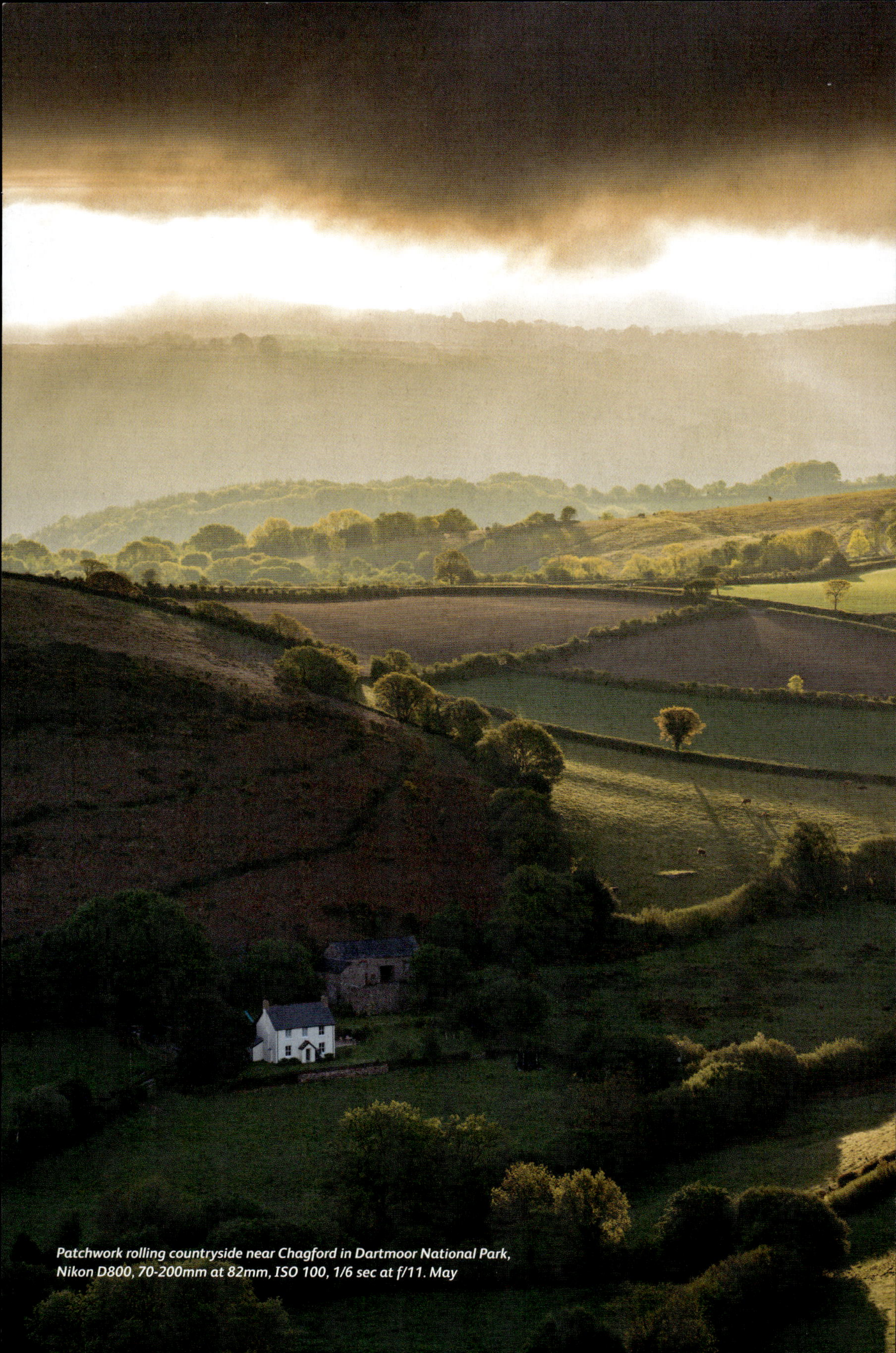

*Patchwork rolling countryside near Chagford in Dartmoor National Park,
Nikon D800, 70-200mm at 82mm, ISO 100, 1/6 sec at f/11. May*

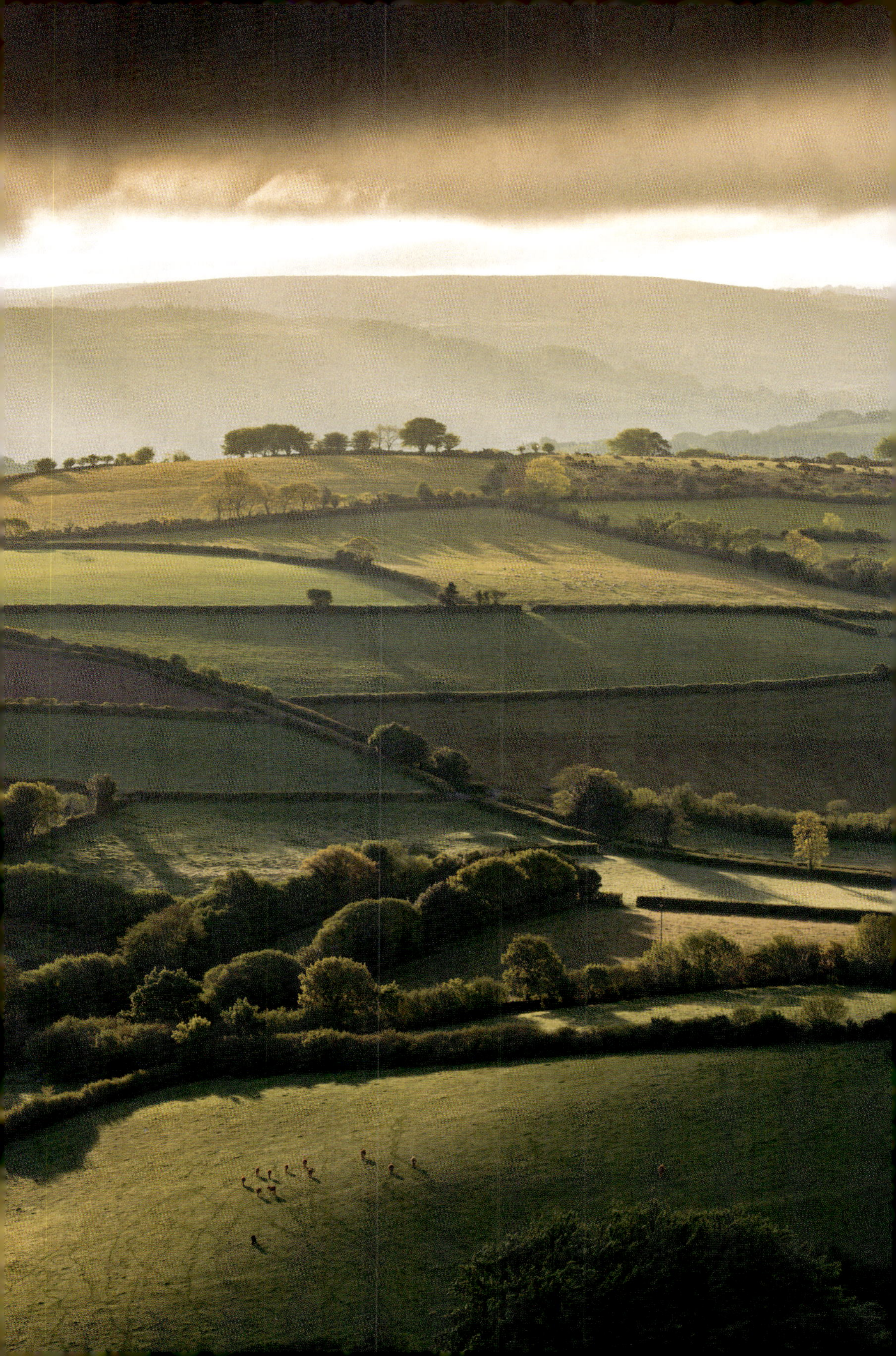

Cornwall and Devon are popular destinations in the summer, attracting millions of holidaymakers. As a result, there is a good network of major roads connecting them with the rest of the UK. Travelling around the area once you get there can take longer than expected, as the country lanes are very narrow and winding.

From the North and East

Visitors to the South West will usually arrive by one of two roads. The majority of people travelling from the north will take the M5 which runs from Birmingham all the way to Exeter in Devon. Those travelling from the east may also join the M5 at Bristol, or alternatively travel along the A303/A30 before it joins the M5 at Exeter. The M5 comes to an end just past Exeter, providing travellers with a choice of two A class dual carriageway roads depending on final destination. The A30 provides the main artery, running right through the centre of Devon all the way down to Land's End at the very western tip of Cornwall. Those travelling to South Devon or South Cornwall, take the A38 towards Plymouth.

Distances and driving times to Exeter

Bristol via M5	80 miles, 1h 35 min
Birmingham via M5	170 miles, 2h 50 min
London via M4 and M5	197 miles, 3h 30 min
Manchester via M6 and M5	241 miles, 4h 20 min
Newcastle via A1(M) and M5	368 miles: 6h 15 min
Glasgow via M74, M6 and M5	445 miles: 7h 15 min

Travelling around Devon and Cornwall

Once you leave the main roads, the South West's minor roads can be somewhat more challenging. Devon and Cornwall are both notorious for their network of very narrow lanes. These lanes, usually accompanied by high banked hedges on either side, meander around, up and over the countryside making it almost impossible to see oncoming traffic until the last minute.

Sat Nav Nightmares: Before heading out plan your route using a map rather than relying on a sat nav, and stick to the main roads where possible. Although a sat nav can be very helpful, it will usually guide you through the most direct route, often along the narrowest lanes. This is particularly important when travelling through Dartmoor and Exmoor. Both national parks contain a maze of of ancient tiny lanes, sometimes requiring fretful crossings over impossibly narrow stone bridges. **You have been warned!**

Livestock on the road: While travelling along any of the South West's rural country lanes be prepared for both wildlife and livestock, as farmers often use minor lanes to move animals between fields. In the National Parks livestock roam freely over the moorland; at any time of the day and night sheep or ponies may be encountered on the roads. This is particularly important when travelling over the moor to capture sunrise. Sheep often sleep on moorland roads during the night.

Land Rover driving along a rural Exmoor road past flowering Rosebay Willowherb wildflowers, Canon 1Ds Mark III, 17-40mm at 36mm, ISO 400, 1/60 sec at f/16. July

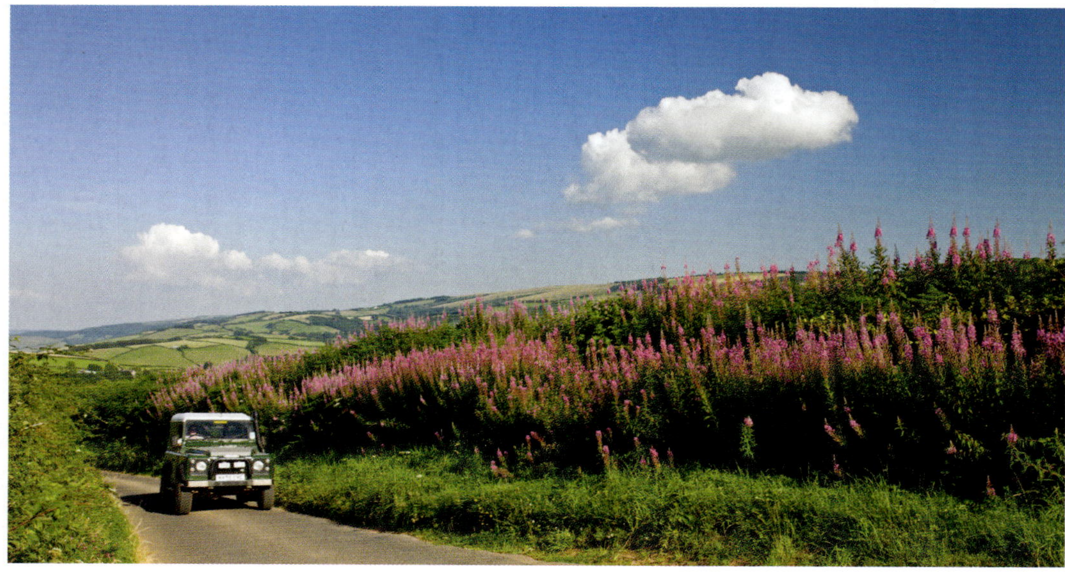

Peak Times

Most tourists visit the South West during the summer and the roads can be very busy, especially near the coast. Allow extra time for both traffic, and for car parking as depending on the location it can be challenging finding a space at the peak times. As you drive along lanes keep a mental note of passing places, you may need to reverse into one at some point.

During sunrise and sunset the roads will of course be far quieter, and the car parks should be empty. Outside of the summer most of the area is quiet on weekdays.

Train

The main rail service connecting Devon and Cornwal is Great Western Trains, formerly First Great Western. The main lines are:

Devon

South Devon Main Line: running between Exeter and Plymouth in south Devon

Avocet Line: running between Exeter and Exmouth in east Devon

Tarka Line: running between Exeter and Barnstaple in north Devon

Riviera Line: running between Newton Abbot and Paignton in south Devon

Cornwall

Cornish Main Line: running between Plymouth and Penzance in west Cornwall

St Ives Bay Line: running between St Erth and St Ives in west Cornwall

Maritime Line: running between Truro and Falmouth in south Cornwall

Atlantic Coast Line: running between Par and Newquay in north Cornwall

Looe Valley Line: running between Liskeard and Looe in south Cornwall

Tamar Valley Line: running between St Budeaux and Gunnislake in south east Cornwall.

Bus

Devon and Cornwall have a good network of bus routes. The main bus companies operating in Devon and Cornwall are Stagecoach and First South West respectively.

By Air

The largest airport connecting travellers with the South West is Bristol, followed by Exeter in Devon and then Newquay in Cornwall.

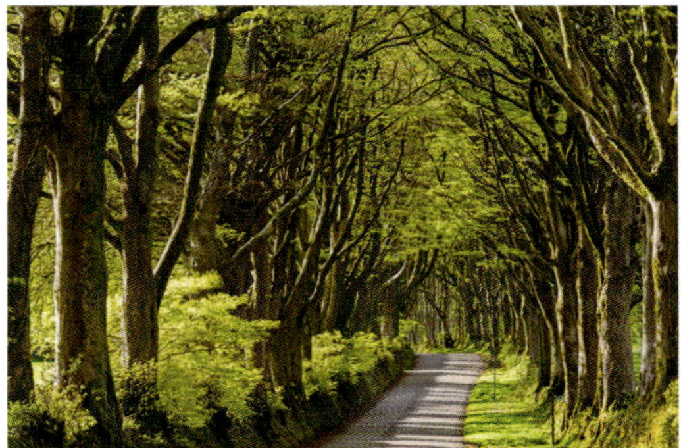

Tree lined country lane in Dartmoor, D800, 70-200mm at 122mm, ISO 100, 0.5 sec at f/13. April

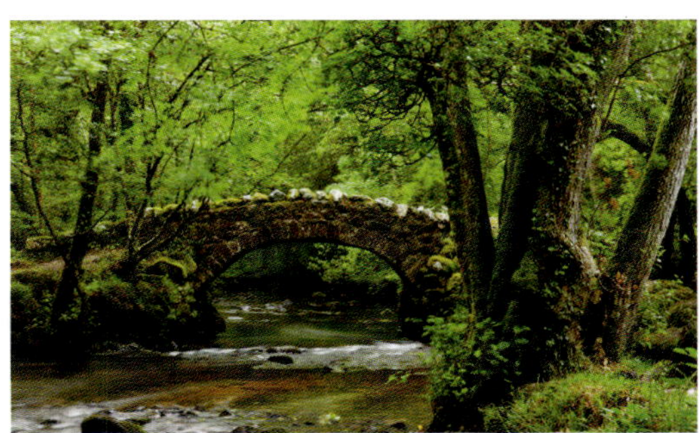

Pack horse bridge crossing the River Bovey in Dartmoor, Canon 1Ds Mark III, 24-70mm at 63mm, ISO 100, 20 sec at f/16. July

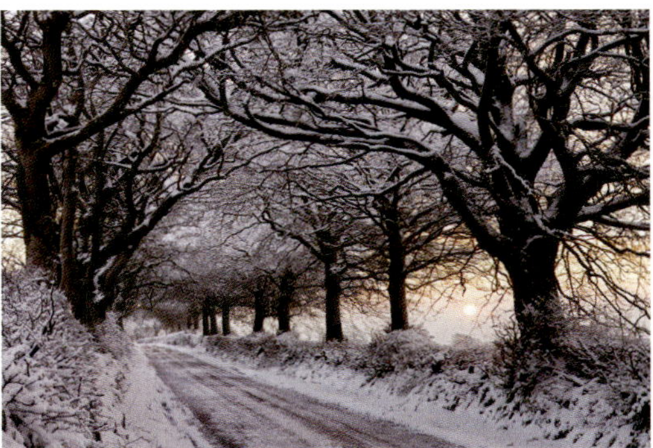

Snow covered Exmoor country lane at sunrise, Canon 1Ds Mark III, 24-70mm at 60mm, ISO 100, 0.6 sec at f/16. January.

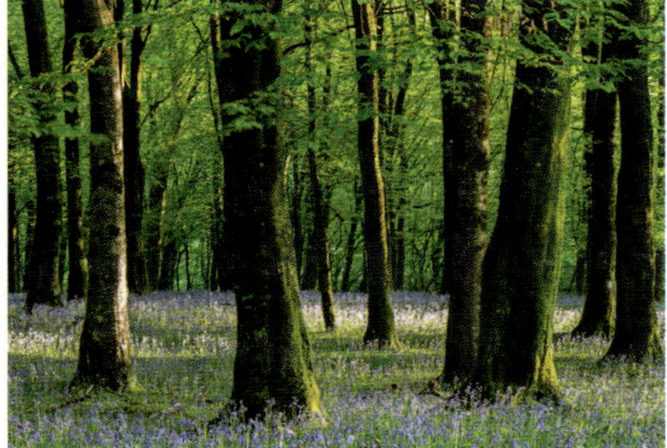

Flowering bluebells in an Exmoor woodland, Nikon D800E, 70-200mm at 95mm, ISO 100, 5 sec at f/13. May

SPRING; March, April, May

Although we associate spring with verdant woodlands, flowering hedgerows and sunny days, for much of March and April the landscape still has a cold and wintry feel. Things really start to change at the beginning of May; this is the time when trees burst into life again with magnificent displays of lime green leaves. Although spring may arrive a little earlier in the South West than the higher elevations of Dartmoor and Exmoor usually ensure they are a couple of weeks behind the surrounding countryside.

When the moment does arrive, there can be no better place to be than in a deciduous woodland, especially one carpeted with beautiful bluebells. Nature's vivid colour combination of lime green and blue is a feast for the eyes, and makes an irresistible subject for landscape photographers. Bluebells are mostly associated with woodlands, but in the South West you can sometimes find large carpets of them flowering out in the open, both on cliff tops and over areas of moorland on both Dartmoor and Exmoor.

Mist floating above Dartmoor's rolling countryside at dawn, Nikon D800, 70-200mm at 190mm, ISO 100, 1/25 sec at f/11. May

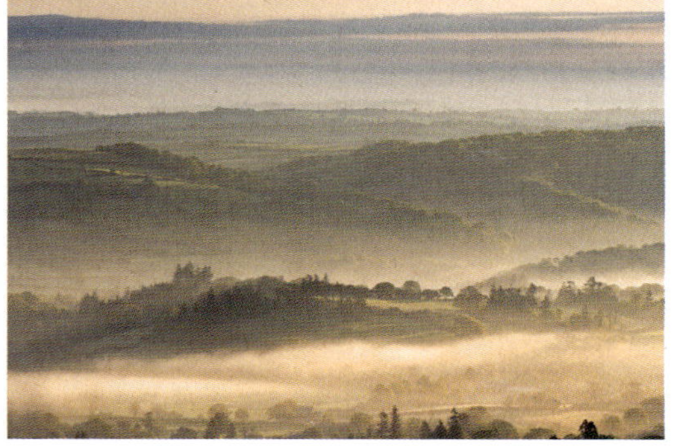

With warm sunny days and still, cool nights, spring can be a wonderful time to photograph mist hanging low over lush spring countryside. With deep valleys and high vantage points to position yourself, the rolling countryside of both Dartmoor and Exmoor make these ideal places for photographing misty mornings.

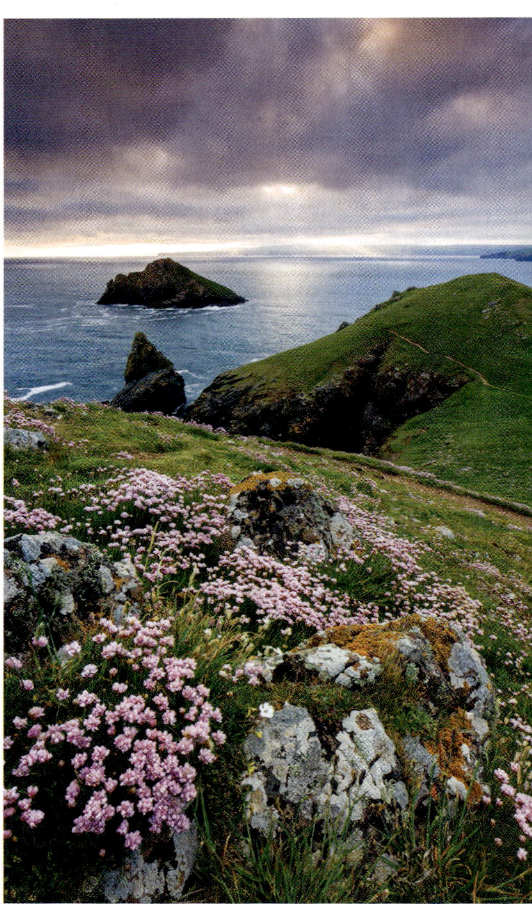

Sea Thrift flowering on the Rumps in Cornwall, Canon 1Ds Mark III, 17-40mm at 22mm, ISO 100, 1.5 sec at f/16. May

Although the coast makes a wonderful place to photograph throughout the year, the best time to shoot from the cliff tops is late May. At this time, headlands all over the Cornish and Devon coastlines are covered in beautiful pink wildflowers. These delicate sea pinks, as well as other wildflowers such as bright yellow kidney vetch, add some lovely colour to foregrounds when shooting from cliff tops.

SUMMER: June, July, August

Summer is the season most people associate with the South West. Visitors flock to Cornwall and Devon over these months, especially during the school holidays. This can make photographing the coast particularly challenging, with beaches busy late into the evening and footprints everywhere spoiling potential compositions. Avoid the popular big beaches and instead head for quiet rocky coves, any location that requires a walk to reach is likely to be far quieter.

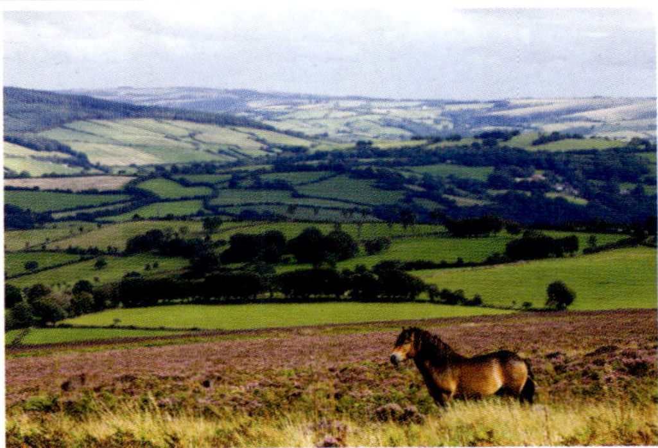

Exmoor pony grazing amongst the heather on Dunkery Hill, Canon 1Ds Mk III, 100-400mm at 150mm, ISO 400, 1/750 sec at f/6.7. August

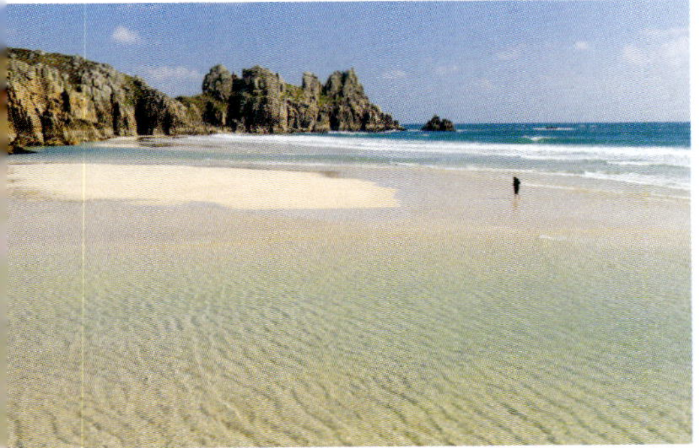

Lone walker on Pednvounder Beach at low tide, Nikon D800E, 24-70mm at 36mm, ISO 100, 1/40 sec at f/10. June

Exmoor and Dartmoor are easier places to find solitude in the summer; aside from some of the popular tourist spots the vast moorland areas are never busy.

The moors look very different at this time of year; the brown hills are replaced with green grasses and large areas of verdant bracken. In late summer sweeping areas of moorland are covered by flowering heather, coating the landscape in a rolling purple carpet.

Exmoor especially is renowned for its heather-covered hills, making August one of the best months to visit the national park. Exmoor's deep wooded combes come into their own during early summer before the lush foliage has faded to dull green. At this time, beautiful ferns spring up around fast flowing rocky streams, contributing to provide irresistible subject matter for woodland photographs. Water levels may be low at this time of year, so time your visit after rain to ensure the rivers and waterfalls are flowing well.

Regardless of your destination, in order to avoid other people as well as the harsh sunlight and hot hazy weather that summer brings, it is always best to head out around sunrise or sunset. With long day lengths making extremely early starts and late finishes, this can be a punishing time of year for landscape photographers.

Beautiful evening sunlight on Exmoor's rolling countryside, Canon 1Ds Mark III, 70-200mm at 200mm, ISO 100, 1/90 sec at f/8

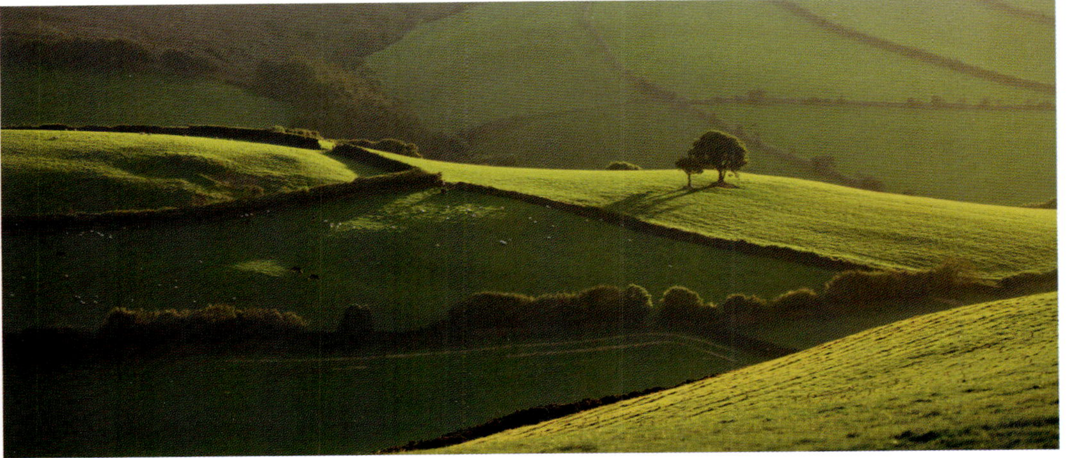

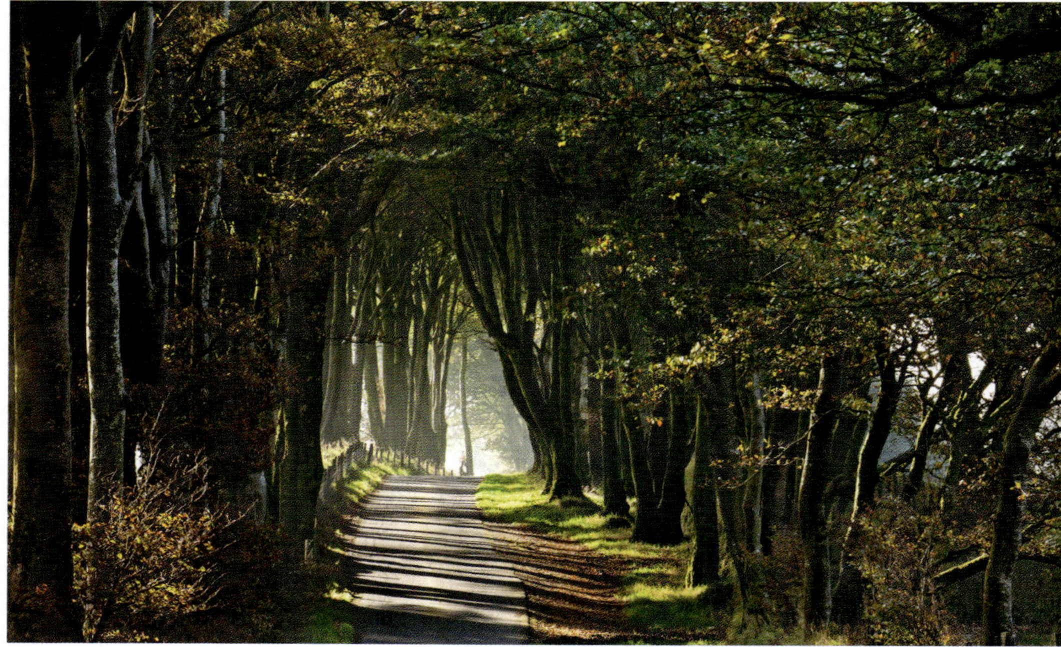

Tree lined narrow country lane in Dartmoor, Canon 1Ds Mark III, 70-200 at 180mm, ISO 100, 0.6 sec at f/16. October

AUTUMN: Sept, Oct, November

Autumn is surely the best season for photography and it is a delightful time in the South West. Early autumn sometimes coincides with a sustained period of good weather, as the UK occasionally enjoys an Indian Summer. With the departure of summer holidaymakers the coast becomes peaceful, with empty beaches and quiet fishing harbours waiting to be photographed.

Sunrise comes later and sunset earlier as the day lengths shorten making landscape photography a more enjoyable experience. But it's the quality of light that really makes autumn special. Gone is the haze of summer, now replaced by crisp clear days with excellent

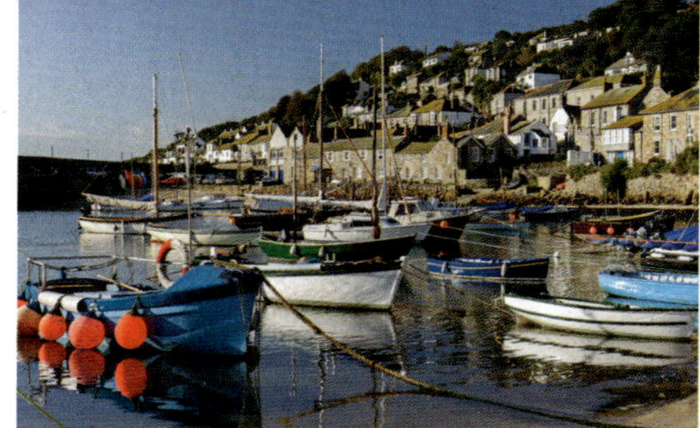

Boats crowd Mousehole's pretty harbour, Canon 1Ds Mark III, 24-70mm at 54mm, ISO 100, 1/15 sec at f/16. September

visibility. Similar to spring, the combination of cold nights and warm still days make September a perfect time to photograph mist-covered countryside.

Moving into October and early November, the landscape is about to undergo its most magnificent transformation of the year. Both national parks boast some incredible locations to photograph autumn colours. Deep wooded valleys with fast flowing rocky rivers such as Watersmeet in Exmoor and Fingle Bridge in Dartmoor make spectacular locations for photography during the autumn when mature deciduous trees overhanging the river banks are resplendent in golden foliage.

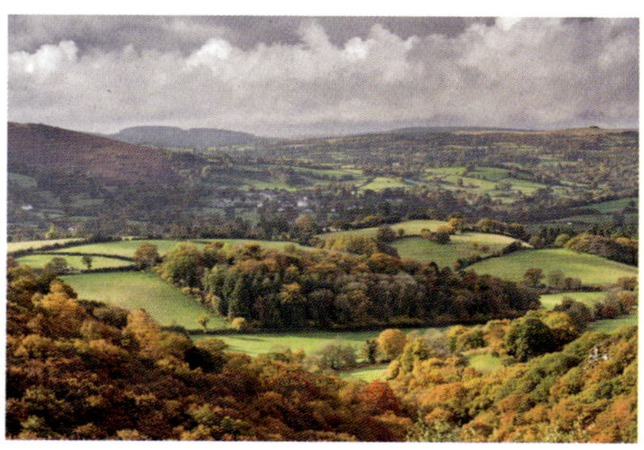

The trees of Dartmoor's Teign Valley in autumnal colour, Nikon D800, 70-200 at 92mm, ISO 100, 1/6 sec at f/13. October

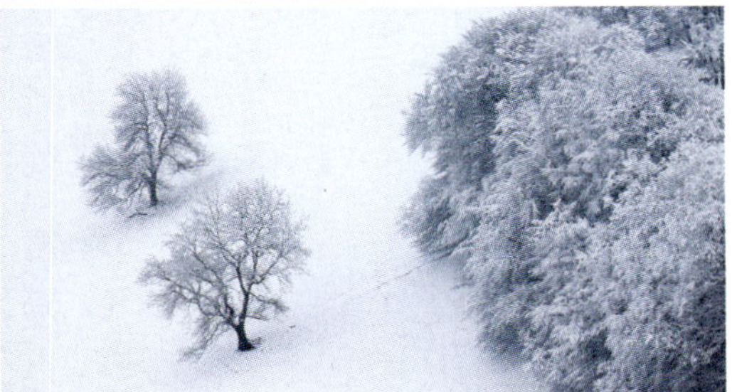

Snowy trees at the Punchbowl in Exmoor National Park, Canon 1Ds Mark III, 70-200mm at 200mm, ISO 100, 1/80 sec at f/13. January

WINTER: December, January, February

Once the autumn colours have faded and all the leaves fallen, some will think the show is over until the following spring. The opposite is true of course, winter is one of the finest times for landscape photography and offers some of the most magical conditions of the whole year.

With higher elevations, the moorland areas are far more likely to experience snowfall throughout cold winter snaps. Snow attracts visitors to the moors, so head up early to ensure the snow is fresh and free from footprints. On frosty mornings, head to high ground on Exmoor or Dartmoor armed with your telephoto lens, and shoot the sugar coated rolling farmland far below. During sustained periods of cold weather you may be lucky enough to encounter hoar frost, which turns trees and bushes completely white.

The coast experiences milder temperatures than inland, with snow and frost far less common. However, the combination of deserted beaches and rough seas make the winter one of the best times to photograph the coast. During winter storms, massive waves crash up against the Atlantic cliffs of Devon and Cornwall offering incredible photographic opportunities for those brave (or crazy) enough to venture out. Take care along the coast in such conditions.

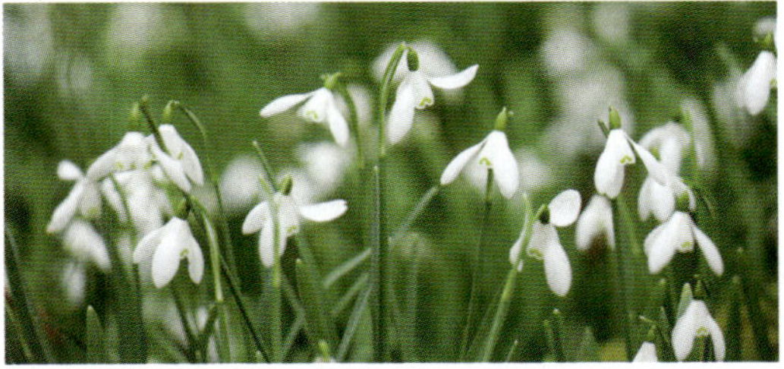

Flowering snowdrops in Snowdrop Valley on Exmoor, Canon 1Ds Mark III, 150mm macro, ISO 100, 1/50 sec at f/4.0. February

As winter gradually releases its grip on the landscape the first wildflowers of the year, snowdrops, signal an impending change to the season. Surrounded by wintry backdrops, these beautiful delicate wildflowers make a real statement of intent. One of the best places to visit and photograph snowdrops is the aptly named Snowdrop Valley, near Wheddon Cross on Exmoor.

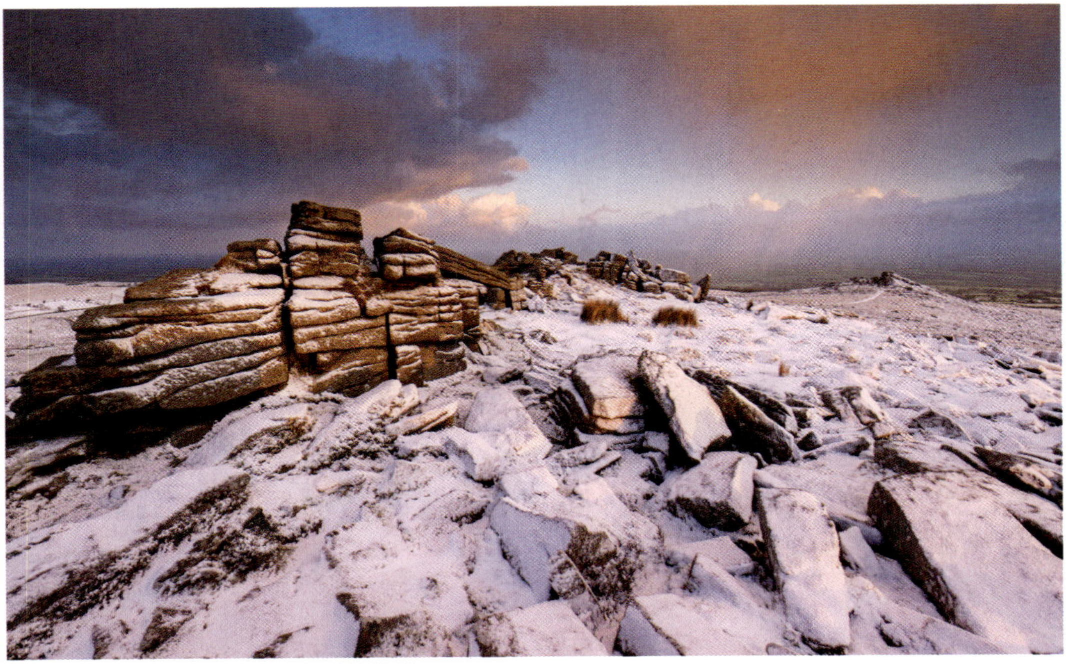

A snow dusted Belstone Tor at dawn, Nikon D800E, 17-35mm at 17mm, ISO 100, ¼ sec at f/11. January

South West Climate and Weather

Climate

The climate of the South West is typified by warm summers, cool winters and precipitation all year round. Cornwall and Devon benefit from being on the eastern edge of the warm Gulf Stream and towns such as St. Ives, Newquay and Ilfracombe have a Mediterranean climate with summer temperatures reaching 30 C (86F). Long days with up to 16 hours of sun mean that summers are great for coastal sunrise and sunset photography. However spring and autumn, or when there are summer storms around, will give that all important cloud on the horizon for the best golden hour photography. An important consideration is that both early spring and autumn are not quite so challenging sleep-wise for golden hour photography. The north coast is generally best for sunsets and the south for sunrises.

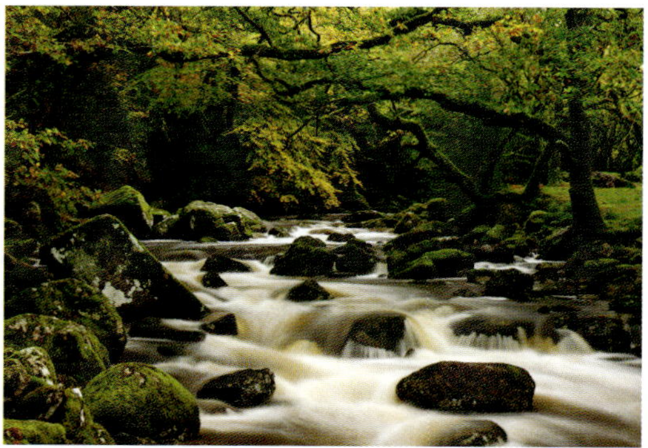

The River Plym running through Dewerstone Wood on Dartmoor, Canon 1Ds Mark III, 24-70mm at 52mm, ISO 50, 5 sec at f/16. October

Rain

Rainfall is less on the coast than on Dartmoor and Exmoor. Rainfall at Princetown, Dartmoor at an elevation of 453m averages over 2,000mm a year, compared to an average of 850mm on the coast. Dartmoor is the highest land in southern England with High Willhays topping out at 2,028ft (618m) and the weather that comes from the maritime west or south-west brings wind, rain and often fog to this high plateau. The moorland areas in both national parks can experience unexpected changes in the weather, so regardless of the season always be prepared for cold wet weather. Even on calm warm days, the exposed peaks can be surprisingly chilly. It will be four degrees colder on Dartmoor than at nearby Plymouth on the coast; so wrap up well before heading up to photograph either of the moors.

Twilight above Trevose Head from Constantine Bay, Nikon D800E, 17-35mm at 20mm, ISO 200, 5 sec at f/11. August.

Snow

While snowfall is fairly infrequent in the South West, the higher elevations of Exmoor and especially Dartmoor will see more than most. In the coldest months from December to March both Exmoor and Dartmoor may experience frost and snow for more than 25 days, whereas the coast with its high winter temperature rarely sees any. Cold snaps can occur at any time throughout the winter, but generally speaking February is best to photograph frosty and snowy landscapes in these two national parks.

Temperature Inversions

Autumn through winter to early spring is the best time for temperature inversions when the land is covered in low mist or fog. If there is a cold, clear and still night, especially after precipitation, there will be a high chance of a misty morning and it will be time to get up high.

Wind

The South West, surrounded by sea on three sides, is the second windiest place in the UK after Western Scotland. Wind speeds can exceed 80 knots in the winter, usually on the exposed Cornish coast. Such storms are impressive but can also be destructive and dangerous. Whilst the coast gets a battering from the wind the upland moors are equally exposed.

Local Weather Forecasts

Met Office Weather Forecast

www.metoffice.gov.uk/public/weather/forecast

BBC Weather

www.bbc.co.uk/weather

Local Radio

BBC Radio Devon, 95.8 / 96.0 / 94.8 / 103.4 / 104.3

BBC Radio Cornwall 95.2 / 103.9

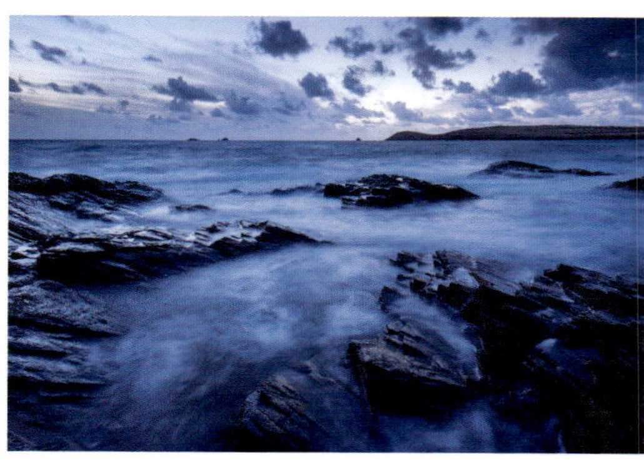

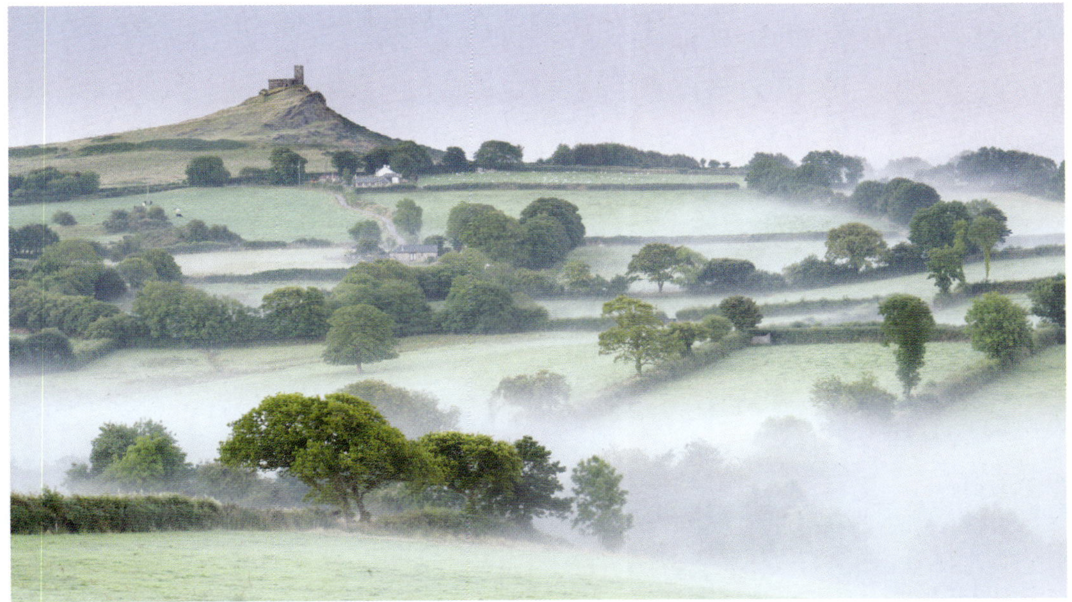

Mist covered rolling countryside near Brentor at dawn, Nikon D800, 70-200mm at 110mm, ISO 100, 5 sec at f/11. August

Upland Averages

Met Office Weather Station averages
Lidcombe, Devon (next to Tarr Steps)
Location:51.086, -3.608
Altitude: 348 m above mean sea level

Coastal Averages

Met Office Weather Station averages
Culdrose, Cornwall (near Lizard Point)
Location: 50.084, -5.256
Altitude: 76 m above mean sea level

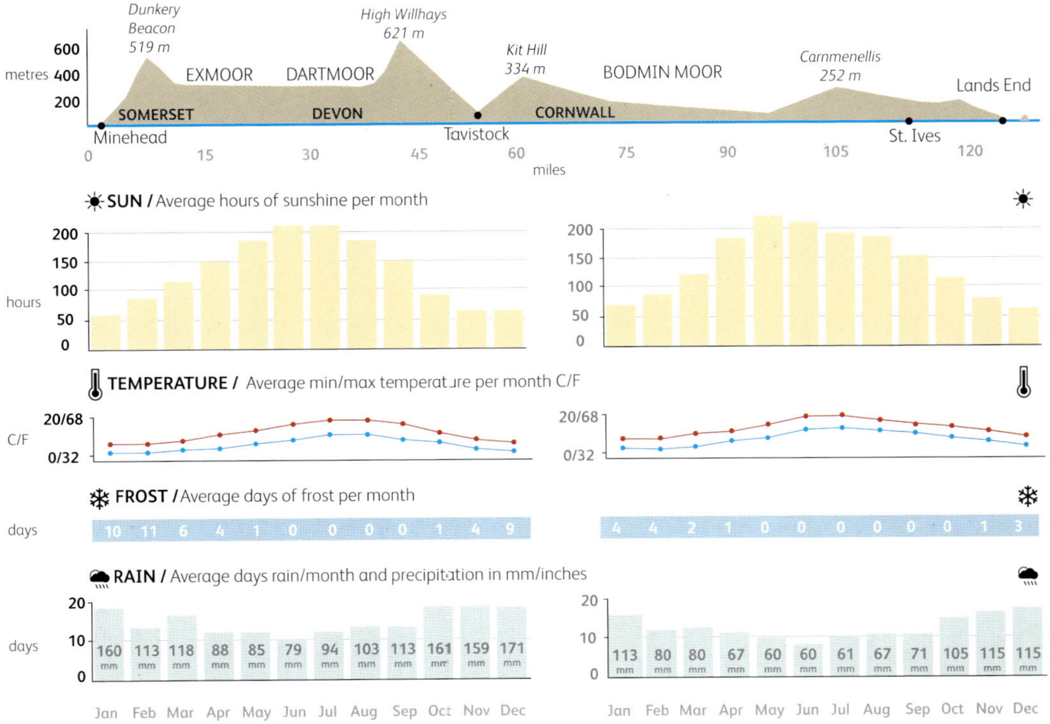

SUN / Average hours of sunshine per month

TEMPERATURE / Average min/max temperature per month C/F

FROST / Average days of frost per month

Upland (Lidcombe) frost days: 10, 11, 6, 4, 1, 0, 0, 0, 0, 1, 4, 9

Coastal (Culdrose) frost days: 4, 4, 2, 1, 0, 0, 0, 0, 0, 0, 1, 3

RAIN / Average days rain/month and precipitation in mm/inches

Upland (Lidcombe) precipitation mm:

Jan	Feb	Mar	Apr	May	Jun	Jul	Aug	Sep	Oct	Nov	Dec
160	113	118	88	85	79	94	103	113	161	159	171

Coastal (Culdrose) precipitation mm:

Jan	Feb	Mar	Apr	May	Jun	Jul	Aug	Sep	Oct	Nov	Dec
113	80	80	67	60	60	61	67	71	105	115	115

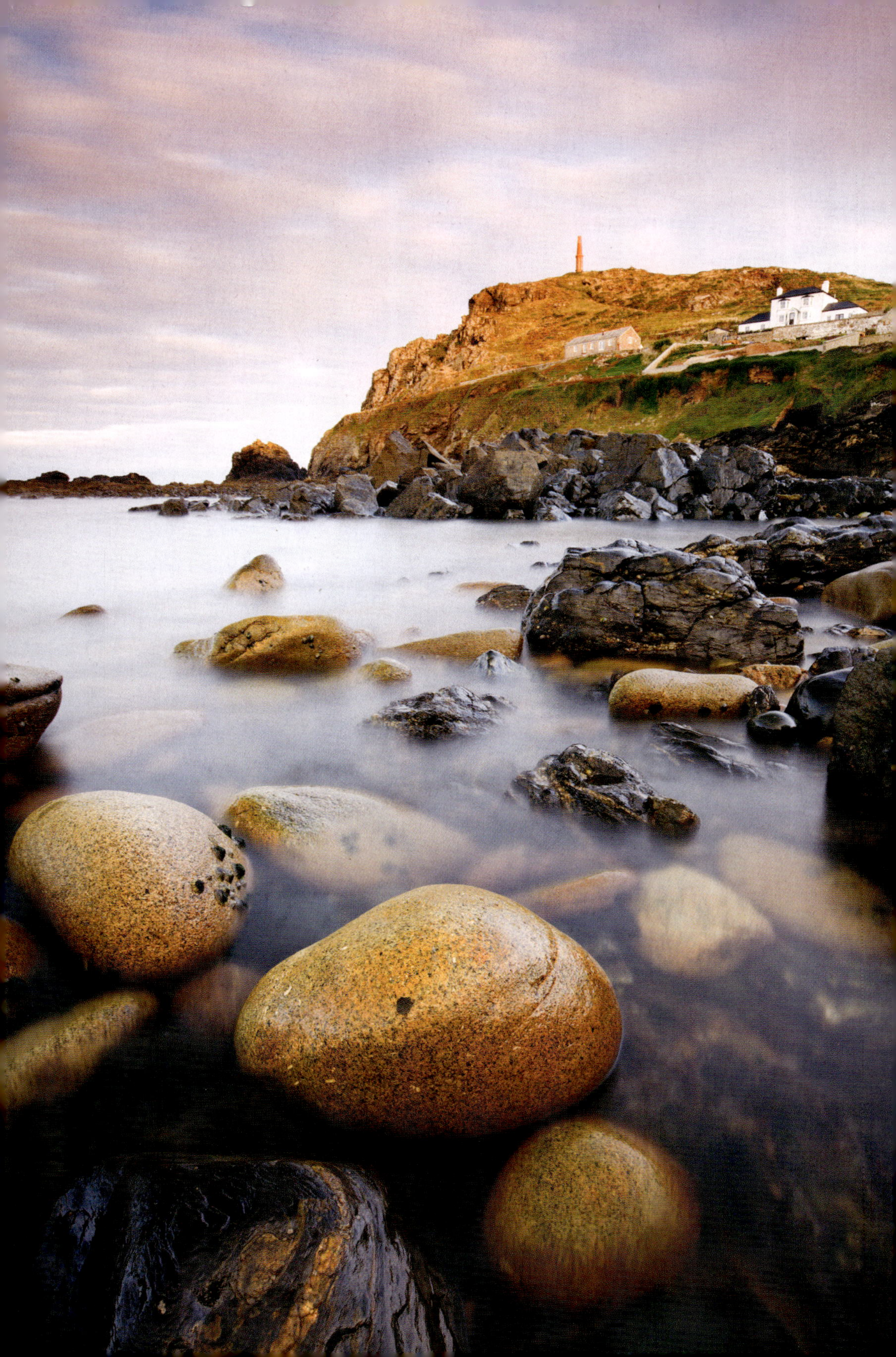

Using this Guidebook to get the Best Images

Great photographs require being in the right place at the right time regardless of whether you are using a digital, film or mobile phone camera. This is what fotoVUE photo-location guidebooks are about – giving you the information and the inspiration to get to great locations in the best photographic conditions.

In the Right Place

Each location chapter in this guide describes a place where you can take great photographs. Comprehensive directions are given including co-ordinates to the nearest car park or lay-by, nearest postal codes for sat navs and smart phones, and an OS map co-ordinate.

Before you set off for a location study a map so that you know where you are going and give yourself plenty of time to get your destination. Also read the **accessibility** notes to check the distances and terrain to the location's photographic **viewpoints**.

Maps

For the best detail, recommended maps for the South West are the OS Explorer Maps (scale 1:25 000). There are 20 maps for the South West in this series so choose your area carefully.

More affordable and covering larger areas, but less detailed, are the OS Landranger maps (scale 1:50 000) which cover the South West in ten maps.

If you are an occasional visitor you may find the OS Tour maps (scale 1:100 000) to Cornwall and Devon and Somerset West adequate.

More details at www.ordnancesurvey.co.uk and online maps at Google and Bing.

At the Right Time

Great photographs usually depend on light and colour. In each location chapter are detailed notes on the best time of year and day to visit a location to get the best photographic results. Good light can occur any time however and often the best times to visit any location is when conditions are rapidly changing like after a storm.

The topography, sun position and the weather determine how the light falls on the land. Use the sun position compass on the front flap of this guidebook for sunrise and sunset times, to find out where the sun rises and sets on the compass (it changes throughout the year) and sun elevation (how high the sun rises in the sky). Useful websites for this include suncalc.org and the Photographer's Ephemeris.

EXIF data on photograph captions

Included in each photo caption is the shooting information. This is taken from the EXIF data recorded in the file alongside each digital photograph taken. EXIF is short for Exchangeable Image File and records a whole host of information about the settings and equipment used to take that photo including shutter speed, aperture, ISO, date and time the image was taken, white balance, and a list of other parameters.

Light conditions and camera exposure vary but hopefully knowing the settings used for all of these photographs will help your own photography.

Responsible Photography

Minimise your impact by following the Country Code: stick to footpaths, close gates, don't climb over fences and don't leave litter. Resist the urge to bend the rules just for a photo; the more people that trample flowers or climb fences, the more restrictions will come into play.

Other Photographers

At some locations you will encounter other photographers. Be courteous and considerate, stay behind them if they are composing a photograph. If someone arrives after you and the light has just been amazing, resist the temptation to tell them that they have just missed the best light ('you should have been here half an hour ago…')

Self Exploration

The interpretation of viewpoints is entirely down to prevailing conditions and your skill as a photographer.

This guidebook will help you get to some of the best photographic locations in the South West. This list is by no means exhaustive, use it as a springboard to discover your own. There are of course many other great places in the South West both known or still waiting to be discovered and photographed. Study a map and look for locations or just follow your nose when conditions are good and discover your own.

The rocky shores of Priest's Cove below Cape Cornwall, Canon 1Ds Mark III, 16-35mm at 20mm, ISO 100, 30 sec at f/16. October

Locations Overview

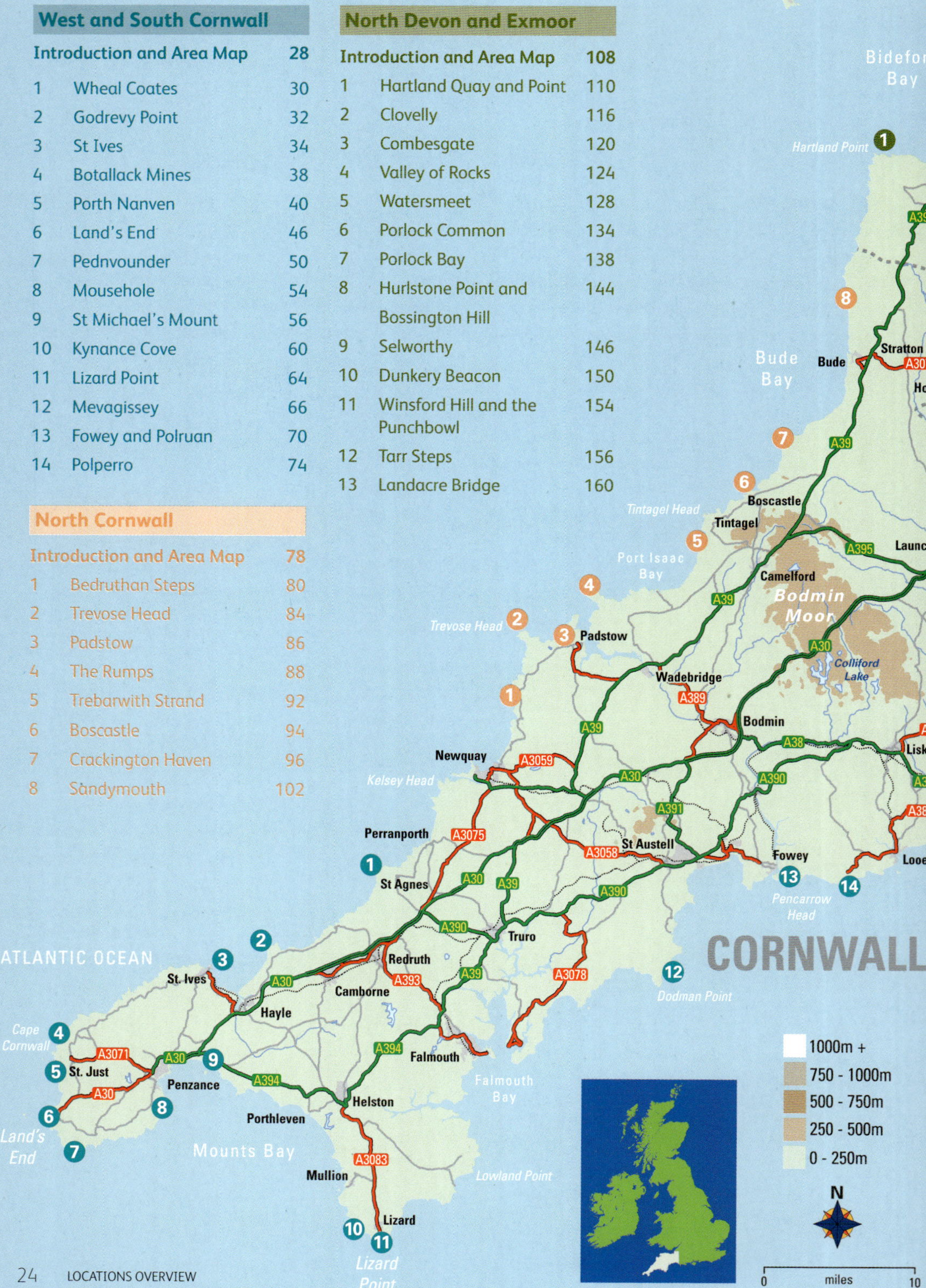

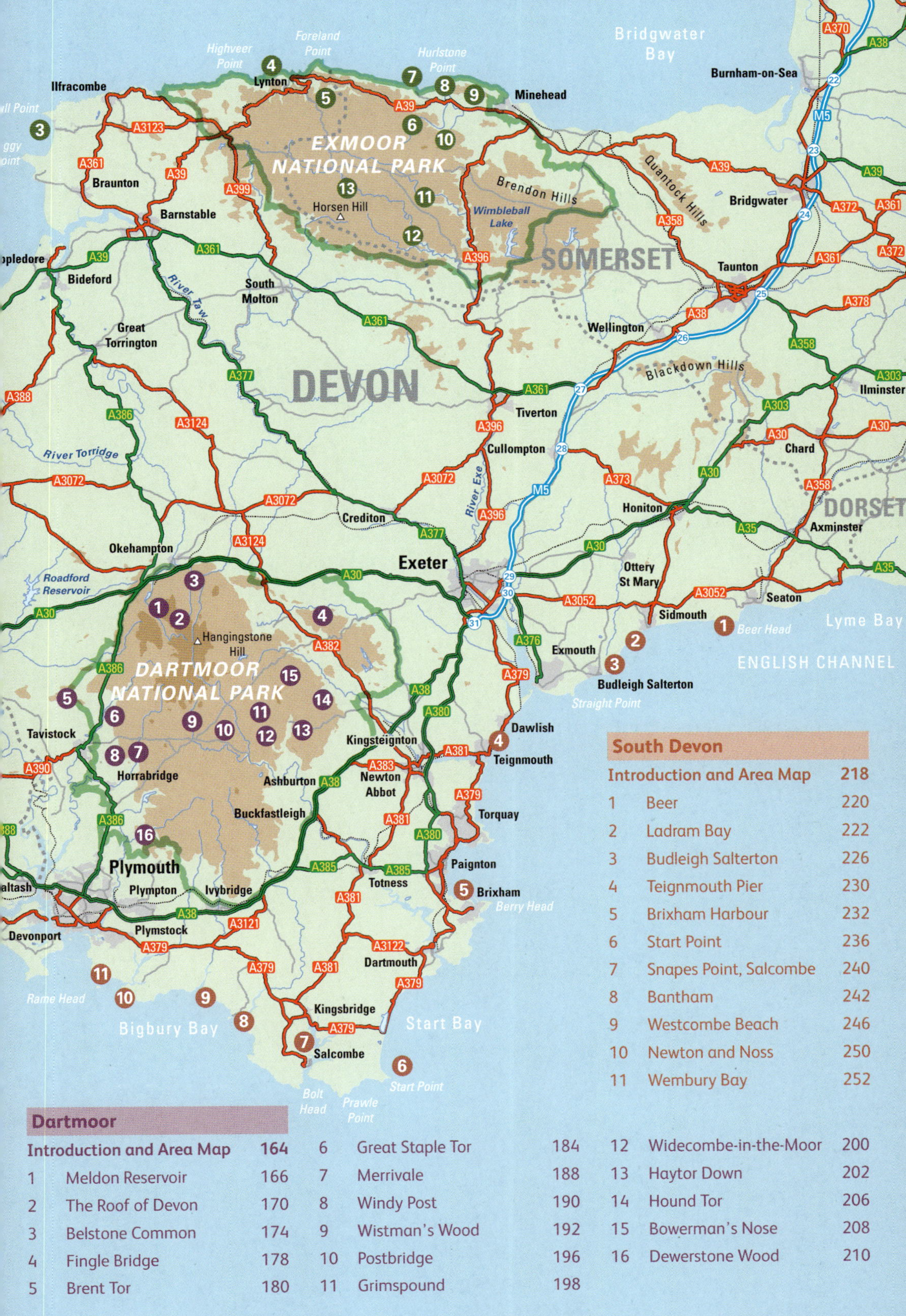

Bridgwater Bay
Burnham-on-Sea
Ilfracombe
Highveer Point
Foreland Point
Hurlstone Point
Lynton
Minehead
Braunton
EXMOOR NATIONAL PARK
Barnstable
Brendon Hills
Wimbleball Lake
Horsen Hill
Bridgwater
Quantock Hills
Bideford
South Molton
SOMERSET
Great Torrington
Taunton
Wellington
DEVON
River Taw
Tiverton
Blackdown Hills
Cullompton
Chard
River Torridge
Ilminster
Crediton
Honiton
DORSET
Okehampton
Roadford Reservoir
River Exe
Exeter
Axminster
Hangingstone Hill
Ottery St Mary
DARTMOOR NATIONAL PARK
Exmouth
Sidmouth
Seaton
Beer Head
Lyme Bay
Budleigh Salterton
Straight Point
Tavistock
ENGLISH CHANNEL
Kingsteignton
Dawlish
Teignmouth
Horrabridge
Newton Abbot
Ashburton
Torquay
Buckfastleigh
Plymouth
Paignton
Plympton
Ivybridge
Totness
Brixham
Berry Head
Devonport
Plymstock
Dartmouth
Rame Head
Bigbury Bay
Kingsbridge
Start Bay
Salcombe
Bolt Head
Prawle Point
Start Point

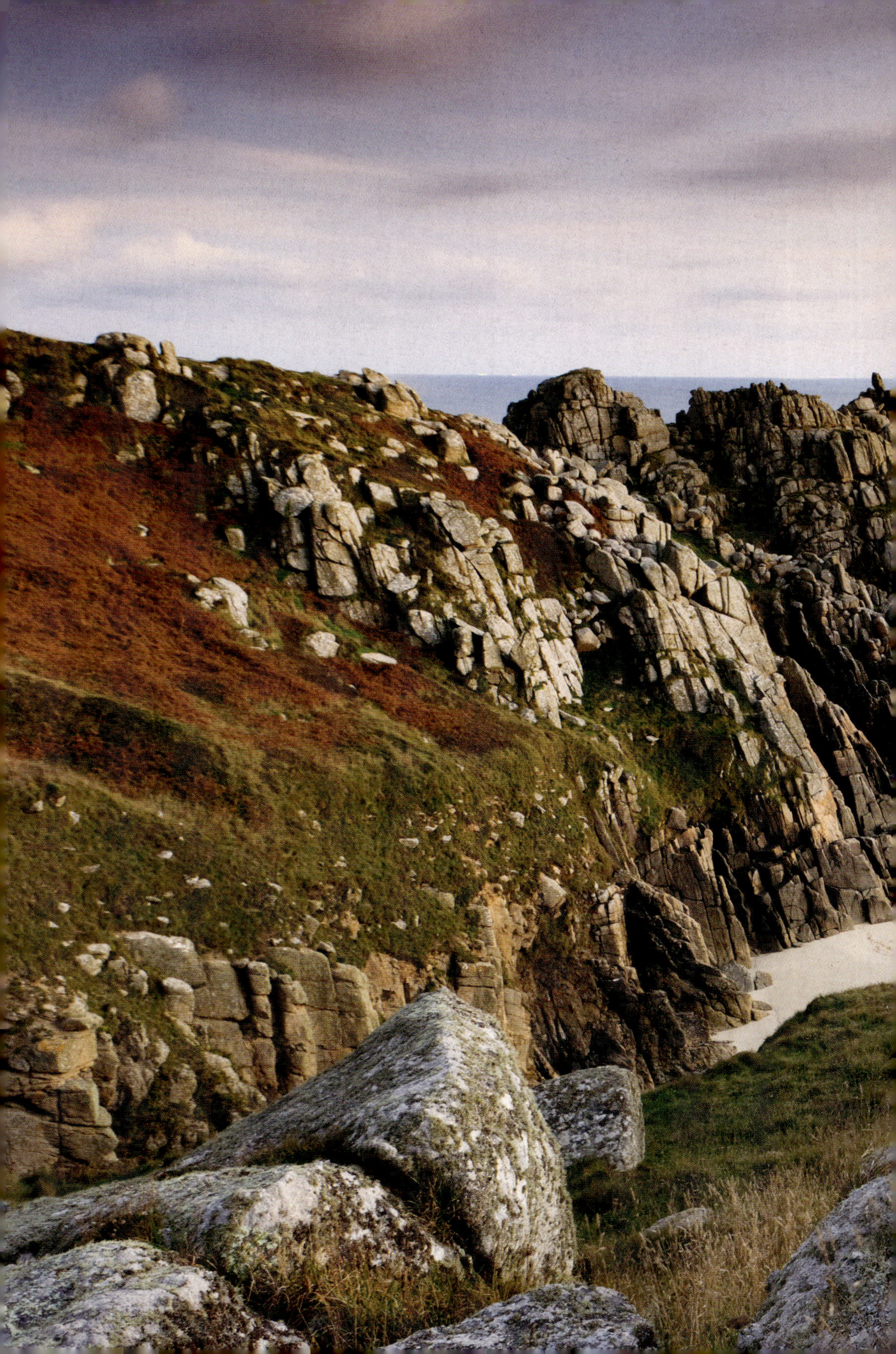

Cornwall

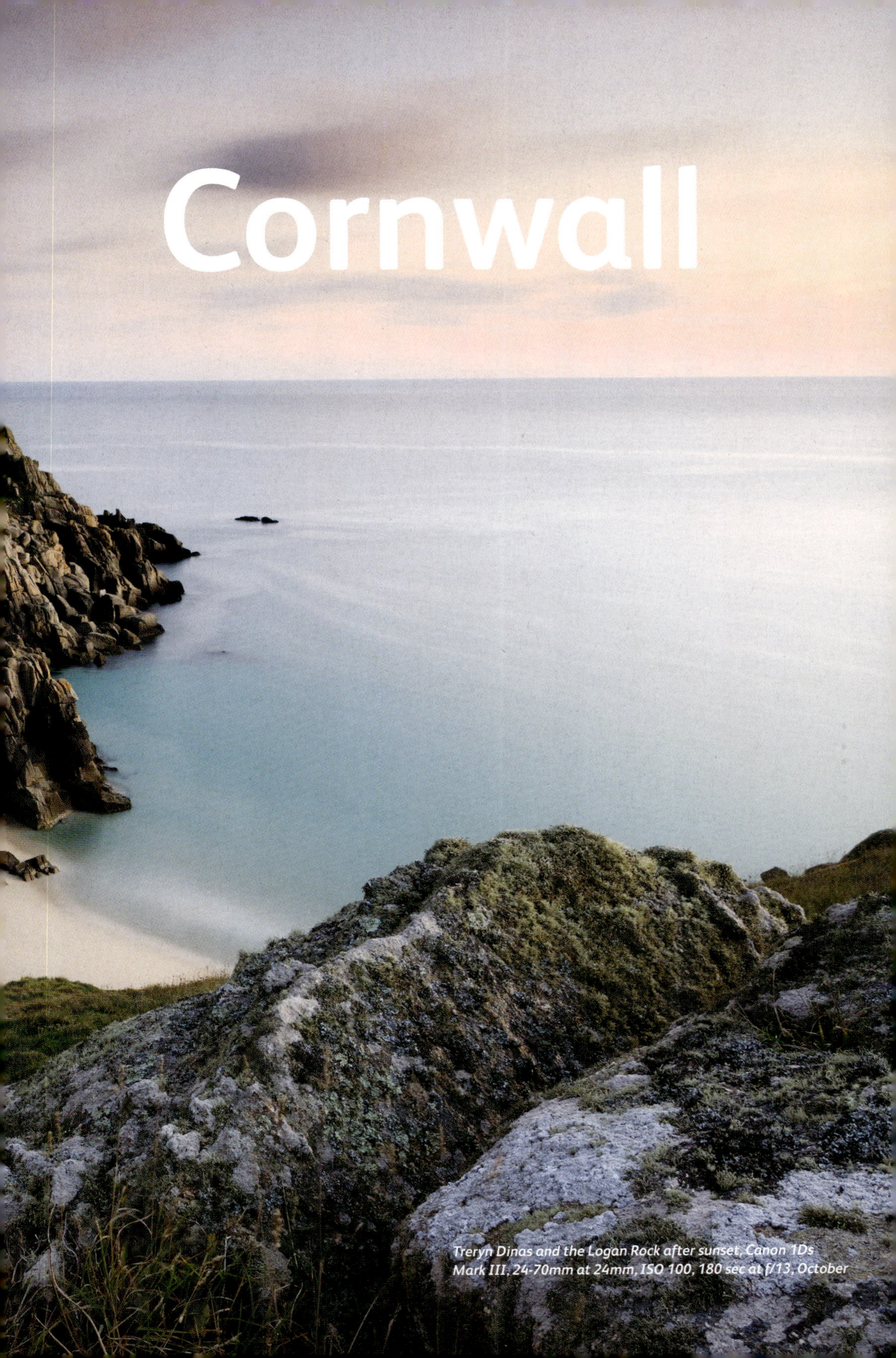

Treryn Dinas and the Logan Rock after sunset, Canon 1Ds Mark III, 24-70mm at 24mm, ISO 100, 180 sec at f/13, October

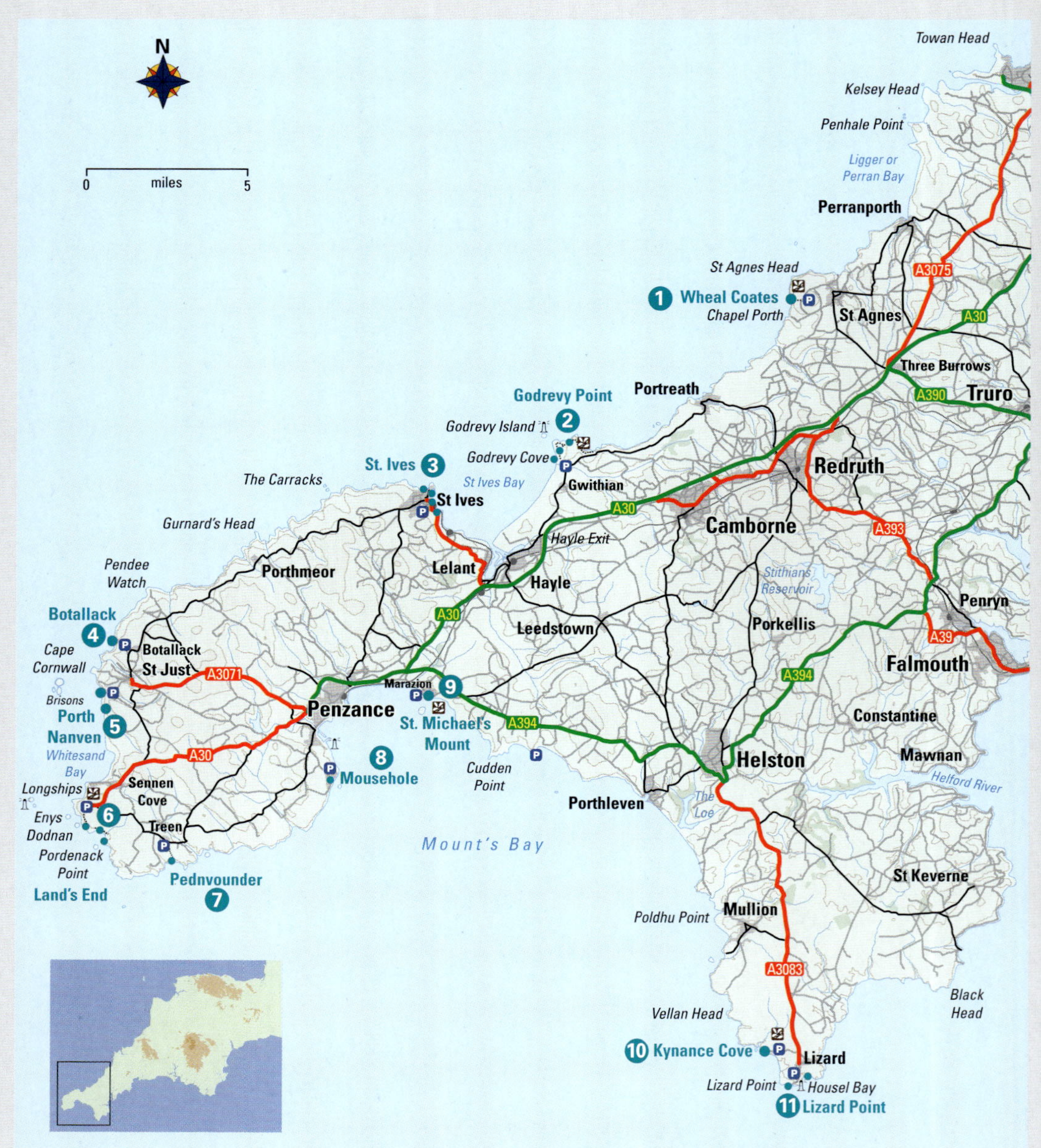

Contains Ordnance Survey data © Crown Copyright and database right (2016), map location overlay © fotoVUE 2016

WEST AND SOUTH CORNWALL

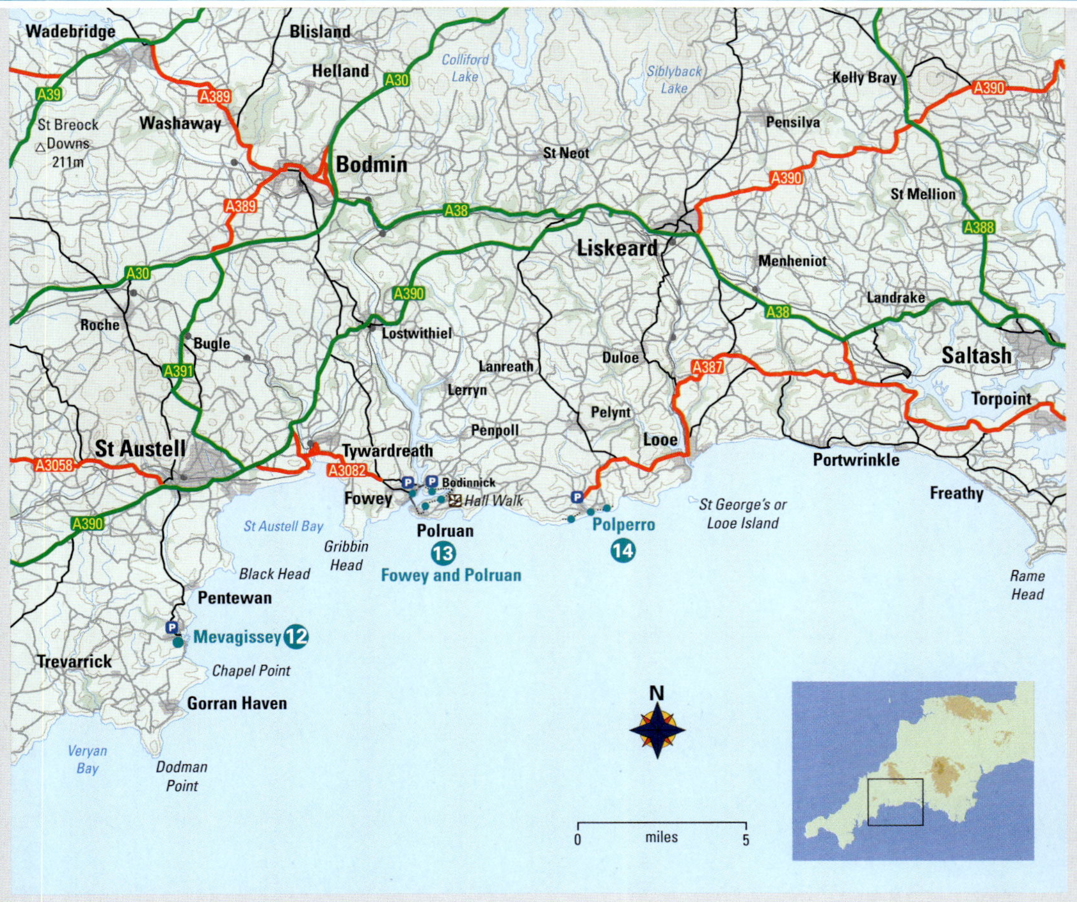

Contains Ordnance Survey data © Crown Copyright and database right (2016), map location overlay © fotoVUE 2016

As you approach the westernmost tip of the Cornish peninsula, the picturesque landscape takes on a wild and more windswept appearance. The land splits into two peninsulas, Penwith and the Lizard, each facing the full force of the Atlantic. The Penwith peninsula is home to two of Cornwall's most famous landmarks; Land's End and St Michael's Mount, both locations high on the list for visitors to the county.

The coast throughout this area is spectacular and always dramatic, with soaring granite cliffs facing angry Atlantic waves. Away from the rugged cliffs, some of Cornwall's most beautiful golden sandy beaches can be found at Porth Leven, Sennen Cove and all around St Ives.

Further south, the geology of the Lizard peninsula is quite unlike Penwith's blocky granite coast. The rocks here are mostly serpentinite, giving the cliffs a distinctive jagged appearance. Notable locations along this stretch of coastline are the beautiful National Trust owned Kynance Cove and nearby Mullion Cove, as well as Lizard Point, the most southerly point of mainland Great Britain.

After rounding the Lizard, the south coast begins its long journey north east towards the border of Devon. Although dramatic cliffs and headlands occur throughout the south coast, generally speaking it has a much softer feel than the exposed Atlantic coastline. Large estuaries and pretty coastal towns such as Fowey, Mevagissey and Polperro add extra flavour to Cornwall's distinctive south coast.

Along with the Crowns mines of Botallack, Wheal Coates is possibly the most photographed of all Cornwall's tin mines. Dramatically located on the cliff tops near St Agnes, it certainly merits such attention.

Several towering buildings make up the former mine, although the undisputed highlight is the Towanroath engine house. Perched precariously near the cliff edge this impressive ruin, complete with chimney stack, is THE iconic tin mine image eternally associated with the Cornish landscape.

When the mine was active the engine house was used to pump water from the 200 metre Towanroath shaft, enabling men to mine a seam of tin just below sea level. But with tin production becoming increasingly sporadic Wheal Coates finally closed in 1913.

What to Shoot and Viewpoints

On first approach from the car park Towanroath engine house seems to be missing from the view. The engine house is set apart from the other buildings, positioned half way down the sloping cliff. As you approach the cliff the chimney stack first appears and then suddenly the magnificent ruin is almost directly below you, with the Atlantic crashing beyond. It is a breathtaking sight to behold for the first time, a view that epitomises the Cornish coast.

This first view is also one of the best, especially in late summer when the steeply sloping cliffs are bursting with colour from flowering heather and gorse. You may find it difficult to pull yourself away but Towanroath works from all angles, both close and far, so it pays to spend some time exploring the potential of the area.

While you are still on the cliffs above the engine house, it is worth walking south a hundred metres or so to gain a view looking northwards towards the mine. You may need to scramble a little to get into position, but it is worth the effort. From this side the engine house looks even more impressive; the chimney is more prominent as is the shape of the tower, complete with three arched windows. This view works particularly well in late afternoon when sunshine lights up the face of the building.

For a very different view head down the cliffs to the footpath below. The coast path runs right alongside the engine house, allowing you to photograph the tower from close quarters. While shooting from this position doesn't give Towanroath the sense of location it deserves, it does permit a more detailed study of the

building itself. The distinctive tin mine shape looks especially prominent against the sky when photographed up close with a wide-angle lens, but unless you are shooting with a tilt/shift lens problems with converging verticals will make the building lean over in your pictures. This can be easily corrected in post processing, but be sure to shoot wider than you wish as the end result will lose space around the frame.

A very different view of Towanroath can be photographed from standing near the coast path on the north side and looking back towards the building. This is also one of the most popular views and works extremely well during early evening when low sunlight warms the cliff and engine house. Careful attention to composition is required when shooting from this viewpoint as the foreground can be somewhat spoilt by unsightly patches of cliff devoid of plants.

For something a little different head back up the cliff on the footpath until you see the ruins of a building looking reminiscent of a long abandoned cottage. This was the calciner, a fundamental part of the mine used for roasting tin to remove impurities such as arsenic. While the calciner doesn't hold anywhere near the same attraction as the iconic engine houses, it does make an evocative feature of this landscape's mining heritage.

How to Get Here

From the A30 junction at Three Burrows take the third exit at the roundabout and follow the B3277 signposted for St Agnes for nearly 3 miles. Take a left at the roundabout and follow the road for another mile. The car park for Wheal Coates is on the left, but it is not signposted and easily missed. Just past the car park is a caravan site, if you see this turn around.

Parking Lat/Long: 50.305452, -5.2277327
Parking Grid Ref: SW 698 505
Parking Postcode: TR5 0NS (nearby Chapel Porth)
Map: OS Explorer Map 104 (1:25 000) Redruth & St Agnes

Accessibility

A wheelchair-friendly track leads to the main cliff top buildings at Wheal Coates, however, Towanroath engine house and the calciner are accessed through uneven tracks. The sloping ground near the footpaths is very loose underfoot, so caution is advised whenever leaving the main tracks.

Best Time of Year/Day

Undoubtedly the best time of year to shoot Wheal Coates is late summer when both heather and gorse are flowering all over the cliffs. Regardless of the season the best time of day to shoot Towanroath is late afternoon or evening when sunshine is illuminating the cliffs and engine house. After the sun has set, the shape of the tin mines look fantastic as silhouettes against a colourful sky.

Opposite: Towanroath engine house at sunset, Canon 1Ds Mark III, 16-35mm at 24mm, ISO 100, 2 sec at f/16, September

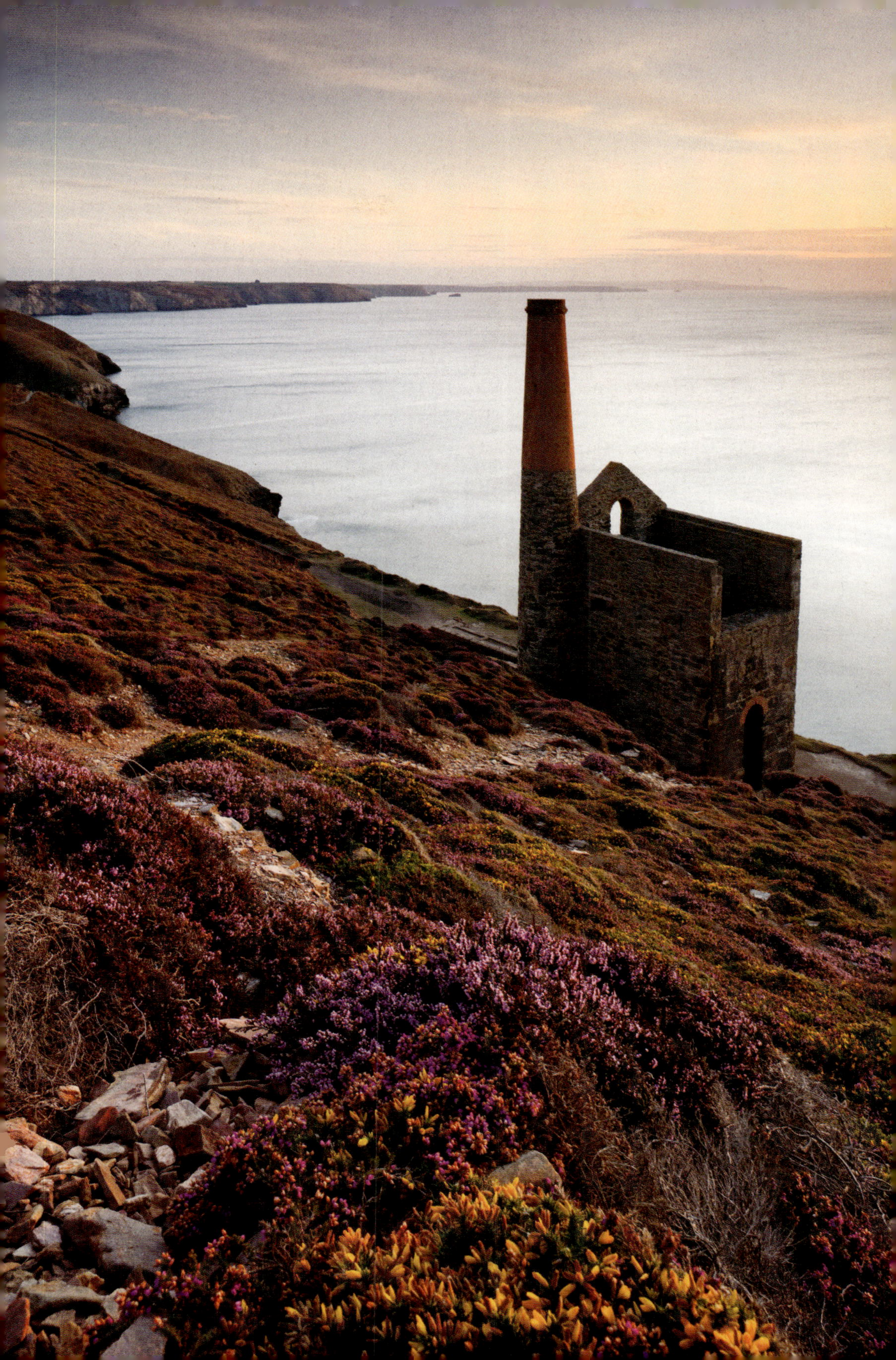

Facing the Atlantic Ocean on the eastern side of St Ives Bay is the craggy headland of Godrevy Point. Located at the north end of Gwithian Beach are some rocky ledges with a large island, home to Godrevy lighthouse, just offshore.

This striking white lighthouse was built in 1859 to warn passing ships of the dangers of a submerged reef known as The Stones. Over the years many ships had foundered here, but it was the high profile sinking of the SS Nile in 1854 with the loss of all on board that resulted in the lighthouse.

The island and nearby coast is a renowned habitat for seabirds including cormorants, fulmar, guillemot, gulls and razorbills. However, the wildlife most associated with Godrevy is the resident colony of grey seals just around the headland at Mutton Cove. From the cliff tops above Mutton Cove seals can often be seen far below basking on the beach. For those seeking a closer encounter, the ledges on the west side of Godrevy Point can offer a great vantage point to watch seals swimming around the rocks. If you are lucky, at high tide you can sometimes see them at really close quarters swimming through the channels between the ledges.

What to Shoot and Viewpoints

Although the cliff top coast path offers elevated vantage points to shoot towards the lighthouse, the lure of shooting from the ledges is hard to resist. The most dramatic shots are usually taken from the ledges; as soon as you reach them you will know why.

There are two areas of ledges, connected by a small sandy beach known as Godrevy Cove. For the best views of the lighthouse it is advisable to shoot from the ledges to the north of the beach, close to Godrevy Point. You can walk along the shore, but an easier walk along the cliff top path will lead you to some steps descending to the northern end of the beach.

From the base of these steps, a rugged area of ledges, rock pools and deep channels stretches out around you. This area is fairly extensive and requires time to fully explore. From this position the island may seem quite insignificant, overwhelmed by the mass of rocks that comprise the ledges.

For the best, uninterrupted views towards the lighthouse walk north over the rocks; within a few minutes the ledge will abruptly give way to a small cove. This elevated viewpoint makes a great position to shoot towards the lighthouse, free from any rocks obscuring the island. On higher tides, several large rocks in front of the ledge make wonderful mini islands, adding strong foreground interest to compositions.

Sunset over the rocky ledges of Godrevy Point, Canon 1Ds Mark III, 24-70mm at 27mm, ISO 50, 2 sec at f/16, October

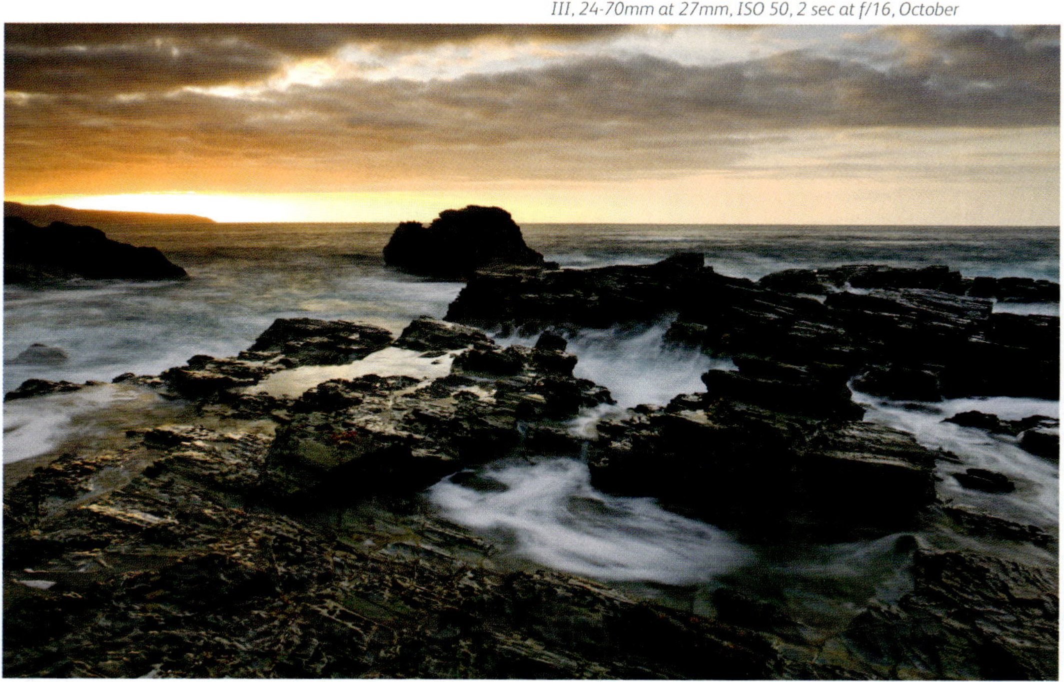

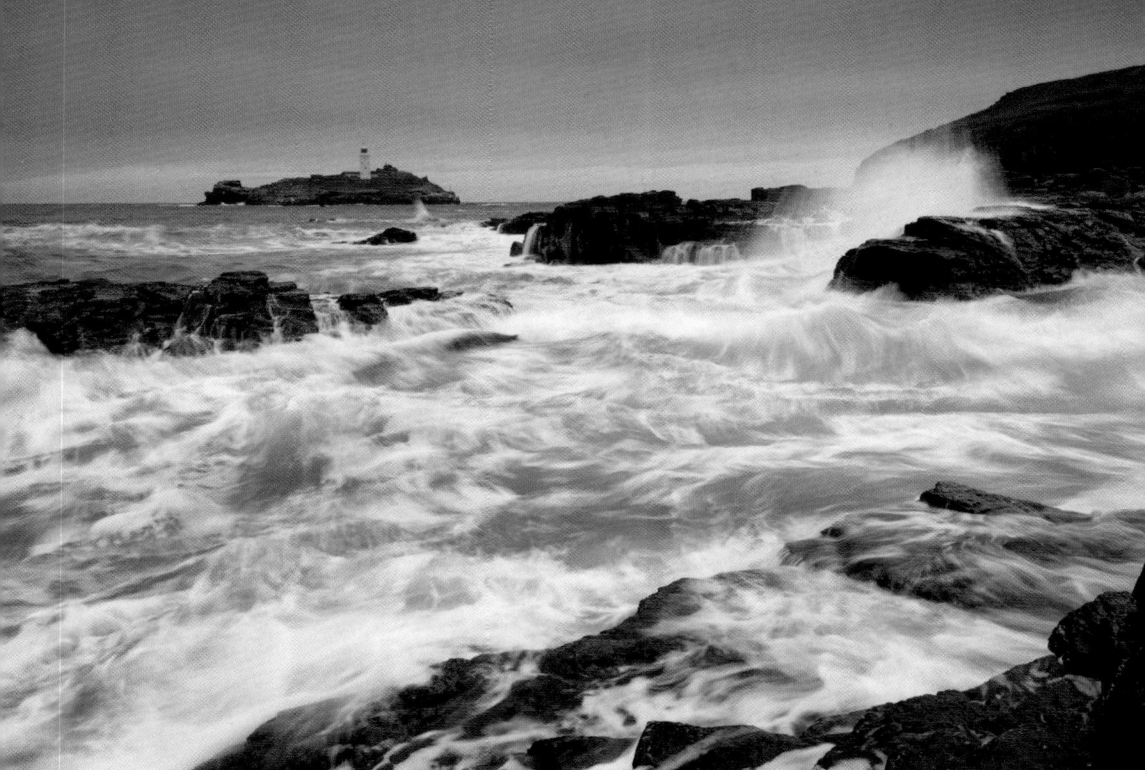

Godrevy Lighthouse and island on a stormy winter evening, Nikon D800E, 17-35mm at 28mm, ISO 400, 0.4 sec at f/11, February

When tide levels are higher, the ledges become easier to photograph from other positions. The wide ledges become separated into a series of channels and mini coves, the water acting as a wonderful simplification subject to any composition. At these times, you can position yourself much further back on the ledge, even as far back as the steps if the tide is very high.

At high tide when waves surge through the channels and crash against the coast, be ready to shoot white water rushing over the ledges or cascading over rocks in a series of waterfalls. Some of the best pictures of Godrevy are captured in such moments. CAUTION: the ledges here are very vulnerable to a pounding from the Atlantic. As photographers, we often feel an urge to shoot from close to the waters edge. But before settling on a position close to the water, watch the area for several minutes and notice how exposed to the waves it is. Be aware of which direction the tide is heading!

As the lighthouse makes for such excellent subject matter there is a tendency to only shoot towards it. But even if the lighthouse wasn't here, the incredible ledges at Godrevy Point would still make it a top location for photography. Once you have photographed the lighthouse, try shooting towards St Ives on the far side of the bay. Being west of Godrevy Point, this direction can offer up beautiful colourful skies around sunset.

How to Get Here

Approaching from the east on the A30, take the Hayle exit and then at the next roundabout turn right signposted Gwithian. Follow this road for 2.5 miles, soon after passing through the village of Gwithian you will see a left turning for Godrevy.

Several National Trust car parks can be found along this road.

Parking Lat/Long: 50.230414, -5.3880414
Parking Postcode: TR27 5ED
Parking OS Grid ref: SW 581 432
Map: OS Explorer Map 102 (1:25 000) Land's End

Accessibility

The ledges are very uneven underfoot and can be slippery in places so good walking boots are recommended. At high tide some rocks can become cut off so know the tide activity at all times and don't put yourself in any areas that could potentially become isolated by the tide. The beach is not suitable for wheelchair users, however there are good views out over the ledges towards the lighthouse from the cliffs near the car park.

Best Time of Year/Day

Godrevy can be photographed equally well throughout the year. Always plan to head out for the afternoon/evening light as the rocks will be lit up by the sun to the west.

The pretty seaside town of St Ives is perhaps the best known and most photographed of Cornwall's fishing villages. St Ives has all the elements that we have come to expect from a Cornish coastal community; pretty whitewashed cottages crowding around narrow winding lanes with a harbour bursting with the colour of many fishing boats. With an oceanic climate, St Ives enjoys some of the mildest winters and warmest summers in Britain.

The unique quality of the light in St Ives is one reason why so many artists have chosen to base themselves here. The opening of the Tate St Ives, a branch of the Tate Gallery, as well as the plethora of galleries in the town centre is evidence that this association shows no signs of diminishing.

What to Shoot and Viewpoints

Viewpoint 1 – View over Porthminster Beach

To fully understand and appreciate St Ives you really need to see it from above. There are elevated areas offering views towards the old part of the town, the best is without question up high above Porthminster Beach.

Great views towards St Ives Head can be achieved from the golden sands of Porthminster, but for the best views head up the coast path running behind the beach. As the path climbs up the cliff side, the view north towards the harbour opens up before becoming obscured by trees. Keep heading up the path and when it crosses a little lane, turn right and continue uphill. Near the top, where the lane joins the A3074, there is a small grassy area clear of trees offering exceptional views over Porthminster towards the harbour.

Sometimes the trees and bushes in this area can become overgrown and clutter the foreground, but with a longer lens and careful attention to composition you should be able to obscure all but one or two twigs, which can be removed later in post processing. Similar views can be achieved along the A3074, but all too often buildings tend to get in the way, partially blocking the view.

With the harbour facing eastwards, this view lends itself to early mornings when a low sun lights up the town. Don't rule out the middle of the day, on a calm summer's day the water is the most brilliant azure colour.

Viewpoint 2 – Harbour

Although it contains fishing boats and stone harbour walls, St Ives is far from a typical harbour. At low tide, water drains from the whole harbour leaving boats stranded on a large sandy beach. Although this allows you to get up close to the colourful fishing boats, unless you are looking to shoot close-up details it is probably best to plan your visit on a mid to high tide.

Most fishing vessels tend to cluster near the harbour wall, known as Smeaton's Pier with the best shots over the harbour usually taken from the pier at dawn or dusk. From this slightly elevated viewpoint you can use a wide angle lens over the boat-filled harbour towards St Ives' church tower on the opposite side of the bay.

For views back towards Smeaton's Pier head around to the opposite side of the harbour. The view is lovely all along the wharf, or standing on West Pier, but does lack foreground. There are some photogenic rocks which make good foreground interest just a little further. After passing West Pier continue along Pendola Walk, keeping a keen eye out for crashing waves if the tide is high, and head along The Warren. Just along this narrow lane, a little cut between houses leads down to a small viewing area where you can find large rocky ledges to shoot from.

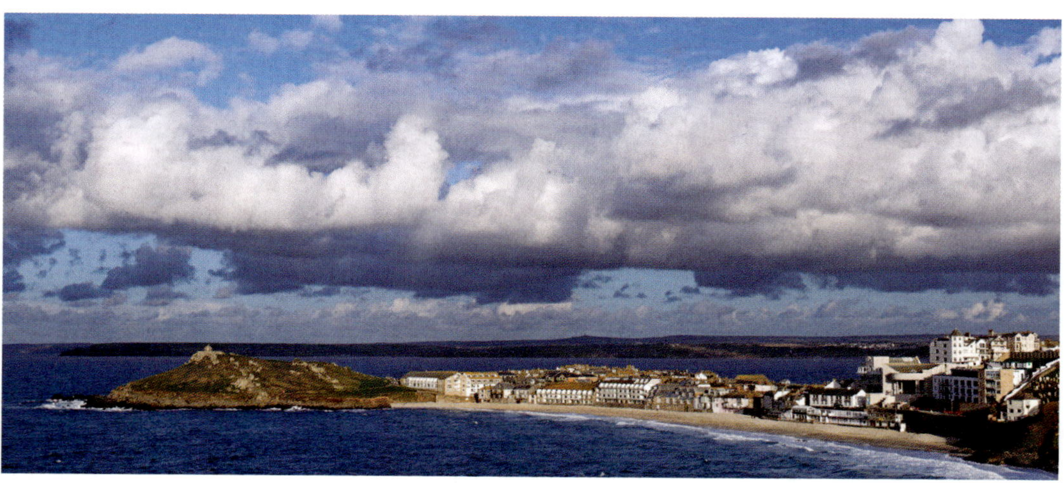

Looking east over Porthmeor Beach from Clodgy Point, Nikon D800E, 24-70mm at 48mm, ISO 100, 1/25 sec at f/11, March

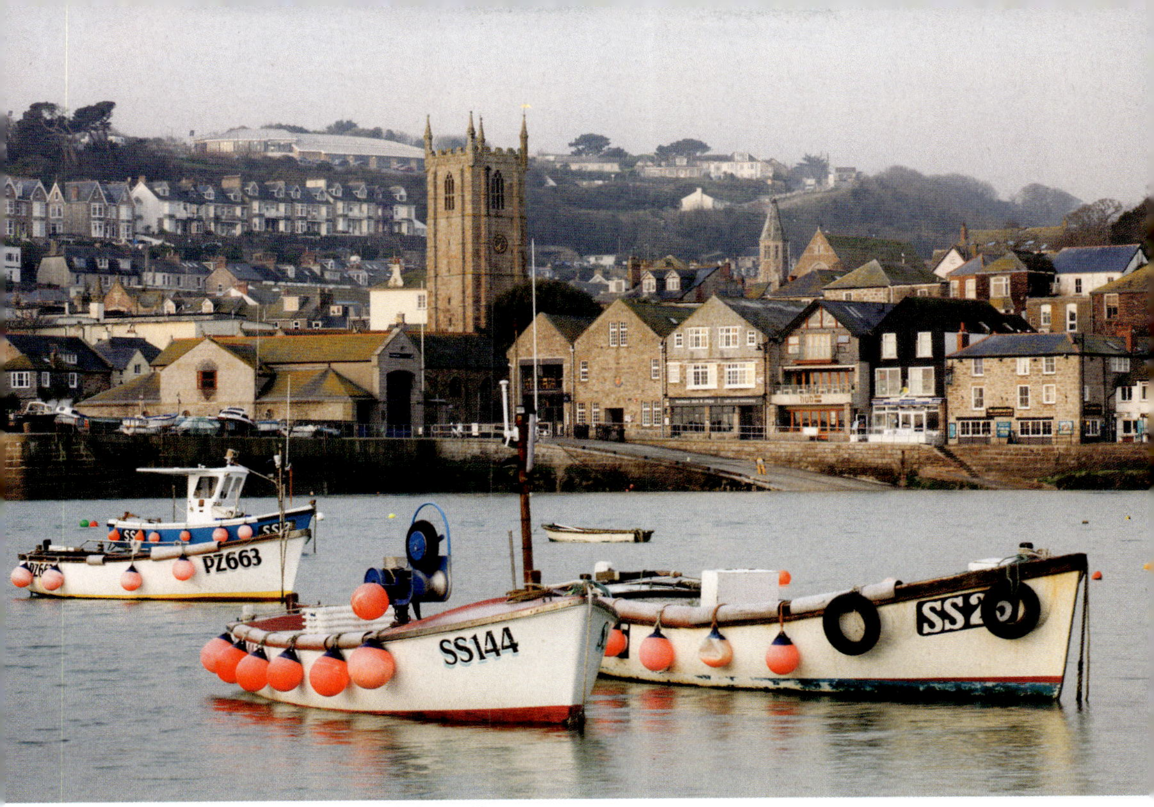

View across St Ive's harbour to Saint Ia's Church, Canon 1Ds
Mark III, 70-200mm at 104mm, ISO 100, 0.5 sec at f/14, March

St Ive's from above Porthminster Beach, Nikon D800,
70-200mm at 78mm, ISO 100, 0.8 sec at f/8, April

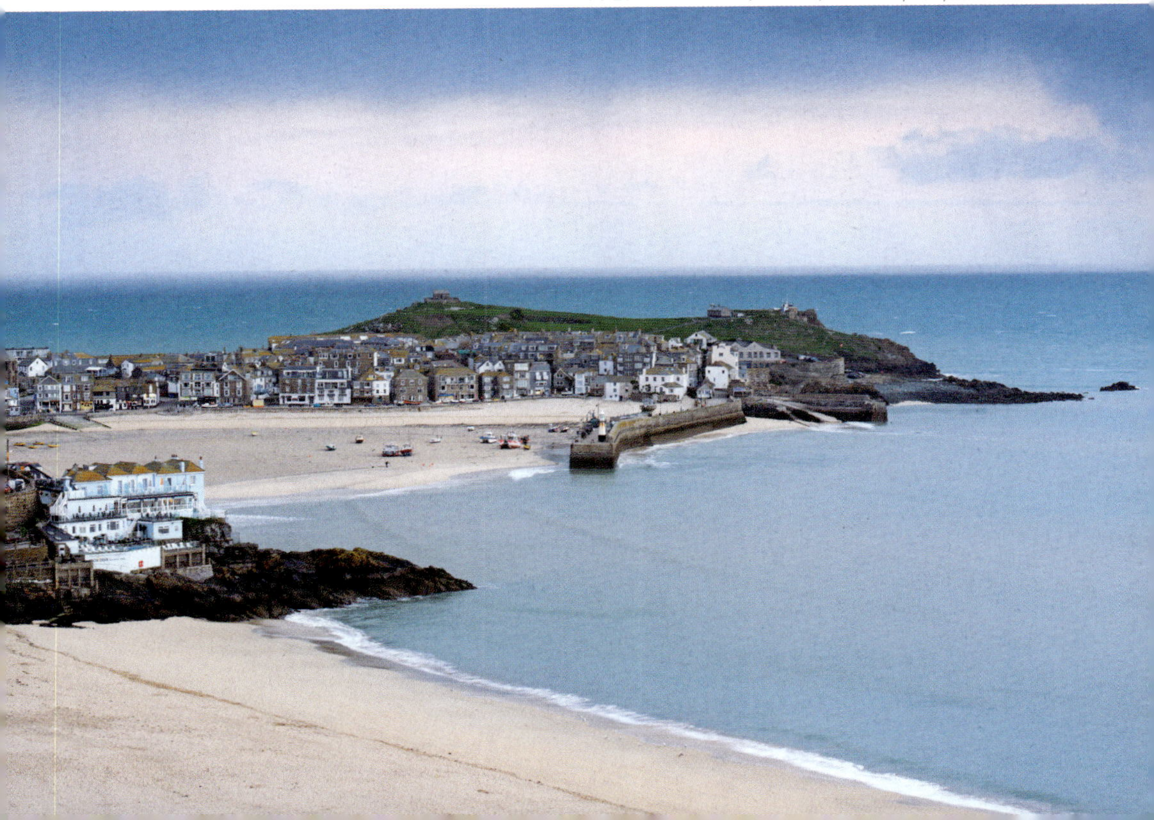

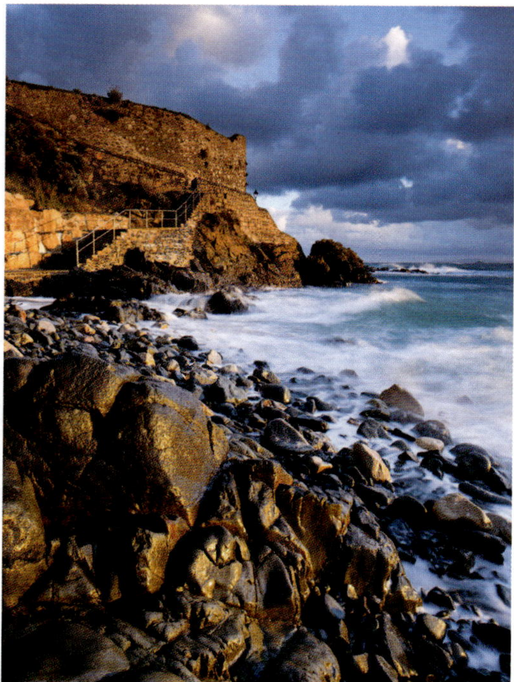

Gorgeous morning light on the rocky coast at Bamalûz Point, Nikon D800E, 17-35mm at 24mm, ISO 100, 1.3 sec at f/13. December

Viewpoint 3 – Porthmeor Beach

Facing the full force of the Atlantic the spectacular Porthmeor Beach has an entirely different feel to it than the sheltered bays on the other side of St Ives Head. This golden sandy beach faces roughly west, making it an ideal location to shoot at sunset.

High up on the beach, especially on the western side, the sandy expanse is broken up by a number of inky black boulders. These provide strong foreground interest when shooting along the beach towards the headland known as The Island, and on a receding tide you will find each boulder surrounded by its own little tidal pool.

If you continue walking past the beach towards Clodgy Point you can achieve excellent wide vistas back over Porthmeor Beach and St Ives. The Tate St Ives overlooks the beach and makes for a great background subject, as does The Island at the eastern edge of the beach.

Several viewpoints near Clodgy Point will allow you to gain suitable elevation to reveal the sea both behind as well as in front of the town.

Viewpoint 4 – Porthgwidden & Bamalûz Beaches

While Porthminster and Porthmeor are by far the biggest and most popular beaches, Porthgwidden and Bamalûz are possibly the best from a landscape photographer's perspective. Both these beaches face east making them ideal sunrise locations and each benefits from areas of rocks, perfect for capturing crashing waves.

Bamalûz is probably the least known of St Ives' many beaches, it is more of a rocky cove, especially at high tide. Squeezed between a harbour wall to the south and Bamalûz Point to the north, the cove is overlooked by steep stone walls and buildings.

All this doesn't sound particularly appealing and yet this beach really does work well in photographs. The beach consists of golden sandy areas but the real interest lies in the rocky shore further up so is ideal to shoot on higher tides. At dawn you can shoot over the shore towards colourful skies, but the beach looks its best after the sun has risen. In those moments after the sun has broken the horizon the wet rocks and stone walls turn to pure gold.

Viewpoint 5 – The Island

At the eastern edge of St Ives with the sea on three sides, the Island makes a great backdrop when viewed from many parts of the town. Perched on the summit a tiny chapel has held a lonely vigil for centuries. When photographed from far away in the town this chapel, dedicated to the fisherman of St Ives, stands head and shoulders above the white washed cottages, appearing as a protective guardian over its inhabitants. From up close it can make a strong photographic subject too; a wide-angle lens allows a simple but effective composition, especially with a good sunset sky beyond.

A footpath offers easy access around the headland but, while the views out to sea are pleasing, they do not offer much photographic potential. From the elevated position of the Island however, you can get great shots looking west over Porthmeor Beach, especially when late sun side lights the buildings facing the beach.

How to Get Here

St Ives is just off the A30 is West Cornwall. Being a popular holiday resort it is well signposted and easy to find. There are several large car parks in the town. A note of caution; some of the lanes leading to car parks are extremely narrow!

St Ives Railway Station
Lat/Long: 50.209098, -5.4782617
OS Grid Ref: SW 519 401
Postcode: TR26 2EQ
Map: OS Explorer Map 102 (1:25 000) Land's End

Accessibility

Being a popular holiday destination, access is excellent throughout St Ives. Most of the viewpoints described here are partially or fully accessible for wheelchair users.

Best Time of Year/Day

With so many beaches facing various directions St Ives can be photographed at any time of day, and at any time of the year. The precise times for each location have been described above. It can be a busy destination throughout the year, but in summer expect large numbers of visitors during the day!

Opposite: Low tide on the sandy Porthmeor Beach, Nikon D800E, 17-35mm at 20mm, ISO 100, 0.8 sec at f/13. December

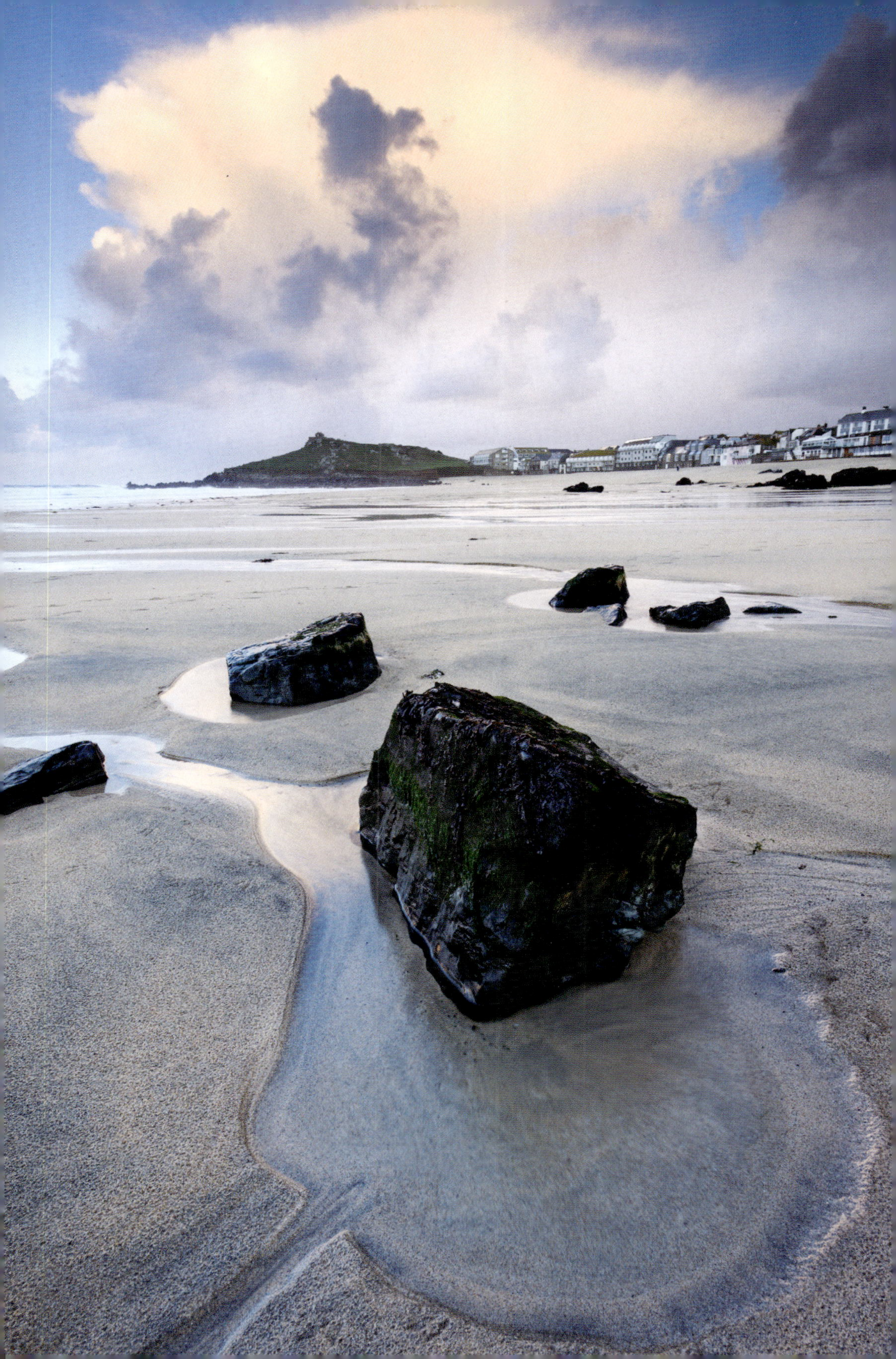

Crumbling ruins of abandoned engine houses form an iconic part of the Cornish landscape; reminders of the county's rich tin mining heritage. Nowhere is this association more evident than on Cornwall's dramatic coastline where engine houses make lonely wardens of the cliff tops, continually withstanding the elements thrown in by the Atlantic Ocean.

Of all Cornwall's remaining engine houses, perhaps none are as dramatically located as the Crown mines of Botallack. The whole area is rich in the remains of mining buildings, mostly on the cliff tops. What makes the Crown mines unusual is their position low down the cliffs, precariously close to the crashing waves of the Atlantic.

The twin engine houses will be familiar to fans of the BBC Poldark series, making many appearances in the show. The mine extends out for about 400 metres under the Atlantic, its deepest shaft being 500 metres below sea level.

What to Shoot and Viewpoints

The engine houses look their dramatic best when photographed from the cliffs immediately to the south. From the South West Coast Path, several smaller trails lead down the cliffs, providing access to a lower viewpoint. From the cliff edge you can gain an unrestricted view into the cove far below the engine houses. The rocky ledges in this cove provide fantastic foreground, especially when fierce waves crash against them, leaving trails of white water surging around the base of the cliffs. Dramatic seas below combined with

View of the Botallack mines from the cliff top coast path, Canon 1Ds Mark III, 70-200mm at 91mm, ISO 50, 1 sec at f/16. April

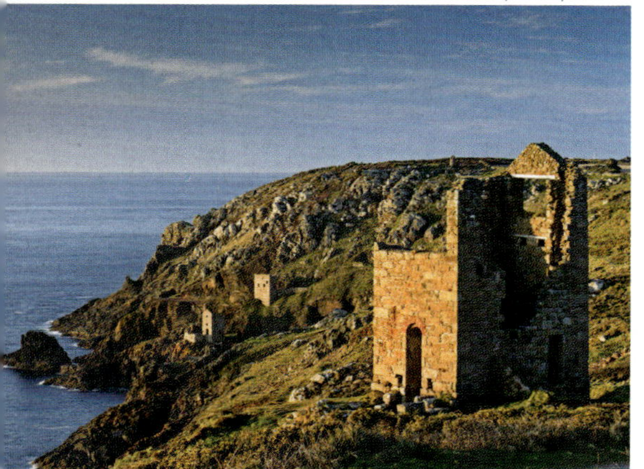

rugged cliffs all around, the Crowns mines epitomise Cornish coastal photograph.

The Crowns can be photographed together with a third engine house from a much less typical viewpoint further away. Heading south along the coast path, you will encounter two more engine houses. Pass by the first and continue to the more ramshackle ruined second building. From this position you can shoot this attractive ruin in the foreground while also including the Crowns' engine houses far away near the base of the cliffs.

Turning around, the path leads right up to the Crowns mines. Just to experience these incredible ruins from up close is reward enough for the walk. Photographing them from this position is much more difficult, and not recommended due to the danger of falling.

How to Get Here

The village of Botallack is only a mile north of St Just, on the B3306. As soon as you see the Botallack village sign, take the left turning. Continue through the village and take the left turning onto a gravel track just before the road bends sharply to the right. Follow the gravel track past some cottages and after a few hundred yards you will find a car park on the right, next to the ruins of Botallack Mine.

Parking Lat/Long: 50.142846, -5.6907525
Parking OS Grid Ref: SW 364 335
Parking Postcode: TR19 7QG (Botallack village)
Map: OS Explorer Map 102 (1:25 000) Land's End

Accessibility

The best viewpoint is only 10 minutes from the car park, although it does involve a steep walk downhill on an uneven footpath. As the cliffs here have sheer drops, and are subject to continual erosion extreme caution should be applied when venturing close to any edge.

Best Time of Year/Day

The coast at Botallack can be photographed at any time of year always in the late afternoon and evening when the sun descends over the Atlantic. At these times, the tin mines and cliffs will glow golden in the late evening sunlight.

This stretch of coastline can be beautiful to visit in late spring, when sea pinks are in flower. These delicate wildflowers make beautiful colourful subjects when photographed in the foregrounds of cliff top seascapes.

Opposite: Crowns engine houses perched precariously on the cliffs, Nikon D800E, 24-70mm at 38mm, ISO 100, 8 sec at f/11. June

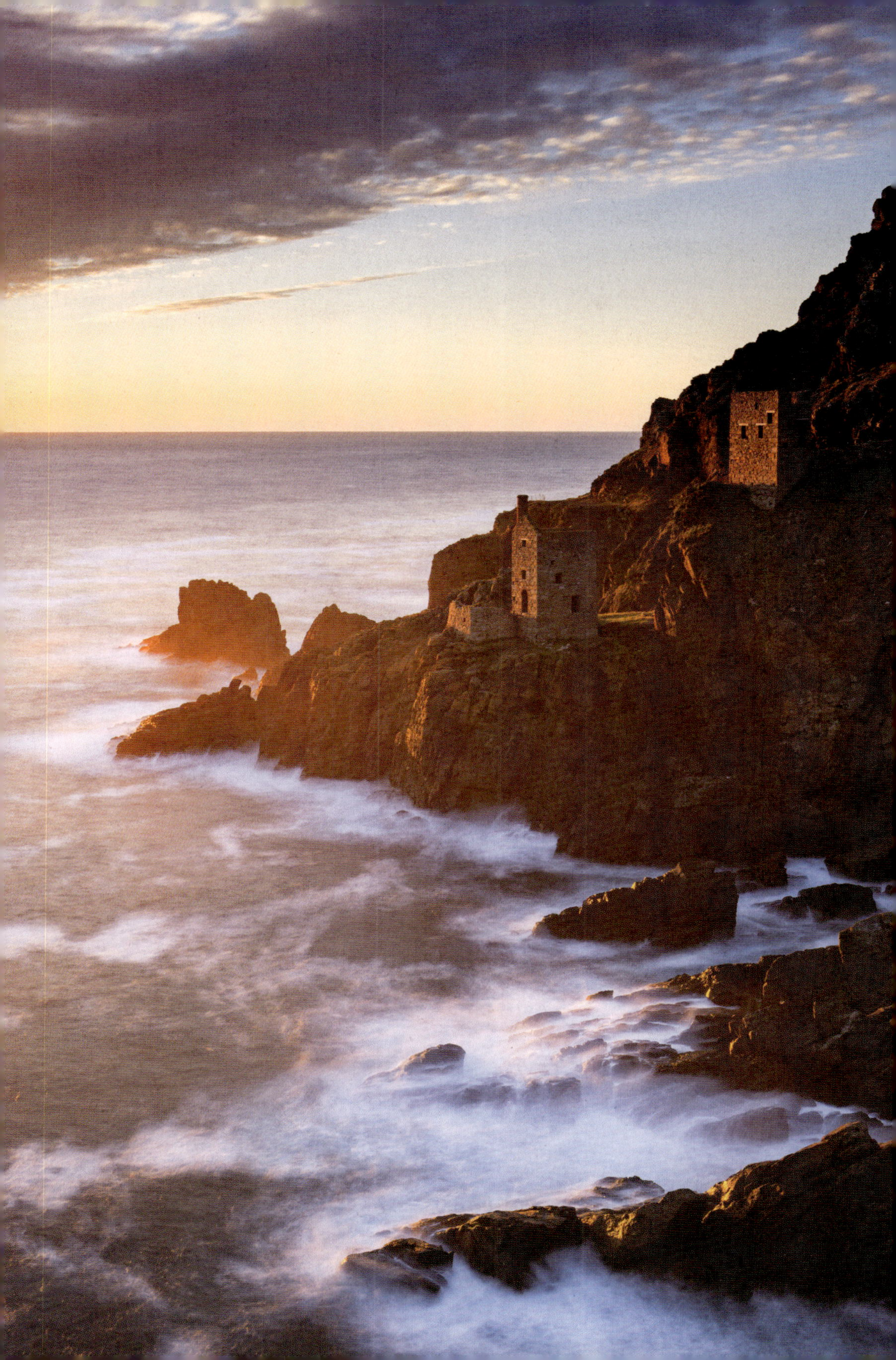

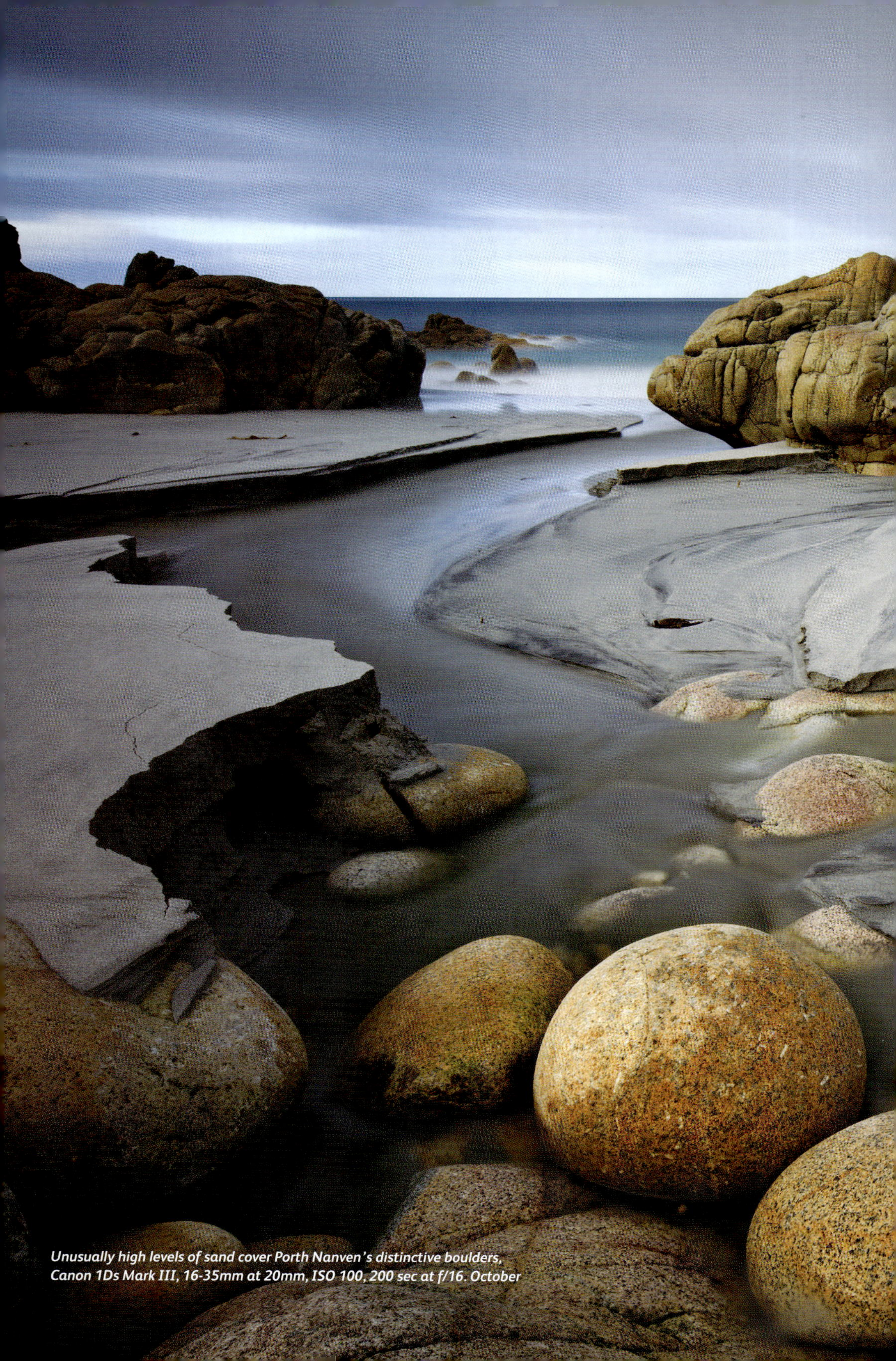

Unusually high levels of sand cover Porth Nanven's distinctive boulders,
Canon 1Ds Mark III, 16-35mm at 20mm, ISO 100, 200 sec at f/16. October

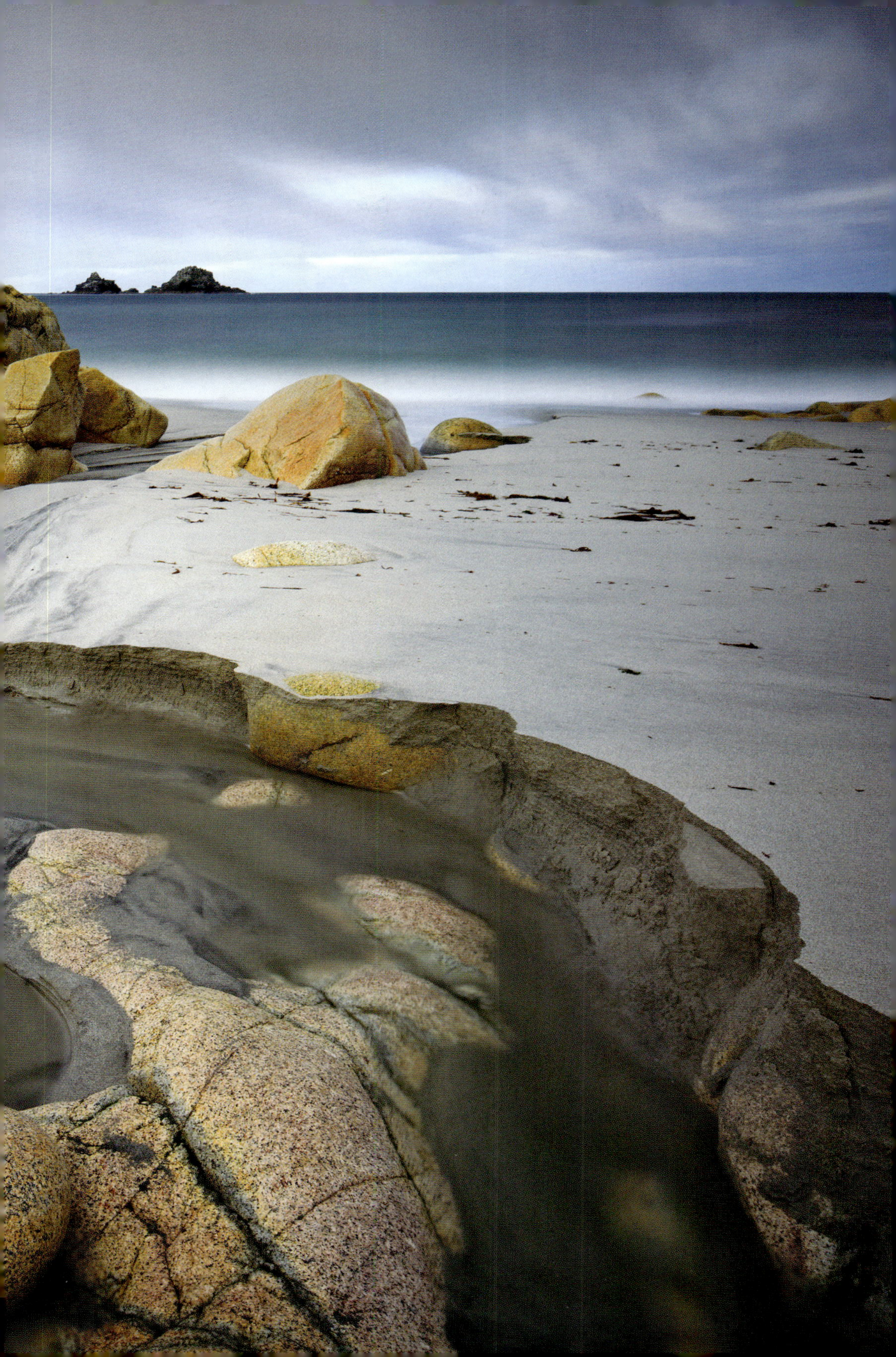

Unless you are a local or a photographer you will probably never have heard of Porth Nanven. This tiny cove on the West Cornish coast seems to have hidden itself from the mass of holidaymakers that descend on Cornwall each summer. Perhaps the absence of a large sandy beach or lack of amenities deters most people. In any case, we should rejoice that the cove has remained so quiet and unspoiled, for this is surely one of the world's most amazing coastal locations for landscape photography.

Porth Nanven has all the ingredients to make a fantastic seascape. The granite here provides wonderful cliffs; crumbled into impressive stacks, or smoothed by waves into gorgeous curves. Off shore, a shapely double island named The Brisons provides a fine backdrop. But what really makes Porth Nanven special is the abundance of large granite boulders shaped by the sea over thousands of years into smooth rounded stones resembling giant dinosaur eggs.

What to Shoot and Viewpoints

Viewpoint 1 – The Cove

Most photographers visiting Porth Nanven will head straight down to the cove. As you reach the beach you have to carefully navigate the boulders to get closer to the water's edge. This isn't as difficult as it may at first look as the boulders are usually not slippery. On rare occasions the beach is covered in sand; although this makes access easier it usually means the beach is less photogenic. The classic viewpoint can be reached by crossing the stream and setting up just in front of the cliff face.

At this position, there are usually fewer boulders leaving space to reveal the beautiful smooth curving ledges.

Viewpoint 2 – Ledges

For something a little different head to the raised ledges on the right hand side of the shore. There is a pathway through the rocks leading away from the cove. Along this path you will find a number of deep rock pools which at sunset can reflect colourful skies. This elevated position also makes a great place for shooting back across the cove in evening sunlight. The low sun setting out to sea can create spectacular rich side-lighting on the granite cliffs and also light up the crashing Atlantic waves.

Heart shaped marking on a granite boulder on the beach, Canon 1Ds Mark III, 16-35mm at 35mm, ISO 100, 0.3 sec at f/16. April

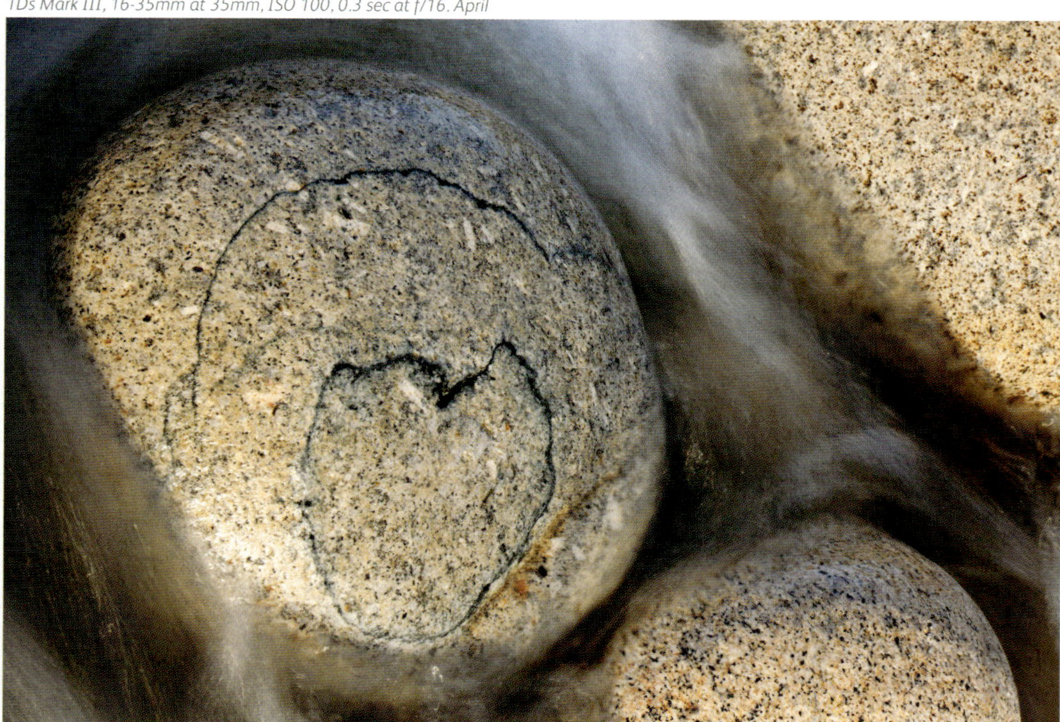

Opposite: Colourful sunset over the Brisons, Canon 1Ds Mark III, 16-35mm at 18mm, ISO 50, 2.5 sec at f/16. September

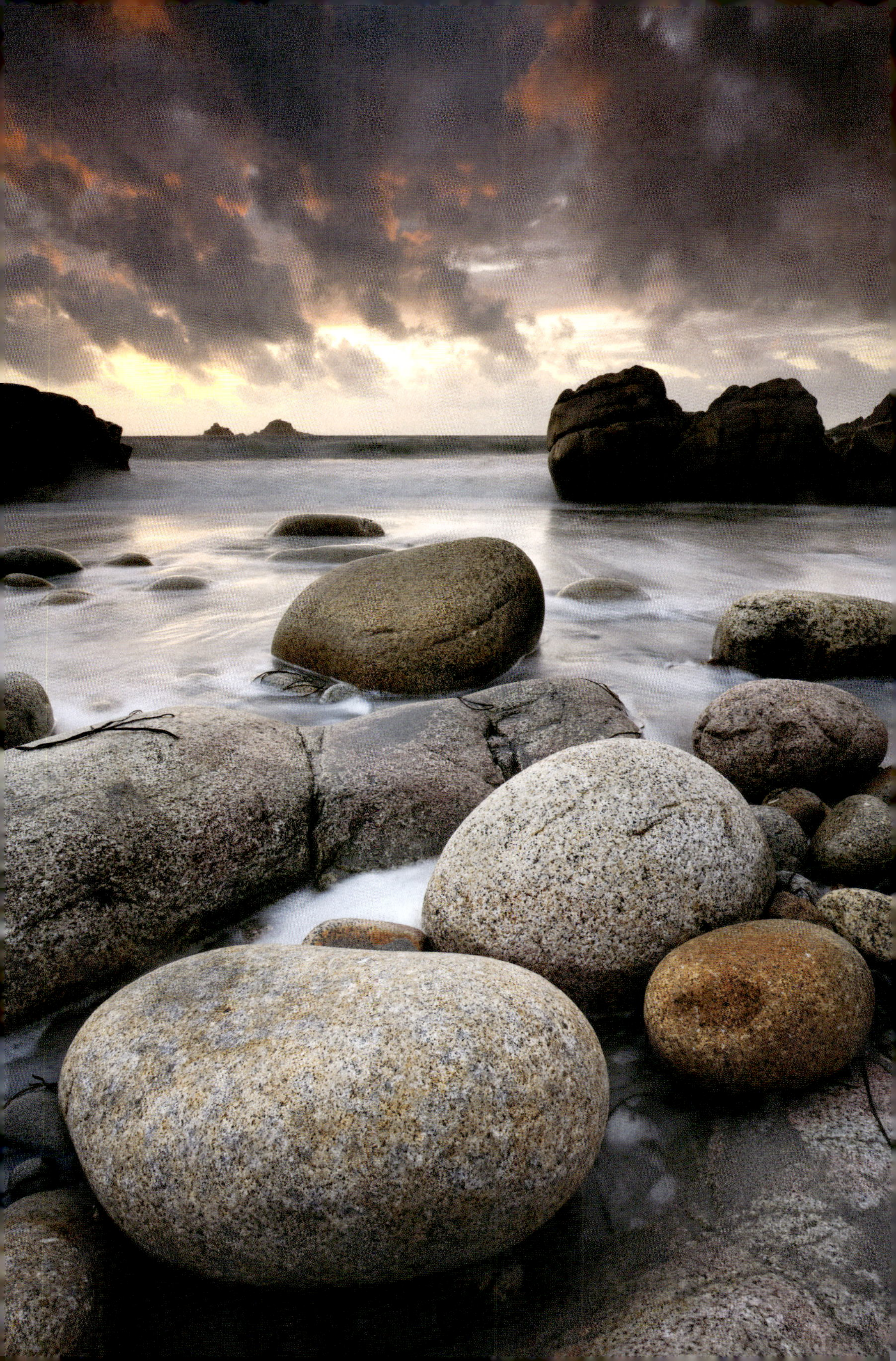

Viewpoint 3 – Nanven

A 10 minute walk over the cliffs to the south of Porth Nanven brings you to an even less visited location. Named on the map as simply 'Nanven', this area has many of the same qualities that make its big brother so popular amongst photographers, yet feels very different. It also takes more effort to reach; at first you need to walk around a narrow coastal footpath before climbing down a little to reach the shore.

When you do reach the shore you will notice the difference immediately. Although there are still rounded boulders here, they are far fewer in number. Instead the whole area is a network of eroded lumpy granite ledges, channels and rock pools, with the occasional boulder here and there. With waves sweeping through the channels and over ledges, there is plenty of material to keep you occupied as you wait for a colourful sunset to develop over the Atlantic.

Opposite: Alternative view of the Brisons from the less visited Nanven, Nikon D800E, 17-35mm at 28mm, ISO 160, 5 sec at f/13.

Classic view of the ledges and boulders of Porth Nanven, Nikon D800E, 17-35mm at 25mm, ISO 50, 20 sec at f/13. December

How to Get Here

From Penzance head west initially on the A30 before turning onto the A3071 towards St Just. After 6 miles you will reach St Just. Drive through the town and turn left into Cape Cornwall Road, and take the second left into West Place then Bosorne Road. Follow the sign for 'Cot Valley' which will lead you out of the town towards Porth Nanven reached in just 5 minutes. The road is narrow and steep with few passing places. Park at the end just above the cove.

Parking Lat/Long: 50.118935, -5.699589
Parking OS Grid Ref: SW 356 308
Parking Postcode: TR19 7NT (nearby YHA hostel)
Map: OS Explorer Map: 102 (1:25 000) Land's End, Penzance and St Ives

Accessibility

There is a small area with parking for several cars just above the cove. From there it is only a few minutes walk down into the cove. As mentioned above, access to the beach involves walking over large boulders so apply caution especially if algae are evident on the rocks. Not suitable for wheelchair users.

Best Time of Year/Day

With the sun descending over the Atlantic Porth Nanven makes an ideal sunset location any time. At high tide most of the cove is under water, so best to visit is when the tide is mid to low, and ideally falling. This ensures the rocks are still wet and sparkling. On windy days when the prevailing wind is blowing in off the Atlantic, sea spray can make it difficult to photograph at Porth Nanven. If possible, plan your visit on a day with low wind.

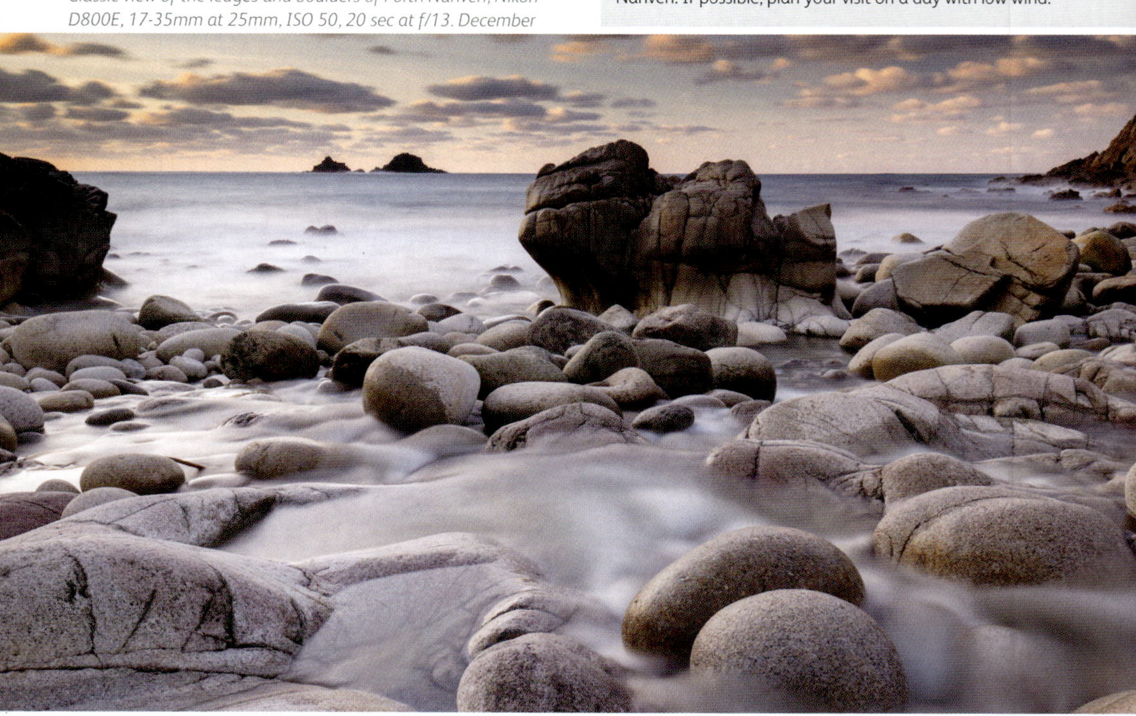

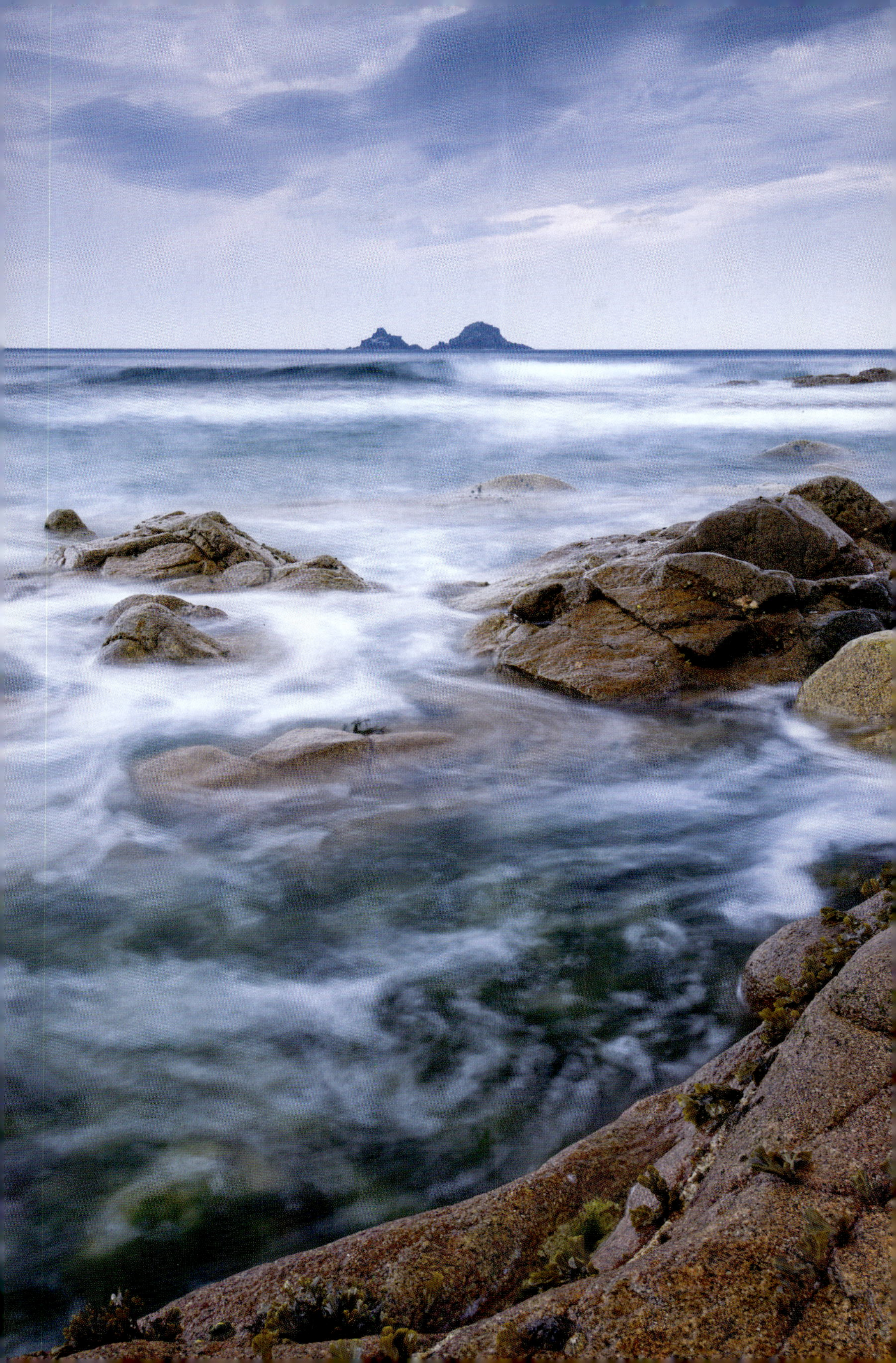

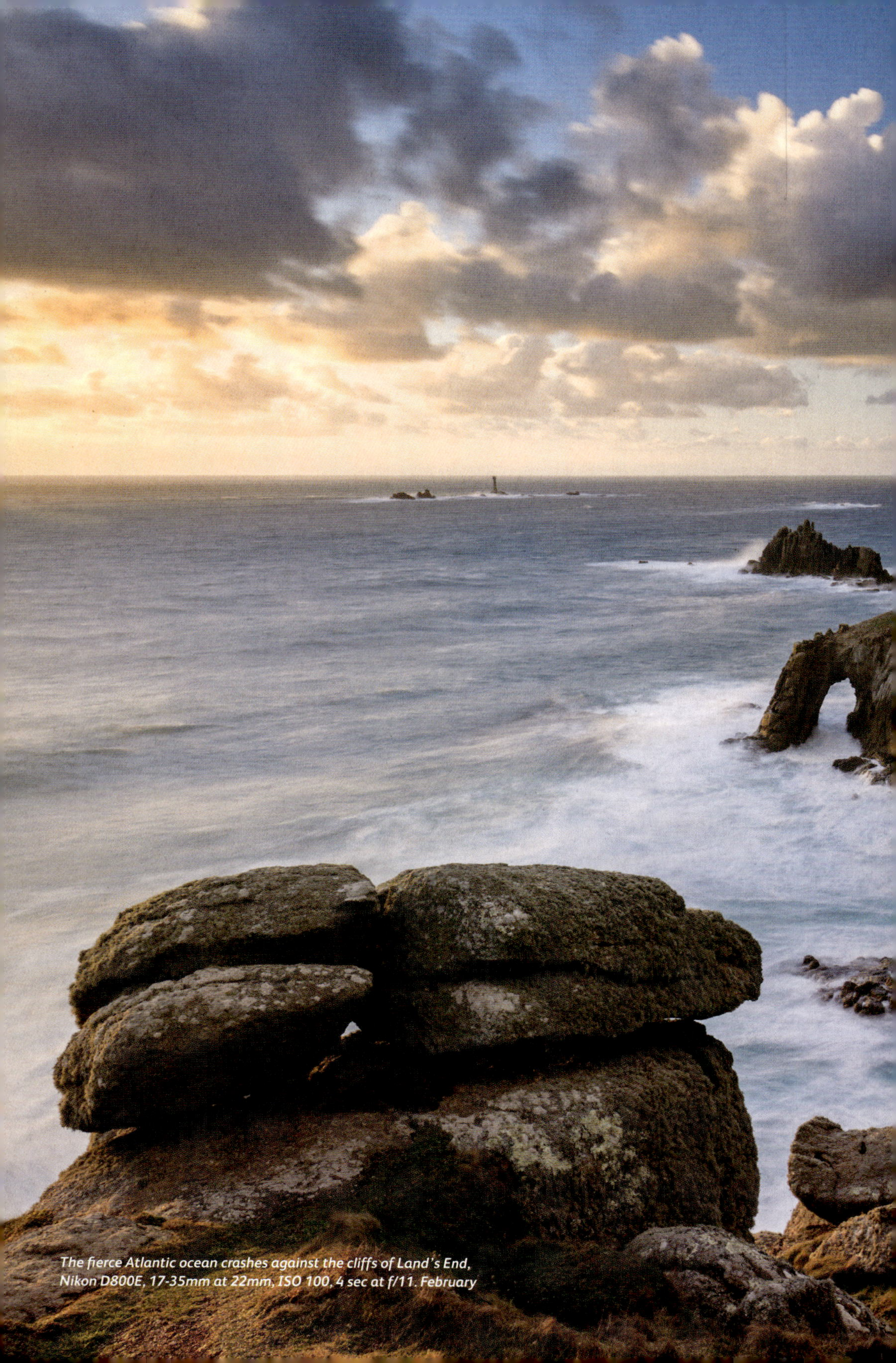

The fierce Atlantic ocean crashes against the cliffs of Land's End,
Nikon D800E, 17-35mm at 22mm, ISO 100, 4 sec at f/11. February

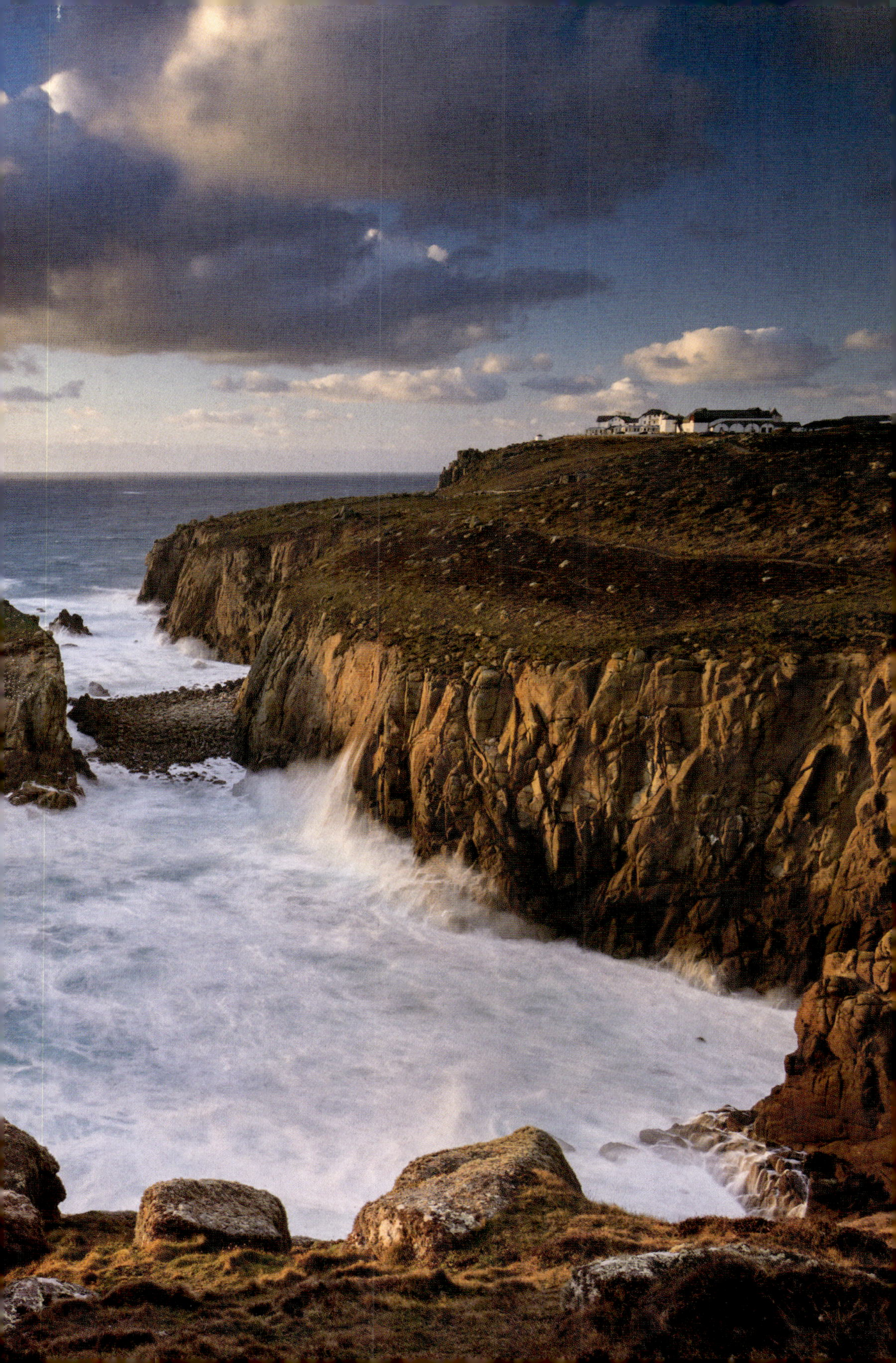

Land's End

Boasting some of the most dramatic cliffs in England, Land's End is much more than just a famous signpost and an under-whelming theme park. Once you get past the commercial buildings the coastal landscape is absolutely exquisite and offers a wealth of viewpoints for seascape photography.

Along with towering granite cliffs, there are several islands just offshore from Land's End which make compelling photographic subjects. Further out to sea, the rocky Longships islets are home to one of the most dramatically situated lighthouses in the UK.

Amid all this spectacular scenery the Atlantic constantly battles with the land, continually sending mighty waves to crash against the cliffs with terrifying force. Fortunately this drama mostly takes place well below the cliff tops, giving you the chance to photograph it in complete safety.

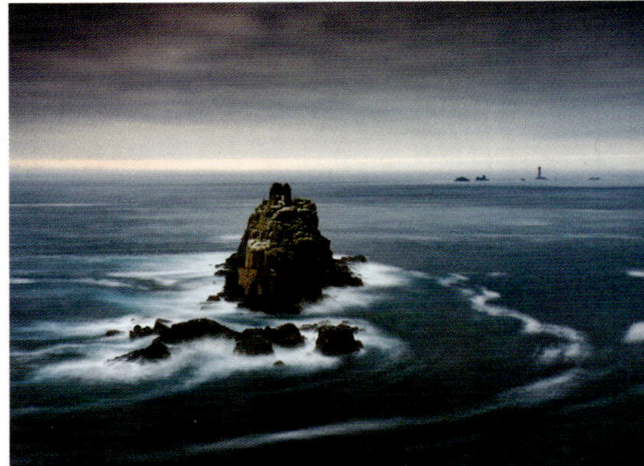

Longships lighthouse and the Armed Knight island, Canon 1Ds Mark III, 17-40mm at 40mm, ISO 50, 20 sec at f/16. May

What to Shoot and Viewpoints

Viewpoint 1 – Enys Dodnan

This is the vista that the majority of landscape photographers visiting Land's End aspire to shoot. From the car park, follow a footpath south for around 15 minutes away from Land's End, which firstly heads past a small tourist farm and then out onto the cliff tops. As the coastal scenery begins to open up, you will get your first view of the magnificent Enys Dodnan island just out to sea to your right. This huge chunk of granite is impressive enough, but as you walk further you will notice the island has an enormous natural arch running through it.

Just behind Enys Dodnan, another islet curiously named the Armed Knight provides a secondary subject. Photographed up close both these islands, together with the shapely granite cliffs of the mainland make a perfectly balanced composition.

If that's not enough the towering cliffs, rugged rocky foreground and distant Longships lighthouse all come together delightfully in the most perfect wide-angle seascape. Even the Land's End cliff top hotel compliments the scenery, adding scale to any picture.

Viewpoint 2 – Pordenack Point

If you can bear to turn your back on the classic view, continue walking away from Land's End. After five minutes you will find yourself looking over an entirely different coastal view. Pordenack Point may not have the arch, lighthouses or island of its more illustrious neighbour but the view is possibly even more dramatic.

Soaring walls of granite rise vertically out of the Atlantic and recede in a series of jagged headlands towards Gwennap Head to the south. When the Atlantic is crashing against the cliffs it is difficult to imagine a more dramatic coastal location anywhere.

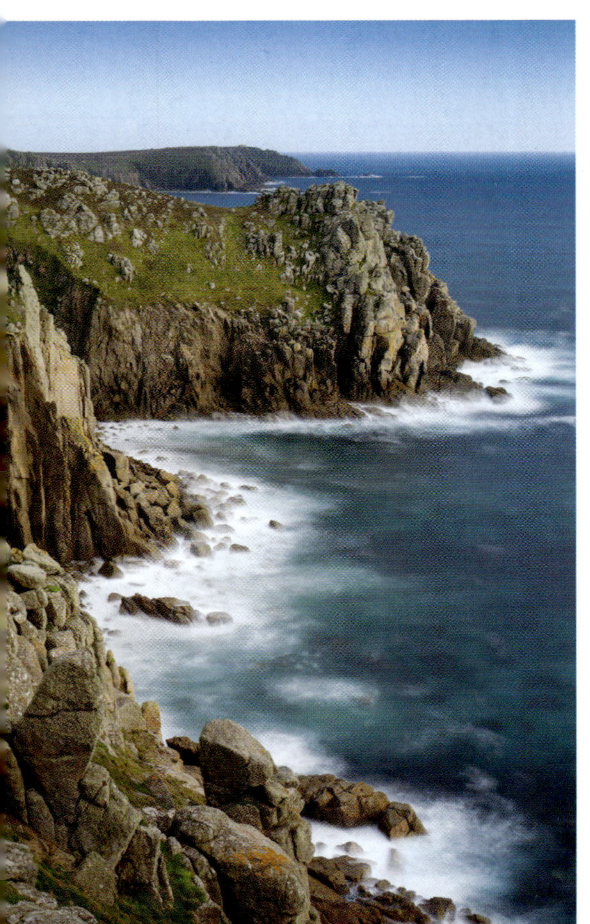

Looking southeast towards Carn Boel and Gwennap Head, Nikon D800E, 24-70mm at 48mm, ISO 50, 15 sec at f/13. September

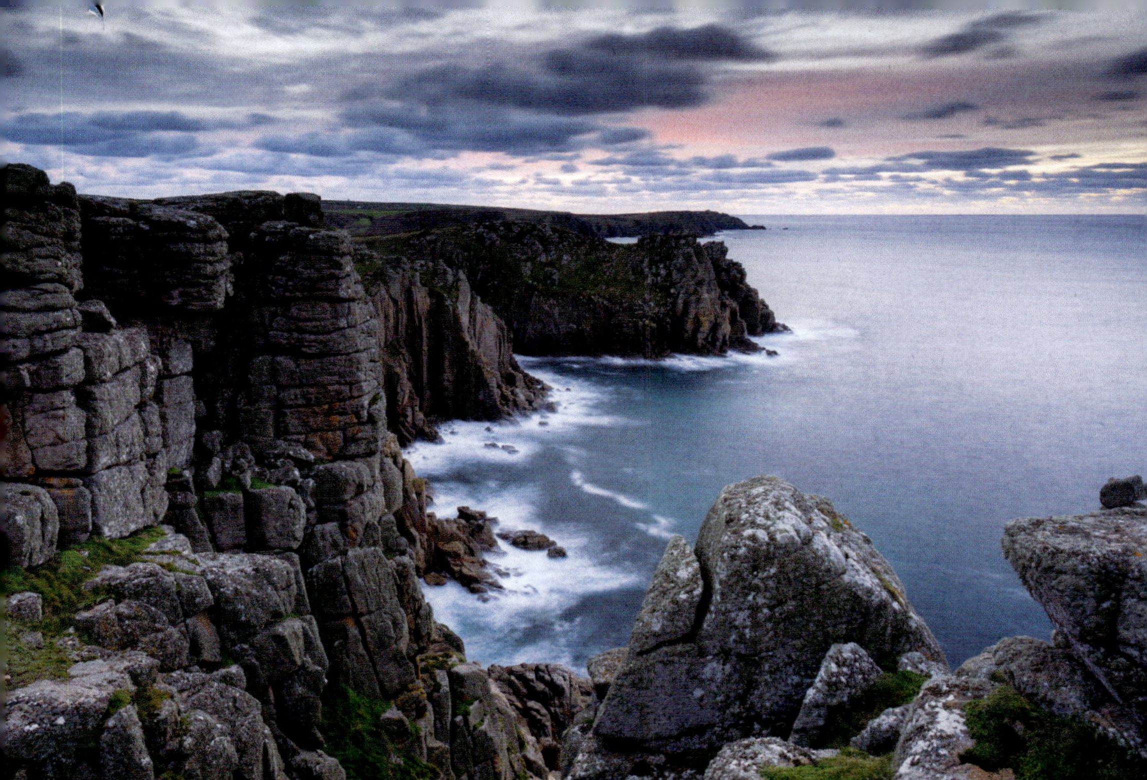

Pink dawn sky above granite battlements of Pordenack Point, Nikon D800E, 17-35mm at 22mm, ISO 100, 25 sec at f/11. December

How to Get Here

From Penzance head west on the A30 following the signs for Land's End. After approximately 10 miles the A30 ends at the gates of Land's End. Through the gates, you will find the car park on the left.

Parking Lat/Long: 50.064771, -5.7127034
Parking OS Grid Ref: SW 344 249
Parking Postcode: TR19 7AA
Map: OS Explorer Map 102 (1:25 000) Land's End

Accessibility

As Land's End is a major tourist destination, facilities are good. There is a large car park, toilets and various places to get food and drink. There are wheelchair-friendly footpaths around the well-known areas near the hotel and famous signpost, however the further you venture the footpaths become uneven and narrow in places.

Best Time of Year/Day

As the sun sets out to sea over the Atlantic, Land's End makes an ideal location to shoot in the evening all year round. Late afternoon/evening sunlight will illuminate the cliffs and islands, turning them to beautiful golden tones. Then once the sun has set, any clouds above the cliffs will be tinged pink. In the summer, if you time your visit well you may be able to shoot the sun setting through the natural arch on Enys Dodnan.

Viewpoint 3 – Armed Knight and Longships Lighthouse

From Land's End on a stormy winter day waves can be seen crashing against Longships lighthouse with tremendous force, sometimes even obscuring the tower completely in explosions of white. With a long telephoto lens, this can make for stunning photos showing the power of an angry Atlantic ocean, as well as the extreme strength of a lighthouse to withstand such force.

Telephoto shots of Longships can be captured from anywhere on Land's End, but for wider pictures showcasing the lighthouse a little more thought is required. The headland at Carn Greeb provides a really interesting vantage point to shoot towards the lighthouse. From this position the Armed Knight makes an intriguing foreground subject which provides an excellent counterbalance to the lighthouse in the background. Often, waves crash around the rocky islet leaving long lines of white foam curving around the island. These white longs make wonderful extra interest to seascape photographs, especially when shooting with a long exposure of several seconds.

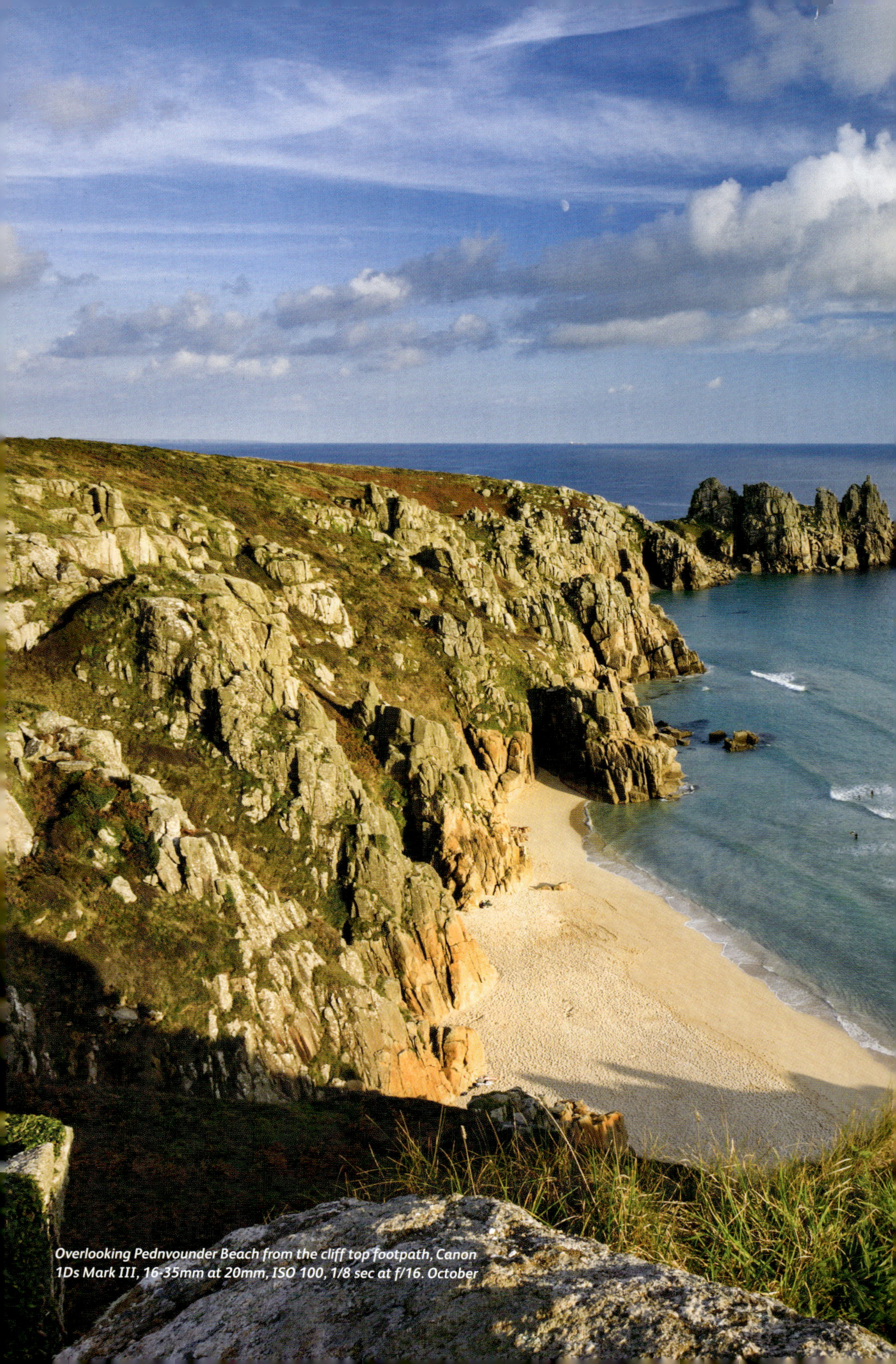

Overlooking Pednvounder Beach from the cliff top footpath, Canon
1Ds Mark III, 16-35mm at 20mm, ISO 100, 1/8 sec at f/16. October

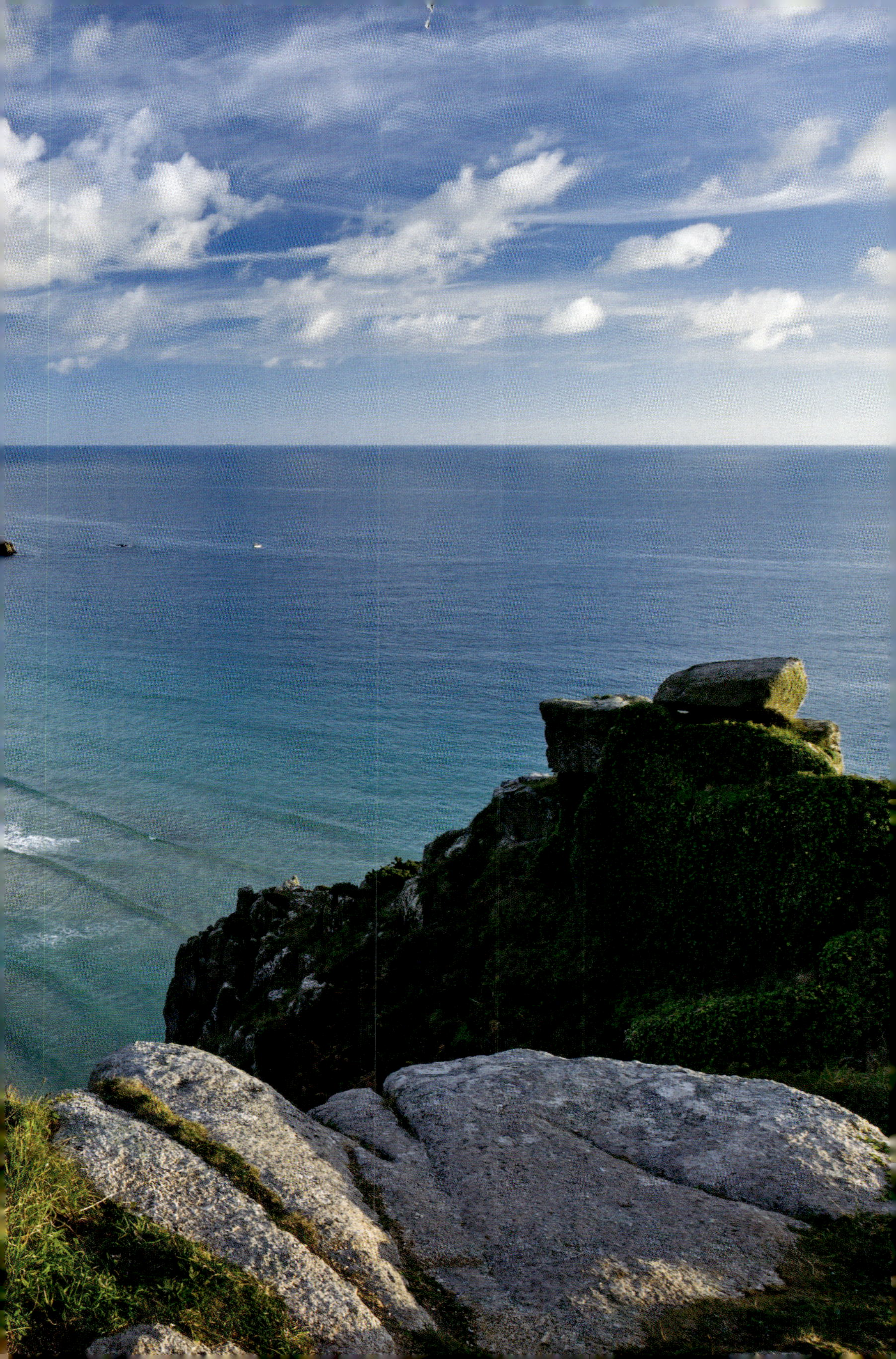

Pednvounder Beach

Just around the corner from the popular Porthcurno beach, neighbouring Pednvounder is a far more secluded location. So much so in fact that Pednvounder is sometimes used an unofficial naturist beach.

This beach has to be one of the finest to be found anywhere in the United Kingdom. Pure golden sand backed by steep granite cliffs, the beach at certain tides surrounds a turquoise tidal lagoon. Beyond the crashing waves a gorgeous granite headland, Treryn Dinas, provides a spectacular backdrop to the beach.

The headland name is often mistaken for Logan Rock, but this single 80 tonne boulder is actually found near the top of the headland. Logan Rock is a finely balanced stone which historically could be rocked by applying just a small amount of pressure. Logan Rock became infamous in the early 19th century when the rock was purposefully dislodged by a Royal Naval Officer, Lieutenant Hugh Goldsmith and his crew. After a public outcry the Admiralty ordered Goldsmith to reposition the rock in its original location. This proved a monumental task involving months of labour.

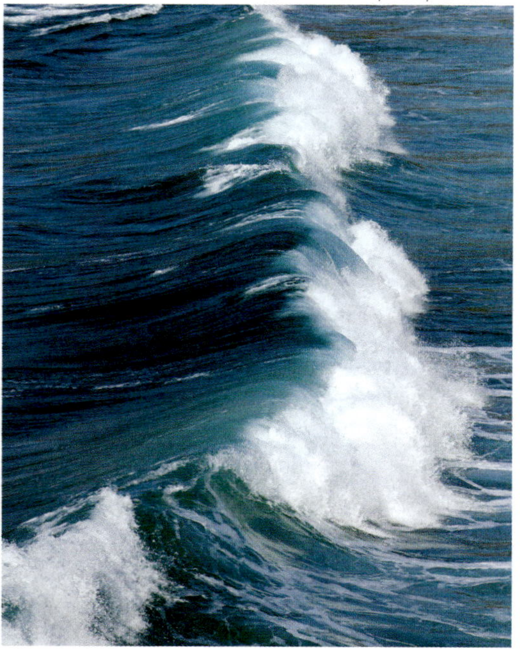

Atlantic roller photographed from Treryn Dinas, Canon 1Ds Mark III, 70-200mm at 200mm, ISO 200, 1/800 sec at f/8. September

What to Shoot and Viewpoints

Viewpoint 1 – Treen Cliff

Pednvounder offers a great many cliff top vistas from which to shoot the beach. The cliffs are connected via the South West Coast Path, so access is pretty much unrestricted. Upon leaving the car park you follow a narrow lane which leads to the cliffs. From here, you can follow the footpath east and walk all the way to the headland at Treryn Dinas. The cliffs offer incredible views of the headland and also back towards Pednvounder.

However most photographers choose to head west from the lane in the direction of Pednvounder Beach. A tiny cliff top footpath winds in the direction of the cliffs, soon opening out to an exposed granite rock which gives the first unrestricted view down onto the beach far below. There is almost no need to go further, this viewpoint has it all. The beach, cliffs and headland are all clearly visible and sit together in a beautiful composition, especially when photographed in portrait orientation.

For those wishing for a wider view of the bay continue along the narrow path for about 5 minutes. Just before the path descends steeply down the cliff there is a rocky summit providing a wonderful picnic spot and photographic viewpoint. This viewpoint gives a much more open view of the whole bay, making it ideal for landscape orientated pictures. On windy days, this makes a wonderful spot to photograph the bay with curving white waves rolling in off the sea.

Viewpoint 2 – The Beach

Access to the beach is far from easy. From the viewpoint mentioned above continue on the footpath as it climbs down through the cliff. The path is steep here and very uneven in places, but only takes around 5 minutes to reach the bottom. The final 10 metres is much more difficult, and involves climbing down a steep section of cliff. This can prove difficult when carrying a heavy camera backpack and tripod.

The main advantage of shooting on the beach is the rippled sand. At low tide beautiful long curving channels of rippled sand stretching far over the beach make wonderful photographic subjects. When photographed with a wide-angle lens, these ripples provide amazing lead-in lines, drawing your eye across the beach to the headland on the horizon.

The lagoon can also make a fascinating subject for photographs. The water colour has to be seen to be believed. It looks truly tropical here, more reminiscent of a Pacific Island atoll than a Cornish beach. A little elevation helps to bring out the colour, so the rocks just above the beach make a great place to compose photographs.

Opposite top: Gorgeous rippled sand on Pednvounder Beach, Nikon D800E, 27-70mm at 24mm, ISO 50, 0.8 sec at f/11. February

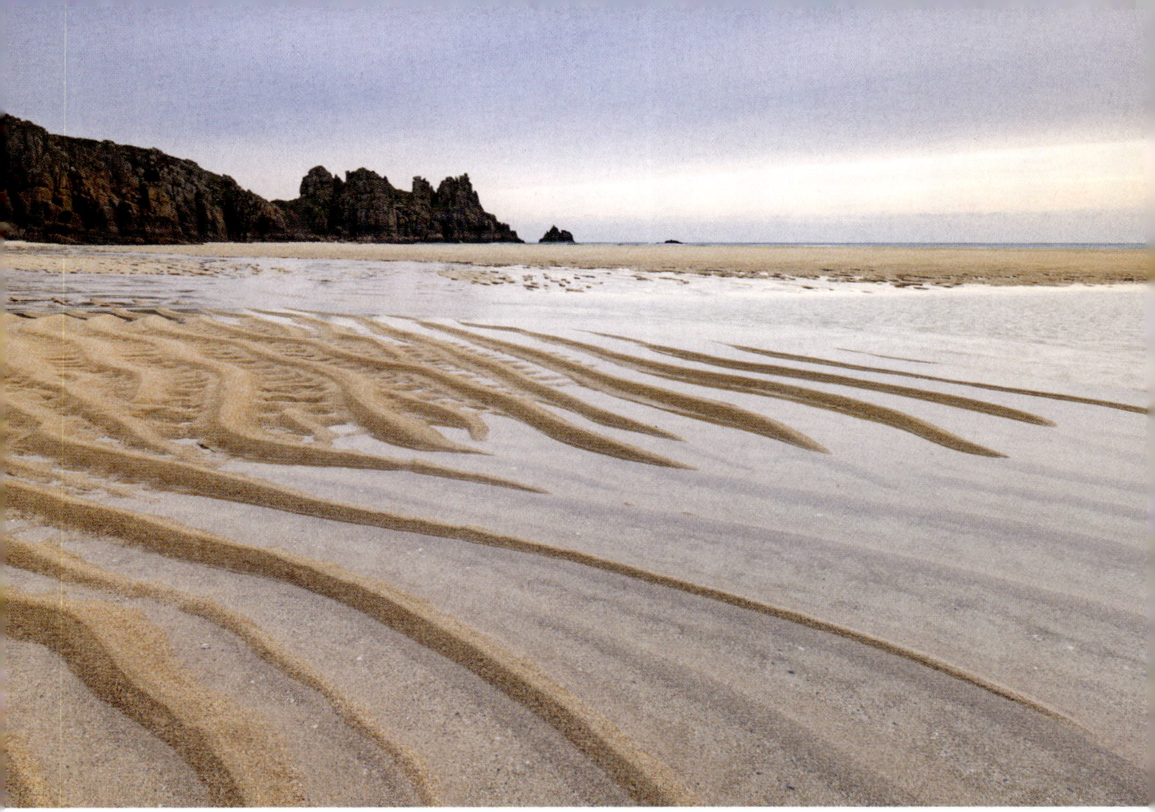

How to Get Here

Head out of Penzance on the A30 in the direction of Land's
End. After around 3 miles, take the left turning onto the
B3283 signposted Minack Theatre. Continue on this road for
approximately 4 miles then turn left following the signpost for
Treen. After driving through the village you will notice a car park
in a farmer's field. Park here and walk out of the car park following
the footpath up past a campsite and onto the cliffs.

Treen
Parking Lat/Long: 50.049851, -5.6406856
Parking OS Grid Ref: SW 394 229
Parking Postcode: TR19 6LQ
Map: OS Explorer Map 102 (1:25 000) Land's End

Accessibility

The walk to the cliffs takes approximately 10 minutes, following
a gravel track and then a well trodden footpath. Once on the cliffs,
several obvious footpaths head off in various directions.
As mentioned above the descent down onto the beach is much
more difficult and involves some scrambling. Alternatively, on a
very low tide you could walk along the beach from Porthcurno.
No wheelchair access.

Best Time of Year/Day

From Treen cliff the view over the beach towards Treryn Dinas looks
roughly in the direction of the sunrise in the autumn and winter,
making this an ideal dawn location at these times. Pednvounder is
also an excellent location year round for late afternoon and evening
visits, as the late sun provides rich side lighting on the granite cliffs.

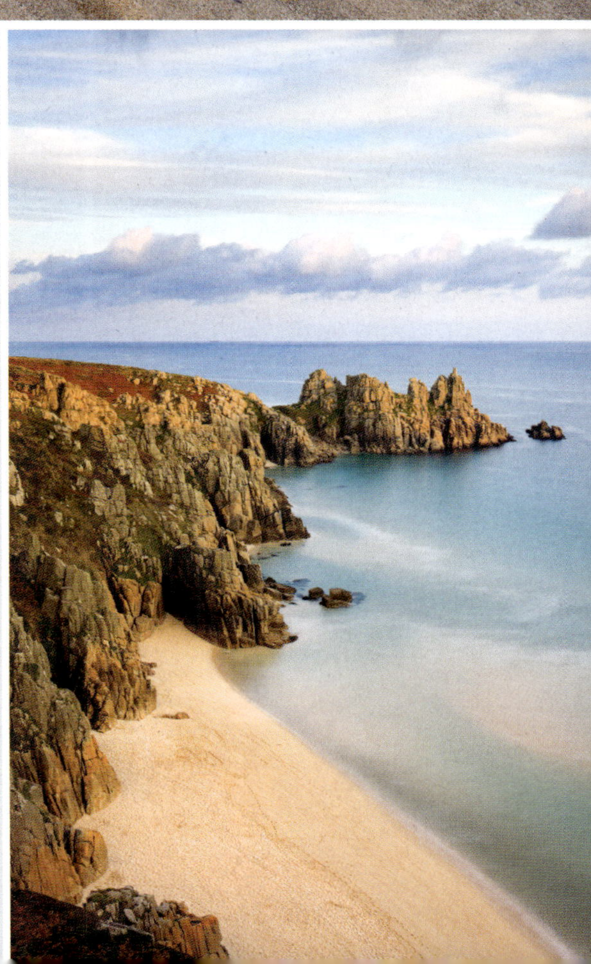

*Late evening sunlight bathes Treryn Dinas in golden tones, Canon
1Ds Mark III, 24-70mm at 38mm, ISO 50, 25 sec at f/16. October*

Close to Penzance in the far west of Cornwall, charming Mousehole is an idyllic Cornish fishing village crowded around a picturesque walled harbour.

Once a bustling port, the sheltered harbour is now mostly occupied with pleasure boats with only a few fishing vessels remaining. The village now thrives as a tourist destination, thankfully one that retains its original character and charm.

In 1595, during the Anglo-Spanish War the Spanish Navy led by officer Carlos de Amésquita destroyed Mousehole, burning the town before going on to burn nearby Penzance and Newlyn. Just one building, a local pub, survived the raid and still stands today. The Keigwin Arms is now a private residence, and commemorates the attack with a plaque bearing the words 'Squire Jenkyn Keigwin was killed here 23 July 1595 defending this house against the Spaniards'.

What to Shoot and Viewpoints

The clamshell-shaped harbour is protected from Mount's Bay by two large stone quays, with just a small opening in-between to allow the passage of boats. While the quays form part of the character and history of Mousehole, photographically speaking they are rather bulky, and when compared with the quaint houses on the opposite side of the harbour aren't particularly photogenic. As both quays serve as car parks this further limits their appeal, so it is advisable to either keep them small in compositions or remove them entirely. The quays do provide excellent elevated vantage points which help to space the boats out when shooting back over the harbour towards the pretty cottages.

'The Mousehole'

One of the best views over the harbour is also probably the first you will encounter. On the northern edge, just in front of the pretty shop 'The Mousehole', a seated area provides an excellent elevated unbroken view over the entire harbour. As the village faces towards the east, this viewpoint works a treat early in the day when the cottages overlooking the harbour bask in rich morning sunlight.

The Beach

For those wishing to get closer to the boats, some steps here lead down to a small sandy beach. Although this sounds appealing, in reality when up close the view becomes cluttered and difficult to compose. The little boats tend to overlap with themselves and the houses beyond, creating a confusing composition. Rather than shoot from up close with a wide-angle lens I would recommend staying a little higher on the beach, or higher still on the harbour wall to benefit from the elevation.

If the tide is low enough you can walk over the sand to the south side of the harbour, being careful of course not to trip over the many rope moorings found in this area. Alternatively, an easier method of access is to wander around the road.

The Wharf

Just past the Ship Inn, the road veers away from the harbour, but on foot you can soon return to the water's edge on The Wharf by taking a left turn past the former Keigwin Arms house.

This is perhaps my favourite area for photographing Mousehole. The stone wharf offers an excellent slightly elevated perspective over the harbour and cottages beyond. Depending on the time of year and weather conditions, boats are sometimes pulled out of the water and left on top of the wharf, providing some very welcome foreground interest.

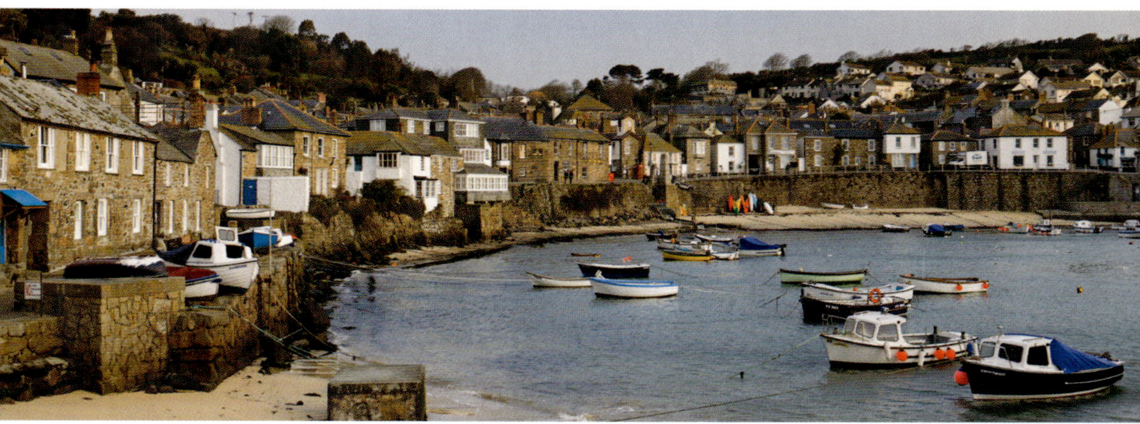

Fishing boats bob and up down in Mousehole harbour, Nikon D800E, 24-70mm at 34mm, ISO 100, 1/13 sec at f/8. April

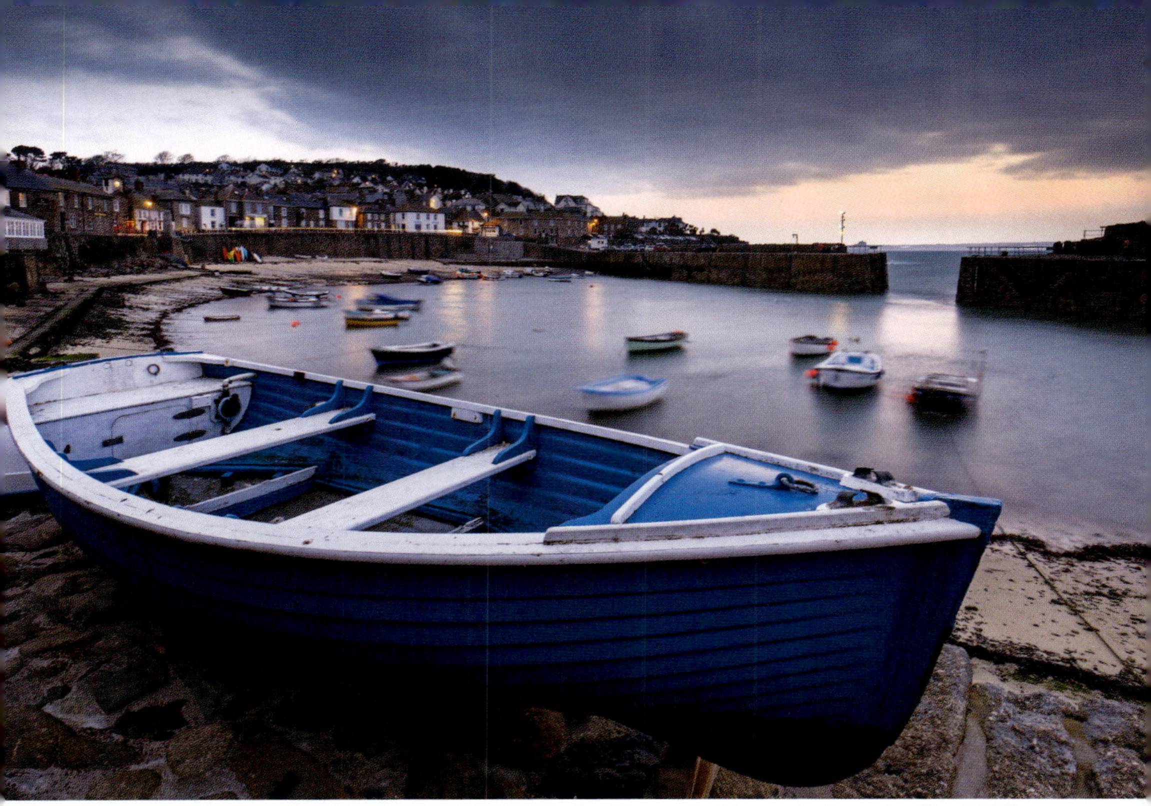

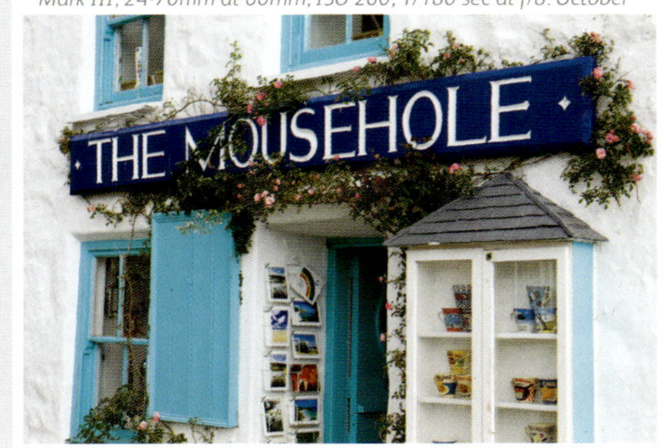

Small boat on the old stone wharf at sunrise, Nikon D800E, 17-35mm at 19mm, ISO 100, 15 sec at f/13. April

How to Get Here

Mousehole is just three miles south of Penzance in West Cornwall. From Penzance take the coast road south, first passing through Newlyn. Before you reach Mousehole you will notice a long stretch of roadside parking. You can park here for free, or alternatively just past the roadside parking there is a large pay and display car park.

Parking Lat/Long: 50.084635, -5.5372213
Parking OS Grid Ref: SW 471 266
Parking Postcode: TR19 6PR
Map: OS Explorer Map 102 (1:25 000) Land's End

Accessibility

There are various car parks in and around Mousehole, however if you prefer to avoid narrow lanes then its best to park on the roadside parking or large car park on the approach to the village. Excellent access is provided all around the harbour, making the place easily accessible for wheelchair users.

Best Time of Year/Day

As Mousehole faces east towards Mount's Bay it works best when photographed from sunrise through to mid morning throughout the year. The tide is an important consideration; at low tide the harbour is all but empty of water so ideally time your visit to coincide with a high tide.

With some careful attention to composition a wide-angle lens allows you to include a boat in your foreground, backed by boats in the harbour and cottages beyond. As your camera will be pointing roughly east-northeast, this makes a great place to shoot at dawn to benefit from a colourful sky and reflection in the harbour water. Although the quays may form a larger part of the frame here than from other viewpoints, the wide-angle composition ensures they stay small and do not overpower the scene. If you choose to shoot at dawn, there is also less chance that the quay car parks will be bustling with distracting cars.

Pretty gift shop overlooking Mousehole's harbour, Canon 1Ds Mark III, 24-70mm at 60mm, ISO 200, 1/180 sec at f/8. October

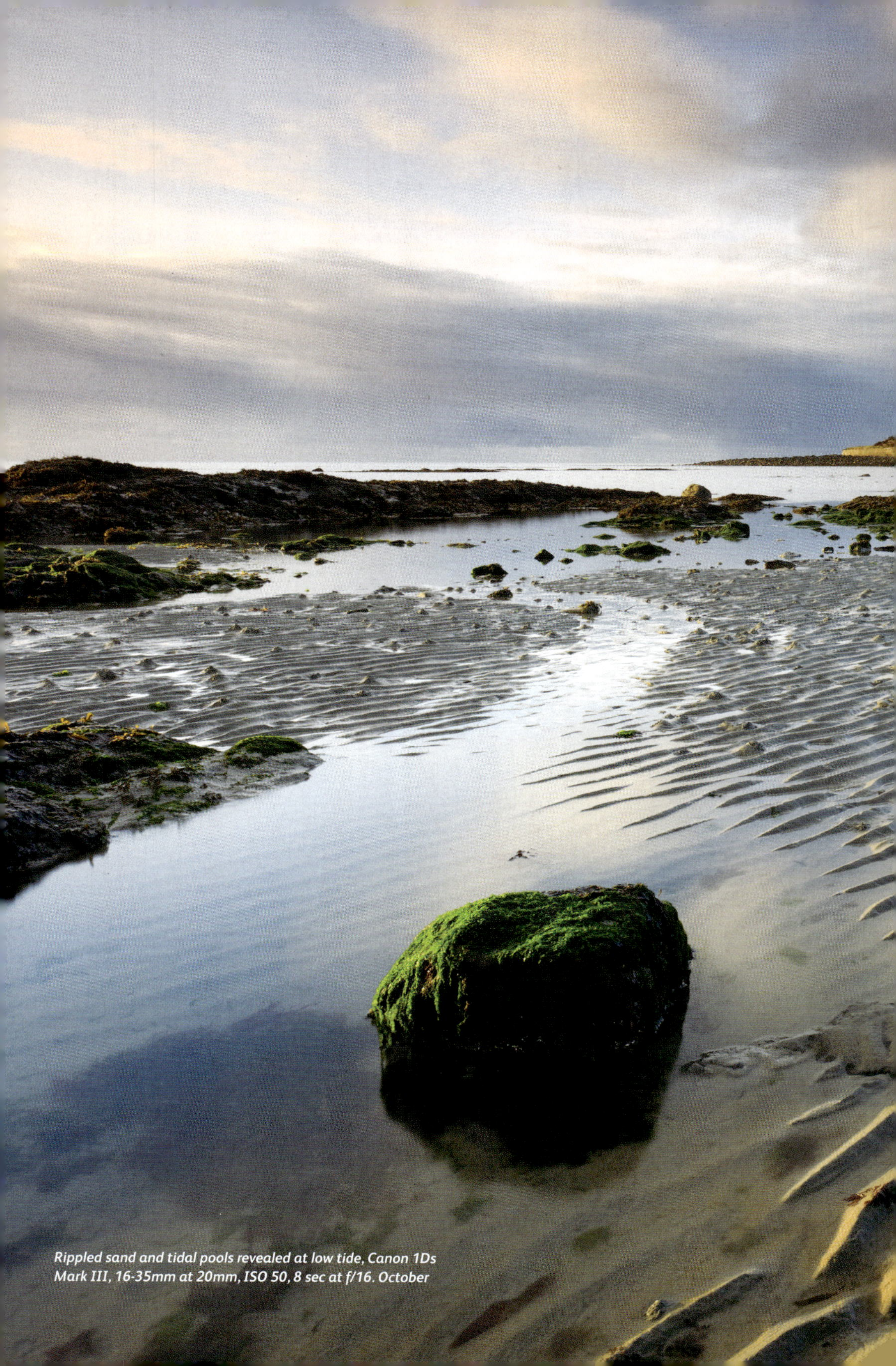

Rippled sand and tidal pools revealed at low tide, Canon 1Ds Mark III, 16-35mm at 20mm, ISO 50, 8 sec at f/16. October

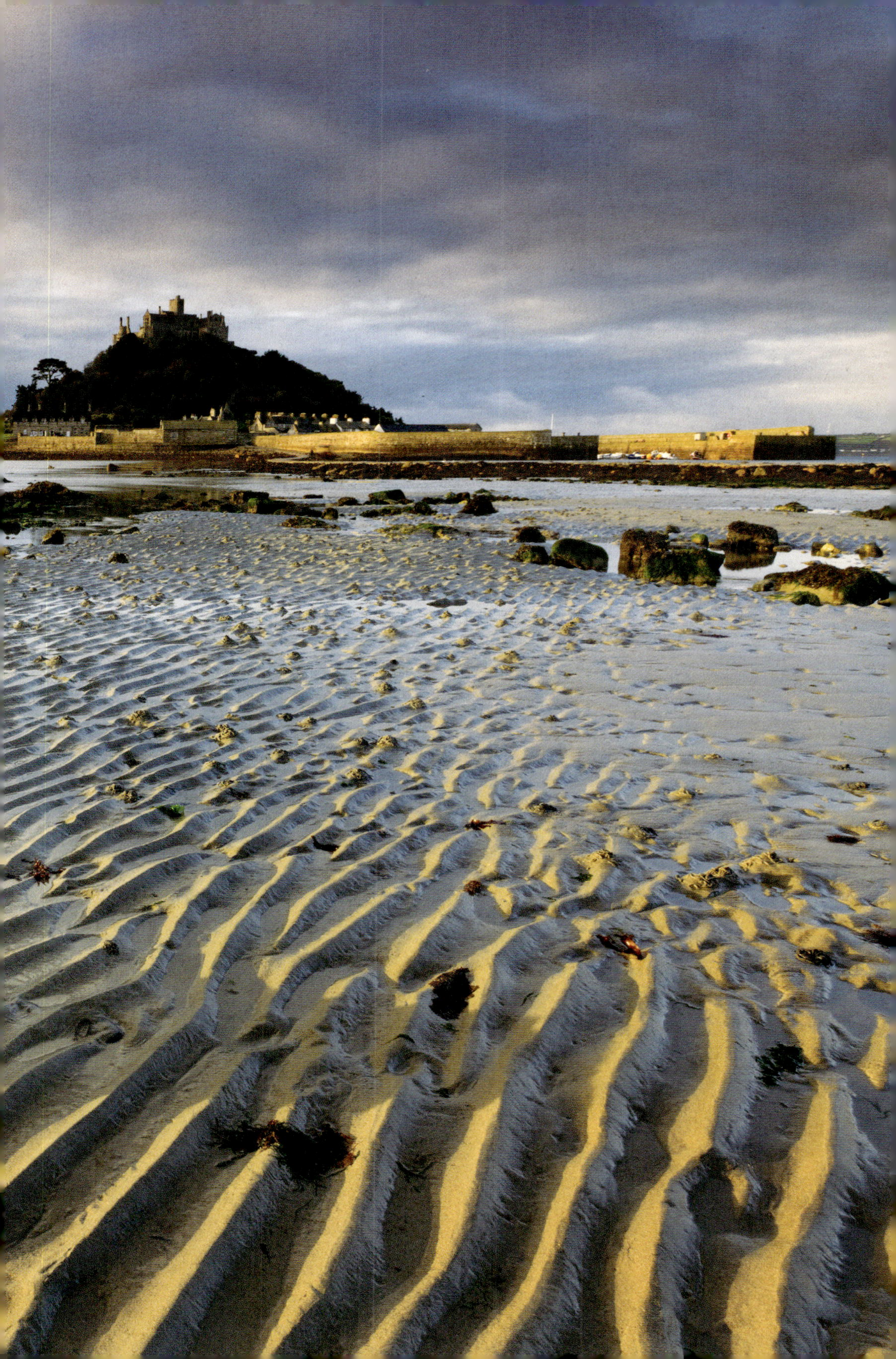

Probably the most famous and instantly recognisable icon of Cornwall's rich landscape, St Michael's Mount has a long history of occupation. A trading port since the Iron Age, the Mount has subsequently been a monastic abbey, a castle and a stately home. The island is now in the care of the National Trust, who also preserve the cottages and small harbour.

The Cornish name for St Michael's Mount, Carrek Los yn Cos, roughly translates to "the grey rock in a wood". This is a curious name indeed for a small offshore island, and suggests a time when Mount's Bay was covered not with water but trees. Fossilised tree remains found at low tide indicate the area was flooded around 1700 BC. Now the island is only connected to the mainland at low tide, accessed via a man-made stone causeway.

What to Shoot and Viewpoints

Viewpoint 1 – The Causeway

Around midway on a falling tide, the famous causeway emerges from Mounts Bay. Little by little the beautiful stone causeway reveals itself, until at low tide you can see it stretching all the way to St Michael's Mount.

The stonework on the causeway is impressive; it consists of rectangular granite blocks mostly golden in colour. As the causeway lies beneath the waves for much of the time it does require regular maintenance, so you can expect the stones to change over time. There are various sections where the stones are noticeably more appealing than others, so if the tide allows it is worth fully exploring the causeway before settling on a viewpoint.

From higher up the beach the causeway appears to run in a very straight line towards the left of the island. As you venture further along the causeway curves to the right in a most attractive fashion, bending back towards the centre of the island.

This section makes the most attractive composition, although it does require a wide-angle lens as you are standing much closer to the Mount. Of course, this viewpoint is very tide dependent and capturing the best photographs takes careful planning. Ideally, you want to shoot this location when the tide is low enough so that the causeway is visible, but with waves still lapping up on either side. If you wait too long, the water will drain away leaving the causeway bordered by rocks and sand, or sometimes unsightly brown seaweed.

Viewpoint 2 – The Beach

The stone causeway makes such an ideal photographic subject, it is very difficult resisting the urge to include it in any photographs of St Michael's Mount.

However, the beach can also provide a wealth of subject matter and offers a less typical shot of the Mount.

To the right of the causeway a wide flat area of sand is broken up only by a series of tidal pools. These pools and sometimes any areas of wet sand can make wonderful subjects for reflecting colourful clouds in photographs captured around dawn and dusk. For a very different view you can ascend the large rock to the right of the causeway and shoot from a slightly elevated position. There are steps leading up onto the rocks offering easy access.

To the left of the causeway the beach tends to be busier making clean compositions more difficult to achieve. There are many low rock ledges and rock pools, which can make lovely photographic interest but are often covered with seaweed. When the tide is low enough some small areas of rippled sand can often be found. These rippled areas of beach look glorious when illuminated by some low side lighting but make sure you arrive early to ensure nobody else leaves footprints in the sand.

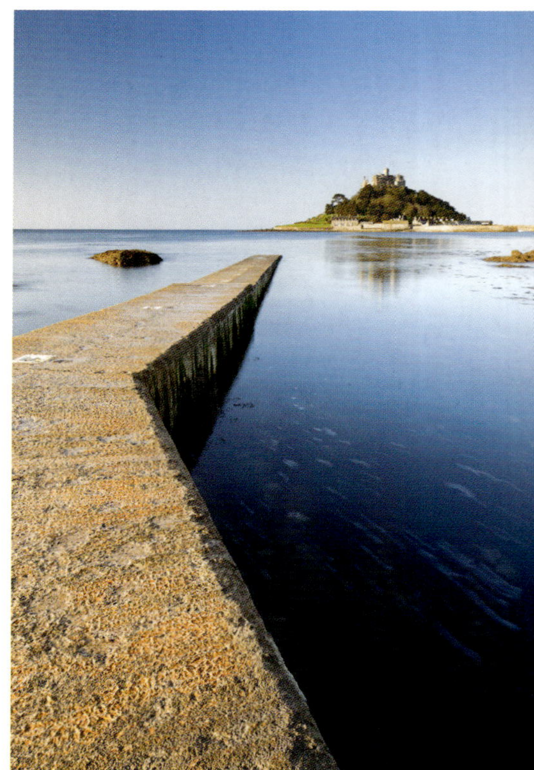

An alternative view of St Michael's Mount from the concrete jetty, Nikon D800E, 17-35mm at 22mm, ISO 50, 2.5 sec at f/11. May

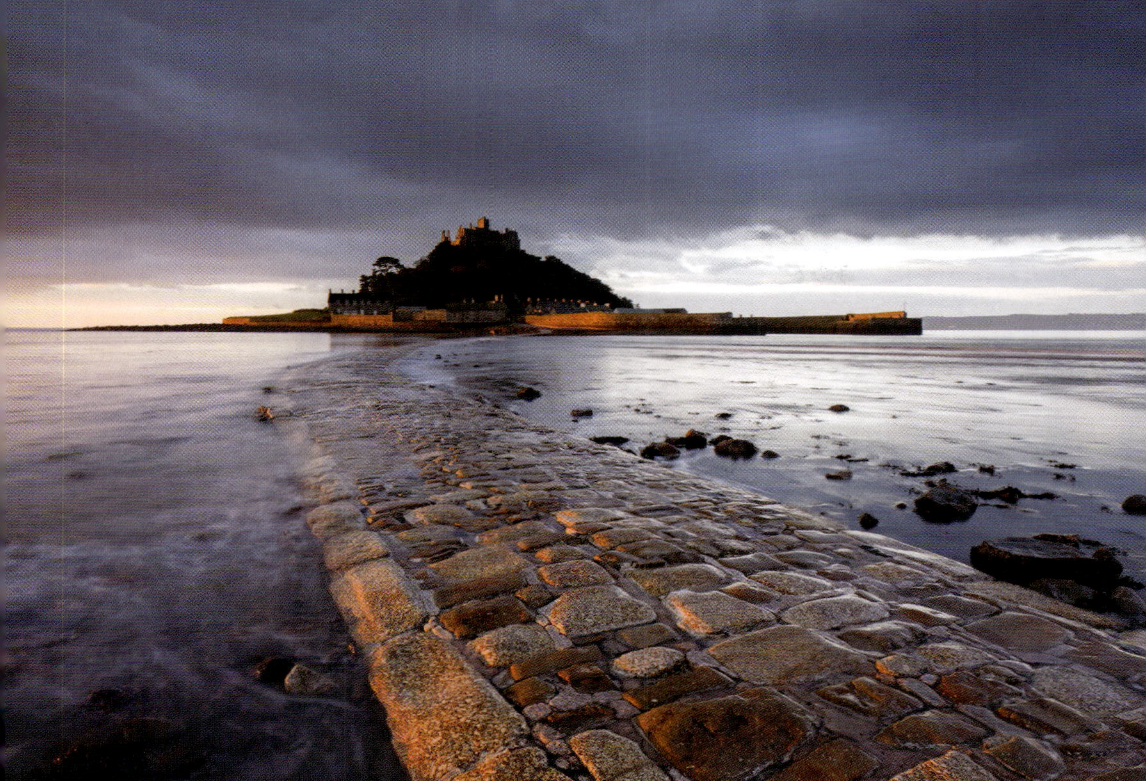

The classic stone causeway at dawn, Nikon D800E, 17-35mm at 20mm, ISO 100, 5 sec at f/11. January

Viewpoint 3 – The Concrete Jetty

With high tide approaching, both the beach and causeway disappear beneath the waves for several hours. At these times you could be forgiven for thinking that St Michael's Mount is not worth visiting, but you would be wrong. The concrete jetty may not sound as romantic as the stone causeway but it is every bit as photogenic, and is at its best approaching high tide.

The jetty can be accessed via some steps from Marazion village, and is used to ferry passengers and staff to and from St Michael's Mount at high tide. Therefore, it can be a busy location during the day but at dawn and dusk it is usually deserted.

Like the causeway the jetty stretches out towards the Mount, but with the addition of a zigzag about half way along to add further interest. To fully appreciate how much this wall of concrete can add to any picture, attach a wide-angle lens to maximize depth. The jetty makes a wonderful lead-in line to a photograph pulling viewers through the scene towards St Michael's Mount in the background.

How to Get Here

From Penzance head east on the A30 for around 3 miles until you reach a roundabout. Take the third exit, signposted Marazion and follow this road for a further mile. When you reach Marazion you will see a car park on the right. Park here, and wander down to the beach. You can't fail to notice St Michael's Mount, the causeway runs directly from the beach below Marazion village centre.

Parking Lat/Long: 50.123467, -5.4738951
Parking Grid Ref: SW517306
Parking Postcode: TR17 0EN (Marazion)
Map: OS Explorer Map 102 (1:25 000) Land's End

Accessibility

The best viewpoints to photograph St Michael's Mount are from the nearby town of Marazion. Marazion has several car parks right next to the beach; from the car park a ramp leads down onto the beach and causeway, which should be suitable for wheelchairs. Unfortunately the concrete jetty is accessible only by steps or a walk over the rocky shore.

Best Time of Year/Day

This location can be photographed with side lighting around dawn and dusk all through the year. However, the best conditions usually occur in winter when the sun's position is better for colours in the sky around sunrise and sunset. As St Michael's Mount is a popular visitor destination, people can often wander along the causeway into your composition. To minimize this, shoot at dawn when there is far less chance of encountering people.

Close to the Lizard, Kynance Cove is a secluded gem of the Cornish coast, considered by some to be among the most beautiful beaches in the world. A popular tourist destination since the Victorian era, the cove is now in the care of the National Trust.

Kynance Cove has is designated a Geological Conservation Review site for its unusual geology. Like most of the Lizard, the main rock is metamorphic serpentinite, formed around 375 million years ago six miles below the earth's surface. Erosion has left behind the islands and sea stacks that make up today's Kynance Cove.

These stacks, with wonderful names such as Asparagus Island, Steeple Rock and The Bishop, are only a part of the fascination of Kynance Cove. Although the main islands are cut off from the shore at high tide, when the sea retreats golden sandy beaches are revealed, with rock pools and deep caves waiting to be explored.

What to Shoot and Viewpoints

Viewpoint 1 – Cliff Top Views

Kynance Cove is best appreciated from a high vantage point. Fortunately with cliffs all along this stretch of coast there is no shortage of opportunities to shoot the cove from an elevated position.

As you approach from the cliff-top car park, your first glimpse of Kynance Cove will be one of the best with the tiny beach, rugged stacks and islands stretching out from the headland surrounded by turquoise ocean.

Some steps lead down towards the cove making for some very good foreground, especially in late May when they are surrounded by flowering sea thrift flowers. Alternatively head closer to the cliff edge for an expansive view of the colourful bay in front of the cove.

While up on the cliffs here, don't forget to look in the opposite direction. The views south towards Lizard Point don't have quite the same appeal as Kynance Cove but still make for beautiful coastal compositions. Of particular interest is the dramatic view over the cliffs towards the towering sea stack named Lion Rock.

For a much less photographed view of Kynance Cove, head down to the café, and then walk up the footpath onto the cliffs just above the beach. From this position you can photograph Kynance Cove with Lizard Point in the distance in an altogether unusual composition that gives prominence to Asparagus Island.

Viewpoint 2 – The Beach

Although the cliff top usually provides the best photographic opportunities a visit to the sandy beach is a must to truly soak up the atmosphere of Kynance Cove. You can get to the rocky shore below the café when the tide is high, but for the true Kynance beach experience you will need to wait for low tide.

Opposite: Coast path steps leading down to Kynance Cove, Canon 1Ds Mark III, 16-35mm at 20mm, ISO 100, 1.3 sec at f/16. May

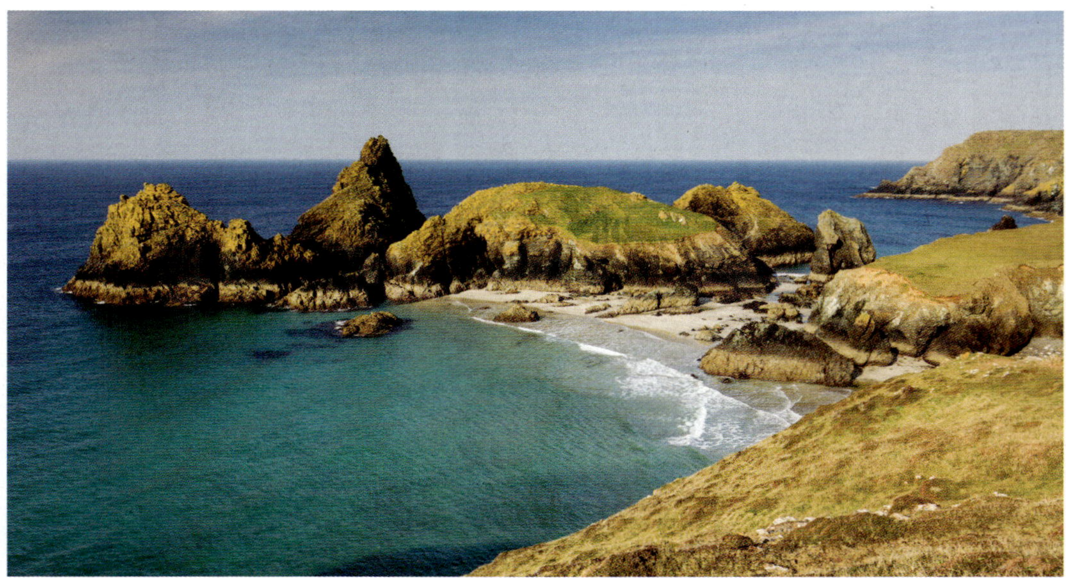

Azure coloured water surrounding Kynance Cove, Canon 1Ds Mark III, 24-70mm at 28mm, ISO 100, 1/8 sec at f/16. April

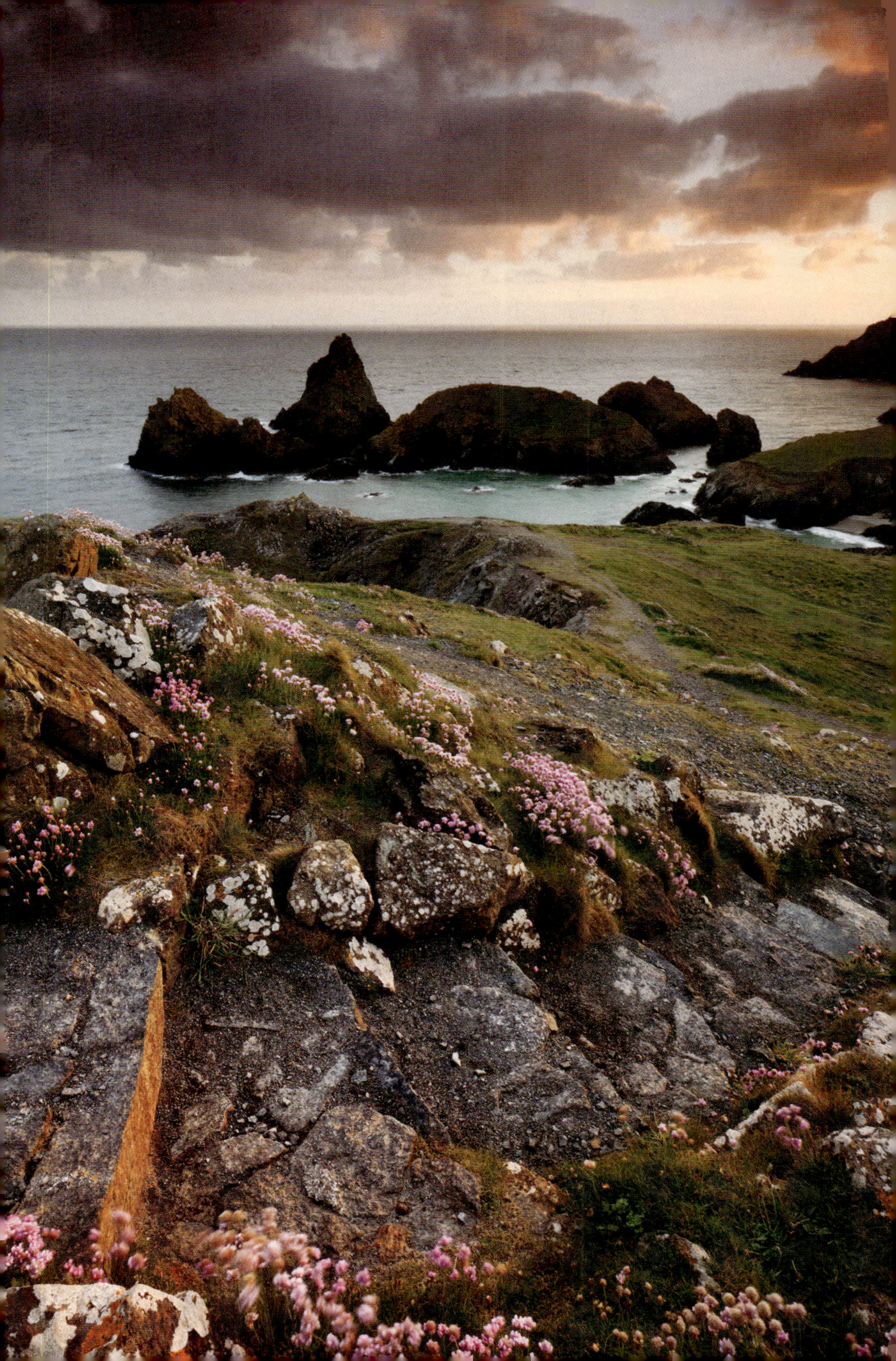

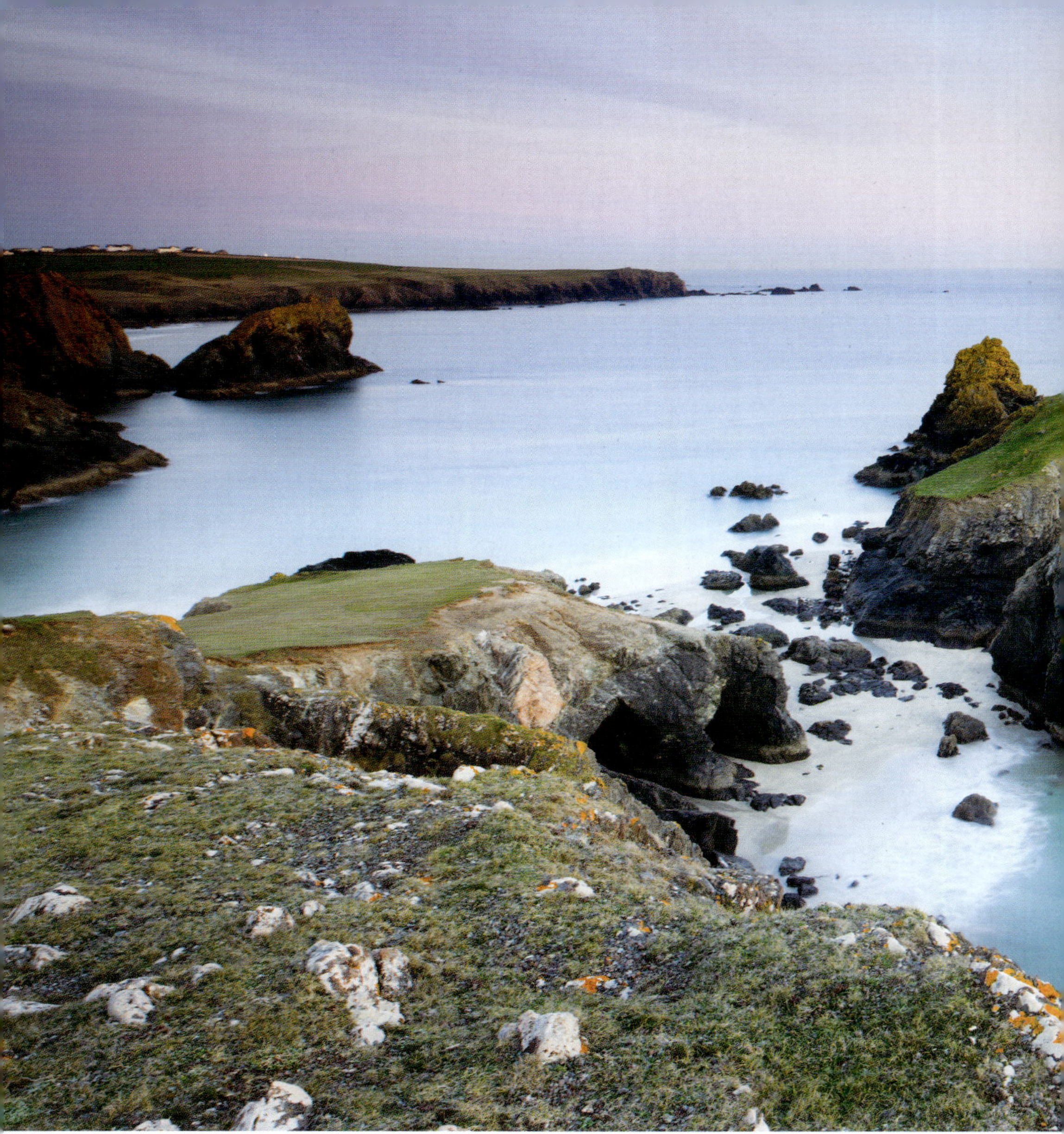

As the tide retreats it is best to be ready and waiting for the first opportunity to get around the cliffs, as the experience of being the first person to walk on the fresh sand is extra special. Tantalisingly the beach reveals itself before you can access it, but a quick removal of shoes and socks, and a wade through a rock pool will ensure you reach the virgin sand before anybody else.

You will find a small beach area with waves lapping against the shore both in front and behind you. Looking to the south, the sandy beach is broken up by small rocks surrounded by photogenic tidal pools, ideal for foreground interest. The background isn't bad either, cliffs and sea stacks make for a dramatic backdrop that ends at Lizard Point just a couple of miles in the distance.

The shore behind you is even more remarkable. While the imposing Kynance Cliff dominates the background, it is an enormous sea stack towering out of the sand on the seashore that commands all your attention. Remember to pack your wide-angle lens if you wish to shoot this stack, but to be completely frank this part of the beach is more an area to experience than a photographic highlight.

Before you leave the beach don't forget to explore the caves. Inside one large cave below the headland, if you time your visit well and are lucky you may experience evening sunshine radiating through a hole in the cliff and illuminating the already turquoise water of a tidal pool. Under such conditions the pool looks absolutely magical, a scene from a fairy tale.

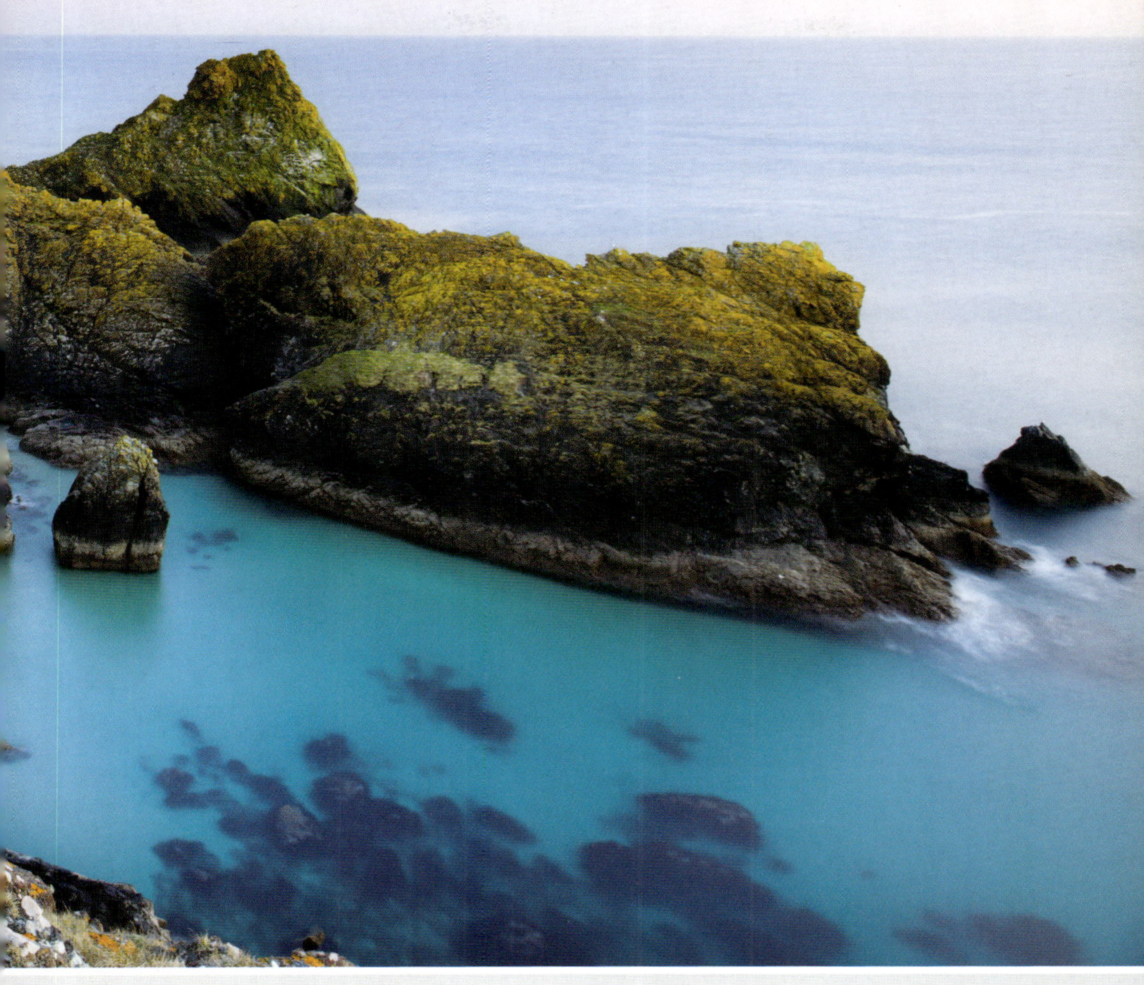

How to Get Here

From Helston head south on the A3083 towards Lizard Point. After 11 miles, take the right turning signposted Kynance Cove, and continue for another mile or so along the National Trust toll road. At the end of this road there is a large National Trust car park.

Parking Lat/Long: 49.974444, -5.2250558
Parking OS Grid ref: SW 688 132
Parking Postcode: TR12 7NT (Lizard Point)
Map: OS Explorer Map 103 (1:25 000) The Lizard

Accessibility

From the car park a surfaced track, suitable for wheelchairs, leads to a cliff top vantage point offering the best views towards Kynance Cove. From here a 15 minute walk down an uneven but well defined footpath leads to the beach.

Best Time of Year/Day

With a variety of viewpoints both on the cliffs and beach, Kynance Cove can be photographed well throughout the year at dawn and dusk. As with most of Cornwall, the cliffs look their best in late spring when wildflowers are abundant.

Twilight above Kynance Cove, looking towards Lizard Point, Canon 1Ds Mark III, 16-35mm at 17mm, ISO 100, 15 sec at f/16. April

Lizard Point

The dramatic Lizard Point is the Lizard Peninsula's equivalent to Land's End. While the latter is the most westerly part of mainland England, Lizard Point is mainland Britain's most southerly point.

The coast off Lizard Point is notoriously hazardous for shipping and has been the site of many disasters. As a result, there has been a lifeboat station on the Lizard since 1859. Such were the dangers of this stretch of water that at one stage three lifeboat stations were operational during the same period. These stations have long since closed, replaced in 1961 by The Lizard Lifeboat Station at nearby Kilcobben Cove.

In addition to the lifeboat station, there has been a lighthouse at Lizard Point since 1619. The current white lighthouse standing on the cliff tops between Lizard Point and nearby Housel Bay has been in operation since 1751 and remains a key focal point of this stretch of coastline.

Moody May evening at Polpeor Cove, Canon 1Ds Mark III, 16-35mm at 33mm, ISO 100, 105 sec at f/8. May

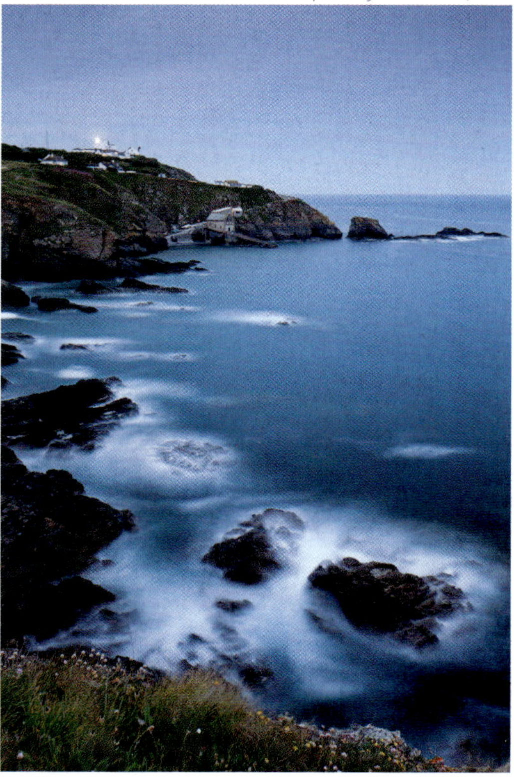

What to Shoot and Viewpoints

Viewpoint 1 – Polpeor Cove

Similar to its illustrious neighbour Land's End, the best views of Lizard Point are achieved from the cliffs. Just below the café and gift shop, rocky Polpeor Cove was the location of the Lizard's original lifeboat station. A slipway descends to a small area of beach alongside the old lifeboat house. Although the lifeboat station closed in 1961, the boathouse forms a permanent association with this area and makes a strong focal point to photographs of the coastline. It can be easily be photographed from either the cliffs or just above on the slipway as part of a dramatic coastal landscape.

For the best views towards Lizard Point, head west on the coast path over the cliff tops. After 250 metres or so, the cliff top vantage point offers a breathtaking view back over Polpeor Cove towards the old lifeboat station. From this position, a commanding view of the headland and lighthouse opens up, with a wealth of rocky ledges and islets adding excellent interest at the base of the cliffs.

While this vantage point easily provides the most dramatic view of the Lizard, perhaps the only disappointment is the lighthouse. From the west the impact of the lighthouse is somewhat diminished by the buildings in front of it. Already a fairly squat tower, the lighthouse is lost in a jumble of buildings on the headland, and unless photographed at twilight when the light is on, it will be almost unrecognisable in a photo to any but the keenest observer.

A much better view of the lighthouse can be achieved from Housel Bay, but before leaving this side it is well worth continuing on the coast path for five minutes to gain views northwards along the cliffs towards Kynance Cove. As you walk along the path you will notice a wealth of rocky islets just offshore, each important enough to command its own name on an Ordnance Survey map. Rocks with names such as Taylor's Rock, Quadrant and Man of War probably all have played their roles in shipwrecks over the years, and all make worthwhile photographic subjects.

Viewpoint 2 – Housel Bay

Retracing your steps to Lizard Point, continue along the coast path eastwards around the outside of the lighthouse. The path passes above Housel Cove, a small sandy beach revealed only at low tide, and continues along the cliff tops on the eastern side of the bay.

From this cliff top position, an altogether different view towards Lizard Point can be photographed. The lighthouse looks so much better from this side, its white tower completely unobstructed.

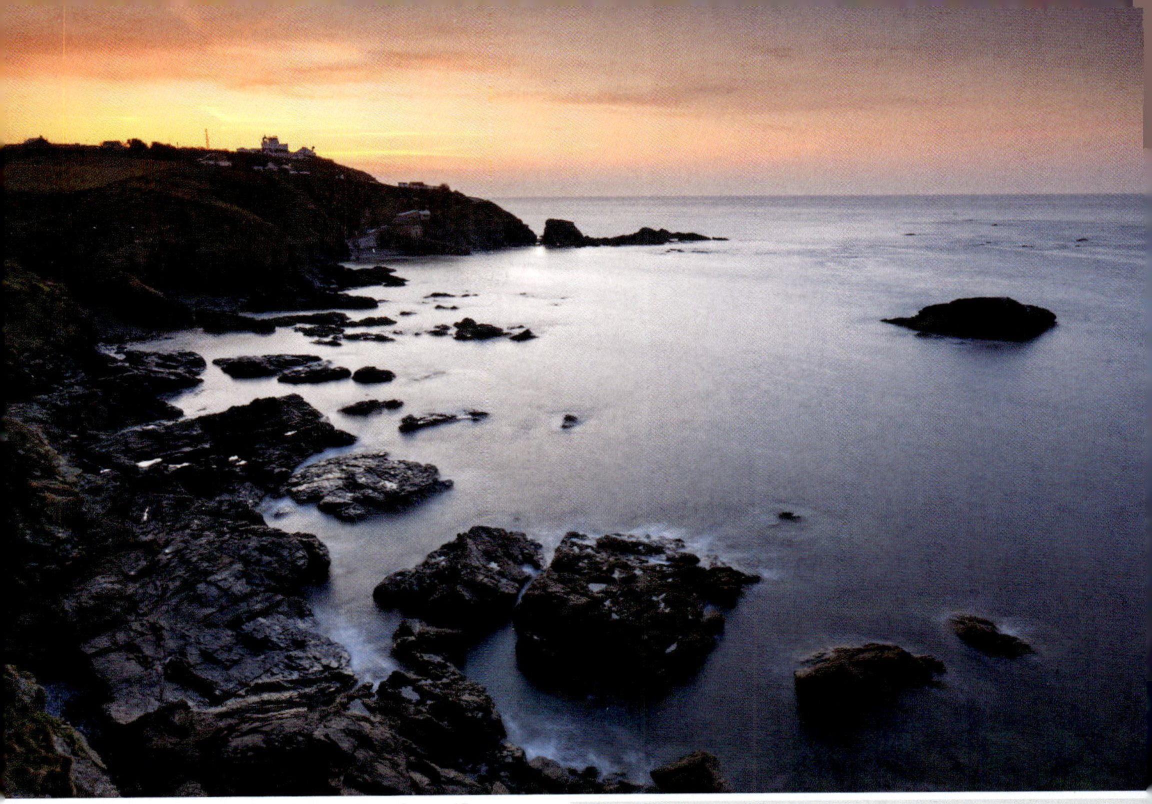

Sunrise above Lizard Point, across Polpeor Cove, Canon 1Ds Mark III, 16-35mm at 23mm, ISO 50, 10 sec at f/16. April

Further along the coast path, before the trail disappears over the next headland some intriguing rocks are exposed on the cliff tops. These outcrops make exceptional foreground subjects when shooting wide-angle compositions back towards Lizard Point.

After photographing the view over Housel Bay it is worth continuing along the coast path to view the modern lifeboat station at Kilcobben Cove. Along the way you pass the historic Lloyds Signal Station building as well as the huts used by Marconi for his groundbreaking wireless signal transmissions in 1901. From the lifeboat station, a series of footpaths and lanes completes a circular walk back to the car park near the lighthouse.

How to Get Here

From Helston travel south on the A3083; after 11 miles you will reach the village of Lizard. Drive through the village for another mile and you will reach Lizard Point. There is a large National Trust car park next to the lighthouse.

Parking Lat/Long: 49.959517, -5.2063555
Parking OS Grid Ref: SW 701 115
Parking Postcode: TR12 7NT
Map: OS Explorer Map 103 (1:25 000) The Lizard

Accessibility

From the car park a 5 minute walk along the road brings you to the cliff top view above the old lifeboat station. This area is suitable for wheelchair access. Access to Housel Bay and to the view of Lizard Point from Polpeor Cove is via the well-defined South West Coast Path footpath.

Best Time of Year/Day

The approximately east/west running coastline make Lizard Point an ideal location for shooting at both sunrise and sunset. The view towards Lizard Point from Polpeor Cove is best photographed at dawn or dusk in the winter months when the rising/setting sun far out to sea will side light the cliffs but not cause any contrast issues. For the view from Housel Bay, a winter sunrise is ideal for the same reasons. Alternatively, if there are clouds in the sky this view can make a colourful sunrise shot at any time of year.

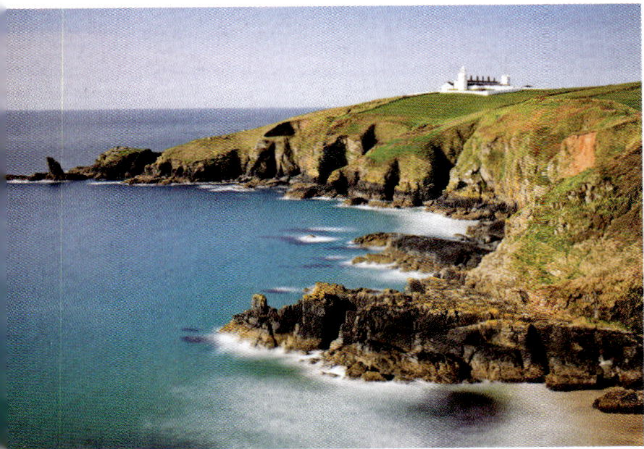

Lizard Point lighthouse from above Housel Bay, Canon 1Ds Mark III, 24-70mm at 42mm, ISO 100, 105 sec at f/16. April

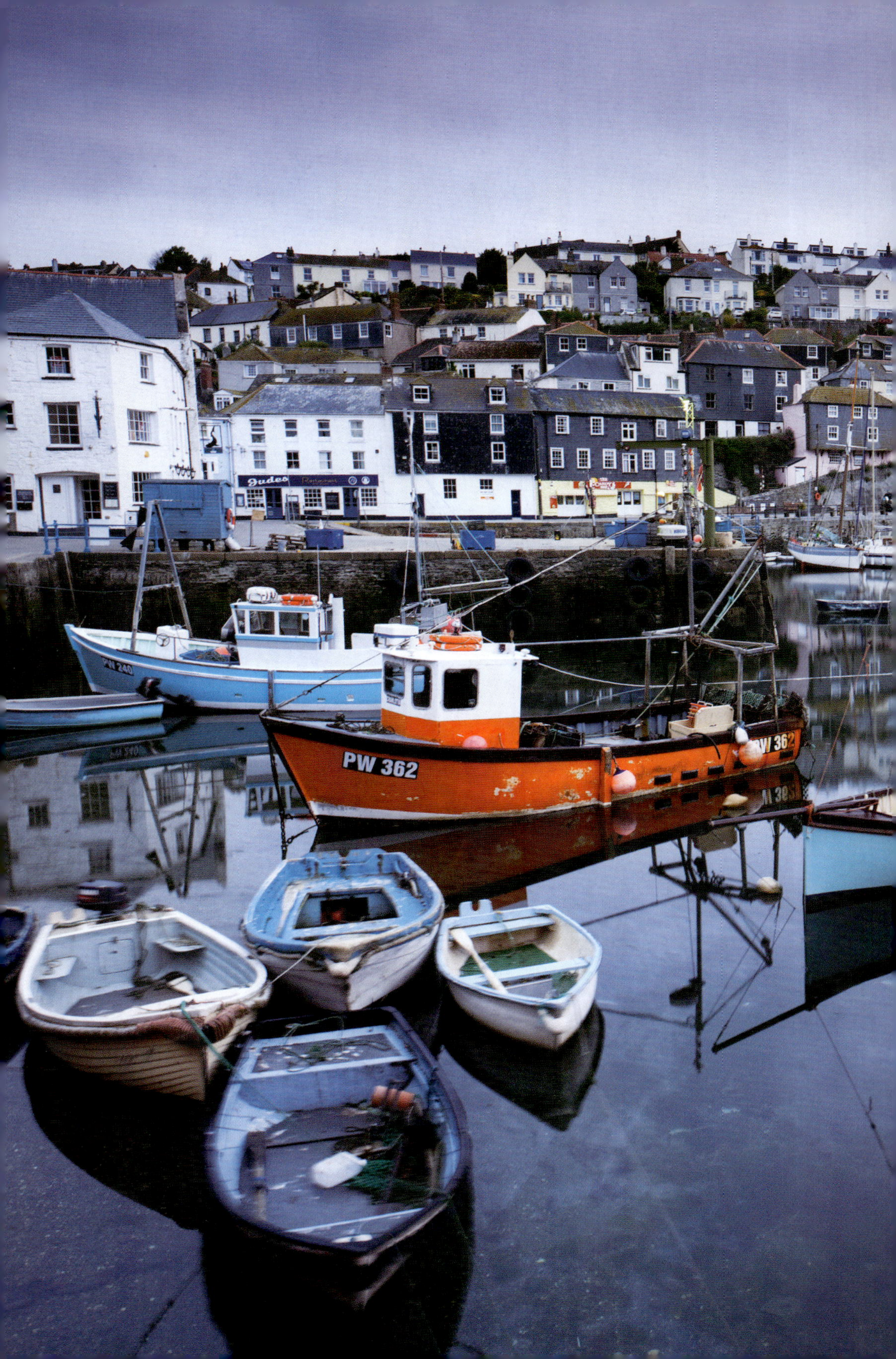

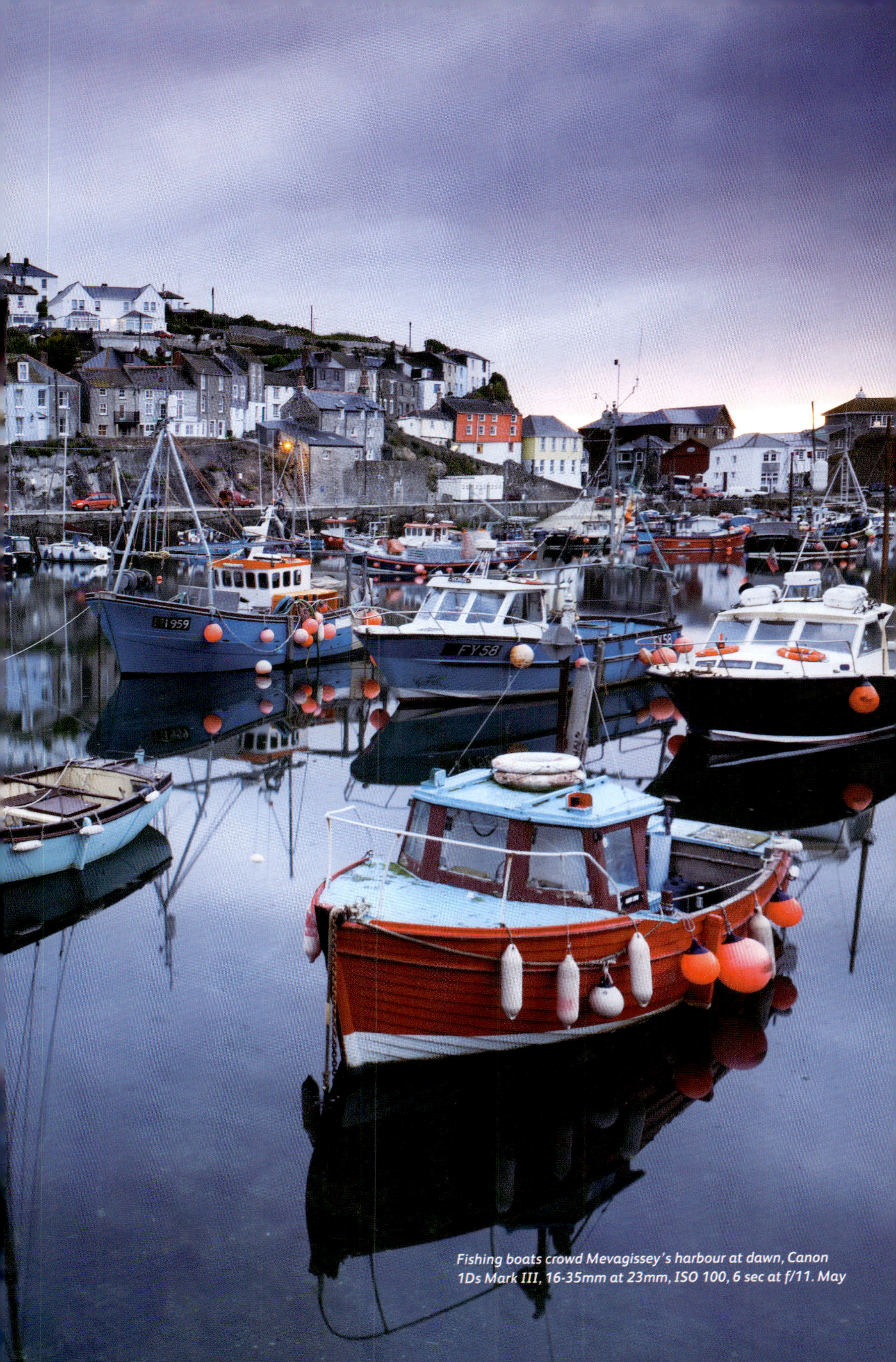

Fishing boats crowd Mevagissey's harbour at dawn, Canon 1Ds Mark III, 16-35mm at 23mm, ISO 100, 6 sec at f/11. May

Mevagissey is an archetypal Cornish fishing village near St Austell on Cornwall's south coast. Inns, cafes and small souvenir shops line the narrow streets in the village centre while rows of houses crowd the steep sloping hills overlooking two picturesque harbours.

Dating back to the early 14th century Mevagissey was originally known as Porthhilly. In the 17th century the village merged with its neighbour, Lamorrick to form Mevagissey, its name derived from the Irish saints, St Meva and St Issey.

Although the fishing industry here is but a shadow of its former self, the harbour is usually bustling with fishing boats as well as several yachts.

What to Shoot and Viewpoints

Viewpoint 1 – Outer Harbour

At over twice the size of the inner harbour, the outer harbour makes a much more challenging subject. Due to its size and location closer to the sea, the water in the harbour is less likely to be still. This can present problems when attempting to photograph the fishing boats at dawn or dusk when a slow exposure will result in the boats blurring. Also, it means there will be less chance of capturing reflections.

Another issue presented by this large harbour is the fishing boats seem too few and far between, and without resorting to your telephoto lens, are often too distant to be photographed effectively.

The inner harbour offers the best potential for photographing the classic harbour scene, so rather than attempting a poor substitute, instead you have to play the outer harbour to its strengths. Above Stuckumb Point on the south harbour wall a small park on Polkirt Hill (SX 016 446) offers some much needed elevation to allow unrestricted views across the village. The panoramic vista from here encapsulates the village, both harbours as well as some of the coast in a delightful view.

Viewpoint 2 – Inner Harbour

With the exception of the park on Polkirt Hill, the best views of Mevagissey are all to be found around the inner harbour. Fishing boats are moored all around the harbour and excellent access to the various quays and wharfs makes it easy to find a good composition.

A particularly pleasing view can be found in the southwest corner of the harbour, standing on West Wharf with your back to the Shark Angling Centre. From this corner the harbour is very sheltered, the glass-like water beautifully reflecting the boats on calm days.

There are always colourful boats in this corner to provide interest throughout the picture, while the backdrop of cottages overlooking the harbour is so typically Cornish.

When the tide goes out the boats become stranded on the mud so it's best to shoot around mid tide. At these times some of the larger boats will become grounded in the low water ensuring you can photograph them in low light without having to worry about the boats moving during a long exposure.

The views from East Wharf are almost as good. Some elegant yachts can often be found on the right side of the harbour, with a multitude of fishing boats clustered on the left side. The houses on the opposite hill are perhaps less photogenic than those behind East Wharf but are by no means an eyesore.

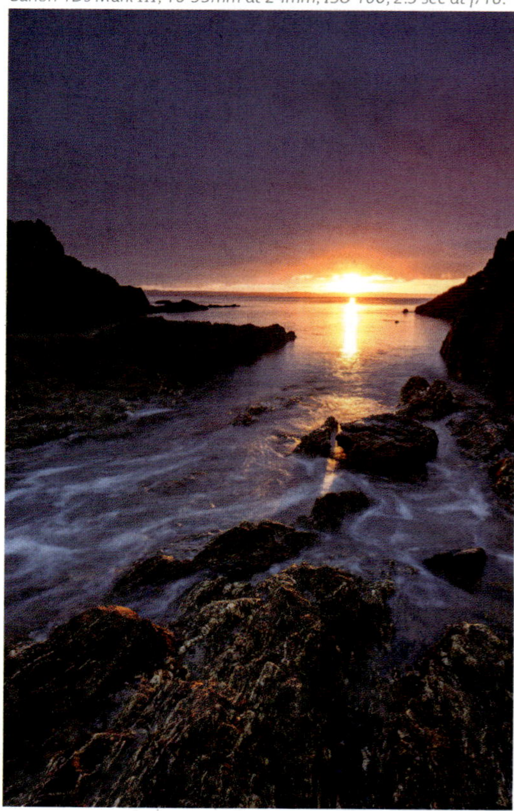

May sunrise from a small area of beach near the harbour, Canon 1Ds Mark III, 16-35mm at 24mm, ISO 100, 2.5 sec at f/16.

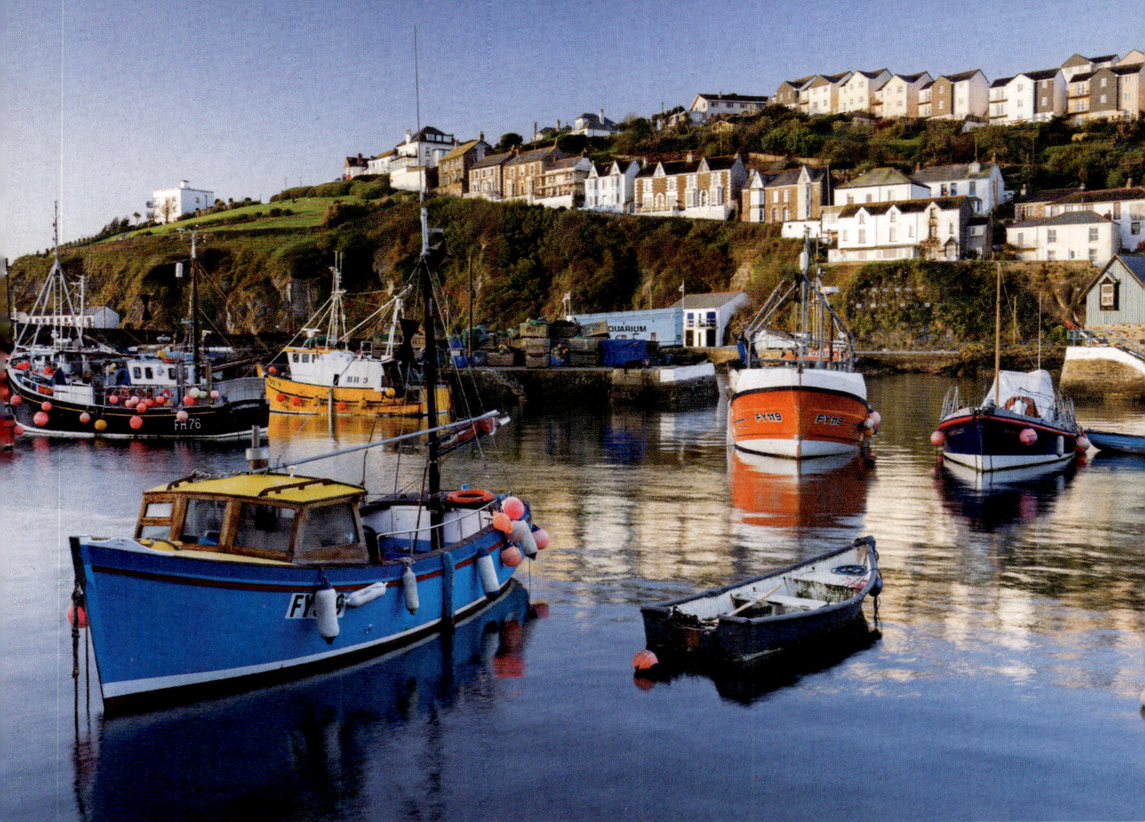

Fishing boats in Mousehole harbour on a tranquil Spring morning, Nikon D800E, 17-35mm at 32mm, ISO 200, 0.3 sec at f/11. May

The challenge with composition is to arrange elements pleasingly within the frame while omitting those that don't complement the picture. In a bustling harbour this may not be easy, but the open views along the wharf will provide you with space to find the right viewpoint.

To help achieve some depth in your composition try heading up the pedestrian path that runs uphill past the cottages that overlook the harbour. The elevation gain enables you to space the boats out in your composition so they aren't squashed behind one another.

If you continue along the East Wharf and out onto the East Quay, you will find a range of fishing paraphernalia piled up on the quayside. Lobster pots, colourful fishing nets, rope and buoys all make wonderful subject matter to capture the essence of this fishing community. The views from here back over the harbour are excellent too.

For something different, walk past the harbour masters office to reach a small area of rocky shore. With jagged ledges stretching out to sea, this little cove makes a fine location for a seascape, especially at dawn on a cloudy day when the skies above can explode with colour.

How to Get Here

Mevagissey can be reached via the B3273, 6 miles south of St Austell.

Parking Lat/Long: 50.272355, -4.7897948
Parking OS Grid Ref: SX 013 451
Parking Postcode: PL26 6UJ
Map: OS Explorer Map 105 (1:25 000) Falmouth & Mevagissey

Accessibility

Several car parks can be found in the village centre, one overlooking the outer harbour. From any of these car parks, the harbours are just a short distance away and easily accessible via roads or pavements.

Best Time of Year/Day

As Mevagissey looks eastwards, the harbours and beach can be photographed very well at sunrise. In autumn and especially winter the position of the morning sun will be ideal for lighting up the photogenic houses above East Wharf. Having said that, with so many possibilities to shoot in different directions, Mevagissey can also be photographed at the other end of the day. Being a popular tourist destination, it is probably best to avoid visiting during the day in the busy summer season when crowds of visitors will be present.

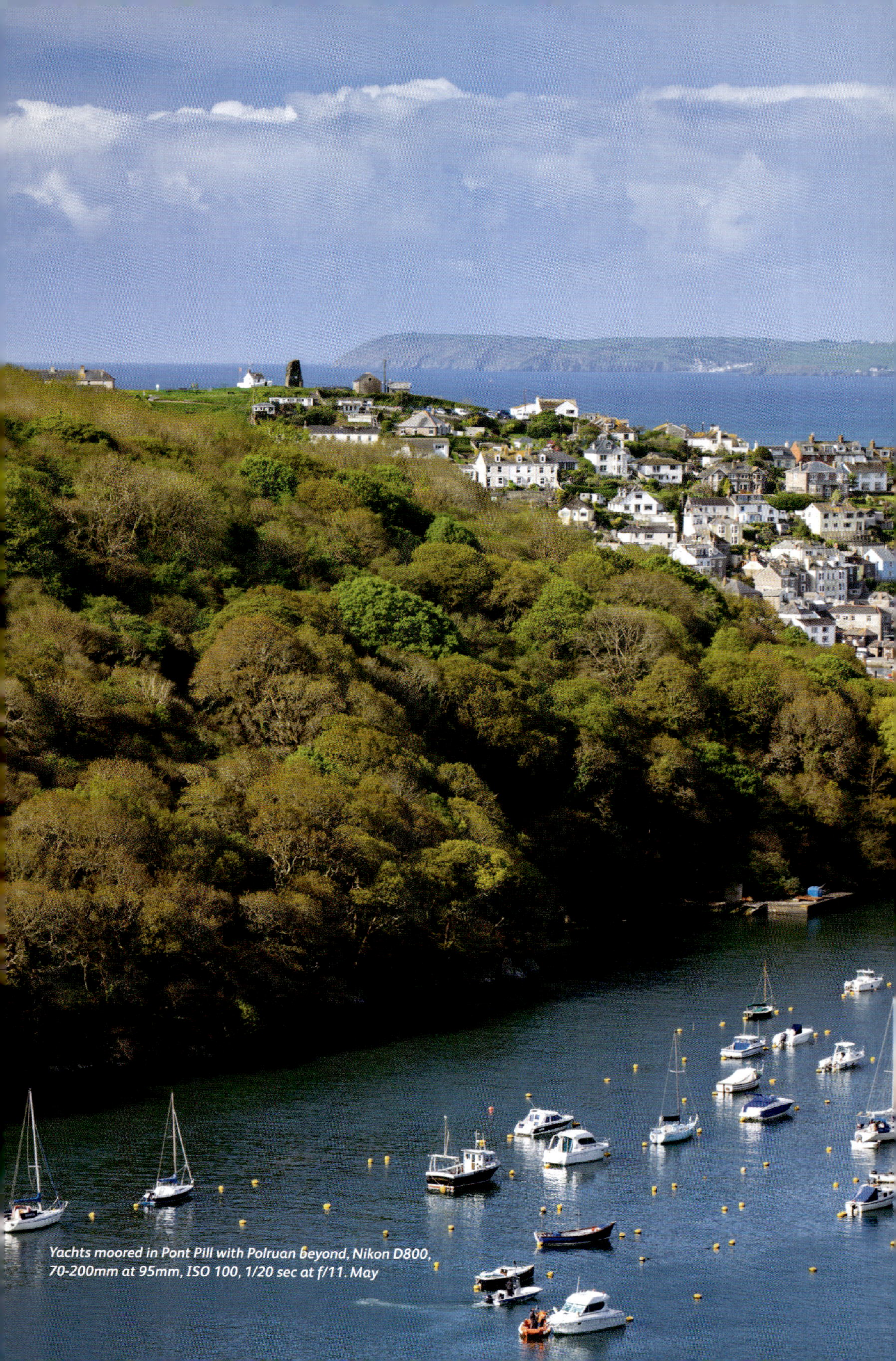

Yachts moored in Pont Pill with Polruan beyond, Nikon D800,
70-200mm at 95mm, ISO 100, 1/20 sec at f/11. May

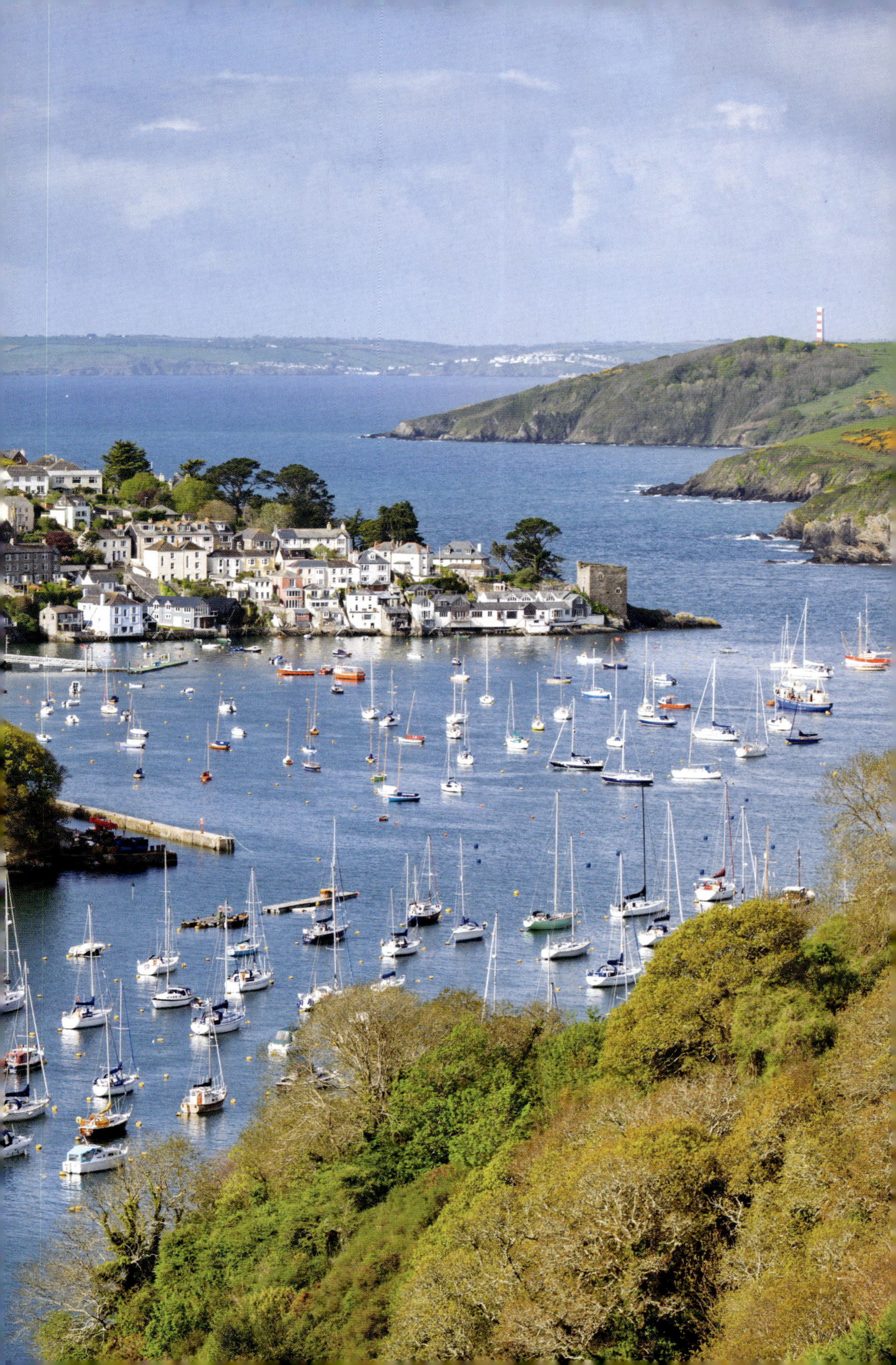

Fowey and Polruan

Fowey and its near neighbour Polruan are picture-postcard communities on Cornwall's south coast. The lesser known of the two, Polruan, is a small fishing village delightfully situated at the mouth of the Fowey Estuary with water on three sides.

Across the estuary the town and port of Fowey has figured much more prominently throughout history. With the estuary offering a natural harbour, Fowey prospered as a trading port with Europe but over the years the town became synonymous with corruption and piracy. During the Hundred Years War, as a reward for providing assistance during the Siege of Calais and the Battle of Agincourt, the port was awarded licence to patrol the coast and seize French vessels.

Sensing an opportunity to profit from this corrupt activity a number of notable privateers acted on this licence in a rather over-enthusiastic way. Over the years, the 'Fowey Gallants' as they came to be known, attacked and seized many foreign ships and some English vessels too. Despite peace being declared with France in 1453, bringing an end to the Hundred Years, piracy continued. Edward IV intervened to bring an end to piracy in Fowey by hanging several pirates and seizing their ships.

On several more occasions over the years Fowey has been a focus for the military. Supportive of Royalists during the English Civil War the area was occupied by Parliamentarian forces in 1644. Near the village of Bodinnick King Charles I narrowly escaped death when a musket fired towards him missed, killing a local fisherman standing close by.

Much later, during the Second World War, Fowey was used by the US army to load ammunition bound for Omaha Beach on D-Day.

What to Shoot and Viewpoints

Although a wander through either Polruan or Fowey will provide plentiful opportunities for photographs, some of the best estuary views can be achieved from Hall Walk.

Owned by the National Trust, the popular Hall Walk runs between Fowey and Polruan, its route taking in glorious views of the estuary, countryside and woodland. To complete the entire circular walk involves catching two ferries, but the best views for photographs can be found on the section near the village of Bodinnick.

A tiny village known for its ferry service to Fowey, Bodinnick was home to the author Daphne du Maurier. Her home 'Ferryside' is fantastically positioned on the shores of the estuary, right alongside the ferry landing, and offers incredible views over to Fowey and Polruan. Just a short walk up the road from the ferry landing, a small inconspicuous footpath sign guides walkers onto Hall Walk. After a hundred metres or so a break in the

Fowey and Polruan separated by the Fowey Estuary, Canon 1Ds Mark III, 70-200mm at 100mm, ISO 100, 0.3 sec at f/16. June

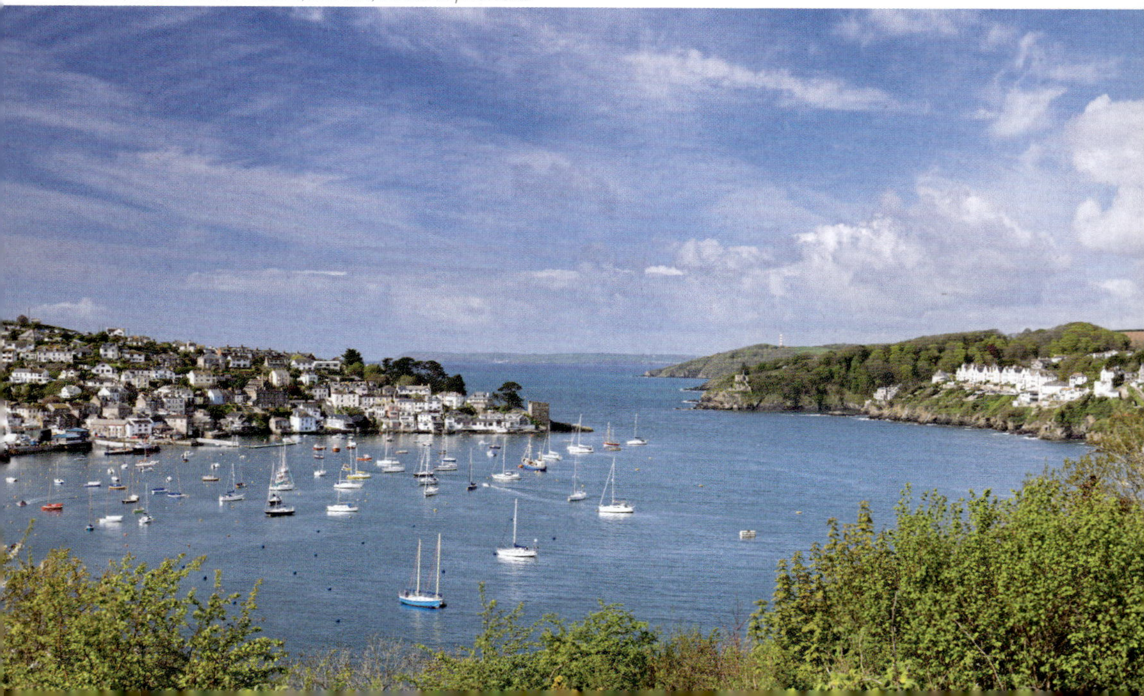

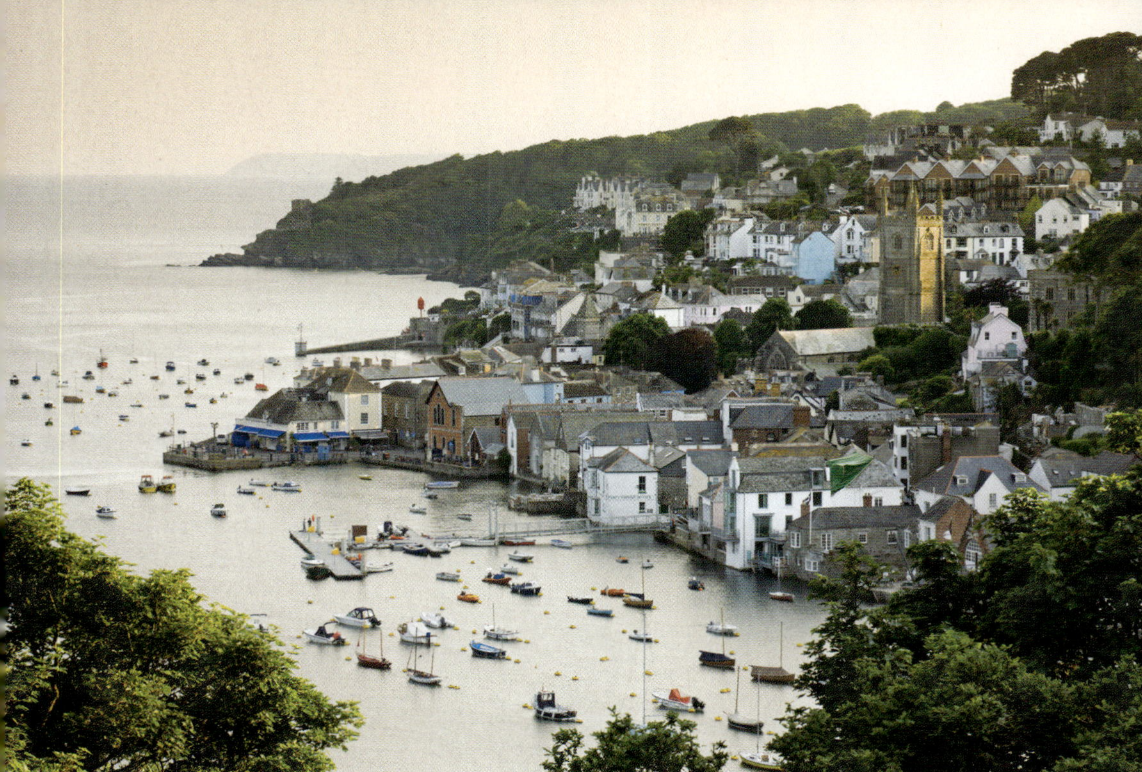

View through trees to the port of Fowey, Nikon D800E, 24-70mm at 45mm, ISO 100, 1/25 sec at f/11. May

trees offers the first glimpse over to Fowey. The elevation here provides a beautiful view of the town with far reaching views beyond to distant Dodman Point.

As you continue along the path, the trees thin out revealing glorious expansive views over the Fowey Estuary. Polruan soon comes into view on the opposite headland behind a sheltered bay dotted with little yachts. From this area, close to where Charles I was almost shot, an extreme wide-angle will enable you to photograph both Polruan and some of Fowey in a single shot. However with such a wide view, to include both villages fully you ideally should stitch several photographs together to make a panoramic.

Further along the path Fowey becomes completely obscured from view, but several new viewpoints offer perhaps the best views towards Polruan. A new channel of water, Pont Pill, is now revealed providing a sheltered natural harbour to dozens of yachts. This channel, together with the steep wooded hills either side make beautiful subject matter to frame the village beyond. Just visible on the opposite headland, the enormous banded Gribbin Daymark tower stands guard over the coast.

How to Get Here

You can either park at Bodinnick itself or park at Fowey and catch the ferry across to Bodinnick. The best approach to Bodinnick to avoid tiny country lanes is via the B3359. Travelling south on the B3359 from Liskeard, you will see a right turn signposted Polruan near the village of Lanreath. Take this turn and follow the road for 5 miles. Just before you reach the village you will see a little car park on the left.

Parking Lat/Long: 50.340831, -4.6307633
Parking OS Grid Ref: SX 129 523
Parking Postcode: PL23 1LX
Map: OS Explorer Map 107 (1:25 000) St Austell & Liskeard

Accessibility

From the small car park at Bodinnick, a 10 minute walk along the road will bring you through the village and onto Hall Walk. Although the walk goes all the way to Polruan, the views described here are all encountered within a mile of Bodinnick. The footpath is very well maintained, but being uneven with some steps is not suitable for wheelchair users.

Best Time of Year/Day

With steep wooded slopes rising up from the banks of the estuary, this location doesn't look its best in the winter when the trees are bare. The best seasons to visit would be late spring, summer and early autumn either early morning or late in the evening to benefit from low rich sunlight.

Perhaps Cornwall's most idyllic fishing village, Polperro is a popular destination for visitors on the south coast. Like many other Cornish fishing villages, rows of whitewashed cottages, originally homes to fishermen, huddle together in close proximity to the pretty harbour. The houses, together with shops and the occasional inn are connected via a network of tiny lanes and alleyways, many too small to even contemplate accommodating a car.

The village has a long association with the sea, with fishing being the main occupation of Polperro families for many centuries. As with many other Cornish fishing communities pilchards (otherwise known as sardines) were the principal catch. Once the fishing boats, known as Polperro Gaffers, returned to the harbour the pilchards would be salted and pressed, with the oil being collected for heating and lighting purposes. However, in the 20th century, with diminishing populations pilchard fishing died out in Polperro. Although some fishing vessels still work out of the harbour catching a variety of fish species, the industry is but a shadow of its former self.

Polperro's other source of income over many years was somewhat shadier. Like many other coastal villages in the South West, Polperro developed a reputation for smuggling. In the 19th century it was estimated that half of all spirits consumed in England had entered the country illegally through smuggling. As a result Parliament formed the Coastguard Service, and ordered coastguards to patrol a network of footpaths all around the coast. Over the years these tracks evolved into the South West Coast Path, preserving unrestricted access to the coastline that we enjoy today.

What to Shoot and Viewpoints

Viewpoint 1 – The Harbour

Without question the highlight of any visit to Polperro is the harbour. Similar to many Cornish coastal villages, the harbour here is tiny and overlooked by picturesque buildings all around, making photographs possible from all directions. In fact, some of the buildings actually form part of the harbour wall.

Walking from the car park your first view of the harbour will be from the west. Protected from the sea by the large stone quay just around the corner the harbour here is very well sheltered, offering good opportunities to shoot

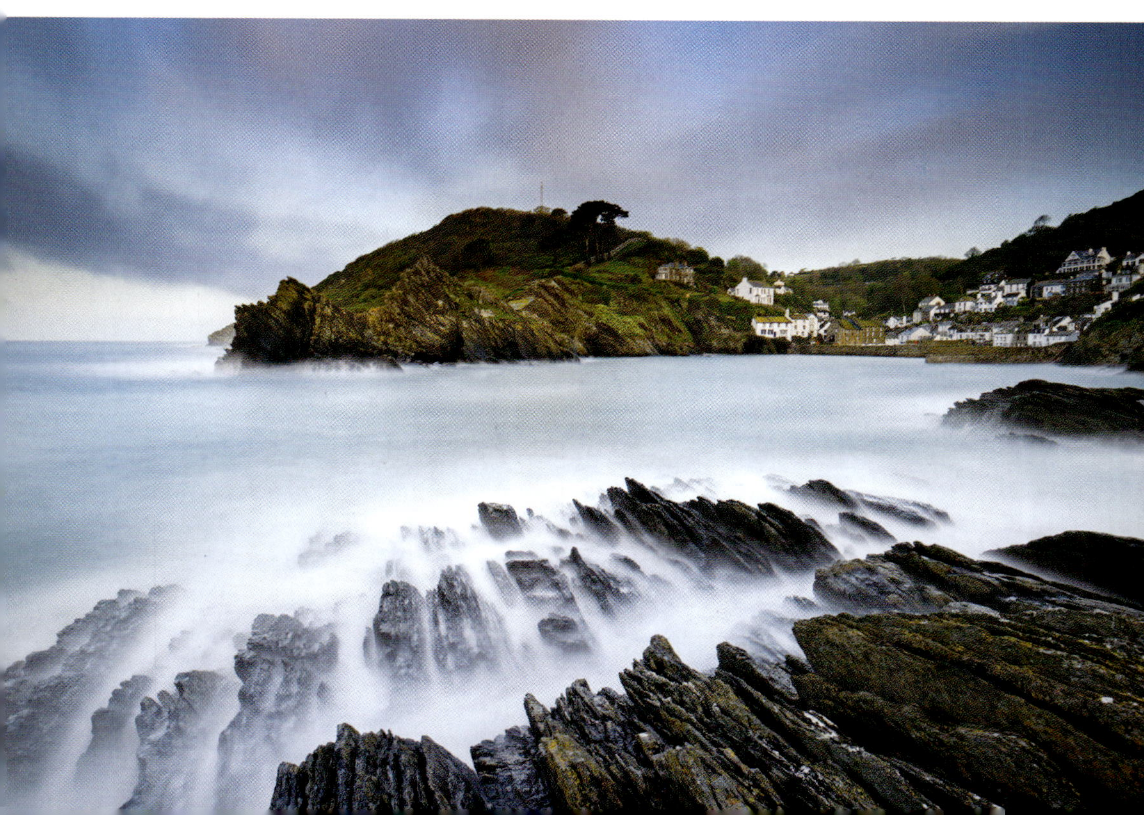

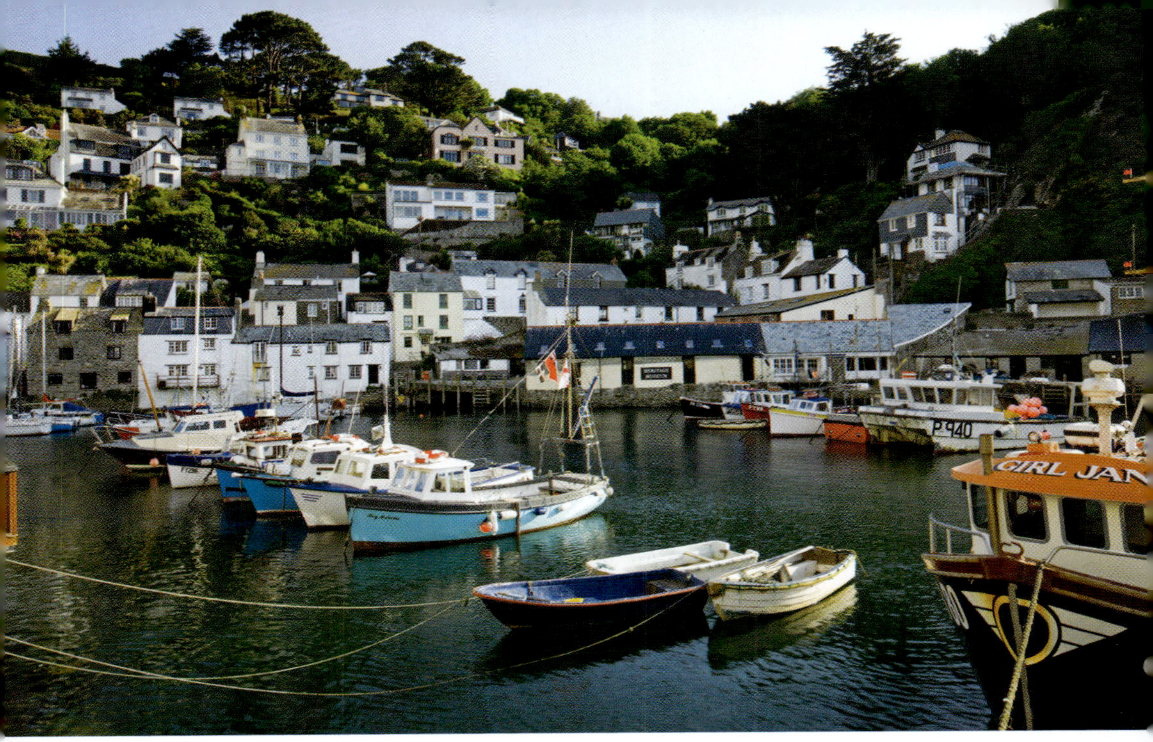

Pretty Polperro harbour on a summer morning, Canon 1Ds Mark III, 16-35mm at 25mm, ISO 100, 1/8 sec at f/16. June

reflections of the colourful boats. Most shots of Polperro harbour are taken from the quayside, near the fish market area. From here, you can gain uninterrupted views across a line of little boats to the harbour and cottages beyond.

On its far side, the cottages that make up the harbour wall restrict access of the view towards the boats. Having said that, there are several areas between buildings where you can gain a good view over the harbour in various directions. Keep a look out for tiny passageways between cottages; several seemingly private alleys are actually public walkways leading to hidden harbour viewing areas complete with benches. An excellent clear view back over the harbour can be gained from just outside the museum. For those wishing to experience the harbour from even closer, a small slipway allows you to get low and close to the small fishing boats usually moored in this area.

Viewpoint 2 – West Cliffs

To gain a good elevated view over the village, look out for coast path sign posts on the west side of the harbour. The path climbs up between some cottages offering glimpses down to the fishing boats below, but the view is too restricted by rooftops and overhead cables to make a good photograph. Instead, continue past the cottages and out onto the headland.

High above on the cliffs, Polperro resembles an idyllic model village. From this elevated viewpoint you get a better appreciation of the village as a whole, the harbour nestled at the bottom of a steep wooded hillside, with newer houses dotted high amongst the rich green slopes.

Opposite: Dramatic ledges beneath the east cliffs, Nikon D800E, 17-35mm at 20mm, ISO 200, 60 sec at f/11. May

Looking in the other direction, a narrow channel between cliffs provides access to the sea. Perched on the headland below, named Peak Rock, a curious building sits alone on the cliffs. Known as the net loft this building, dating back to the 1800's, was used for storing the pilchard nets and sails. It is believed that the building occupies the site of a much older chapel and possibly even a lighthouse.

The net loft, headland and village are very spaced out from this viewpoint; so much so that it is impossible to include them all in a single picture. The only way to achieve this would be to capture a series of images, to then be stitched together into a panoramic format.

Boats moored safely in Polperro harbour, Nikon D800E, 17-35mm at 17mm, ISO 100, ¼ sec at f/11. May

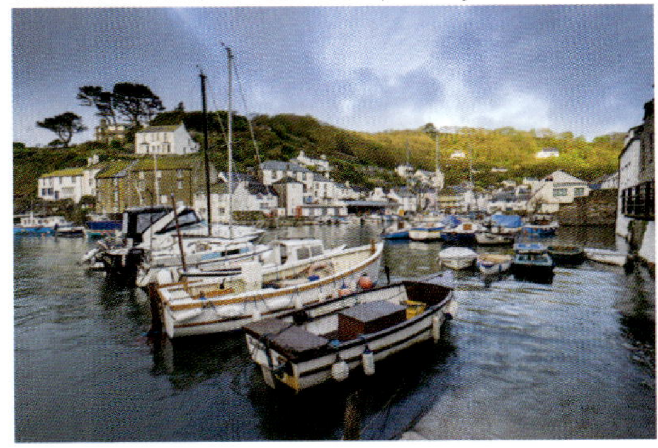

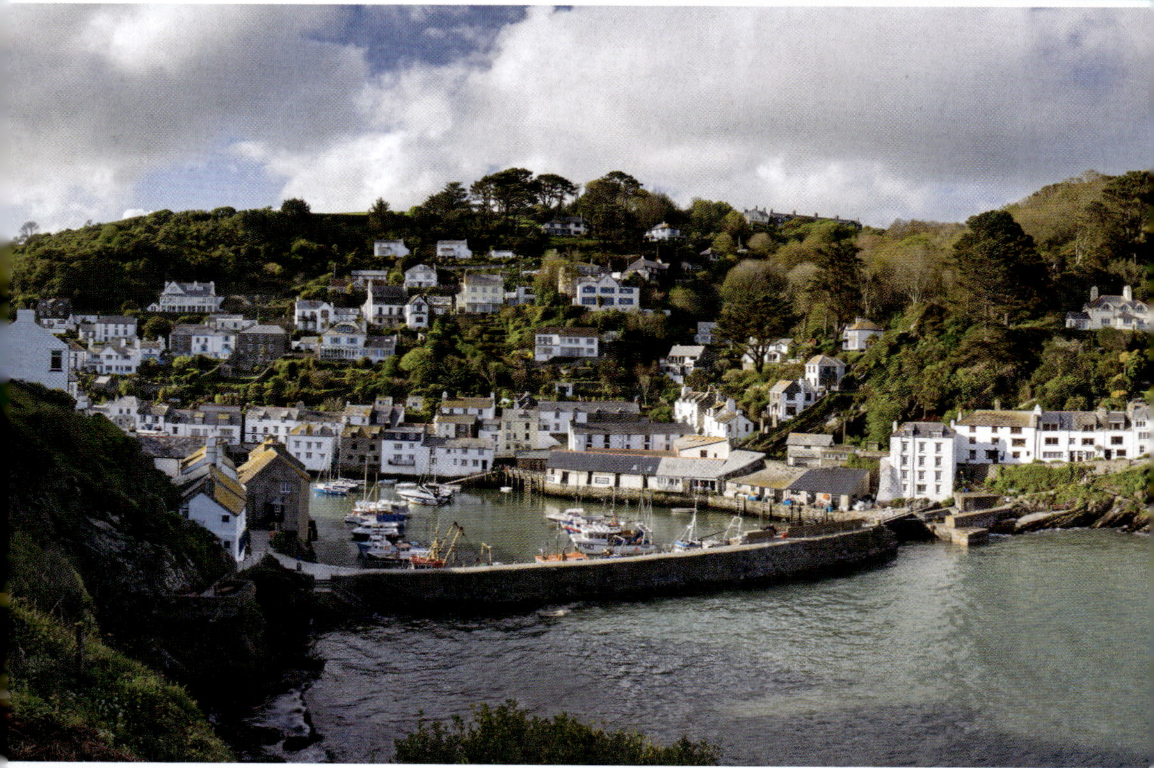

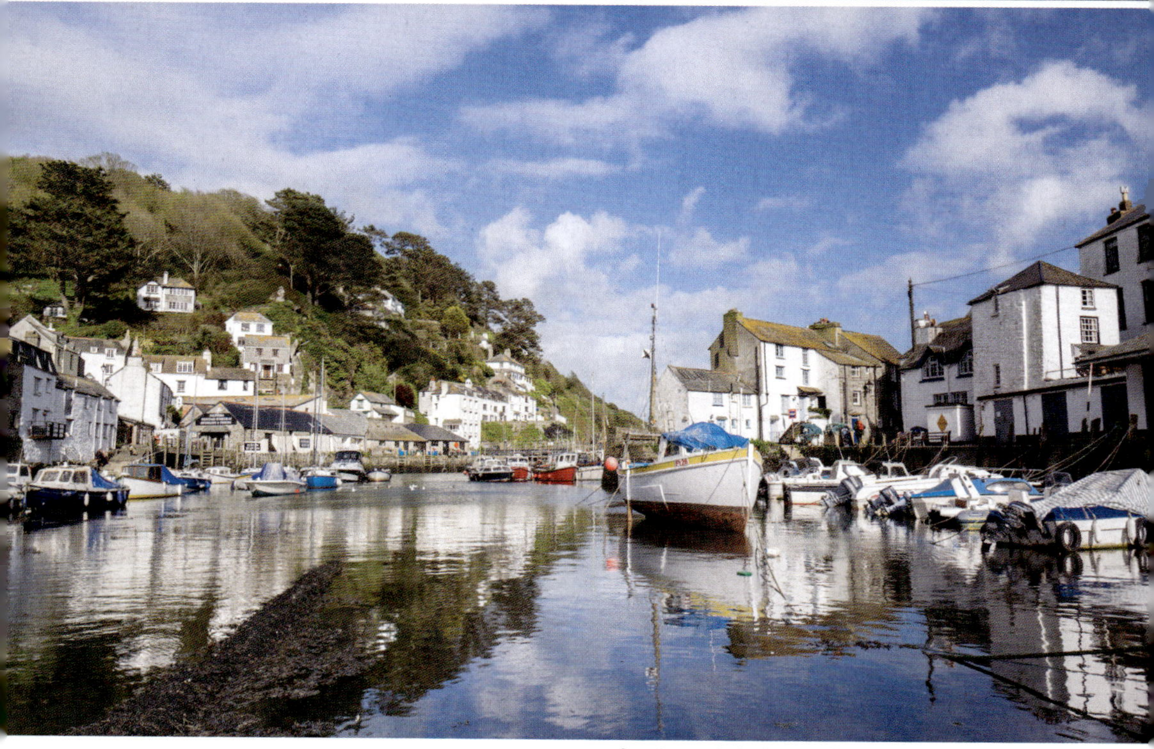

Standing in the harbour itself at low tide, Nikon D800E, 17-35mm at 24mm, ISO 100, 1/25 sec at f/11. May

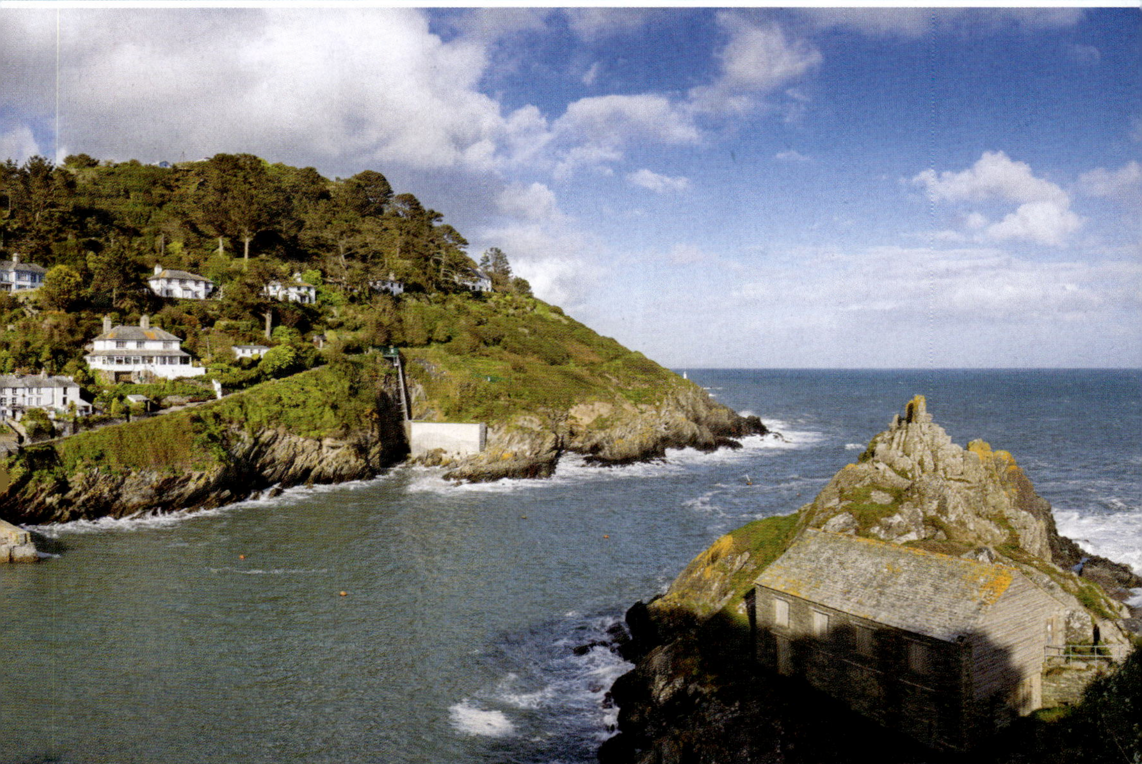

Panoramic view down towards Polperro from the cliffs to the west, Nikon D800E, 17-35mm at 20mm, ISO 100, 1/15 sec at f/11. May

Viewpoint 3 – East Cliffs

From below the east cliffs a much less typical and dramatic view of the village and coastline can be photographed. Head eastwards out of the village on the South West Coast Path in the direction of Talland Bay. Once past the houses follow a small track winding down through vegetation on the cliff side. Soon you will find yourself standing on some very jagged ledges, with row upon row of sharp vertical rocks pointing upwards. You need to be very careful on these ledges; they are difficult to walk upon and are close to some vertical drops into the sea. Also, be extra careful not to get caught by some unexpectedly large waves crashing over the rocks.

Once you are safely in position, you can fully appreciate the opportunities this view creates. Photographed as part of a wide-angle composition the foreground rocks make fantastic subjects, especially when waves are crashing over them. The real benefit of this viewpoint though is how it enables you to emphasise the dramatic geographical setting where Polperro is located. For the effort in getting into this position, your photographs from here reward you with a completely different view of Polperro, very different from the pretty picture postcard fishing village usually conveyed in photographs.

How to Get Here

Polperro lies just 5 miles west of the town of Looe on the A387. Vehicle access is restricted through Polperro from April to September. Even outside of those times, it is unadvisable to drive into the village as the roads are extremely narrow and no car parking is available. There is a large pay and display car park just before you reach the village.

Parking Lat/Long: 50.336938, -4.5223318
Parking OS Grid Ref: SX 206 516
Parking Postcode: PL13 2PL
Map: OS Explorer Map 107 (1:25 000) St Austell & Liskeard

Accessibility

A 15 minute walk from the car park along a road with a gentle gradient offers convenient access to the harbour. Away from this main route, some of Polperro's alleys and lanes are very steep, and together with the coast path are not accessible for wheelchair users.

Best Time of Year/Day

With views in many directions Polperro can be photographed well at either end of the day. For the harbour, try to plan your visit to coincide with a higher tide as at low tide the water drains from the harbour. It is not advisable to visit during the day, especially in the summer months when the village will be busy with visitors. As Polperro lies within a wooded valley, it is advisable to visit from late spring to early autumn when the valley slopes are verdant.

North Cornwall – Introduction

Dramatic cliffs, crashing Atlantic waves and pristine sandy beaches; these are the ingredients that make North Cornwall one of the UK's most spectacular coastal locations.

The beaches along the seaside of North Cornwall draw visitors every summer, eager to enjoy the sun and surf that this coastline offers in abundance. From Bude near the Devon border down to Newquay and beyond every beach is a winner for both holidaymakers and photographers alike, consisting of golden sands and dramatic cliffs.

Without question one of North Cornwall's most photogenic locations is the stretch of coastline between charming Padstow and its noisier neighbour Newquay. Around Trevose Head alone no less than seven glorious sandy beaches can be found, the difficulty for any visitor is choosing which beach to visit.

Away from the beaches, the cliffs are no less spectacular and thanks to the South West Coast Path are freely accessible to visitors. One highlight of this area is the incredible Bedruthan Steps, a dramatic series of rock stacks running parallel to the cliffs. At high tide these stacks take a pounding from the fierce Atlantic rollers, while at low tide they become stranded on one of the most beautiful beaches to be found anywhere.

In a county renowned for its tin mining past, the Towanroath Engine House at Wheal Coates is perhaps the most iconic and recognisable reminder of Cornwall's mining heritage. This abandoned building, now preserved by the National Trust, guards the cliff tops overlooking the Atlantic and is the subject of countless iconic Cornish postcards.

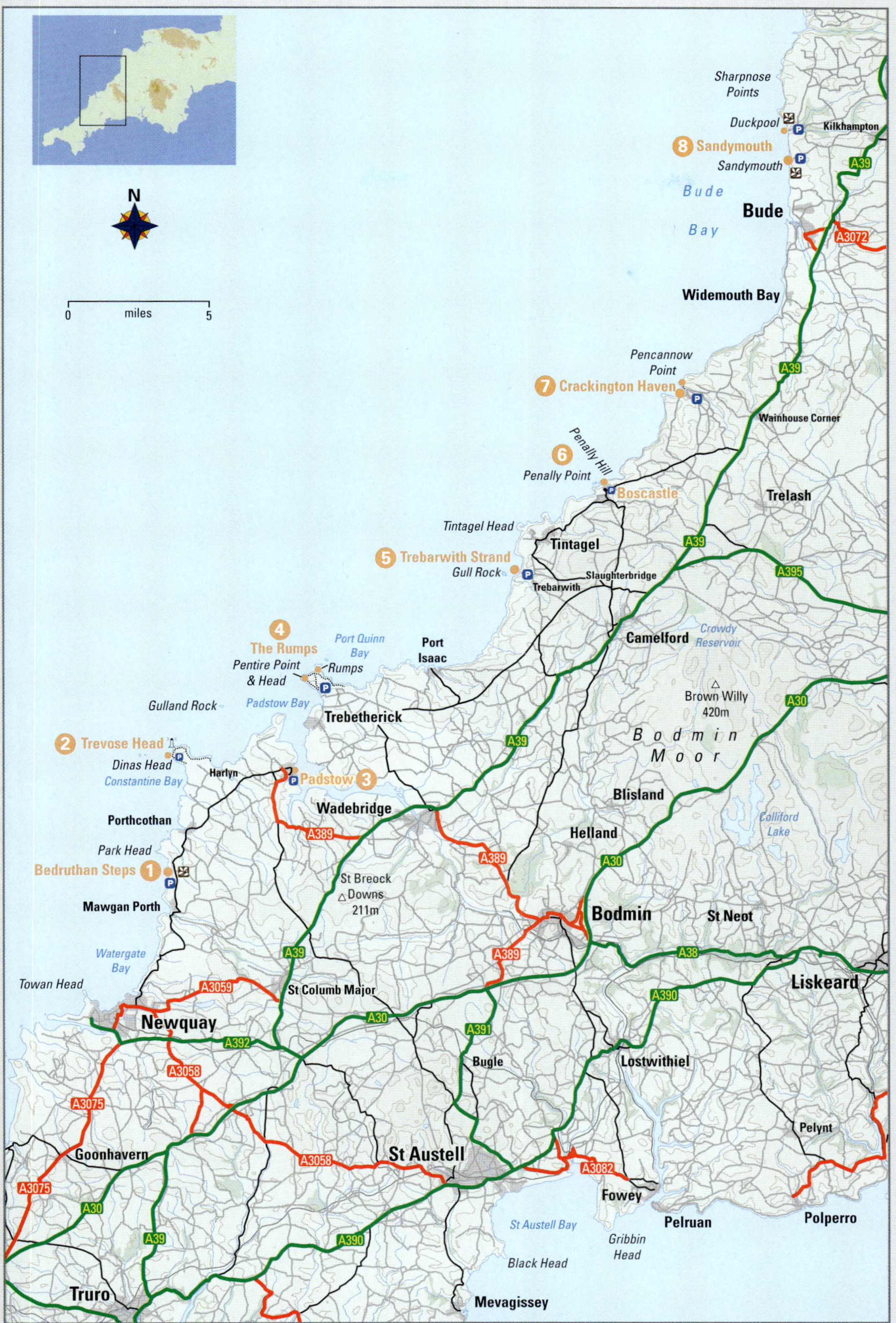

N
0 miles 5
Sharpnose Points
Duckpool
Kilkhampton
A39
8 Sandymouth
Sandymouth
Bude Bay
Bude
A3072
Widemouth Bay
Pencannow Point
7 Crackington Haven
A39
Wainhouse Corner
Penally Hill
6
Penally Point
Boscastle
Trelash
Tintagel Head
Tintagel
A39
5 Trebarwith Strand
Gull Rock
Slaughterbridge
A395
Trebarwith
4
The Rumps
Port Quinn Bay
Camelford
Crowdy Reservoir
Pentire Point & Head
Rumps
Port Isaac
Brown Willy 420m
A30
Gulland Rock
Padstow Bay
Bodmin Moor
Trebetherick
A39
2 Trevose Head
Blisland
Colliford Lake
Dinas Head
Harlyn
P Padstow 3
Helland
Constantine Bay
Wadebridge
A389
Porthcothan
A389
Bodmin
St Neot
Park Head
St Breock Downs 211m
Bedruthan Steps 1
A30
Mawgan Porth
A389
A38
Watergate Bay
A39
Liskeard
Towan Head
A3059
St Columb Major
A390
Newquay
A30
Pelynt
A392
A391
A3058
Bugle
Lostwithiel
A3075
A3058
St Austell
A3082
Goonhavern
Fowey
Polperro
A3075
Pelruan
A30
St Austell Bay
Gribbin Head
Truro
A39
A390
Black Head
Mevagissey

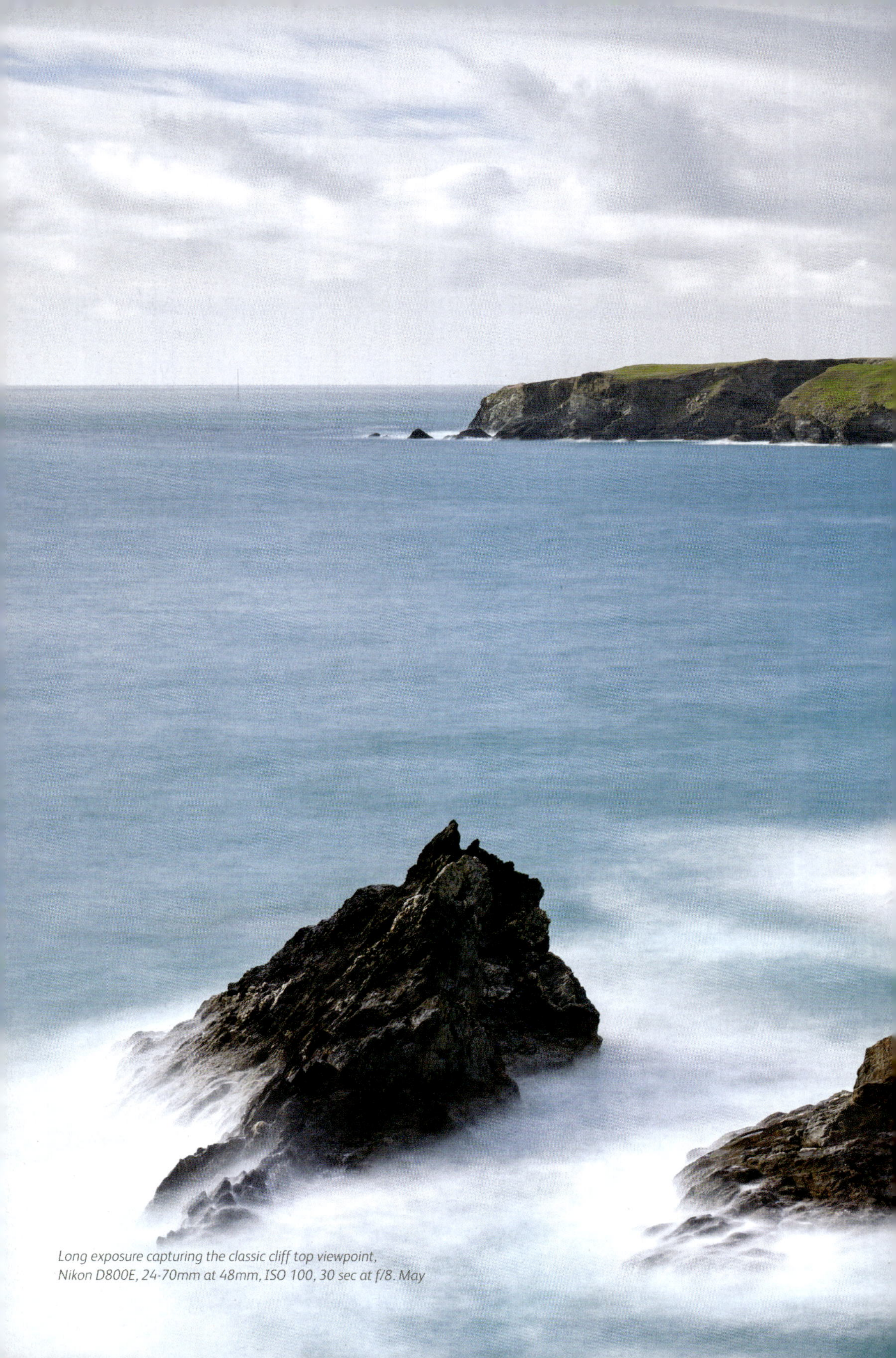

Long exposure capturing the classic cliff top viewpoint,
Nikon D800E, 24-70mm at 48mm, ISO 100, 30 sec at f/8. May

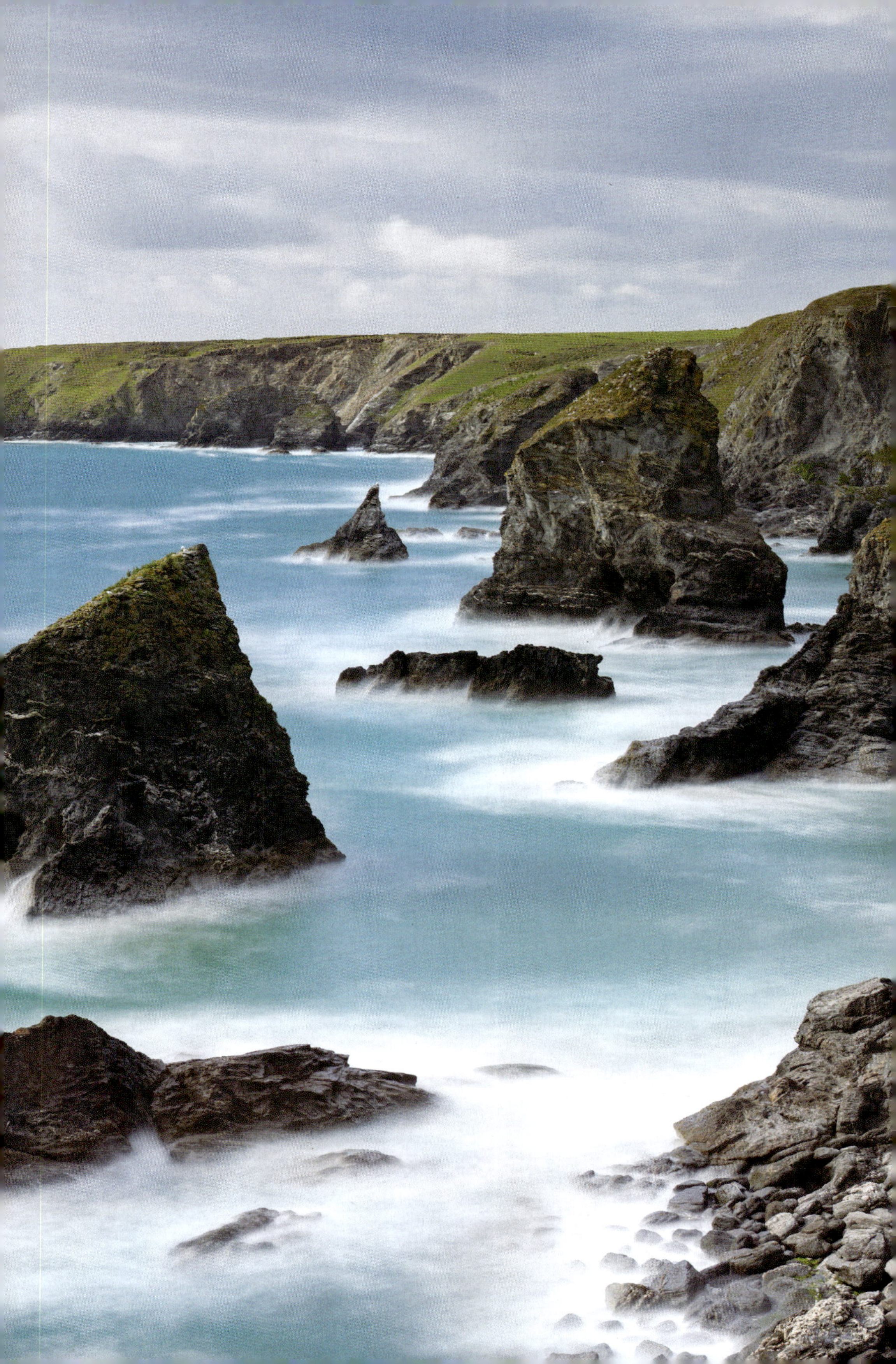

One of Cornwall's most dramatic vistas, Bedruthan Steps is an undisputed highlight of the Cornish coast. The cliff top viewpoint has been the subject of countless postcards dating back to the Victorian era, and remains a popular attraction for visitors to North Cornwall today.

The view from the cliffs to the south looking north over the beach towards Park Head is a typically rugged Cornish coastal view. The giant stacks and towering cliffs are regularly pounded by crashing Atlantic waves. For such a hostile and seemingly inaccessible stretch of coast, the most surprising aspect of Bedruthan Steps is the transformation it undergoes with a retreating tide. Unlike similar stretches of coastline, with the outgoing tide a beautiful beach is revealed at the base of the cliffs, leaving the stacks stranded in golden sand.

A steep staircase cut into the cliffs provides access to the beach below.

What to Shoot and Viewpoints

Viewpoint 1 – From the Cliffs

The classic view is best reached from the National Trust car park at nearby Carnewas. Close to the car park Carnewas Point offers a first glimpse of spectacular far-reaching coastal views towards Bedruthan Steps and distant Trevose Head. Past this viewpoint a well-maintained path descends some wide low steps ending directly above Bedruthan Steps.

The classic view over the beach is photographed from this viewpoint, close to the wooden fence. To the left you will notice a fenced-off path leading up to a higher vista. This once was a popular photographic viewpoint complete with benches but thanks to a cliff fall is no longer safe to access. Fortunately from the lower viewpoint the view is better, so there is no need to take risks crossing the barrier.

Thanks to the access provided by the coast path, Bedruthan Steps offers so much more than one cliff top view. The footpath north of the main viewpoint is particularly interesting, especially in late spring when the cliffs are awash with colourful sea pink wildflowers.

Sea thrift wildflowers flowering on the cliff tops in late Spring, Nikon D800E, 17-35mm at 19mm, ISO 50, 15 sec at f/13. May

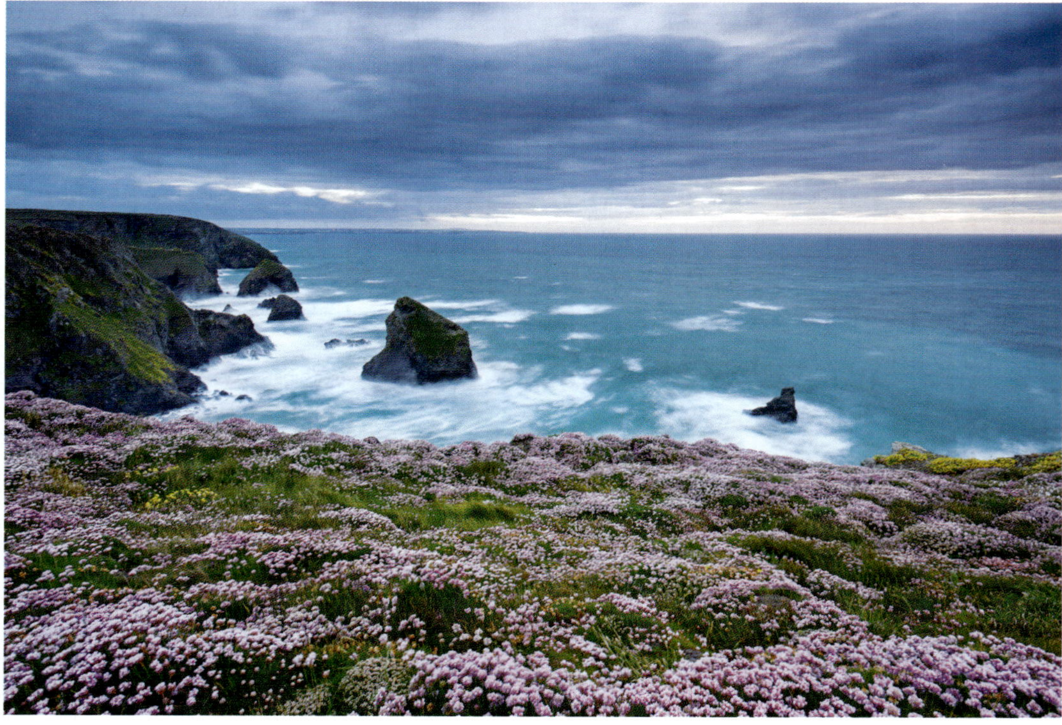

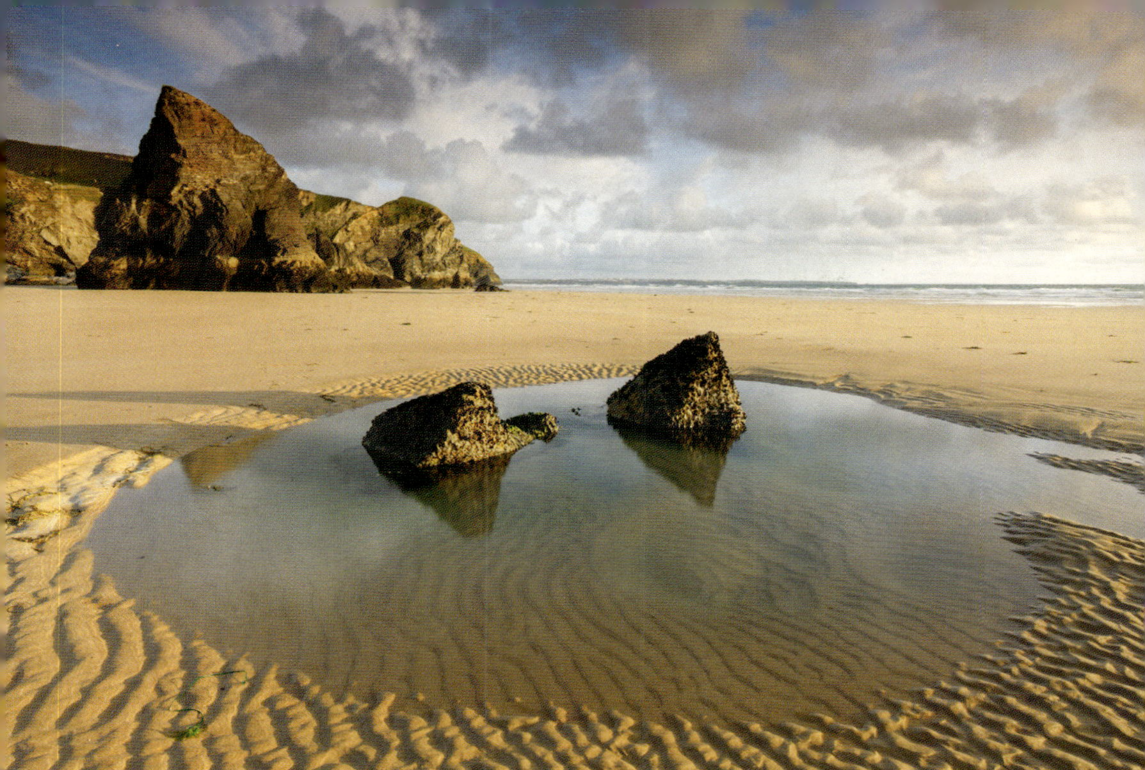

During low tide a glorious golden sandy beach is revealed, Canon 1Ds Mark III, 16-35mm at 20mm, ISO 100, 0.5 sec at f/16. May

Viewpoint 2 – On the Beach

The best time to head to the beach is as the tide retreats. If you can be one of the first people on the beach at this time you will benefit from having clean sand, free from footprints. More importantly by arriving at this time you won't have to worry about being cut off by the tide.

Take your time descending the steps to the beach. They are in a safe condition and offer handrails most of the way down, but are still very steep and can appear quite daunting. Once you reach the beach allow plenty of time to look for compositions; there are lots of areas to explore.

As the sea stacks are to be found north of the steps, it is natural to head in this direction. Most of the stacks are so large you will need a wide-angle lens to capture them in their entirety; to help you achieve this try and get as far up the beach as you can.

If you get to the beach soon after the tide has uncovered the sand, you will find tidal pools and channels of water all around, making excellent reflective foreground subjects. Alternatively rippled sand always looks great in photographs, especially when side lit by late sunshine.

Once you have settled on a composition it is probably best to be patient and wait for the optimum moment (usually at sunset) rather than scouting for other viewpoints. This location is unsurprisingly popular with visitors and photographers alike; if you leave a viewpoint the chances are it may be spoilt with footprints upon your return.

How to Get Here

Bedruthan Steps is just off the B3276 about halfway between Newquay and Padstow. A signpost from the road leads to the National Trust car park at Carnewas.

Parking Lat/Long: 50.481466, -5.0320119
Parking Grid Ref: SW 849 69
Parking Postcode: PL27 7UW
Map: OS Explorer Map 106 (1:25 000) Newquay & Padstow

Accessibility

The track from the National Trust car park to Carnewas Point is suitable for wheelchair users. After this point, steps prevent wheelchair access to the classic Bedruthan Steps view. The walk from the car park to the main viewpoint takes approximately 10 minutes, and accessed via a well-maintained track. The staircase to the beach is very steep and long, requiring stamina to climb back up. The staircase to the beach is closed through the winter months (November to February).

Careful planning for the tide is important for every trip down to the beach at Bedruthan Steps, as it is easy to become cut off. The incoming tide creeps around the sea stacks, cutting you off from the steps before you have realised you are in any danger.

Best Time of Year/Day

Like most locations on the North Cornwall coast, Bedruthan Steps is best visited in the afternoon/evening when the sun sets out over the Atlantic. Photographs from the cliffs look incredible at any time of year but are especially pleasing in late spring when the cliffs are carpeted with wildflowers. The beach cannot be reached during the winter months.

Situated close to Padstow on the dramatic North Cornwall coast, the Trevose Head promontory stretches out into the Atlantic Ocean. From the coast path on a clear day there are far-reaching views along the coast for many miles; as far as Pendeen in the south and Hartland Point to the north.

Perched on the northwest extremity of the headland, a lighthouse has offered guidance to passing ships since 1847. Until it was commissioned there had been no lighthouse between Land's End and Lundy Island, making this stretch of Atlantic coast particularly treacherous for ships passing through the Bristol Channel.

Carpets of wildflowers on Dinas Head, Canon 1Ds Mark III, 17-40mm at 29mm, ISO 100, 4 sec at f/16. May

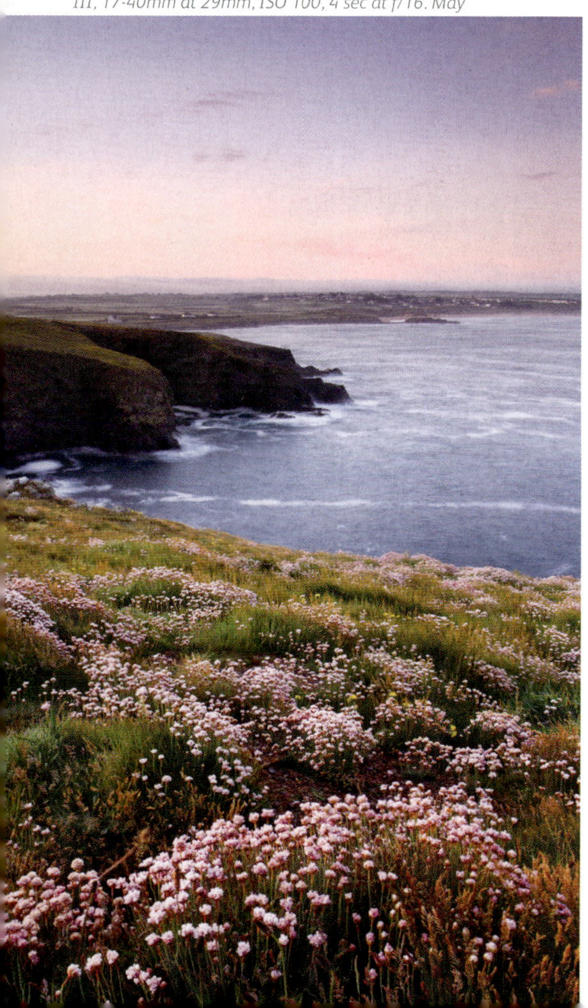

What to Shoot and Viewpoints

Although the headland makes a good backdrop to pictures captured from the beaches and cliffs to the south, the lighthouse itself is all but obscured from view by a smaller promontory called Dinas Head. This little headland pokes out like a giant nose from Trevose Head and hides the lighthouse beyond it.

Fortunately, the South West Coast Path provides access to walk around the perimeter of Trevose Head, and a short detour onto Dinas Head offers one of the finest and most dramatic lighthouse views to be found anywhere along the Cornish coast. Viewed from Dinas Head the lighthouse makes an unmistakable cliff top subject overlooking Stinking Cove, an unappealing name that does nothing to convey the magnificence of this location.

Stinking Cove

The small cove is enclosed on three sides by steep cliffs and ledges, and due to its west facing position at the tip of the headland is very exposed to the Atlantic. Waves regularly surge around the rocks and crash against the cliffs, creating explosions of white water far below. White water adds a dramatic impact to seascapes especially when photographed with a long exposure of anything from several seconds to minutes. Stinking Cove therefore makes a particularly good location for this style of photography.

Although the view to the lighthouse can be photographed just a short walk away from the cliff top car park, for the best viewpoint head down the cliffs a little. The rocky cliffs slope gently here, allowing you to position yourself several metres down the cliff for a viewpoint that overlooks the cove. Although it is relatively easy to get to this lower position, be aware that the rocks here are often loose making it slippery. Once in position this lower viewpoint will allow you to include some of the ledges below at the base of your frame, effectively linking up the cliffs all around your picture.

Dinas Head

The view south from Trevose Head is far reaching but not anywhere near as dramatic, yet with the right conditions is certainly worth photographing. Standing on the top of Dinas Head, the view encompasses the beaches that hug the western side of Trevose Head, namely Booby's, Constantine and Treyarnon Bays. This view works particularly well in late spring, when a wide-angle lens allows you to fill the foreground with the beautiful sea pink wildflowers that carpet the cliff tops of Dinas Head.

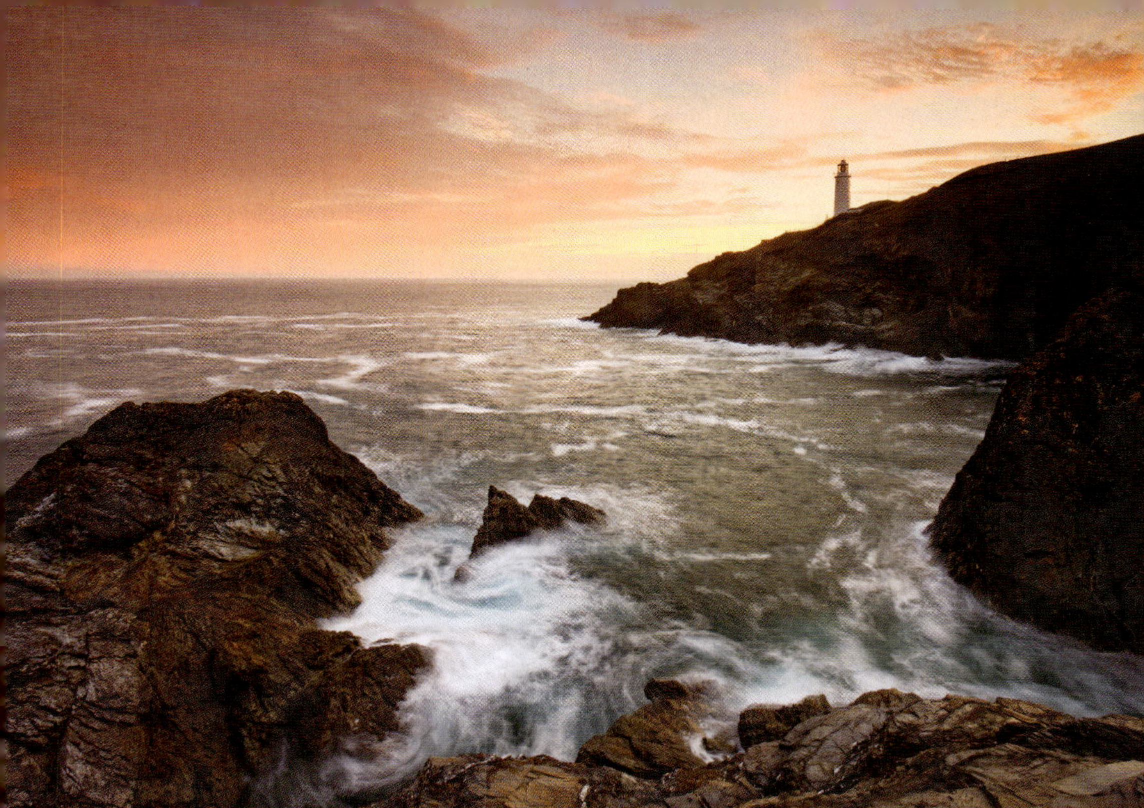

Beautiful sunrise above Stinking Cove, Canon 1Ds Mark III, 17-40mm at 20mm, ISO 100, 3 sec at f/16. May

How to Get Here

Head west out of Padstow on the B3276 for 2 miles, before taking the right hand turn towards Harlyn. Drive through Harlyn village and turn right, then right again, now following the signs for Trevose Head. Soon after passing Harlyn Sands Holiday Park you will arrive at a private toll road. Purchase a ticket at the pay and display machine, and then continue up to the cliff top car parking area.

Parking Lat/Long: 50.540406, -5.0236441
Parking Grid Ref: SW 851 763
Parking Postcode: PL28 8SH
Map: OS Explorer Map 106 (1:25 000) Newquay & Padstow

Accessibility

From the car park, follow a path down to an old quarry and then continue out onto Dinas Head. The lighthouse will come into view almost immediately; to gain an uninterrupted view of the lighthouse over Stinking Cove veer to the right onto some slate cliffs. Although the cliffs are just a few minutes from the car park, good walking boots are recommended as the loose stones on the rocks may make them slippery.

Best Time of Year/Day

As the lighthouse faces west, it makes an ideal location for late afternoon/evening and sunset photographs. The sun sets further to the northwest in the summer, giving the best chances of sunlight fully illuminating the dark cliffs that surround the cove. Providing there are clouds in the sky, the sun's position at this time of year will also provide the best opportunity for a colourful sunset. Having said that, this view can be photographed well throughout the seasons, especially on a dark moody winter day when waves crash against the cliffs with tremendous force.

Time your visit to avoid low tide. A particularly jagged rocky islet makes a wonderful feature to any photographs of the cove, but at low tide this rock is less impressive when lower water levels remove its island status.

Padstow

Situated on the west bank of the Camel Estuary, popular Padstow is one of the visitor hotspots of North Cornwall. Like many Cornish fishing towns and villages along the coast, Padstow with its lovely harbour is picture-postcard material.

With its sheltered location by the only estuary on the rugged north coast of Cornwall, Padstow was a thriving port dating back to the medieval era, important for trading and ship building. Like many of Cornwall's coastal communities, the principal industry up until recent years was fishing. Padstow now prospers as a major visitor destination, popular due to both its spectacular natural surroundings and, in more recent years, the influence of its best known inhabitant, celebrity chef Rick Stein. Although some trawlers remain in the pretty harbour, the fishing fleet has in the main been replaced with sparkling modern yachts.

Surrounded by some of Cornwall's finest beaches and rugged coastline, Padstow often gets overlooked by photographers. But, in the right circumstances the harbour makes a beautiful place to spend time with your camera.

What to Shoot and Viewpoints

It's really all about the harbour. The town is typically Cornish, with narrow streets, whitewashed cottages and rows of little gift shops and galleries. The streets are wonderful for browsing, but the harbour has a natural lure for any photographer.

Unlike most other Cornish fishing towns, the inner harbour at Padstow is enclosed by a tidal gate. This not only ensures that there is always a sufficient water level for photographs of the harbour, but also keeps the water sheltered and therefore often reflective. A walkway over the top of the gate also enables you to access every side of the harbour to maximize photographic opportunities.

The large trawlers are usually to be found moored alongside the south quay of the inner harbour, close to the harbour master's office. Being so large, these boats can often dominate photographs of the harbour, but are easily avoided in compositions.

Smaller fishing boats tend to be moored alongside the south quay a little further to the west, while a marina near the north quay is always busy with photogenic yachts.

Viewpoint 1 – South Quay

Perhaps the best location to shoot from is on the south quay to the left or right of the trawlers. From here the yachts in the small marina are lined up in a very pleasing arrangement, while beyond on the north quay a row of old iconic buildings sit sandwiched between the harbour and a line of trees.

Between these shops and cafes sits Abbey House, one of Padstow's most important buildings and reputably one of the oldest houses in Cornwall. Whether photographed as a background to a harbour shot or as a subject in its own right, Abbey House is a fascinating building and, like the harbour, is part of the fabric of Padstow. Dating back to the 15th century, Abbey House at one point was the Guild House of the Padstow merchants. A tunnel connecting Abbey House and Prideaux Place, supposedly used for smuggling, was for many years rumoured to exist but has never been found.

Viewpoint 2 – The Strand

For some variations in viewpoint head west along the south quay. The smaller fishing boats just below the quay are far easier to include in the foreground of a photograph than the huge trawlers to the right.

The Strand connects both quays and also offers a wonderful place from which to shoot the north quay from a very different angle. The road at the northwest corner of the harbour affords a very pleasing view of the moored boats and buildings along the north quay. As you are looking roughly eastwards this viewpoint works especially well on a colourful cloudy sunrise, but is best avoided if no clouds are in the sky.

Viewpoint 3 – North Quay

With many immediately recognisable buildings lining the south quay such as the Old Customs House, it is worth continuing onto the north quay to photograph back across the harbour. Typically a much busier composition, due to the quantity of buildings and boats on this side, the vista really benefits from a still harbour to bring some simplicity to an otherwise cluttered view. This panorama is ideally positioned to take advantage of early morning sunlight and therefore can be photographed just after capturing sunrise from the nearby viewpoint on the Strand.

Top: Tranquil morning overlooking Padstow harbour, Nikon D800E, 24-70mm at 36mm, ISO 100, 1.3 sec at f/11. June

Middle: The Old Custom House, now a classy harbour front inn, Nikon D800E, 70-200mm at 98mm, ISO 100, 1/8 sec at f/8. March

Bottom: Wide angle reflections in Padstow harbour, Canon 1Ds Mark III, 16-35mm at 23mm, ISO 100, 1/8 sec at f/16. May.

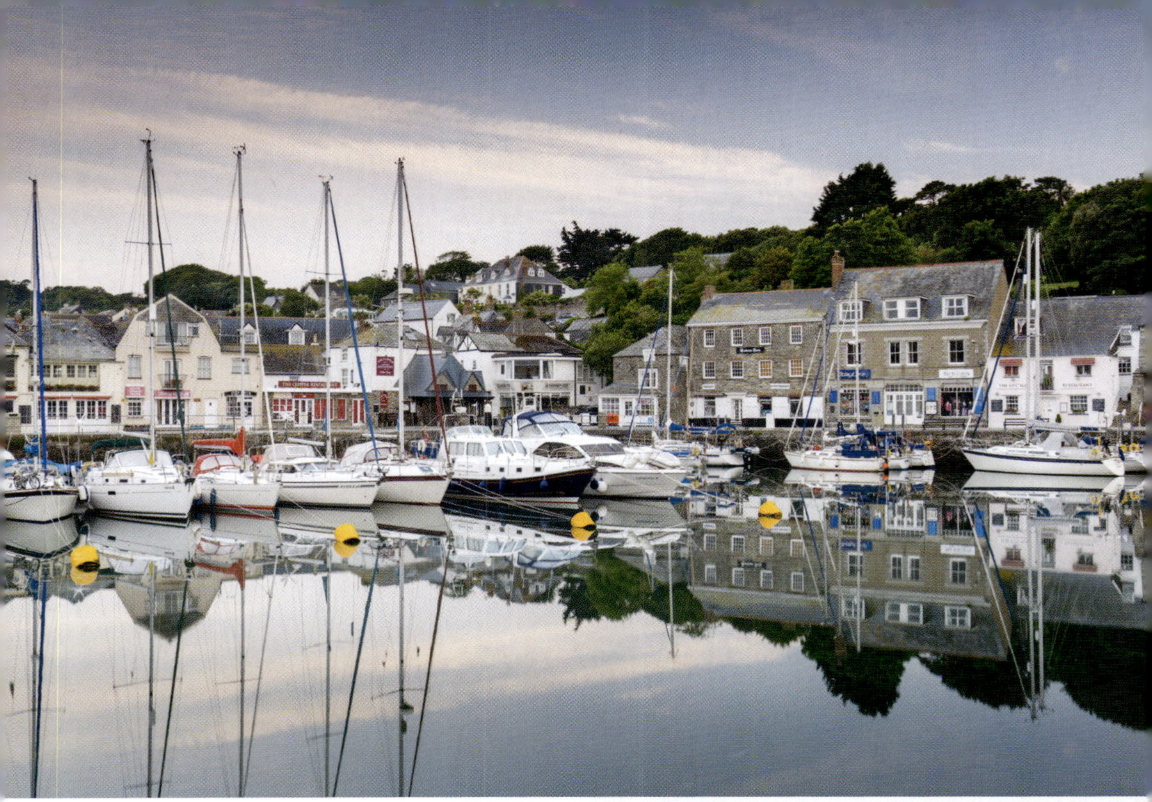

How to Get Here

Padstow is located approximately 8 miles from Wadebridge in North Cornwall. Head west out of Wadebridge on the A39. After two miles, turn right onto the A389 and follow this road all the way to Padstow.

Parking Lat/Long: 50.543109, -4.9367196
Parking Grid Ref: SW 920 753
Parking Postcode: PL28 8AF
Map: OS Explorer Map 106 (1:25 000) Padstow

Accessibility

The large car park behind the south quay is only metres from the harbour. From the car park, you can easily walk around the entire harbour in 5–10 minutes. As the quaysides are all paved roads, all the views of the harbour described above are wheelchair friendly.

Best Time of Year/Day

Due to its immense popularity Padstow is a very busy town throughout the year, but especially in the summer months. To avoid cars and hundreds of people milling around on the quays it is always best to visit at dawn, regardless of the season.

Fortunately the sun's position during sunrise and early morning is ideal to shoot the various views over the harbour, and this is also the best time to ensure still reflective water. Even at this early time you still need to keep an eye out for photographic eyesores spoiling the view, such as delivery vans and rubbish lorries but your chances of capturing a photograph are much better.

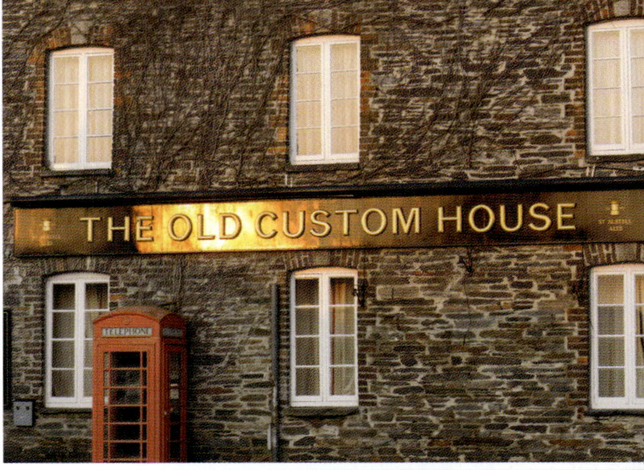

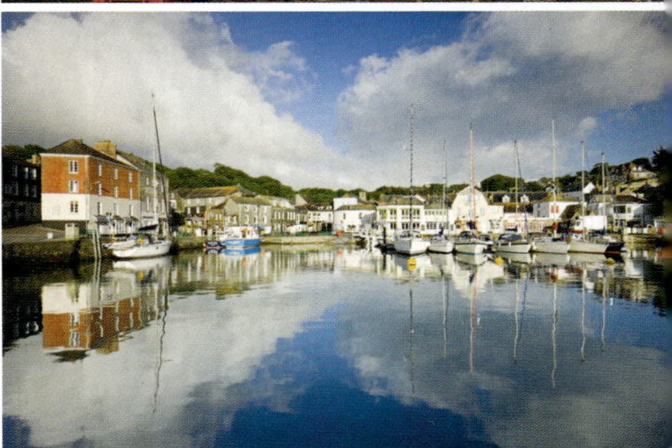

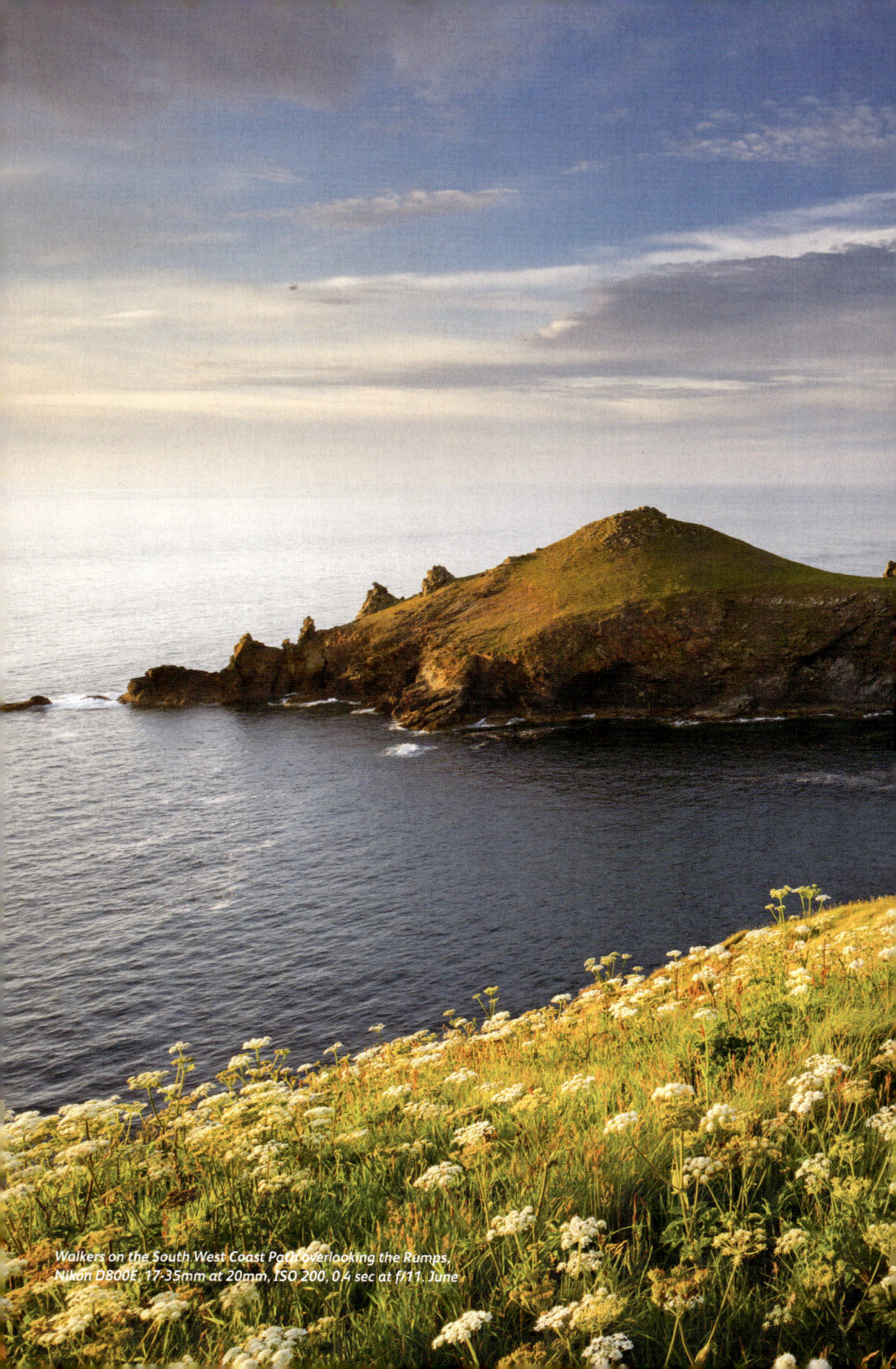

Walkers on the South West Coast Path overlooking the Rumps.
Nikon D800E, 17-35mm at 20mm, ISO 200, 0.4 sec at f/11. June

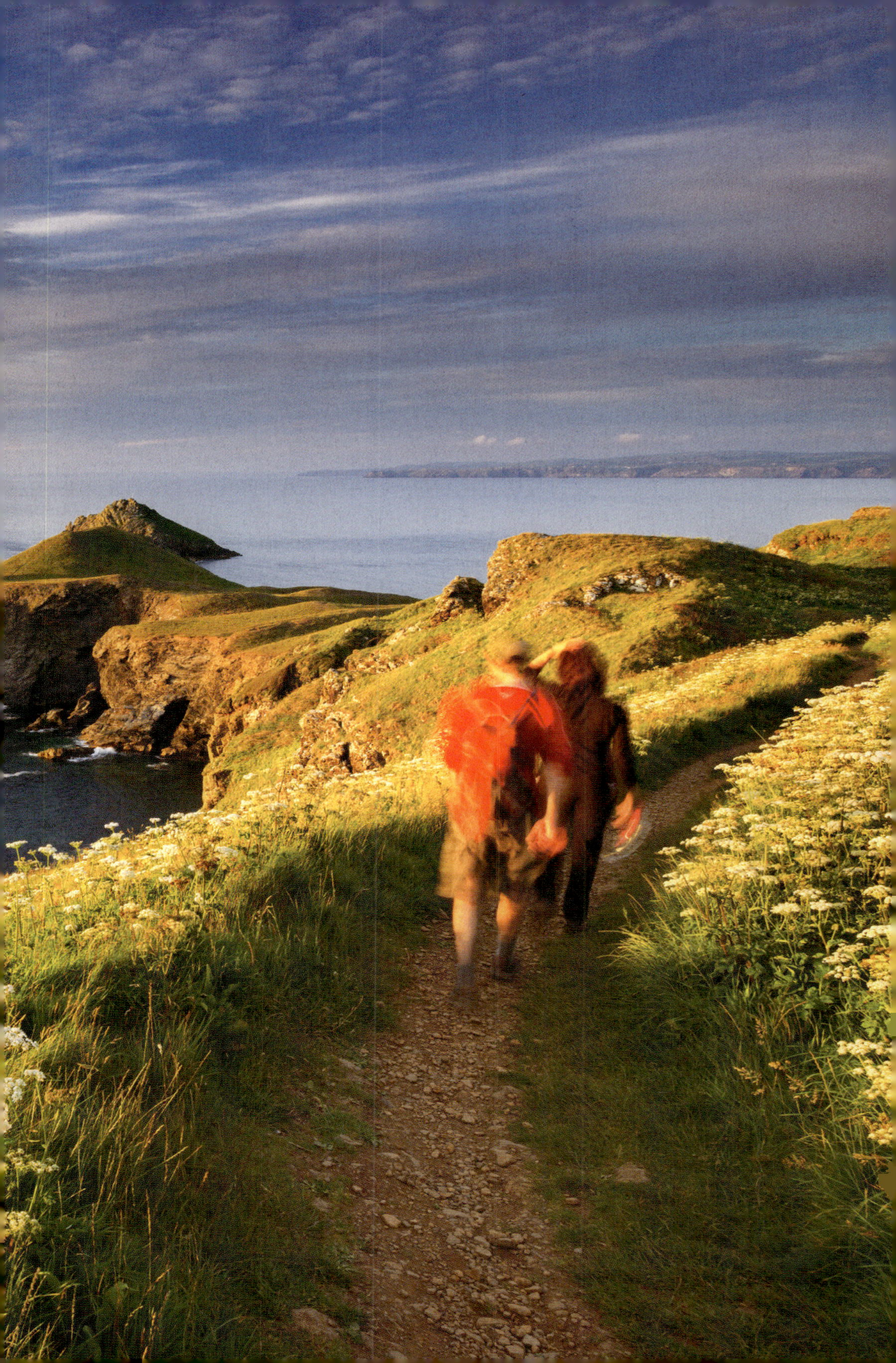

Just around the corner from the Camel Estuary the Rumps is a spectacular and unusual promontory in North Cornwall consisting of twin headlands connected to Pentire Head via a narrow strip of land.

The geology makes the Rumps a natural defensive fortification, most likely the main reason for the siting of an Iron Age fort. Earth ramparts, once covered in wooden palisades, are still evident today on the narrow entrance to the promontory.

What makes the Rumps different fro the rest of the dramatic north Cornish coastline is the accessibility to viewpoints. As the promontory stretches out into the sea, you can reach amazing lofty viewpoints to shoot both towards the headland and from it back along the coast.

The Rumps offers one of the most breathtaking coastal walks to be found in Cornwall. Yet, despite being close to the ever-popular Padstow, it is off the beaten track for many visitors and remains a quiet crowd free place to wander.

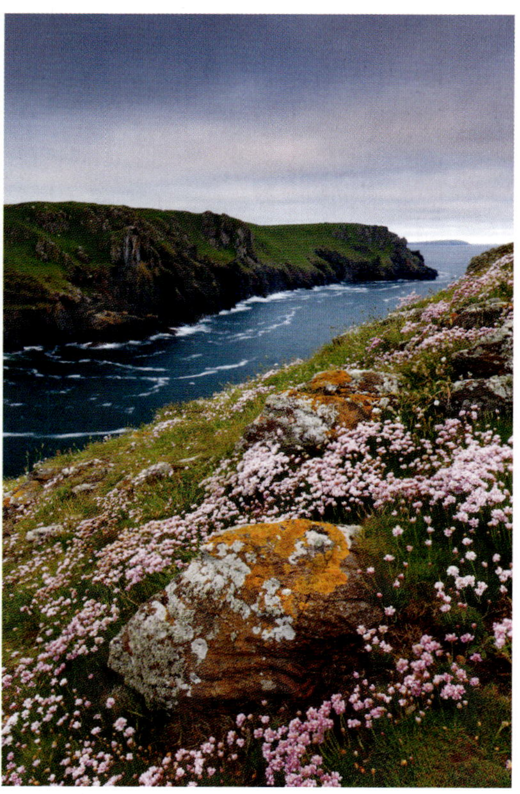

What to Shoot and Viewpoints

Viewpoint 1 – Towards Rumps Point

The view most associated with the Rumps can be photographed just to the southwest on Pentire Head looking out towards the promontory. From the cliffs here the view over the sea towards Rumps Point is really rather special. The elongated headland stretching westwards resembles a great sleeping dinosaur, the cliffs rising up to a peak before sloping down a jagged ridge all the way to the sea.

The effort involved to achieve this view is minimal. If you approach the Rumps on the South West Coast Path from Pentire Point, the view towards the promontory will be directly in front of you. You don't even need to leave the footpath; in fact many of the best shots include the footpath as a leading line.

With the background speaking for itself, your choice of viewpoint will be determined by the availability of suitable photographic subjects in the immediate vicinity to make up your foreground. Fortunately there is no shortage of candidates in this regard. In spring look out for wildflowers, especially bluebells, which grow in patches over these cliffs followed shortly after by beautiful delicate sea pinks. At any time of year, the pale algae-covered rocks all over these cliffs make wonderful subjects especially when illuminated by late evening sunshine.

Viewpoint 2 – On the Rumps

To make the most of this dramatic coastline a trip onto the Rumps is required. Despite the previous view being high on most landscape photographers' lists, pictures captured from the Rumps itself are far less common.

A short walk along the coast path brings you past the Iron Age earthworks and onto the promontory. Before heading up high, wander over to the cliff edge and look westwards. The vista along the coast is particularly impressive, revealing the spectacular cliffs of Pentire Head looking towards Trevose Head and Gulland Rock in the distance.

After taking in this view, continue out over the promontory and follow the path up onto Rumps Point, the name of the western headland. A few minutes walking to reach the top will reward you with a tremendous view stretching eastwards. From this elevated position you get to experience so much more of the Rumps than is possible from Pentire Head.

Flowering sea pinks on the headland at dawn, Canon 1Ds Mark III, 17-40mm at 27mm, ISO 100, 3 sec at f/16. May

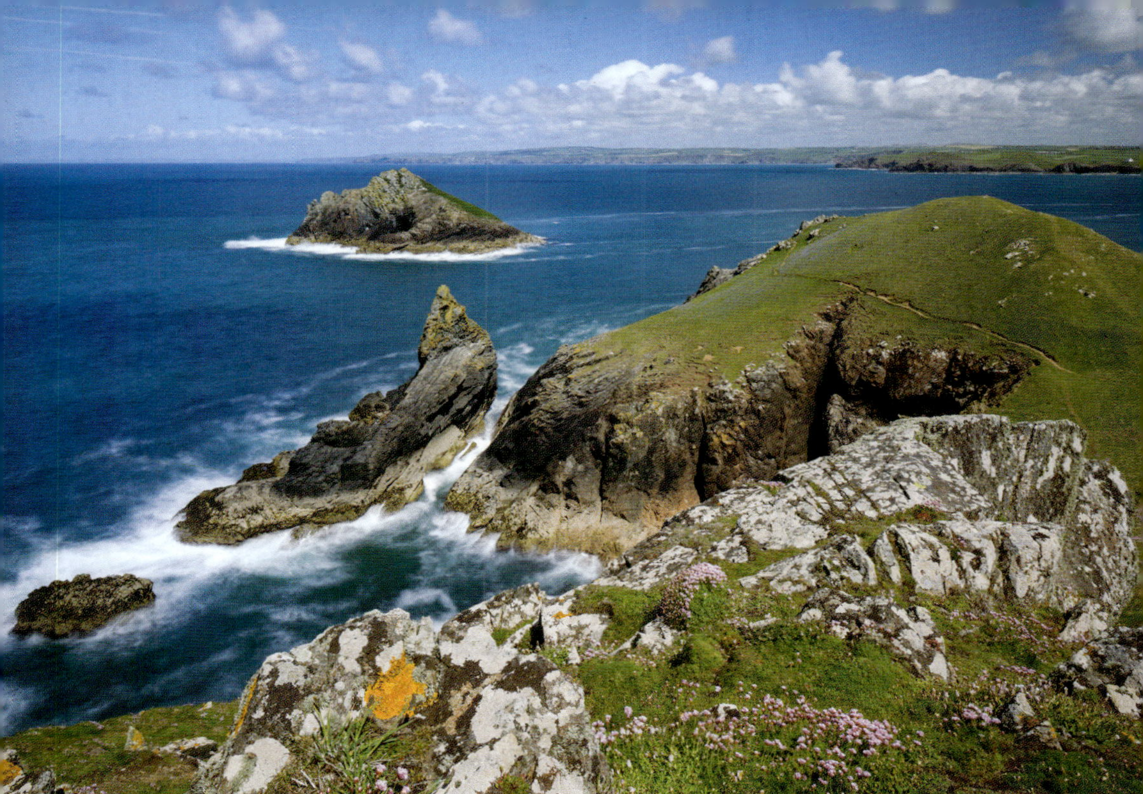

Seven Souls Rock and The Mouls, Nikon D800E, 17-35mm at 24mm, ISO 50, 8 sec at f/14. May

Far below, almost hugging the headland is Seven Souls Rock, a triangular islet named after a shipwreck where seven lives were lost. Seven Souls Rock together with a smaller neighbour form a dramatic barrier for waves rolling in off the Atlantic, and as a result look very photogenic when surrounded by crashing white water. Several hundred metres offshore another island, named The Mouls, further enhances the drama clearly evident along this rugged stretch of coast. From your lofty viewpoint high up on Rumps Point all of these photographic riches can be included in an incredibly strong seascape composition.

How to Get Here

From Wadebridge head north on the B3314. After 5 miles, just as the main road bends to the right, take the left turning signposted Polzeath. Head down this country lane, and turn left at the junction. After one mile, take the right turn towards New Polzeath and keep driving along this road until you see a sign for Lundynant Caravan Site. Take a right here onto a narrow lane and follow this for around half a mile to the car park.

Parking Lat/Long: 50.585863, -4.9170851
Parking Grid Ref: SW 936 803
Parking Postcode: PL27 6QY
Map: OS Explorer Map 106 (1:25 000) Newquay & Padstow

Accessibility

The South West Coast Path follows the perimeter of Pentire Head, offering spectacular coastal views all along. A more direct footpath from the car park crosses several fields before arriving on the cliff tops in perhaps the best viewpoint from which to shoot the Rumps. The footpaths are not suitable for wheelchairs.

Best Time of Year/Day

The Rumps can be photographed equally well at any time of the year, but spring is perhaps the best time when wildflowers can be found carpeting the cliff tops. For a very different feel, try visiting in winter to witness the power of the Atlantic crashing against the cliffs. The Rumps are usually photographed in the evening, when the cliffs are side lit by the setting sun.

Located just south of Tintagel on the rugged North Cornwall coast, Trebarwith Strand makes a wonderful location for dramatic seascape photography. At low tide the location is no more than a small rocky cove backed by crumbling slate cliffs, but when the sea retreats a wide stretch of sandy beach is revealed. Just offshore, the unmistakable Gull Rock Island makes a glorious photographic subject.

What to Shoot and Viewpoints

Viewpoint 1 – High Tide

Although high tide severely restricts the accessibility of Trebarwith Strand, this is the best time to shoot. As so often happens the rising tide transforms the potential of the location; water covers all the sand and many rocks, simplifying the subject matter and making compositions stand out.

If you know this beach at low tide, you will be surprised at how different it looks now. Where before this view would have been cluttered by a mass of dark rocks and busy beach, now a narrow slate ledge surrounded by waves points out towards Gull Rock on the horizon. Comprised of eroded slate, this ledge makes tremendous foreground interest, especially when wet from incoming waves.

For a slightly different but no less dramatic viewpoint head up to the higher ledges on the right hand side of the cove. Just past the beach toilets, several crude steps have been cut into the slate offering an easy method of climbing onto this higher ledge. From here, you gain an alternative less photographed viewpoint shooting towards Gull Rock.

When shooting at high tide extreme caution should be applied; large waves and slippery wet rocks can make both these ledges dangerous. Make sure you are familiar with the tide at all times, and only venture as far down the ledges as is safe.

Viewpoint 2 – Low Tide

Low tide provides access to the sandy beach. There is nothing that can ruin a beach photograph more effectively than well-trodden sand, so try and time your trip so that you can be the first person onto the beach as the tide recedes. Once you reach the sand, just in front of the ledges you will find many tidal pools. These pools always make wonderful foregrounds to any photograph, especially at sunset when they can reflect colourful skies.

A small stream cuts through the ledges, rushing beneath a tiny natural slate bridge on its passage to the sea. Dependent on water levels several tiny waterfalls can be photographed around this area cascading into rock pools.

To the right and left sides of the beach many dark slate rocks dotted around the sand can offer great picture

The delicate natural bridge near the beach, Canon 1Ds Mark III, 17-40mm at 21mm, ISO 100, 6 sec at f/13. February

Low tide reveals a gorgeous sandy beach, Canon 1Ds Mark III, 16-35mm at 26mm, ISO 100, 10 sec at f/16. September

This water eroded channel makes a great subject, Canon 1Ds Mark III, 17-40mm at 20mm, ISO 100, 8 sec at f/13. February

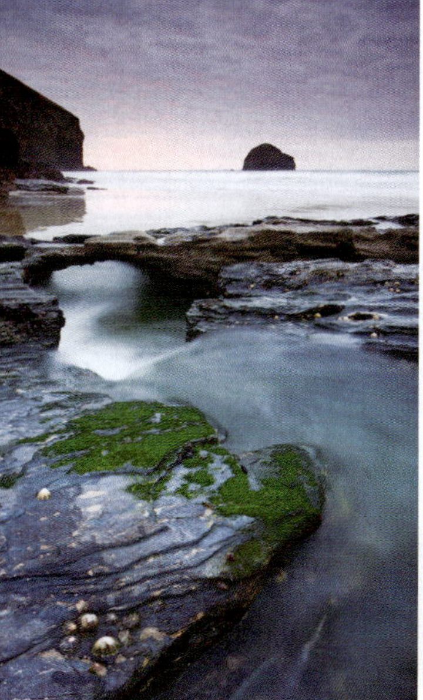

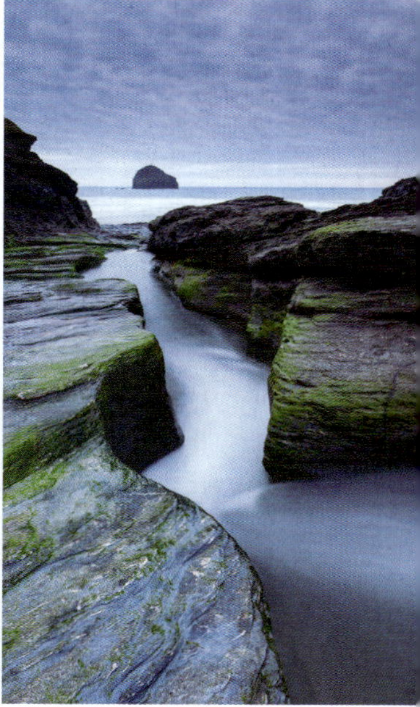

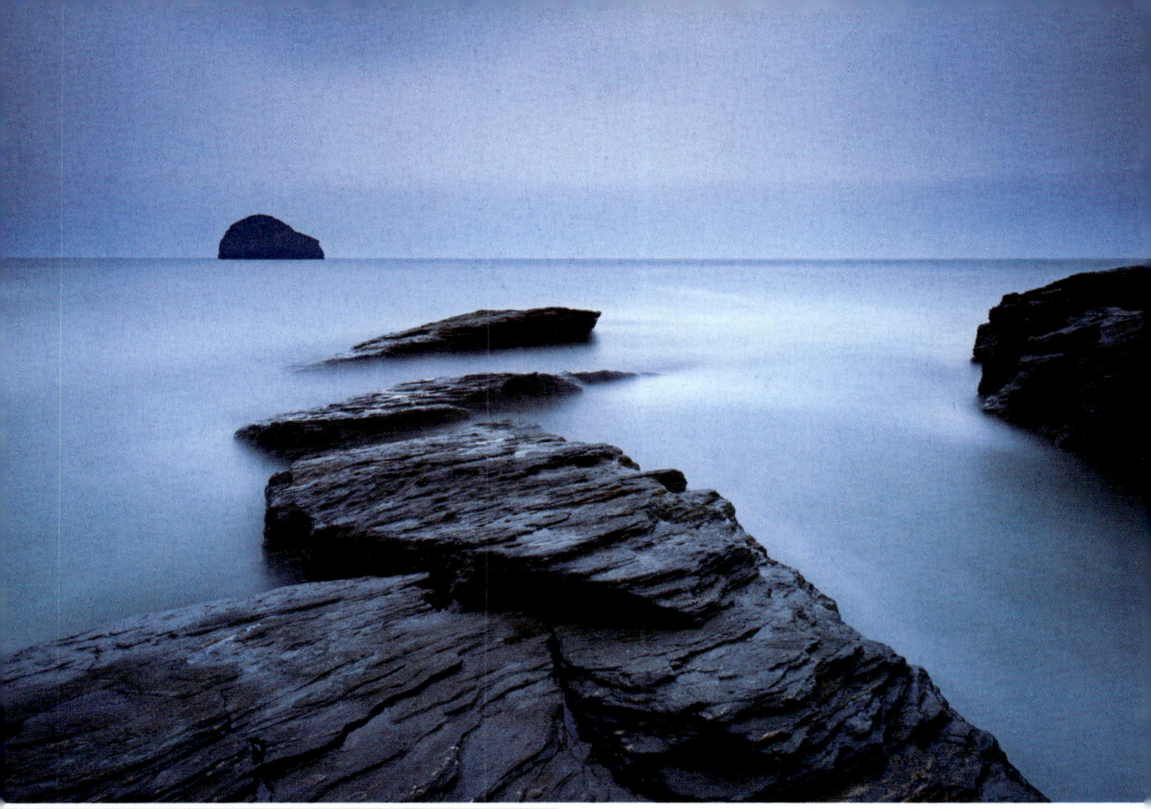

*Gull Rock from the highly photogenic slate ledges at high tide,
Nikon D800E, 17-35mm at 25mm, ISO 200, 180 sec at f/11. June*

How to Get Here

From Launceston head west on the A30 for 2 miles
before picking up the A395 exit signposted North
Cornwall. Stay on this road for 10.5 miles until it meets
the A39 Atlantic Highway. Turn left onto the A39 and
then after 1.4 miles turn right following the signs to
Tintagel. You will pass through the village of Slaughter
Bridge, then turn right following the signs to Trebarwith
Strand. After 5 miles you will see a car park on the right.

Parking Lat/Long: 50.644676, -4.7552153
Parking Grid Ref: SX 053 864
Parking Postcode: PL34 0HB
Map: OS Explorer Map 111 (1:25 000) Bude, Boscastle
& Tintagel

Accessibility

A road leads from the car park right to the beach.
In order to reach the beach you need to walk over a wide
area of slate rocks. As mentioned above at low tide you
can walk past the ledges and onto a sandy beach, while
at high tide you are restricted to standing on the ledges.
Not wheelchair friendly.

Best Time of Year/Day

As this stretch of coast faces west over the Atlantic,
Trebarwith Strand is best visited in the evening when
the sun sets over the sea. To increase your chances
of avoiding people walking into your pictures and/or
leaving footprints plan your visit to avoid weekends
and holidays, especially the busy summer months.

potential, still wet and glistening from the retreating tide.
Find rocks close to the water's edge, wait for a wave to
roll in and then take your photograph as each wave drags
back into the sea.

Alternatively, for a minimalist picture stand in a sandy
area away from the rocks and shoot out towards Gull
Rock. With both careful positioning and timing, when the
waves retreat you should be able to capture the island
with its reflection in the sheen on the wet sand.

*Summer sunset over the Atlantic , Canon 1Ds Mark III,
17-40mm at 19mm, ISO 100, 8 sec at f/22. June*

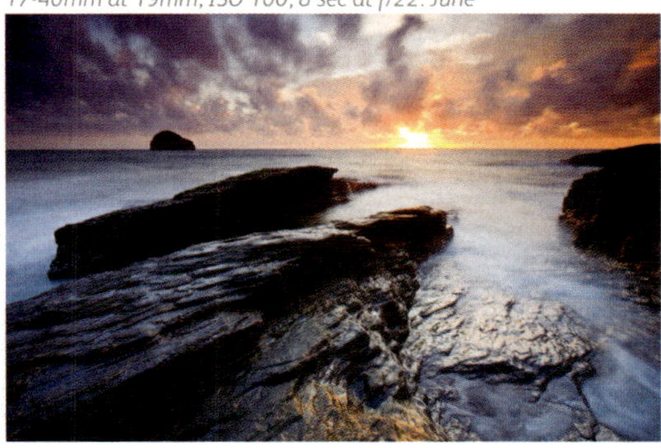

A narrow curving inlet between steep cliffs makes Boscastle an ideal sheltered natural harbour on the otherwise exposed Atlantic coast. Being the only harbour for many miles along this rugged stretch of coast, Boscastle used to be a small yet busy port, importing coal and exporting slate. Now only a few fishing boats remain, and the village is a popular visitor destination.

What to Shoot and Viewpoints

Viewpoint 1 – The Village from Penally Point

From the village car park an easy 15 minute walk along the north side of the river brings you to Penally Point, a windswept slate promontory at the head of the harbour.

Whenever shooting the coast, there is a natural tendency to compose pictures looking out towards the sea. The headland offers a variety of elevated positions from which to shoot the coastline and sea, but one of the best views from here is looking back inland. From this viewpoint the harbour, complete with old stone walls guides your eye along the valley towards the village in the distance.

The background falls nicely into place with any composition from here, but the real work comes from finding some suitable foreground.

Fortunately Penally Point provides some wonderful foreground to work with. The rocky headland is eroded magnificently in this area, offering jagged crumbling layers of slate stretching out towards the harbour.

Viewpoint 2 – Boscastle Harbour from Penally Hill

Without doubt the greatest view from Boscastle, and perhaps the finest cliff top view in Cornwall is from the cliff tops on Penally Hill. Heading back from Penally Point, follow the footpath that veers up hill for around 10 minutes. Upon reaching the top head you will notice a mast. Head towards the mast, close by an exposed slate ledge offers the most magnificent view over the harbour that you could wish to find.

Far below, the inlet snakes around the cliffs before reaching the sea in the most perfectly balanced composition imaginable. The whole scene seems to fit together like a jigsaw puzzle, with fishing boats and offshore islands providing added interest and scale. With so many strong elements the challenge is fitting them all in. To include both the boats on the left and the island (Meachard Rock) on the right of the same picture a wide-angle lens is required.

Towards Boscastle harbour from Penally Point, Canon 1Ds Mark III, 17-40mm at 29mm, ISO 100, 0.5 sec at f/16. February

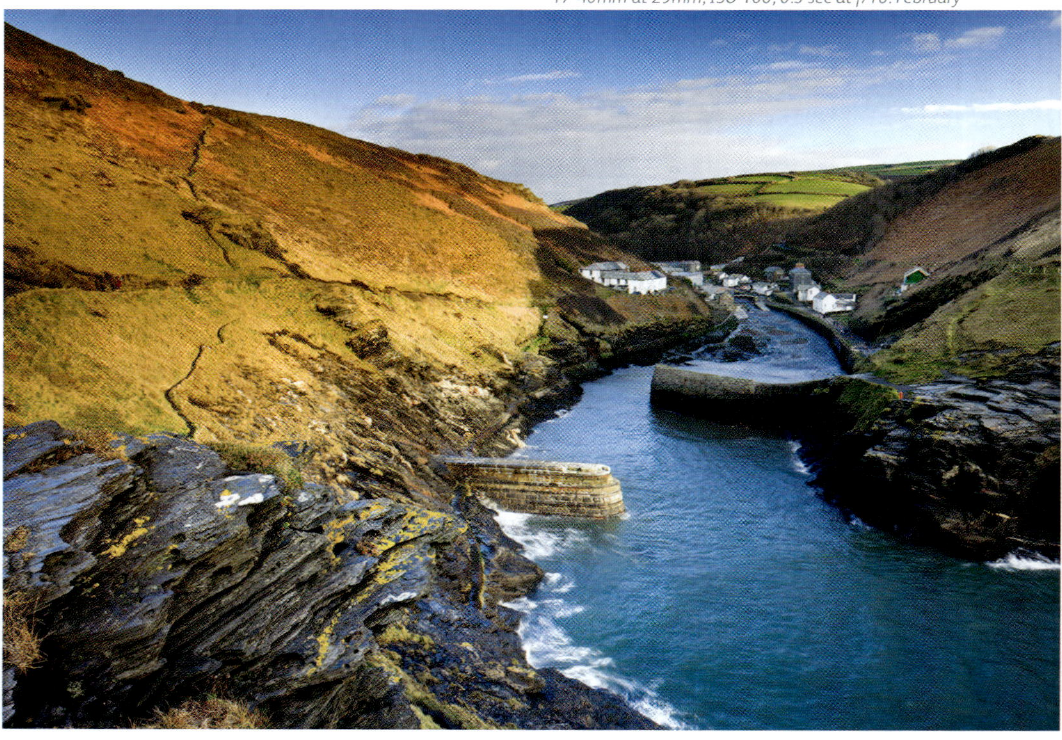

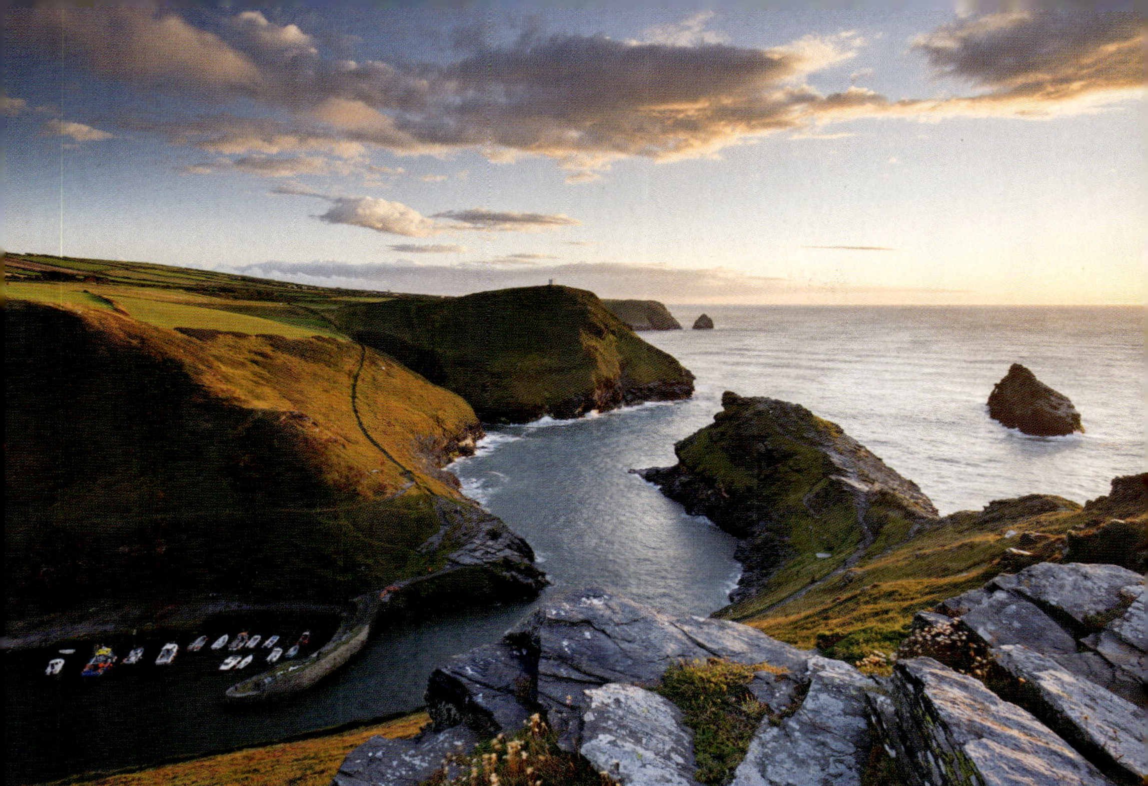

Overlooking the harbour from Penally Hill at sunset, Nikon D800E, 17-35mm at 20mm, ISO 100, 0.8 sec at f/11. August.

Forward Planning

Although the scenery is eye watering enough to make a fantastic photograph almost any time, a little bit of planning before your trip can reap dividends. Firstly, plan to arrive on a mid to high tide. When the tide is low, the harbour all but drains of water leaving the boats stranded in sand. Ideally you not only want water filling the channel, but also waves crashing against the cliffs to add extra drama. Be careful when it's very windy, this viewpoint is very exposed and it will be difficult to keep your tripod steady in windy conditions. Finally, time your visit in late afternoon/evening when the low sun setting over the Atlantic will paint the cliffs with warm light.

Viewpoint 3 – The North East Coast

With such a strong viewpoint you may find it difficult to drag yourself away. But if you are able to spare a few minutes, a one minute dash to the other side of the headland will give you a very different vista of the rugged North Cornish coast. This new view of the coast stretching in a northeast direction towards distant Cambeak may not have quite the same appeal as Boscastle, but it still makes a worthwhile additional photograph when the conditions are right.

How to Get Here

Boscastle is around 20 miles from Launceston on the North Cornwall coast. From Launceston, head west on the A30 for a couple of miles before taking the A395 junction signposted North Cornwall. Follow this road for 10 miles and then turn right onto the A39. Take the second left, and follow the road signs the rest of the way to Boscastle. As you descend into the old village you will see the harbour to your left. Keep going until you reach a large car park on the right.

Parking Lat/Long: 50.690459, -4.6940795
Parking Grid Ref: SX 099 913
Parking Postcode: PL35 0HD
Map: OS Explorer Map 111 (1:25 000) Bude, Boscastle & Tintagel

Accessibility

Both viewpoints can be reached within 15 minutes from the car park, following clearly defined footpaths. The paths are uneven in places so good walking boots are recommended. Neither path is suitable for wheelchair users, but good views towards the cliffs and harbour can be achieved from the village.

Best Time of Year/Day

Spring and summer evenings are the best times to shoot from Penally Hill. At these times the sun sets further to the north, so late evening sunshine will glow against the cliffs. The view to the village from Penally Point also works well when photographed late in the day, but due to the position of the sun is more suited to autumn or winter.

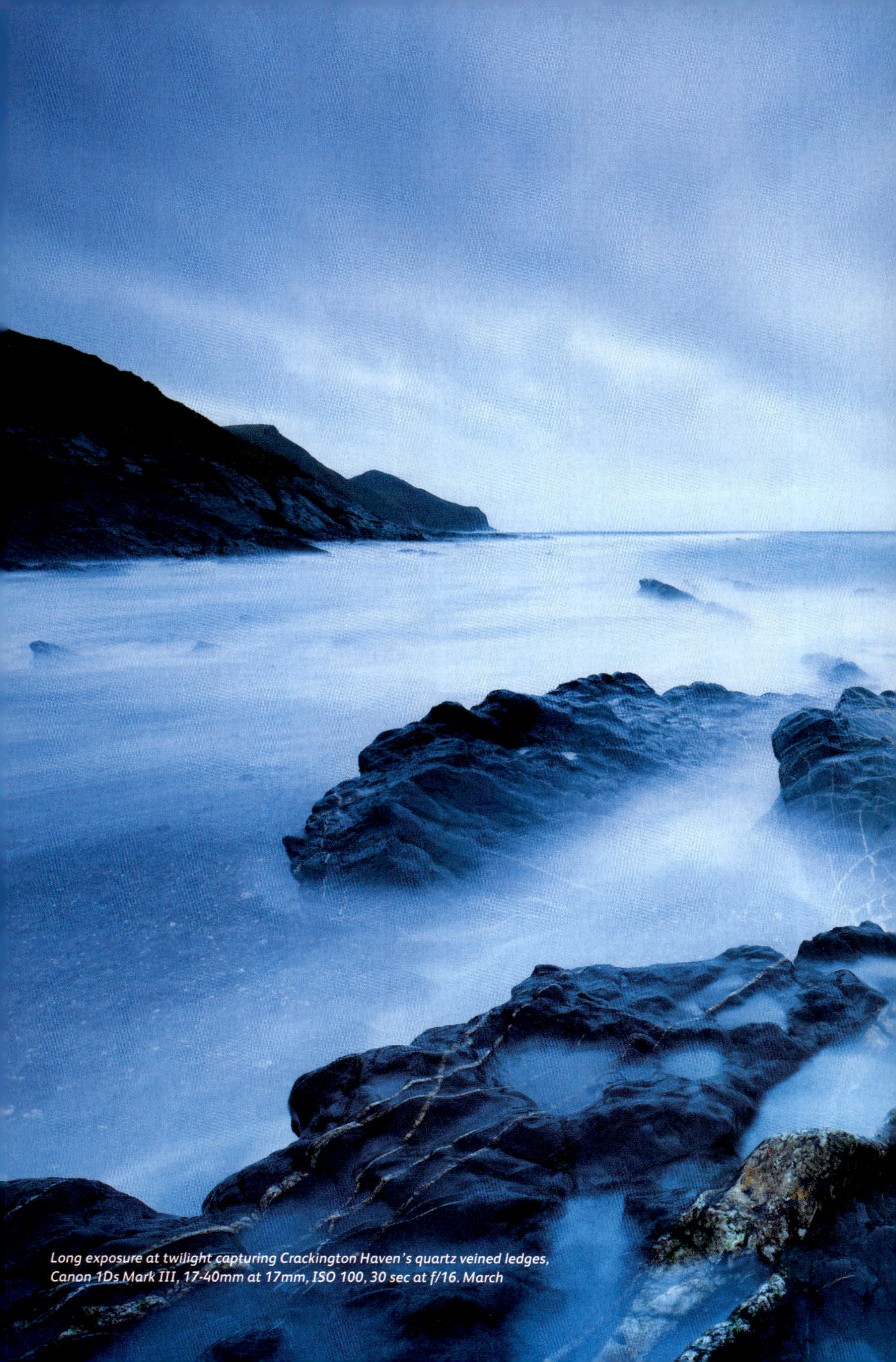

Long exposure at twilight capturing Crackington Haven's quartz veined ledges, Canon 1Ds Mark III, 17-40mm at 17mm, ISO 100, 30 sec at f/16. March

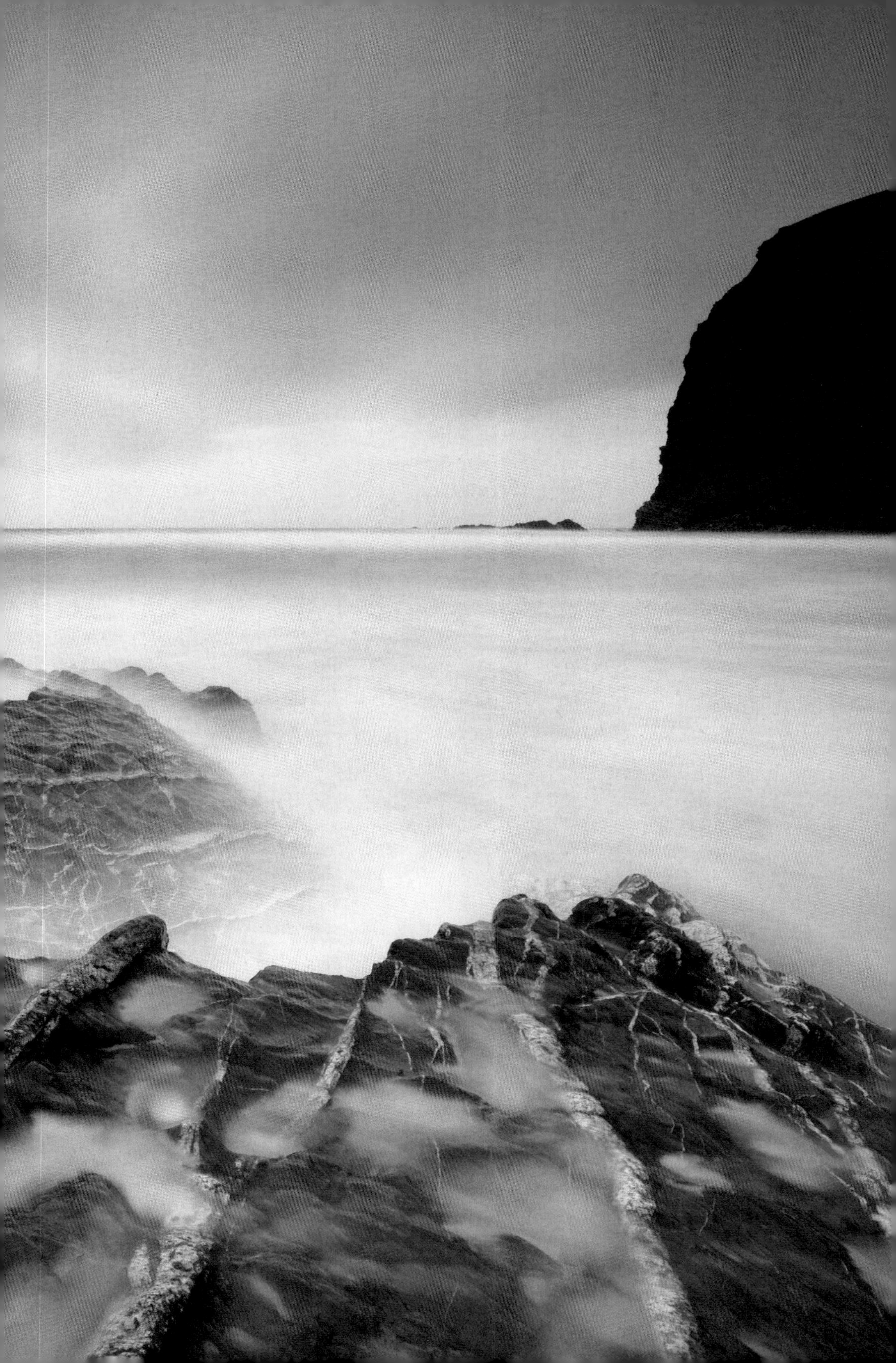

Crackington Haven is a typical North Cornish beach. Imposing cliffs on either side shelter a long narrow beach comprised of sand and rocks. At low tide in the summer the beach is a popular destination for holidaymakers. But it's in the winter when the beach is deserted and Atlantic rollers pound against the shore that Crackington Haven has the most appeal for photographs.

The towering cliffs have very visible folded sedimentary rock formations and the beach itself is covered with spectacular quartz-veined boulders and ledges. The area is so renowned for its geology that it gives its name to the Crackington Formation, a sequence of carboniferous sandstones and grey shales.

What to Shoot and Viewpoints

Viewpoint 1 – Low Tide

There is a wealth of ledges and boulders to photograph high up on the beach. While these all make irresistible subjects for photographs, the sheer number of them on show at low tide make it difficult to find clean and simple compositions. Best to leave these objects for higher tides and instead head down the beach.

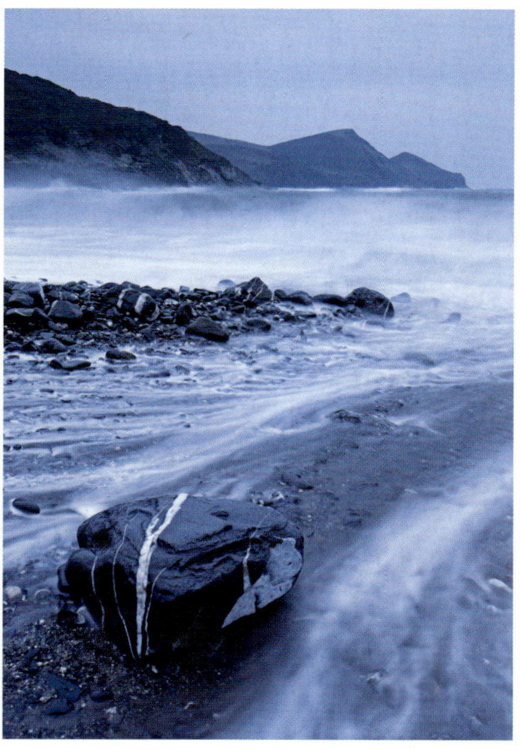

When the tide is low, an expansive area of sand is revealed. Clean sand always makes an ideal subject to simplify compositions. Keep an eye out for tidal pools that form around solitary rocks trapped in the sand. These pools can make beautiful foreground subjects and are good for reflecting colourful skies. Such pools are usually found on either side of the beach, closer to the ledges and cliffs.

In the middle of the beach a wide area of rocky ledges seem set too low in the sand to be particularly photogenic. However, if you time your visit to catch the tide just beginning to rise, these ledges look beautiful as an emerging lagoon gradually floods them.

When the tide is very low, you may encounter a wide area of large ripples in the sand, each one trapping a pool of seawater. This network of pools creates a series of repeating patterns throughout the lower beach and makes for wonderful photographs.

Whether you are looking to photograph pools, ledges or rippled sand, your images will usually require a background element to complete the scene. With impressive headlands on either side of the beach, this shouldn't be a problem. Yet Pencannow Point, directly to the north is rather difficult to photograph. This massive wall of rock close to the beach is very dominant in any photograph and often overpowers the foreground, leaving an unbalanced picture. To further complicate matters, the huge cliff makes it difficult to use graduated filters when attempting to control exposures. Luckily the shapely headland to the southwest, Cambeak, suffers from no such compositional problems, partly due to its distance. Therefore, most photographs from Crackington Haven look out in this direction, often avoiding Pencannow Point entirely.

Viewpoint 2 – High Tide

As the incoming tide rushes up the beach, the mass of rocks are soon hidden beneath the water. Before the tide reaches its highest point several ledges near the southern side of the beach, previously a bit cluttered to photograph, now take on a new significance. The layers of folded rock, crisscrossed with quartz veins make amazing subjects with water rushing between them; a wide-angle lens gives the veins the attention they merit.

From this viewpoint higher up on the beach, Pencannow Point is slightly less dominant and so can be included in a composition more effectively. A super wide-angle lens allows you to photograph the headlands on either side of the beach in a single frame.

CAUTION: When the tide is high enough to wash over the best quartz-veined ledges, it is also high enough to cut you off. When standing up on the ledge, the waves will

Gorgeous quartz veined boulders can be found high up the beach, Nikon D800E, 17-35mm at 26mm, ISO 200, 4 sec at f/13. February

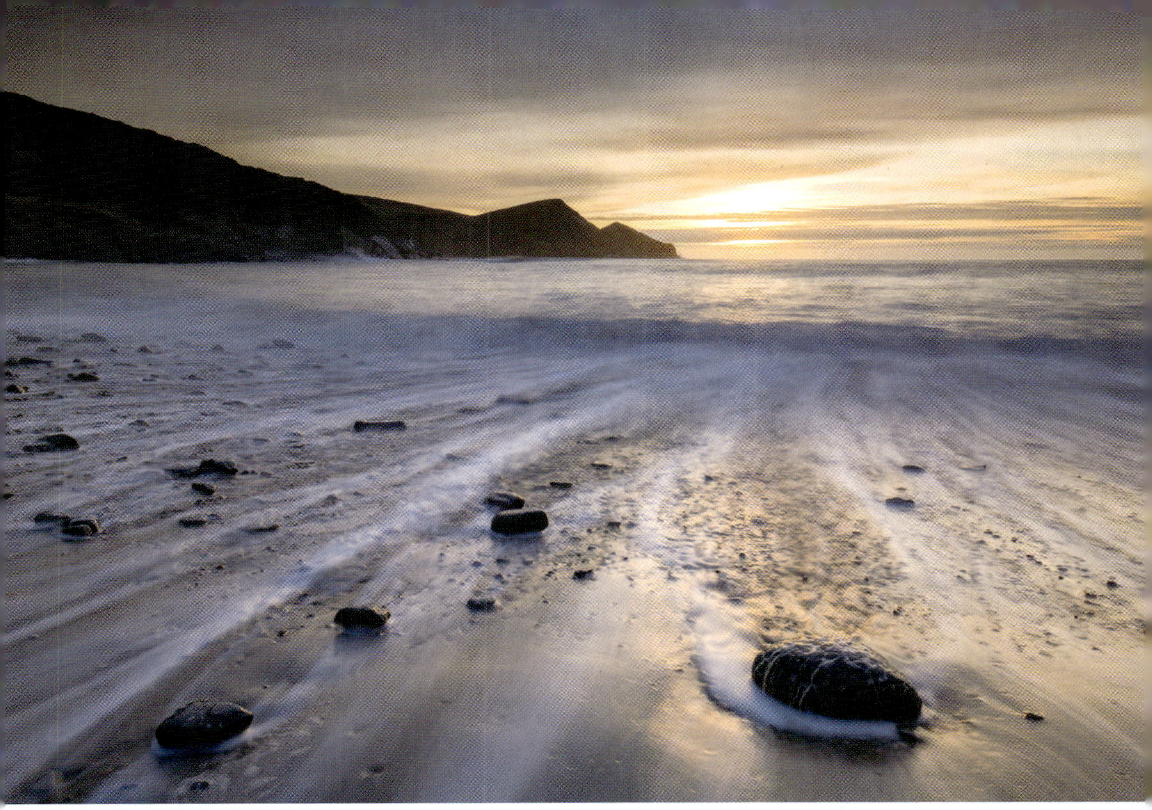

High tide at Crackington with sunset over Cambeak, Nikon D800E, 17-35mm at 20mm, ISO 100, 3 sec at f/11. March

Coast Path high above Crackington Haven beach, Nikon D800E, 17-35mm at 22mm, ISO 100, 1/5 sec at f/11. August

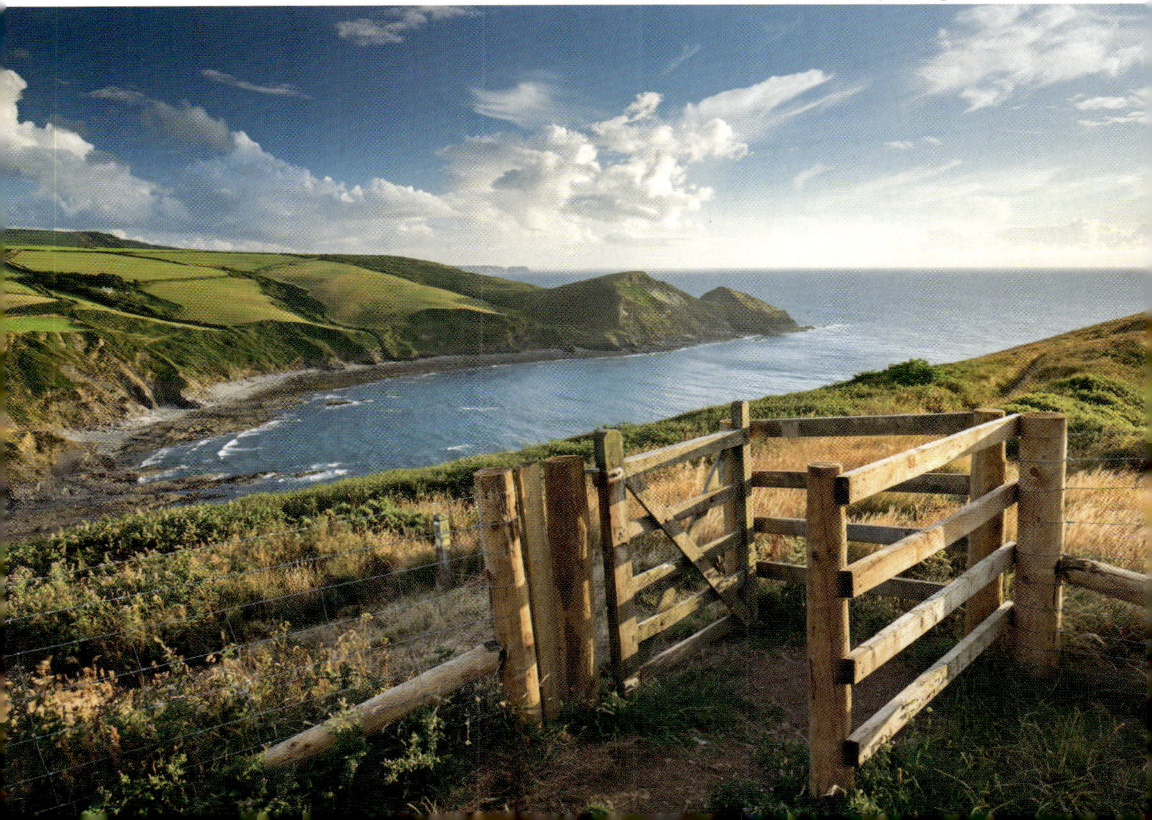

surge around you, turning your viewpoint into an island. Providing you don't spend too long taking photographs, you will easily be able to make a quick retreat between waves. Of more concern with this viewpoint is the exposure to occasional large waves. With the tide this high, every few minutes a surprisingly large wave will crash over the rocks you stand upon, potentially damaging your gear or worse.

When the tide reaches its highest point, you can still shoot Crackington Haven well. High up on the beach, there is a plethora of quartz-veined boulders which make excellent foreground subjects. For dramatic shots, wait for a wave to crash over the boulders and then shoot when the water rushes back into the sea. As the water retreats past the boulders, it creates a white blur around each stone. With an exposure of several seconds, these white water trails look marvellous and add excellent atmosphere to photographs.

Viewpoint 3 – Pencannow Point

The coast path provides access to the cliffs on either side of Crackington Haven. By following the footpath up to Pencannow Point you can gain an expansive vista over the sweep of Tremoutha Haven, the rocky cove adjacent to Crackington Haven, and over rolling farmland to Cambeak. While perhaps not as enticing as the seascape photographs that can be captured on the beach, the cliff tops do offer very different and less photographed viewpoints.

How to Get Here

Crackington Haven is on Cornwall's north coast, around 11 miles south of Bude. From Bude, head south on the A39, after 8 miles take the right turn at Wainhouse Corner signposted Crackington Haven and follow the lane all the way to the village.

Parking Lat/Long: 50.741078, -4.6312412
Parking Grid Ref: SS 144 967
Parking Postcode: EX23 0JG
Map: OS Explorer Map 111 (1:25 000) Bude, Boscastle & Tintagel

Accessibility

A beach car park is just across the road from the beach. From the car park, it is only a 5 minute walk before you are standing at some of the best beach viewpoints. Welly boots are recommended for all beach photography, as they will enable you to get into positions without having to worry about getting wet feet. The stones and boulders high up on the beach prevent the beach being wheelchair friendly.

Best Time of Year/Day

Although this isn't one of Cornwall's most popular beaches, it does attract holidaymakers in the summer. For that reason it is best avoided during the day, and people will still be on the beach in the evenings. Even when people have left the beach, their footprints will still be visible in the sand until the next high tide. At high tide, you shouldn't experience such issues so will be free to shoot.

Generally speaking, as with many of Cornwall's beaches Crackington Haven is best visited in the quieter seasons when less people are around. Due to the position of the sun, it makes an ideal sunset location.

Intriguing ledges high up on the beach, Canon 1Ds Mark III, 17-40mm at 17mm, ISO 100, 120 sec at f/11. March

Opposite: Pencannow Point looking north, Nikon D800E, 17-35mm at 32mm, ISO 100, 0.8 sec at f/14. August

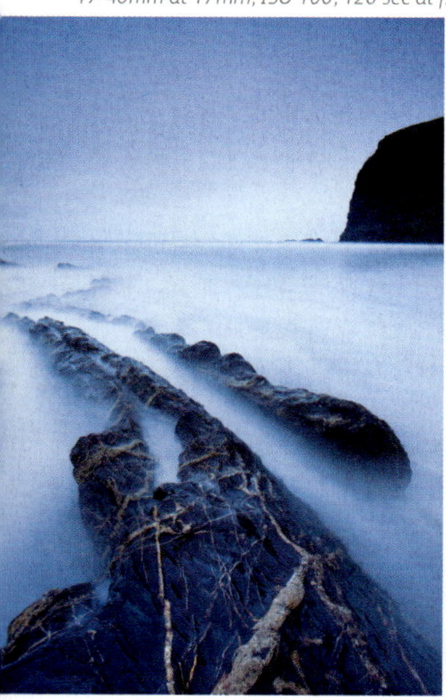

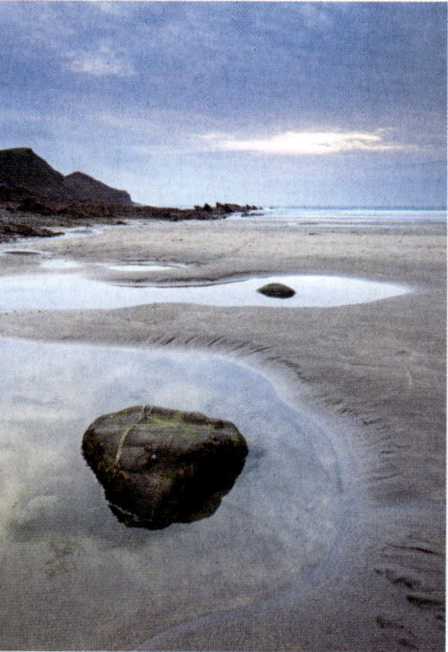

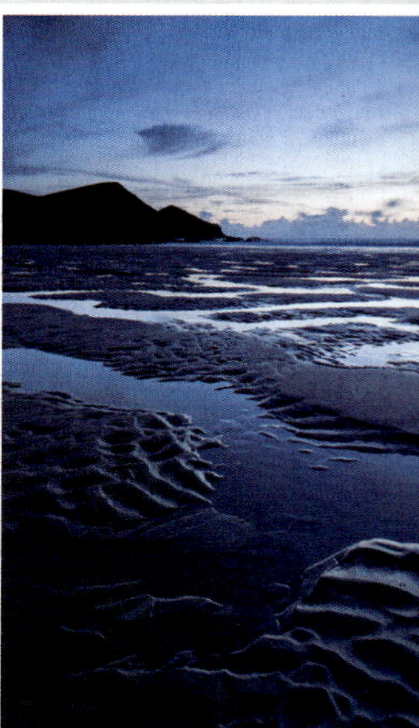

Tidal pools offer some variety to the rugged ledges, Nikon D800E, 17-35mm at 28mm, ISO 100, 6 sec at f/13. July

Sand patterns at low tide during twilight, Nikon D800E, 17-35mm at 24mm, ISO 200, 30 sec at f/13. August

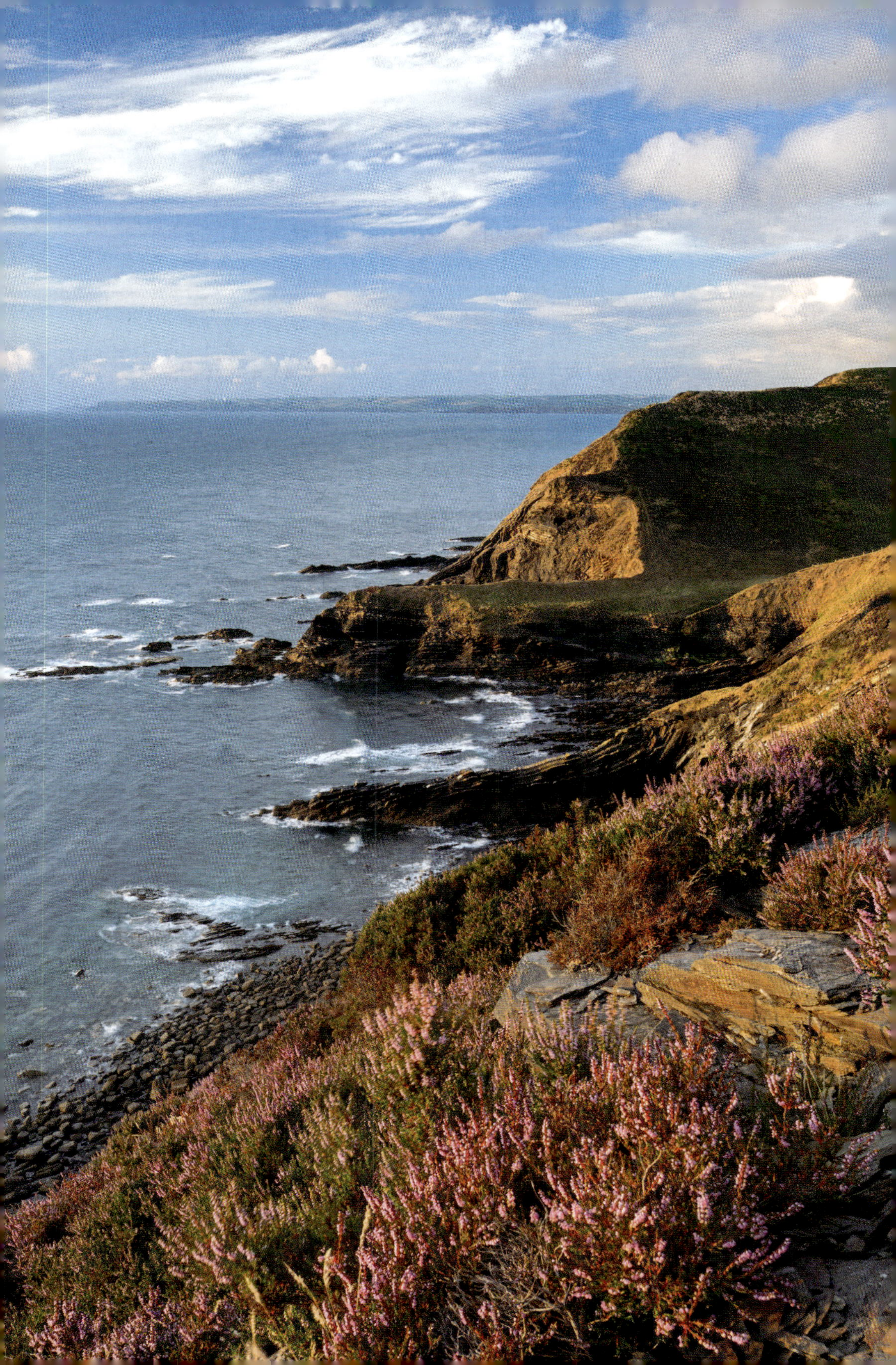

Located on the North Cornish coast, close to the Devon border, Sandymouth and Duckpool are two rugged beaches in the care of the National Trust. This dangerous stretch of Atlantic coast has long been hazardous for passing ships; with rough seas and jagged rocks it's easy to see why.

These dramatic beaches are great to explore with a camera, Sandymouth in particular is a popular location for landscape photographers. Less than a mile to the north of Sandymouth, neighbouring Duckpool is a less visited beach which retains a feeling of remote isolation.

What to Shoot and Viewpoints

Viewpoint 1 – Sandymouth

First time visitors to the beach will be surprised by the deep orange coloured cliffs. These characteristic cliffs make a fascinating subject in their own right; the heavily eroded sedimentary cliffs have been sculpted into appealing irregular shapes, resembling mini orange mountains. But it is the cliff faces themselves that offer the most appeal. Bright orange chunky layers of sedimentary rock descend diagonally into pale circular pebbles on the beach below, providing incredibly contrasting colours and shapes. When photographed up close these can make excellent abstract subjects.

Initial impressions of Sandymouth will be influenced by the tide. At high tide, the beach is reduced to a small area of pebbles, leaving the real potential of Sandymouth hidden beneath the incoming waves. By far the best time to visit is on a mid tide, ideally going out so the sand is left clean and footprint free.

If you plan your trip to coincide with a falling tide, you will encounter a wide expanse of sandy beach, broken up by a plethora of long low ledges stretching out towards the ocean. This may initially seem a little overwhelming, with ledges everywhere where do you set up? The best thing to do is arrive early and spend time exploring.

Most visitors to Sandymouth will be concentrated near the car park, so personally I would wander down the beach a little further to find some isolation. Generally speaking the north is more rocky and rugged making it perfect when the tide is a little higher. To the south, there are more sandy areas broken up by ledges and tidal pools which work well with a lower tide. Try to avoid low tides however as the ledges will be separated from the sea by a large area of unbroken sand.

It is difficult to be more specific as the sand levels can change over time and with the seasons. So, on a repeat visit you may find a favoured ledge has disappeared completely underneath the sand.

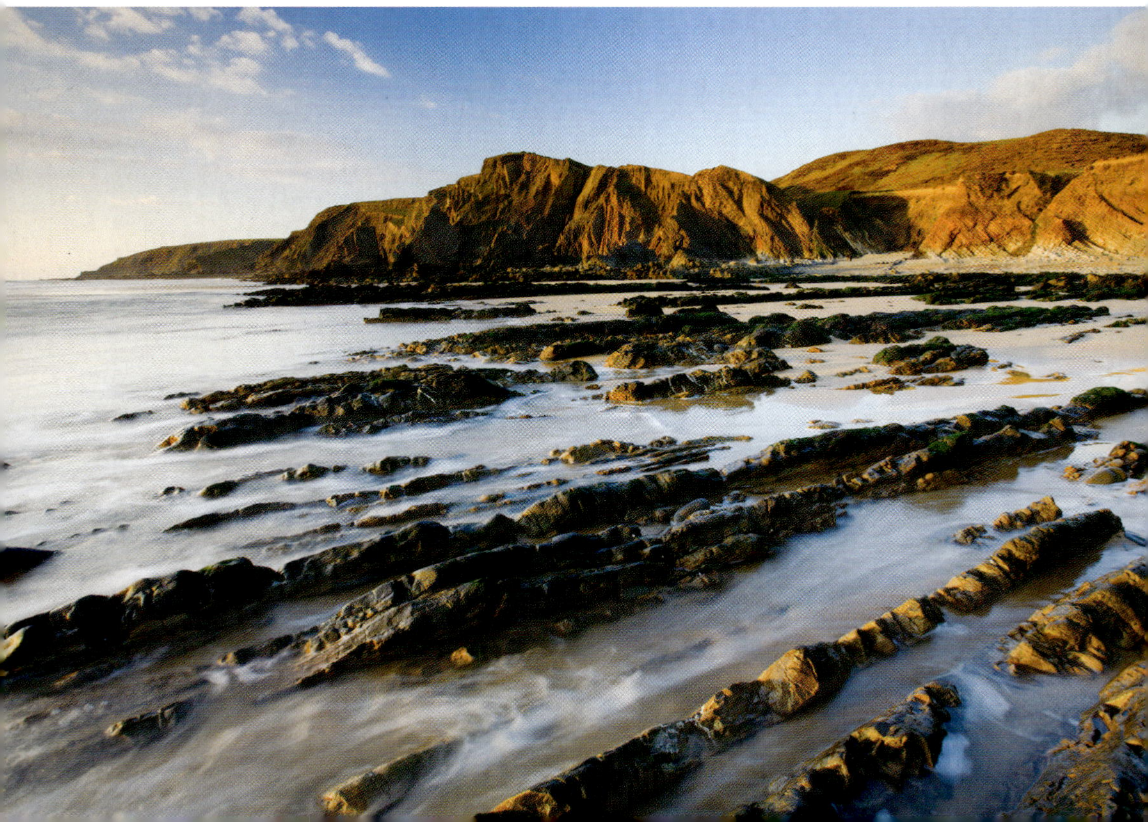

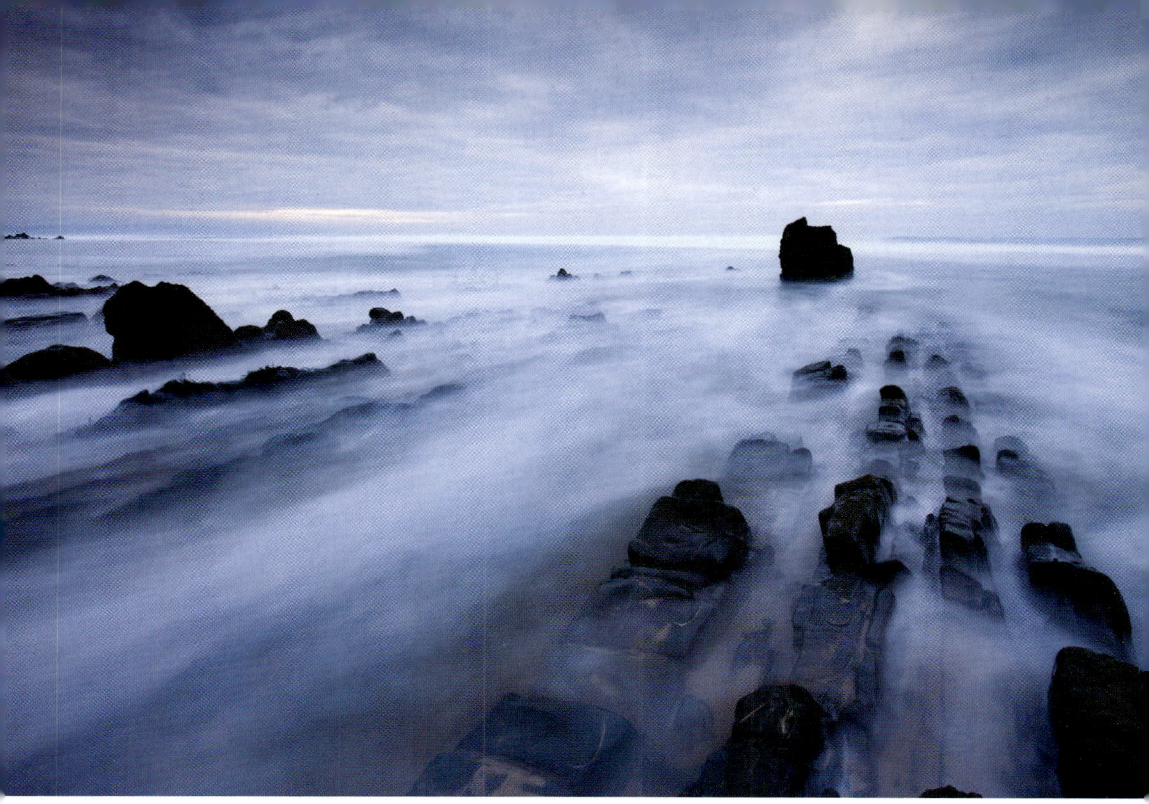

*Some of Sandymouth's dramatic ledges stretching out to sea,
Canon 1Ds Mark III, 17-40mm at 20mm, ISO 100,
30 sec at f/19. November*

How to Get Here

Both Sandymouth and Duckpool are about 15 minutes drive
north of Bude. Head north on the A39 and just before you reach
Kilkhampton take the left hand turning signposted Stibb. Continue
through Stibb and you will notice a left turning signposted
Sandymouth. For Duckpool, continue for another mile and you
will see a left turning signposted Duckpool. The beach and car
park is half a mile down this narrow lane.

Parking Lat/Long: (Sandymouth) 50.861513, -4.5548108.
(Duckpool) 50.877685, -4.5482036
Parking Grid Ref: SS 203 100 (Sandymouth), SS 203 117
(Duckpool)
Parking Postcode: EX23 9HW (Sandymouth Holiday Park),
EX23 9JN (Coombe, near Duckpool)
Map: OS Explorer Map 126 (1:25 000) Clovelly & Hartland

Accessibility

There are car parks just a few minutes walk from both beaches.
Welly boots are recommended for all beach photography, as
they will enable you to get into positions without having to worry
about getting wet feet. Pebbles high up on both beaches restrict
wheelchair access.

*Opposite: The distinctive coloured cliffs glow warmly with late
afternoon sunshine, Canon 1Ds Mark III, 17-40mm at 19mm,
ISO 100, 1.5 sec at f/16. April*

Best Time of Year/Day

Both Sandymouth and Duckpool face west which makes them
ideal locations to photograph at late afternoon and sunset. Both
locations can offer excellent photographic opportunities throughout
the year, but bear in mind in summer there may be holidaymakers
around. Time your visit to coincide with a falling tide to increase
chances of the beaches being clean from footprints.

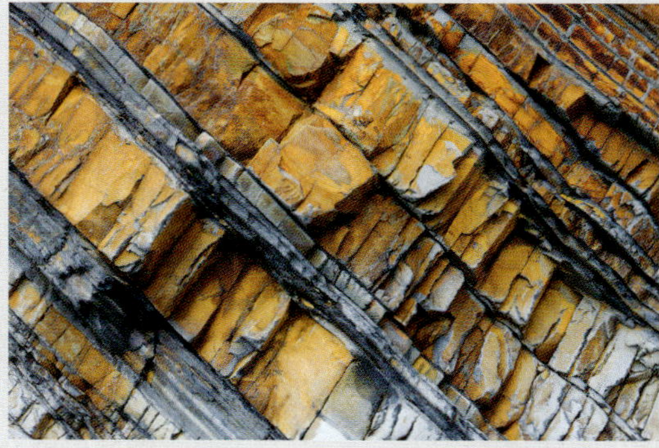

*Detailed shot of cliff face showing the inclined layers, Canon 1Ds
Mark III, 24-70mm at 51mm, ISO 100, 0.7 sec at f/22. March*

Viewpoint 2 – Duckpool

Despite its name conjuring up images of pleasant English village ponds there is nothing sedate about Duckpool. While the geology of the coastline is almost identical to Sandymouth the beach has a more remote and wild feeling about it. Along this popular stretch of coast you are quite likely to enjoy an evening at Duckpool all to yourself.

Like Sandymouth, Duckpool is best avoided on a high tide when water covers the dramatic ledges, and on a low tide when the beach can be golden sand and little else. Therefore a mid tide is ideal, where the ledges look photogenic with waves rushing between and over them. The main bay contains numerous ledges to photograph, including a large distinctive jagged ledge running down the centre of the beach. One potential challenge you face when shooting this area is the large Steeple Point cliff, just to the north of the beach. Being so close to the beach this enormous cliff has a tendency to dominate compositions and is best avoided.

A clamber over some rocks and boulders to the south will take you around the headland and onto a remote area of the beach that is far enough away from Steeple Point to reduce its dominance in pictures. In this area, diagonal shark fin like rocks protrude out of the ledges and make fascinating subjects. There is little sand to be found in this part of the beach, so it can make compositions feel rather busy with lots of boulders, rocks and ledges everywhere. As always, water provides the simplification factor necessary for clean compositions so look for rock pools to place in your foreground. Alternatively wait for the tide to be high enough for water to lap around the rocks, but don't wait too long as this area could become cut off with an incoming tide.

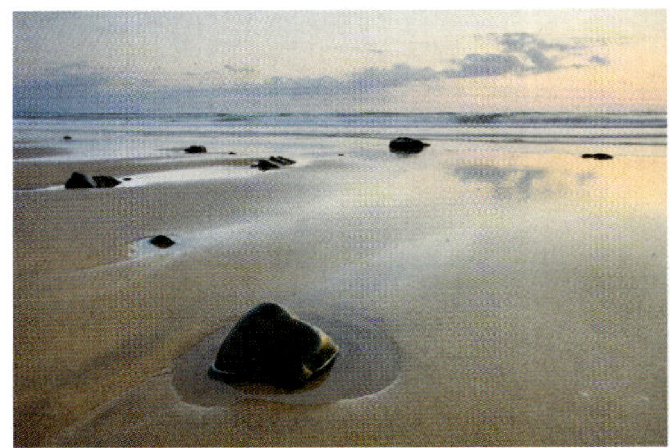

Sandymouth features large areas of golden sand at low tide, Canon 1Ds Mark III, 17-40mm at 27mm, ISO 100, 1.5 sec at f/16. April

Wet ledges make fascinating photographic subjects in low light, Canon 1Ds Mark III, 17-40mm at 17mm, ISO 50, 60 sec at f/19. March

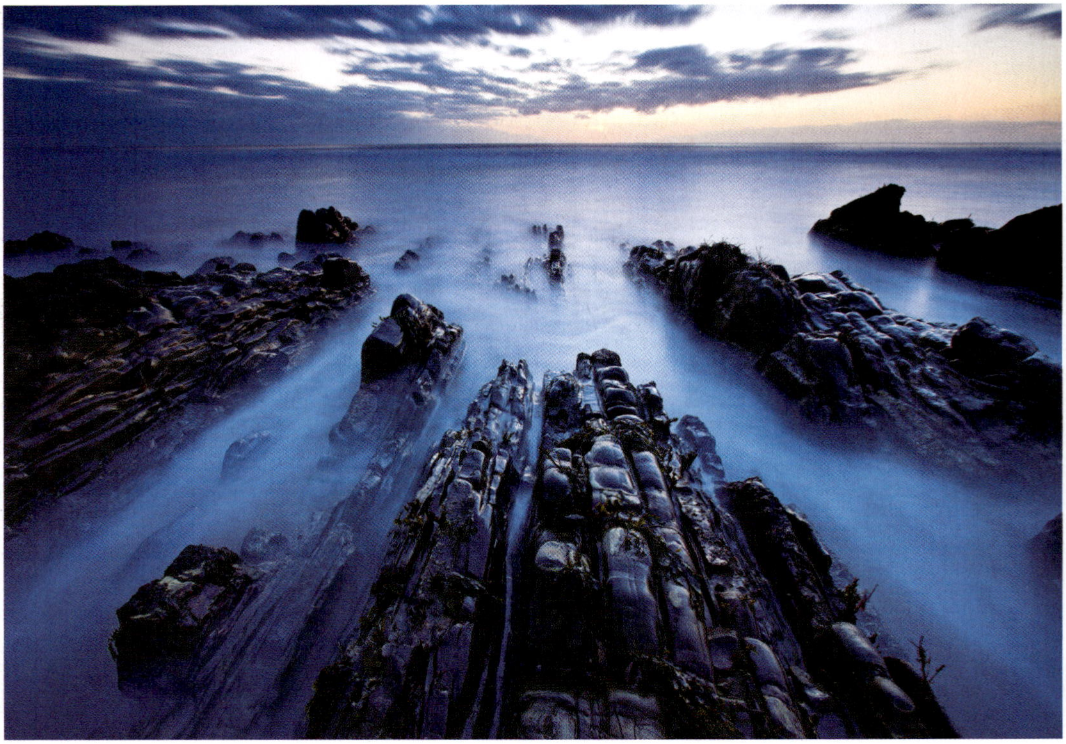

Jagged upright ledges at Duckpool, Canon 1Ds Mark III, 16-35mm at 25mm, ISO 100, 8 sec at f/16. March

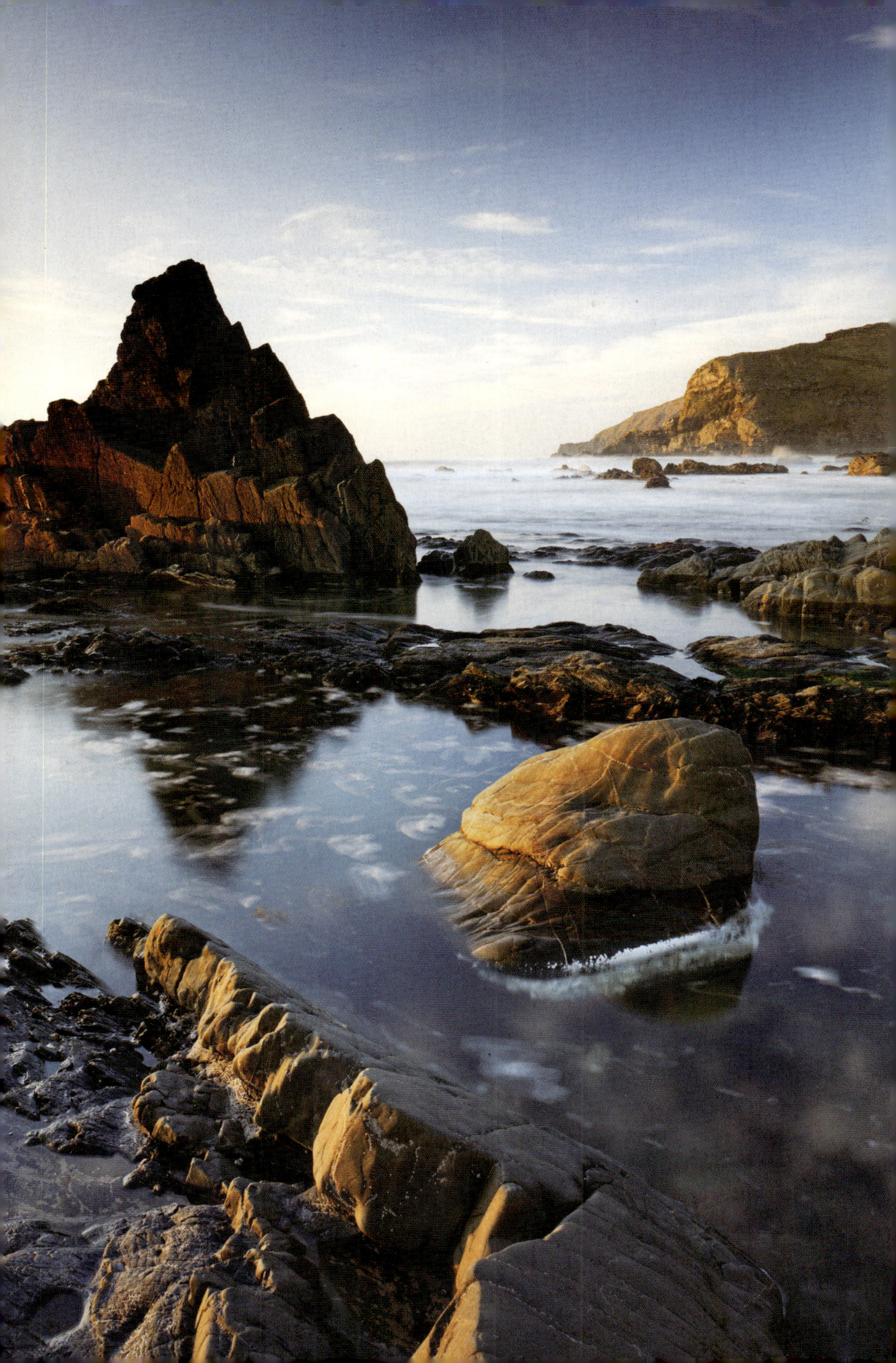

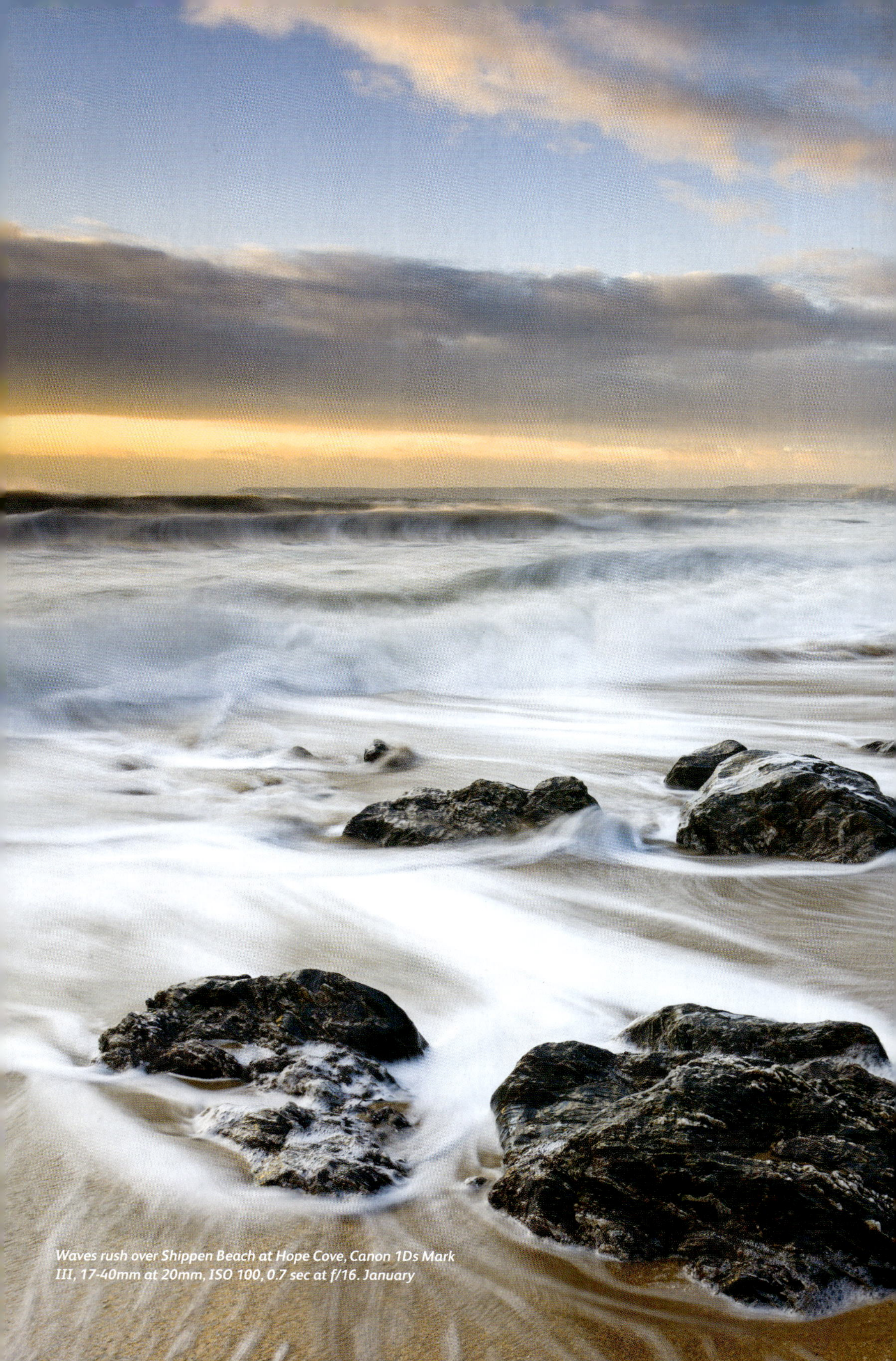

Waves rush over Shippen Beach at Hope Cove, Canon 1Ds Mark III, 17-40mm at 20mm, ISO 100, 0.7 sec at f/16. January

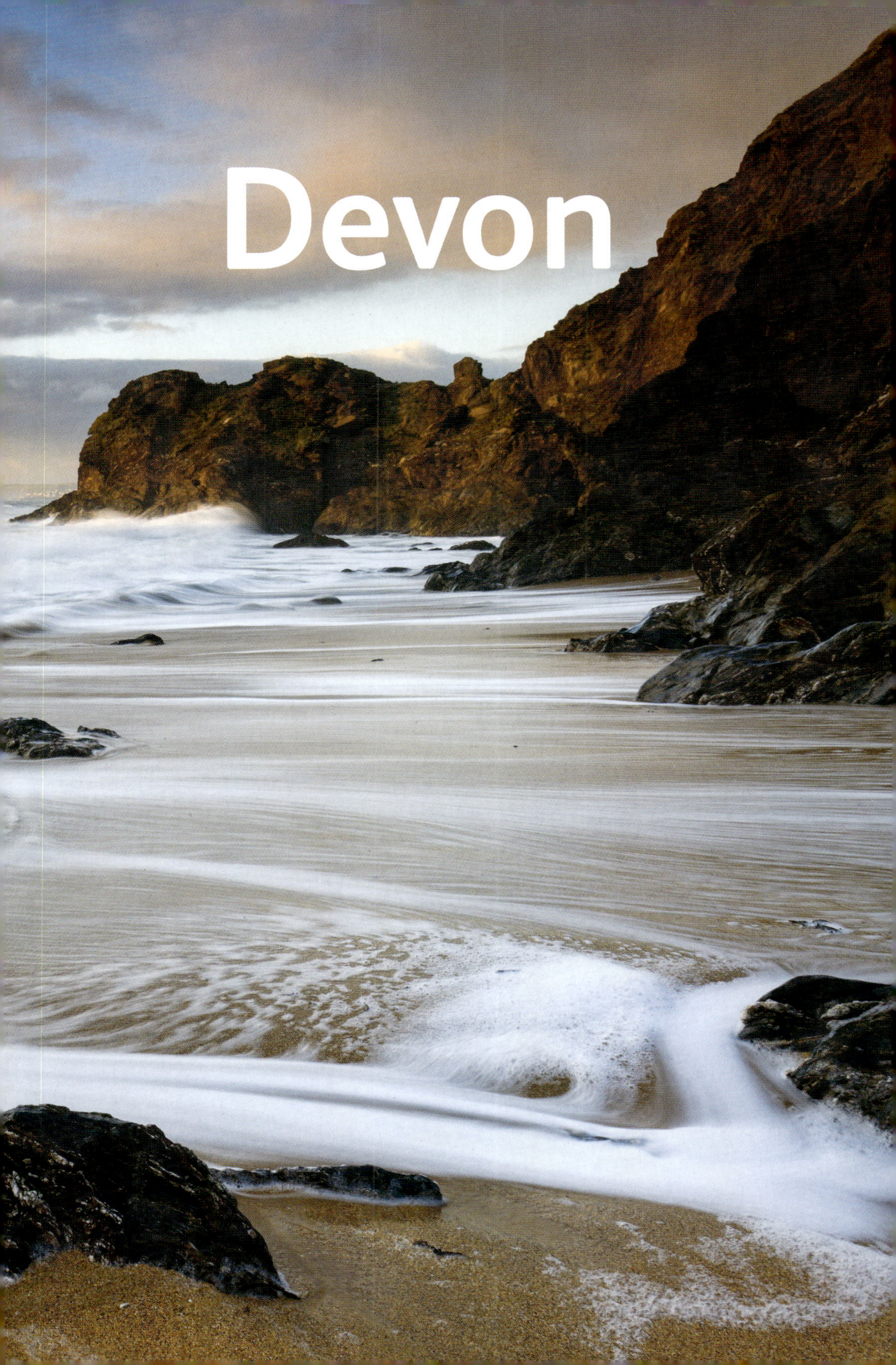
Devon

NORTH DEVON AND EXMOOR

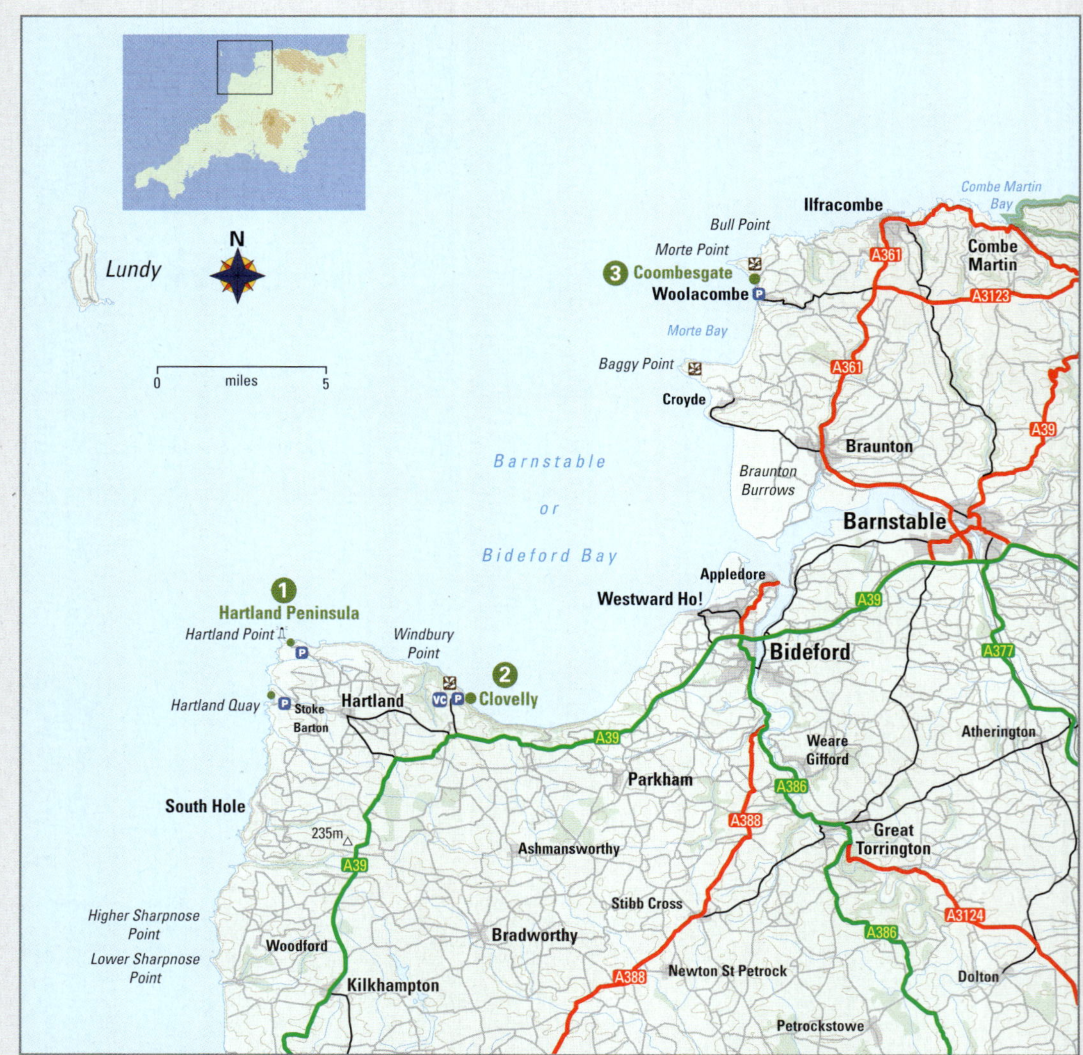

Contains Ordnance Survey data © Crown Copyright and database right (2016), map location overlay © fotoVUE 2016

Devon's north coast shares many similarities with neighbouring Cornwall; sweeping sandy beaches and towering cliffs are to be found in abundance along this coast. Away from the towns this area has the same wild remoteness that is to be found all along the Atlantic coast, and forms a large part of its appeal.

Our chapter begins with the incredibly rugged Hartland Quay close to the Cornish border, and then sweeps around the coastline following some beautiful beaches before reaching Exmoor. At Exmoor, things change quite suddenly and dramatically. Although already high, the cliffs surge upwards making them the highest cliffs in England. With such high cliffs and fewer openings to the sea, much of the Devon stretch of the Exmoor coast is the remotest in England. Eventually, Devon gives

way to Somerset and before long a wide pebble beach at beautiful Porlock Bay replaces the towering headlands of before.

Although one of the UK's least visited national parks Exmoor surely boasts some of the greatest variety. As well as its incredible coastline the National Park, which straddles both Devon and Somerset, is famous for rolling moorland, idyllic rural countryside and wooded combes. Although being fairly close in proximity to neighbouring Dartmoor, the national parks bear little similarity. Exmoor features far larger areas of rolling countryside, and while it still contains large areas of moorland the distinctive heather covered hogsback hills have no granite tors in sight.

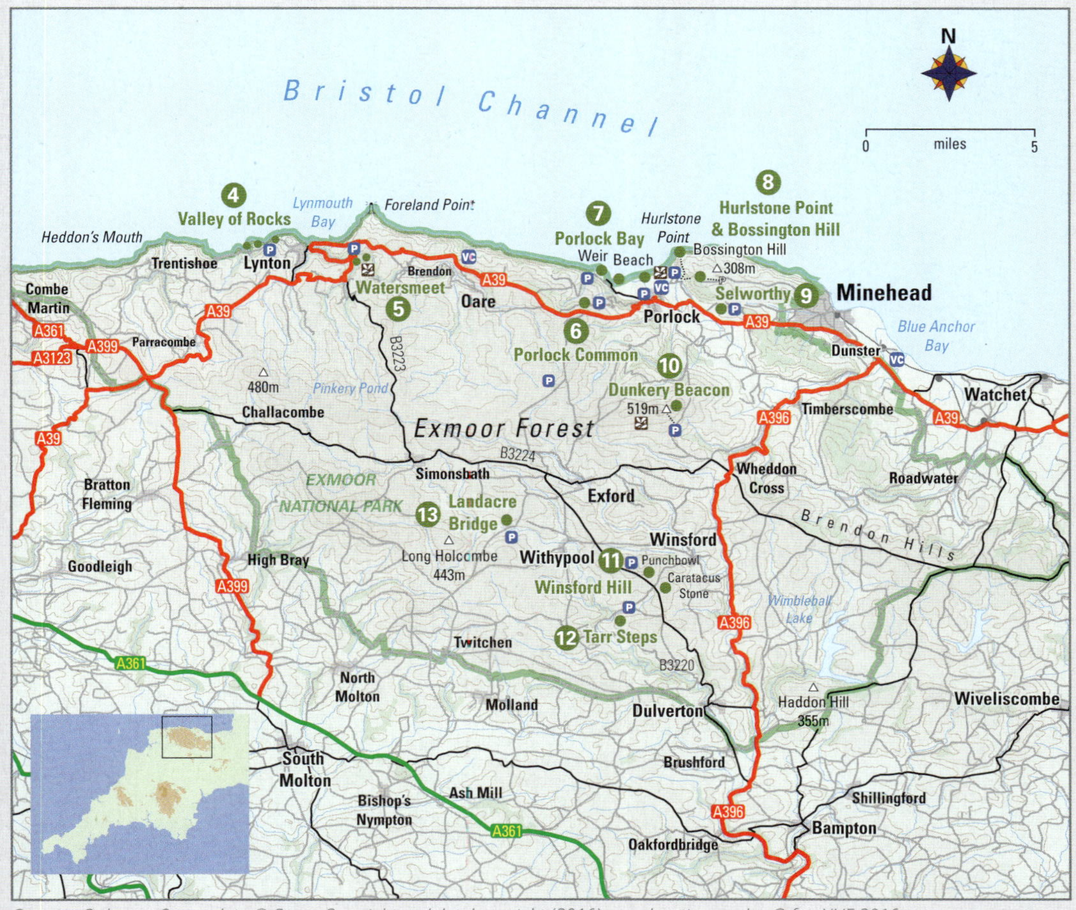

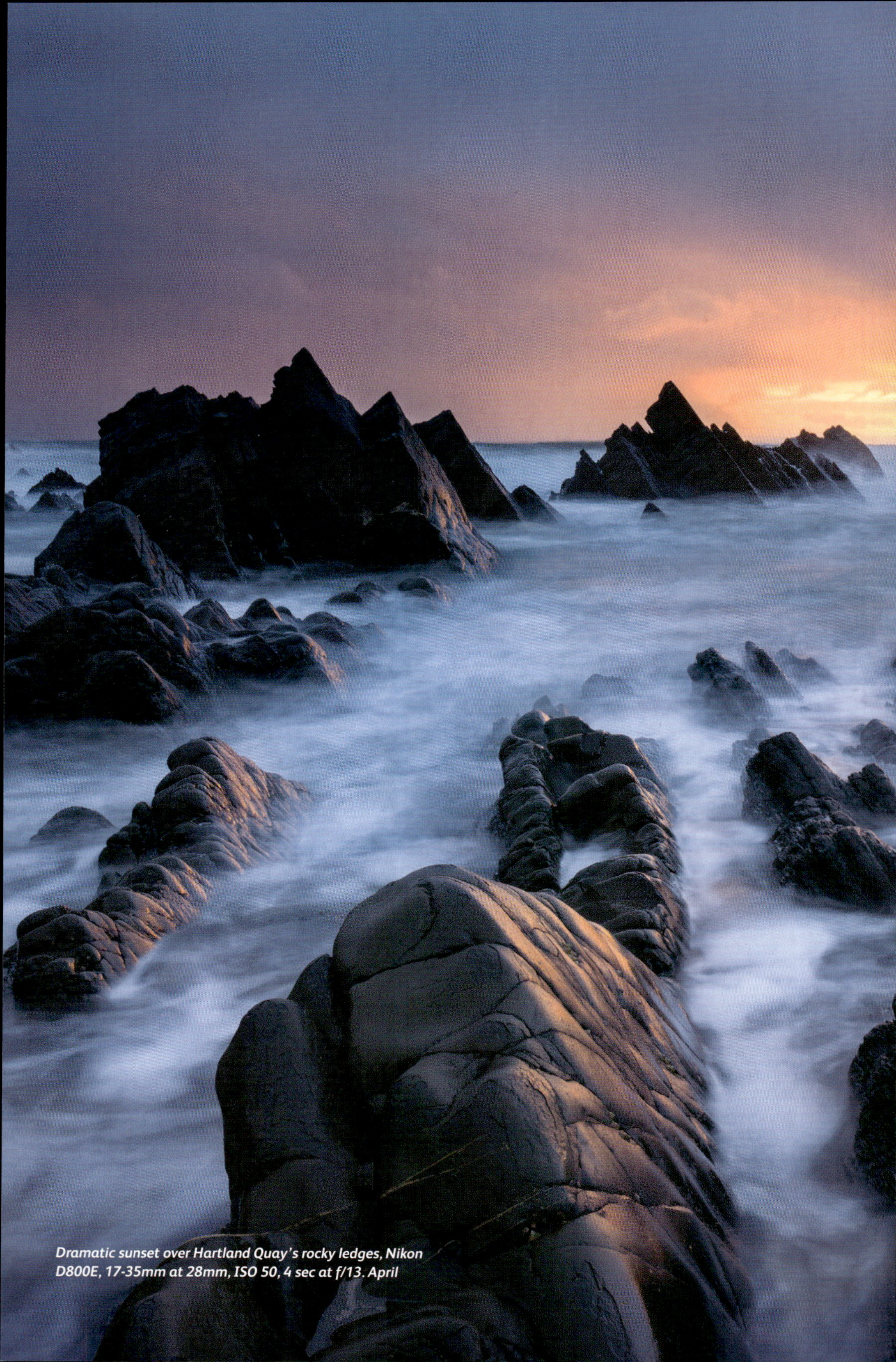

Dramatic sunset over Hartland Quay's rocky ledges, Nikon D800E, 17-35mm at 28mm, ISO 50, 4 sec at f/13. April

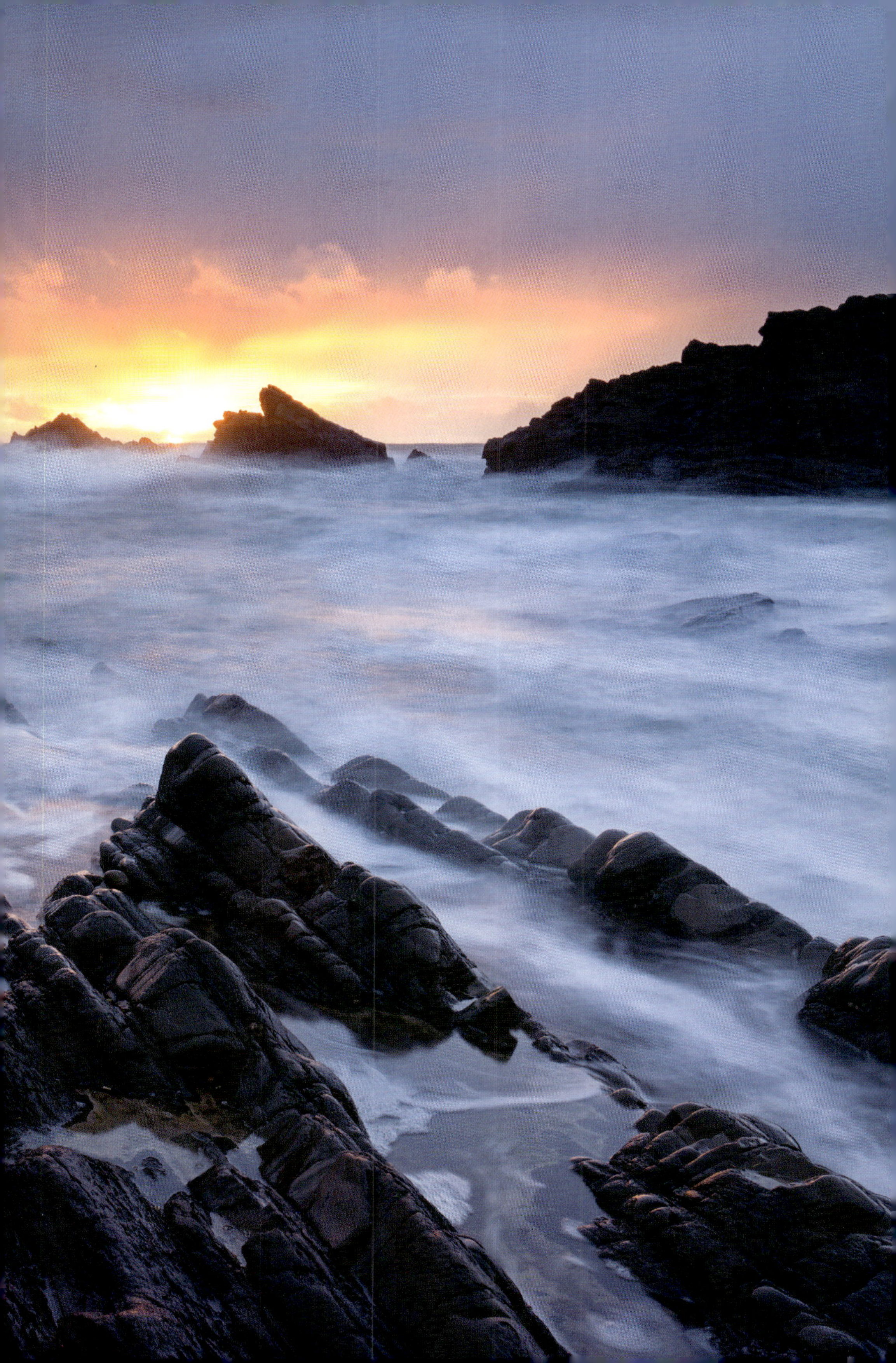

Located on the north coast, Hartland Peninsula is Devon's equivalent to Land's End in Cornwall. In many ways, the coastline here is even more dramatic than its Cornish counterpart, and over the years has been every bit as hazardous for shipping. Although there are many places to explore in the vicinity, from a photographic perspective two areas attract the most attention, Hartland Quay and Hartland Point.

Although the name suggests a bustling harbour, Hartland Quay offers no such shelter for passing boats. A stone harbour was built in the late 16th century but fierce Atlantic storms swept it away in 1887 and it was never rebuilt. A few miles to the north, Hartland Point provides a lonely outpost for the Hartland Point Lighthouse.

What to Shoot and Viewpoints

Viewpoint 1 – Hartland Quay; Towards Screda Point

The cliff top paths above Hartland Quay, adjacent to the car park, provide fantastic vantage points from which to shoot a series of dramatic headlands receding into the distance towards Cornwall. From this position, the nearest and most prominent headland, Screda Point, makes a striking subject for cliff top shots. Screda Point lies just to the south of Hartland Quay, connected to the latter via a rugged beach bursting with rocky ledges. A sheer rock wall juts out into the sea, at its end several enormous triangular stacks stretch out even further.

As incredible as the backdrop is, it's the foreground that keeps people returning to shoot this vista. In late spring, many of the cliffs around Devon and Cornwall look their best with colourful patches of pink sea thrift wildflowers springing up all around. This cliff top vantage point is especially good for these delicate wildflowers, with large clumps flowering all around this area. Many other wildflowers are flowering on the cliffs at this time but it's the sea pinks that steal the show, creating a stunning foreground to compliment the dramatic backdrop.

View north towards Hartland Point, Canon 1Ds Mark III, 16-35mm at 27mm, ISO 50, 30 sec at f/16. April

Opposite: Looking south to Screda Point, Nikon D800E, 17-35mm at 22mm, ISO 100, 15 sec at f/14. May

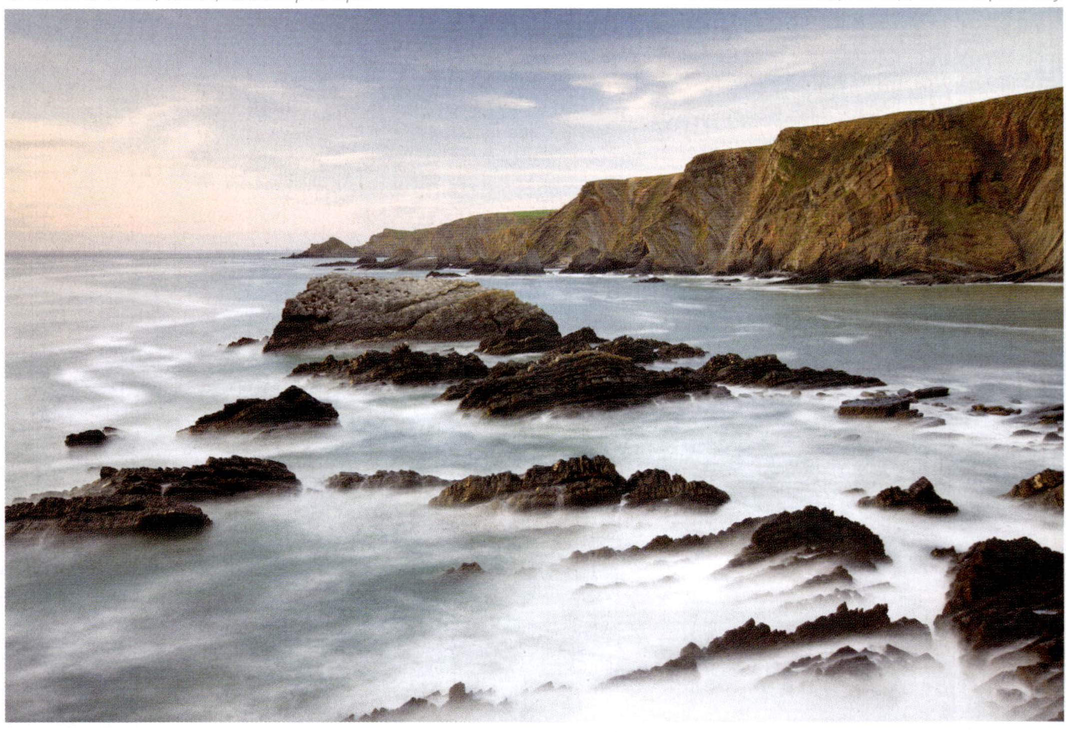

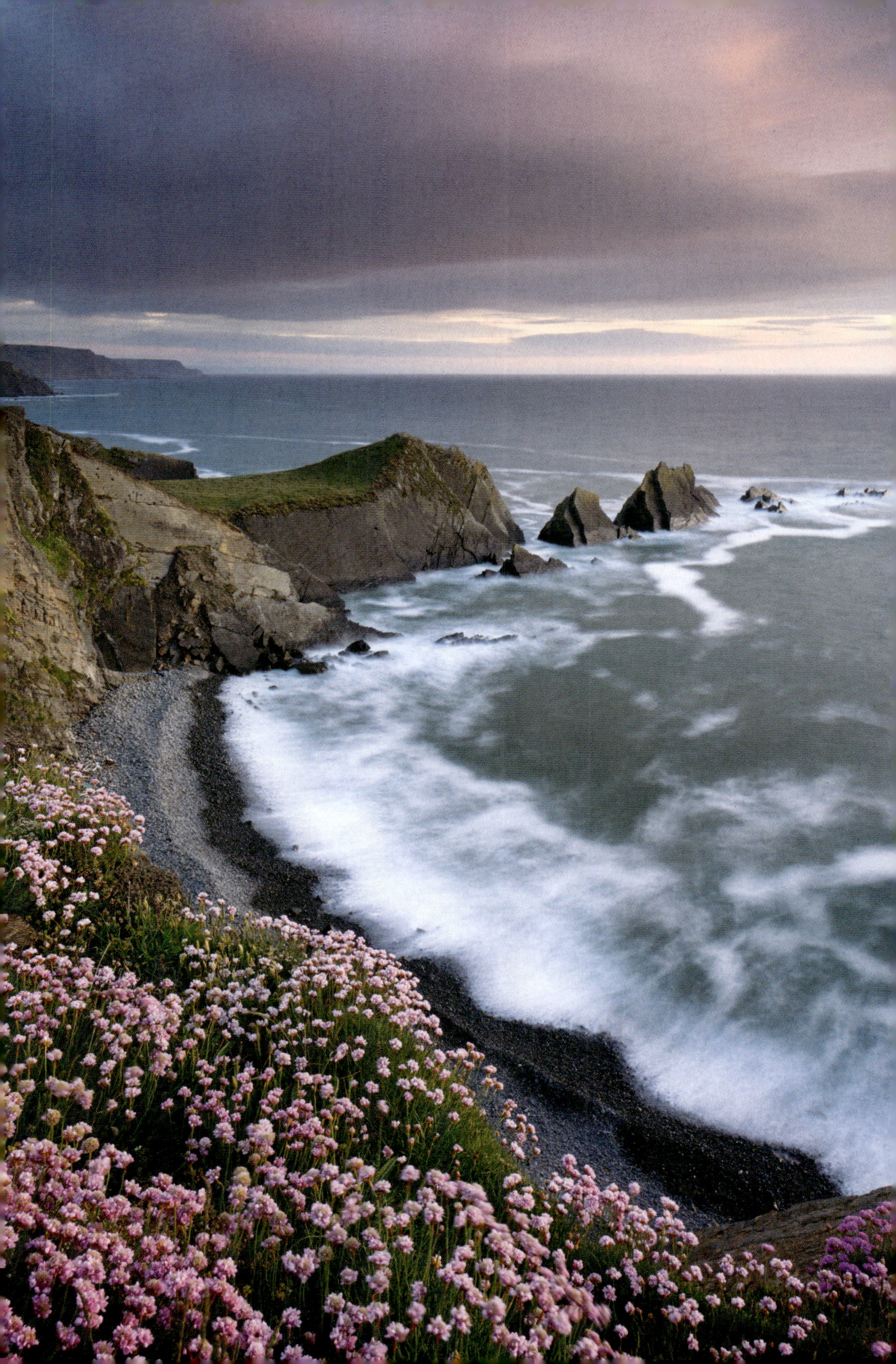

Viewpoint 2 – Hartland Quay Beach

To try some very different photographs from the cliff top vantage point head past the hotel and down the stone slipway. Just to the left of the wall the seashore is about as rugged as can be, with a host of spectacular jagged rocks and ledges forming an almost alien landscape. This area is very tide dependent; if the tide is too high you won't be able to get below the wall, while a low tide will reveal a massive expanse of dark rocks too busy to photograph well. A mid tide is ideal, as waves rush to and fro breaking up the mass of dark rocks in the frame.

NOTE: Caution is advised when venturing to this location at any time; the ledges are slippery and sharp in places making it a difficult place to walk. When waves crash against these rocks this can be an especially perilous place to photograph, so keep your wits about you and don't take unnecessary risks.

When the tide drops further, a sandy beach is revealed with tidal pools and rocks offering countless photographic possibilities. For some of the best viewpoints head around the shore to stand on the far side of the beach, where several long straight ledges stretch out into the water. When photographed with a wide-angle lens these ledges make an incredibly appealing foreground, acting as lead-in lines to draw the eye over to the rocky headland beyond. With the sun setting out to sea directly in the frame this is a good area to stand for sunset and twilight. Position yourself on one of the ledges, and wait for the waves to surge up through the rocks. Once a wave has reached its furthest point, an exposure of several seconds will enable you to capture some beautiful motion as it rushes back into the sea.

Viewpoint 3 – Hartland Point

A couple of miles to the north the coastline makes an abrupt turn eastwards at Hartland Point. This point marks the meeting place of the Bristol Channel and the Atlantic Ocean, and is home to the dramatically positioned Hartland Point Lighthouse. Upon reaching the point for the first time, you could be forgiven for not noticing the lighthouse. It lies near the base of a 325 foot cliff, almost hidden from view and completely inaccessible to the public.

To achieve the best vantage point from which to photograph the lighthouse, follow the coast path westwards from the car park for 5–10 minutes. When you reach a stile, a gap in the cliff hedge nearby will reveal a vista northwards towards the lighthouse far below and distant Lundy Island beyond. Another more open view can be achieved just a little further along, right beside a memorial stone to the Glenart Castle, a hospital ship that sank nearby after being torpedoed in the Second World War.

Although these two viewpoints are probably the most open, achieving good photographs of the lighthouse is challenging. If you are shooting with a tripod, it is difficult to position the camera high enough to avoid overgrown cliff-side bushes creeping into the frame. To make matters worse, with the tripod fully extended the exposed position of this lofty viewpoint often makes it difficult to capture a sharp picture.

Although the lighthouse can make a worthwhile shot, the experience of standing on these dramatic cliffs is the real reward for your endeavour. This location was known to the Romans as the promontory of Hercules; standing on the high cliffs on a stormy day it's easy to see how it got its name.

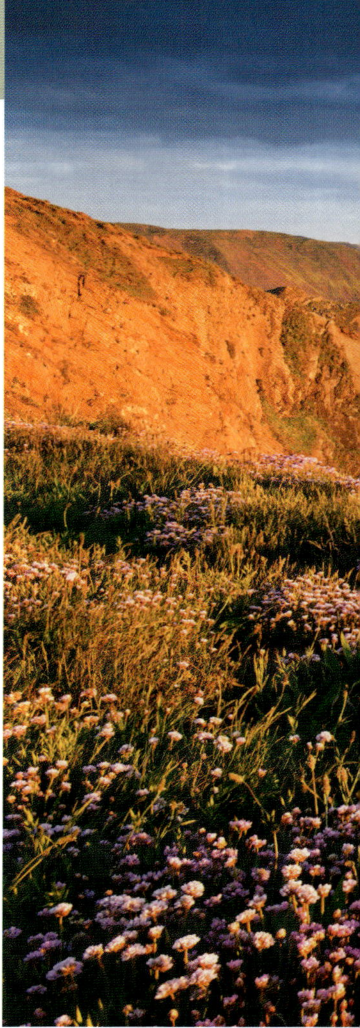

Sea pink wildflowers on the cliffs above Screda Point, Nikon D800E, 17-35mm at 20mm, ISO 100, 6 sec at f/14. May

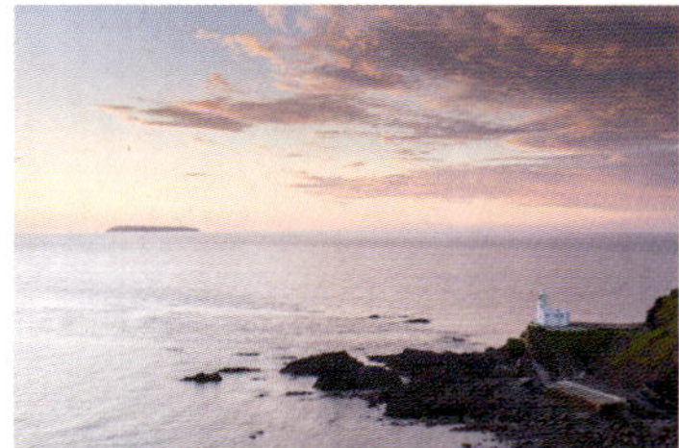

Sunset over Hartland Point Lighthouse, Nikon D800E, 24-70mm at 40mm, ISO 200, 1/3 sec at f/11. May

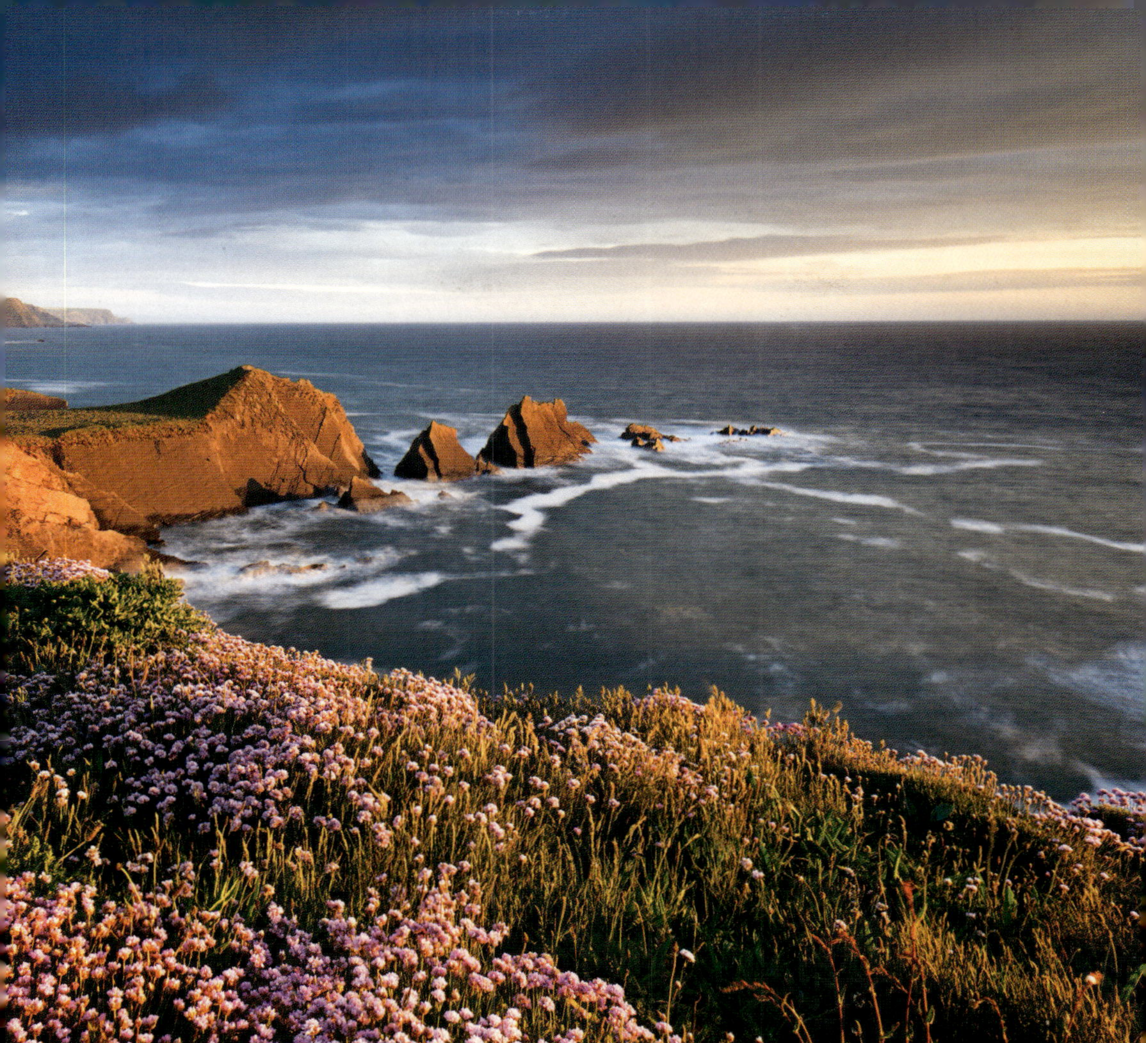

How to Get Here

Hartland Quay and Point are both 16 miles west of Bideford in North Devon. Follow the A39 to Higher Clovelly and then take the right turning onto the B3248 signposted Hartland. After a couple of miles, a right turning will take you to Hartland Point and its lighthouse (VP3).

For Hartland Quay (VP 1 and 2), stay on the B3278, passing through the villages of Hartland and Stoke before arriving at Hartland Quay. Both locations are accessed via private toll roads which lead to sizable car parks.

Parking Lat/Long: 50.994190, -4.5335903 (Hartland Quay), 51.019683, -4.5192948 (Hartland Point).
Parking Grid Ref: SS 223 247 (Hartland Quay), SS 234 275 (Hartland Point)
Parking Postcode: EX39 6DU (Stoke village)
Map: OS Explorer Map OL126 (1:25 000) Clovelly & Hartland

Accessibility

From the car park at both Hartland Quay and Point, impressive views can be photographed almost immediately with little walking. Hartland Quay has three car parks, one at the top of the cliffs, one near the middle and one near the bottom. For the vista of Screda Point you can park no more than a couple of metres away from the viewpoint, making this vista achievable for people of all abilities. The lower car park is paved, providing wheelchair access past the hotel to various elevated views of the coast.

Best Time of Year/Day

Hartland Quay and Point can be photographed at any time of the year. Facing west it is best photographed in the evening for late sunshine and sunset colours. For those wishing to photograph the wildflowers, plan to visit from mid May to early June.

It's normally Cornwall that springs to mind when there is mention of picturesque coastal fishing villages. Yet, one of the West Country's most beautiful and best known examples is in neighbouring Devon. Nestled into a steep wooded valley overlooking the Bristol Channel, the village of Clovelly is perfect picture-postcard material. Pretty whitewashed cottages and small shops crowd either side of a tiny cobbled lane that descends rather steeply down to a tiny harbour, complete with fishing boats.

Clovelly owes much of its fortune to this cobbled lane. Being so steep and narrow, the lane escaped the modernisation that swept the country's roads with the arrival of the motor car, ensuring that Clovelly retained its old world charm.

The village is managed by the Clovelly Estate Company; visitors are charged an admission fee which contributes to the continual restoration programme required to maintain the buildings.

Opposite: Fishing boats in the harbour at high tide, Canon 1Ds Mark III, 17-40mm at 27mm, ISO 100, 0.5 sec at f/13. September

Cobbled steps leading to the harbour, Canon 1Ds Mark III, 17-40mm at 22mm, ISO 100, 0.3 sec at f/16. September

What to Shoot and Viewpoints

Viewpoint 1 – The Cobbled Lane

The steep cobbled lane is one of the main focuses of Clovelly. The lane at first descends in a fairly straight direction past cottages and shops before a series of steps zigzags around some more houses just above the harbour.

The best place on the higher straight section to position yourself is near the New Inn Hotel. You will see a sign for the inn hanging above you, at this point the lane narrows significantly. As well as shooting wide-angle from here, try attaching a telephoto lens and shooting from further uphill. The longer focal length will compress the elements in your photo, effectively pulling the buildings closer together and emphasising the gradient of the lane.

Further downhill at the zigzags, views of the sea and harbour begin to open up. These elevated views over whitewashed houses to the little harbour can make for some great pictures.

The whole route down is very picturesque although it can be difficult to photograph. The main issue is avoiding people in your pictures; the popularity of Clovelly ensures that there is a near continuous flow of visitors walking up and down the lane during the day. The best time to visit is early or late in the day but even at these times you may need to be patient.

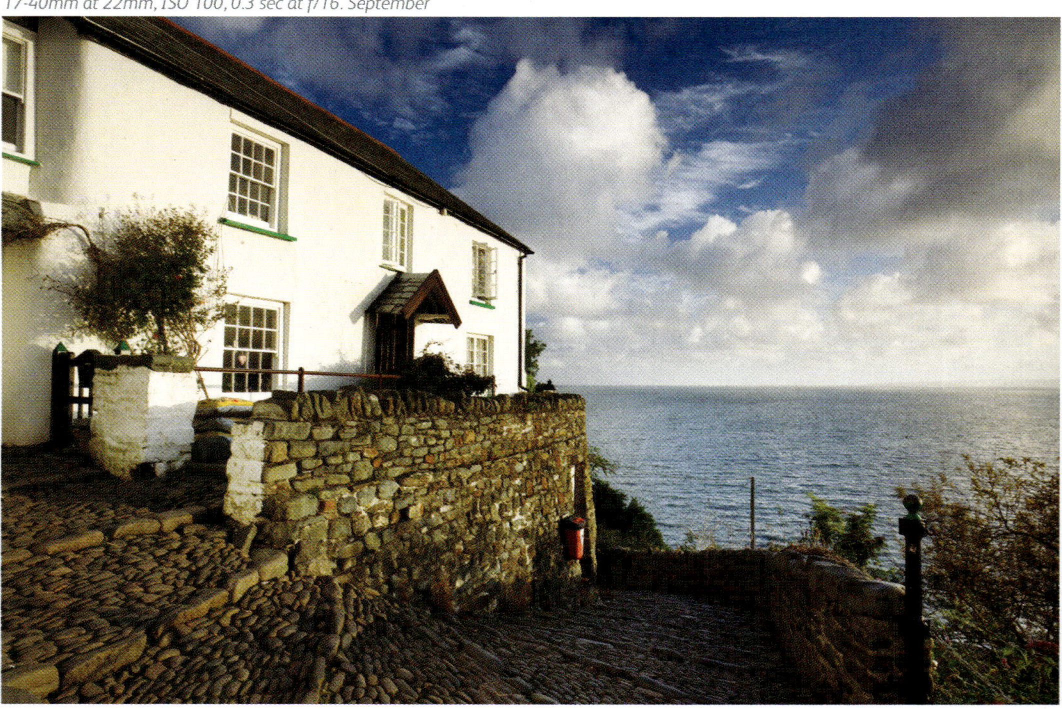

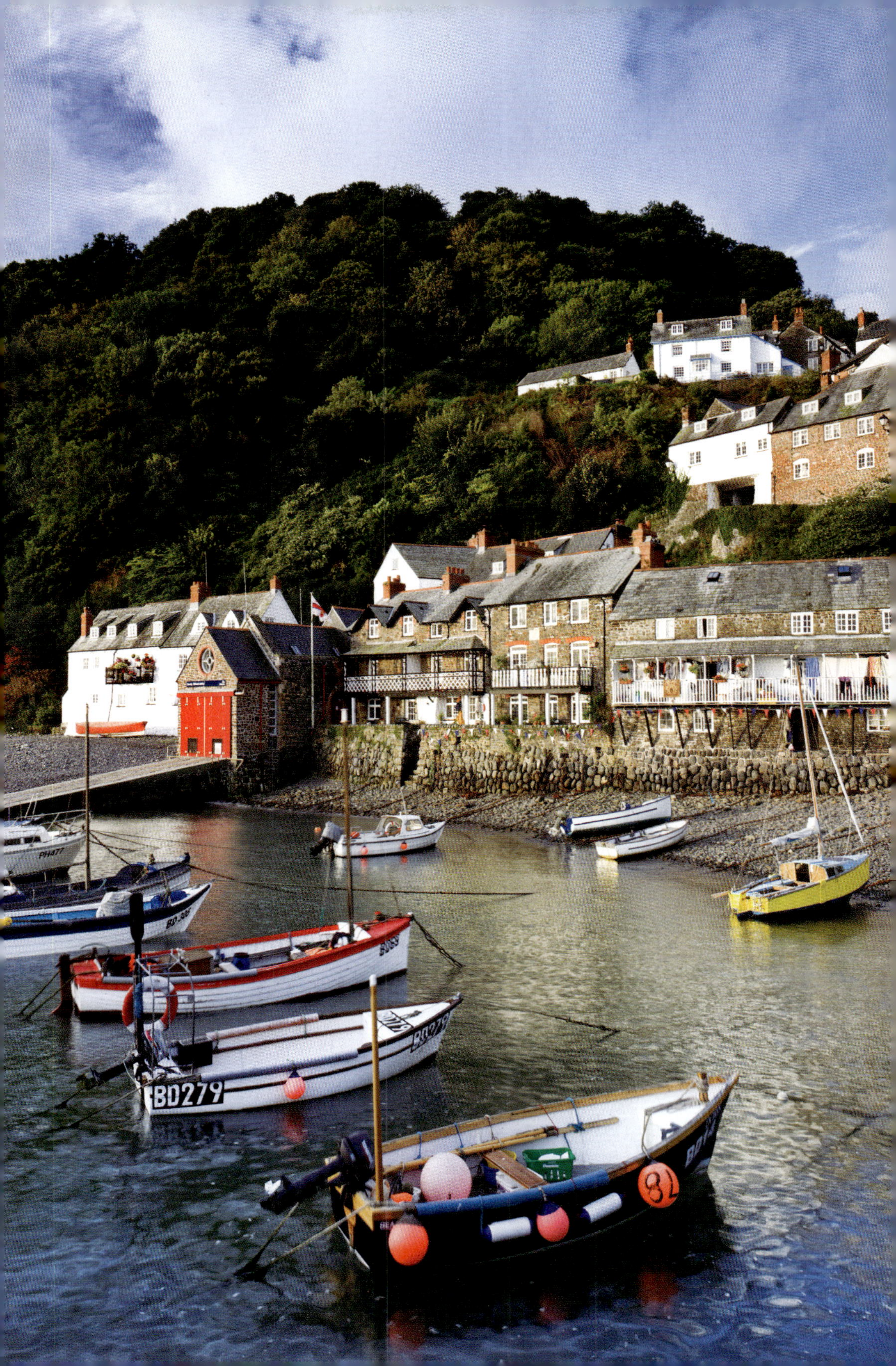

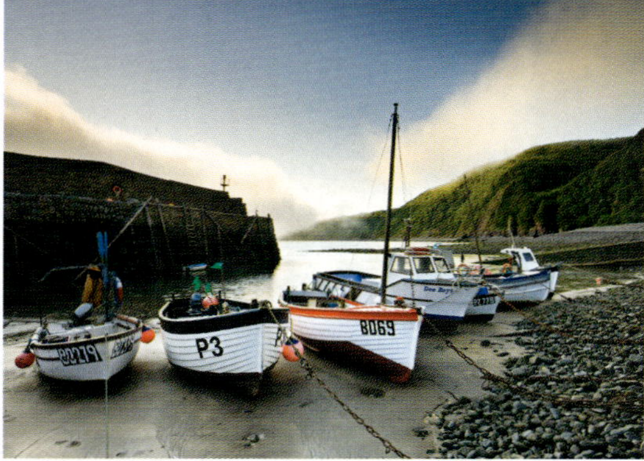

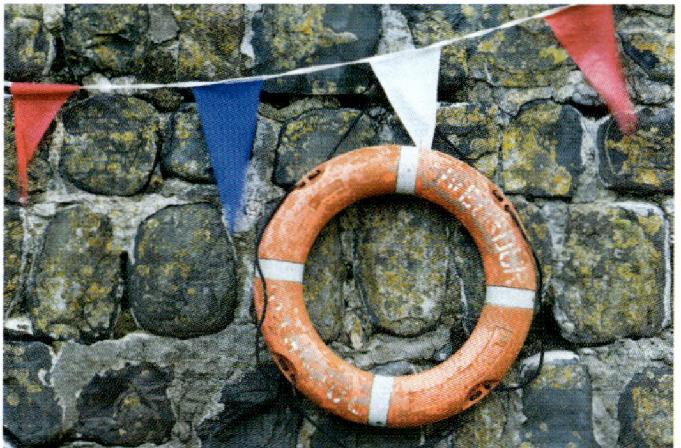

Viewpoint 2 – The Harbour

Once at the shore, the old harbour wall is an obvious draw. From the wall you can get a classic shot of the village clustered around the boats on the foreshore. Try to time your trip to coincide with a high tide, the boats tend to look better when bobbing around in the water. With a super wide-angle lens, it's possible to include the attractive curving stone harbour wall in the foreground.

When the tide is lower, head down to the beach to shoot the boats pulled up high on the shore. Just above the beach there are several picturesque old fishing cottages; a wide-angle lens will enable you to photograph both the fishing boats and these cottages backed by dense wooded cliffs beyond.

As well as making a great vantage point to shoot the village, the harbour wall offers a wonderful photographic subject in its own right, especially for close-up shots. The old wall with its steps, wooden posts and blocks of stone has plenty to keep your camera busy, all helping to capture a real flavour of this old fishing community.

Opposite: Steep narrow cobbled lane in Clovelly, Canon 1Ds Mark III, 70-200mm at 122mm, ISO 100, ¼ sec at f/16. September

Left: Various views around Clovelly's harbour

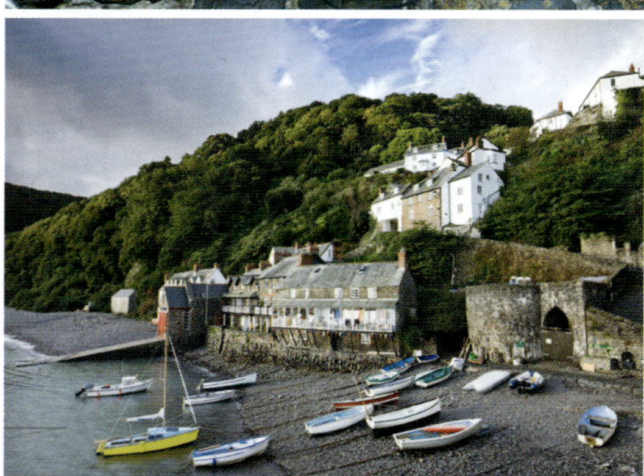

How to Get Here

From Barnstaple head west on the A39 for around 17 miles. At the village of Higher Clovelly, turn right at the roundabout following the signs for Clovelly. Follow this road for another mile and you will reach the village car park and Visitor Centre.

Parking Lat/Long: 51.000915, -4.4096494
Parking Grid Ref: SS 314 249
Parking Postcode: EX39 5TA
Map: OS Explorer Map 126 (1:25 000) Clovelly & Hartland

Accessibility

The village is accessed via the Visitor Centre by paying an admission fee. For those wishing to avoid paying an entrance fee or to arrive out of usual opening hours, you can access the village freely on foot using the South West Coast Path. The cobbled lane is extremely steep and unsuitable for wheelchair users. For an additional fee, a Land Rover shuttles visitors to the harbour via a service road.

Best Time of Year/Day

Clovelly is at its best in late spring and early summer when the wooded cliffs are verdant with lush green foliage. However, unless you wish to photograph lots of people try to avoid visiting during the daytime. Sunrise and early morning is undoubtedly the best time to visit, when the village is quiet and the position of the low sun over the sea will illuminate the cottages.

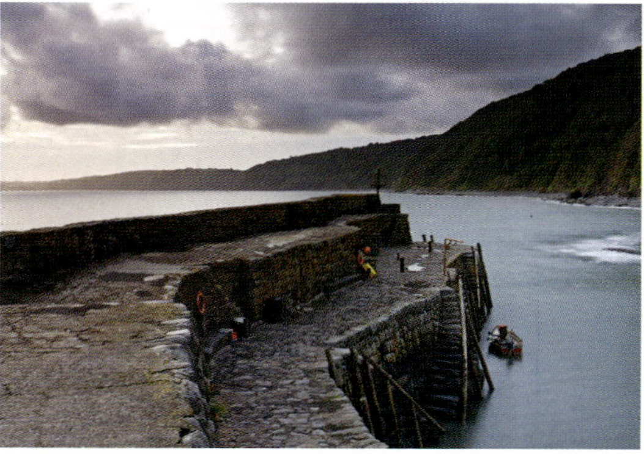

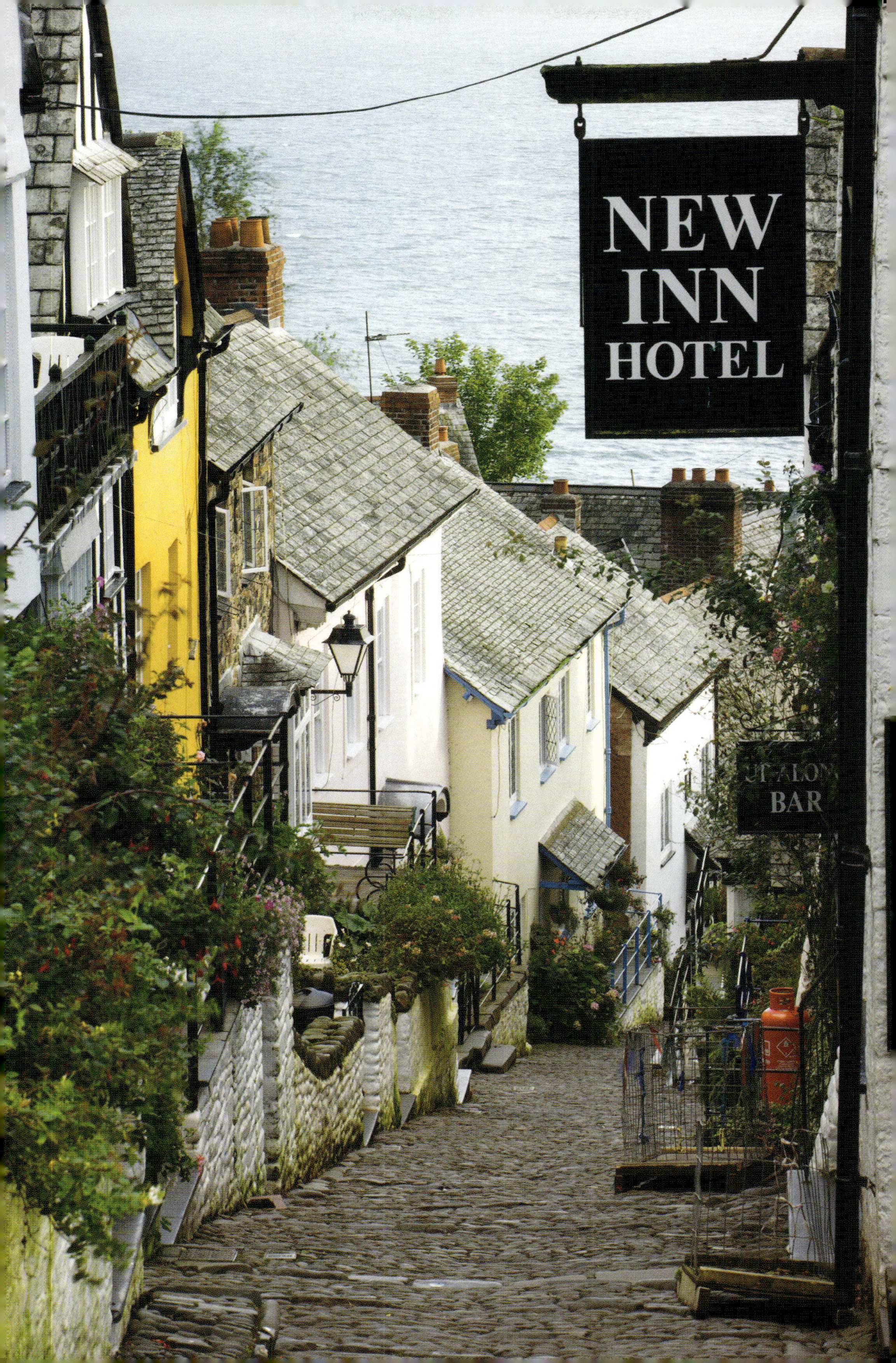

NEW
INN
HOTEL
BAR

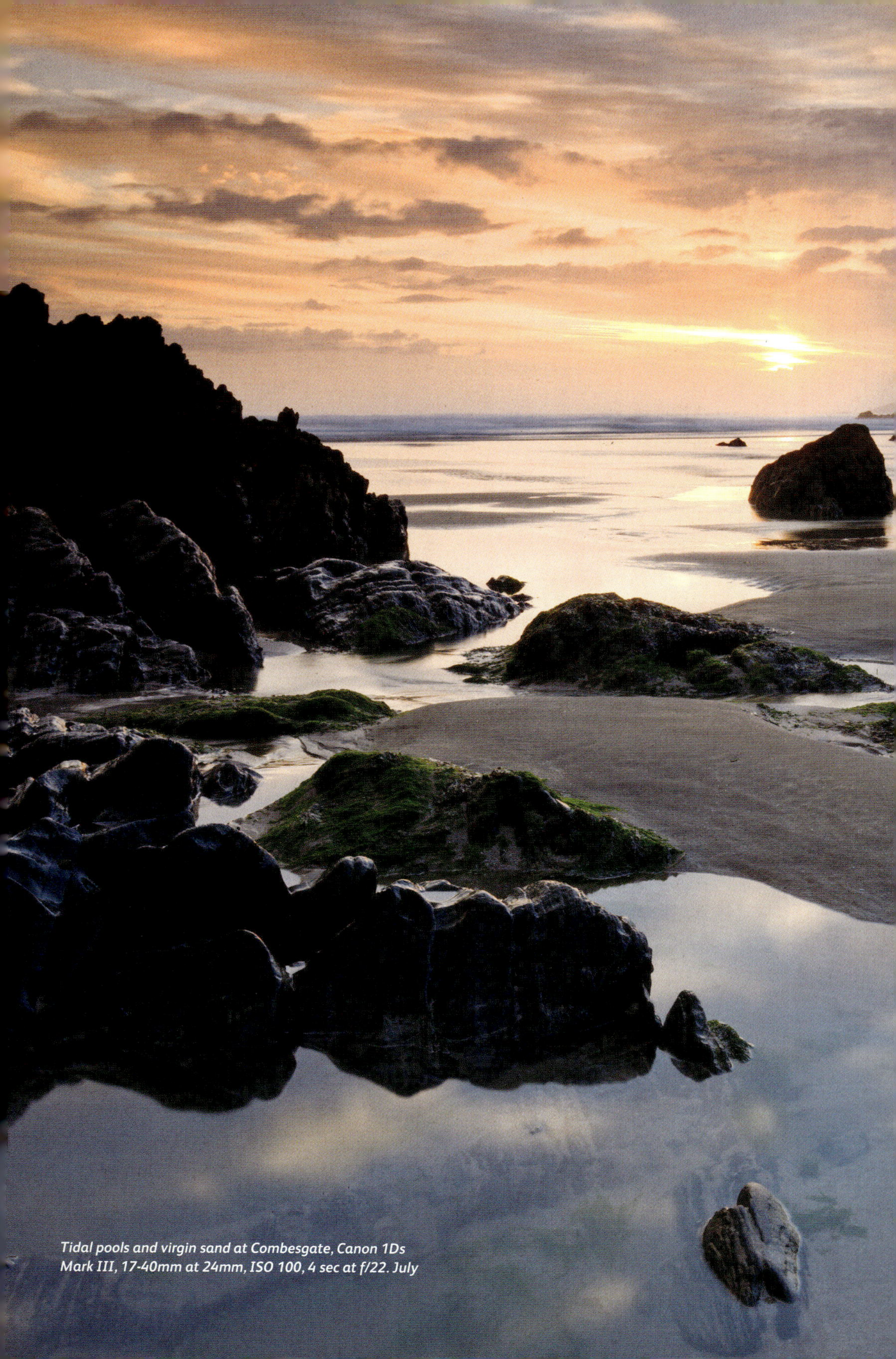

Tidal pools and virgin sand at Combesgate, Canon 1Ds Mark III, 17-40mm at 24mm, ISO 100, 4 sec at f/22. July

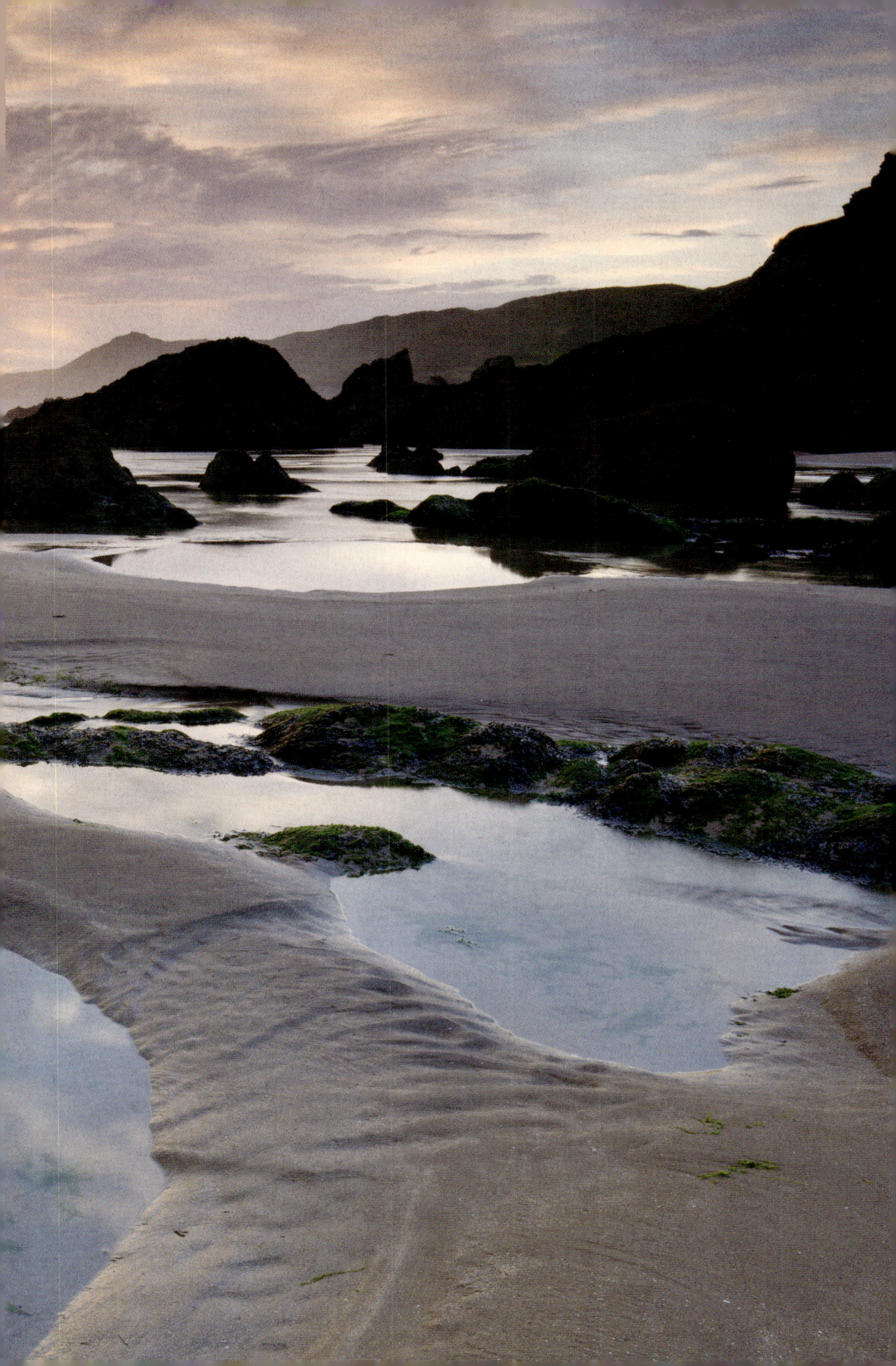

3

Combesgate Beach

Combesgate lies just to the north of one of Devon's best-loved beaches, the beautiful Woolacombe Bay. This stretch of the north Devon coast is popular with holidaymakers, dominated by both Woolacombe and its near neighbours, Croyde and Saunton Sands. While the sweeping expanse of golden sands make these beaches ideal for summer tourists, Combesgate offers much more dramatic scenery for landscape photographers.

What to Shoot and Viewpoints

With nearby Woolacombe attracting all the attention Combesgate seems quite an insignificant beach, one that can easily be overlooked. Indeed, if you peer down from the cliff tops at high tide there is barely any beach at all, the crashing Atlantic waves almost reaching the base of the cliffs.

However, venture down the steep steps to reach the beach on a lower tide and you will soon recognise its appeal for photography. Unlike Woolacombe's clean sandy beach, Combesgate is far rockier, with stony debris high up on the beach and sand lower down in channels between large jagged outcrops.

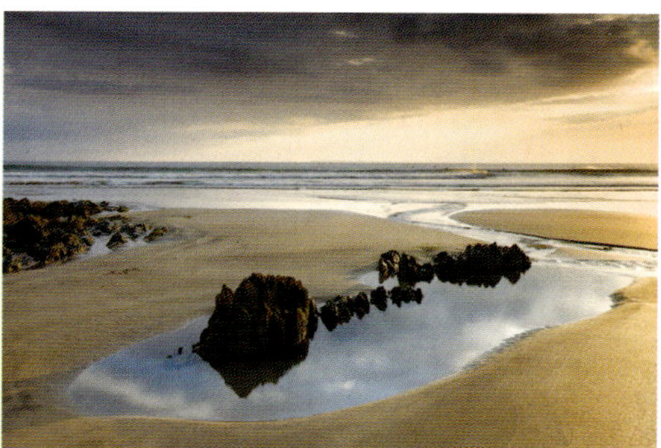

Low tide at Combesgate, Canon 1Ds Mark III, 16-35mm at 35mm, ISO 100, ¼ sec at f/16. June

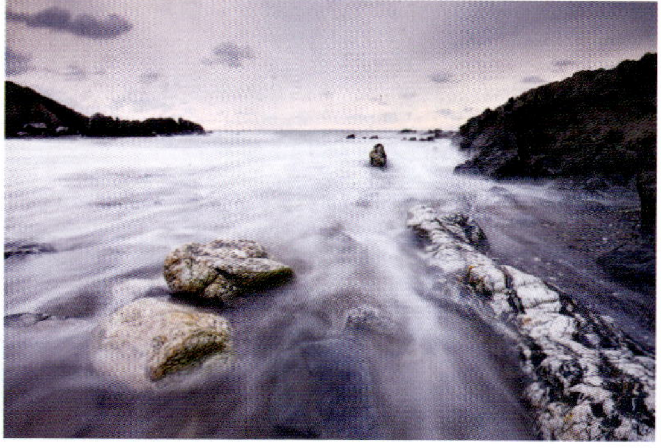

Rocks and Golden Sand

The rocks and outcrops are mostly comprised of slate which protrude almost vertically in dramatic layers. While these sharp rocks make access challenging, they offer great photographic potential as well as providing good opportunities to shoot from a higher vantage point where required.

In and around these outcrops, the angular rocks contrast with soft golden sand, which helps to prevent large masses of rock from overwhelming compositions by bringing both simplicity and balance in colour. Further down the beach, the channels become wider expanses of sand at low tide, broken up with beautiful tidal pools and heavily eroded low ledges.

Although the large outcrops and rocky debris higher up the beach can make good subject matter for photos, the lower section offers simpler and cleaner compositions. Aim to visit on a mid to low tide, ideally with the tide retreating so the sand will be fresh and clean from footprints. Your own footprints may also become a problem, so be careful where you wander on the sand.

Tidal Pools

Look for an interesting tidal pool to include in a wide-angle composition. The pools make excellent foregrounds helping to bring balance to a picture by reflecting the sky's colours in the water. There are plenty of pools in this area, each forming around the smaller rocky outcrops and ledges that occur lower down the beach. As it points in a westerly direction Combesgate makes an ideal beach to shoot late in the day, especially at sunset. From a compositional point of view the beach lends itself to shooting in this direction, with the rugged Morte Point headland adding some extra interest in the background. If you are shooting at low tide and are positioned far enough down the beach, you can also shoot southwards and benefit from Baggy Point as a distant backdrop. On a cloudless evening this can be a good alternative to shooting westwards directly into the sun, and will ensure your chosen foreground benefits from some rich side lighting.

Surfers

This stretch of Atlantic coastline is a popular surfing destination; at low tide you can usually find surfers at Combesgate or nearby Barricane Beach. Whether photographed with a telephoto lens riding a wave, or standing on a beach watching the sunset surfers make excellent photographic subjects that help to capture a real flavour of this coastline.

Left: High tide at Combesgate, Canon 1Ds Mark III, 17-40mm at 17mm, ISO 100, 8 sec at f/16. November

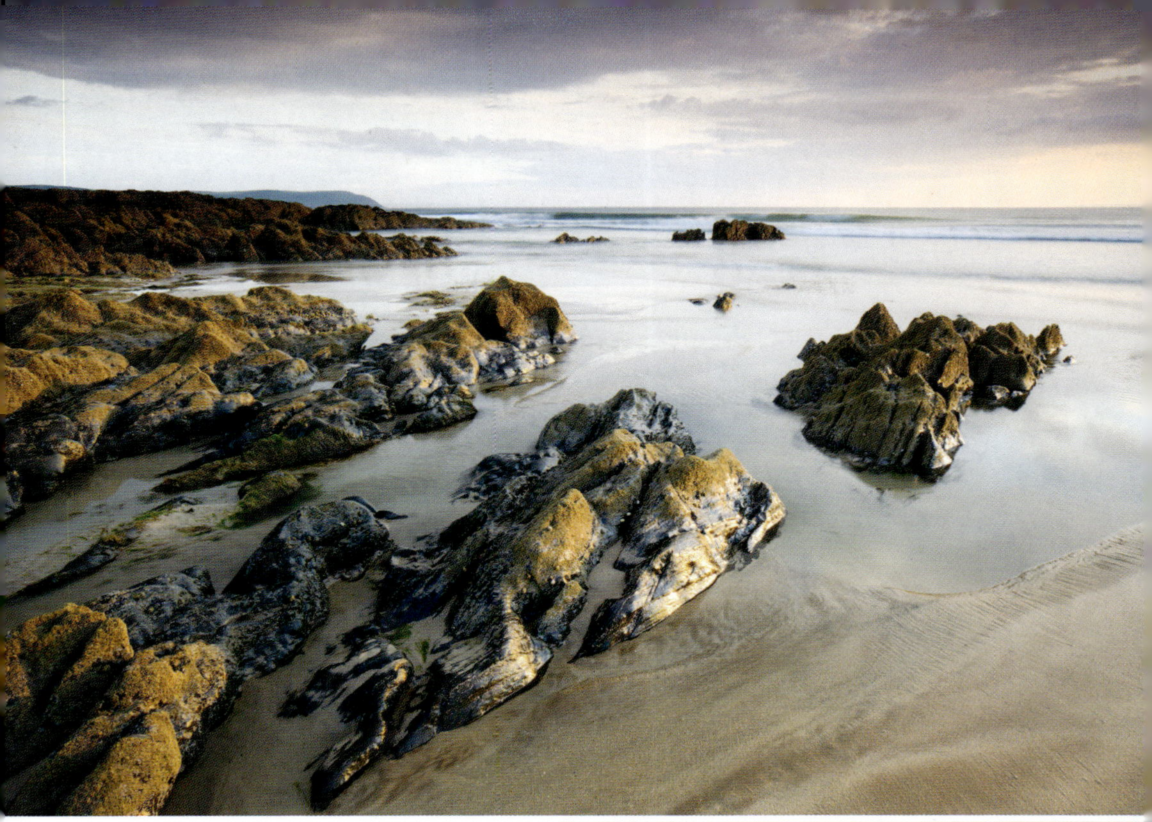

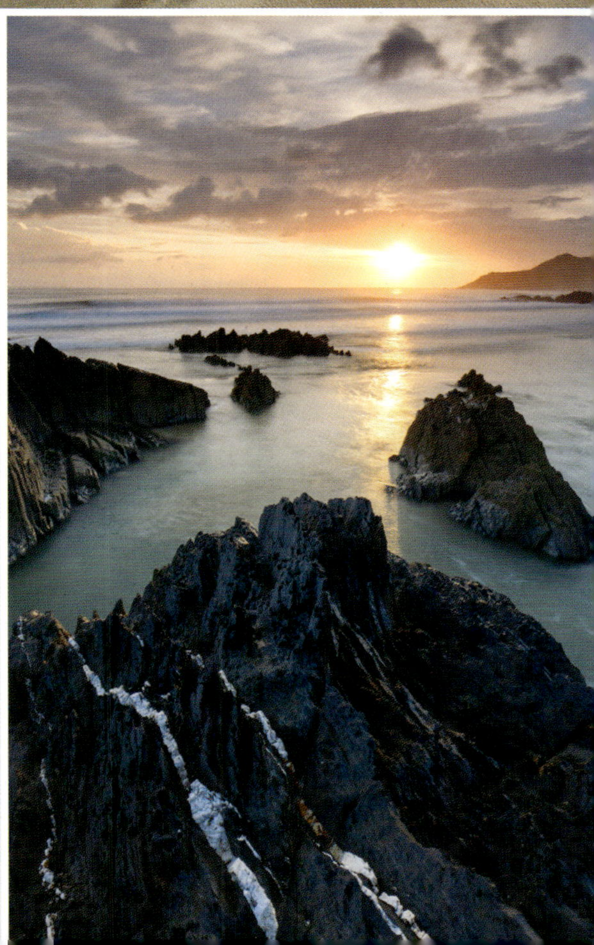

How to Get Here

Combesgate Beach is 13 miles north west of Barnstaple on the North Devon coast. From Barnstaple, head west on the A361 towards Braunton. Pass through Braunton and continue on the road, following signs for Woolacombe. When you reach Woolacombe, you will find Combesgate Beach to the north of the main beach. The beach is directly below the Watersmeet Hotel.

Parking Lat/Long: 51.177241, -4.2121464
Parking Grid Ref: SS 453 443
Parking Postcode: EX34 7EB
Map: OS Explorer Map 139 (1:25 000) Bideford, Ilfracombe and Barnstaple

Accessibility

Combesgate is reached via a steep set of steps, making access impossible for wheelchair users. During low tide the beach can also be accessed from nearby Barricane Beach.

Best Time of Year/Day

Being a coastal location seasonality isn't particularly important, and with the sun always setting out to sea Combesgate Beach can be photographed equally well throughout the year. However, the entire southwest coastline can be busy with holidaymakers in the summer months, so if you are looking for solitude plan to visit in the winter.

Above: There is a wealth of rocky ledges on the beach, Canon 1Ds Mark III, 16-35mm at 23mm, ISO 50, 2 sec at f/16. June

Right: Sunset just off Morte Point, Canon 1Ds Mark III, 17-40mm at 19mm, ISO 100, 6 sec at f/22. July

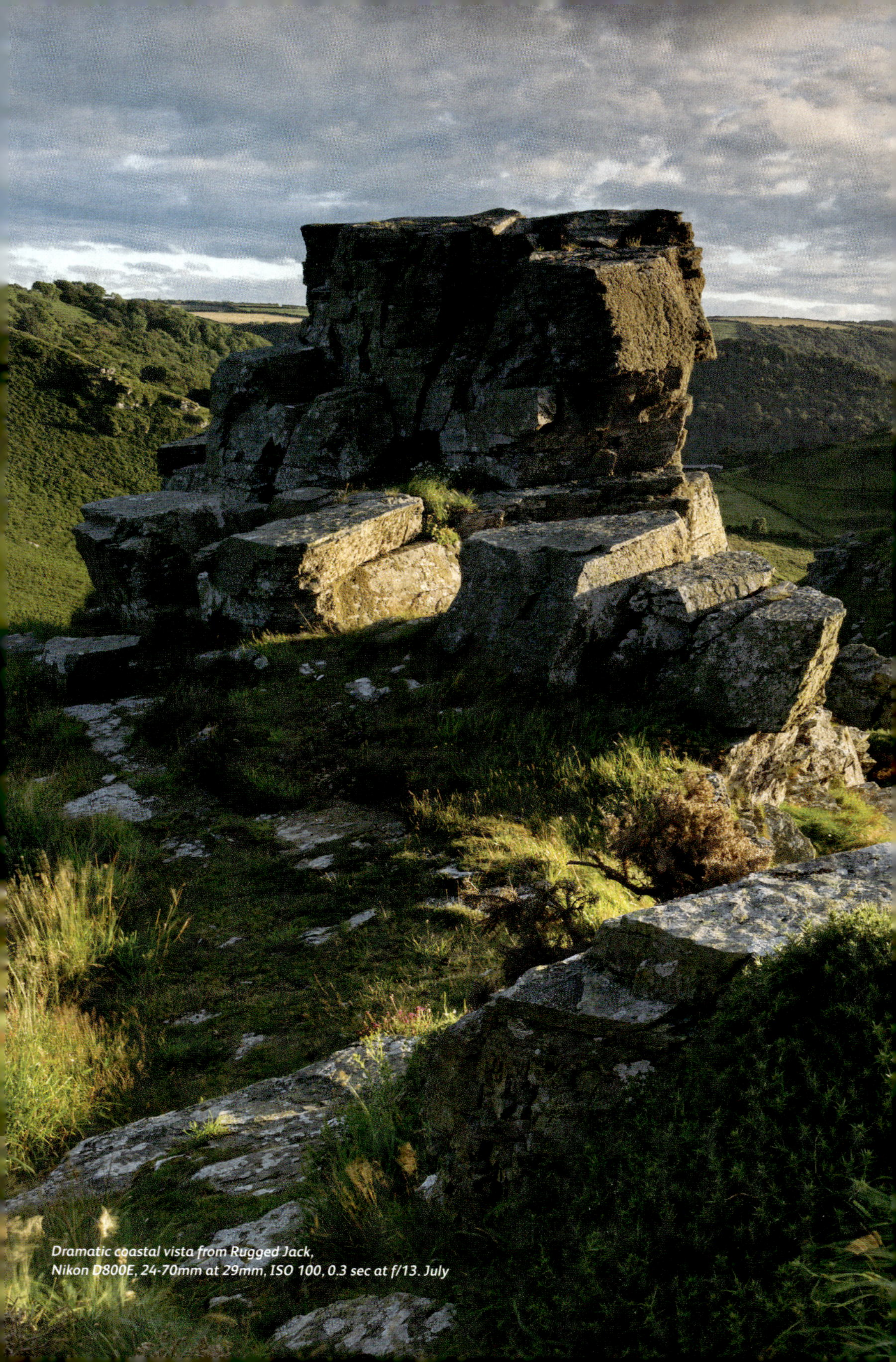

*Dramatic coastal vista from Rugged Jack,
Nikon D800E, 24-70mm at 29mm, ISO 100, 0.3 sec at f/13. July*

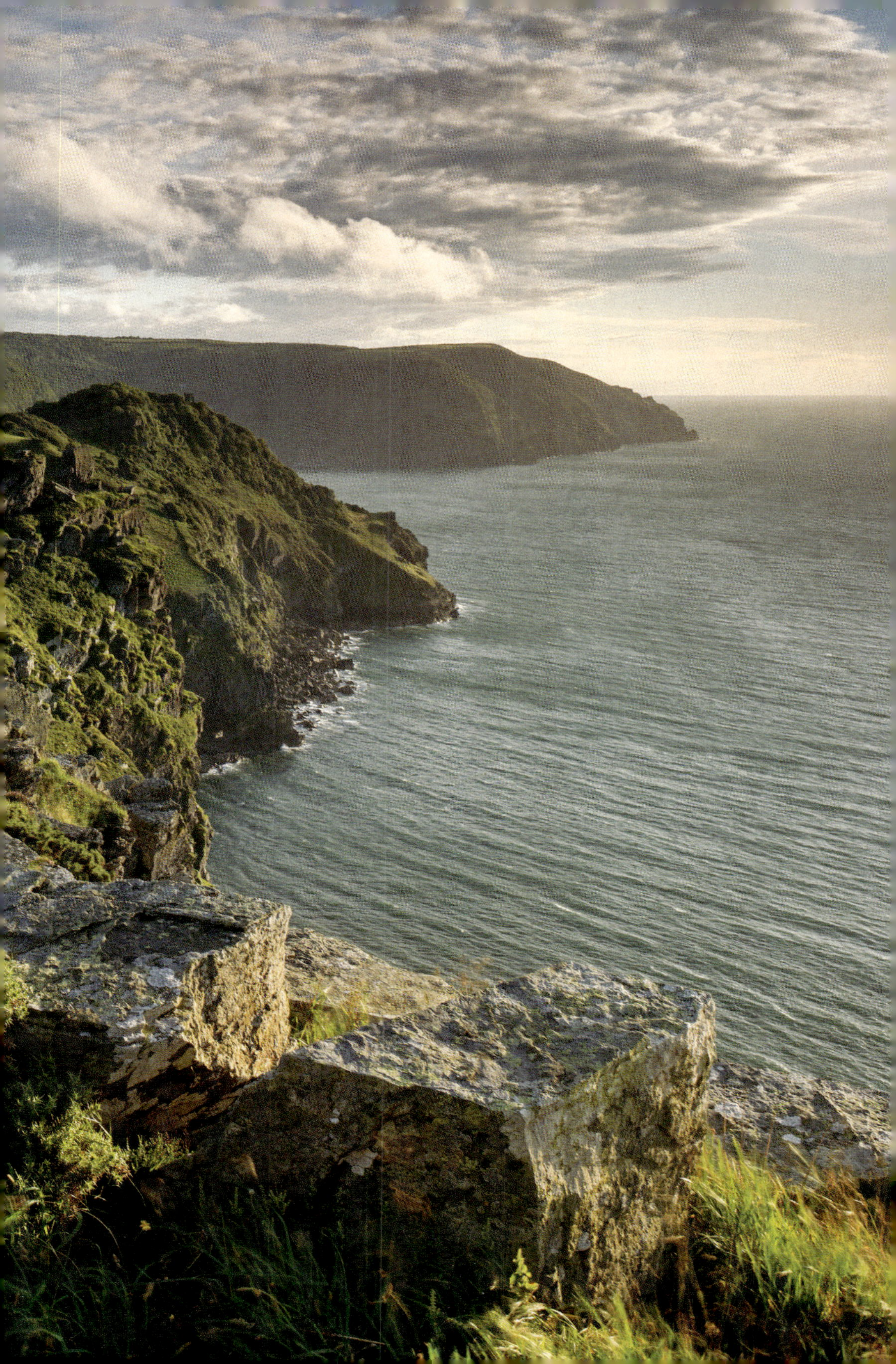

Valley of Rocks

The rugged terrain of the Valley of Rocks is quite out of place in Exmoor's otherwise gentle rolling landscape. This dry valley running alongside the towering cliffs of the North Devon coast is one of Exmoor's most dramatic locations. And yet, surprisingly it is just around the corner from the town of Lynton. An easy ten minute stroll will bring you into this tremendous valley.

Sadly the bottom of the valley has lost its sense of wilderness thanks to a cricket pitch, road and large car parks. These can all become problematic when trying to capture the natural ruggedness of the location. There are however many elevated parts of the valley, served by a network of accessible paths, where it's possible to exclude the less photogenic man-made objects.

What to Shoot and Viewpoints

Viewpoint 1 – Castle Rock

Although many of the best viewpoints are to be found at higher elevations, one of the most popular vistas is also the simplest to get to. An easy two minute walk west from the car park brings you to a tarmac footpath which cuts into the seaward side of the steep cliffs. The footpath isn't for the faint hearted; the cliffs fall away almost vertically to one side of the path all the way to the sea far below.

From the footpath you have an unrestricted viewpoint from which to shoot the magnificent Devon coastline including the dramatic Castle Rock cliff in the foreground.

Feral goats on the cliff tops, Canon 1Ds Mark III, 70-200mm at 70mm, ISO 100, 1/90 sec at f/5.6. August

Viewpoint 2 – Hollerday Hill

To better appreciate the valley the best place to photograph is from Hollerday Hill. At over 240 metres, Hollerday Hill offers commanding views over the Valley of Rocks and the coastline beyond and makes a fantastic location to appreciate, and photograph, the full extent of this unusual rocky landscape.

From the car park a footpath zigzags up the side of the hill with amazing vistas opening up as you climb, so there is no need to venture to the very top. As you are looking straight down the valley from here, the cricket pitch and car park are very evident in the frame. To get around this problem, try using a telephoto lens and close in on the peaks, or alternatively seek out some foreground interest, which with careful positioning can be used to hide any unsightly objects beyond. Luckily there are plenty of jagged rocks jutting out of the hill that can work wonders for blocking out the cricket pitch.

If you are lucky you may even get to photograph some of the valley's wildlife. There is a resident herd of feral goats living among the rocky terrain. These goats can be easily seen roaming all over the valley, and make fantastic subjects when perched on a rocky outcrop.

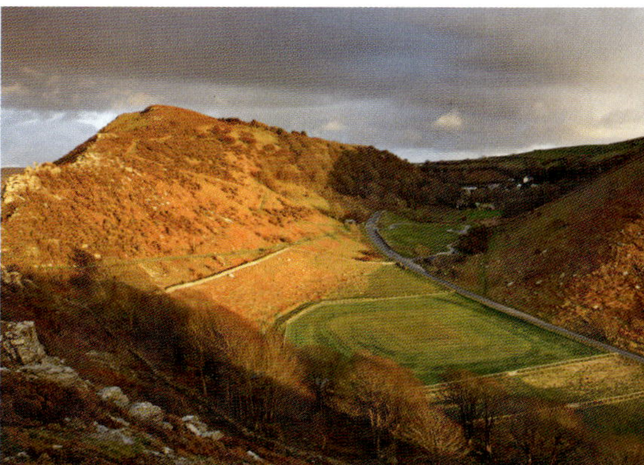

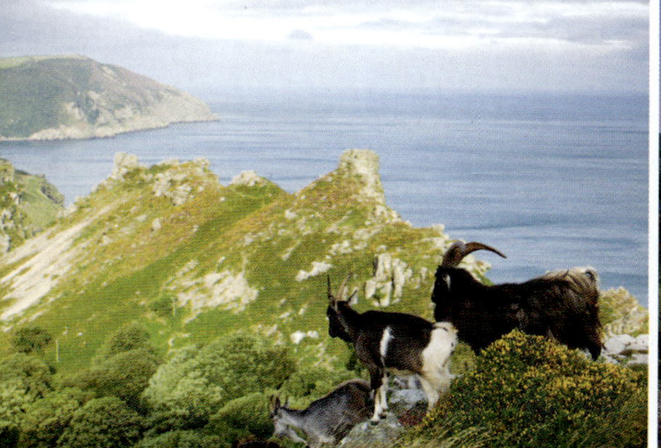

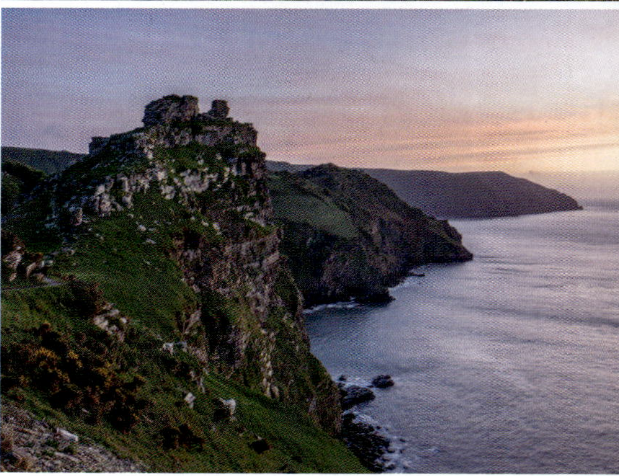

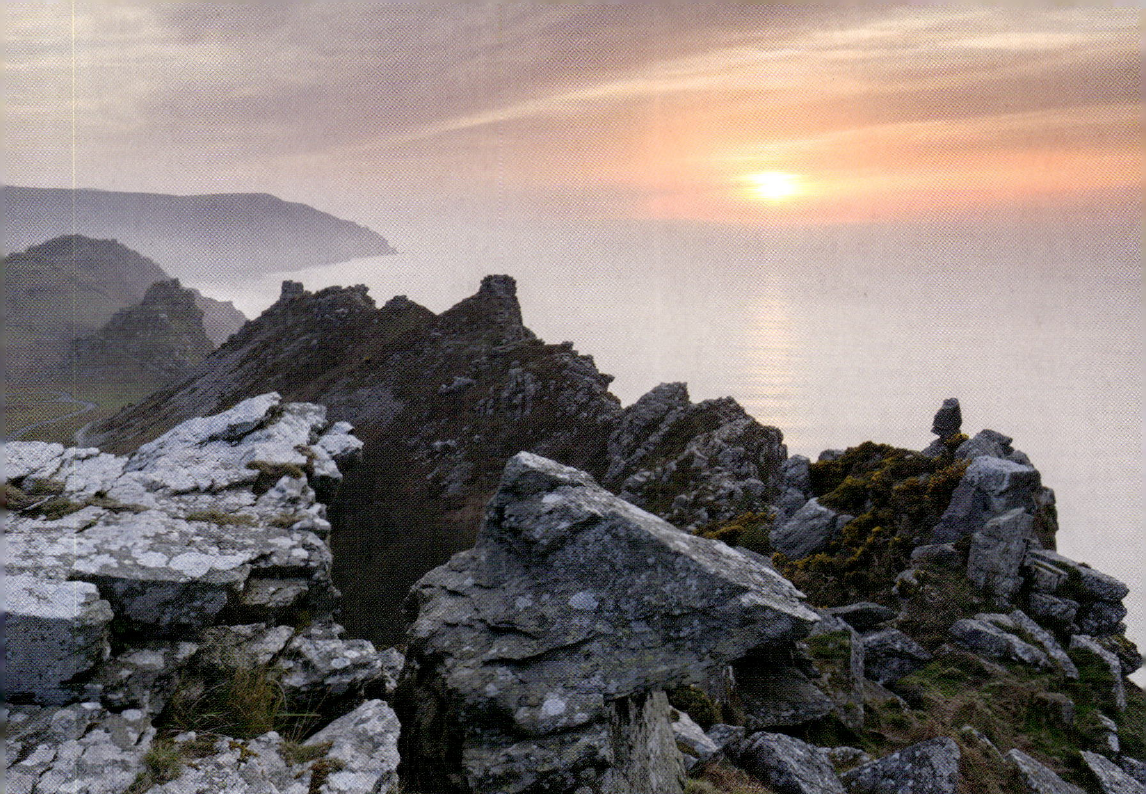

Sunset over Valley of Rocks from Hollerday Hill, Nikon D800E, 24-70mm at 36mm, ISO 100, 2.5 sec at f/14. April

Viewpoint 3 – Rugged Jack

Just to the east of Castle Rock a long jagged ridge, aptly named Rugged Jack, stretches along the seaward edge of the valley. From the tarmac footpath at the eastern edge of the ridge you can climb up onto Rugged Jack to get some incredible, and less typical shots of the surrounding scenery. There isn't a footpath as such, but an uneven rocky trail leads over to the western end of the ridge. This is by no means an easy walk, and involves a little clambering over rocks to get into position, but the end result is definitely worth the effort.

From this high position you can gain an amazing vista over the soaring North Devon cliffs. Even the towering Castle Rock is far below. In the opposite direction the rocky ridge makes an intriguing foreground with Foreland Point, complete with its lighthouse, far away in the background.

CAUTION: with an almost vertical drop of 150 metres to the sea, this isn't a location to visit on a windy day. Even without wind, extreme caution should be applied when venturing anywhere along this ridge.

Opposite top: View of the valley and cricket pitch, Canon 1Ds Mark III, 24-70mm at 27mm, ISO 100, 1.6 sec at f/16. March

Opposite below: Sunset skies above Castle Rock, Valley of Rocks Nikon D800E, 17-35mm at 35mm, ISO 400, 1/6 sec at f/11. May

How to Get Here

Being so close to the towns of Lynton and neighbouring Lynmouth, the Valley of Rocks is an easy location to find. Once you reach Lynton, drive straight through the town centre and almost as soon as you leave the town behind, you will find yourself entering the valley. There are two large car parks, one on the left and a second further down just past the cricket pitch on the right.

Parking Lat/Long: 51.232399, -3.8519740
Parking Grid Ref: SS 707 497
Parking Postcode: EX35 6EQ (Lynton)
Map: OS Explorer Map OL9 (1:25 000) Exmoor

Accessibility

There is a network of footpaths running around the Valley of Rocks offering good access to viewpoints. The most popular route for walkers is the tarmac footpath that runs along the outside of the cliffs below Rugged Jack and continues along the coast to Lynmouth. For a circular loop of the valley, head along this footpath and then take a second path which diverts to the right. This path heads between a gap in the cliffs, offering elevated viewpoints from which to shoot the valley, and runs along the base of Hollerday Hill eventually joining the road. The whole loop is suitable for wheelchair users. There are also public toilets here.

Best Time of Year/Day

With so many viewpoints facing differing directions, Valley of Rocks can be photographed well at both dawn and dusk. Midsummer sunset would usually be the most suitable from each viewpoint as the sun sets over the sea, casting warm side lighting onto the cliffs in the late evening.

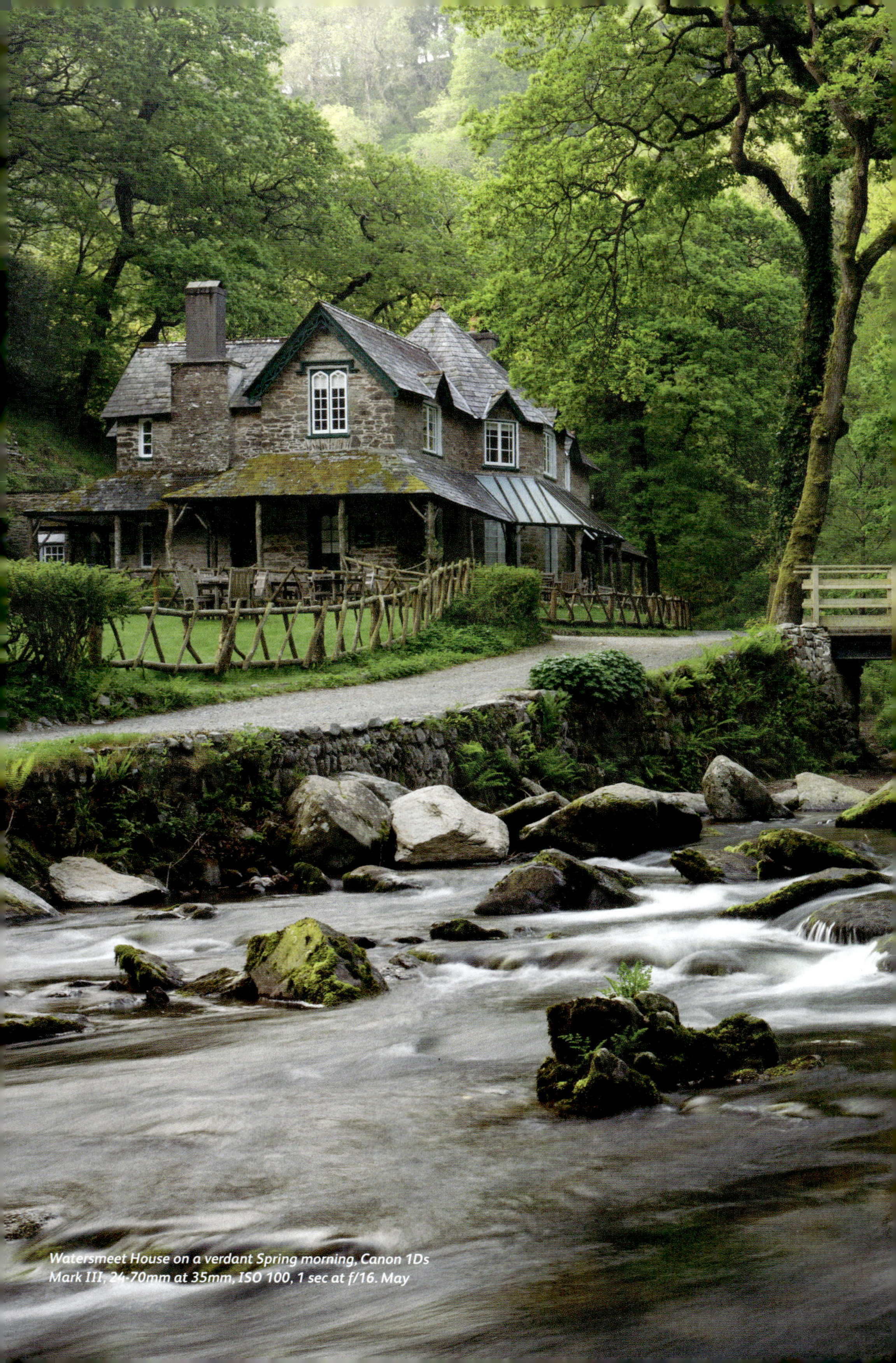

Watersmeet House on a verdant Spring morning, Canon 1Ds
Mark III, 24-70mm at 35mm, ISO 100, 1 sec at f/16. May

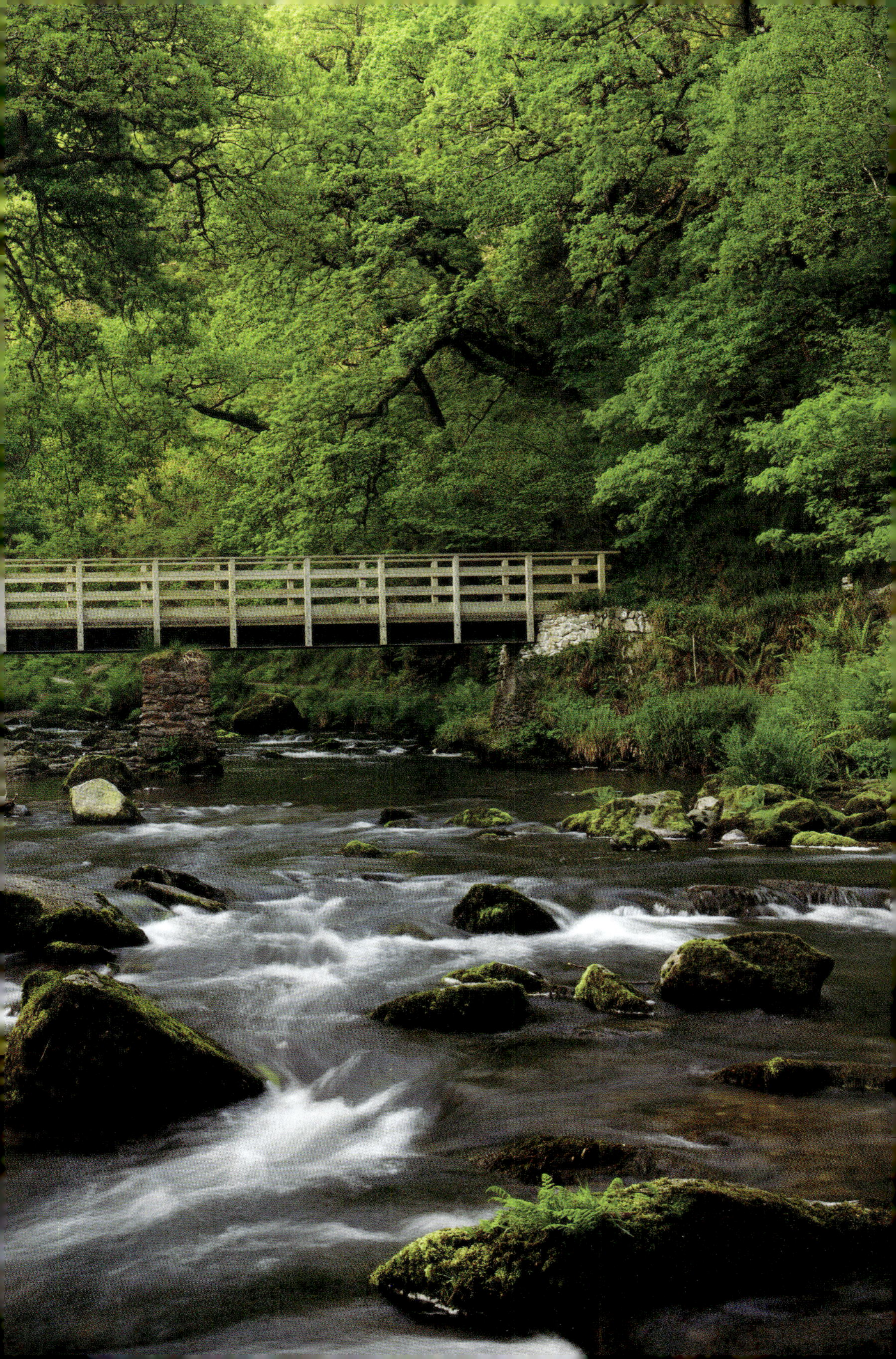

Watersmeet is one of Exmoor National Park's most well-known beauty spots. An excellent network of footpaths follows two rivers, Hoar Oak Water and the East Lyn, through many miles of steep wooded valleys near the North Devon coast. The two rivers converge at Watersmeet and then meander the remaining mile or two to reach the sea at nearby Lynmouth.

Now in the care of the National Trust, Watersmeet is a very popular destination for visitors. As well as being the starting point for many walks there is a photogenic former fishing lodge, now a National Trust tearoom, which makes Watersmeet a wonderful place to relax with a cream tea and enjoy the beautiful surroundings.

What to Shoot and Viewpoints

With many miles of footpaths running either side of the two rocky rivers opportunities for great photographs are endless. This whole area requires many visits to truly explore the potential of the place.

Elegant waterfall on Hoar Oak Water, Canon 1Ds Mark III, 70-200mm at 131mm, ISO 100, 2 sec at f/11. May

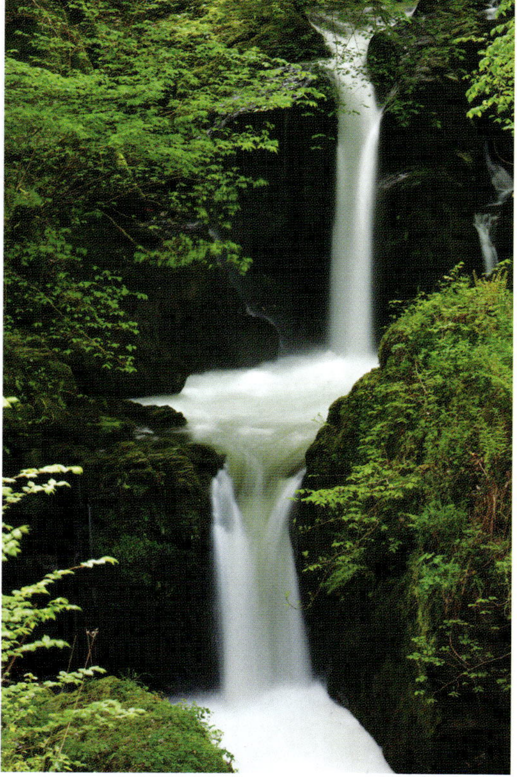

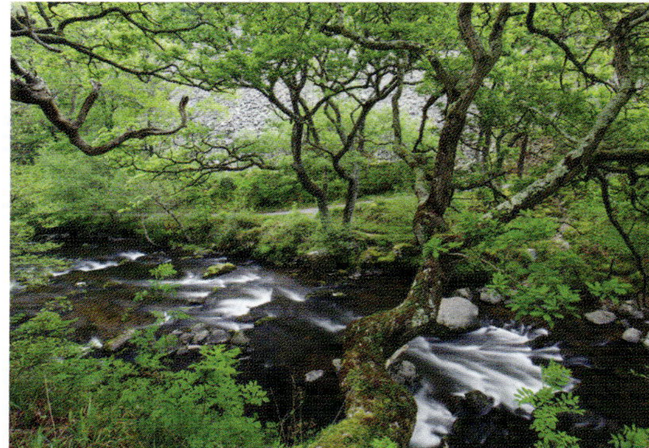

East Lyn River flowing towards Lynmouth, Canon 1Ds Mark III, 17-40mm at 21mm, ISO 100, 2 sec at f/16. May

Viewpoint 1 – Waterfalls

Although both fast-flowing rivers rush and tumble in dramatic fashion through channels between large rocks there aren't many true waterfalls. Several exceptions however are to be found along Hoar Oak Water, very close to the old fishing lodge.

The first is easy to find, and passed by every visitor walking down from the roadside car park making this possibly the most photographed view at Watersmeet. When you reach the bottom of the steep gorge, a wooden footbridge crosses Hoar Oak Water. The bridge provides the perfect platform to photograph the river as it cascades down through a series of impressive falls.

The other waterfall is less photographed but even more impressive. After crossing the footbridge, turn right and climb the steep steps back up the gorge. At the top of the steps follow the wide footpath in a southerly direction, keeping the river on your right. After a few minutes walk you will see a much smaller path veer off to the right. This leads down to a small railed-off viewing area above an elegant waterfall. The river cascades vertically through a narrow drop for several metres before plunging into a pool. A second waterfall drops further before the river continues its journey towards Lynmouth.

When photographed together, surrounded by woodland foliage this double waterfall makes a lovely picture, especially in springtime when the new leaves are lime green. The challenge of this shot always arises from the restricted viewpoint the platform offers. Sometimes the trees and bushes in front of the railings are overgrown, making a clean shot of the waterfall next to impossible. In this scenario, there is no alternative viewpoint to shoot from forcing you either to compromise or walk away without a photograph.

East Lyn River during autumn, Nikon D800E, 24-70mm at 34mm, ISO 100, 4 sec at f/13. November

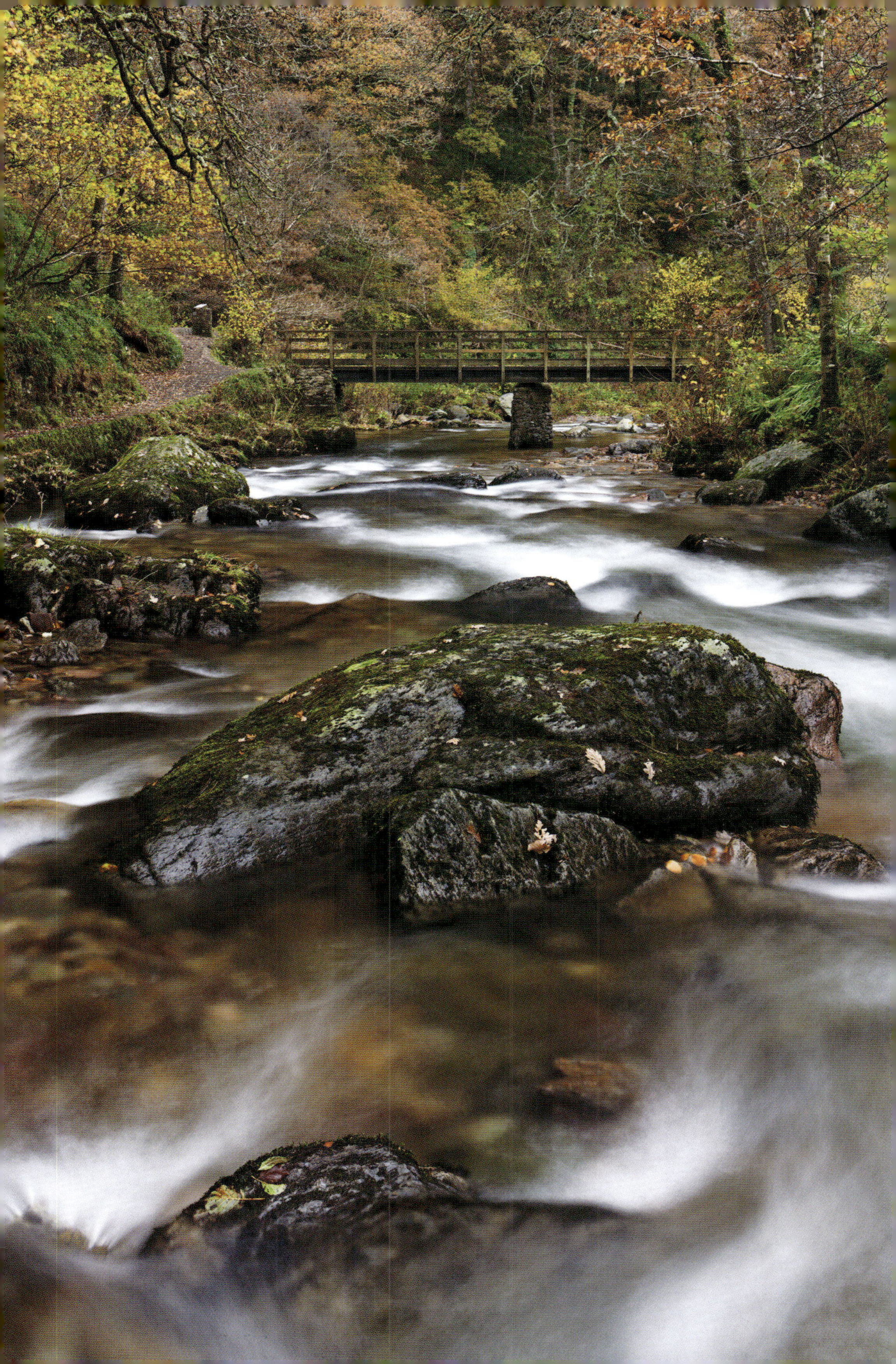

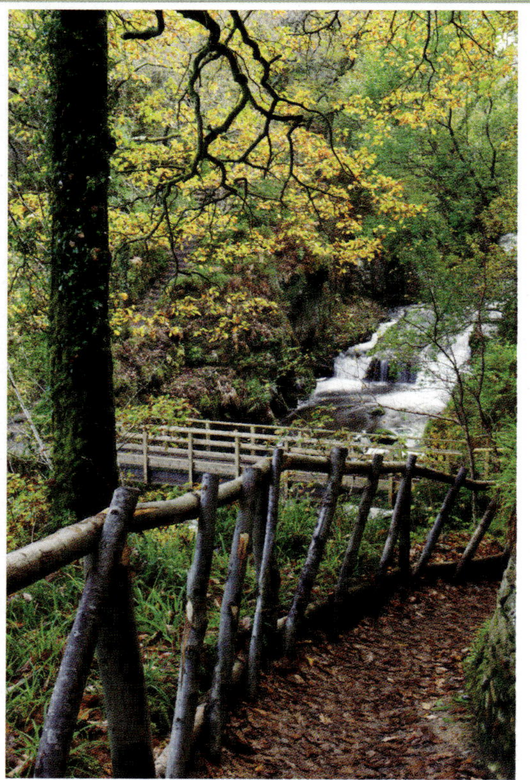

Viewpoint 2 – Watersmeet House

Built in the 1830's the old fishing lodge (Watersmeet House) is a grand old building which works extremely well when photographed in its river setting surrounded by woodland. Although it is now both a tearoom and information centre, the building still retains its Victorian charms and looks very authentic. If you choose to photograph it during the day you may find the view spoilt somewhat by visitors, but early mornings and evenings will see the area deserted.

The best view of Watersmeet House is from across the East Lyn River, on the footpath below the car park. Before you reach the footbridge you will find a path on the left which leads down to the west side of the river. This path offers an excellent slightly elevated view towards the lodge. Alternatively if you wish to get lower to emphasize the fast flowing water in the foreground of your photo, just continue down the path and you will soon reach the riverbank.

Left: Footpath leading to Watersmeet, Canon 1Ds Mark III, 24-70mm at 38mm, ISO 100, 4 sec at f/16. October

Below: Blustery autumn day in Barton Wood, Nikon D800E, 24-70mm at 48mm, ISO 100, 10 sec at f/13. November

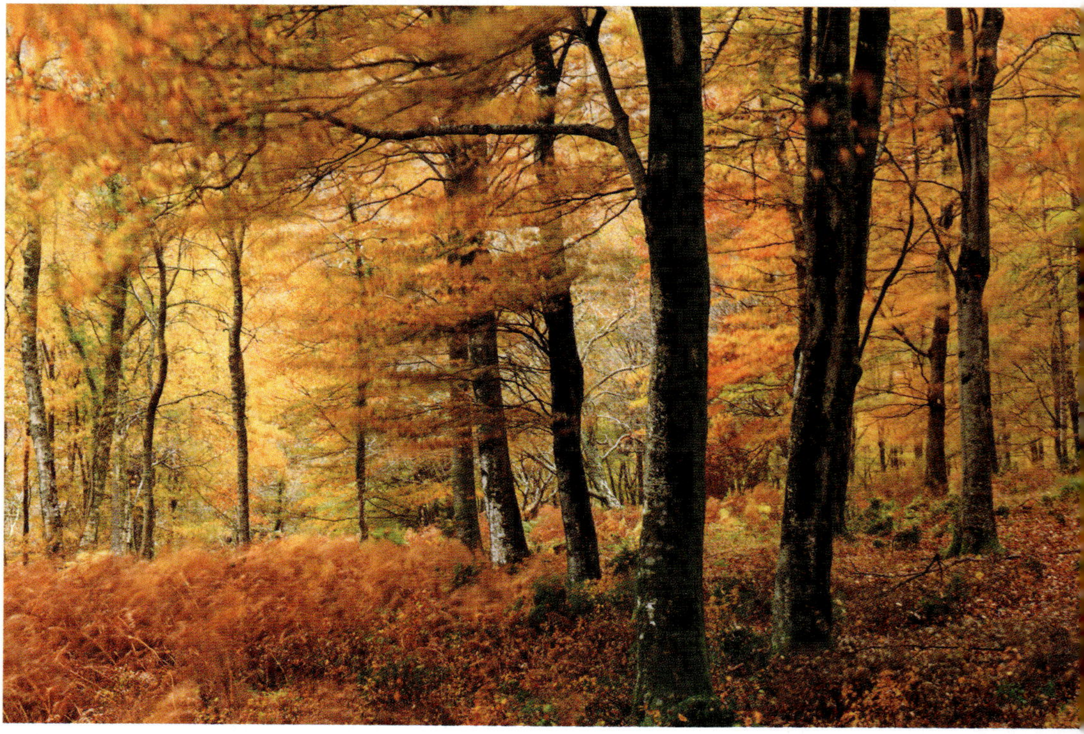

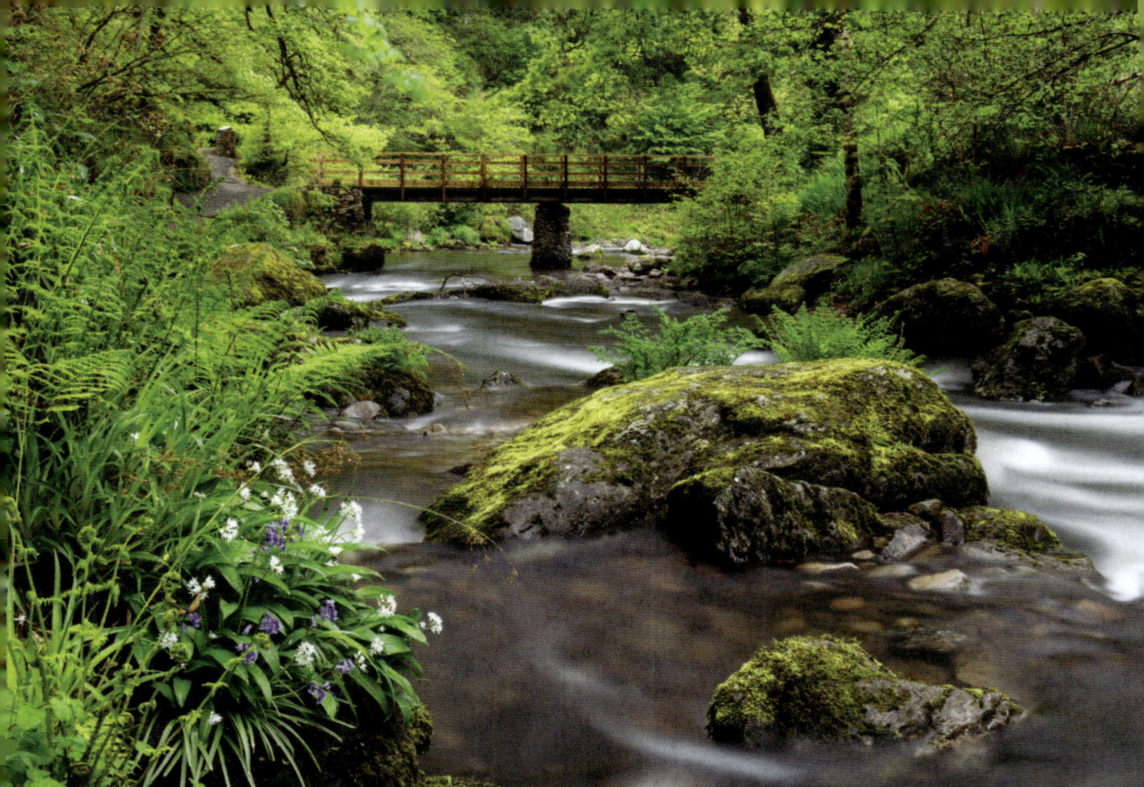

Spring wildflowers on the banks of the East Lyn River, Nikon D800E, 24-70mm at 38mm, ISO 400, 20 sec at f/14. May

How to Get Here

Watersmeet is just 2 miles from Lynmouth on Exmoor's North Devon coast. From Lynmouth take the A39 out of the village; after a few minutes this narrow winding road will pass a car park on your right. Park here, cross the road and pick up the footpath down through the woods.

Parking Lat/Long: 51.223634, -3.8000020
Parking Grid Ref: SS 744 487
Parking Postcode: EX35 6NT
Map: OS Explorer Map OL9 (1:25 000) Exmoor

Accessibility

The roadside car park offers plenty of parking, but this is almost at the top of the valley. A steep walk down through well-maintained gravel footpaths is required to reach the rivers at Watersmeet. A note of caution for National Trust members; although Watersmeet is a National Trust location the car park is operated by the local council, so you will need to purchase a ticket.

Mobility parking can be arranged in advance with the tea room at Watersmeet House.

The gravel paths following the rivers are very well maintained, but uneven in places and in some areas climb steeply up the valley sides.

Best Time of Year/Day

As with all areas of deciduous woodland, the best times of year are usually autumn and spring. In both these seasons the trees are going through extreme changes, the results of which are very appealing to photograph. Personally, I feel spring is the best season for this area; the verdant colours on the fresh spring leaves brings the whole area to life.

Whichever season you decide, it is best to time your visit after a period of rainy weather so that the rivers are rushing with good water levels. Avoid sunny days when both visitor numbers and harsh sunlight make photography difficult. A great time to visit this kind of location is on a showery day, when wet leaves give your photographs a lovely saturated look.

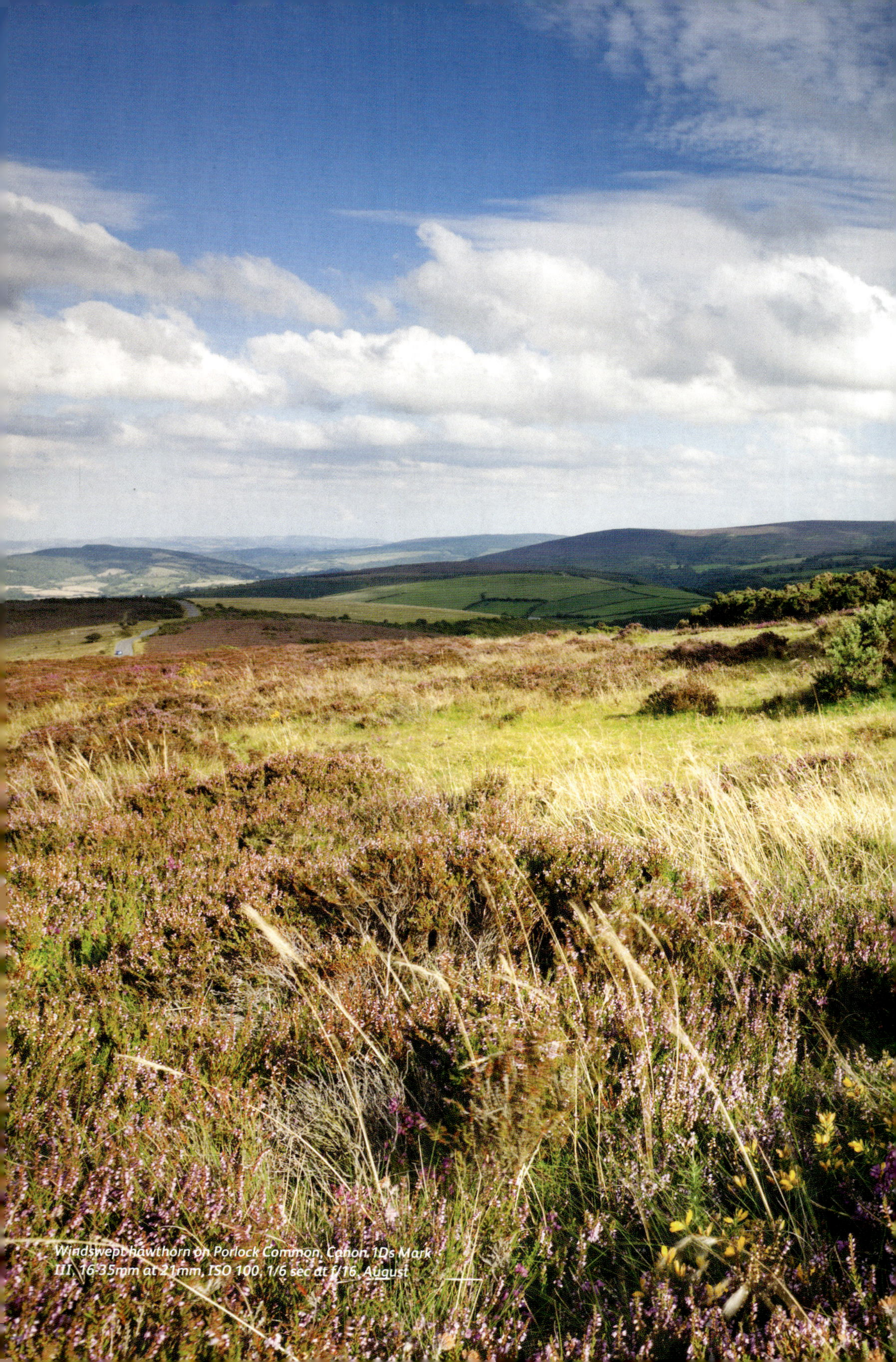

Windswept hawthorn on Porlock Common. Canon 1Ds Mark III, 16-35mm at 21mm, ISO 100, 1/6 sec at f/16, August

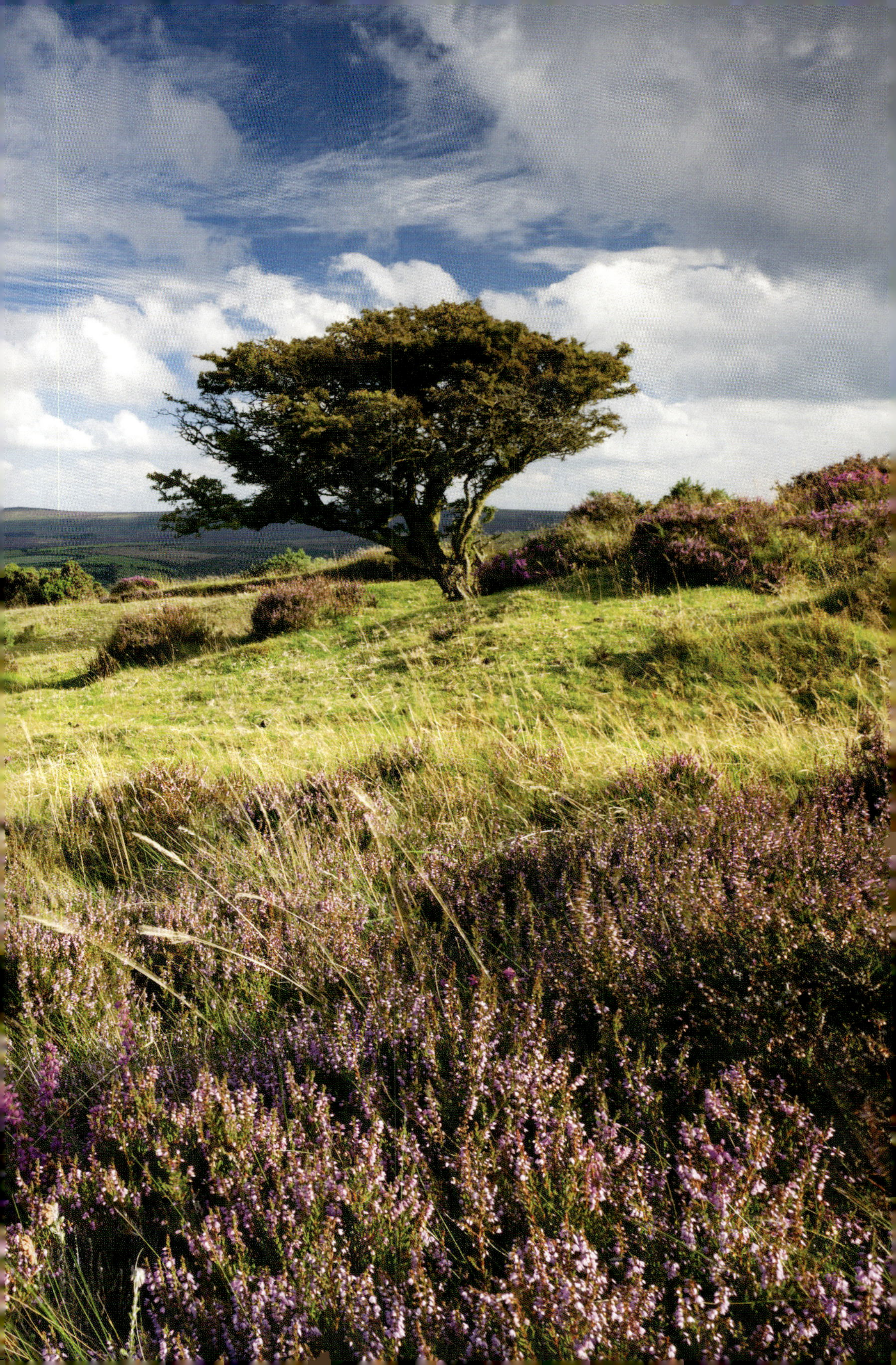

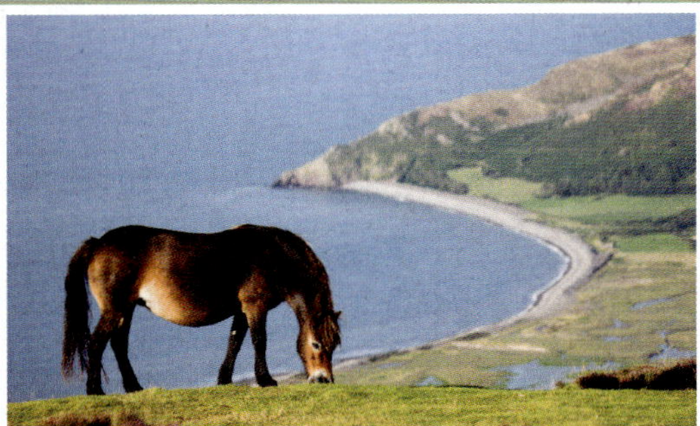

Exmoor Pony with Porlock Bay far below, Canon 1Ds Mark III, 100-400mm at 180mm, ISO 400, 1/250 sec at f/5.6. August

Although only a couple of miles from its low-lying village namesake, Porlock Common is up on Exmoor's high rolling moorland. The infamous road up Porlock Hill connects the village and the common. With an elevation gain of almost 400 metres in less than two miles this is one of the steepest main roads in England.

From this high viewpoint the curve of Porlock Bay and Hurlstone Point are visible far below, and on a clear day you can easily see the cliffs of South Wales across the Bristol Channel.

What to Shoot and Viewpoints

The obvious view from Porlock Common is looking northwards facing the channel. As well as the sea, this view takes in heather-covered moorland overlooking patchwork rolling countryside. You can also see a wooded combe (narrow valley) cutting into the farmland below. This rich variety of scenery is what makes Exmoor so unique and is difficult to achieve anywhere else in the National Park quite so effectively in one view.

Hawthorn Trees

To effectively convey wide landscape vistas into a photograph you need to find something close by to place in the foreground. Porlock Common has several photogenic hawthorn trees dotted around, their exposed position high up on the moor giving them an appealing windblown appearance.

There is one hawthorn in particular that garners most attention from photographers, mainly due to its position on a sloping area of moorland with the grand coastal view beyond. The appeal of this hawthorn is further enhanced by the circular patch of grass growing around the tree, holding back the heather which covers the surrounding moorland. From the main car park this tree is out of view, but can be found with a simple five minute walk northwards down a moorland path.

Another photogenic hawthorn can be found closer to the car park, close to the edge of the road. When shooting from the south, the road is completely hidden from view, leaving you with a classic windswept tree moorland photograph. Although it is very distant, the background view of Dunkery Beacon, the highest point in Somerset is no less impressive.

Heather in August

Both the above views look their best in late summer when colourful heather blankets the landscape. When photographing during this time, shoot with a wide-angle lens and tilt your camera downwards slightly to give emphasis to the blanket of purple in your foreground.

A few hundred metres to the west of the main car park, several more hawthorns can be found growing near the road. In this area of the common the landscape falls away quite steeply just beyond the trees which makes it easier to prominently feature the rolling countryside and sea as a colourful backdrop to the moorland foreground.

Exmoor Ponies

As well as the trees Exmoor ponies are regularly encountered in this area of the moor. Synonymous with the Exmoor landscape, these hardy ponies are Britain's oldest breed of native horse, and make wonderful photographic subjects.

How to Get Here

Porlock Common is seven miles west of Minehead in the north of Exmoor National Park. From Minehead, head west along the A39, passing through the village of Porlock. The road then climbs up Porlock Hill and directly through the common. The main car park can be found on the right side of the road, opposite a left turning signposted Exford.

Parking Lat/Long:
Parking Grid Ref: SS 856 464
Parking Postcode: TA24 8QD (Porlock village)
Map: OS Explorer Map OL9 (1:25 000) Exmoor

Accessibility

The A39 main road runs through Porlock Common, with several car parks along the route. Far-reaching views over the Bristol Channel can be photographed from each car park. For the best viewpoints, you need to walk for 5–10 minutes over moorland footpaths.

Best Time of Year/Day

Flowering heather all over Porlock Common makes this an ideal location to visit in late summer (August), either at dawn or dusk. The hawthorn flowers in May. This moorland can look beautiful during a cold winter morning when the landscape, and ideally the trees, is coated in thick hoar frost.

Opposite: Carpet of flowering heather on Porlock Common, Nikon D800E, 17-35mm at 32mm, ISO 200, 1/40 sec at f/13. August

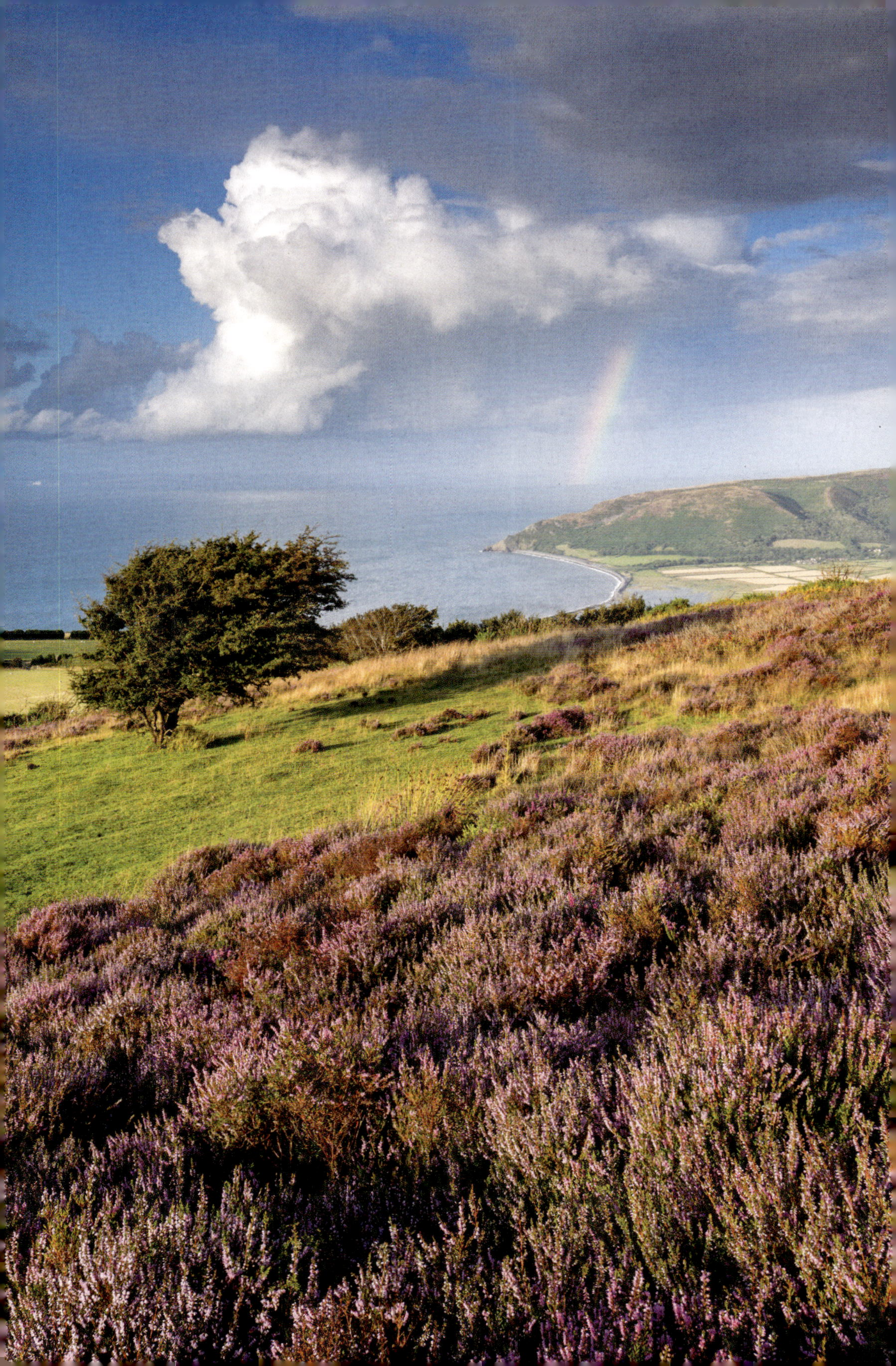

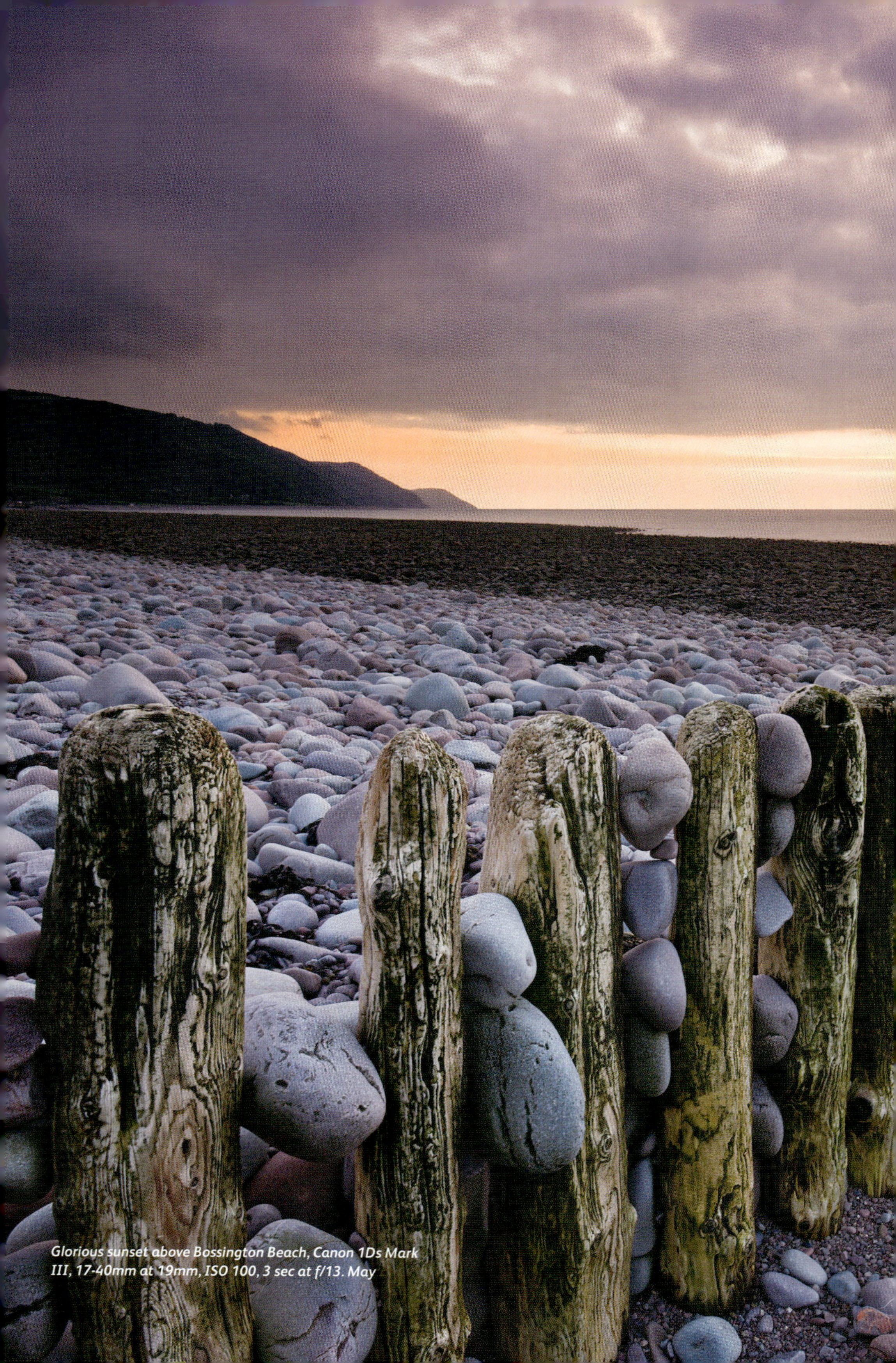

Glorious sunset above Bossington Beach, Canon 1Ds Mark
III, 17-40mm at 19mm, ISO 100, 3 sec at f/13. May

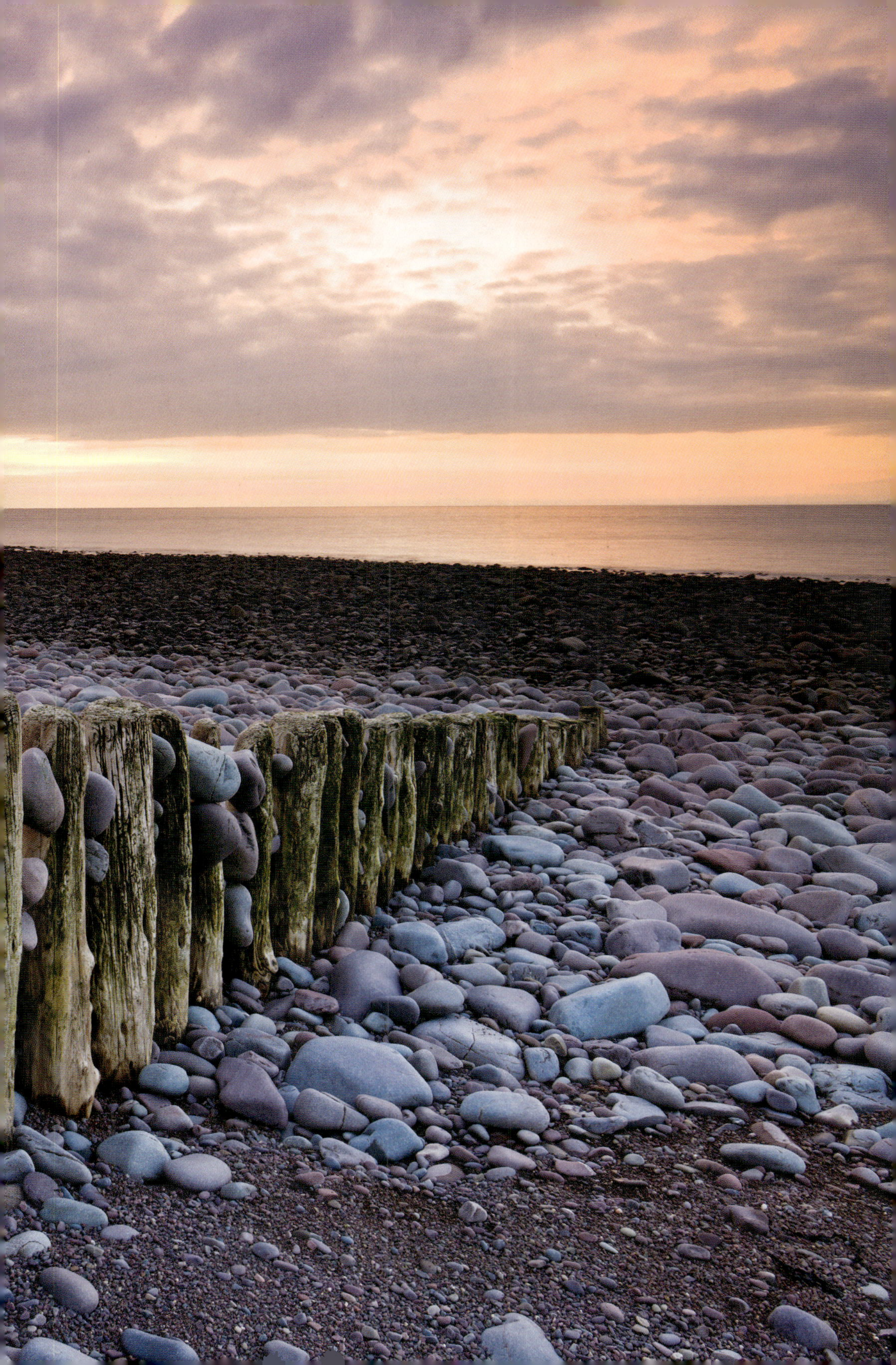

At Porlock Bay Exmoor's high rolling hills give
way to the wide Vale of Porlock, before briefly
rising again at Bossington Hill. The valley issues
out into the sea at Porlock Bay, where
an enormous sweeping shingle beach absorbs
the energy of the breaking waves.

The shore comprises two very similar beaches,
Bossington on one side and Porlock on the other,
with the pretty harbour village of Porlock Weir at
the western end of the beach. This area of the
national park is one of Exmoor's most popular
for visitors and thanks to the weathered wooden
groynes is also one of its most photogenic.

While the beach commands the most interest,
Porlock Weir is also worthy of attention. A small
settlement gathered around a tiny harbour,
Porlock Weir has somehow avoided modern
development and remains a charming and
picturesque sleepy coastal village.

What to Shoot and Viewpoints

Viewpoint 1 – Porlock Weir

Porlock Weir's main point of interest for photographers
is its little harbour. The state of the tide is important here
to get the harbour at its best. The area has the second
largest tidal range in the world. When the tide is low the
harbour is completely dry, very muddy and not
particularly photogenic.

The Harbour

Approaching from the village car park, straight away you
will see a small harbour-like sheltered bay. This small bay
isn't the main harbour but is picturesque and is usually
home to several yachts. Standing in front of the hotel,
you can achieve some good compositions of these
moored yachts with the distinctive thatched 17th century
Gibraltar cottages as a backdrop.

Continue to walk around the road and cross over the
narrow footbridge, you will see the main harbour
to the left crowded with various small boats.

Porlock Weir harbour can be photographed from all
directions. The bridge makes a good location to shoot
over the harbour towards sunset, alternatively continue
over the bridge and turn left walking in front of the

*Boats moored in the sheltered lagoon beyond the harbour, Nikon
D800E, 17-35mm at 19mm, ISO 400, ¼ sec at f/11. July*

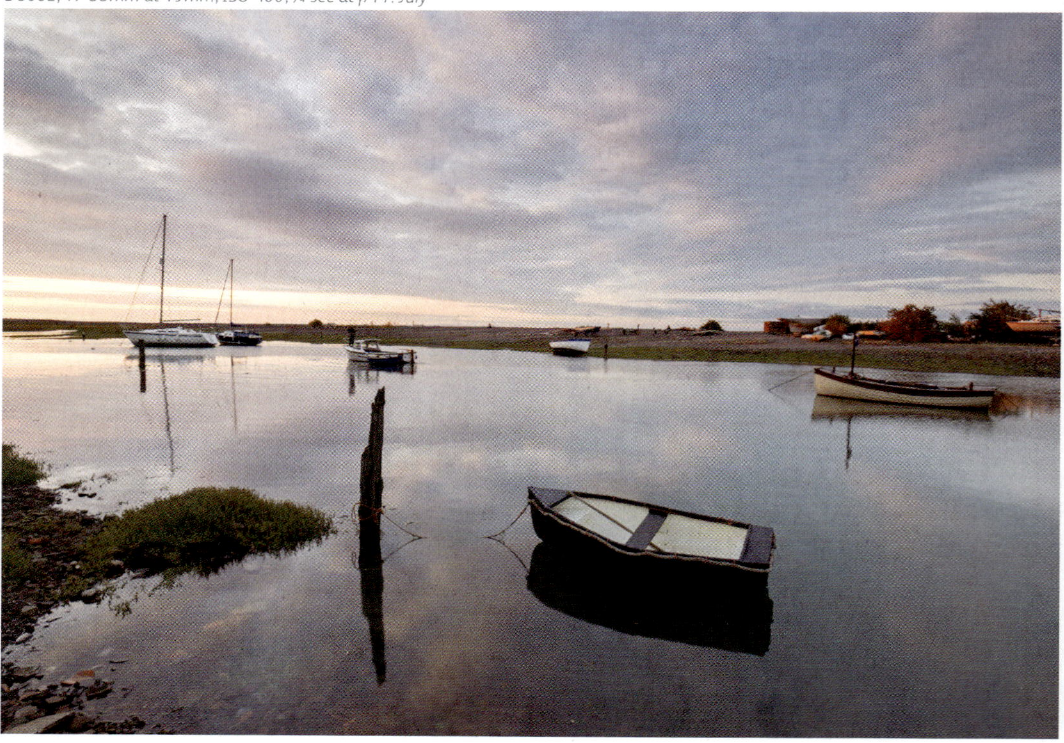

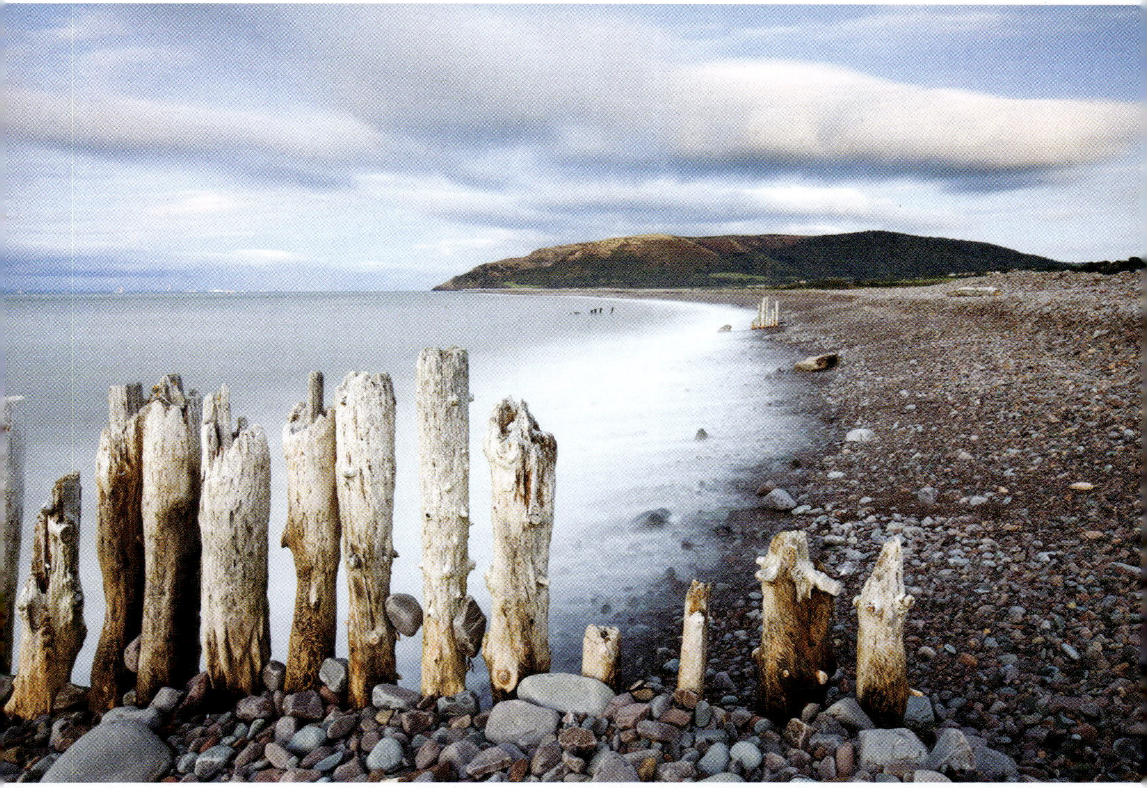

Porlock Beach looking towards Bossington Hill, Canon 1Ds Mark
III, 16-35mm at 23mm, ISO 100, 60 sec at f/13. September

Gibraltar cottages to shoot back towards the hotel.
This view works particularly well after dawn, especially
in the spring when rich early sunshine shines on the
buildings and the lime green wooded hill beyond.

Just past the harbour, at high tide a shallow lagoon
forms where you can usually find several boats moored.
Photographs from this area capture a more peaceful
atmosphere than the busy little harbour. Providing
there is no wind, this lagoon provides good reflections
of the boats and colourful sunset skies.

Viewpoint 2 – Porlock Beach

Without any obvious focal point the huge expanse of
grey rounded rocks that comprise Porlock Beach would
make it a very difficult photographic subject. Thankfully
the wooden groynes provide the necessary ingredient to
add some magic to an otherwise fairly ordinary beach.
These wooden posts provide two essential services; they
protect the coast from erosion due to longshore drift,
and make superb photographic subjects.

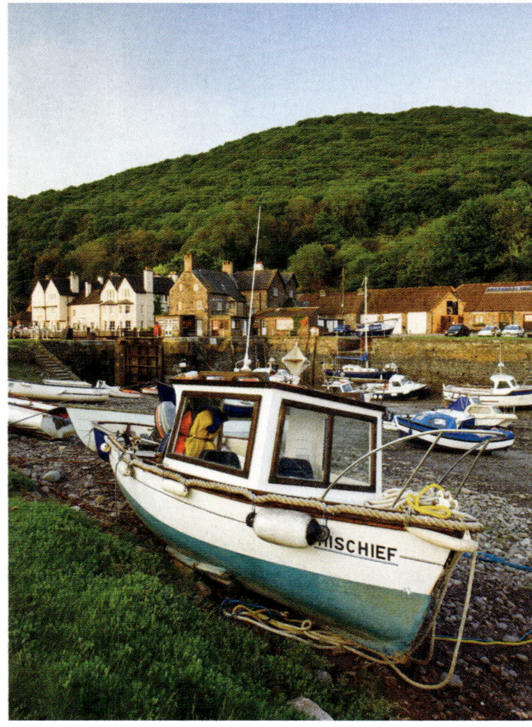

Low tide in Porlock Weir harbour, Canon 1Ds Mark III,
17-40mm at 26mm, ISO 100, 1 sec at f/16. May.

The Groynes

Like many areas that suffer from coastal erosion, both Porlock and Bossington have several groynes stretched out over the beach. The groynes are very weather worn with the constant battering throughout the year from the sizeable stones, and many are completely submerged each day by the extreme tides. As a result they have a delightfully ramshackle appearance, and often line up in a rather haphazard order, both of which made them ideal photographic subjects.

The groynes look good photographed in a variety of ways, the key is getting close enough so they feature prominently in the foreground. Such a close viewpoint usually involves wet feet from incoming waves, so wellies are a prerequisite for this location. From up close the repeating vertical lines of each weathered post make very appealing subjects and work especially well when photographed stretching diagonally through the frame as a lead-in line.

Considering the Tide

The groynes look their best when photographed with water around them or near them. As most are fairly high up the beach, a higher tide is required to achieve this. Several visits may be required to get a good understanding of when a particular set will look its best. Generally speaking aim to visit just when the tide is starting to go out. This way, the water will hopefully be lapping around the posts, and the nearby pebbles will be wet and shiny from the retreating tide.

The stones on the beach are continuously shifting. Sometimes the same area of beach may be at a different level. Most likely when you visit the groynes will probably look very different to the pictures on these pages.

When shooting the posts of Porlock Beach, you can use either Bossington Hill as a backdrop, or back towards Porlock Weir and the wooded hills beyond. Your choice of background subject may be determined by what's happening in the sky, fortunately this location can be photographed equally well at either end of the day.

Weathered groynes on Bossington Beach, Canon 1Ds Mark III, 16-35mm at 31mm, ISO 100, 20 sec at f/16. March

Post-sunset pinks above Porlock Bay, Canon 1Ds Mark III, 16-35mm at 25mm, ISO 100, 30 sec at f/16. September

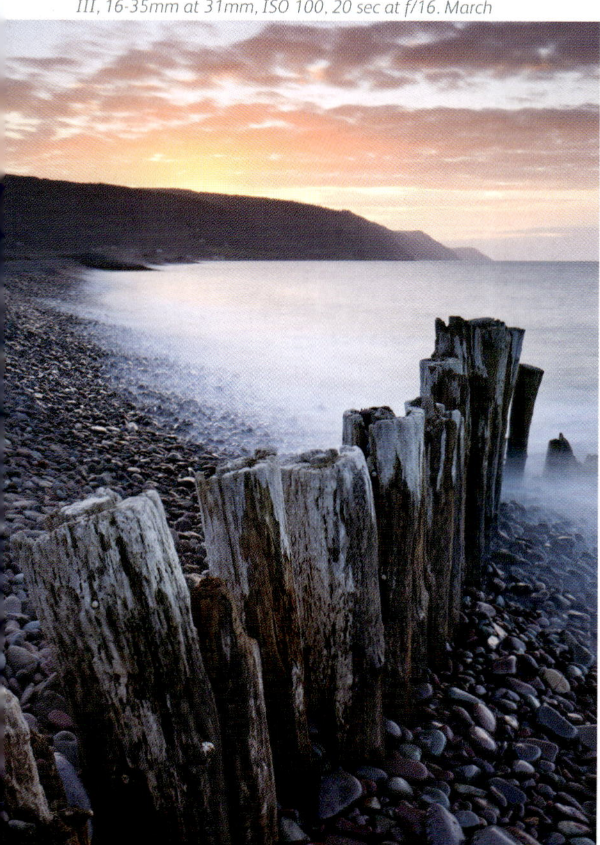

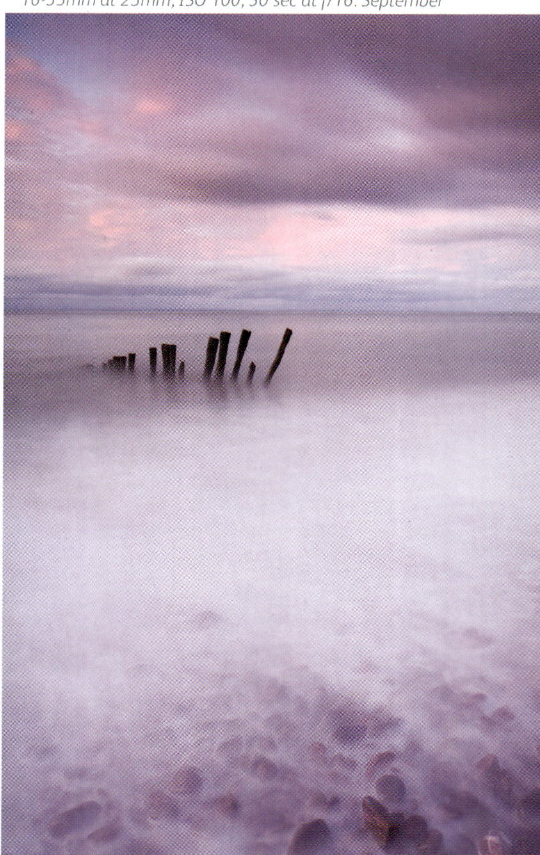

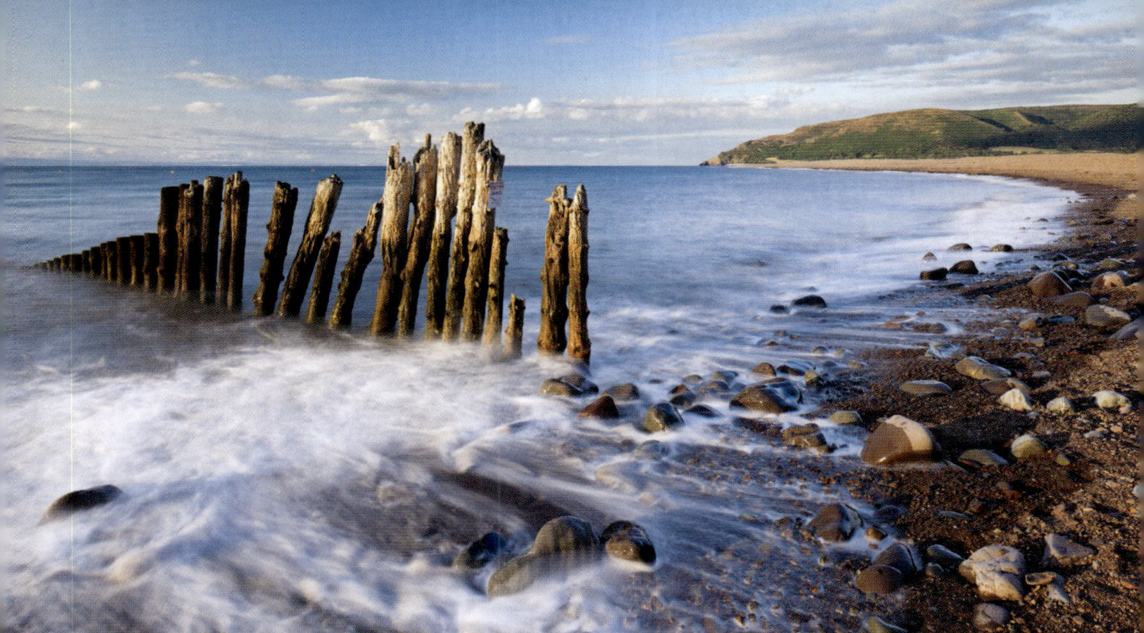

Waves wash against the shore at Porlock Beach, Nikon D800E, 17-35mm at 20mm, ISO 50, 2.5 sec at f/11. July

Viewpoint 3 – Bossington Beach

Very similar to Porlock Beach, Bossington has more groynes to offer and possibly a better backdrop. Being further round the bay to the east, this is primarily a sunset location and benefits from a more open view of the towering Exmoor cliffs receding to the west.

Accessing the beach from the National Trust car park at Bossington, you need to walk westwards along the beach for 15 minutes before you reach the first groyne. From here you will see several more in the distance.

Your choice of posts will be influenced by their physical appearance and also the tide height. In addition look out for groynes where pebbles have become wedged between the posts. These groynes with lodged pebbles are worth looking for as they make very appealing subjects for both wide landscapes and abstract close ups.

The shore tends to be steeper at this end of the beach, making it more difficult to judge the optimum tide height. Like Porlock Beach you really need to arrive when the tide is high to make the most of the posts, but you will find that you need to work very quickly. Compositions appear and then disappear again in just a few minutes as the tide changes so rapidly, so be prepared to work quickly!

While you are at Bossington, you can't miss the old stone pillbox partially submerged into the shingle high up on the beach. As an alternative to shooting the posts this relic from the Second World War makes a very worthwhile subject to photograph.

How to Get Here

Bossington is approximately 5 miles west of Minehead on Exmoor's north Somerset coast. From Minehead, follow the A39 for 4 miles until you reach Allerford. Turn right here and follow the small lane for another mile until you reach Bossington. Park in the National Trust car park in the village on the right hand side.

For Porlock Weir stay on the A39 until you reach Porlock. Take the right turn from Porlock signposted Porlock Weir and follow this smaller lane for another 2 miles before you reach the village.

Parking Lat/Long: 51.220507, -3.5807826 (Bossington), 51.218081,-3.6265210 (Porlock Weir)
Parking Grid Ref: SS 897 480 (Bossington), SS 865 478
Parking Postcode: TA24 8HQ (Bossington), TA24 8PB (Porlock Weir)
Map: OS Explorer Map OL9 (1:25 000) Exmoor

Accessibility

Visitors to Porlock Weir and Beach can park in the large village car park. From here there is good access around the village and harbour, both suitable for wheelchair users. Several groynes can be found at the start of Porlock Beach just behind Gibraltar cottages. A 20 minute walk around the beach from the car park will bring you to several more groynes. From Bossington, walk out of the National Trust car park and turn right initially following a small lane which soon becomes a footpath. After 15 minutes the path will open out on the beach. From here turn left and walk for another 15 minutes to reach the first groyne.

Best Time of Year/Day

Porlock Bay is best avoided on a low tide, and is probably at its best at or around high tide. All three viewpoints are suited to visits later in the day and at sunset; Porlock Weir and Beach also work very well at sunrise. The only seasonal factor to consider when visiting these locations is the foliage on the hill beyond Porlock Weir. In the winter, this wooded hill can look quite bare and unappealing.

Hurlstone Point and Bossington Hill

Hurlstone Point is a headland at the western tip of Bossington Hill that provides the best viewpoint from which to appreciate the grand sweep of Porlock Bay. Voted one of England's favourite views by readers of Country Life magazine, and with the South West Coast Path passing right by, it has long been a popular photo stop-off for walkers.

While the lookout at Hurlstone Point is perhaps best known to photographers, Bossington Hill is worth the small effort. The summit is almost 200 metres higher than Hurlstone and affords some excellent views westwards over the Vale of Porlock.

What to Shoot and Viewpoints

Viewpoint 1 – Hurlstone Point

The best approach to Hurlstone Point is from the National Trust car park at Bossington. Cross the footbridge at the back of the car park and follow the path to the left. After 20 minutes the path will begin to climb through the trees and up onto the moorland.

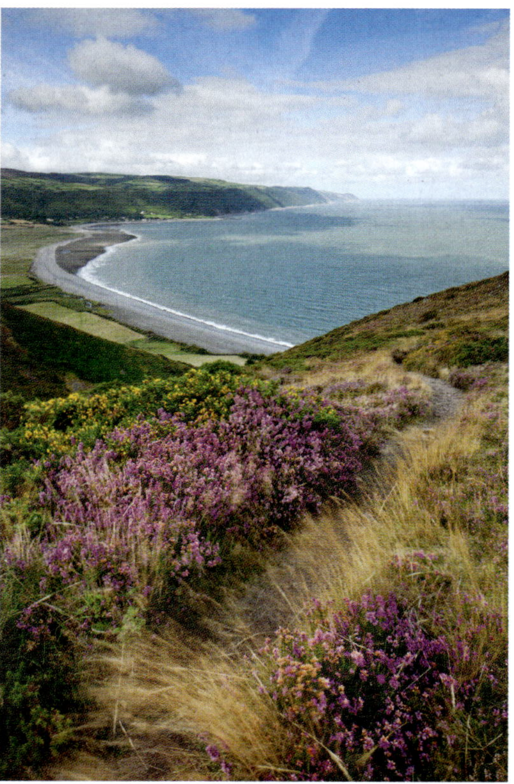

The main viewpoint is another 10 minutes walk when you will soon notice the old coastguard building.

This blocky stone building isn't the most attractive for photographs, but does provide shelter for setting up your camera on windy days. The main viewpoint over Porlock Bay is just in front of the lookout shelter. A better angle over Porlock Bay can be achieved by climbing up the hillside a little. This allows the beach to sweep through the frame at a more exaggerated angle.

This higher view also has better foreground than the standard viewpoint below. Outcrops of rock give welcome rugged foreground interest. This is a good technique to help viewers engage with your pictures, especially with grand vistas such as this where a photograph cannot convey anywhere near as effectively as being there.

With the view facing towards the southwest this location can work well around sunset in early spring and late summer when the sun sets over the sea just to the right of the distant headlands.

Viewpoint 2 – Bossington Hill

Due to its much larger size Bossington Hill offers many more possibilities to capture unique views over the surrounding countryside. Typically most cameras are still pointed in a south westerly direction over the Vale of Porlock but a good network of footpaths provide access to many different vantage points.

For Bossington Hill, park in the hilltop car park near Selworthy Beacon. From here follow the footpath in a northerly direction; this will soon swing to the northwest in the direction of Hurlstone Point. This path leads directly past some very photogenic large areas of heather with far reaching views beyond. You will see other footpaths heading off in many directions, including the South West Coast Path which leads down to Hurlstone Point.

Bossington Hill looks its best during summer when the hills are awash with the colour of flowering heather and gorse. Unlike the common heather growing on many other parts of Exmoor, vibrant bell heather grows up here, turning Bossington Hill bubblegum-pink.

With a network of useful footpaths up on the hilltop explore the smaller narrow paths and look for areas where these run through clumps of heather or grasses. With a wide-angle lens, turn the path into a lead in line to guide the eye towards the distant backdrop.

To photograph in the direction of the Vale of Porlock there is an excellent circular path around Bossington Hill, about 50 metres below the summit. The hill drops steeply away to one side giving uninterrupted wide vistas of the valley beneath you. This footpath generally works best in the afternoon/evening when the valley floor is side-lit with late sunshine.

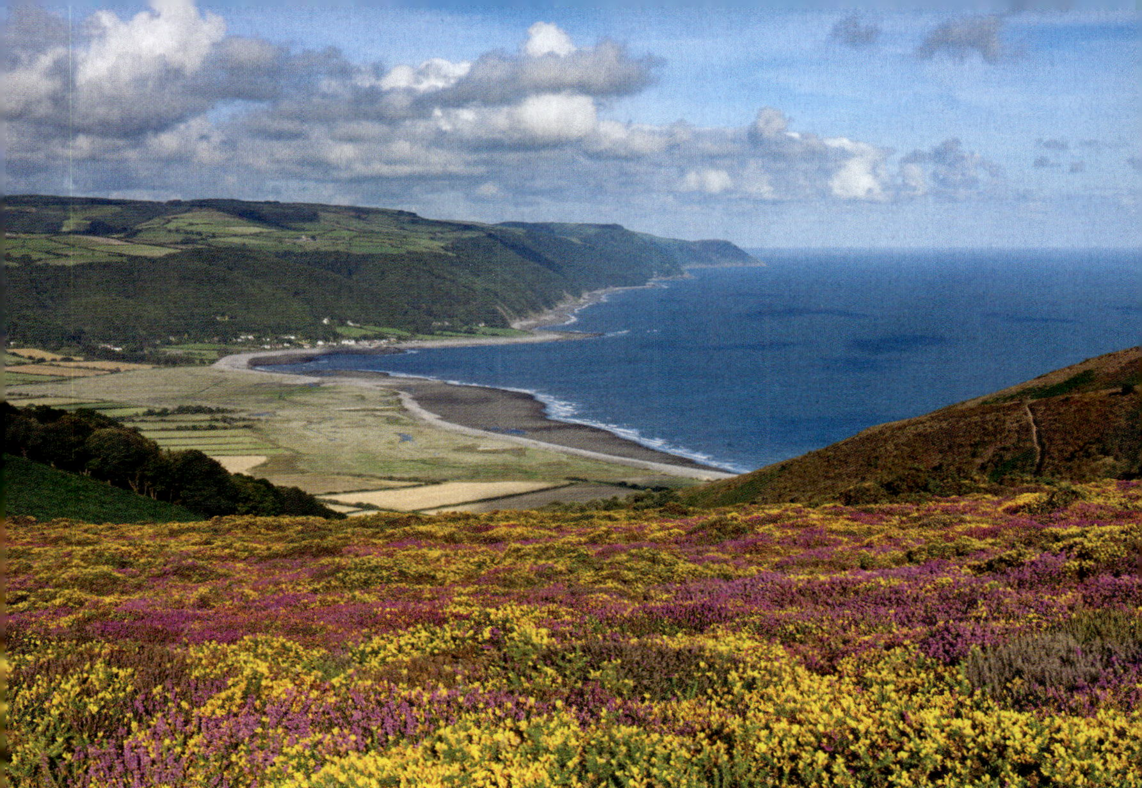

Carpets of pink bell heather mixed with yellow gorse, Canon 1Ds Mark III, 24-70mm at 55mm, ISO 100, 1/25 sec at f/16. August

How to Get Here

Hurlstone Point and Bossington Hill are both approximately 5 miles west of Minehead on Exmoor's north Somerset coast.

For Hurlstone Point park in the National Trust car park in the village of Bossington. From Minehead, follow the A39 for four miles until you reach Allerford. Turn right here and follow the small lane for another mile until you reach Bossington. Park in the National Trust car park in the village on the right hand side.

While you can reach Bossington Hill from the same car park, there is also a car park on top of the hill. For this car park leave the A39 at the Alcombe roundabout, taking the exit onto Alcombe Road towards Minehead town centre. When you reach the town centre, follow Park Street round to the left, and then take the second right up Western Lane. Follow this road north, taking the fifth turning left onto Moor Road. This road will head out of the town, winding up to the top of North Hill and then leading all the way over to Bossington Hill. At the end of the road you will find a large car park.

Parking Lat/Long: 51.220507, -3.5807826 (Bossington), 51.218079, -3.5606527 (Bossington Hill)
Parking Grid Ref: SS 897 480 (Bossington), SS 911 477 (Bossington Hill)
Parking Postcode: TA24 8HQ (Bossington), TA24 8RY (Minehead)
Map: OS Explorer Map OL28 (1:25 000) Dartmoor

Accessibility

The paths are over rough ground and are unsuitable for wheelchairs.

Best Time of Year/Day

Both Hurlstone Point and Bossington Hill are best suited to evening visits. To include the sun setting over the sea time your visit for early spring or late summer. The bell heather on Bossington Hill flowers earlier than common heather does on other parts of Exmoor, so visit early in August to make the most of the colours.

Opposite page: Cliff top coastal footpath on Bossington Hill, Canon 1Ds Mark III, 16-35mm at 23mm, ISO 100, 0.4 sec at f/16. August

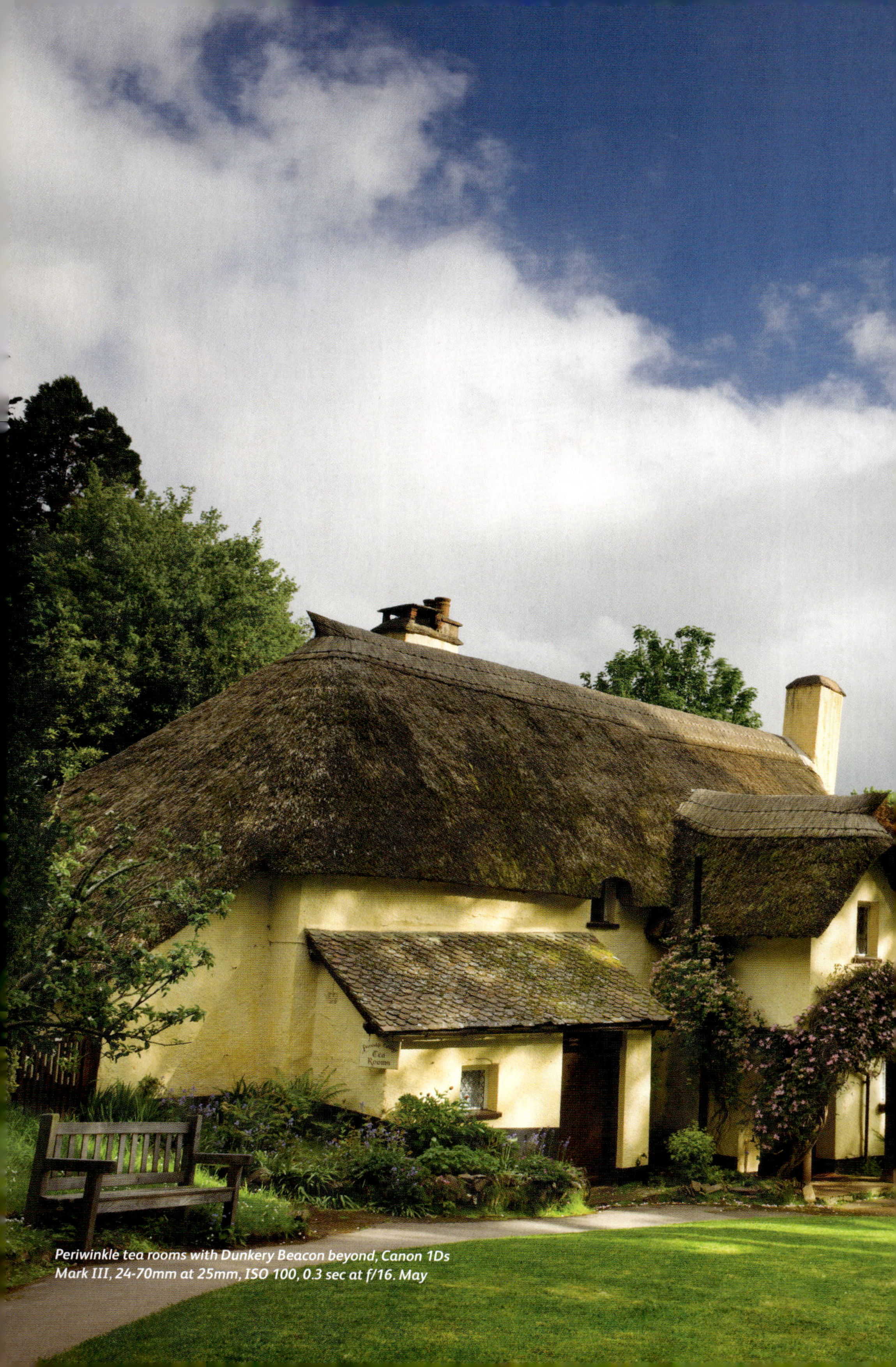

Periwinkle tea rooms with Dunkery Beacon beyond, Canon 1Ds Mark III, 24-70mm at 25mm, ISO 100, 0.3 sec at f/16. May

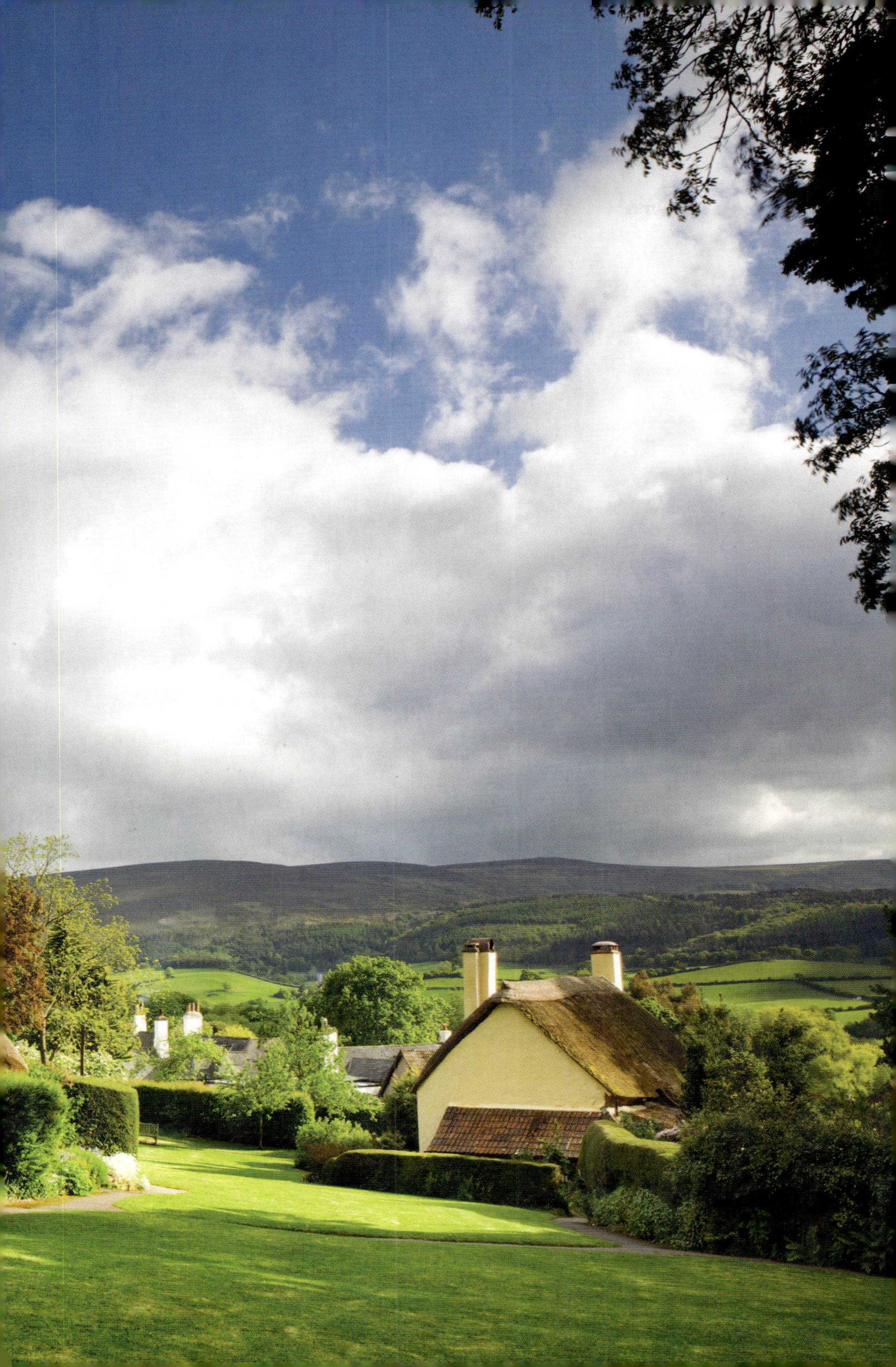

With its pretty thatched cottages and perfectly manicured lawns Selworthy presents itself as the idyllic English village. Prior to the mid 19th century the village would have looked very different indeed. In 1828 Selworthy was rebuilt by the local landowner St Thomas Acland as a model village, to provide housing for aged and infirm workers of the Holnicote Estate.

In 1944 the Holnicote Estate, including the village of Selworthy, was donated to the National Trust by Sir Richard Acland.

What to Shoot and Viewpoints

Although around a dozen cottages remain at Selworthy, most of these are surrounded by private gardens and are inaccessible to the public. Fortunately, the most photogenic area of the village, which also contains the prettiest thatched cottages, is freely available for visitors to wander around.

As you approach from the car park you will first notice two tiny cottages, one of which is now a National Trust shop at the top of the village, nestled against the steep wooded hill beyond. Both these houses are worth photographing, but just around the corner the best viewpoint is waiting. Just as the path reaches the woodland, swing around to the left where a lawned area opens up. On the left a beautiful large thatched cottage, now the award winning Periwinkle Tea Rooms, makes a wonderful photographic subject. Several other cottages are visible from this viewpoint, together with a gorgeous rolling countryside view beyond.

To fully appreciate the view over the Vale of Porlock, head up to the whitewashed church just above the car park. From here you can photograph far-reaching views across the hilly patchwork countryside towards Dunkery Beacon, the highest point in Somerset.

Selworthy's unusual church is one of the few buildings to predate the 1828 rebuild, and dates back to the 15th century. Its distinctive white colouring and elevated position makes it an easily recognisable landmark visible from far away on the other side of the valley.

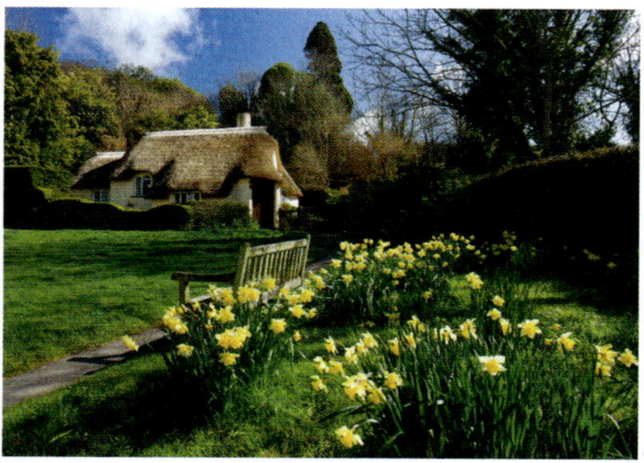

Early Spring daffodils on Selworthy's green, Canon 1Ds Mark III, 17-40mm at 21mm, ISO 200, 1/15 sec at f/16. March

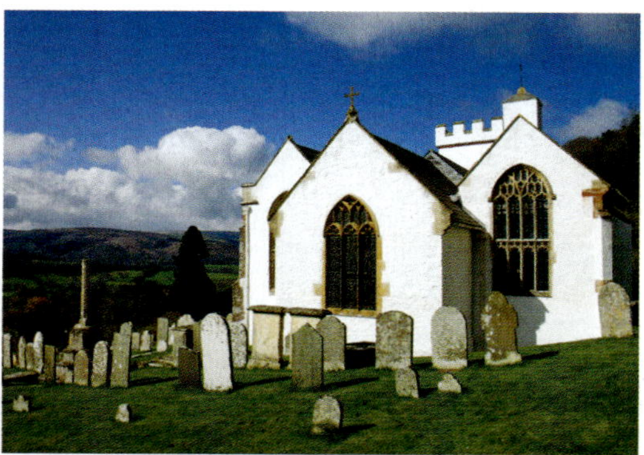

Selworthy's unusual whitewashed church, Canon 1Ds Mark III, 24-70mm at 27mm, ISO 200, 1/250 sec at f/16. March

How to Get Here

From the M5 take the Bridgwater exit and head west on the A39 following the directions to Minehead. When you reach the turn off to Minehead, continue on the A39 for another 4 miles until you see a right turn to Selworthy. Head up the hill and into the village. When you reach the church, park in the small car park on the right.

Parking Lat/Long: 51.209614, -3.5494429
Parking Grid Ref: SS 920 467
Parking Postcode: TA24 8TW (Selworthy village)
Map: OS Explorer Map OL9 (1:25 000) Exmoor

Accessibility

From the car park cross the road and walk back past the church. Go through the gate to the right of the memorial cross and follow the path. It is no more than 100 yards to the best viewpoints, the path is wheelchair friendly all the way.

Best Time of Year/Day

As with many locations popular with visitors in order to avoid people getting in your photographs it is advisable to shoot early or late in the day. Late afternoon and early evening are ideal as sunlight will still be bathing the cream walls of the tea room. The rolling countryside will look its best at this time also.

The village looks beautiful from early spring (March) when many daffodils are flowering, right through to early autumn before the leaves have fallen.

Alternatively head up early on an autumn morning to shoot the countryside appearing through a blanket of low mist.

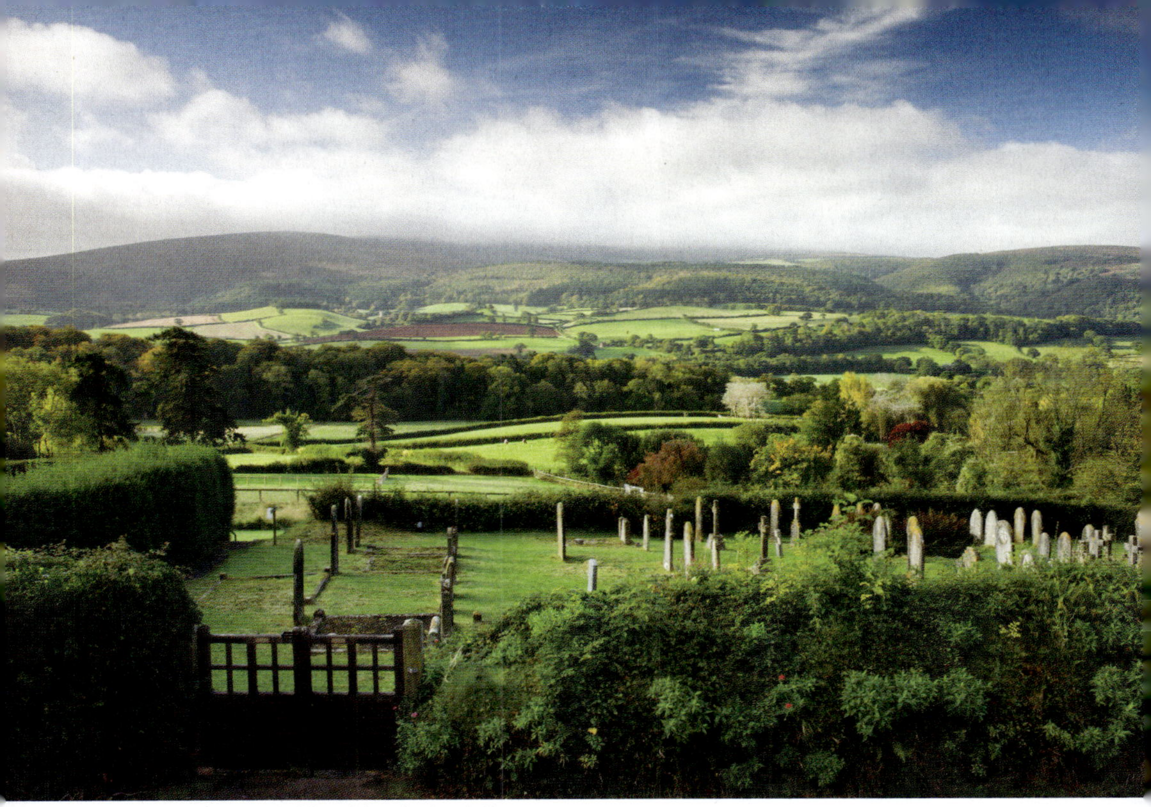

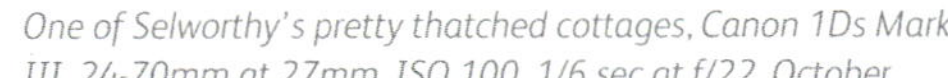

*Stunning views can be photographed from Selworthy church, Canon
1Ds Mark III, 24-70mm at 28mm, ISO 100, 0.7 sec at f/22. October*

*One of Selworthy's pretty thatched cottages, Canon 1Ds Mark
III, 24-70mm at 27mm, ISO 100, 1/6 sec at f/22. October*

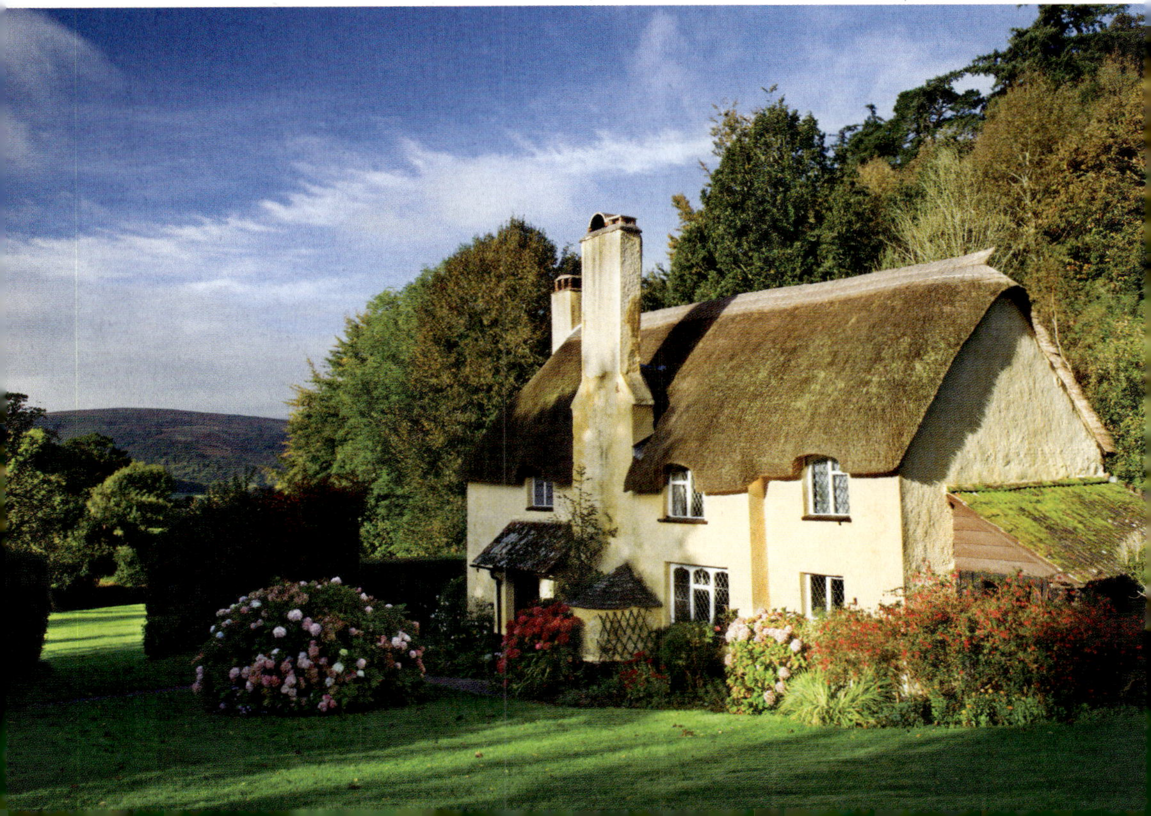

Located on the summit of Dunkery Hill up on Exmoor's rolling moorland, Dunkery Beacon, at 519m/1,702ft, is not only Somerset's highest point, but also the highest point in southern England outside of Dartmoor. This large hill is visible from many miles around, making it a prominent feature in many photographs captured around the national park.

Dunkery Hill and much of the surrounding landscape was donated to the National Trust. A large stone cairn was erected on its summit in 1935 to commemorate this donation.

What to Shoot and Viewpoints

Being such a prominent feature within Exmoor, Dunkery Beacon is an obvious place to head to for visitors to the national park. Access is simple, there is a small road passing up over the hill with several parking areas relatively near the summit.

From these parking areas, far-reaching views can be enjoyed over Exmoor's rolling countryside to the east. However, a 15 minute walk provides more impressive views in all directions. On a clear day you can see the Brecon Beacons, Bodmin Moor, and Cleeve Hill in Gloucestershire.

Armed with a telephoto lens this can be an excellent place to position yourself for compressed countryside landscapes. The view towards Porlock Bay is particularly impressive, encompassing rolling moorland and Exmoor's characteristic deep wooded combes. Alternatively shoot in a southeast direction over the pristine patchwork farmland near Wheddon Cross. Whichever direction you choose to point your camera, this area is an ideal place to stand at dawn, when atmospheric mist can hang low in the distant valleys all around.

Top left: Dusting of snow on Dunkery Beacon, Canon 1Ds Mark III, 17-40mm at 19mm, ISO 100, 1/15 sec at f/16. December

Top right: Exmoor pony amongst the heather, Canon 1Ds Mark III, 100-400mm at 285mm, ISO 400, 1/500 sec at f/5.6. August

Bottom left: Mammatus clouds above Dunkery Hill at sunset, Canon 1Ds Mark III, 17-40mm at 19mm, ISO 100, 6 sec at f/22, August

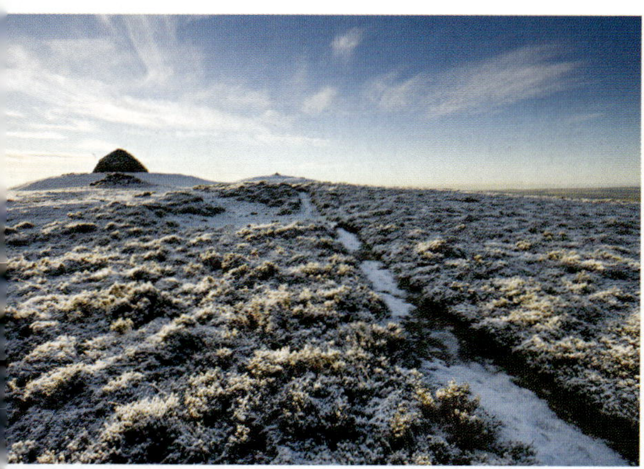

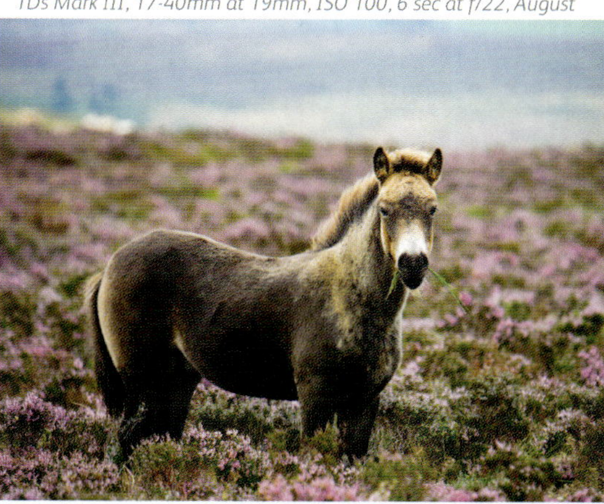

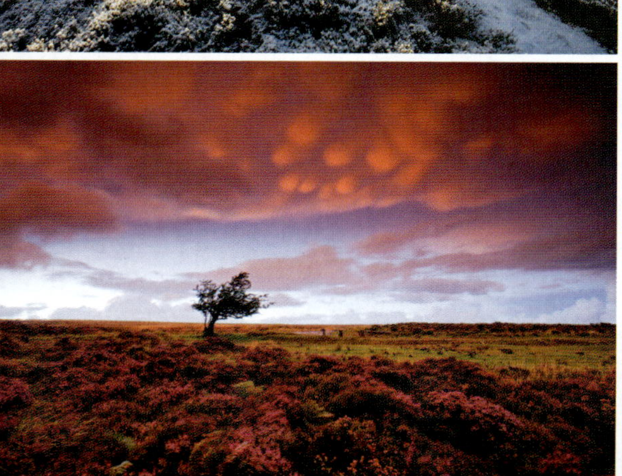

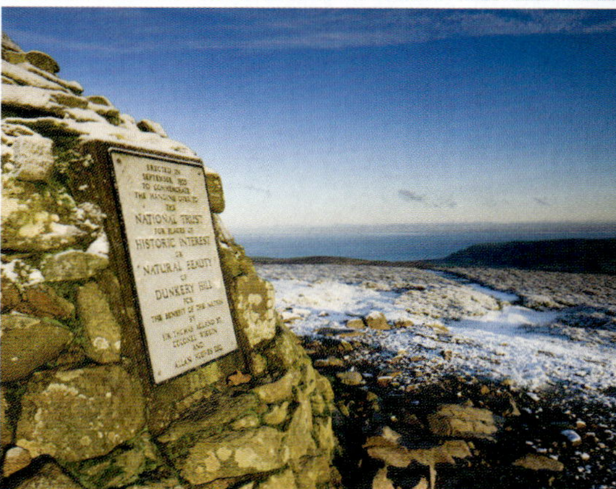

Above: Cairn on the summit of Dunkery Beacon, Canon 1Ds Mark III, 17-40mm at 25mm, ISO 100, 1/15 sec at f/16. December

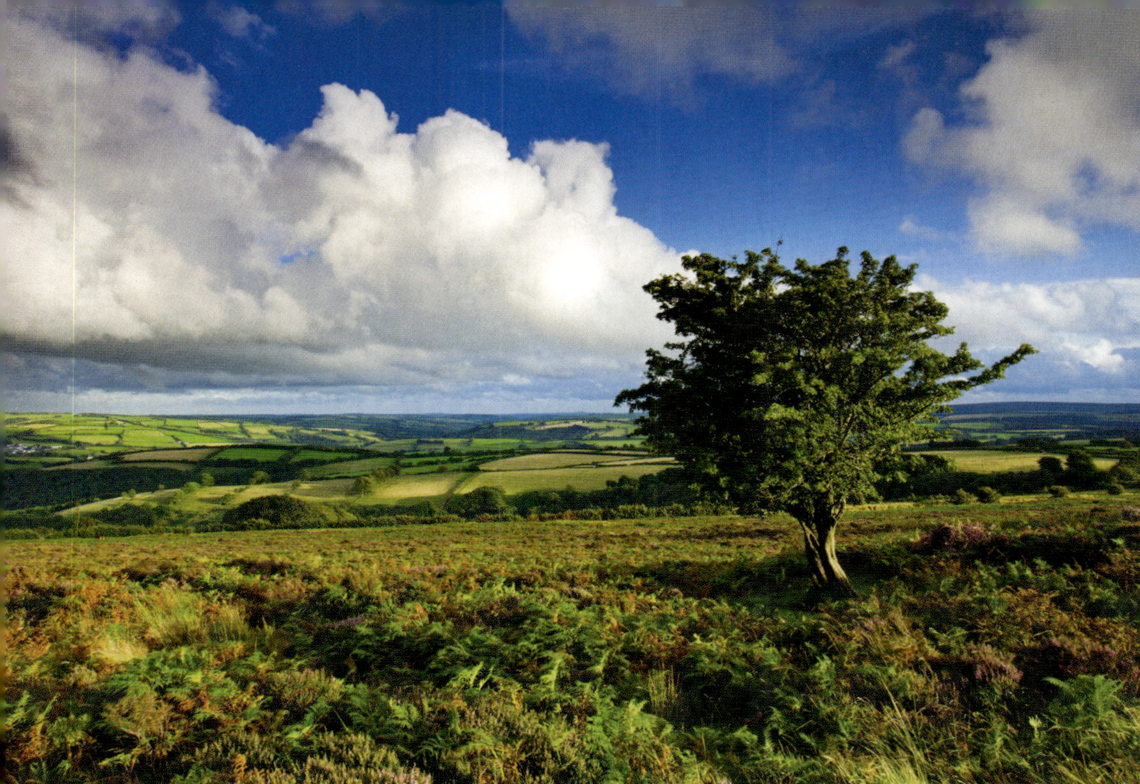

Hawthorn tree on the moorland below Dunkery Beacon, Canon 1Ds Mark III, 17-40mm at 23mm, ISO 100, 1/8 sec at f/22. August

Away From The Summit

While the backdrop is clearly impressive from the summit, the immediate foreground is less interesting. A wide grassy area surrounds the cairn, making photographs of the summit itself quite plain and unappealing. A more effective composition can be achieved by positioning yourself a bit further away, amongst the heather that surrounds the summit. Even if you aren't visiting during the summer when the heather is in flower, the plants still add interest to the scene. Several footpaths can be found winding throughout the heather; these make excellent lead in lines to compositions, drawing the eye towards the cairn in the background.

Near The Parking Area

Back near the parking area, there are several small photogenic trees growing by the roadside. As mentioned previously, with the absence of large rocky areas on Exmoor's rolling uplands, trees become of prime importance for adding interest to moorland photographs. The trees tend to be hawthorn (they flower in May/June), which seem to thrive on these areas of high moorland, gaining an appealing windswept appearance due to their exposed position. Don't worry that the trees are close to the edge of the road. With a careful composition you can either exclude the road completely, or minimise its importance in the frame. Alternatively, use the road as a focal point in the composition.

How to Get Here

Dunkery Beacon is in the north of Exmoor National Park, close to the village of Wheddon Cross. From Wheddon Cross, head west on the B3224 for about a mile. As the road bends around to the left, take the right turning signposted Dunkery Beacon. Continue along this lane, passing over a cattle grid and climbing up onto the moor. After about two miles, you will see a small parking area to the right of the road.

Parking Lat/Long: 51.165812, -3.5688995
Parking Grid Ref: SS 904 419
Parking Postcode: TA24 7DT (Wheddon Cross)
Map: OS Explorer Map OL9 (1:25 000) Exmoor

Accessibility

From the car park, a 15 minute walk is required to reach the top of Dunkery Beacon, via a well-defined but uneven moorland footpath. The car park itself offers excellent far reaching views of the surrounding landscape.

Best Time of Year/Day

Like most of Exmoor's moorland areas, Dunkery Beacon is carpeted in heather, and looks its best during late summer (August/early September) when the heather is in flower. Alternatively head up to the moor during a cold winter snap, when the high elevation can leave Dunkery Beacon sugar coated with frost or fresh snowfall.

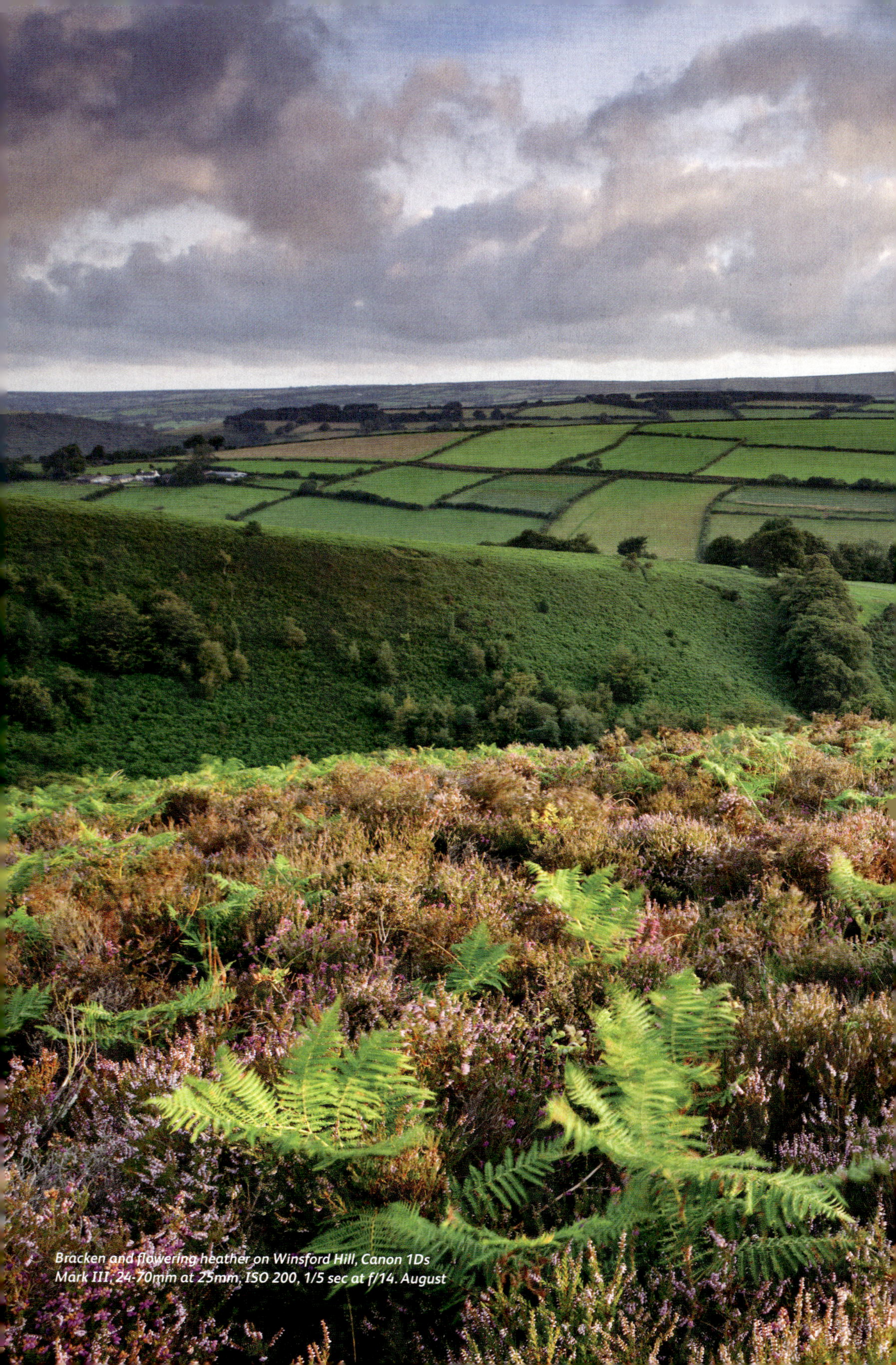

Bracken and flowering heather on Winsford Hill, Canon 1Ds Mark III, 24-70mm at 25mm, ISO 200, 1/5 sec at f/14. August

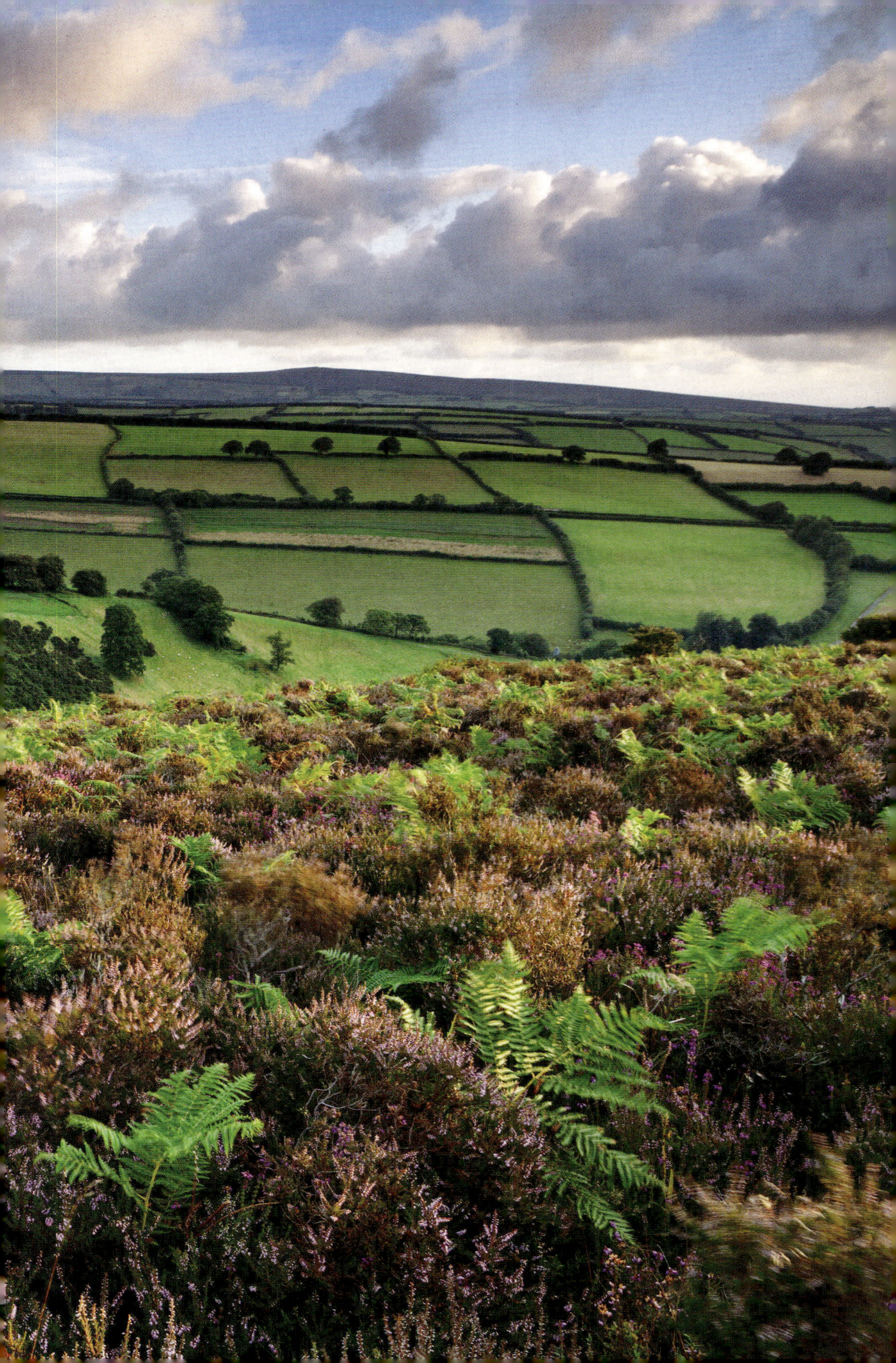

Winsford Hill is an elevated area of open moorland in the south of Exmoor National Park. With a summit in excess of 400m/1300ft the hill makes a wonderful vantage point from which to shoot Exmoor's picturesque patchwork rolling countryside. Although the hill is expansive, most photographic attention is drawn towards the Punchbowl, a photogenic steep valley cut into the side of the hill.

What to Shoot and Viewpoints

The Punchbowl

The highlight of Winsford Hill is undoubtedly the Punchbowl. Approaching from the moorland hilltop, the landscape suddenly plunges steeply over 100 metres. For little effort you get a tremendous far-reaching view, initially taking in the Punchbowl and then mile upon mile of lush green rolling fields.

A number of hawthorn trees grow on the edge of the Punchbowl, which can add some good immediate interest. These trees are particularly effective to help reflect the seasons when shooting the Punchbowl throughout the year. Visit in early June to find the hawthorns covered in white blossom. Visit in October to find them covered with deep red berries. On a cold winter morning they may be covered with hoar frost or snow.

In late spring vibrant green bracken springs up on the steep slopes of the Punchbowl, turning deep green in summer and then warm copper in autumn. In late summer Winsford Hill, as with all of Exmoor's upland areas undergoes a transformation when the landscape turns purple with flowering heather. At these times, shoot with a wide angle lens to fully showcase the beautiful distinctive colours that Exmoor is famous for. On the eastern slopes of the Punchbowl, there is an area where heather and bracken grow together. The vibrant colours of each plant complement one another well and provide a gorgeous foreground to images of the rolling countryside towards Dunkery Beacon.

This location makes a wonderful vantage point to shoot with a telephoto lens. For photographic subjects look for single trees in far off fields and repeating patterns made by distant hedgerows, or isolated farmhouses surrounded by fields. With such a high vantage point there are lots of possibilities for telephoto shots from the Punchbowl.

Point of interest – Caratacus Stone

An ancient inscribed standing stone can be found on the moorland, believed to have been erected in the 6th century. The inscription appears to read 'CARATACI NEPVS' which translates to 'grandson or immediate descendent of Caratacus', a British chieftain notable for resisting the Roman invasion in the 1st century.

A relic of such importance deserves to be photographed, but frustratingly the Caratacus Stone makes a very challenging subject. Over a hundred years ago a shelter was built around the stone to protect it from the elements. This shelter now bears more resemblance to a bus shelter than an ancient memorial! However, despite the photographic limitations the stone remains an important historical feature and is worth visiting while you are up on Winsford Hill.

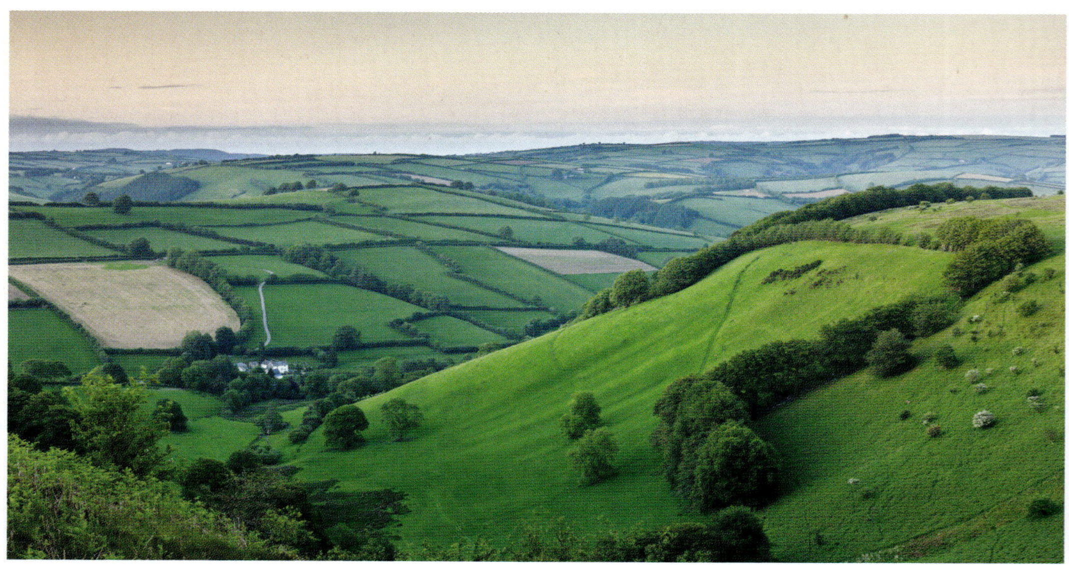

Beautiful rolling farmland beyond the Punchbowl, Canon 1Ds Mark III, 24-70mm at 48mm, ISO 200, 1.5 sec at f/13. June

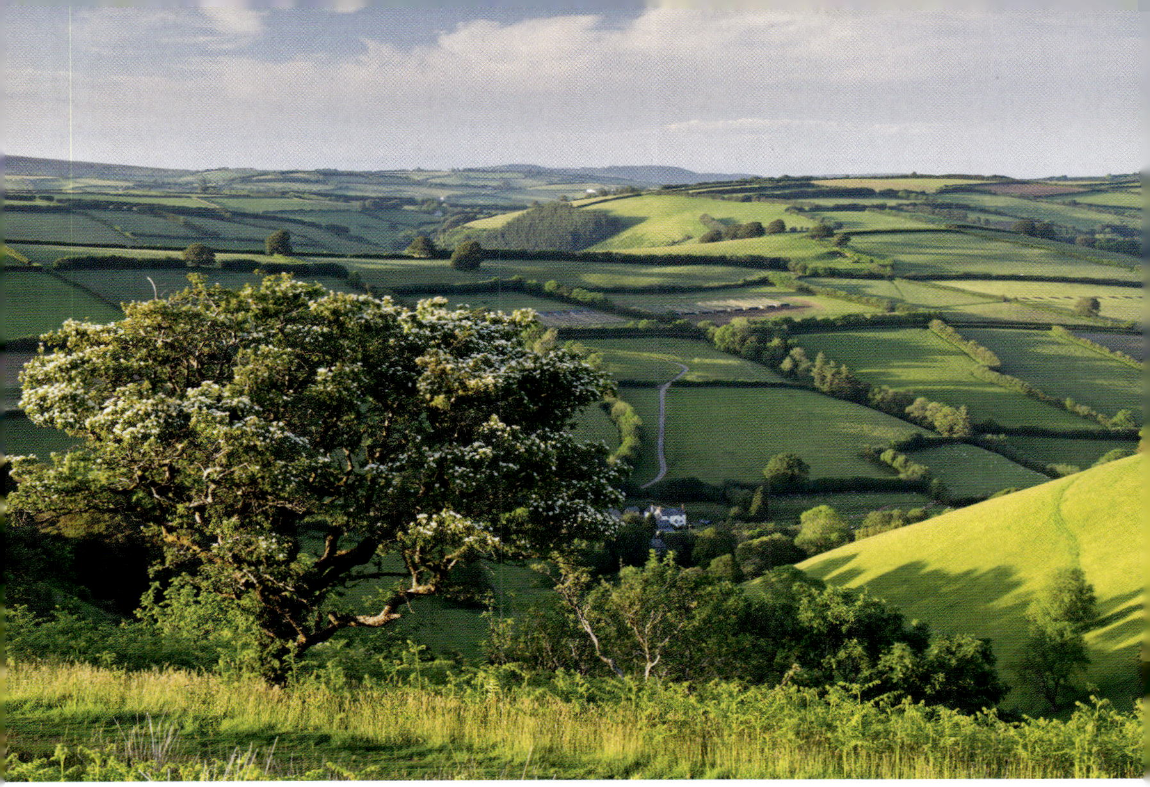

Hawthorn in Blossom in late Spring, Nikon D800E, 24-70mm at 70mm, ISO 100, 0.4 sec at f/13. June

Wintry scenes in the Punchbowl, Canon 1Ds Mark III, 70-200mm at 94mm, ISO 100, 1/40 sec at f/16. January

How to Get Here

Winsford Hill falls within the Somerset side of Exmoor National Park, close to Dulverton. From Dulverton head north on the B3223 for approximately 5 miles; the road passes right over the Winsford Hill where there is a small parking area. The views down to the Punchbowl are just north of the road.

For the Caratacus Stone drive from Winsford Hill summit southeast for half a mile to a junction, turn left here and park in a lay-by. Follow the path to the stone.

Parking Lat/Long: 51.091034, -3.5876986 (Caratacus Stone), 51.096096, -3.6036698 (Punchbowl)
Parking grid ref: SS 889 337 (Caratacus Stone), SS 878 342 (Punchbowl)
Parking Postcode: TA24 7JE (Winsford village)
Map: OS Explorer Map OL28 (1:25 000) Dartmoor

Accessibility

A road runs up and over the crest of Winsford Hill, with several parking areas providing easy access to the best viewpoints. Although good views can be achieved from these parking areas, both the Punchbowl and the Caratacus Stone require a short 5 minute walk over uneven moorland tracks.

Best Time of Year/Day

With colourful purple heather carpeting the moorland in late summer, this is the obvious time to visit Winsford Hill. However, the moorland can be photographed well throughout the seasons. For the best quality light, aim to visit at either end of the day.

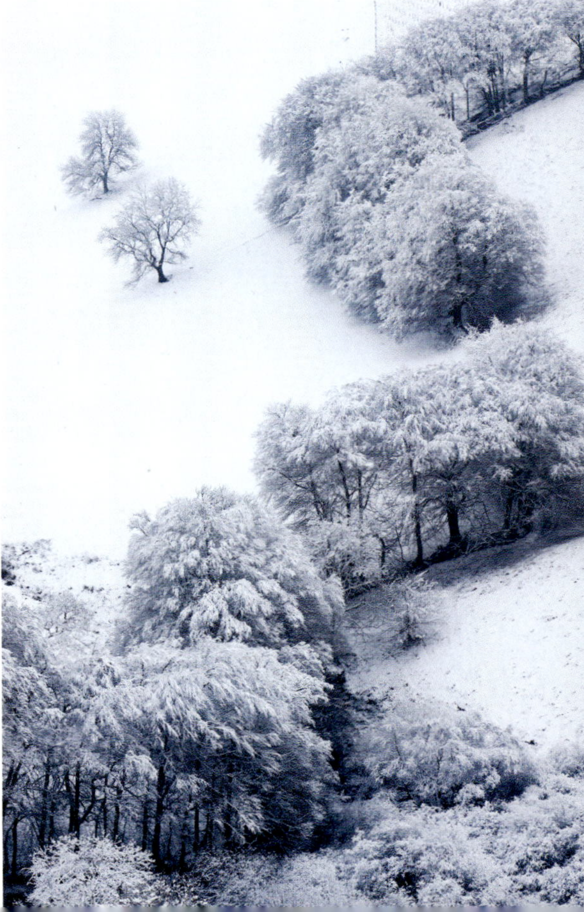

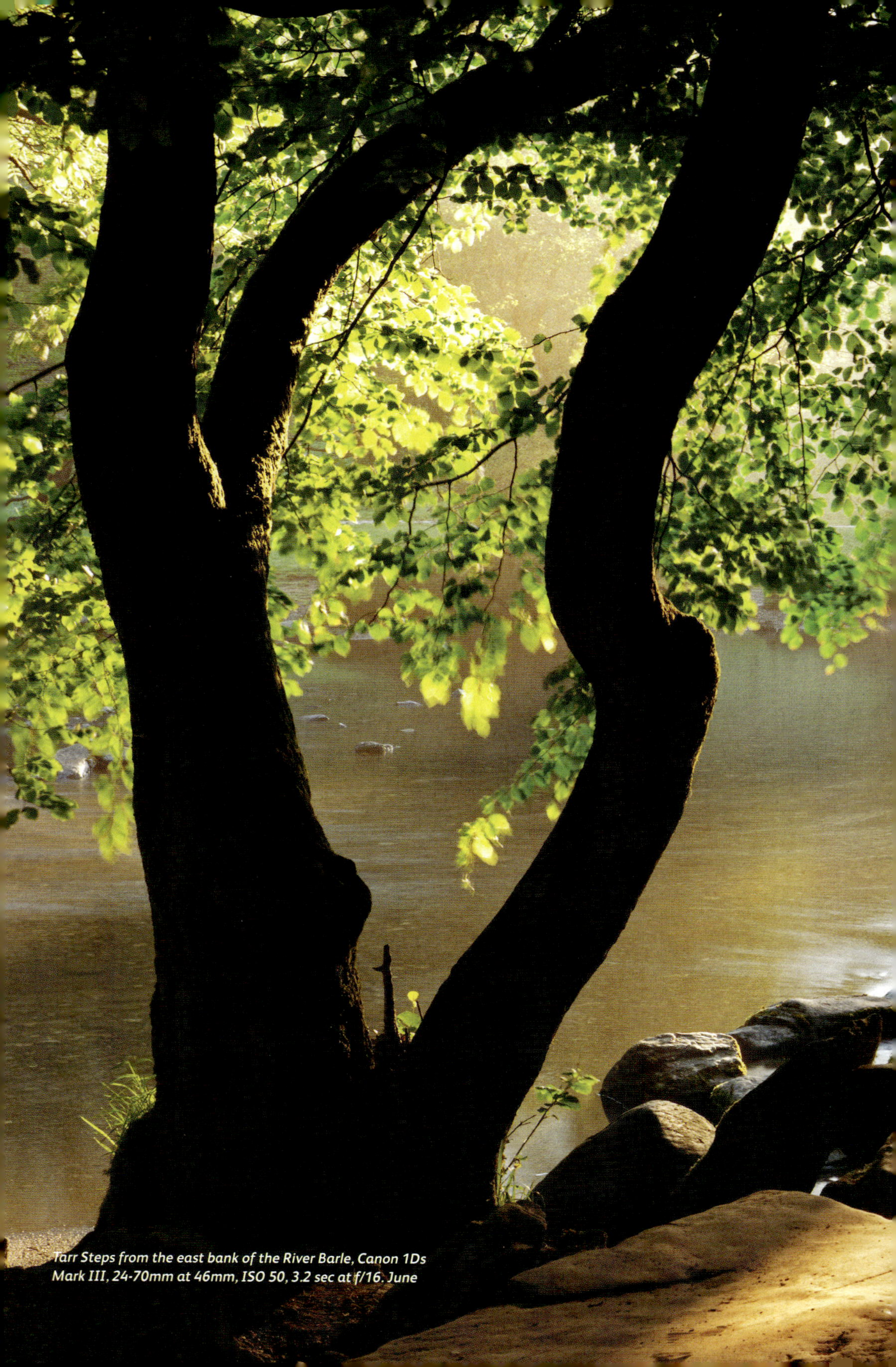

Tarr Steps from the east bank of the River Barle, Canon 1Ds Mark III, 24-70mm at 46mm, ISO 50, 3.2 sec at f/16. June

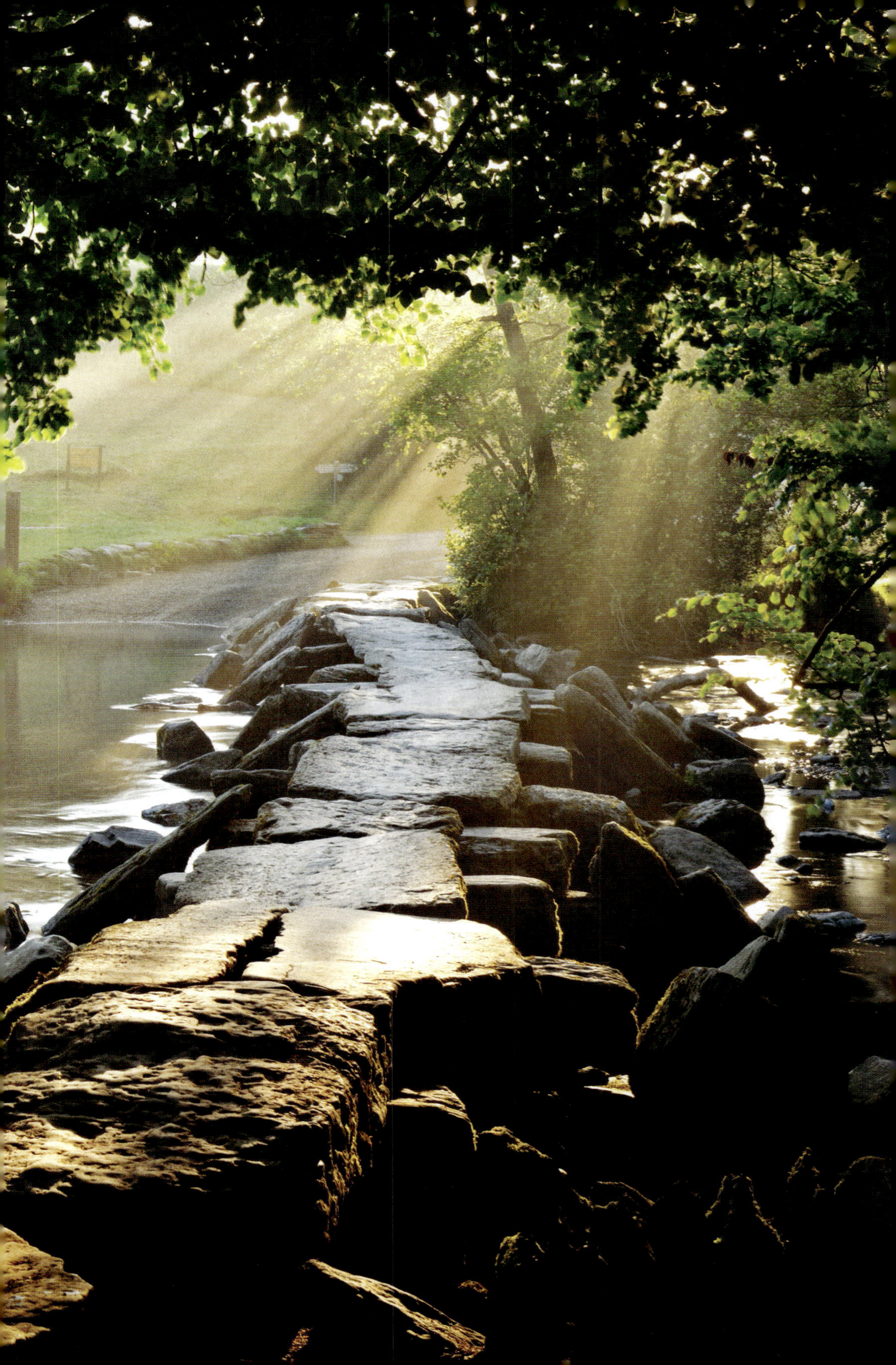

Crossing the River Barle in deepest Exmoor, Tarr Steps is an ancient clapper bridge, stretching across the river like an enormous centipede. The bridge is a simple design, comprised of giant slabs laid over piled-up rocks.

Question marks remain over the age of the bridge; some believe it was a medieval construction while others consider it far older, dating back to the Bronze Age. Whichever theory is correct, Tarr Steps is pretty old and, at 50 metres in length, it is the widest clapper bridge in Britain.

One local myth suggests that the bridge was built by the Devil, so that he could sunbathe on the giant slabs away from the cover of the trees. The Devil forbade any locals to cross the bridge on punishment of death. Any doubts to the seriousness of the Devil's threat were put aside when an unfortunate cat, sent across the bridge by the locals, was vaporised in a puff of smoke.

In desperation the frightened locals turned to their parson to tackle the Devil head on. Upon setting foot on the bridge the Devil appeared and confronted the parson, intimidating the religious man through a ferocious tirade of abuse. Resisting the urge to turn and flee, the parson instead responded in similar fashion. His cursing so impressed the Devil that he decided to allow people to pass over the bridge freely from that point.

Due to its simple construction and low position the bridge is very vulnerable to flood damage and has been washed away many times over the years. The most recent of which occurred in the winter of 2012, when half of the bridge was washed downstream during a period of heavy flooding. To enable Tarr Steps to be rebuilt after flooding each rock is now numbered so it can be authentically reassembled like an enormous puzzle.

What to Shoot and Viewpoints

Being so long, the bridge makes a difficult subject when photographed side on. Far more dynamic photographs can be achieved by standing close to the bridge on either riverbank and shooting along it. Both banks offer great viewpoints, but most photographers prefer to shoot from the west side.

West Bank

The first challenge to photograph from this viewpoint is crossing the bridge; it isn't slippery but is quite uneven and does deter some people. Once you reach the far side the picture potential will be immediately evident. The unusual bridge makes a wonderful subject as it stretches over the river. An attractive mature beech tree stands alongside the bridge, its branches bending over the enormous slabs. During spring and autumn the leaves make a wonderful colourful frame around the bridge and help to hide some of the less photogenic lawned area on the opposite river bank.

Sometimes the bridge's sandstone slabs can appear a bit too dry and pale, standing out too much from the lush woodland surroundings. To remedy this plan your visit on a rainy day when wet the rocks look darker and much more in keeping with the rest of the scenery. Also, on rainy days foliage will appear more saturated, especially if you use a polariser to cut through any reflections on wet leaves.

East Bank

Although this view is probably the best, it is definitely worth crossing back over the bridge and shooting from the other bank. The background is preferable from this side, especially during late autumn when the beech tree mentioned above adds a lovely splash of colour beyond the bridge. By positioning yourself just to the right you can emphasise the curve of the bridge. This section of the river is a ford and is therefore usually quite shallow; if you bring a pair of wellies you will be able to wade into the water a little to gain a better angle from which to shoot the bridge.

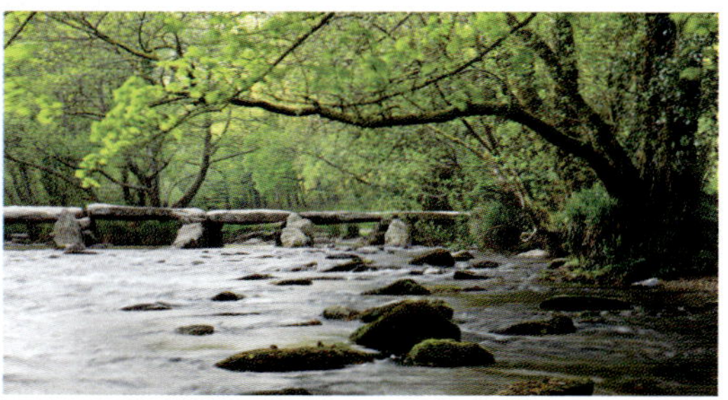

Opposite top: Autumn colours on the east bank of the Barle. Canon 1Ds Mark III, 24-70mm at 70mm, ISO 100, 6 sec at f/22. October.

Opposite left: A tiny whirlpool and waterfall, Canon 1Ds Mark III, 17-40mm at 40mm, ISO 100, 3 sec at f/19. May

The ancient clapper bridge photographed from downstream, Canon 1Ds Mark III, 24-70mm at 70mm, ISO 200, 0.7 sec at f/22. May

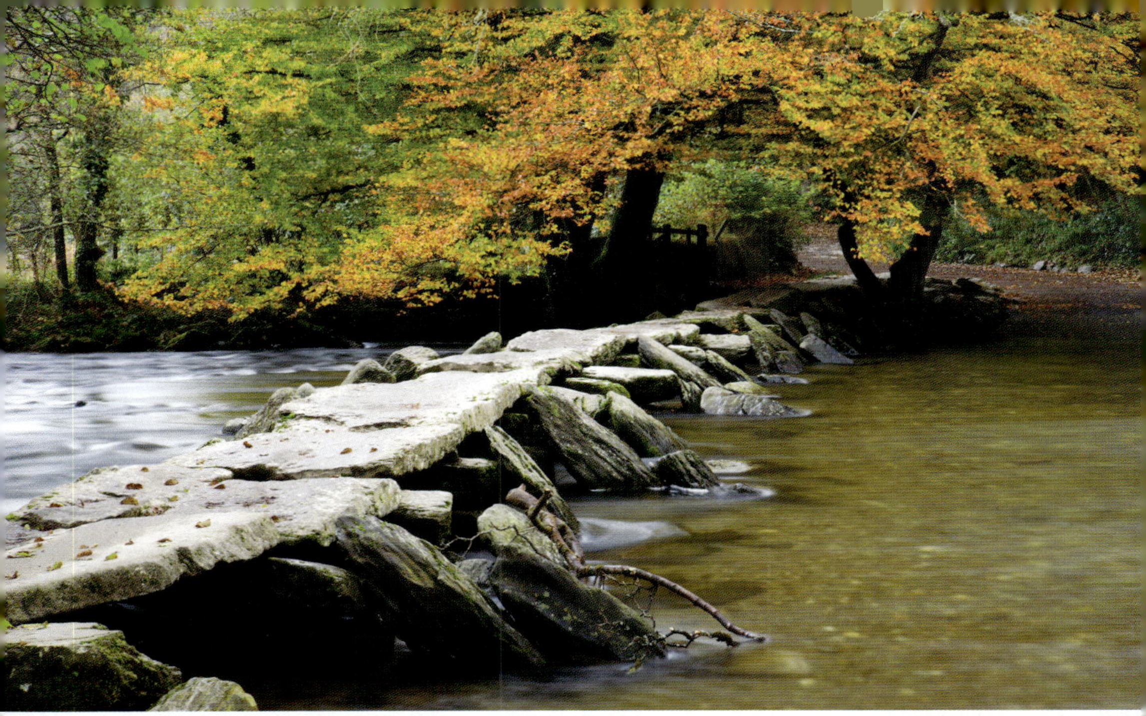

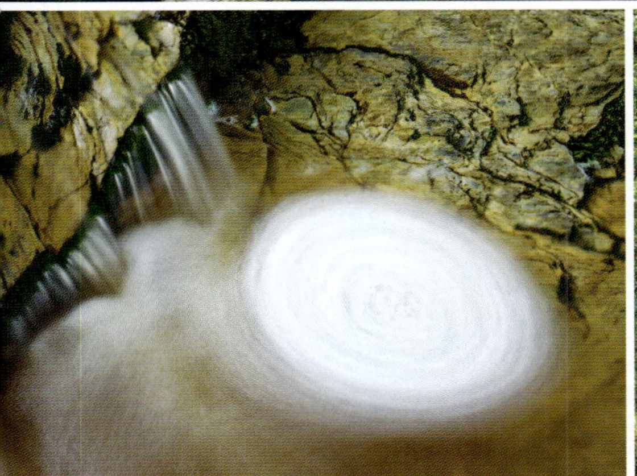

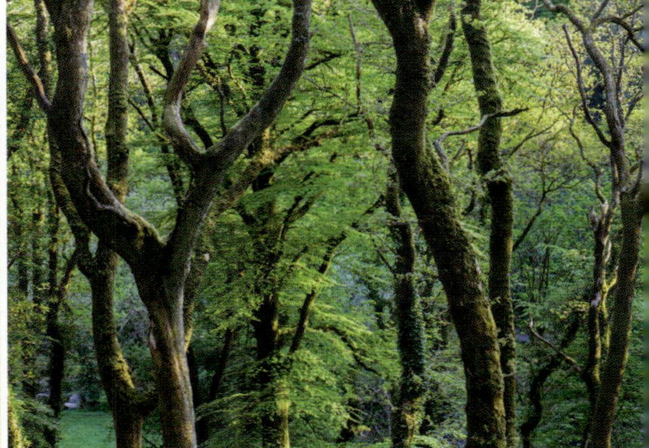

How to Get Here

Tarr Steps is best approached from the east of the River Barle. You can reach the bridge from the west via the village of Hawkridge but there is no parking on this side and, unless you have a 4x4, it is not advisable to cross the ford. To avoid the ford approach from Dulverton – 15 minutes drive to the east. In the centre of Dulverton you will see a signpost for Tarr Steps and the B3223. This narrow road passes through the village and follows the River Barle for a mile before climbing up onto the moor. After 5 miles turn left to Tarr Steps and follow the lane until you reach a car park on the left.

Parking Lat/Long: 51.079818, -3.6102450
Parking Grid Ref: SS 873 324
Parking Postcode: TA22 9PY
Map: OS Explorer Map OL9 (1:25 000) Exmoor

Knaplock Wood on the banks of the River Barle, Canon 1Ds Mark III, 24-70mm at 70mm, ISO 100, 6 sec at f/22. May

Accessibility

From the car park, a 5 minute walk downhill through a field leads you to Tarr Steps. A second car park is restricted for vehicles displaying disabled permits and can be found right beside the bridge. This makes the west viewpoint accessible for wheelchair users but the uneven stone slabs on the bridge make the opposite bank unsuitable.

Best Time of Year/Day

As the bridge is surrounded by deciduous woodland, the area is probably best avoided in the winter months when the trees are bare. Late spring, when new leaves are lime green, or late autumn when the leaves are turning are both ideal times to visit. Tarr Steps is a popular location for visitors; unless you want to photograph people walking on the bridge it is best avoided during the daytime on holidays and weekends. To avoid people try arriving early or late in the day, or alternatively visit on a rainy day.

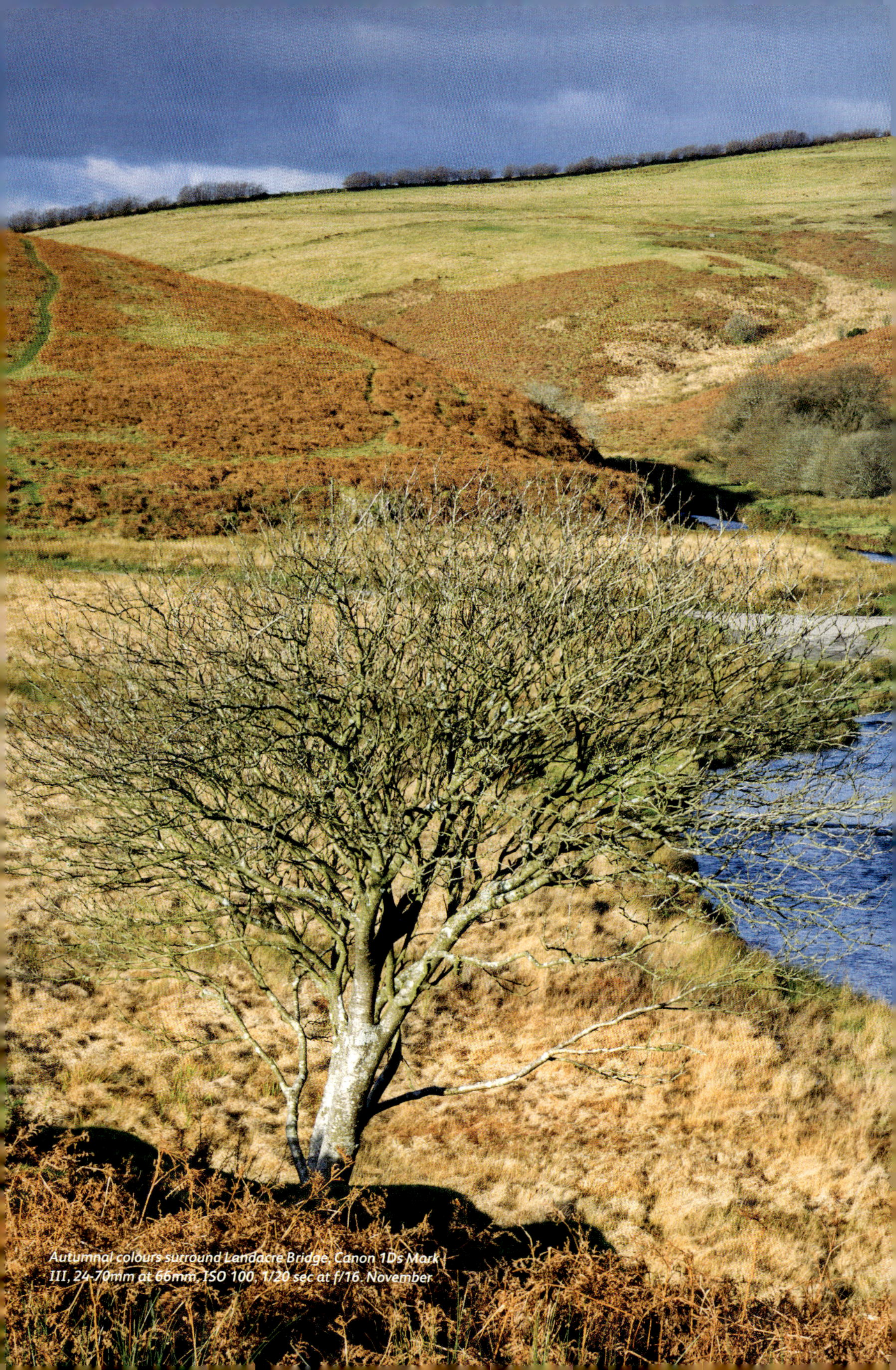

Autumnal colours surround Landacre Bridge. Canon 1Ds Mark
III, 24-70mm at 66mm, ISO 100, 1/20 sec at f/16. November

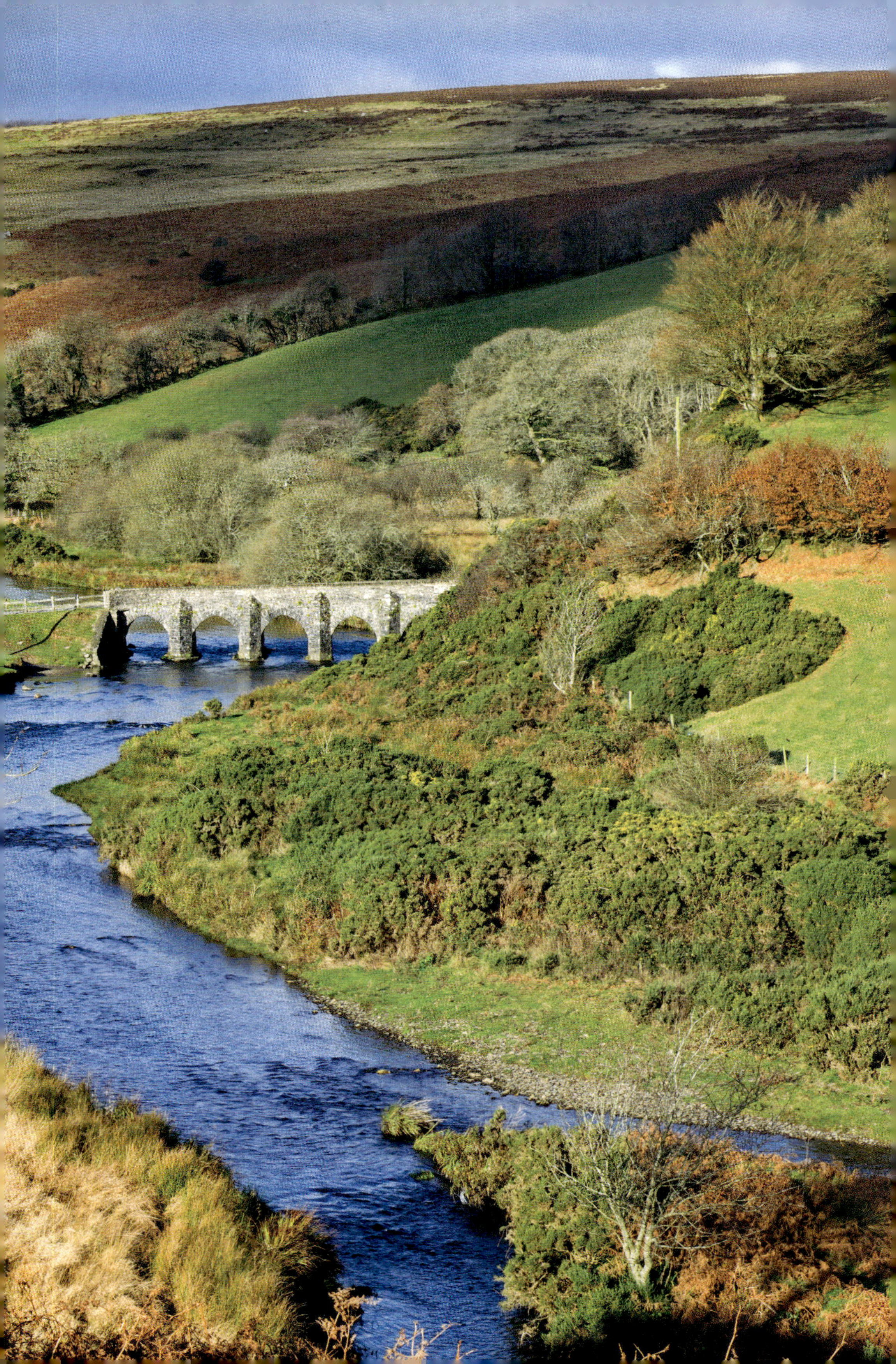

⑬ Landacre Bridge

Unlike Dartmoor with its characteristic granite tors, Exmoor's gentle rolling moorland areas are generally less inspiring for photography. The key to photographing Exmoor's moorland areas is firstly finding and then building compositions around unique features in the landscape. Distinctive valleys, beech tree hedges and stone cairns can all help to identify different areas of the moor; on Withypool Common the prominent feature is Landacre Bridge.

This beautiful old stone bridge spans the River Barle on the edge of Withypool Common. An important and instantly recognisable feature within Exmoor, this medieval bridge is a scheduled ancient moment with a Grade II* listed building status.

Below top: Frosty Withypool Common early morning, Canon 1Ds Mark III, 24-70mm at 38mm, ISO 100, 0.7 sec at f/16. December

Below bottom: The bridge and river in springtime, Canon 1Ds Mark III, 24-70mm at 48mm, ISO 100, 1/8 sec at f/16. June

Below: Spring greens on the shores of the River Barle, Canon 1Ds Mark III, 24-70mm at 42mm, ISO 50, 1.6 sec at f/16. June

What to Shoot and Viewpoints

Close Up

The five ornate arches that comprise the bridge are best appreciated from up close, and can be photographed from the riverbank on either side of the bridge. When the water levels are low, you can wade to the opposite bank to get a fresh perspective. However, a large part of the appeal with Landacre Bridge lies with its setting. This grand old bridge seems quite out of place in a lonely windswept part of the moor; in order to reflect this you need to be able to photograph the bridge within the landscape.

Up High and Close

The simplest way to achieve this is to gain some elevation. Walking over to the northern side of the bridge immediately gives the desired results. Just over the bridge, the road bends sharply to the right and begins to climb uphill. Probably due to this difficult approach and the fact that the bridge is quite narrow, you occasionally can be disappointed to find the stonework damaged in places from vehicles. Almost as soon as the road bends to the right, climb up onto the bank and you should gain an impressive clear view of the bridge and river, with the rolling moorland beyond.

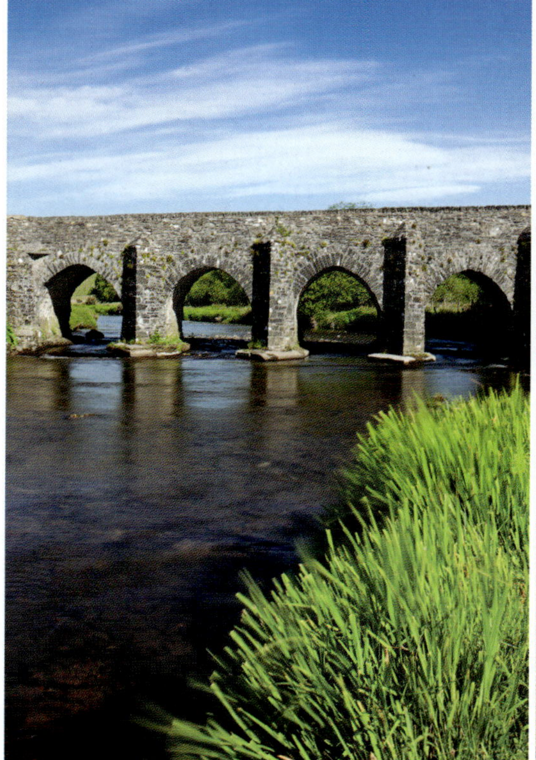

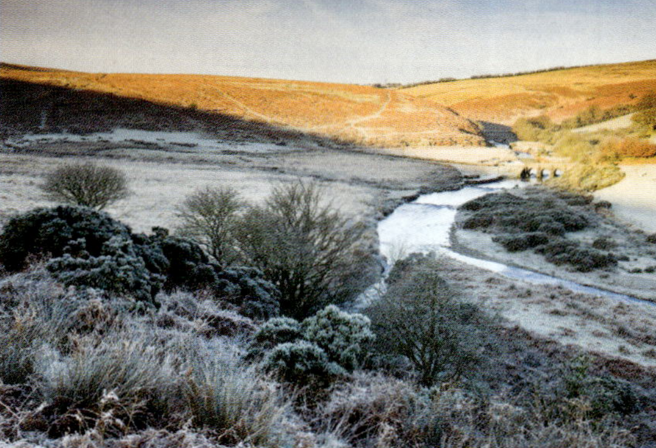

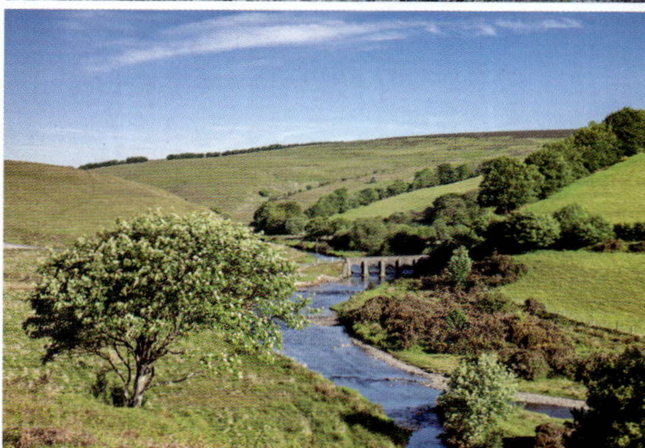

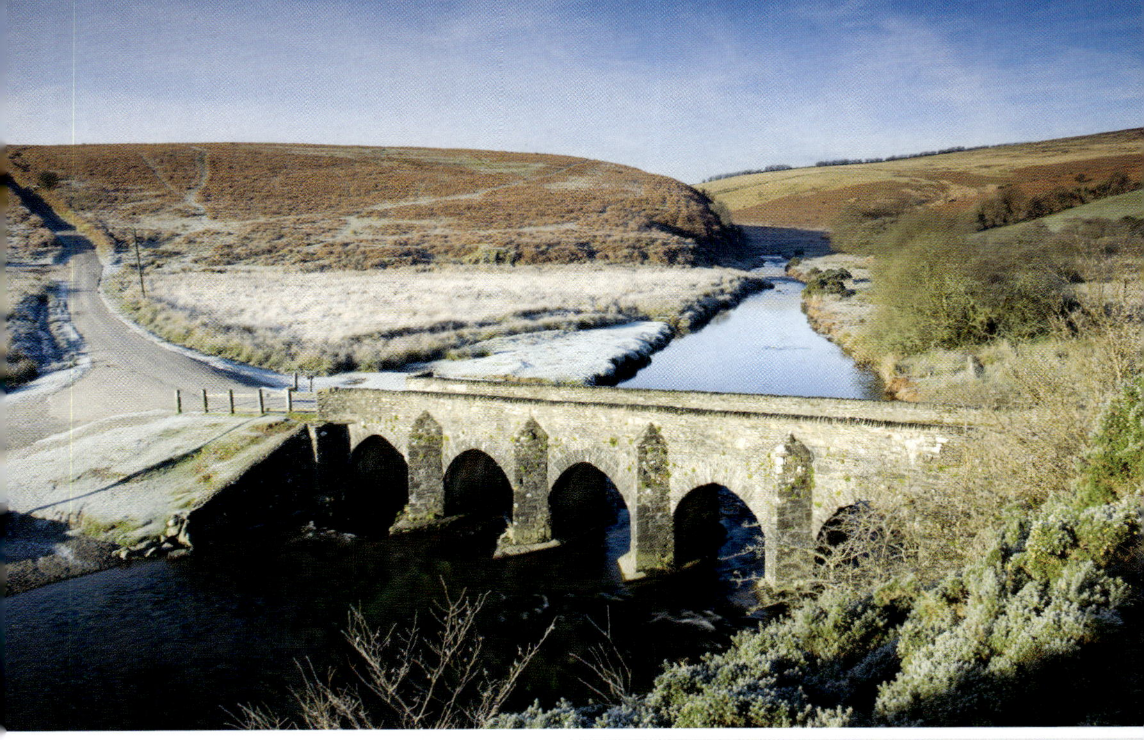

The bridge from the side of the road, Canon 1Ds Mark III, 24-70mm at 28mm, ISO 100, ¼ sec at f/16. December

From this viewpoint the bridge clearly takes prominence in the frame, and also gives it a real sense of location with its moorland surroundings. To benefit from sunlight illuminating the bridge, aim to shoot this location from early to mid morning, depending on the season.

Further Away

Although the bridge becomes much less prominent, my favourite viewpoint for shooting Landacre Bridge is from much further away. Walk back to the southern side of the bridge, and along the road. When you get to the second small parking area, turn left and walk over the open moorland. You will soon pick up a footpath which leads eastwards over the moor towards Withypool. Within minutes the path begins to climb, affording some wonderful elevated views back towards the bridge.

From this higher viewpoint a more ambitious landscape can be achieved. The bridge now appears much smaller, sandwiched between the rolling moorland, allowing the beautiful Exmoor landscape to become the star attraction. When photographed with a wide-angle lens, include the sweep of the River Barle to guide the eye towards the bridge. For added interest, there are several trees on this small hill which further help to add some very welcome interest to an otherwise open moorland.

How to Get Here

Landacre Bridge is on the edge of Withypool Common, within the Somerset section of Exmoor National Park. To reach the bridge from Dulverton, head north on the B3223 for 9 miles, and then take the left turning signposted Landacre. The bridge can be found just 2 miles along this small road.

Parking Lat/Long: 51.111006, -3.6941886
Parking Grid Ref: SS 815 360
Parking Postcode: TA24 7SD (Landacre Farm)
Map: OS Explorer Map OL28 (1:25 000) Dartmoor

Accessibility

There is a small parking area beside the bridge, and another a short walk away. From both parking areas you can be in position to shoot the bridge within a few minutes. The higher viewpoint is about 5 minutes walk and can only be accessed by following a moorland footpath over rough ground.

Best Time of Year/Day

Visiting the moor in more than one season will reward you with very different images of Landacre Bridge. Of course the bridge won't change, but the river and surrounding moorland will look completely different at certain times of year. The landscape undergoes it biggest change in winter, especially in periods of snow.

However it is a difficult location to access in snow. A much easier and no less photogenic option is a frosty morning. Even without the luxury of frost or snow it is still worth visiting Landacre Bridge on a winter morning. At this time of year the moorland grasses and decaying bracken have turned copper, giving the landscape a distinctive appearance so different to the greens of summer.

Dartmoor – Introduction

At over 350 square miles, Dartmoor National Park contains southern England's largest remaining area of wilderness. The landscape is most famous for its vast areas of windswept rolling moorland, crested by hundreds of remote granite outcrops known as tors. This dark brooding landscape with its dramatic weather has for long been associated with many myths and legends; haunting tales of headless horseman, hell hounds and many stories of the Devil himself have made the moor an ominous location for superstitious visitors over the years. Taking inspiration from such legends, Arthur Conan Doyle's famous novel, The Hound of the Baskervilles was largely based on Dartmoor,

Although Dartmoor is closely associated with its characteristic open moorland, the National Park includes a gentler side which may elude first time visitors; large areas of patchwork rolling countryside are interspersed with idyllic villages while fast moving rocky rivers rush through verdant deep wooded valleys.

While much of Dartmoor's moorland is now remote and empty, evidence is spread all over the moor of previous human habitation. Megalithic stone circles, standing stones and stone rows can be found throughout the moor, as well as remains of Bronze Age settlements and smaller hut circles, all pointing to a time when the climate was far more forgiving than the present day. In fact Dartmoor contains the highest concentration of Bronze Age artefacts in Europe; put a pin anywhere on an Ordnance Survey map of Dartmoor and you will be close to some ancient remnants of the past.

DARTMOOR

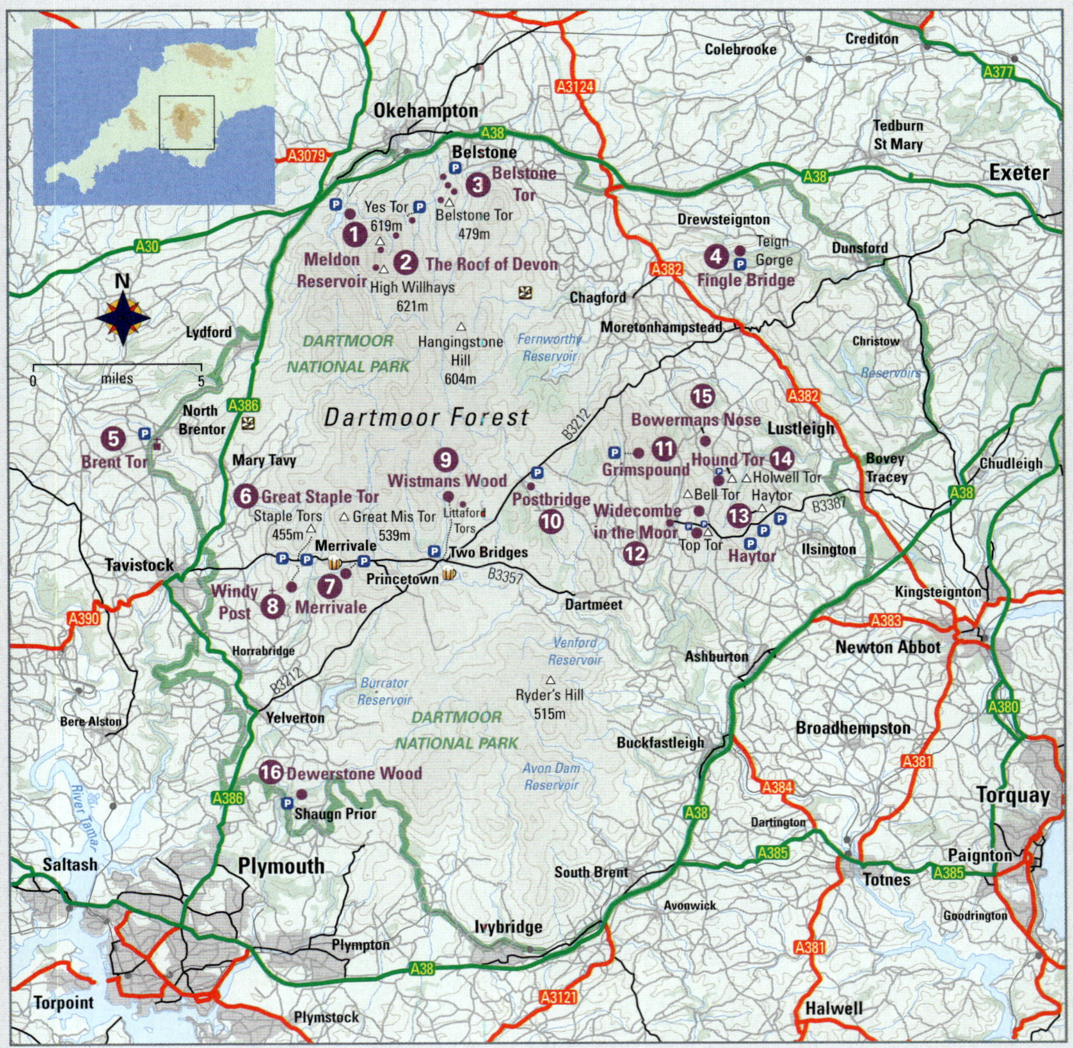

Colebrooke
Crediton
A377
A3124
A38
Okehampton
Tedburn St Mary
Belstone
Exeter
Belstone Tor
3
Yes Tor
619m
Belstone Tor
479m
A38
Drewsteignton
1
Teign Gorge
4
Meldon Reservoir
2 The Roof of Devon
High Willhays
621m
Fingle Bridge
Dunsford
A382
Chagford
Christow
Moretonhampstead
Reservoirs
DARTMOOR NATIONAL PARK
Hangingstone Hill
604m
Fernworthy Reservoir
Lydford
N
15
Dartmoor Forest
Bowermans Nose
Lustleigh
miles
0   5
A382
North Brentor
A386
B3212
11
14
Bovey Tracey
5
Mary Tavy
9
Grimspound
Hound Tor
Holwell Tor
Chudleigh
Brent Tor
Wistmans Wood
Postbridge
Bell Tor
Haytor
A38
6 Great Staple Tor
Staple Tors
455m
Great Mis Tor
539m
Littaford Tors
10
13
Widecombe in the Moor
Top Tor
Haytor
B3387
Ilsington
Tavistock
Merrivale
Two Bridges
12
Kingsteignton
Windy Post
Princetown
B3357
7
8 Merrivale
Dartmeet
Newton Abbot
A383
A390
Horrabridge
B3212
Venford Reservoir
Ashburton
A380
Burrator Reservoir
Ryder's Hill
515m
Bere Alston
Yelverton
DARTMOOR NATIONAL PARK
Buckfastleigh
Broadhempston
A381
16 Dewerstone Wood
A386
Avon Dam Reservoir
Torquay
Shaugh Prior
A384
Dartington
River Tamar
A38
A385
Saltash
Plymouth
South Brent
Totnes
A385
Paignton
Plympton
Avonwick
Goodrington
Torpoint
Ivybridge
A381
A38
Plymstock
A3121
Halwell

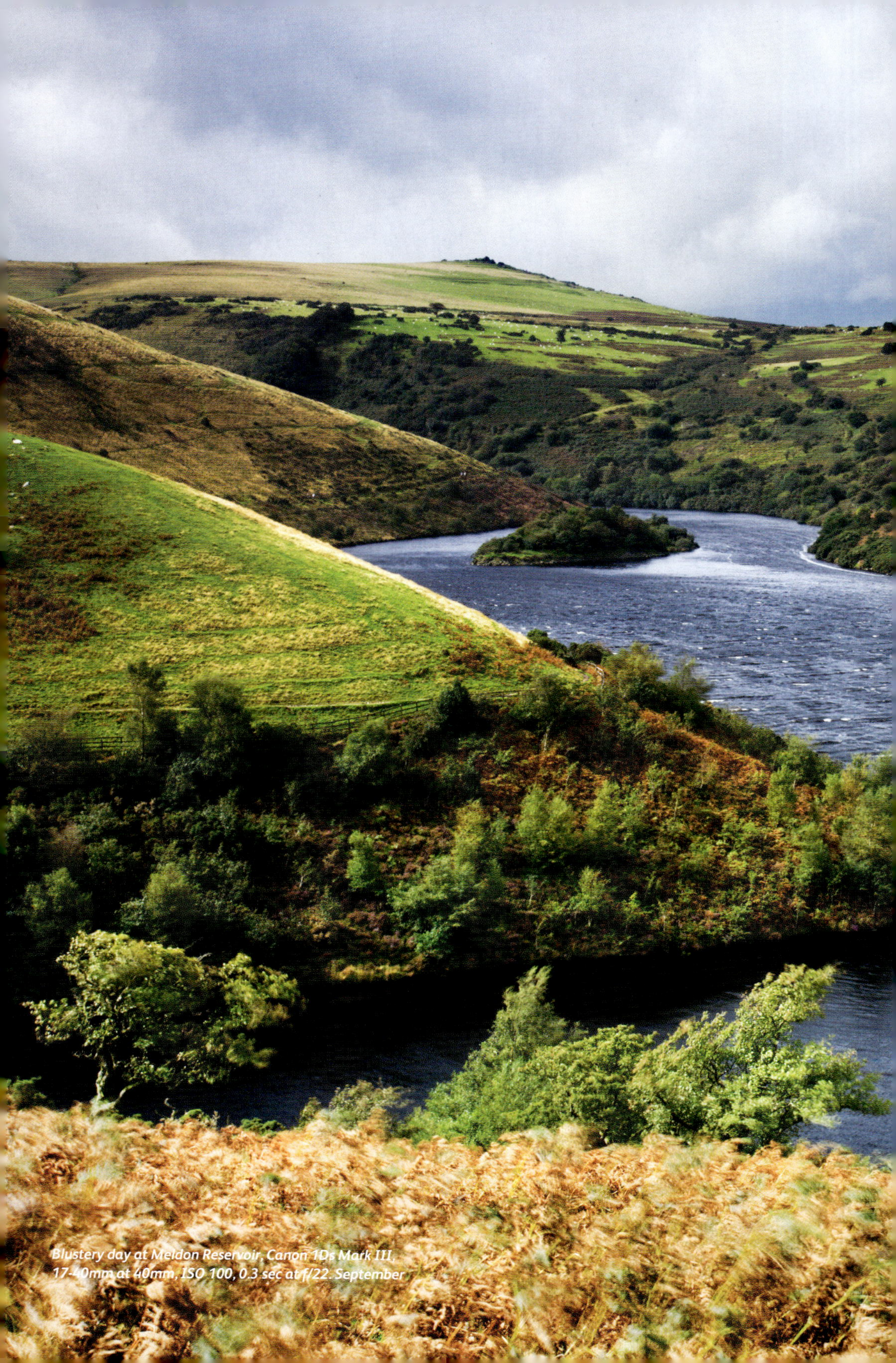

Blustery day at Meldon Reservoir. Canon 1Ds Mark III,
17-40mm at 40mm, ISO 100, 0.3 sec at f/22. September

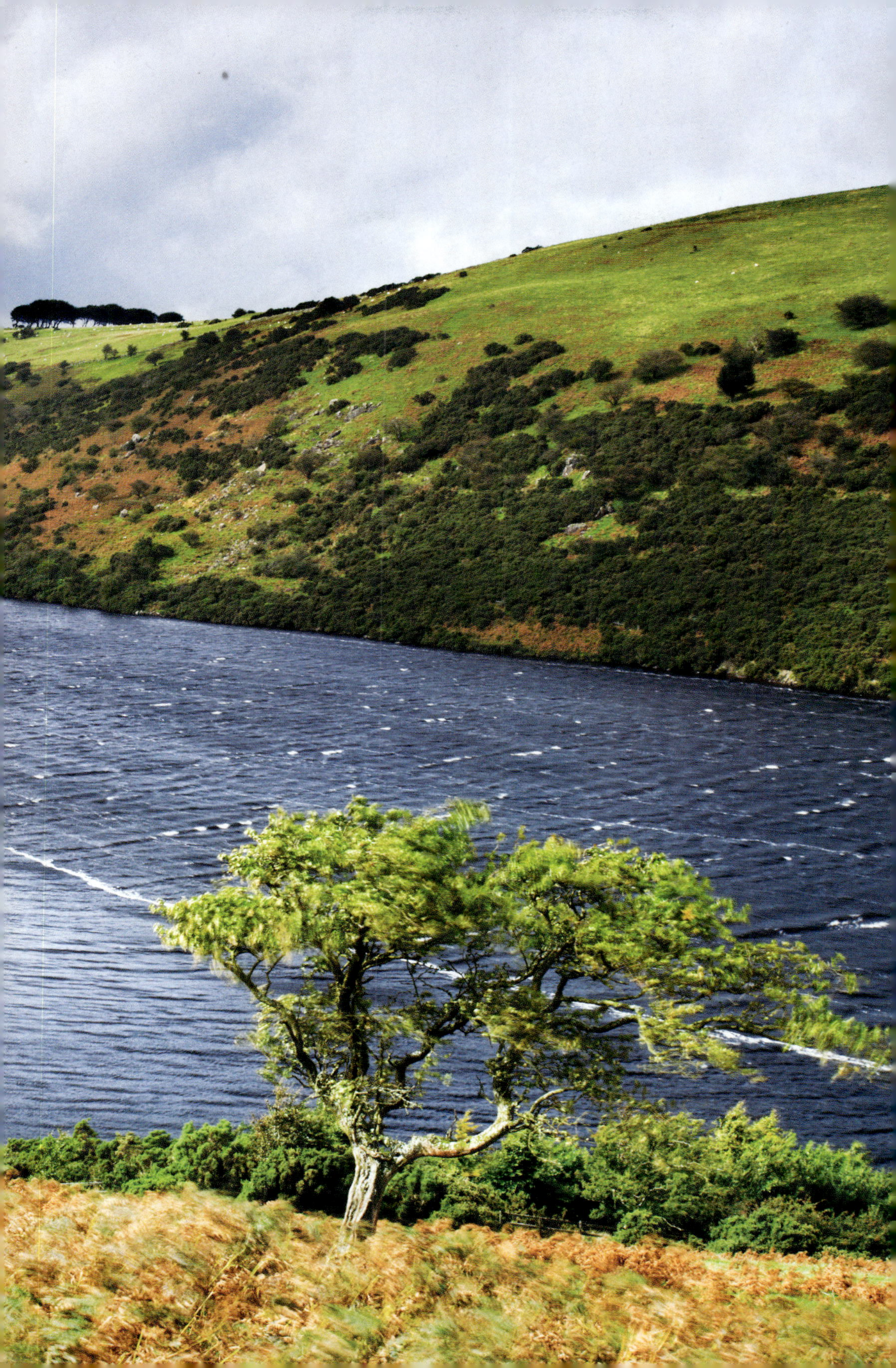

Completed in 1972, Meldon was the last of eight reservoirs to be created within Dartmoor National Park. Located in the West Okement valley and surrounded by the steep rolling hills of the northern moor, Meldon is one of the most photogenic lakes in Devon. Due to its steep sloping sides this is a difficult location to shoot from the shore, but with open moorland surrounding the lake, many elevated viewpoints are achievable.

What to Shoot and Viewpoints

Viewpoint 1 – The Dam

A short walk from the car park and you find yourself crossing the impressive dam at the northern end of the reservoir. At over 55 metres high, the dam provides an excellent lofty vantage point to look north over the valley towards Meldon Viaduct. In order to photograph the dam itself, continue to the far side and turn left, and walk up onto the open moorland. As you climb higher the view of the dam really opens up; when the water levels are high the water rushing out of the dam looks impressive.

Viewpoint 2 – Hawthorn Trees

Turning right after crossing the dam, a footpath circles the entire lake. After following this path for 5 minutes, a second footpath veers sharply to the left climbing up Longstone Hill heading in the direction of Yes Tor. Longstone Hill provides an ideal vantage point to capture expansive photographs of Meldon Reservoir. Weathered and windblown hawthorn trees are scattered all over the hill, making fantastic foreground subjects.

Viewpoint 3 – The Island

Near the southern end of the lake a beautiful circular (presumably man-made) large island makes a very welcome photographic subject. The island can be photographed from many viewpoints along the footpath, but probably the most photogenic angle is from the south west side of the lake. From this viewpoint, the lake curves around the steep valley in a very pleasing way, with the island the undisputed highlight of any composition.

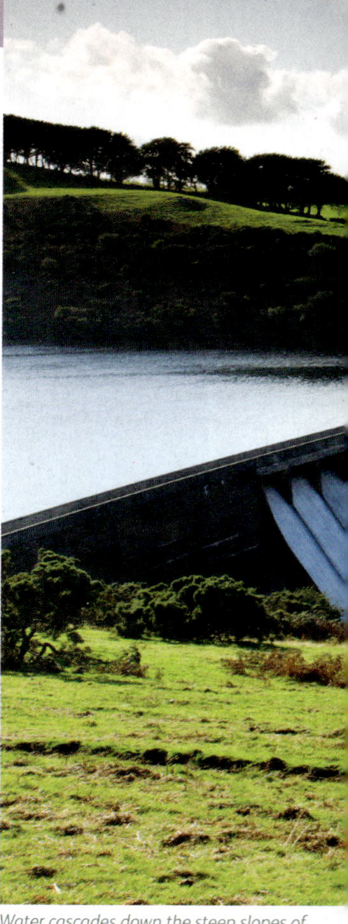

Water cascades down the steep slopes of the dam, Canon 1Ds Mark III, 17-40mm at 29mm, ISO 100, 0.3 sec at f/22. September

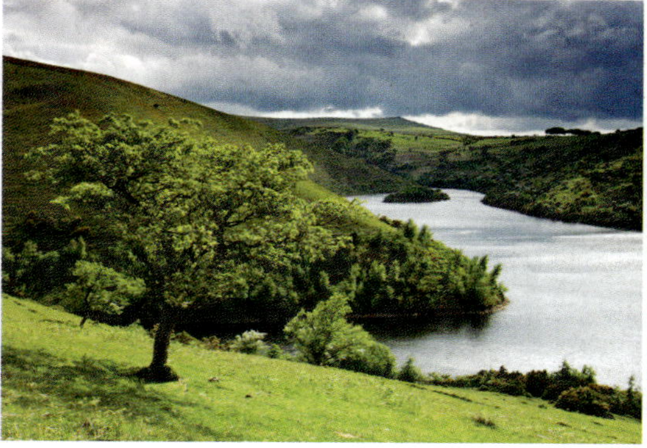

Hawthorn tree with vibrant spring foliage, Canon 1Ds Mark III, 17-40mm at 40mm, ISO 100, 1/30 sec at f/13. May

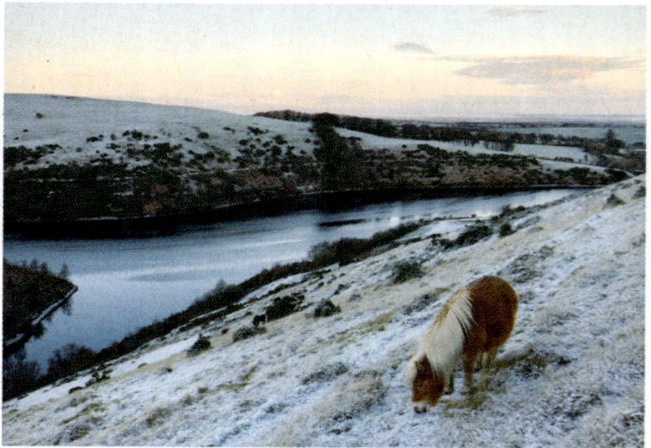

Shetland pony grazing on the snowy moor above the reservoir, Canon 1Ds Mark III, 24-70mm at 34mm, ISO 200, 1/10 sec at f/11. November

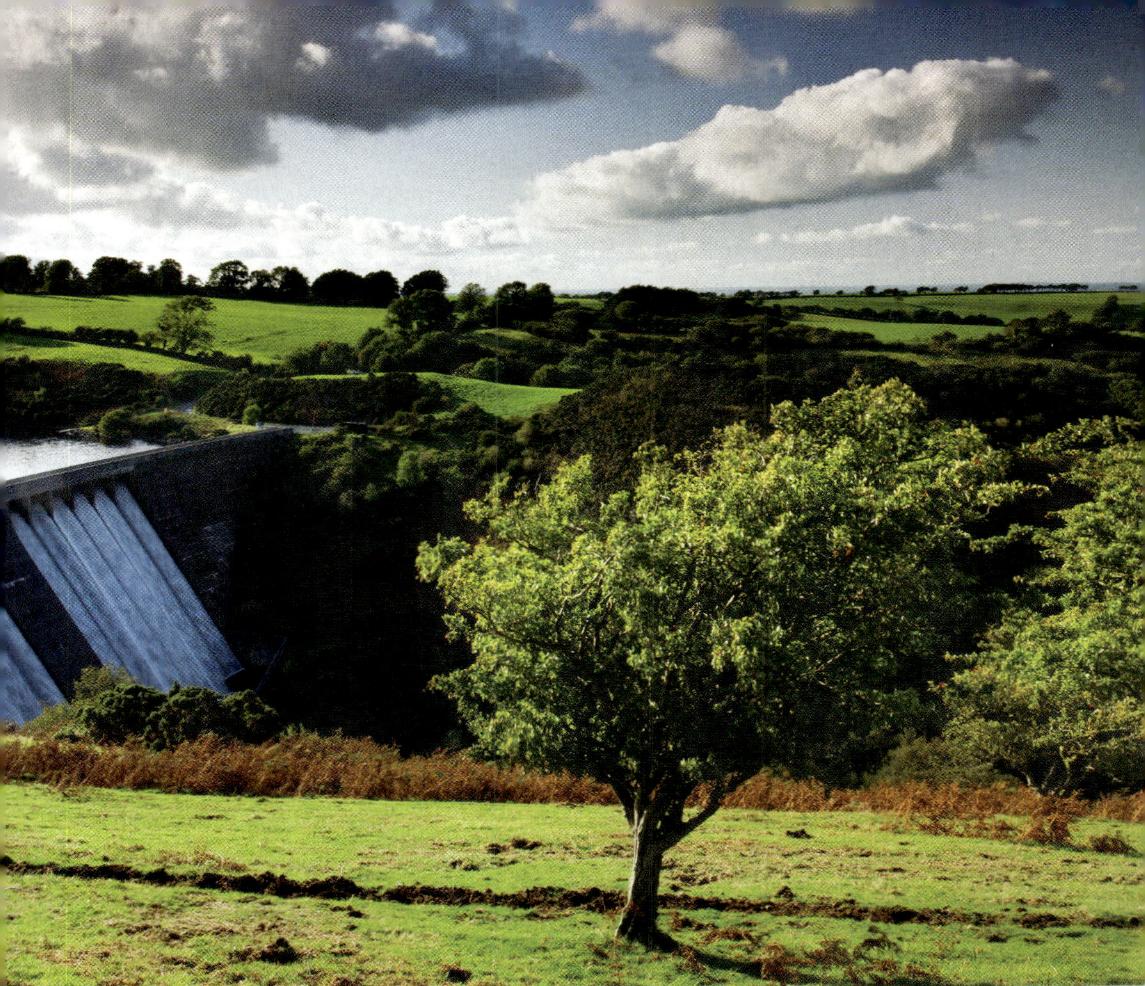

How to Get Here

From Exeter head west on the A30 towards Cornwall. After around 25 miles take the junction signposted Sourton. Head back onto the A30 heading back towards Exeter, but take the first exit signposted Okehampton. At the end of the slip road, turn right and follow the road for about a mile. Immediately after you drive underneath an old railway bridge turn left, the dead end lane stops at Meldon Reservoir. When you reach the reservoir, you will find a large car park, with public toilets.

Parking Lat/Long: 50.712228, -4.0421740
Parking Grid Ref: SX 562 917
Parking Postcode: EX20 4LU (Meldon village)
Map: OS Explorer Map OL28 (1:25 000) Dartmoor

Accessibility

Meldon Reservoir is a popular walking location with well-maintained footpaths. The path encircling the lake is around 2.5 miles in length and is mostly fairly level with several inclines. In some places the path is quite narrow and uneven under foot. On the western side of the lake the path can become quite muddy after rainy periods. The full path is not suitable for wheelchairs users, however the initial section crossing the dam and beyond will be accessible.

Best Time of Year/Day

Due to the steep hills surrounding the lake, sunrise and sunset are not ideal as much of the valley will be in darkness. The viewpoints covered above work extremely well with afternoon sunshine. Plan to visit late in the afternoon for a better quality of light but before the low sun fills the valley with shadow.

The lake looks beautiful and very different throughout the seasons. In winter, this is a very accessible location and like everywhere can look very appealing during periods of snow. Late spring sees the hawthorn trees come into flower, while in summer flowering rhododendron and bracken gives the moorland surrounding the lake a very different look. One less appealing factor to the summer is the water levels; as the levels will be significantly lower the steep rocky shores will be evident reminding any observer of the man made origins of this lake. Autumn is appealing too, not only should the water levels have recovered but as the bracken dies off the steep hills turn brown and shine golden in the evening light.

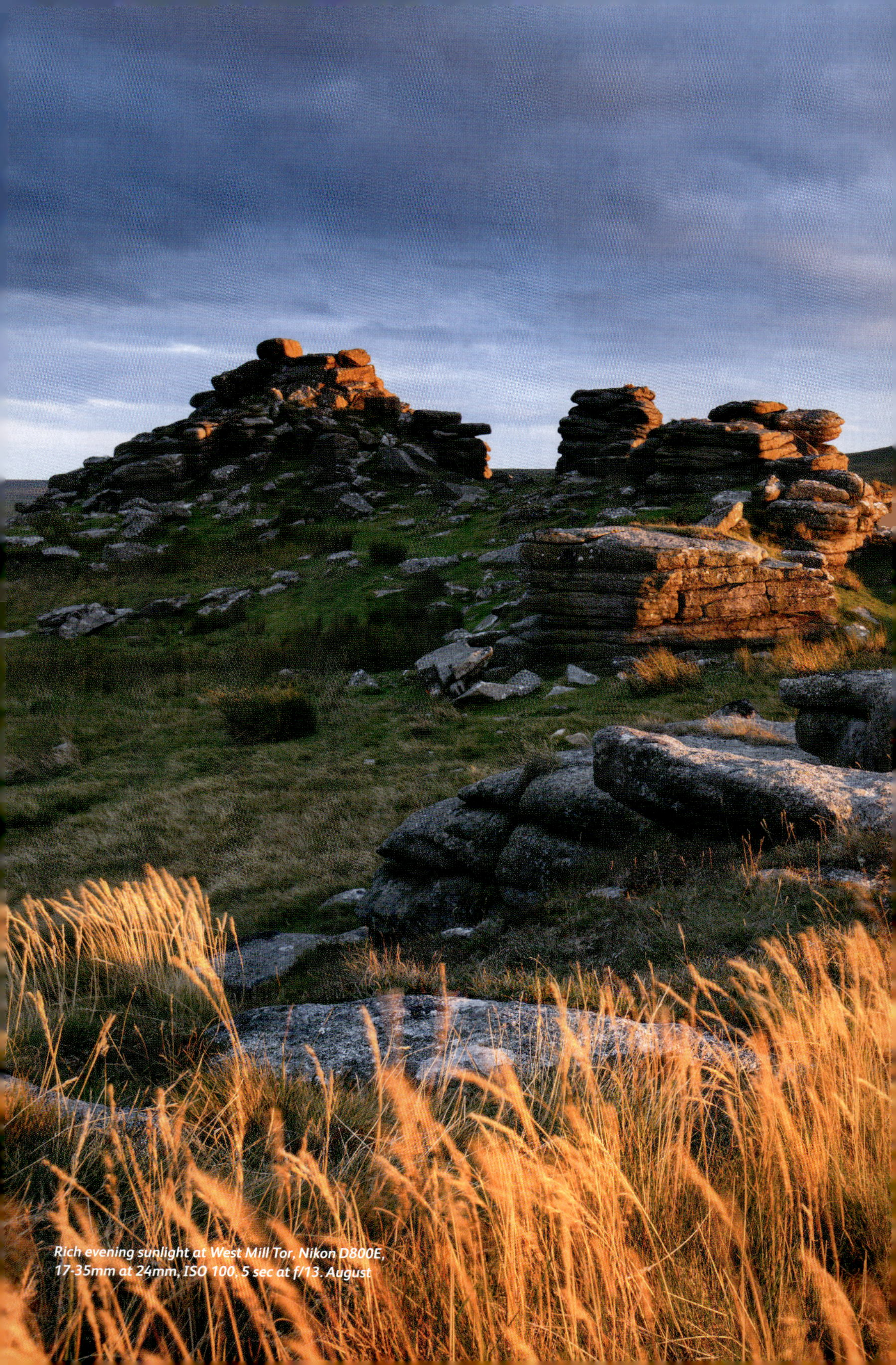

Rich evening sunlight at West Mill Tor, Nikon D800E,
17-35mm at 24mm, ISO 100, 5 sec at f/13. August

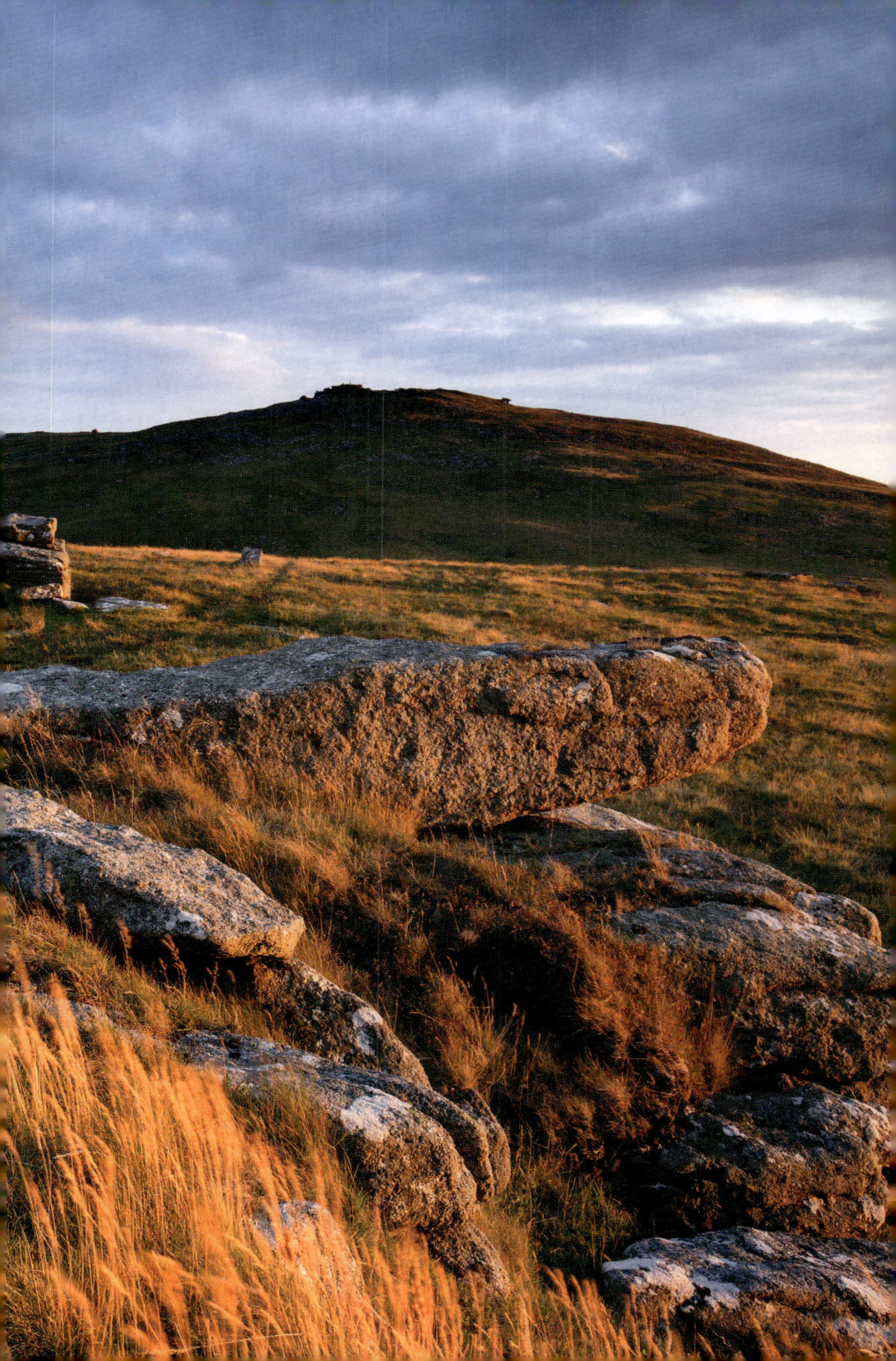

Located in the more remote northern part of Dartmoor, 'the roof of Devon' is the informal name given to a ridge connecting the two highest points of the moor: Yes Tor and High Willhays. Both peaks are over 600 metres (1900ft), making them the highest points in England south of the Peak District. High Willhays beats Yes Tor by just over two metres to claim the crown of highest point, but Yes Tor is by far the more photogenic of the two.

This area forms part of the Okehampton Ranges which have been used by the Ministry of Defence for nearly 150 years for live firing exercises.

What to Shoot and Viewpoints

For the simplest approach to Yes Tor and High Willhays, head up past the Okehampton Army Camp. A private road allows public access when the ranges are not in use. This road climbs high onto the moor, with a parking area at approximately 415 metres leaving only around 200 metres to reach the highest point. This route passes two other tors that are well worth photographing on your way up to the summit.

Viewpoint 1 – Rowtor

Even with its 468 metre elevation, Rowtor (SX592916) is only a ten minute walk from the parking area. Despite being the lowest of the local tors, the views from here are still incredible. To the north the rolling Devon farmland stretches as far as you can see, while in the other direction the view of windswept moorland makes a great contrast.

There are several smaller granite outcrops spread out around this area, all of which offer good potential for photographs. While the large bulky tors look more impressive, the smaller ones such as Rowtor often make the best photographs. Spend time walking around to find compositions; the spread-out nature of the rocks here makes it relatively simple to find subjects to place in the fore, mid and backgrounds.

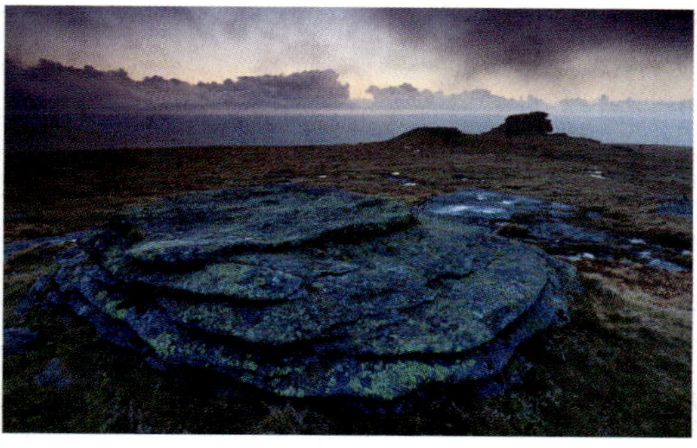

Viewpoint 2 – West Mill Tor

To reach West Mill Tor (SX 587 909) from Rowtor, follow the MOD track for another 20-30 minutes. The path climbs another 100 metres and is fairly steep in places but it's well worth it. West Mill Tor is arguably the most impressive tor in this area.

The tor is much larger than Rowtor with several distinctive peaks arranged in close proximity along a ridge running in a northerly direction. This makes it ideal to visit early morning or late evening when rich side lighting glows on the face of the rocks.

The tors here are easily climbed, each offering possibilities to shoot fresh angles from elevated viewpoints.

Viewpoint 3 – Yes Tor

A path leads down from West Mill Tor and then climbs up to the summit of Yes Tor (SX580901). Alternatively, retrace your steps back to the MOD track for the next 100 metre climb. You will see the impressive tor looming above you, but the track will at first appear to lead you away from it. Stay on the track, it soon bends back around and climbs up the hillside to almost reach Yes Tor before bending away again towards High Willhays.

You will feel a sense of achievement on reaching the top and immediately recognise why this area is known as the roof of Devon. The far reaching views down over Dartmoor and Devon's rolling countryside are truly spectacular.

On its eastern face the tor is a high wall of rock, which makes photographing difficult from this side. The higher west side is much more gentle, and you can easily climb onto the rocks to gain a superb vantage point over the moorland below. The best views are looking towards the moorland to the east and south.

There are a few unsightly objects which tend to get in the way of some shooting angles. The first is the large flagpole positioned on the main outcrop. There is also a small building and a trig point but with careful attention to composition all can be avoided easily enough.

Viewpoint 4 – High Willhays

High Willhays (SX580891) is just 5 minutes walk to the south of Yes Tor. The moorland here slopes far more gradually, so you don't have the impressive dramatic vistas that you see from Yes Tor. Also, and unusually for Dartmoor, there isn't a lot of granite here; just a couple of small outcrops, one featuring a stone cairn celebrating its status as the highest point.

Without nearby Yes Tor, it would barely merit a visit let alone a considered landscape photograph. However, after making the effort to reach Yes Tor, its worth the extra few minutes walk if only to say you've visited the highest point in Southern England.

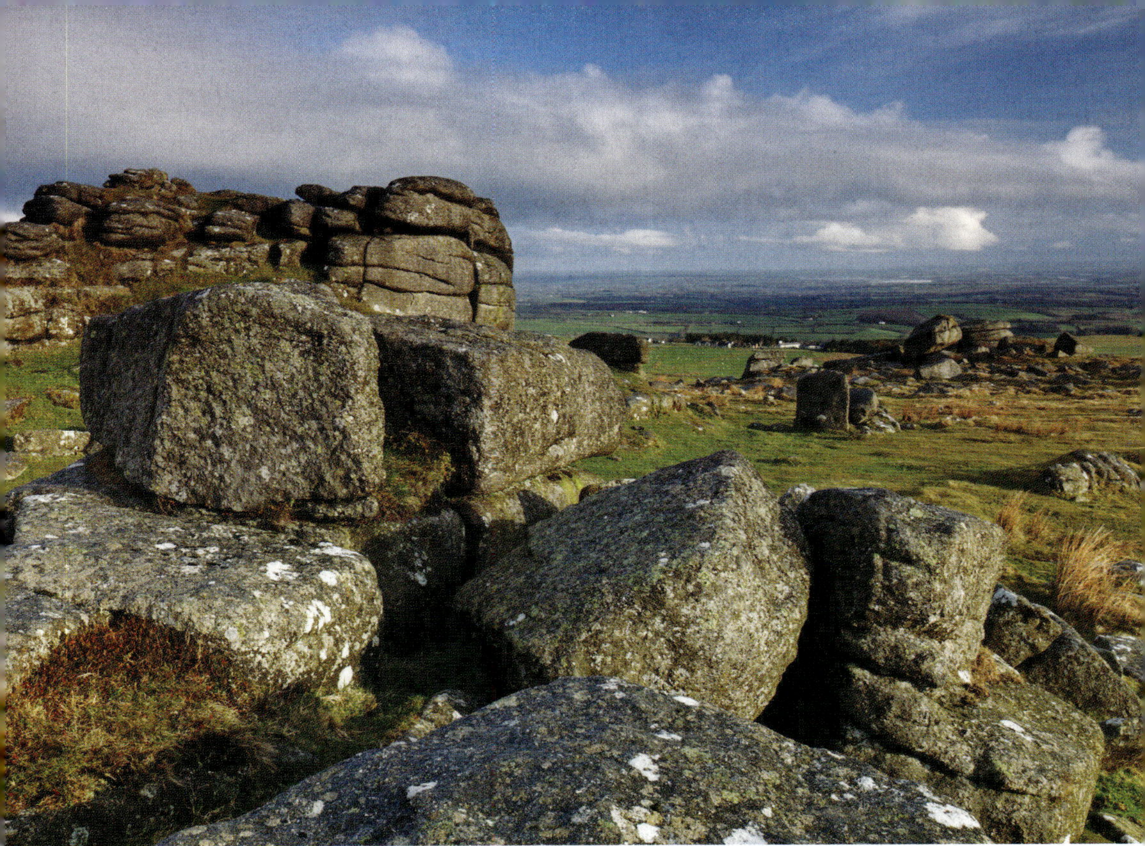

How to Get Here

These tors are near the northern edge of Dartmoor, about three miles from the town of Okehampton. Drive into Okehampton along Fore Street. At the traffic lights in the town centre, take the turning signposted in red 'Camp'. Head up this road and take the third right onto Station Road, again following the 'Camp' sign. Follow the road all the way up the hill and onto the moor. Stay on the road as you pass the camp, soon the road will swing around to the left and you will cross a cattle grid and a small bridge. Stay on this road for another half a mile and you will come across a large gravelled parking area on the right.

Parking Lat/Long: 50.713352, -3.9886068
Parking Grid Ref: SX 597 923
Parking Postcode: EX20 1QP (Okehampton Camp)
Map: OS Explorer Map OL28 (1:25 000) Dartmoor

Accessibility

A public road climbs up onto the moor and leads to Okehampton Army Camp. From here a private army road provides access further up onto the moor when the ranges are not in use. Just under a mile further along this road, a large gravelled parking area makes an ideal set off point.

It is a round trip of just over 4 miles on tracks and good footpaths from the parking area to High Willhays and back.

Firing Times

Access is allowed to this area when there is no firing. The firing programme for the following week is published in local newspapers, at Information Centres, is available on freephone 0800 4584868 and BBC Radio Devon broadcasts daily updates. Also Google 'Okehampton firing times' or visit www.dartmoor.gov.uk to find out when the area is open. Red flags will be flown from Yes Tor and nearby summits to indicate when live firing is taking place.

Best Time of Year/Day

The tors make great photographic subjects year round, so anytime of year can work well providing the Ranges are open. As each of these viewpoints is located at such a high elevation, there are few other landmasses around to restrict the sunlight, making these areas excellent for both sunrise and sunset photographs. However, it is worth checking the weather forecast carefully before your visit as on gloomy days this high part of Dartmoor can be lost in low cloud, particularly Yes Tor and High Willhays

Opposite: Twilight at High Willhays, south England's highest point, Canon 1Ds Mark III, 24-70mm at 24mm, ISO 100, 3.2 sec at f/16. April

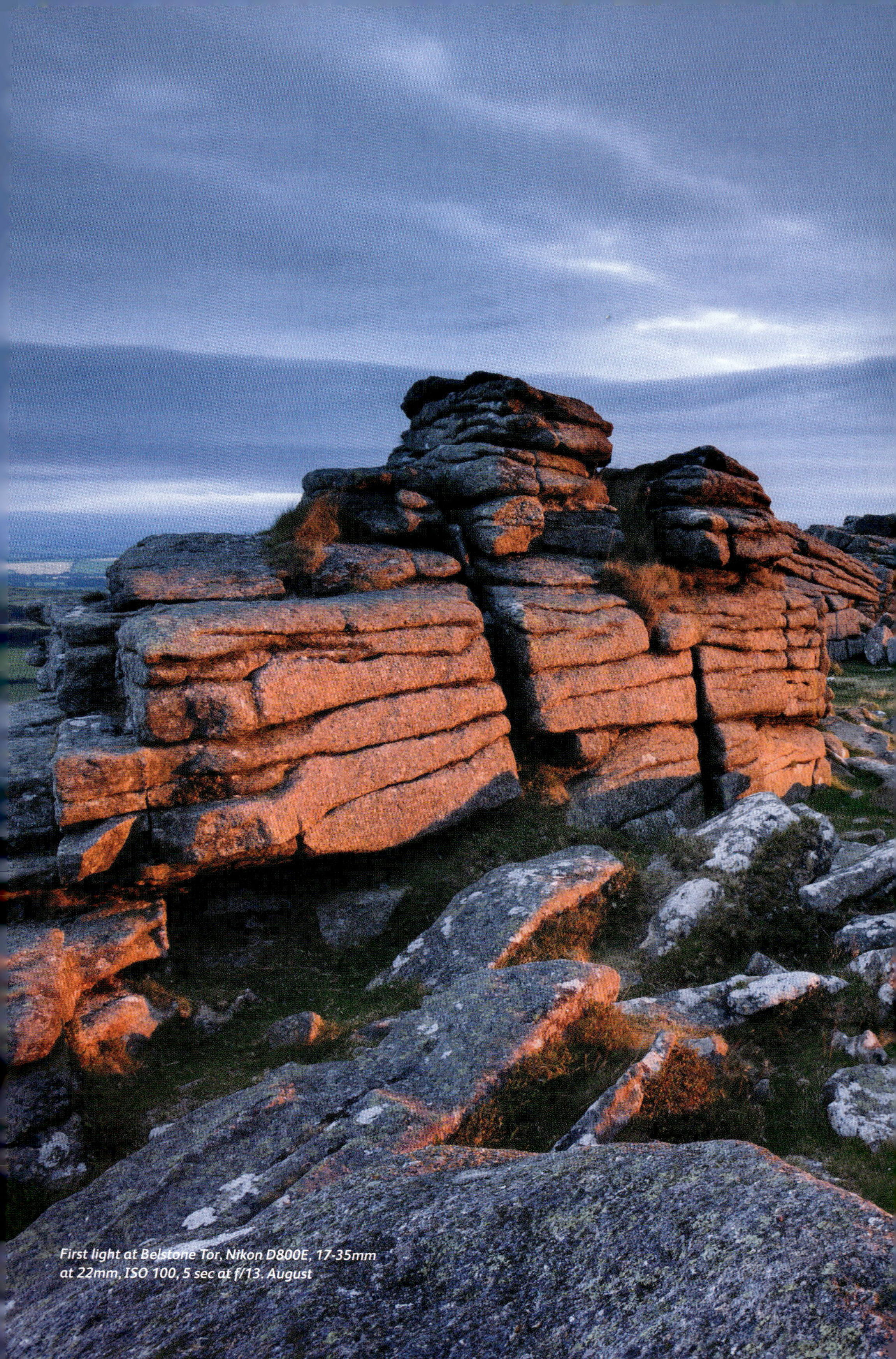

First light at Belstone Tor, Nikon D800E, 17-35mm at 22mm, ISO 100, 5 sec at f/13. August

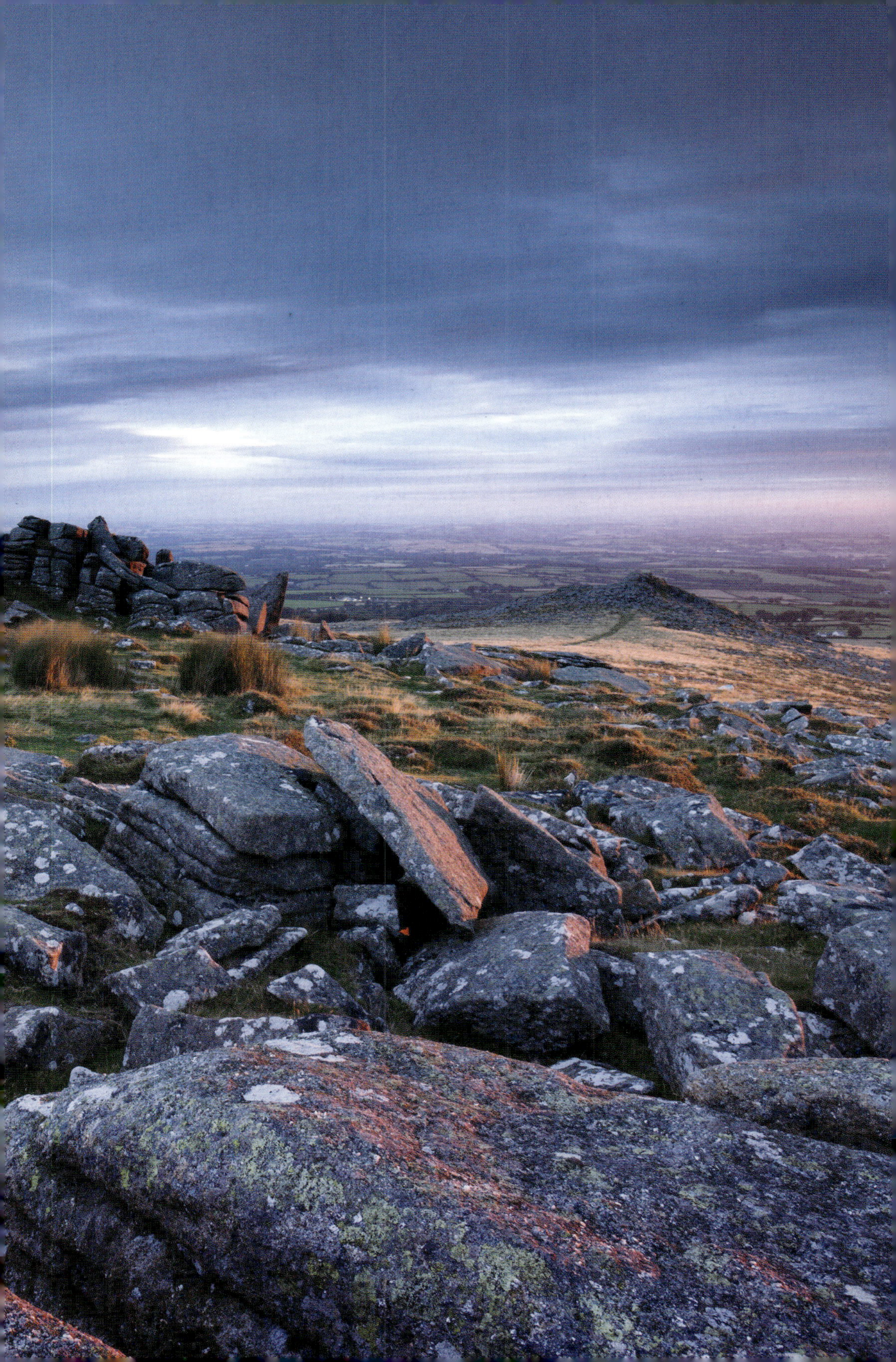

Belstone Common connects a series of rugged granite outcrops in the north of Dartmoor and offers an excellent starting point for exploring the northern moor. From the highest point there are spectacular views in all directions. Belstone makes an ideal location for those wishing to find an accessible tor in a less crowded area.

What to Shoot and Viewpoints

This is a two mile round trip if you visit all the viewpoints.

Viewpoint 1 – Ladybrook Tor

A mere ten minute walk from the parking area brings you to Ladybrook Tor. This first outcrop you reach has plenty of interest to photograph, but for only another 5 minutes walking uphill the rocks are far more interesting. A series of piled up granite rocks run from north to south along the ridge of the hill. The rocks here are generally more broken up than the lower area, offering countless opportunities for unique compositions. Possibly the best compositions will be looking northwards down the ridge and over the rolling Devon countryside.

Viewpoint 2 – Belstone Tor

Another five to ten minutes uphill leads you to the highest part of Belstone Common (SX 614 920) one mile from the car park. At the summit the ridge flattens onto a wide plateau comprised of both larger granite tors and scattered rocks, known as *clitter*. With so much rocky debris here there is a wealth of both foreground and mid-ground potential, while the background all around is a feast for the eyes. To the east neighbouring Cosdon Hill dominates the skyline; over this hill the sun rises throughout the year. To the north, the view down over Devon's patchwork countryside is even more impressive due to the extra elevation. The lower outcrop now gives a mini-mountain backdrop in front of the countryside beyond. To the west a dramatic view over moorland and rolling fields ends at Yes Tor and High Willhays.

Viewpoint 3 – Rabbit Rock and Irishman's Wall

Close to the summit of Belstone Tor stands a very photogenic granite outcrop unofficially known as Rabbit Rock. When photographed from the southern side the shape of the rabbit complete with ears can be seen quite clearly, at least by some.

Nearby, the tumbledown stone Irishman's Wall runs up and over the moor. The true history of this wall is now lost to legend, but one story tells of a group of Irish men who built the wall in an attempt to enclose some common land. The people of Belstone had other ideas and one night ventured onto the moor to knock the wall down.

Whatever the origins, the wall now provides a wonderful photographic subject offering a great lead-in line. When photographed from the north, it can be included in a composition together with Rabbit Rock.

Viewpoint 4 – Towards Higher Tor

A few metres walk south from Rabbit Rock, the plateau suddenly descends several metres in a vertical granite wall. This position provides an excellent viewpoint for shooting over the south into the heart of Dartmoor's moorland. The vista takes in Higher Tor in the mid distance, before stretching out over moorland towards Steeperton Tor and beyond. This vast area of wilderness forms part of the MOD's Okehampton Ranges, used as a firing range with restricted access.

Viewpoint 5 – The Nine Maidens

On the way back down from Belstone Tor, a five minute diversion brings you to the Nine Maidens, a small megalithic cairn circle. Smaller than stone circles, cairn circles such as this one were built in the Bronze Age to surround burial sites. In a wild moorland setting surrounded by dramatic peaks the Nine Maidens provides an extremely photogenic subject.

Opposite: Early morning light bathes the tor in golden tones, Canon 1Ds Mark III, 16-35mm at 16mm, ISO 100, 1 sec at f/16. December

A light dusting of snow on the Nine Maidens cairn circle, Nikon D800E, 17-35mm at 28mm, ISO 100, 1/15 sec at f/11. February

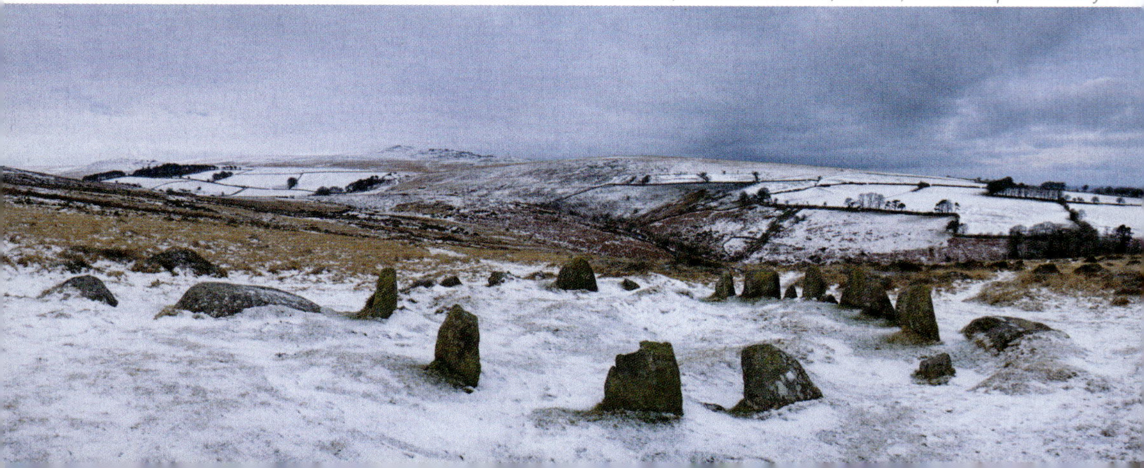

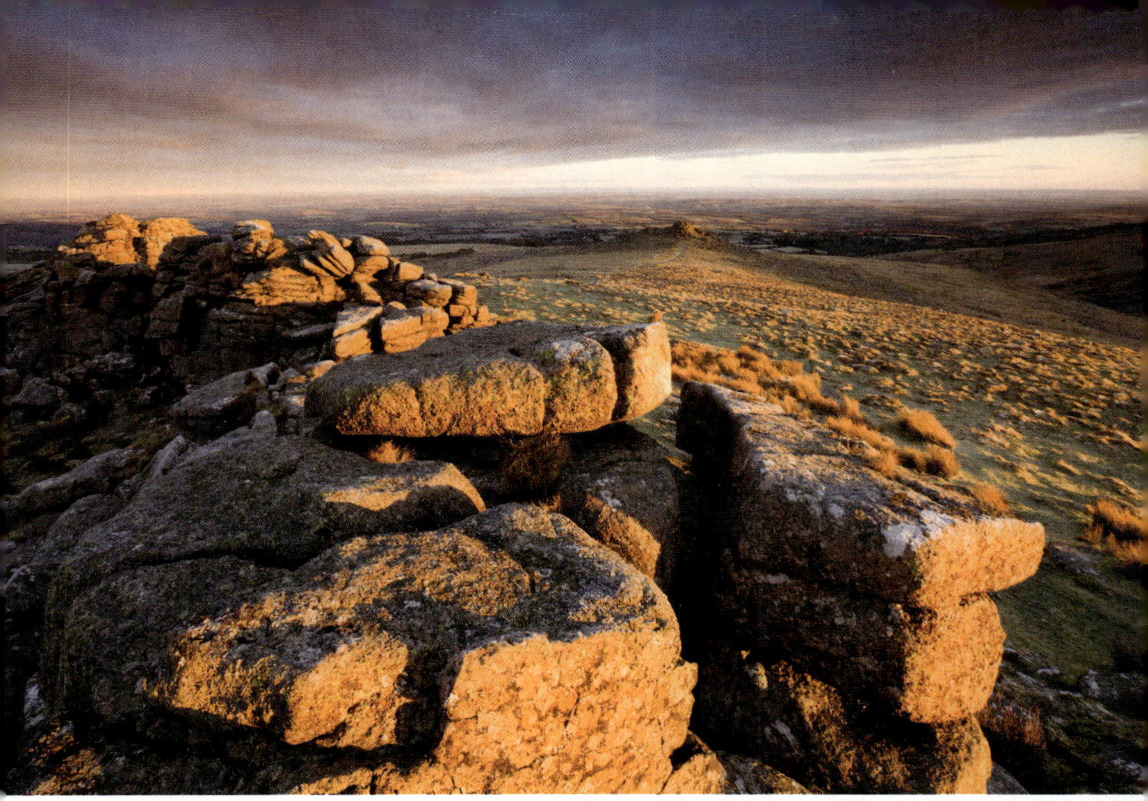

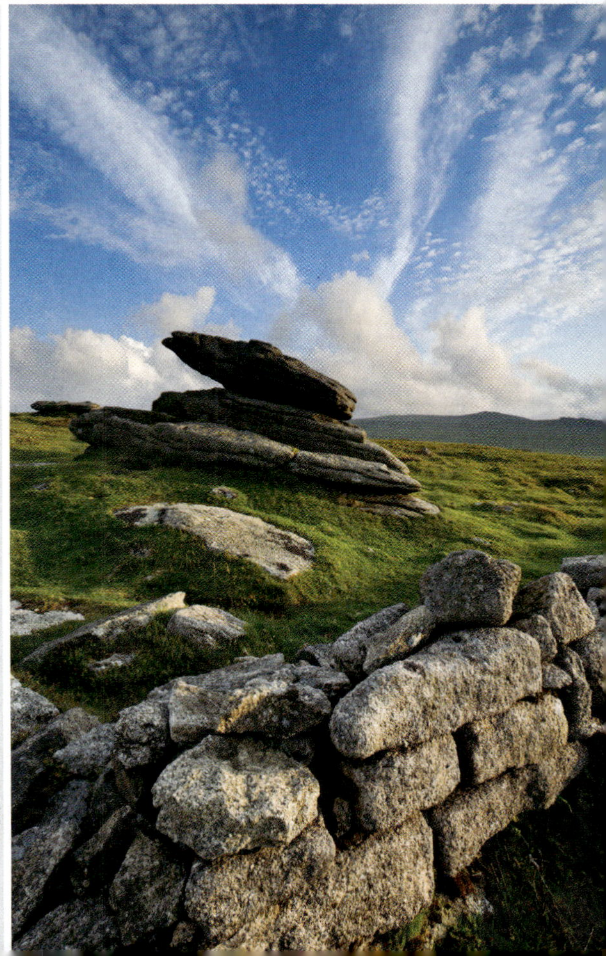

How to Get Here

From Exeter head west on the A30 towards Cornwall. After 20 miles you will see a Services sign, plus an exit for Belstone. Take this junction and then turn left past the services and take the first right signposted Belstone. Continue through the village passing the standing stone on your left. After several hundred yards you will find a small parking area opposite a South West Water building.

Parking Lat/Long:50.721628, -3.9571787
Parking Grid Ref: SX 617 934
Parking Postcode: EX20 1QZ (Belstone village)
Map: OS Explorer Map OL28 (1:25 000) Dartmoor

Accessibility

From the car park, the walk to the summit of Belstone Tor gains about 120m in elevation and typically would take between 20-30 minutes. The first section of the walk has a very gentle incline, followed by a fairly steep ascent as you climb onto the tor. As the walk is over open moorland there aren't predefined footpaths as such, but the route up onto the tor is very obvious. The ground is very rocky throughout and boggy in places, so good walking boots are recommended. Not suitable for wheelchairs.

Best Time of Year/Day

Due to its high elevation and geology Belstone Common is a perfect photographic viewpoint at all times of the day. However, for the best light plan to visit at either sunrise and sunset. In summer, the moorland is covered with verdant bracken; this turns to beautiful brown tones in autumn and winter. Due to its high elevation and relatively easy access, Belstone Common can be a great place to photograph winter snow.

Right: Rabbit Rock and Irishman's Wall, Nikon D800E, 14-24mm at 18mm, ISO 100, 1/10 sec at f/10. June

Fingle Bridge

Set deep at the base of the steep-sided Teign Gorge, Fingle Bridge is one of Dartmoor's most popular beauty spots. Originally used by packhorses carrying corn and wood over the River Teign, the narrow bridge now provides access to a National Trust car park for any drivers brave enough to cross in their vehicles.

Surrounded by deciduous woodland, the 17th century stone bridge makes a lovely photograph in its own right, but the River Teign is the real star of the show. One of Dartmoor's larger rivers, the Teign offers countless photographic opportunities as it meanders beneath the canopy of trees.

What to Shoot and Viewpoints

Upstream

With footpaths either side of the river, there are a whole host of viewpoints from which to capture individual river pictures. One of the best viewpoints can be reached by crossing Fingle Bridge and following the riverside footpath upstream. After only five minutes walk, a treeless stretch of river bank provides an open view of the river flanked by woodland. The river here is wide, deep and sheltered, making this an excellent place to capture reflections of the trees in the slow moving water.

Further upstream the Teign turns into a more typical Dartmoor river, wide and shallow with fast flowing white water surging past scattered boulders. These moss covered boulders make wonderful foreground objects for photographs, especially during autumn when adorned with colourful fallen leaves. A pair of wellies will enable you to wade out into the river to get nice and close to the most attractive boulders.

From Higher

As well as following the riverbank the footpaths sometimes climb high into the woods. You can use these opportunities to shoot trees and woodland scenes from elevated viewpoints, reducing the chances of any ugly white patches of sky creeping into photographs.

A mile or so further upstream will bring you to a wooden footbridge. You can cross the river here and wander back to Fingle Bridge on the opposite bank. Alternatively, after crossing the bridge take the footpath directly ahead to climb up to the top of the gorge. This higher footpath, running just below the impressive Castle Drogo, also returns to Fingle Bridge but offers some very different scenery to shoot. From this high elevation, far reaching views open up over the wooded gorge, then across gorgeous rolling Dartmoor countryside towards the distant moor. This area can make for a fantastic photographic viewpoint on misty mornings.

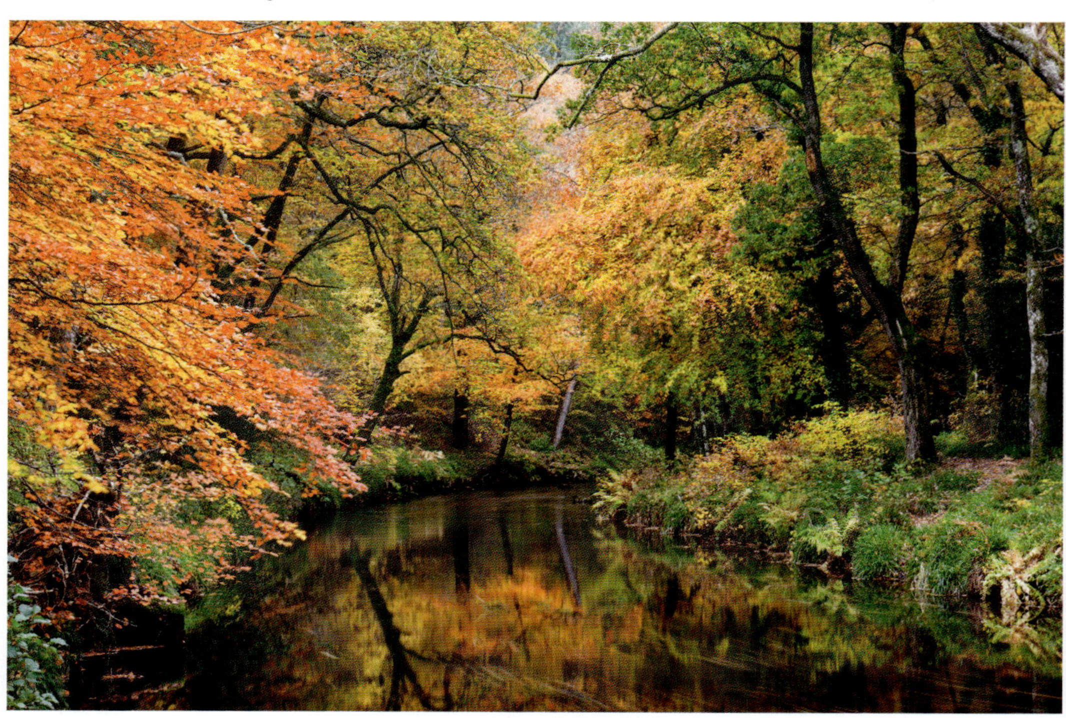

Autumnal foliage above the banks of the River Teign. Canon 1Ds Mark III, 24-70mm at 70mm, ISO 100, 5 sec at f/16. November

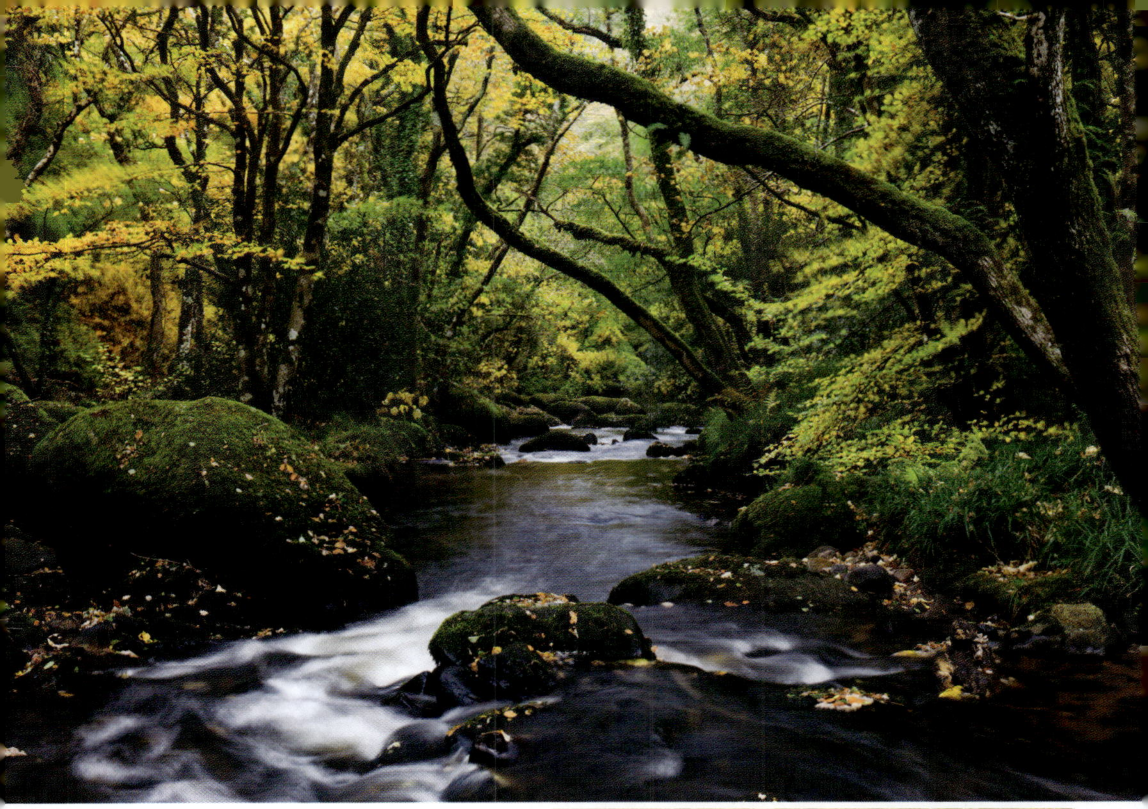

How to Get Here

Heading westwards from Exeter, take the Whiddon Down exit off the A30, and turn left at the first roundabout, signposted Moretonhampstead. After a few hundred yards take the left turning signposted Drewsteignton. Follow this country lane for nearly four miles, then when you arrive at Drewsteignton, instead of following the road left into the village go straight ahead. A sign for Fingle Bridge guides you down a steep narrow lane for approximately half a mile until you reach the bridge.

Parking Lat/Long: 50.695628, -3.7804576
Parking Grid Ref: SX 744 898
Parking Postcode: EX6 6PW
Map: OS Explorer Map OL28 (1:25 000) Dartmoor

Accessibility

The footpaths are very well maintained but uneven underfoot so good walking boots are recommended. The paths do have some fairly steep uphill sections especially on the north bank.

Best Time of Year/Day

As with most woodlands, the best time to visit this area is autumn. Timed right, a late autumn visit to Fingle Bridge will reward you with some of the finest autumnal colours to be found anywhere in Dartmoor. Wet overcast days are ideal as the light is even and rain can help to saturate the foliage, giving you vibrant pictures.

Late spring and early summer are also wonderful times to visit when trees are verdant with lime green leaves, while the river banks burst to life with wildflowers and ferns.

Top: A small section of the River Teign above Fingle Bridge, Canon 1Ds Mark III, 24-70mm at 40mm, ISO 100, 2 sec at f/16. October

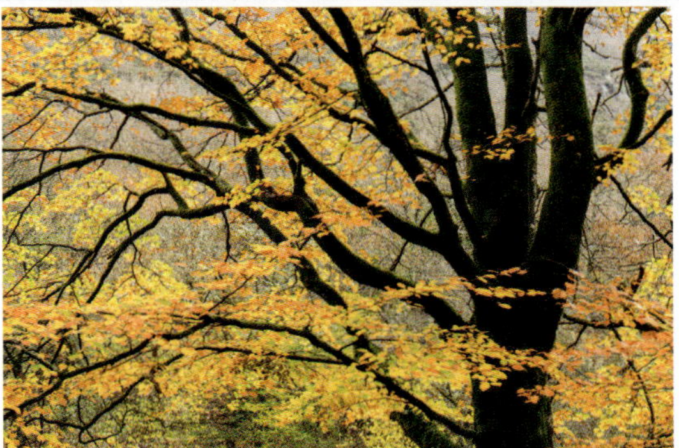

Moss covered beech tree with autumnal gold foliage, Nikon D800E, 24-70mm at 48mm, ISO 200, 1.3 sec at f/13. November

Fingle Bridge Inn beyond the ancient stone bridge, Nikon D800E, 24-70mm at 48mm, ISO 50, 1 sec at f/11. October

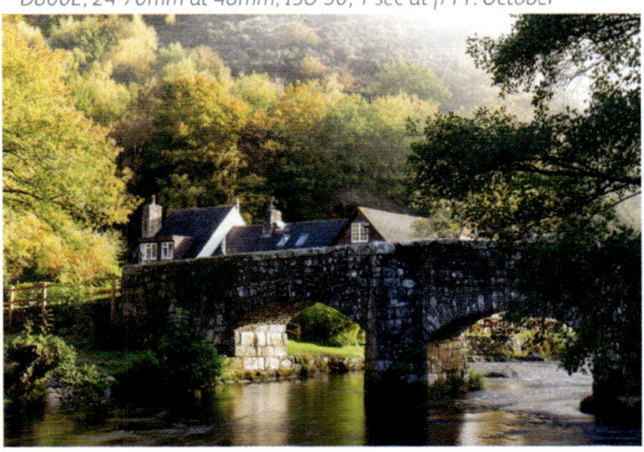

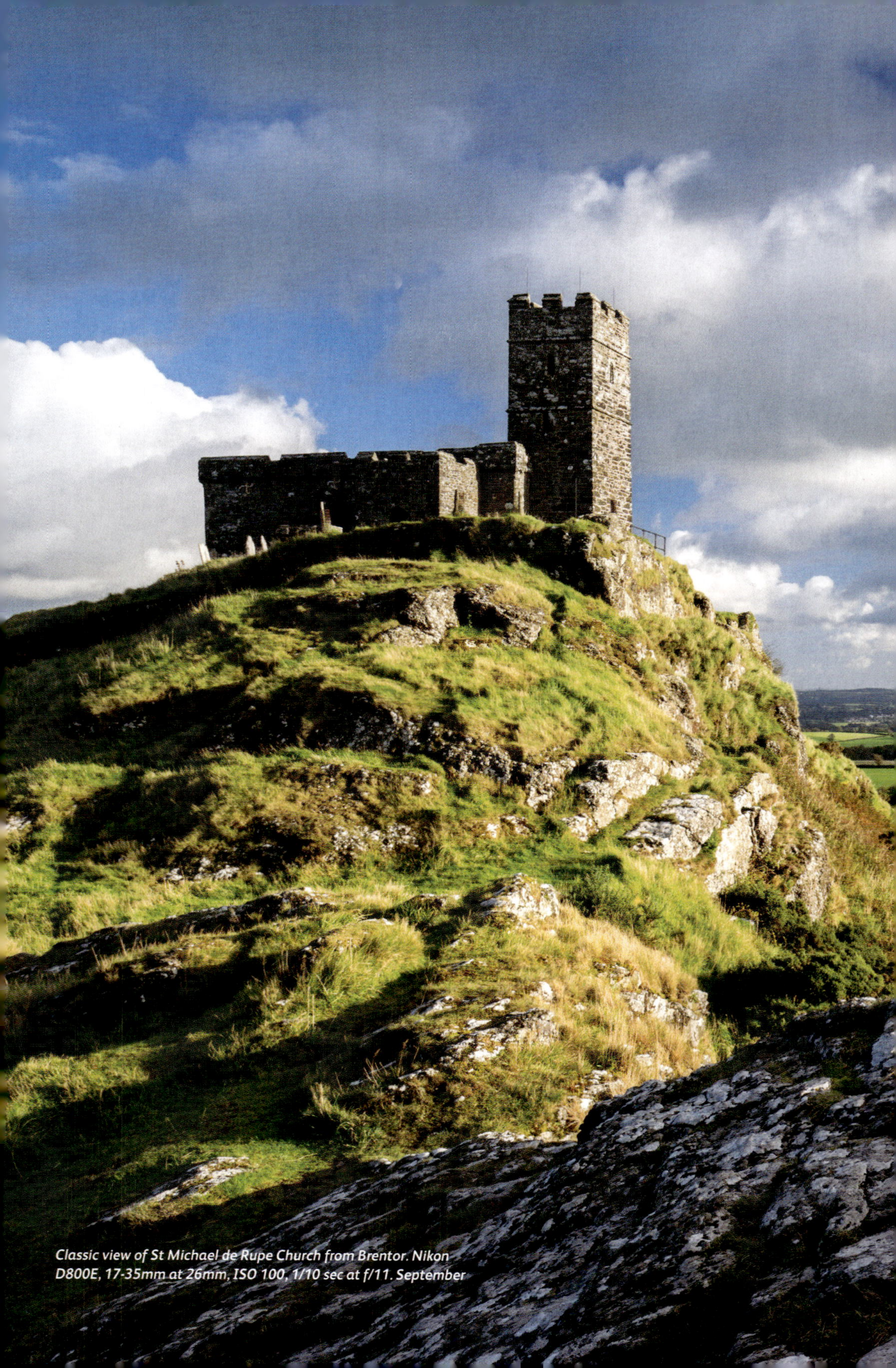

Classic view of St Michael de Rupe Church from Brentor. Nikon D800E, 17-35mm at 26mm, ISO 100, 1/10 sec at f/11. September

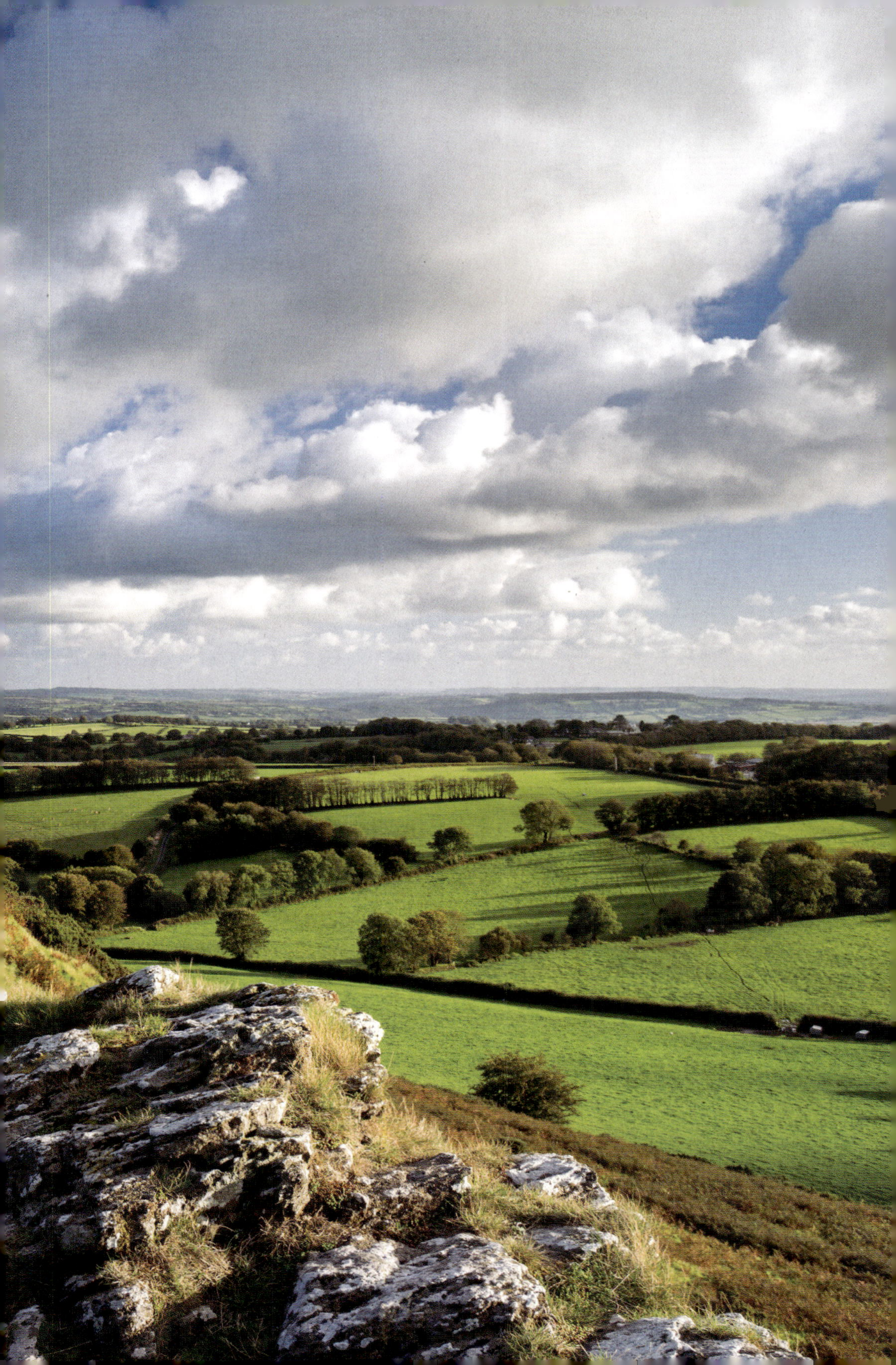

Surrounded by gentle rolling countryside on the western fringes of Dartmoor, Brent Tor is a striking landmark visible from many miles all around. The tor sits on top of the remains of an ancient weathered volcano. Perched on top since the 13th century is the tiny church of St Michael de Rupe which is still used for special services by parishioners of the village of Brentor.

Many local legends are associated with how the church came to be built upon Brent Tor. One tells of a local wealthy merchant whose ship was caught at sea during a terrible storm. Fearing death was upon him, the merchant vowed that were he to be saved he would build a church on the highest land he saw. So, true to his word, the merchant started to build the church but on hearing this news the devil had other ideas and each night would climb Brent Tor and break up all the building work. This continued for many days until St Michael himself confronted the Devil and chased him away from Brent Tor for good.

From a photographic perspective Brent Tor is an un-missable stop off on any trip to Dartmoor.

What to Shoot and Viewpoints

Viewpoint 1 – Views from the Tor

From the car park, cross over the road and pass through a stile. Follow a winding grass path up the side of Brent Tor, in approximately 15 minutes you will reach the church.

A short steep climb up Brent Tor rewards you with breathtaking 360 degree views of the surrounding countryside. With good light you can point the camera in any direction and capture a beautiful picture. Patchwork green fields surround the tor on all sides and stretch off in every direction, so your choice of subject really depends on the position of the sun. The view north east is particularly pleasing, encompassing the village of Brentor with a rolling moorland backdrop complete with distant tors cresting the horizon.

Some of the finest pastoral countryside can be photographed roughly to the north. Late in the day, this view is accentuated by low sunshine and long shadows stretching over the farmland.

Remember to bring a telephoto for these rolling countryside shots. A long focal length has the effect of compressing all the elements in the picture, like stacking the fields on top of each other in a series of layers.

Viewpoint 2 – St Michael de Rupe Church

Despite all the lovely countryside surrounding the tor, most photographers climbing Brent Tor do so with the aim of photographing the little church. When standing on the tor the church can be photographed from both its north and south side. From the south, a wide angle lens will allow you to include all the church in a composition, but from this side the building does appear somewhat blocky and slightly too dominant in the frame. It is also difficult to appreciate the church's lofty position.

Fortunately a second slightly lower outcrop on a ridge to the north provides the perfect position to photograph the church in its magnificent setting. From this viewpoint the church perches beautifully on the crest of the tor, surrounded by far reaching views to Devon's lush patchwork farmland. The exposed rocks all along this ridge are coated with lichen and make an intriguing foreground to wide angle compositions. By positioning your camera close to the edge of the ridge the steep sided slope of the tor is revealed as is the rolling fields below, further emphasising the elevated position of the church.

All you need now is to wait for some sunlight to give the scene some magic. When late afternoon/evening sunlight glows on the side of both the tor and church, there simply isn't a better location in Dartmoor to be standing.

How to Get Here

Exit the A30 at Sourton Down and take the A386 south towards Tavistock. After approximately four miles turn left towards Lydford. Drive through the village and follow the road for another five miles towards Brentor. Before long Brent Tor will be visible in the distance, when you reach the tor take a right turn and park in the car park on the left.

Parking Lat/Long: 50.604405, -4.1655993
Parking Grid Ref: SX 469 805
Parking Postcode: PL19 0NF
Map: OS Explorer Map 108 (1:25 000) Lower Tamar Valley & Plymouth

Accessibility

There is a good path from the car park up to the tor and church. This location is suitable for wheelchair users, but does have an incline up grass to the church.

Best Time of Year/Day

The views of, and from the church can be photographed at any time of year. Evening light is always best for shooting the church from the lower outcrop, and is also an ideal time to shoot the rolling countryside. Alternatively try heading up to Brent Tor at dawn on a misty morning to shoot low lying mist hanging over the rolling fields.

Opposite: Rainbow descending into church tower, Canon 1Ds Mark III, 24-70mm at 30mm, ISO 100, 1 sec at f/16. April

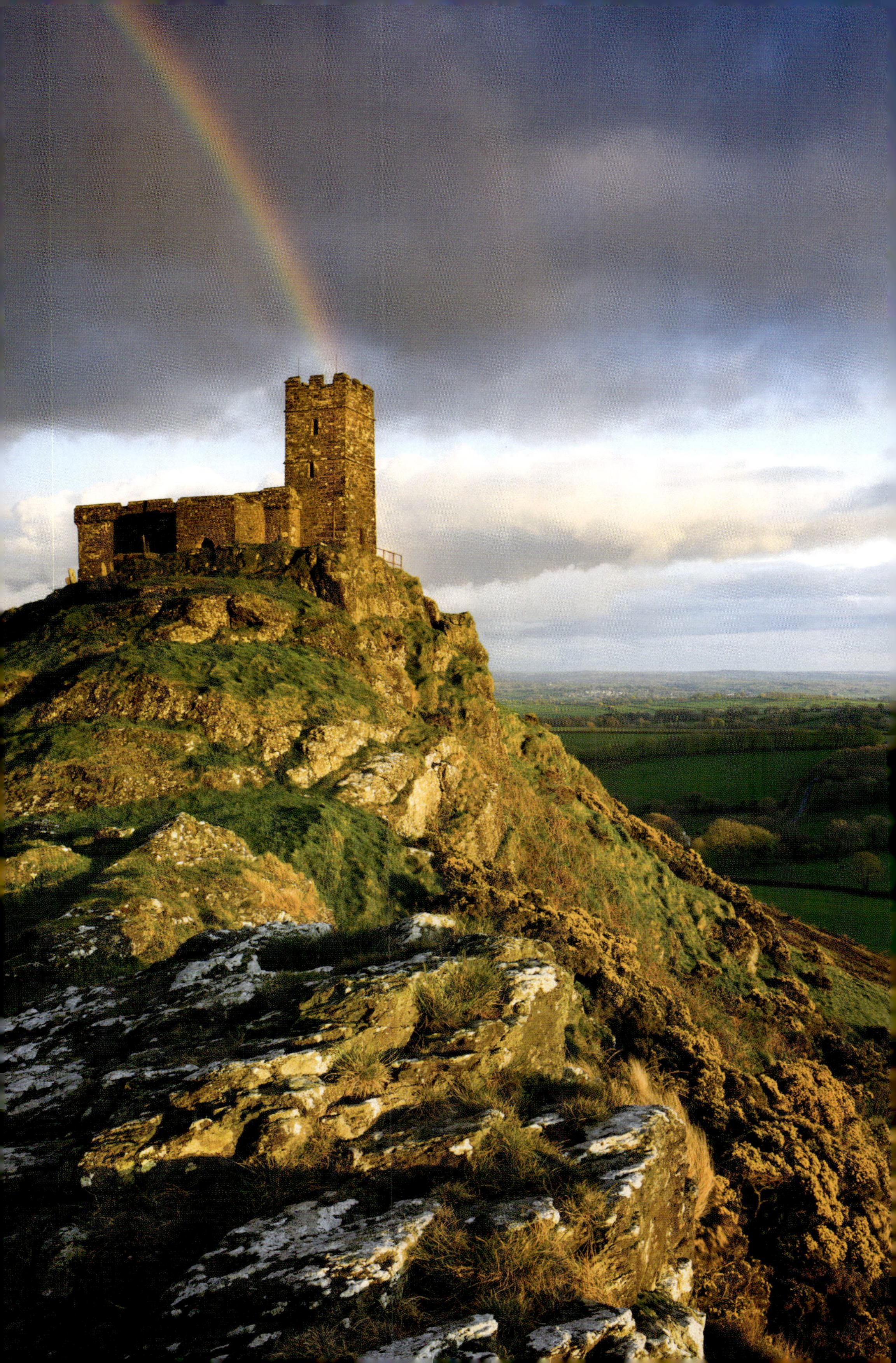

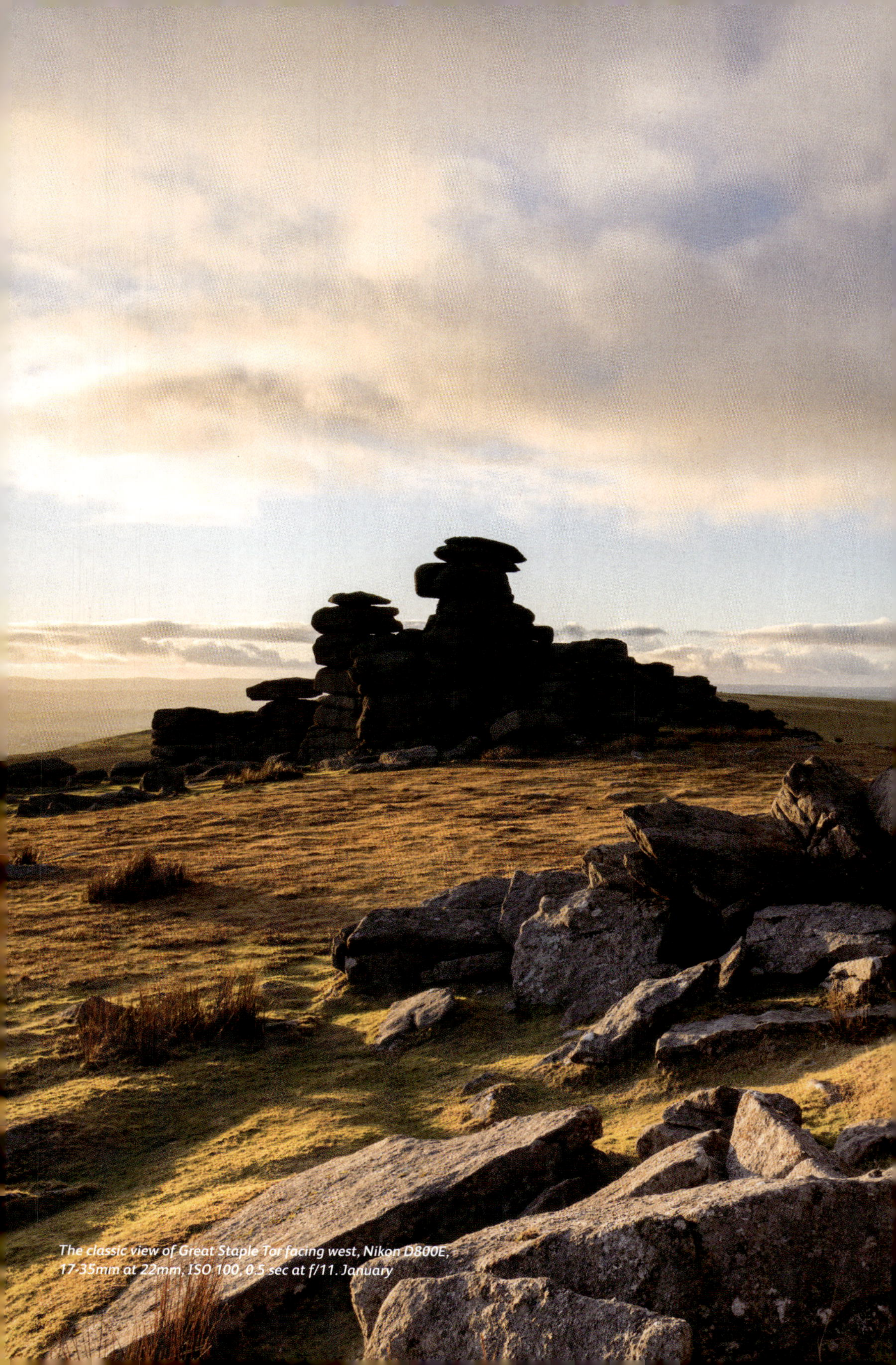

The classic view of Great Staple Tor facing west, Nikon D800E,
17-35mm at 22mm, ISO 100, 0.5 sec at f/11. January

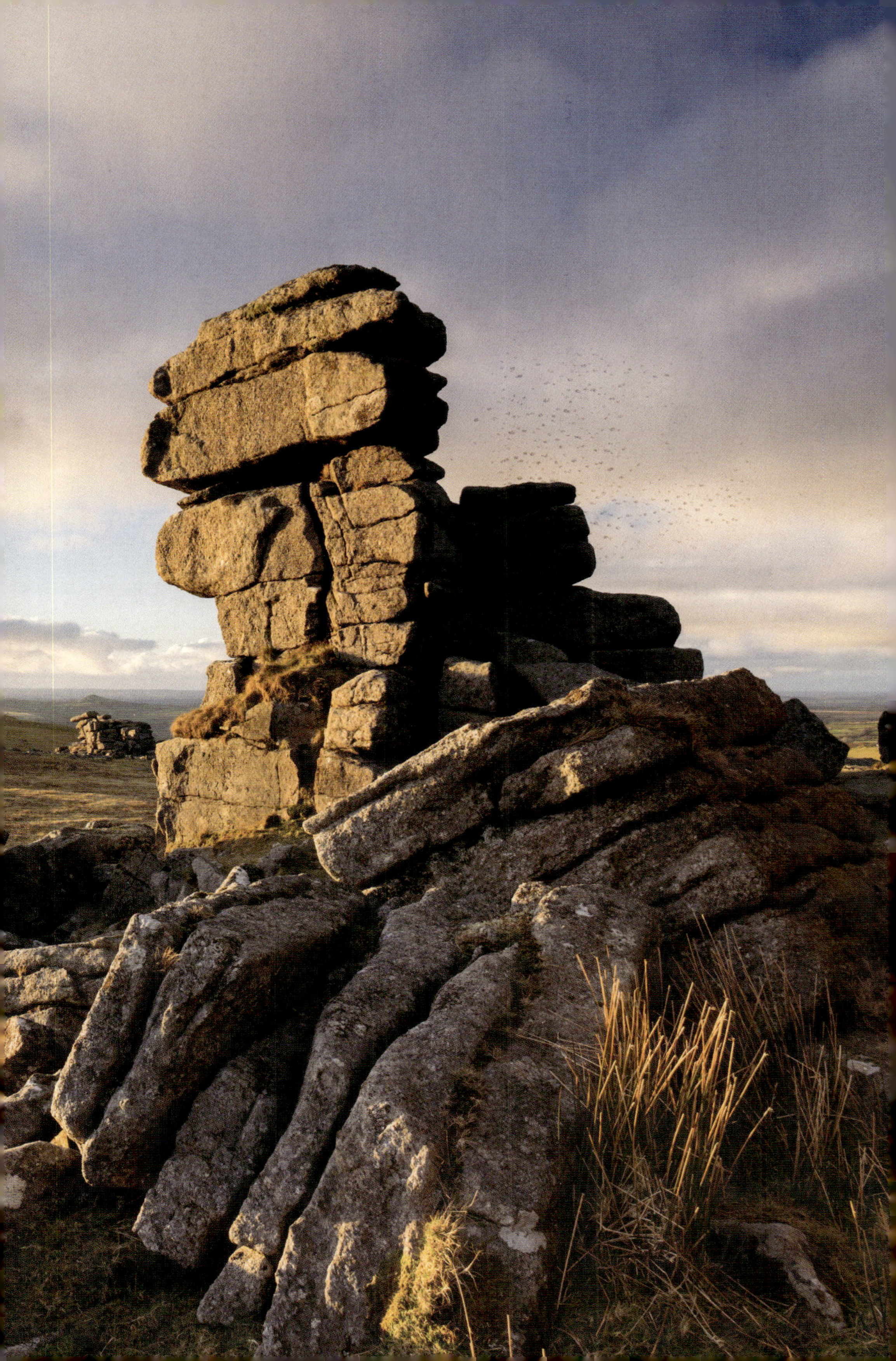

Of all Dartmoor's many granite outcrops, Great Staple Tor is arguably the most photogenic. Its distinctive stacks are instantly recognisable and make dramatic photographic subjects, drawing photographers from far and wide to capture their windswept beauty.

What to Shoot and Viewpoints

Viewpoint 1 – Classic View 1

From either car park on the B3357 take paths north of the road onto the moor toward the tors.

On the way up to Great Staple Tor (SX542760) you will pass both Little and Middle Staple Tors (SX540756), the latter of which is worth an exploration in its own right. But don't spend too long here, the main tor unquestionably is the highlight and is only another five minutes wander uphill. When you reach Great Staple Tor (455m/1492ft), you will notice two tors with a wide flat area of moorland in between. Head to the tor on the right with the large pillar, and look back in the direction of the other tor. This is the classic viewpoint that so many photographers aspire to shoot, and for very good reason. The subject matter and composition work together in a way that is as good as anything you will find over the whole moor.

The keener eyed will spot Brentor Church on the horizon; with a long enough telephoto this can make a great shot in its own right, however the lure of the foreground rocks is difficult to avoid.

Viewpoint 2 – Classic View 2

Another, equally impressive photograph of Great Staple Tor's distinctive stacks can be achieved by simply walking over to the other tor and shooting back towards the first. Walk behind the two largest stacks and climb up onto the tor, then shoot back towards the first pillar, so that all three feature prominently in your composition. The weathered rocks piled on top of each other stand out perfectly, especially when late evening sunshine glows against the granite.

Viewpoint 3 – Towards Great Mis Tor

As the stacks of Great Staple Tor make such wonderful subjects for photographs, you could be forgiven for thinking that they should be included in any composition from this location. However, this area is so rich in photographic potential that time should be spent to fully appreciate what is on offer. One such area to explore is the tor just behind the first pillar. The expansive rocky terrain offers many interesting rock formations to utilise in wide-angle pictures, from layered bulky granite to scattered broken rocks. On the horizon to the north west Great Mis Tor makes a recognisable background subject to complete a wild and remote moorland scene.

How to Get Here

From Tavistock head up onto the moor on the B3357 heading towards Two Bridges. As the road climbs onto the moor you will pass a cattle grid and a large car park on the right. You can either park here, or continue a hundred yards or so and find a smaller car park on the left hand side.

Parking Lat/Long: 50.557327, -4.0523132
Parking Grid Ref: SX 533 752
Parking Postcode: PL20 6ST (Merrivale)
Map: OS Explorer Map OL28 (1:25 000) Dartmoor

Accessibility

The route up from the smaller car park is a 3/4 mile, 20 minute uphill walk, gaining around 120 metres in elevation. A path leads from either car park and heads in the direction of Great Staple Tor. Although the path continually climbs, it is a relatively easy walk over moorland. There will be some clambering over rocks, so like most moorland locations good walking boots are recommended. This location is not accessible for wheelchair users.

Best Time of Year/Day

Winter is an excellent time to visit Great Staple Tor. On a winter afternoon the setting sun will cast beautiful side lighting on the stacks when shooting the main classic viewpoint. A colourful sunrise at any time of year can make a beautiful background to the silhouetted stacks when shooting from the second classic viewpoint. With so much interest to shoot, Great Staple Tor is worthwhile visiting throughout the seasons.

Frost covered granite slabs at dawn, Nikon D800E, 17-35mm at 24mm, ISO 100, 6 sec at f/11. December

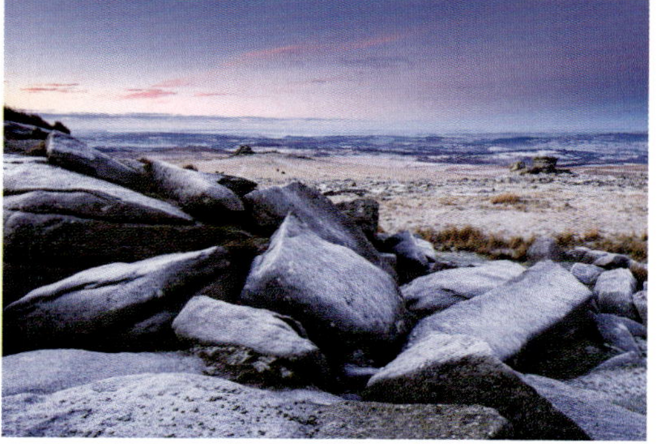

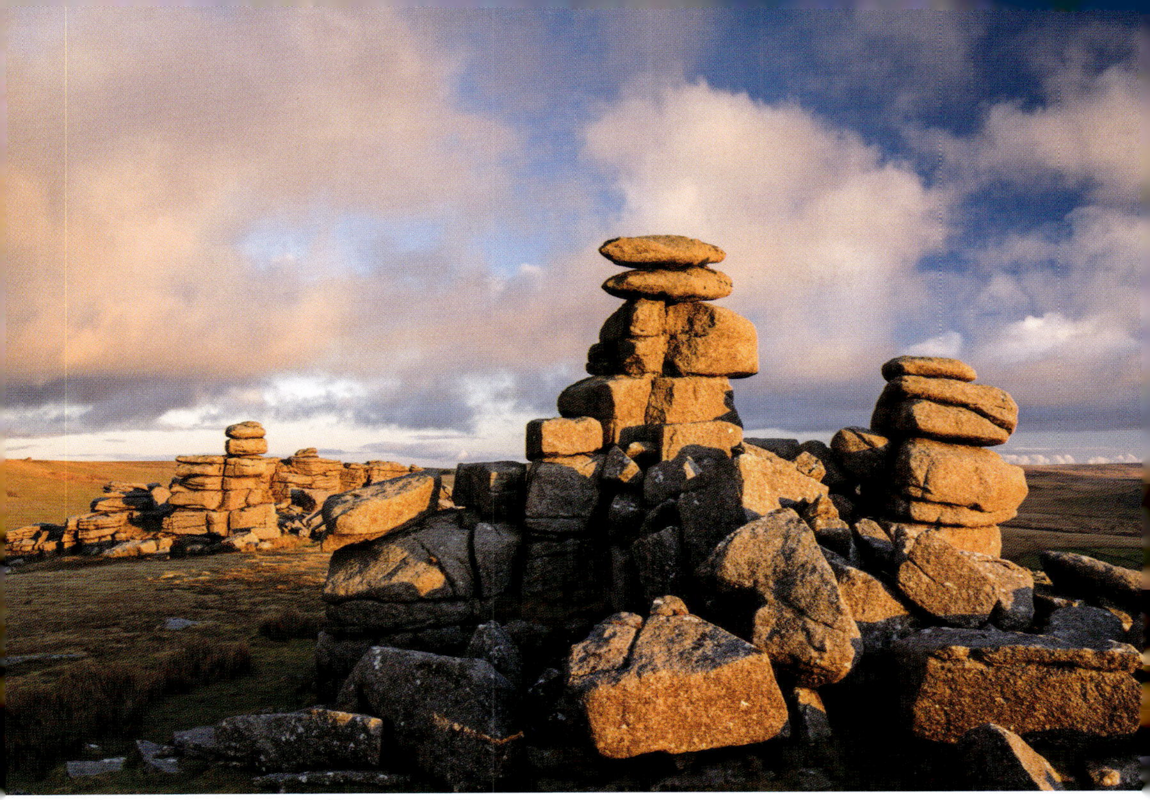

Above: The second classic viewpoint looking eastwards, Nikon D800E, 17-35mm at 26mm, ISO 100, 0.8 sec at f/11. January

Snow covered moorland at dawn, Nikon D800E, 17-35mm at 35mm, ISO 100, 1/5 sec at f/13. January

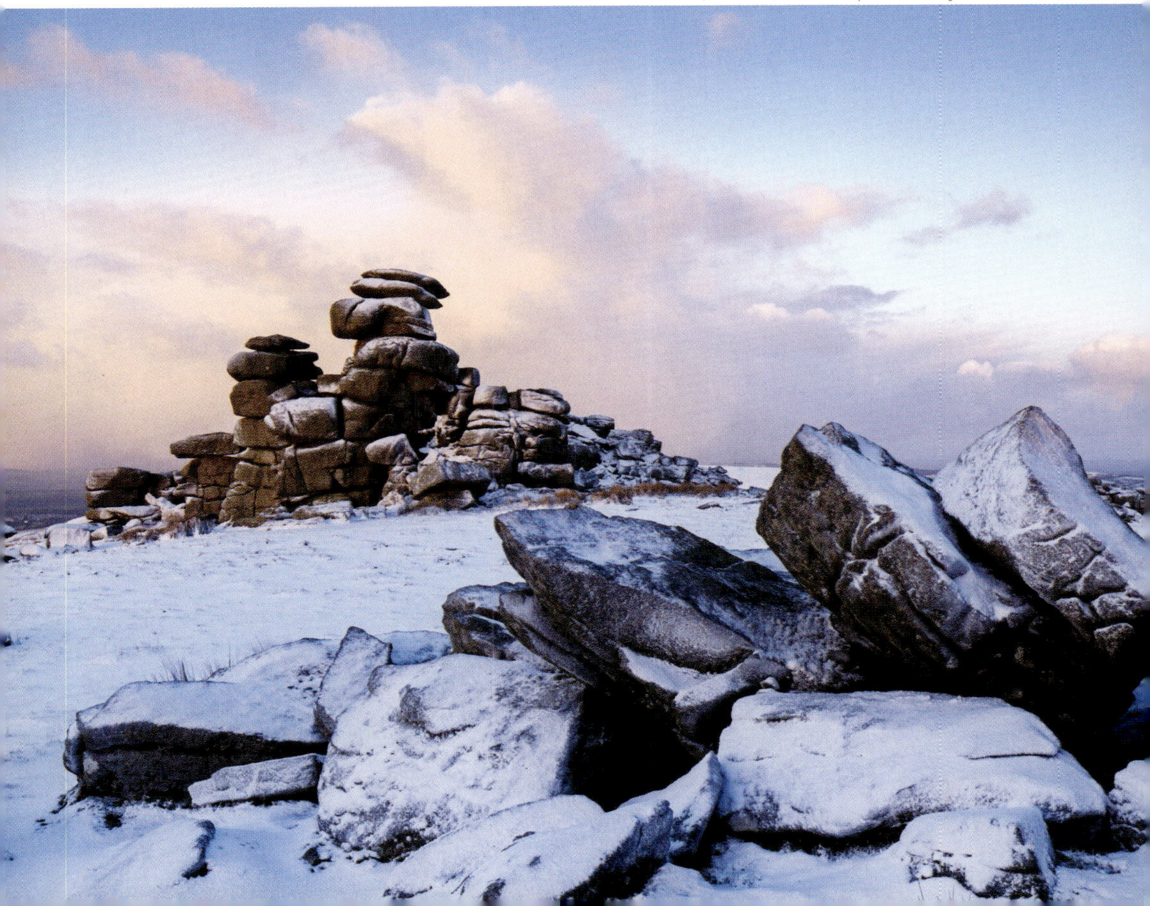

Although most of Dartmoor is made up of windswept inhospitable moorland, it is surprisingly rich in the remnants of megalithic human occupation. The National Park contains the largest concentration of Bronze Age remains in the country. A brief scan of an Ordnance Survey map will reveal a wealth of artefacts all over the moor, from standing stones, stone circles, hut circles and stone rows.

One of the most well known areas to view and photograph these ancient relics is Long Ash Hill near the hamlet of Merrivale. Although there are larger and more impressive megalithic areas to visit on Dartmoor, Merrivale is one of the most accessible, lying close to the B3357 main road.

What to Shoot and Viewpoints

A brief 5-10 minute walk up onto the moor from the car park will bring you to Merrivale's prehistoric site. There is an abundance of ancient remains spread over the moor comprising burial cairns, a stone circle and a particularly impressive menhir (tall standing stone), but the three stone rows command the most attention.

The head of the main stone row, facing west, Canon 1Ds Mark III, 17-40mm at 30mm, ISO 100, 0.7 sec at f/16. October

How to Get Here

To reach Merrivale Stone Rows by car, head east on the B3357 from Tavistock for four miles. After passing through the hamlet of Merrivale the road begins to climb a hill; park in the rough car park on the right.

Parking Lat/Long: 50.557327, -4.0523132
Parking Grid Ref: SX 553 750
Parking Postcode: PL20 6ST (Merrivale)
Map: OS Explorer Map OL28 (1:25 000) Dartmoor

Accessibility

Despite being quite close to the car park, as the site is located on the moor Merrivale is not suitable for wheelchair users.

Best Time of Year/Day

The stone rows can be photographed equally well throughout the seasons. As they point towards the west, the rows make ideal subjects for sunset shots, backed by colourful cloud filled skies or visit early when low sunlight glows warmly over the landscape. At these times, golden light illuminates the stones and clearly defines them from the surrounding moorland, while long deep shadows stretching across the grass accentuates their size and stature.

Opposite top: Isolating a smaller section of a Merrivale stone row, Nikon D800E, 24-70mm at 48mm, ISO 100, 0.4 sec at f/14. July

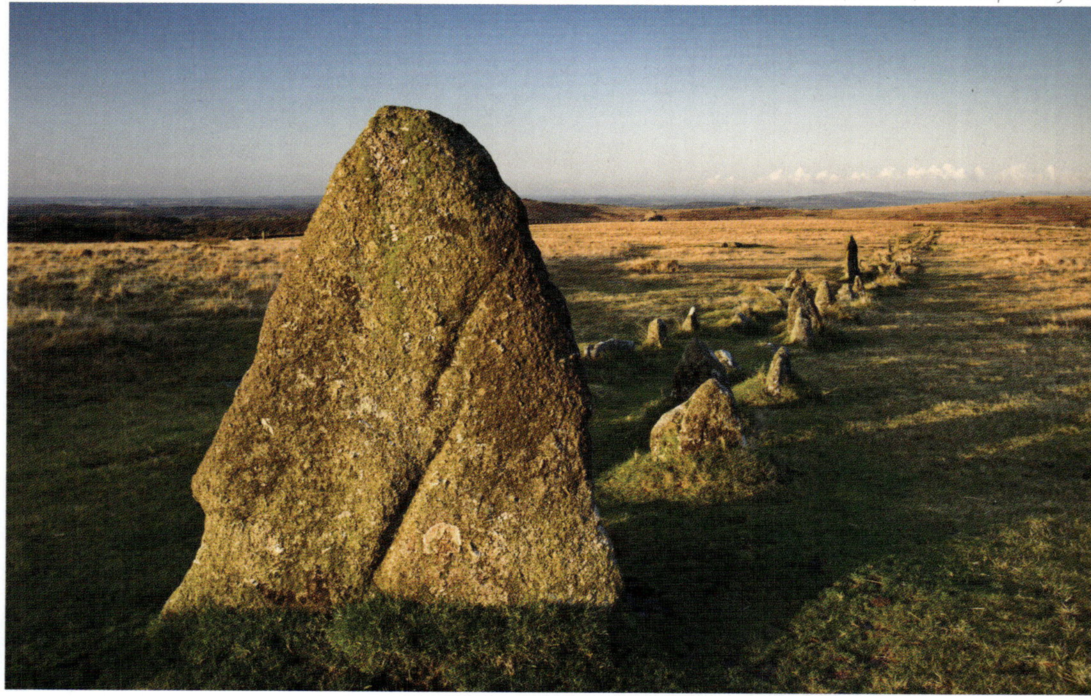

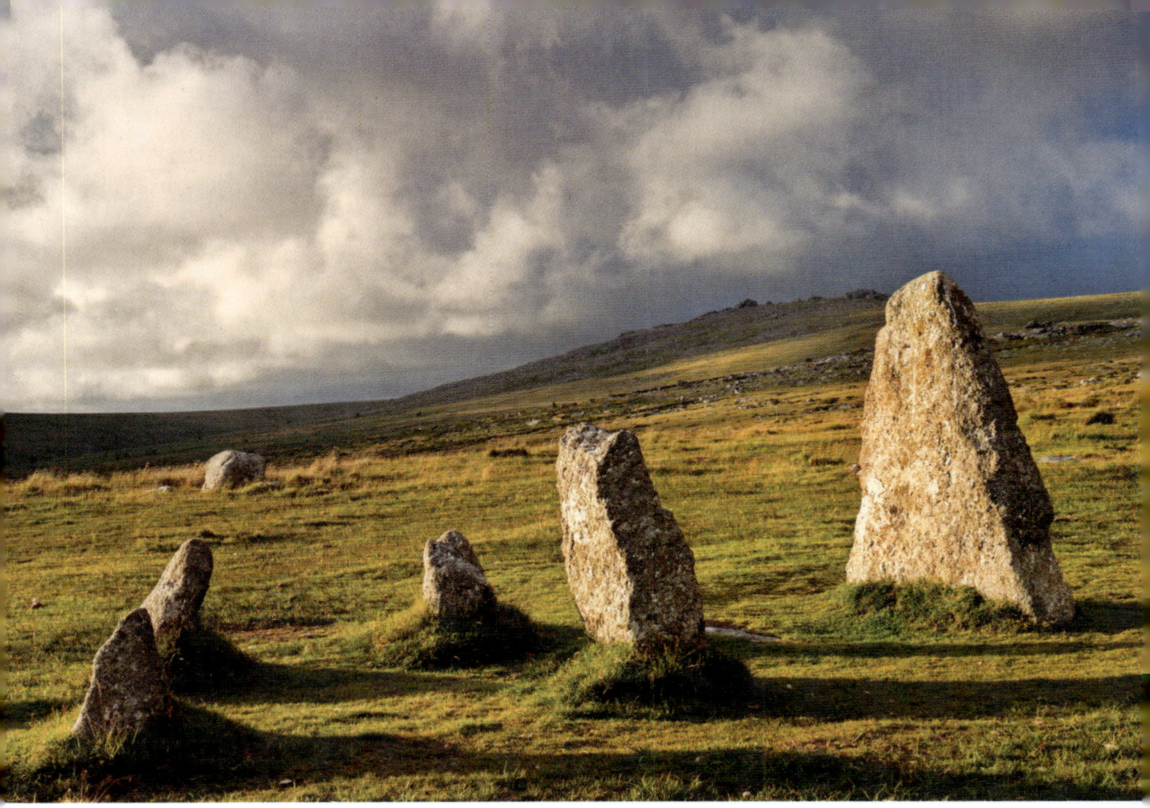

Rows of Standing Stones

Of the three rows, most attention is drawn to two double rows of standing stones running parallel in a westerly direction, either side of a small stream. The southern row is the more impressive of the two, comprising approximately 200 stones running in straight lines for over 250 metres. The second row is slightly shorter, but still measures approximately 180 metres in length. The stones vary in size, with the largest being around half a metre in height.

The size of the rows makes them fascinating curiosities to behold, but photographing them can be particularly challenging. The largest stones can be found on the southern row, at its eastern extremity. Here a large triangular blocking stone seems to purposefully indicate the end (or beginning) of the stone row, and being potentially the most photogenic part of the row makes an ideal subject to head to with your camera.

The biggest challenge with photographing the row is solely down to composition. While the most impressive feature of the stone row is clearly its length, the relatively small height of the stones makes it difficult to convey this effectively. Without careful consideration to composition the row begins impressively with the dominant triangular blocking stone, and then soon fades away into nothingness, swallowed up by the relatively flat moorland all around.

Try to isolate a group featuring an odd number of standing stones, ideally three or maybe five. To make the stones large and imposing in the frame, shoot from close range with a wide angle lens. A low viewpoint will make the stones look larger and far more dominant in the photo than they really are.

To the north Great Mis Tor makes a fantastic rugged backdrop to pictures of the stone rows, be aware that cars travelling along the B3357 will be visible, time your shot to exclude them. To the south Kings Tor is equally dramatic, both helping to convey the wild and remote surroundings in which these ancient monuments were built.

Three stones with Great Mis Tor beyond, Nikon D800E, 17-35mm at 25mm, ISO 100, ¼ sec at f/14. July

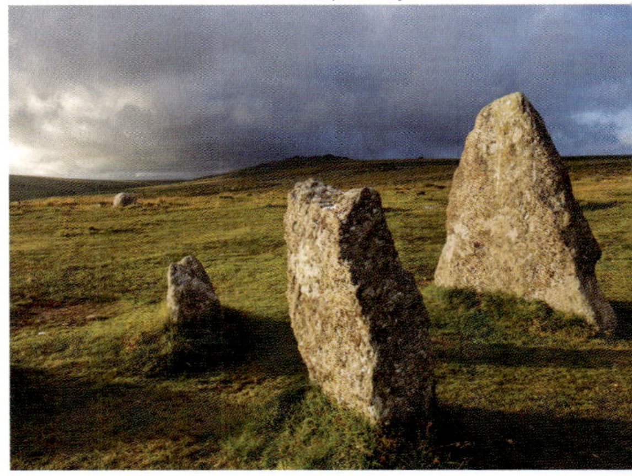

Ancient stone crosses are as much a part of Dartmoor's identity as its famous tors. The leaning Windy Post, correctly known as Beckamoor Cross, is one of the better known. Dating from the 15th Century, it is thought that this weathered medieval cross may have replaced a much earlier version.

The purpose of Windy Post is unknown, but it may have served as a marker on a medieval monastic route between Buckfast and Tavistock Abbeys. The cross' nickname suggests it gets its lean from being so openly exposed to the elements on the wild moorland. In reality it has probably been pushed out of position by animals using it as a scratching post.

Windy Post benefits from the man-made stream, known in the West Country as a leat, running alongside it. The Grimstone & Sortridge Leat was created over 700 years ago to carry water to the manor houses of Grimstone and Sortridge. Today it is the last remaining of Dartmoor's leats to supplement drinking water, supplying approximately 35 houses and farms.

A short walk over the moorland takes you to Feather Tor.

What to Shoot and Viewpoints

Viewpoint 1 – Windy Post

This post makes a difficult subject to photograph on its own. Luckily this is where the Grimsbridge & Sortridge Leat helps out. Just about every photograph of Windy Post includes the leat; in fact you even could argue that the leat is the main subject as the cross always takes a background role.

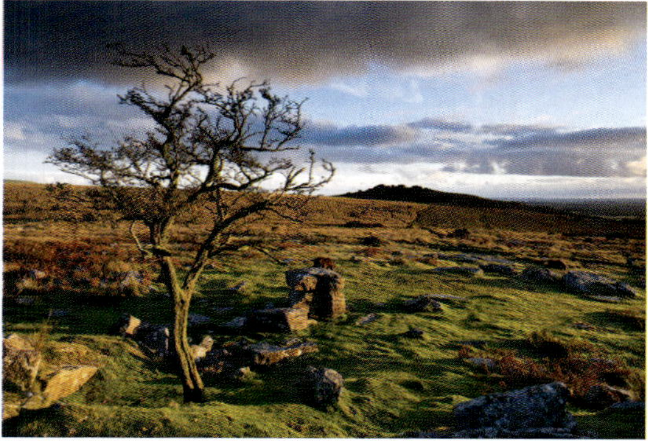

Fortunately, as the little stream rushes past the cross it tumbles down over some granite slabs in a very pleasing cascade. When water levels are high, a second smaller series of waterfalls are sometimes created as the water tumbles over lesser granite rocks. Using a low position the waterfall makes a mouth-watering leading line drawing the eye in towards the cross in the background.

Viewpoint 2 – Feather tor

One of Dartmoor's less impressive granite outcrops, Feather Tor on its own wouldn't merit an entry but being positioned so close to Windy Post it makes a worthwhile bonus excursion after visiting the cross. A hop over the leat followed by an easy 5 minute amble over moorland brings you to Feather tor.

While the tor is under-whelming it is the single hawthorn tree that grabs the attention of most who visit this location. This tree, crooked and misshapen by strong moorland winds, stands completely alone next to the tor and makes for an evocative photographic subject on the otherwise barren landscape.

The tree is equally photogenic from a number of angles; choice of viewpoint really depends on the time of day and available light. In late afternoon and evening the view south to Pew tor can look particularly appealing with low side lighting illuminating both the tree and landscape

How to Get Here

From Tavistock head towards Two Bridges on the B3357. After driving up Pork Hill you cross a cattle grid heralding your arrival on the moor. A large car park will appear on the right, continue 200m beyond to a second smaller parking area on the left. Cross the road and head down into the small valley to the south, and up the other side. You will soon notice the leat running southwards; a level ten minute walk you bring you to the cross.

Parking Lat/Long: 50.557656, -4.0697908
Parking Grid Ref: SX 534 751
Parking Postcode: PL20 6ST
Map: OS Explorer Map OL28 (1:25 000) Dartmoor

Accessibility

Depending on the weather and time of year, the moor can be wet and muddy so it is advisable to wear sturdy walking boots. Not suitable for wheelchairs.

Best Time of Year/Day

Windy Post makes a great late afternoon/evening subject when both the waterfall and cross are bathed in rich side lighting. Feather Tor works equally well at this time of day. Alternatively, Windy Post works very well on a dark moody day. The most important thing to bear in mind when shooting Windy Post is the water level. In the summer when water levels are low, the waterfall may disappear. At these times the location loses much of its appeal.

Looking towards Pew Tor from Feather Tor, Nikon D800E, 17-35mm at 24mm, ISO 400, 1/40 sec at f/8. Handheld. September

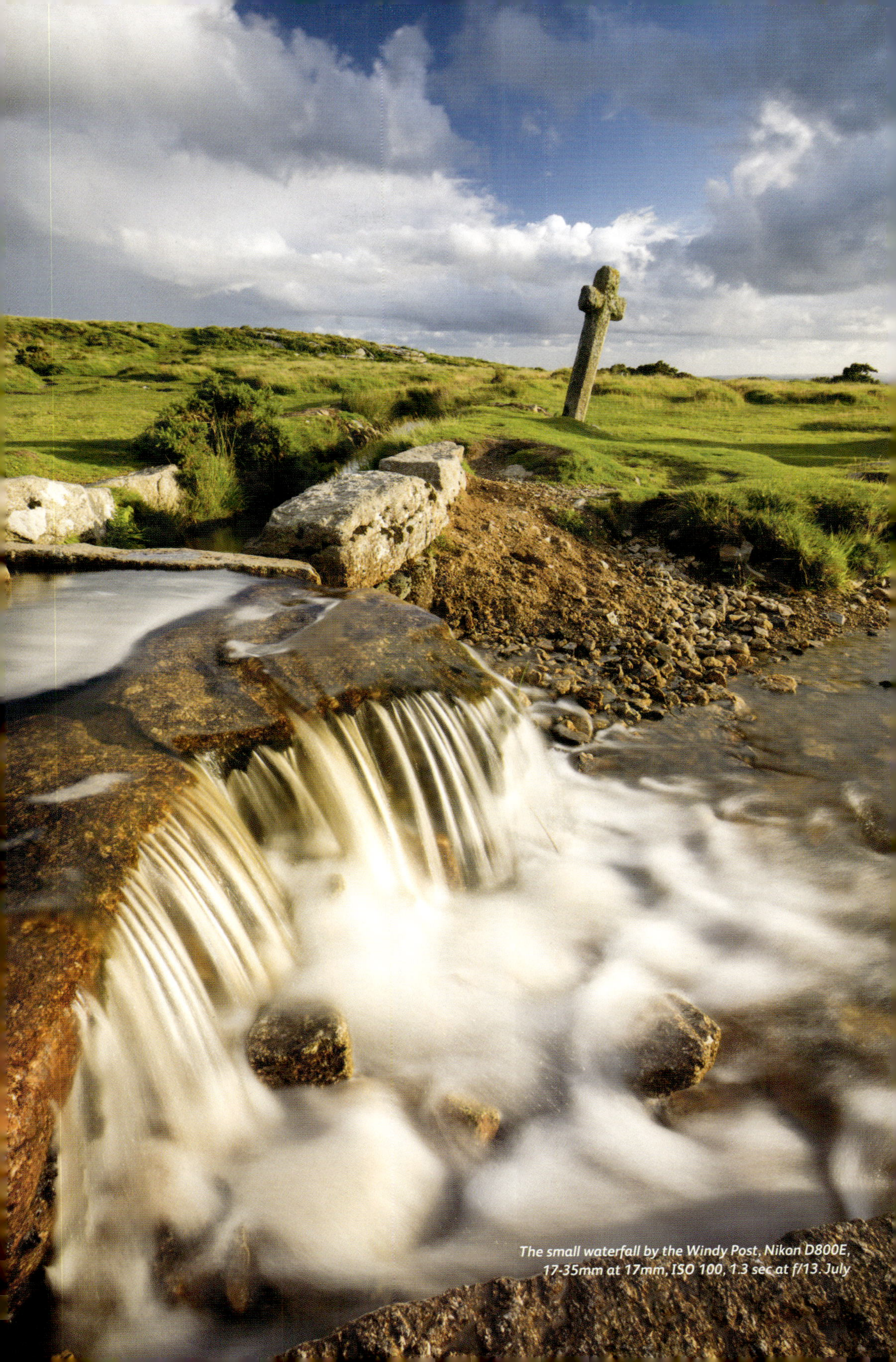

The small waterfall by the Windy Post, Nikon D800E,
17-35mm at 17mm, ISO 100, 1.3 sec at f/13. July

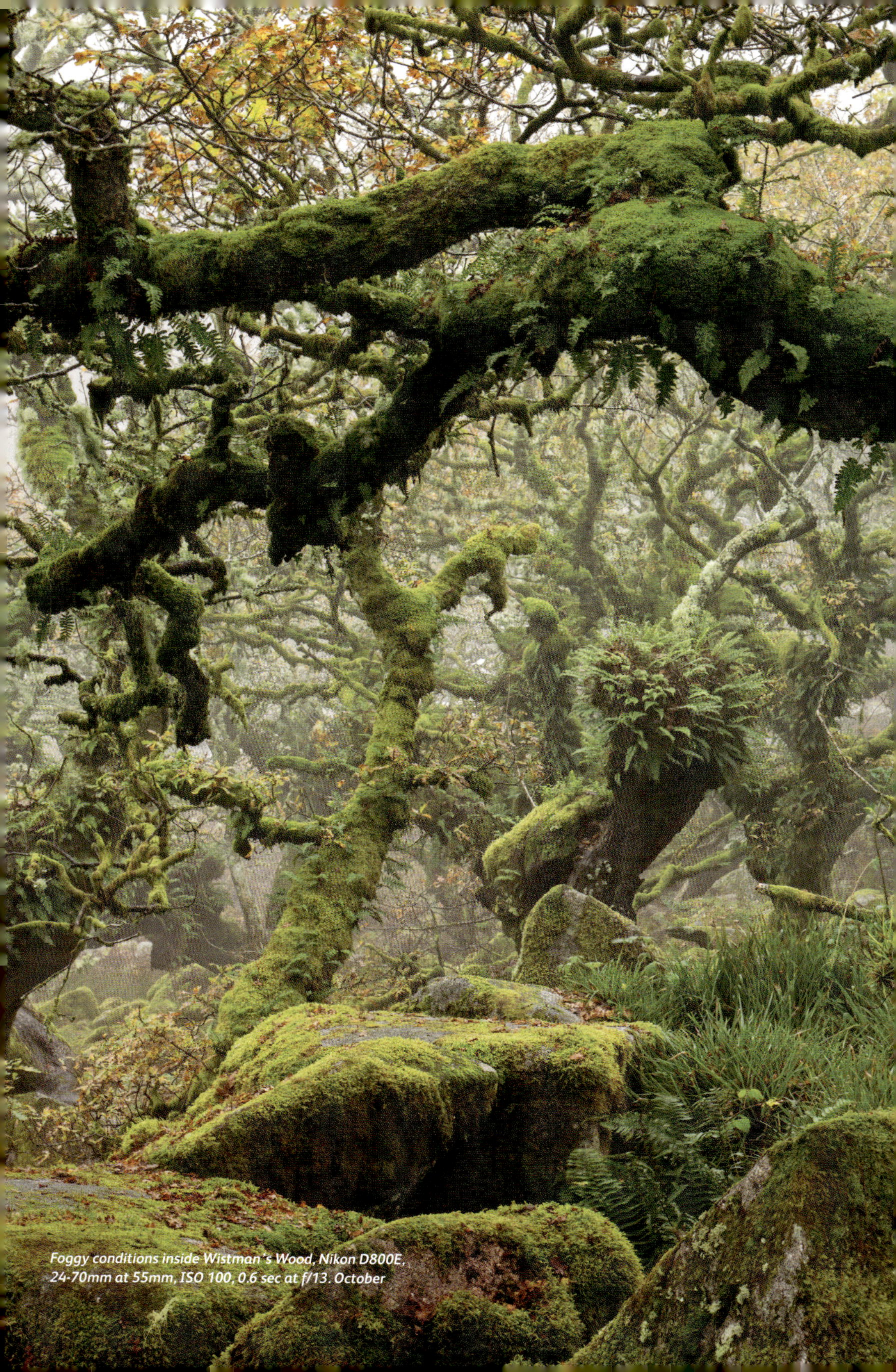

Foggy conditions inside Wistman's Wood, Nikon D800E,
24-70mm at 55mm, ISO 100, 0.6 sec at f/13. October

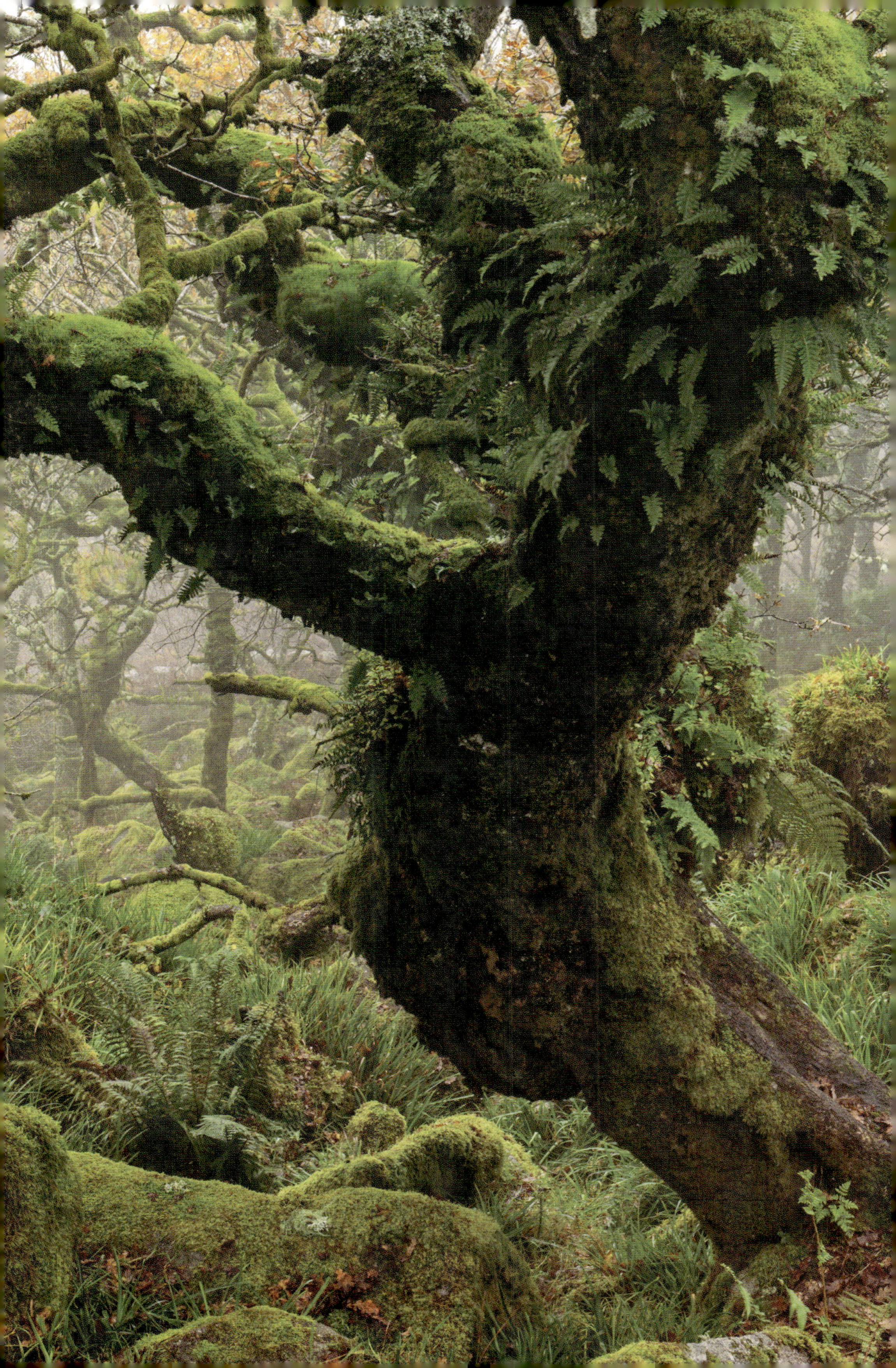

Hidden in a valley surrounded by wild moorland, Wistman's Wood is a place of mystery, intrigue and wonderful photographic opportunity.

Reputed to be the most haunted location on Dartmoor, Wistman's Wood has long been associated with myth and legend. Tales of druids, ghosts, hell hounds and even the Devil himself are woven into the history of the area. While all this may sound somewhat far-fetched to the 21st Century visitor, when you step into the wood for the first time it is easy to see how these stories arose. Stunted oak trees grow in twisted and tangled shapes over huge granite boulders, with both rocks and wood coated in thick green moss and lichens. The woodland oozes atmosphere and can carry a very real sense of foreboding.

What to Shoot and Viewpoints

Viewpoint 1 – Wistman's Wood

The wood is split into three areas: north, middle and south groves. In total it covers around 9 acres in a thin strip hugging the side of the valley. Most visitors approach from the south and may initially feel somewhat underwhelmed by their first sight of the woodland.

From a distance it doesn't look much, a squat collection of bush-like trees surrounded by moorland.

Once inside however your opinion will immediately change as you venture into a mystical world. Compared with a typical oak forest the trees are small, around 6 metres in height, giving the woodland a cramped and claustrophobic feel. Twisted and tangled branches stretch above and all around, bearing more resemblance to Middle Earth's Fangorn Forest than Dartmoor!

The most accessible part of the wood is the south grove, where many of the oldest trees can be found. Just to the north, the woodland becomes very dense, with a fenced area restricting access. Further north the trees are younger and grow straighter and taller than in the other groves.

Despite the tremendous appeal to photographers, Wistman's Wood is a difficult location to photograph well. The gnarled intertwined trees are beautiful but chaotic, making compositions very busy and confusing.

The best photographs are usually captured on overcast days when contrast is less of an issue. Visit Wistman's Wood on a foggy day for a real treat; as well as enhancing the atmosphere, fog softens the impact of the chaotic trees, simplifying compositions while reducing contrast even further.

Part of the challenge of photographing the wood is getting into position. The jumble of boulders makes it very difficult to walk around, and extreme care should be taken

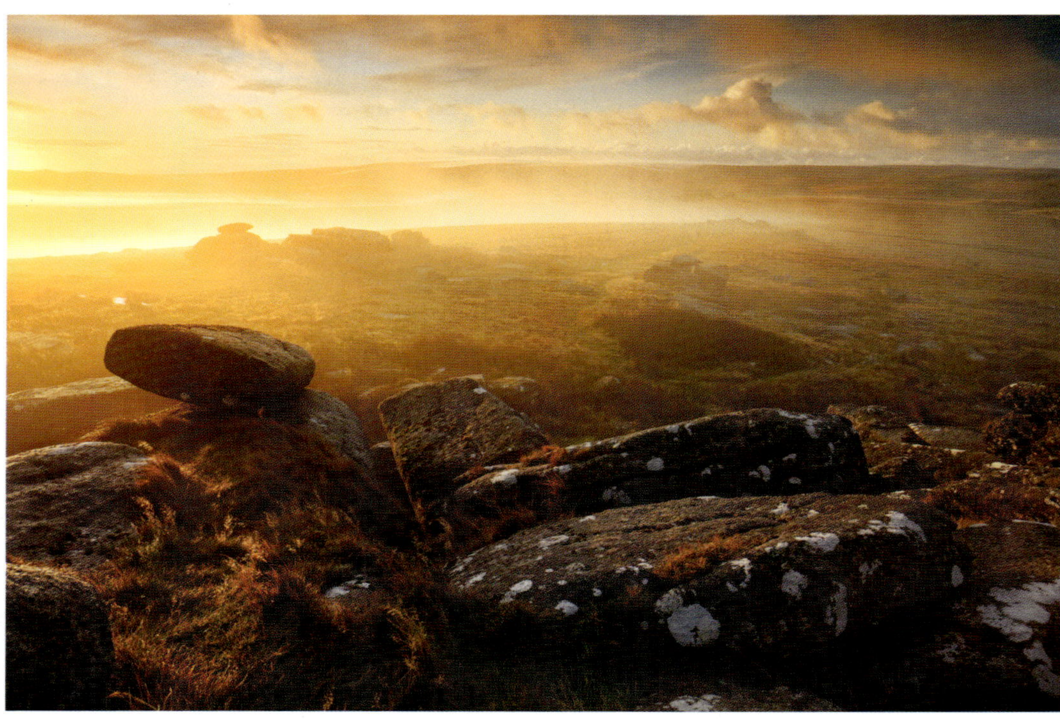

A glorious misty dawn at Littaford Tors, Nikon D800E, 16-35mm at 23mm, ISO 100, 0.5 sec at f/16. October

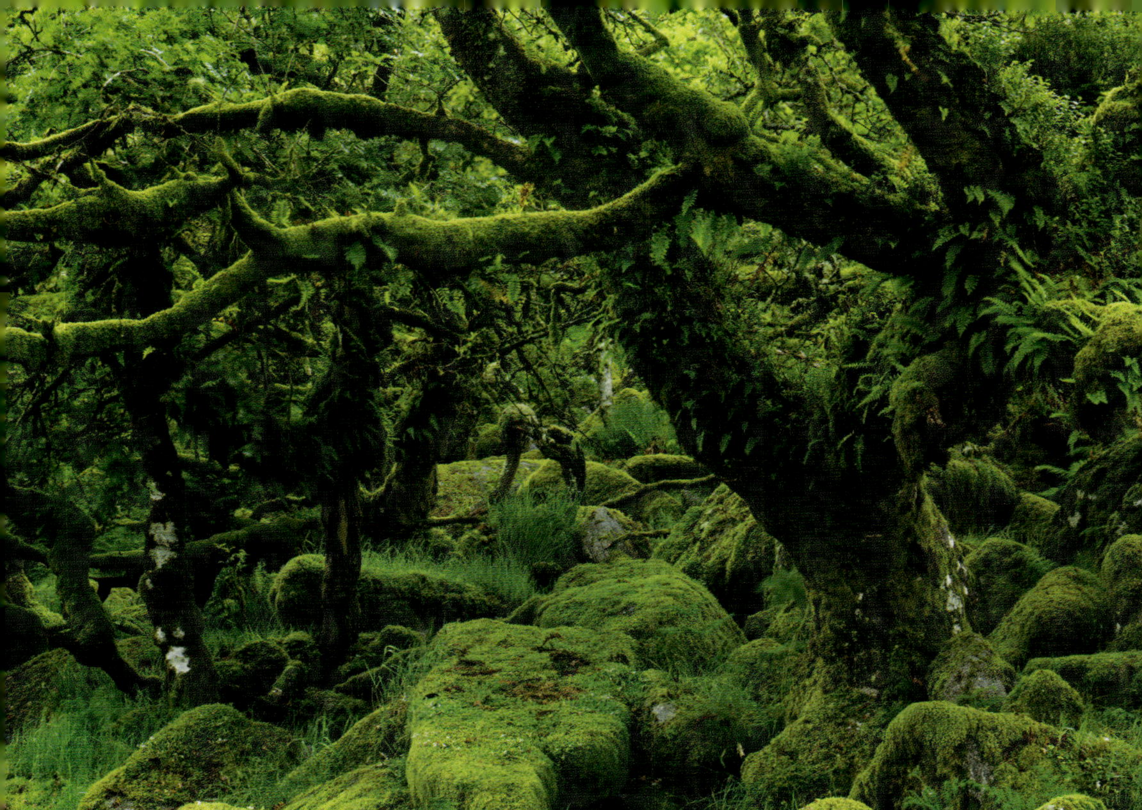

Verdant scene inside Wistman's Wood in mid summer, Nikon D800E, 24-70mm at 62mm, ISO 100, 4 sec at f/14. July

to avoid damaging the delicate moss and lichens growing on the boulders, many of which are rare species. Although there is no path as such, several areas in the south grove offer good access to some of the most twisted trees without clambering over boulders, making this the recommended area for photography.

Viewpoint 2 – Littaford Tors

After making the journey to reach Wistman's Wood, several photogenic tors can be reached with only a quick diversion. The simplest to reach is Littaford Tors, which lies just above Wistman's Wood at the top of the hill. The granite outcrops on Littaford provide an excellent moorland alternative that can save a wasted journey if conditions in the woodland are less than ideal.

How to Get Here

Wistman's Wood can be reached on foot from Two Bridges in Dartmoor National Park in Devon. To reach Two Bridges by car, head east on the B3357 from Tavistock. The road climbs up onto the moor and passes straight through Two Bridges after 8 miles. When you reach Two Bridges park in the little car park on the left directly opposite the Two Bridges Hotel. From here, head north through a gate and follow the footpath for 1.25 miles to reach the woodland.

Parking Lat/Long: 50.558157, -3.9651235
Parking Grid Ref: SX 609 750
Parking Postcode: PL20 6SR
Map: OS Explorer Map OL28 (1:25 000) Dartmoor

Accessibility

From the car park at Two Bridges, follow the uneven moorland footpath north for 1.25 miles to reach Wistman's Wood. The path continues along the moorland just to the east of the woodland, and provides the simplest method of accessing each grove. The footpath and woodland is not accessible by wheelchair users.

Best Time of Year/Day

Under the right conditions the woodland can be photographed well at any time of year. Summer can be a particularly good season as the woodland is at its most verdant, with ferns springing up around the boulders and hanging from branches. At this time of year, the thicker leaf coverage also helps to prevent ugly white patches of sky from creeping into compositions and spoiling the atmosphere in photographs. Although autumn may seem an obvious time to shoot a typical woodland, Wistman's may be the exception. The leaf coverage in this ancient woodland is quite thin, and as a result autumnal foliage is a far less important consideration when photographing these trees.

Postbridge

Surrounded by wild moorland the hamlet of Postbridge lies in the very heart of Dartmoor. This is a popular location for visitors to the National Park, partially because of the nearby visitor centre but mainly due to the clapper bridge that spans the East Dart River.

This ancient structure dating from the 13th Century was originally used by pack horses laden with tin to cross the river on their way to Tavistock. A larger bridge was built alongside the original in the 18th Century, this is still used to carry the B3212 road across the river.

Hoar frost on the banks of the East Dart River, Nikon D800E, 17-35mm at 30mm, ISO 100, 1/10 sec at f/11. December

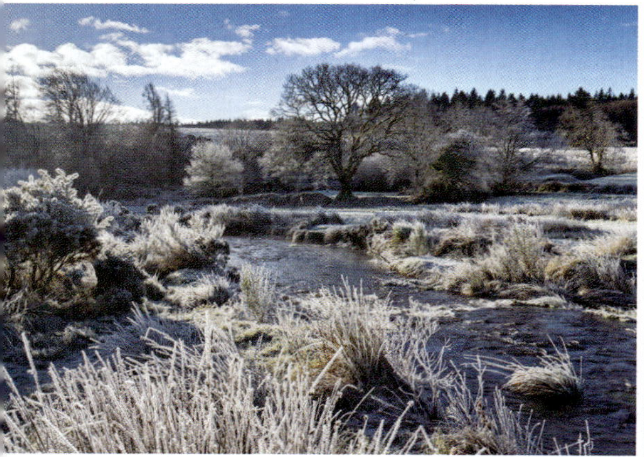

The pretty clapper bridge on a summer evening, Nikon D800E, 17-35mm at 30mm, ISO 100, ¼ sec at f/11. July

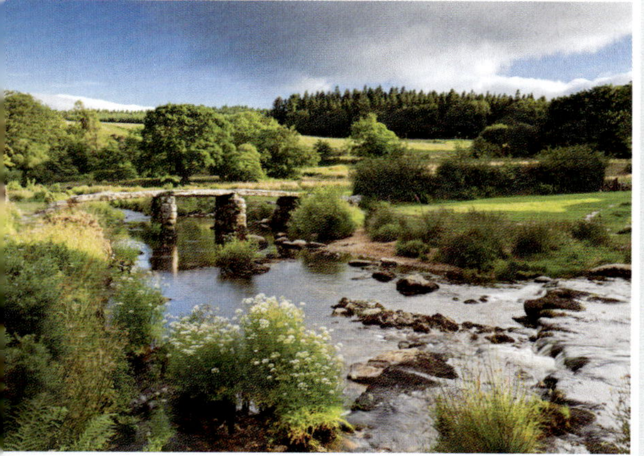

What to Shoot and Viewpoints

Although the newer bridge is very photogenic in its own right, the clapper bridge does tend to get lost when they are photographed together. Therefore, unless you specifically want to capture both bridges in one photograph it is best to stand in front of the road bridge and shoot downstream.

By doing this, the ancient bridge will be surrounded by countryside and trees, capturing its peaceful origins with barely a hint of its present location by a busy road. The bridge can be photographed on either side of the river with probably the best view on the eastern side as it gives a lovely vista not only of the bridge but also the scenery behind. As the road bridge is narrow and fairly busy with traffic it is not advisable to shoot from the bridge.

How to Get Here

Postbridge is a hamlet in the heart of Dartmoor in the county of Devon 12 miles east of Tavistock. Take the B3357 out of Tavistock signposted to Princetown. Continue 8.1 miles to Two Bridges and just after the hotel turn left on the B3212 signed for Postbridge in 3.6 miles. There is a car park at the visitor centre on the left hand side.

Parking Lat/Long: 50.593510, -3.9133430
Parking Grid Ref: SX 646 788
Parking Postcode: PL20 6SY
Map: OS Explorer Map OL28 (1:25 000) Dartmoor

Accessibility

This clapper bridge is one of Dartmoor's most accessible photographic locations. There is a large car park in the National Park visitor centre on the opposite side of the road. From this car park, cross the road and follow a wheelchair friendly path to the western river bank. The other river bank involves a descent down several steep steps from the road, or alternatively a walk over the clapper bridge itself. Unfortunately neither of these are suitable for wheelchairs.

Best Time of Year/Day

For the best chance of avoiding people standing on and around the bridge, it is advisable to visit this location either early morning or late evening.

In early summer the countryside and river banks surrounding the bridge look beautiful during the evening with rich sunlight kissing the vibrant grasses, bracken and wildflowers. For a very different feel, try visiting on a cold winter morning when frost or snow can transform the location into a winter wonderland.

The East Dart River flowing swiftly in Spring, Canon 1Ds Mark III, 17-40mm at 28mm, ISO 200, 1/10 sec at f/13. May

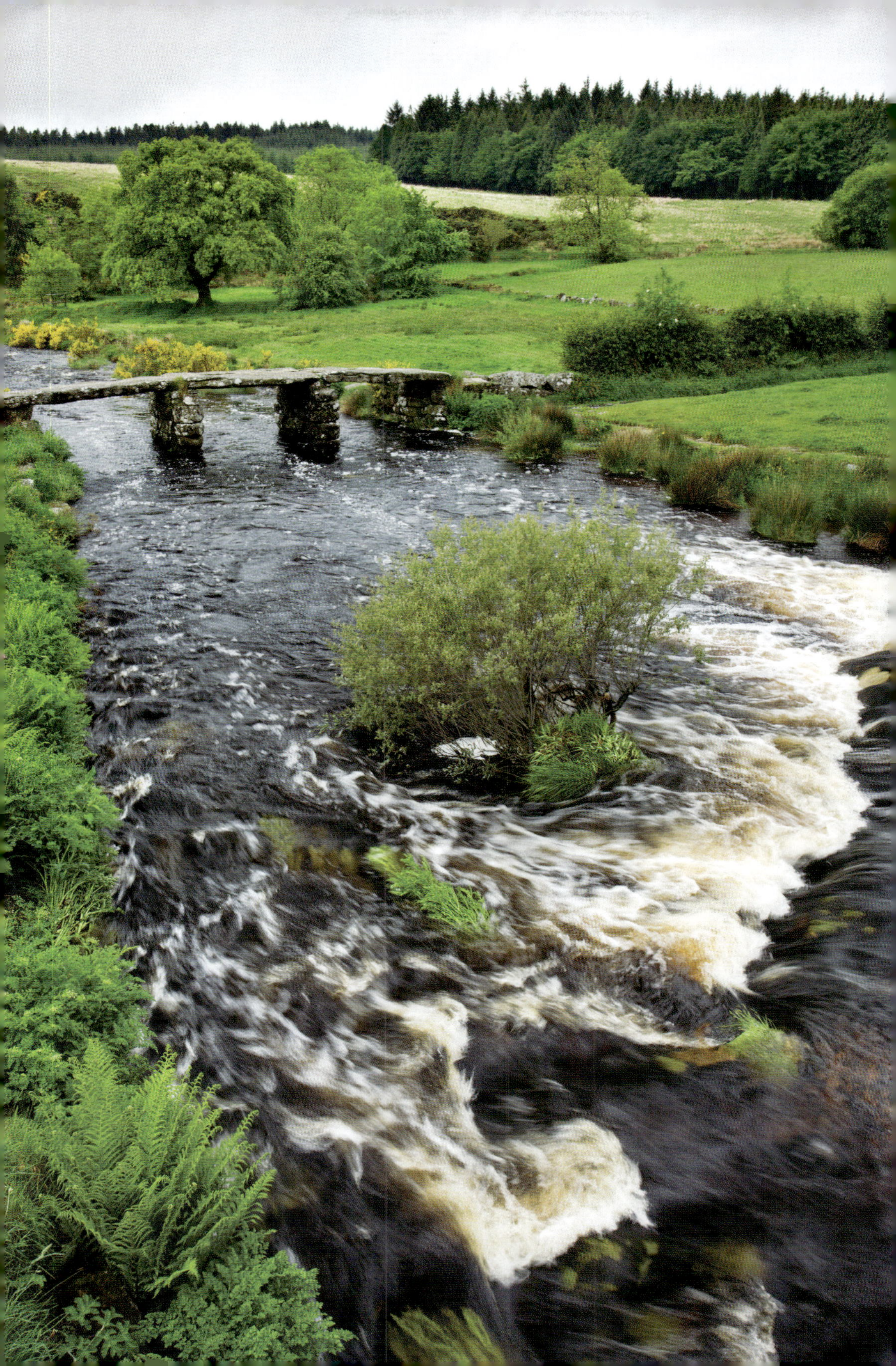

Grimspound

Dating back to the Bronze Age, the remains of Grimspound are amongst the largest and best known of Dartmoor's prehistoric settlements. A huge circular stone wall surrounds a collection of hut circles, the stone remains of ancient dwellings occupied as far back as 1300 BC.

Located in a valley overlooked by nearby Hookney and Hameldown Tors, the settlement could have served little purpose as a defensive fortification. It is believed that the large stone wall provided protection from predators roaming the moor as well as a barrier to prevent livestock roaming .

After a substantial archaeological excavation in the Victorian era, large parts of Grimspound, including sections of the wall and several hut circles were reconstructed. The settlement that we see today therefore is only part authentic.

What to Shoot and Viewpoints

Most visitors approach Grimspound from the west. A path leading up from the parking area passes through a gap in the large stone wall. As soon as you pass inside the settlement you will notice the hut circles in front of you. Several buildings appear to be much better preserved and therefore command the most attention. Without doubt, these are the reconstructed hut circles but nevertheless make for better photographs. Many of the authentic ruins are more difficult to photograph, being ramshackle and overgrown with heather and grass.

The hut circles do make very appealing photographic subjects and are small enough to be captured in their entirety for incredible foreground interest as part of a wider moorland image. Some huts have upright granite stones marking an entrance way, and one even features a porch to keep the harsh wind from entering the building. To the right of the entrance, a raised stone area would have served as a bed.

The wall makes for a more challenging photographic subject due to its immense size. Although no more than a metre in height, the wall is easily three metres in depth comprising piles of stones without any obvious points of interest. Although it can be photographed well under the right conditions with careful attention to composition, the obvious solution is to head to the main entrance. This can

The circular settlement is clearly visible from Hookney Tor, Canon 1Ds Mark III, 17-40mm at 21mm, ISO 100, 1.5 sec at f/16. January

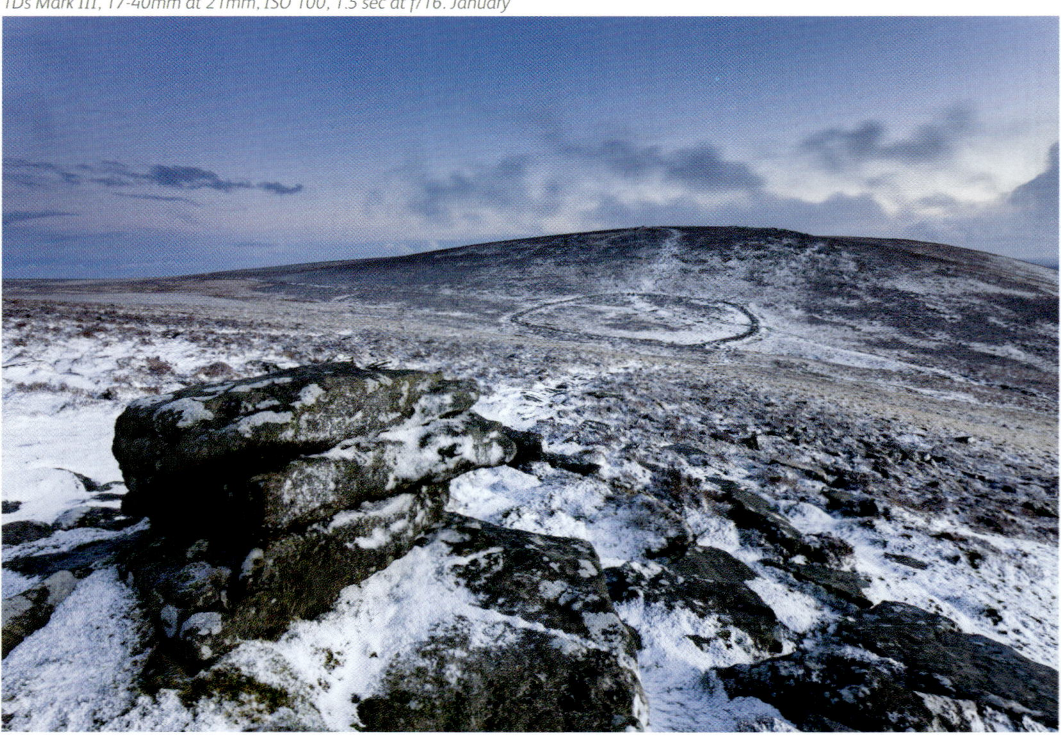

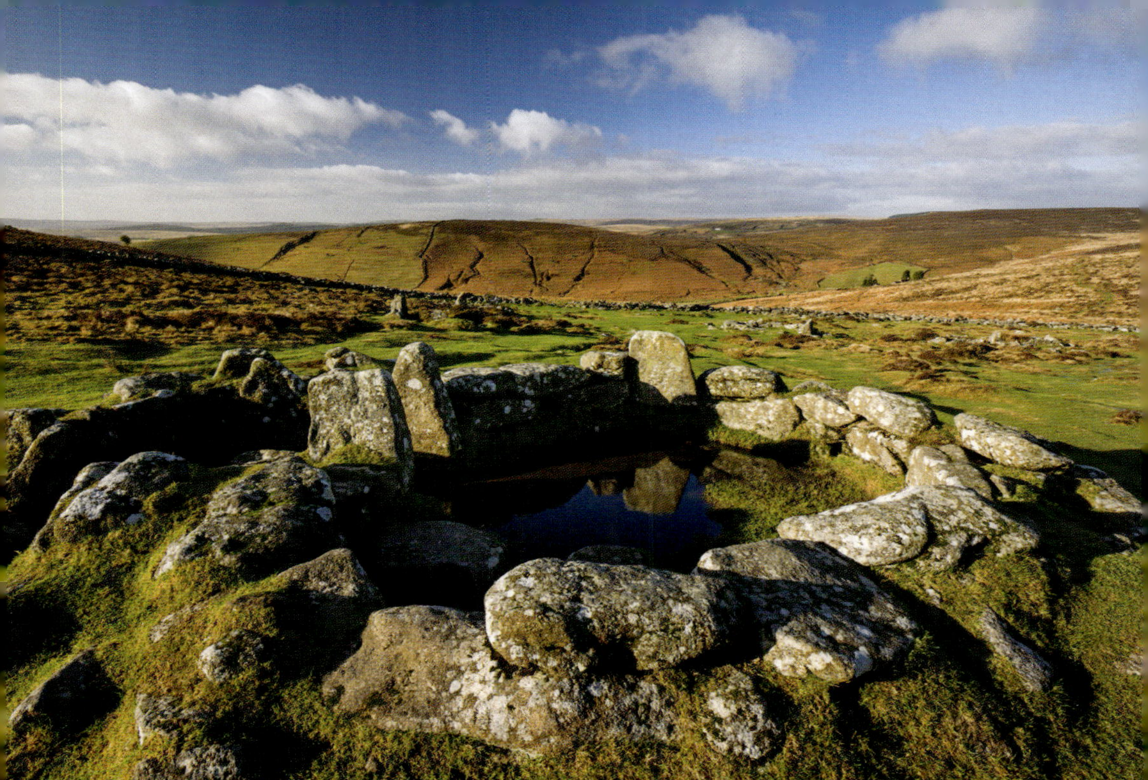

One of Grimspounds many hut circles, Nikon D800E,
17-35mm at 17mm, ISO 100, 1/6 sec at f/13. January

be found on the southern perimeter of the wall, and is one of the highlights of Grimspound.

At nearly two metres wide, the entrance is a well-preserved feature of the settlement. Large granite blocks stand guard either side of a paved corridor nearly two metres wide, with views into Grimspound and beyond towards Hookney Tor.

To fully appreciate the scale of Grimspound you need to photograph it from above. While Hameldown Tor offers elevation, the view from Hookney Tor is far better. An easy path leads from the settlement up to the tor, climbing around 50 metres to reach the summit. From this new perspective, the huge perimeter wall easily distinguishes Grimspound from its moorland surroundings.

From this distant perspective the settlement doesn't make a particularly strong picture in its own right, but when incorporated as a background element into a wider landscape it works incredibly well. Fortunately the gran te outcrops that comprise Hookney Tor offer a wealth of excellent subjects from which to fill the foreground.

How to Get Here

Grimspound is approximately 6 miles south west of Moretonhampstead in Dartmoor National Park. Take the B3312 west from Moretonhampstead. After five miles take the left lane, signposted Grimspound. After one mile, you will see a lay-by on the right hand side. Park here, cross the road and follow the path up to the settlement.

Parking Lat/Long: 50.613154, -3.8429725
Parking Grid Ref: SX 697 808
Parking Postcode: PL20 6TB
Map: OS Explorer Map OL28 (1:25 000) Dartmoor

Accessibility

A 300 metre gentle uphill moorland path leads from the parking area to Grimspound. The settlement is not suitable for wheelchairs.

Best Time of Year/Day

Grimspound can be photographed year round with the best light usually on offer in the evening. The ancient settlement looks especially photogenic during wintertime when sugar coated by early morning frost or dusted with snow.

As its full name indicates, the charming village of Widecombe is located on Dartmoor surrounded by wild moorland. The village is best known thanks to a 19th Century Devon folk song 'Widecombe Fair', which featured the popular character 'Old Uncle Tom Cobley'.

Although the village itself is photogenic, the star attraction of Widecombe is the impressive church of St Pancras. Known informally as the 'Cathedral of the Moors' the church boasts an impressive tower 40 metres in height, which makes a striking landmark visible from many miles around.

What to Shoot and Viewpoints

Viewpoint 1 – Village Green

The village green makes an excellent viewpoint from which to photograph the church up close. Apart from a stone wall and the occasional passing car the viewpoint is free from any distracting elements, allowing you to compose a clutter-free composition of the church. You can use the spreading branches of several mature trees around the green to frame the tower, while on sunny days the shadows from the branches stretching over the grass make interesting foreground subjects.

As the tower is so tall, photographs of the church will invariably be distorted, resulting in the tower leaning heavily. You can get around this by shooting with a perspective control lens, but it is also possible to correct in post processing software. Just be sure to keep some free space around the edges of the frame, as the correction will require cropping into the image.

The real appeal comes with shooting the church tower from a distance as part of a wider landscape. The surrounding moor offers elevated vantage points from which to shoot the village and its surrounding farmland.

View down towards Widecombe from Bell Tor, Canon 1Ds Mark III, 17-40mm at 24mm, ISO 100, 0.3 sec at f/22. July

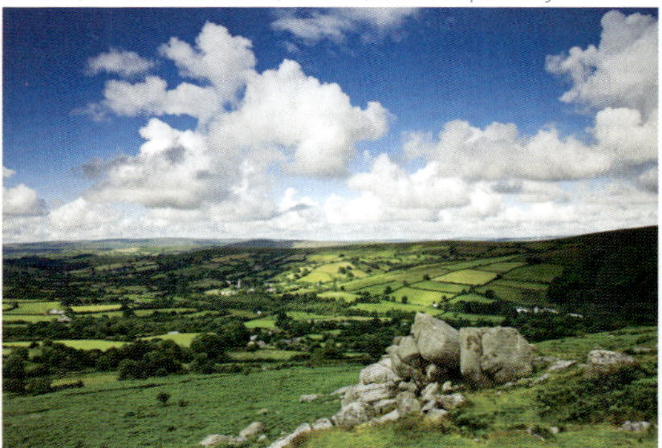

Viewpoint 2 – Top Tor

Probably the most popular viewpoint to shoot from is the roadside car park near the B3387, the main approach into Widecombe. From this car park, or from higher up on Top Tor, you can achieve a clean shot of the church backed by rolling green fields. As Widecombe is fairly distant from this viewpoint, you will ideally be shooting with a telephoto lens to prevent your subject becoming lost in the landscape. A lens with a focal length of between 70-200mm is ideal for this kind of photography.

Viewpoint 3 – Bonehill Rocks

A similar view towards Widecombe can be achieved from Bonehill Rocks. The vista here looks south west towards the church, the main benefit of this viewpoint being the appealing angle of the tower from this direction. For those wishing more elevation, a 5-10 minute stroll up the moorland path will lead you to Bell Tor or higher still Chinkwell Tor.

Opposite top: The view from near Top Tor, Nikon D800, 70-200mm at 122mm, ISO 200, 1/30 sec at f/8. February

Church of St Pancras from the village green, Canon 1Ds Mark III, 17-40mm at 33mm, ISO 100, 1/10 sec at f/16. April

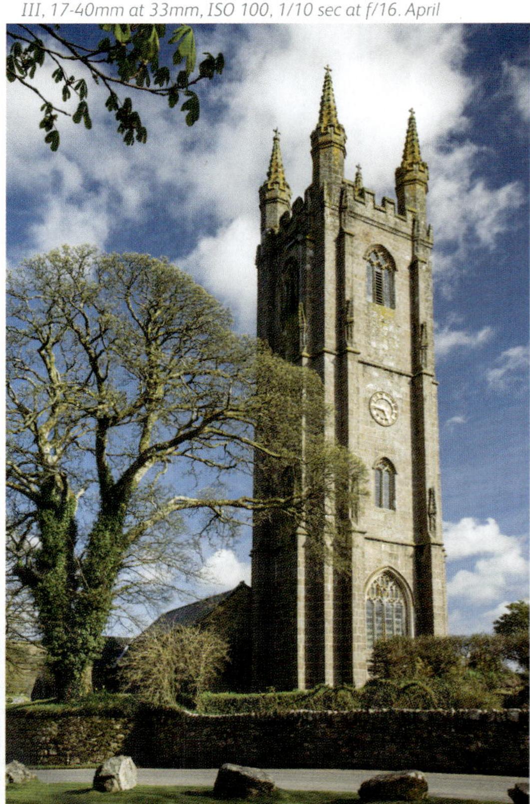

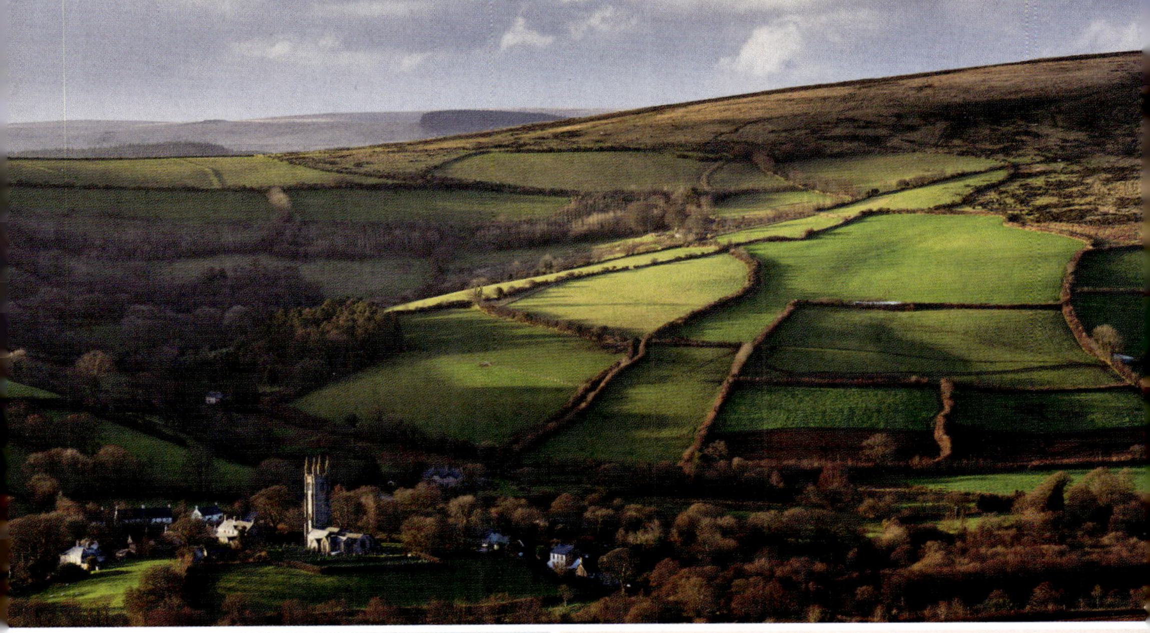

How to Get Here

The nearest town to Widecombe-in-the-Moor is Bovey Tracey
(7 miles). From Bovey Tracey, head west on the B3387. After just
three miles you will climb up onto the moor, passing Haytor on
your right. Continue for another 4 miles to reach Widecombe.

Parking Lat/Long:
50.577296, -3.8119447 (village car park)
50.576730, -3.7883735 (Top Tor car park)
50.583080, -3.7915599 (Bonehill Rocks car park)
Parking Grid Ref:
SX 718 768 (village car park)
SX 734 767 (Top Tor car park)
SX 732 774 (Bonehill Rocks car park)
Village Parking Postcode: TQ13 7TA
Map: OS Explorer Map OL28 (1:25 000) Dartmoor

Accessibility

Several car parks in the village are just metres away from the
village green. The countryside view towards the village can be
photographed from the car park below Top Tor. From the car park
at Bonehill Rocks a 5 minute walk over the moorland will bring you
to some excellent vantage points.

Best Time of Year/Day

This location can work equally well at any time of year, and
depending on your viewpoint, any time of day. The landscape looks
very different throughout the seasons; whether you prefer to shoot
it in snow, frost, autumn colours or summer greens is purely down to
preference. As it sits in a valley Widecombe can be subject to misty
mornings in the spring or autumn months. If a misty morning is
predicted, head to one of the moorland vantage points for dawn.
Providing conditions are right, the sight of the church tower poking
through a sea of mist is an unforgettable sight, and makes
a spectacular photograph.

*Misty morning from Bonehill Rocks, Canon 1Ds Mark III, 70-
200mm at 200mm, ISO 100, 1/13 sec at f/10. September*

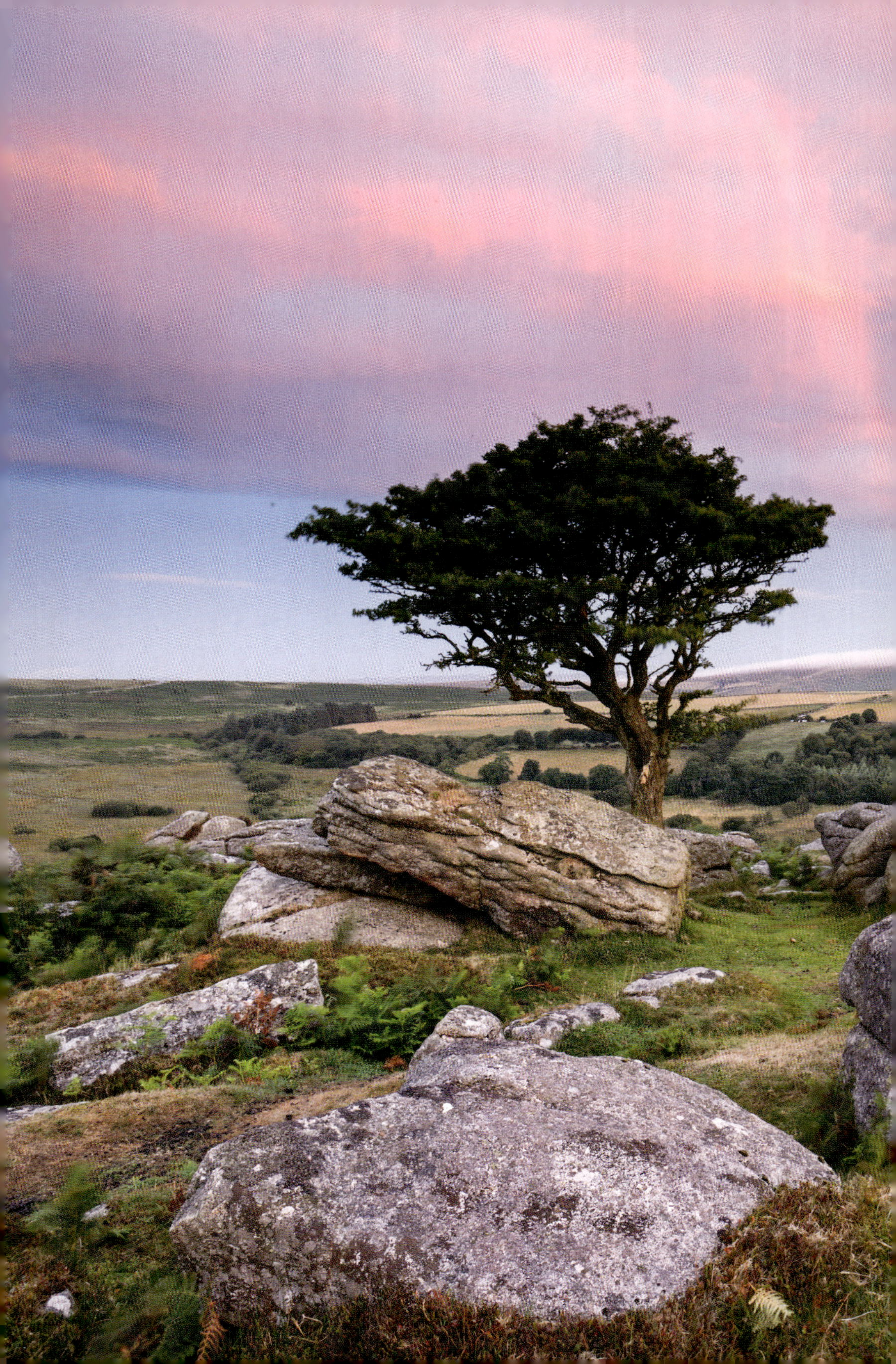

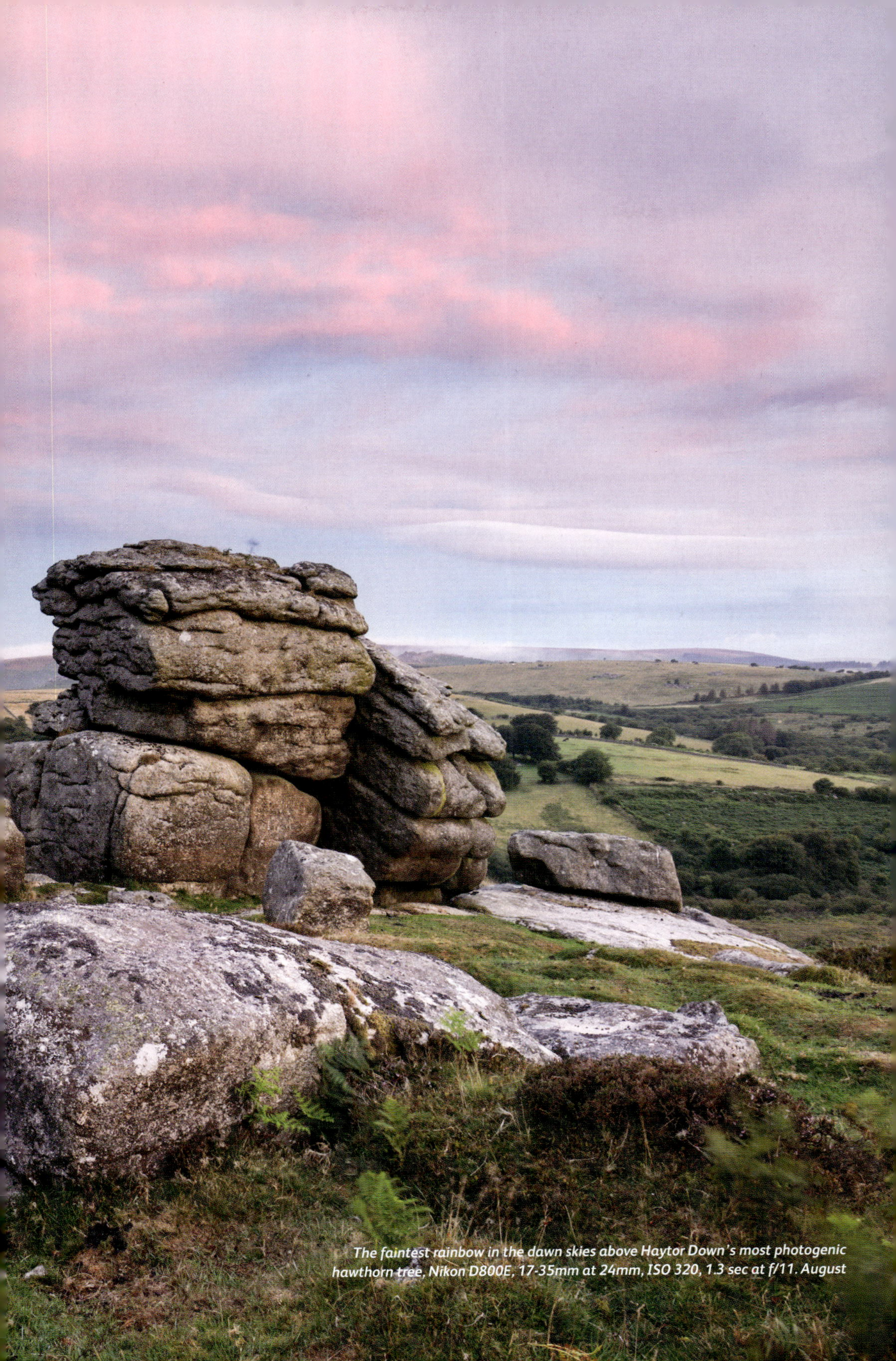

The faintest rainbow in the dawn skies above Haytor Down's most photogenic hawthorn tree. Nikon D800E, 17-35mm at 24mm, ISO 320, 1.3 sec at f/11. August

Haytor Down

Located on the eastern edge of Dartmoor, Haytor Down is a huge double peaked tor visible for many miles to the south and north of the National Park. This area is rich in prehistoric history, with Bronze Age hut circles spread over the moor. In the 19th Century quarrying left a more visible mark on the area; granite from Haytor was used in the construction of the London Bridge, now situated in Arizona.

Haytor Down rocks make a strong focal point from both near and far, while several other photogenic tors are just a short walk away. It's a popular place and you may have to share the place with others.

What to Shoot and Viewpoints

Viewpoint 1 – Haytor Rocks

Haytor Rocks can be reached with a ten minute walk from the main visitor centre car park, or a five minute walk from another large car park closer to the summit.

The tor is split into two huge granite outcrops, separated by a wide grassy avenue. From close up the eastern section is larger and more impressive; its vertical walls of granite giving a very distinctive shape quite unlike other Dartmoor tors. While still a very substantial tor in its own right, the western section has a more sloping approach, making it an ideal platform to stand upon to gain some elevation when shooting back towards the other outcrop.

The tor's distinctive shape changes quite dramatically when viewed from different angles. Some of the best views can be gained from a little further away on the moor where the characteristic shape of Haytor Rocks can be best appreciated. There is a plentiful supply of rocks scattered over the moorland to utilise as foreground interest, or alternatively photograph from one of the larger outcrops such as Holwell Tor.

Viewpoint 2 – Holwell Tor

Although Haytor Rocks is the highlight of this area for the majority of visitors, for photographers Holwell Tor is a better alternative to the immense Haytor Rocks, its various outcrops offering more potential for compositions. Located to the north of Haytor Rocks, Holwell Tor enjoys wonderful far reaching views over the Holwell Valley towards one of Dartmoor's largest outcrops, Hound tor. Alternatively, attach a telephoto lens to gain a closer view of Hound Tor and its neighbour Greator Rocks.

Midway between Holwell and Saddle Tor, several unnamed tors are worth exploring. The most well known of these boasts perhaps Dartmoor's most photographed tree. Sometimes referred to as Holwell Tor and occasionally Saddle Tor, the little granite outcrop with its accompanying hawthorn tree doesn't merit a name on the Ordnance Survey map, yet remains an ever popular subject for photographers.

The small windswept tree adds some welcome variety to this typically moorland view and makes a perfect companion to the squat granite tor, each complementing without overpowering the other. The tor and tree can be photographed well from various angles, your choice of viewpoint will depend on the sun's position at the time of your visit.

Opposite top: Haytor Rocks at dawn, Nikon D800E, 17-35mm at 19mm, ISO 100, 1/5 sec at f/11. January

Ponies shelter beside a tor to escape a summer downfall, Nikon D800E, 17-35mm at 32mm, ISO 100, 0.3 sec at f/11. August

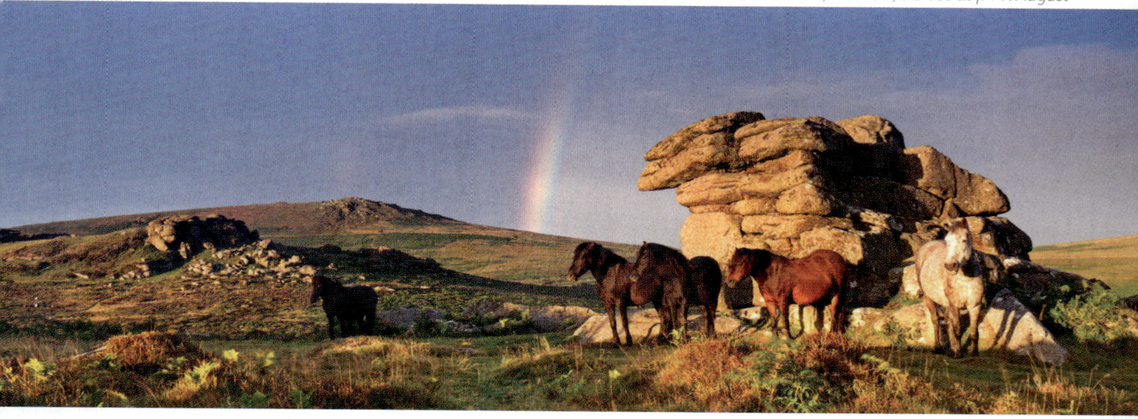

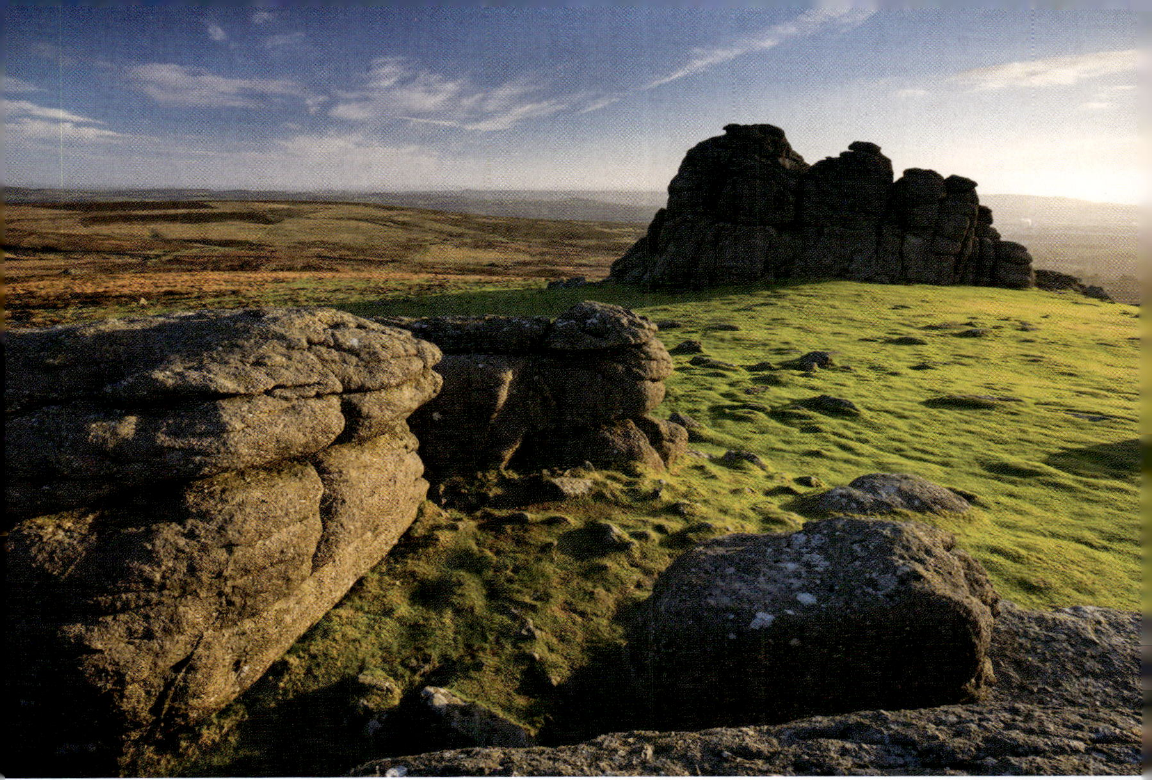

How to Get Here

Haytor Down is approximately four miles west of Bovey Tracey in Dartmoor National Park. Take the B3387 west out of Bovey Tracey; after two miles the road begins to climb steeply up towards the moor. Continue for another two miles; you will soon see Haytor Rocks in front of you. The visitor centre car park will be on your left.

Parking Lat/Long: 50.580675, -3.7452221
Parking Grid Ref: SX 765 771
Parking Postcode: TQ13 9XT (Haytor Vale)
Map: OS Explorer Map OL28 (1:25 000) Dartmoor

Accessibility

Three sizeable car parks positioned at various points along the B3387 ensure excellent access for Haytor Down. From each car park, paths lead over open moorland to the various tors. Although the paths are well defined with only gentle gradients, they are nevertheless over rough moorland and are not wheelchair friendly. Views of Haytor Rocks however can be achieved from each of the three car parks, with the main visitor centre car park offering probably the best angle on the tor.

Best Time of Year/Day

Haytor Down can offer wonderful photographic possibilities throughout the year. Every season brings something different to the moor, from carpets of bluebells in the spring, to golden bracken in autumn. Winter can be an exceptional time to shoot Haytor Down. Although snowfall is an infrequent occurrence in the southwest, areas such as Haytor Down on Dartmoor's high moorland will occasionally receive a dusting of snow during a cold snap. Providing the roads are kept clear during periods of snow the moor is a magical place to photograph.

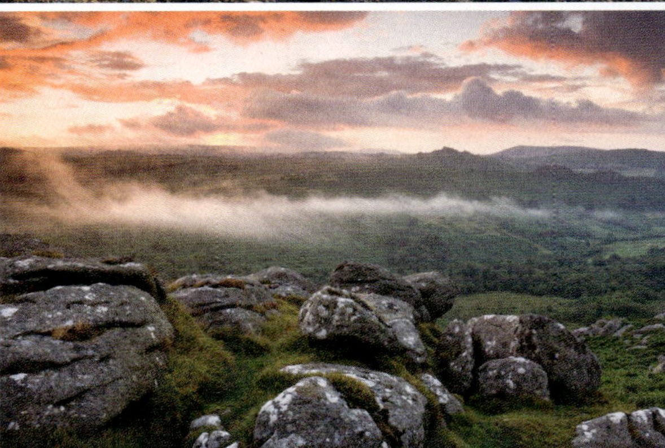

Looking towards Hound Tor from Holwell Tor, Canon 1Ds Mk III, 24-70mm at 28mm, ISO 100, 1.6 sec at f/16. July

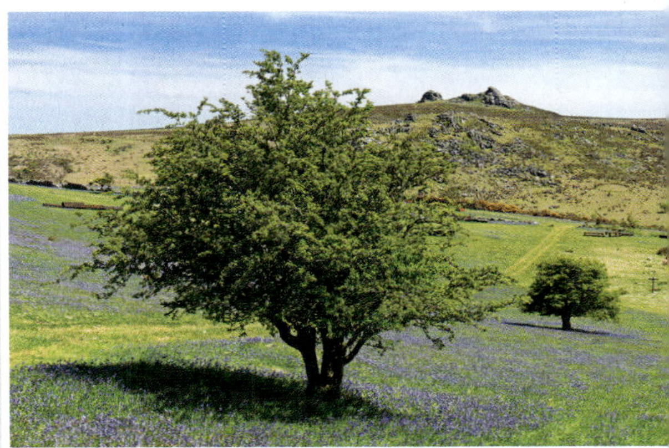

Bluebells on Holwell Lawn, with Haytor Rocks behind, Nikon D800E, 24-70mm at 58mm, ISO 100, 1/15 sec at f/13. June

According to Dartmoor folklore the huge outcrops at Hound Tor contain the petrified remains of Bowerman's hunting hounds, mentioned in the Bowerman's Nose description (p.208). Local superstition seems to associate itself with Hound Tor; stories of ghosts and mysterious black dogs are commonplace. It is even thought that the tor provided the inspiration for Arthur Conan Doyle's 'The Hound of the Baskervilles'.

Contrary to what the legends may lead you to believe, Hound Tor is a must for any Dartmoor visitor. Surely one of the largest and most impressive of Dartmoor's tors, it is also very accessible. Hound Tor is one of the National Park's most popular locations, especially for rock climbers who test their skills on the tor's steep walls.

What to Shoot and Viewpoints

The tor comprises two huge granite masses separated by a wide avenue, plus a series of smaller outcrops. With such rich potential there are countless opportunities for compositions at every turn, resulting in Hound Tor not having a single classic 'photographers' viewpoint typical of many other tors.

With so much rock on offer, you could be forgiven for at first feeling somewhat overwhelmed by Hound Tor. To simplify things slightly, rather than walking through the avenue between the two main rock masses, instead walk around the southern perimeter of the tor. There are several smaller outcrops to be found on this side which are especially photogenic. These mini tors featuring some intriguing pillars usually make for better pictures and being located slightly lower than the main tor can be photographed in front of a dramatic background. When shooting from this side, the obvious direction to shoot is south east towards Haytor Rocks, the characteristic shape making an excellent and recognisable background.

Next, continue to the eastern side of the main tor, where several other smaller outcrops can be found. Although these tors are not as impressive as those to the south, the moor slopes downhill quite significantly here, making it very easy to create a composition that includes both the granite rocks and the distant lush rolling countryside and woodland of Lustleigh Cleave.

To photograph the main rock masses that make up Hound Tor, it is a good idea to get some elevation. The southern rock mass provides the easiest access route to gain a higher vantage point, although there may still be some scrambling involved. From up here the main tor is rendered smaller in the frame and doesn't overwhelm the composition, while the height enables you to include a wonderful rolling backdrop to complete the picture.

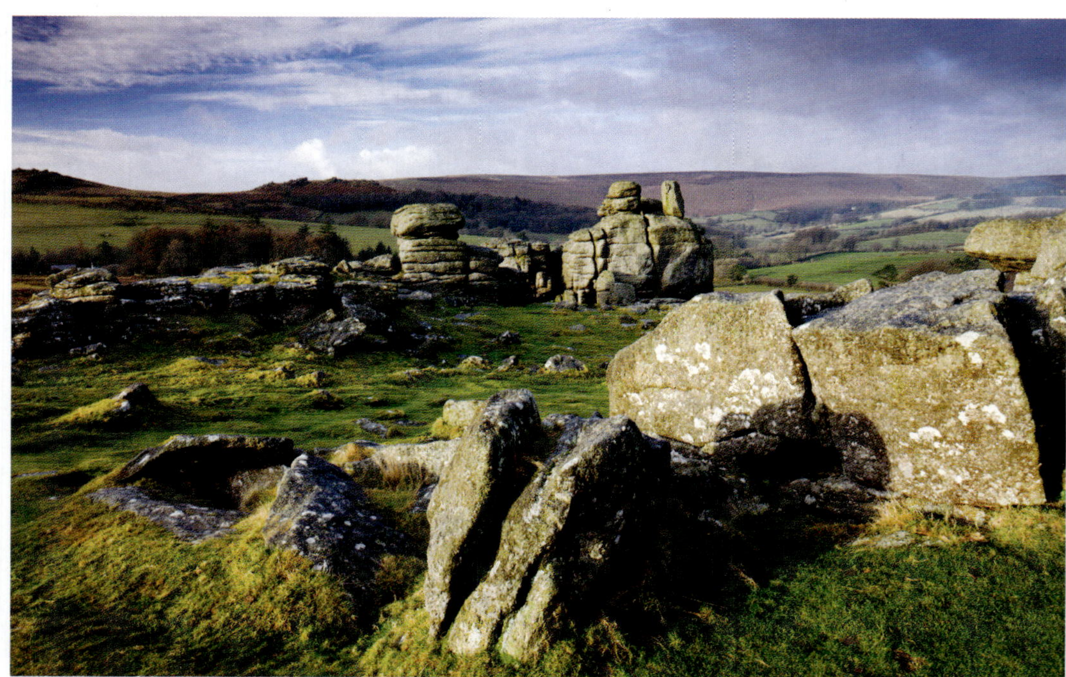

Granite outcrops on the southern side of Hound Tor, Canon 1Ds Mark III, 17-40mm at 28mm, ISO 100, 0.5 sec at f/16. December

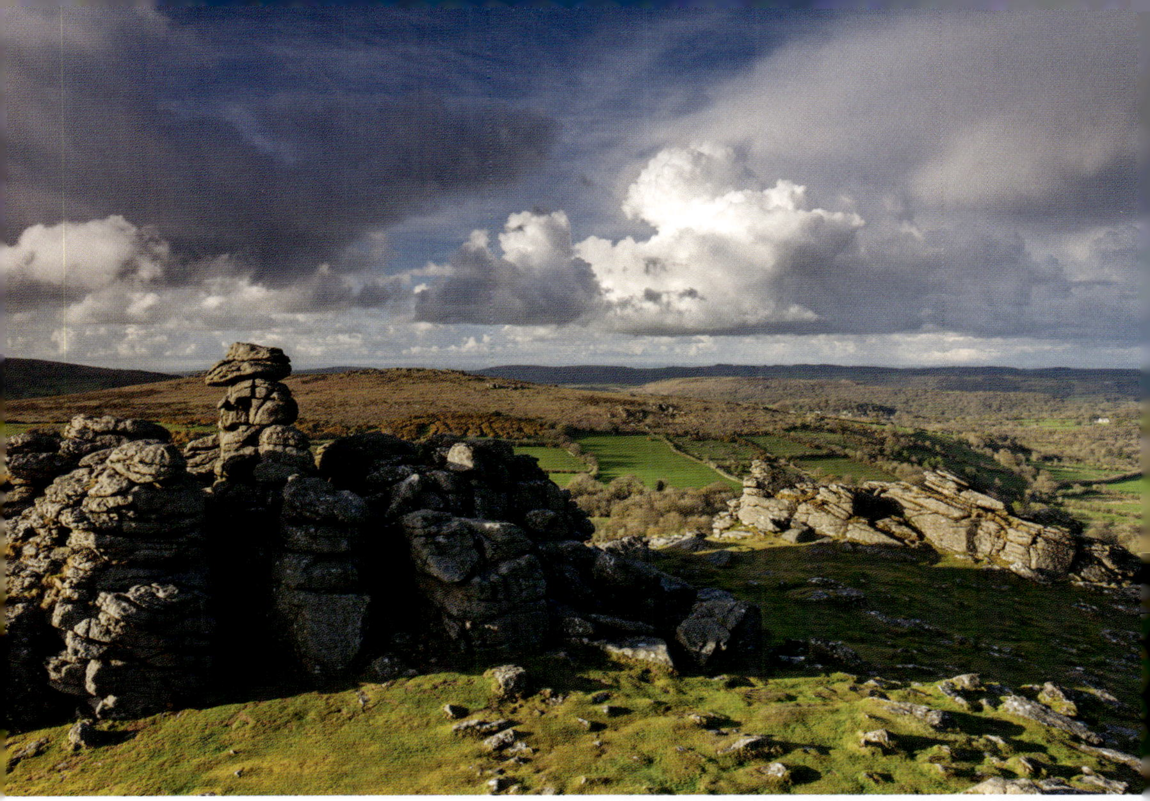

View over Hound Tor northwards, Canon 1Ds Mark III,
17-40mm at 24mm, ISO 100, 1/6 sec at f/13. April

For something a little different follow the path to the
south east of the tor. After a few hundred metres you will
come across the deserted village of Hundatora. Compared
with the Bronze Age settlements to be found all over the
moor this village is relatively modern, dating back only
to the Medieval era.

Clearly visible amongst the moorland are the walled
remains of houses, including four Dartmoor longhouses
and several farm buildings. It is believed the village was
occupied until the late 14th or early 15th Century, and
then abandoned either due to Dartmoor's deteriorating
climate or possibly the Black Death.

How to Get Here

Hound Tor is 8 miles from Bovey Tracey in Dartmoor National Park.
From Bovey Tracey, head west on the B3387 towards Haytor Vale.
After climbing up onto the moor you will pass Haytor and then
cross over a cattle grid. The road bends to the right, heading in the
direction of Widecombe-in-the-Moor. In a few hundred yards take
the right hand turning signposted Hound Tor. After a few minutes
you will see Hound Tor, and its large car park signed off to the right.

Parking Lat/Long: 50.599028, -3.7822795
Parking Grid Ref: SX 739 792
Parking Postcode: TQ13 9XQ
Map: OS Explorer Map OL28 (1:25 000) Dartmoor

Accessibility

From the large car park, the tor can be reached via a ten minute
gentle uphill walk across the open moorland. As the moorland is
rough and uneven, Hound Tor is not accessible for wheelchair users.

Best Time of Year/Day

Like other moorland areas of Dartmoor, Hound Tor can be
photographed equally well throughout the seasons. As the tor
offers viewpoints in all directions both sunrise and sunset are
suitable, although dawn would be my preference. Try to avoid
visiting during the day in the summertime, as visitor numbers
can make photographing the tor a frustrating experience.

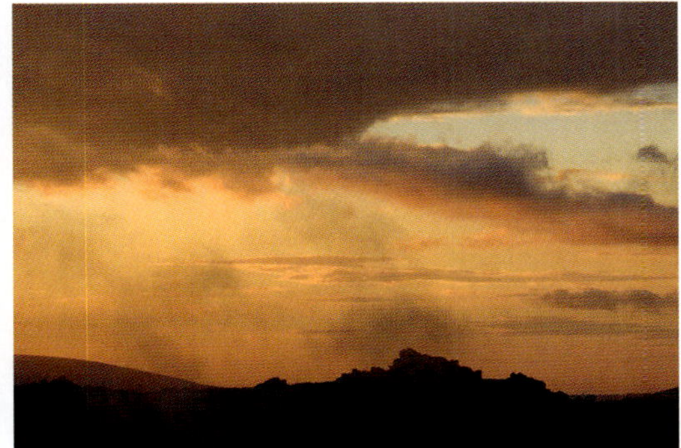

Sunset over Hound tor, photographed from Holwell Tor, Canon 1Ds
Mark III, 70-200mm at 163mm, ISO 100, 1/30 sec at f/16. July

In Dartmoor folklore Bowerman the Hunter, together with his pack of hounds, would roam all over the moor hunting prey. One day, while chasing a hare he stumbled upon and startled a coven of witches. After Bowerman and his hounds had charged past in pursuit of the hare, the angry witches plotted their revenge. One of the witches changed appearance to a hare, and lured Bowerman and his hounds to chase her over the moor. This pursuit lasted for many hours before an exhausted Bowerman was enticed behind a tor where the remaining witches lay in wait. The witches chanted a powerful spell, petrifying Bowerman into the pillar of granite we recognise today as Bowerman's Nose. The hounds were equally unfortunate, their stony figures can still be found nearby in the shape of Hound Tor.

Legend aside, Bowerman's Nose is a wonderfully picturesque and instantly recognisable Dartmoor feature, often appearing in local calendars and postcards. Located on the slopes of Hayne Down in the heart of Dartmoor, the granite stack makes an imposing photographic subject as it stands guard over surrounding moorland backed by distant rolling countryside.

What to Shoot and Viewpoints

There really is only one place from which to shoot Bowerman's Nose. The stack offers little potential from any angle apart from on the gentle slopes of Hayne Down. Don't let that dissuade you from visiting however, the view from Hayne Down is tremendous, and one of the most famous vistas in Dartmoor.

This is a quiet location, you won't find crowds of tourists here, just the occasional dog walker or lone photographer. This only adds to the special feeling of the place.

Although the viewpoint is restrictive, your choice of positioning makes a dramatic difference to Bowerman's Nose photographs. By venturing close and shooting wide-angle, the stack dominates the composition, standing up high above the surrounding hills. With a colourful sunset or if you are shooting a night sky this can make a terrific viewpoint. Alternatively, walk a little further uphill and shoot the stack in the context of its environment. By doing this, you achieve a very different picture, the stack sits below the horizon and is therefore surrounded by countryside.

As with most of Dartmoor's tors, sunlight bathing against the granite will transform this view and, in this case, bring the Bowerman back to life.

Illuminated by rich side lighting on a winter afternoon, Nikon D800E, 24-70mm at 45mm, ISO 100, 0.3 sec at f/11. January

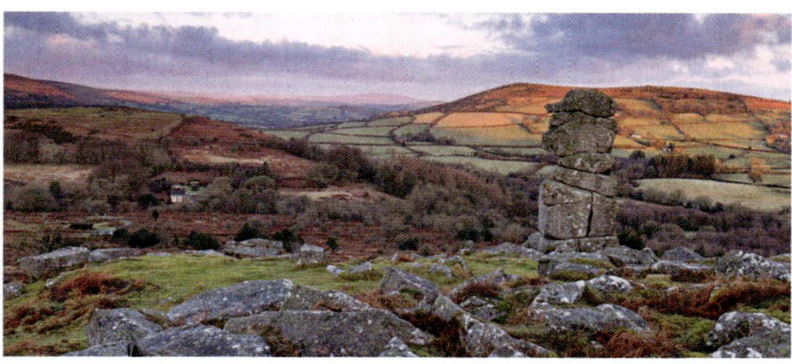

First light on a chill winter morning, Nikon D800E, 24-70mm at 32mm, ISO 100, 2.5 sec at f/11. January

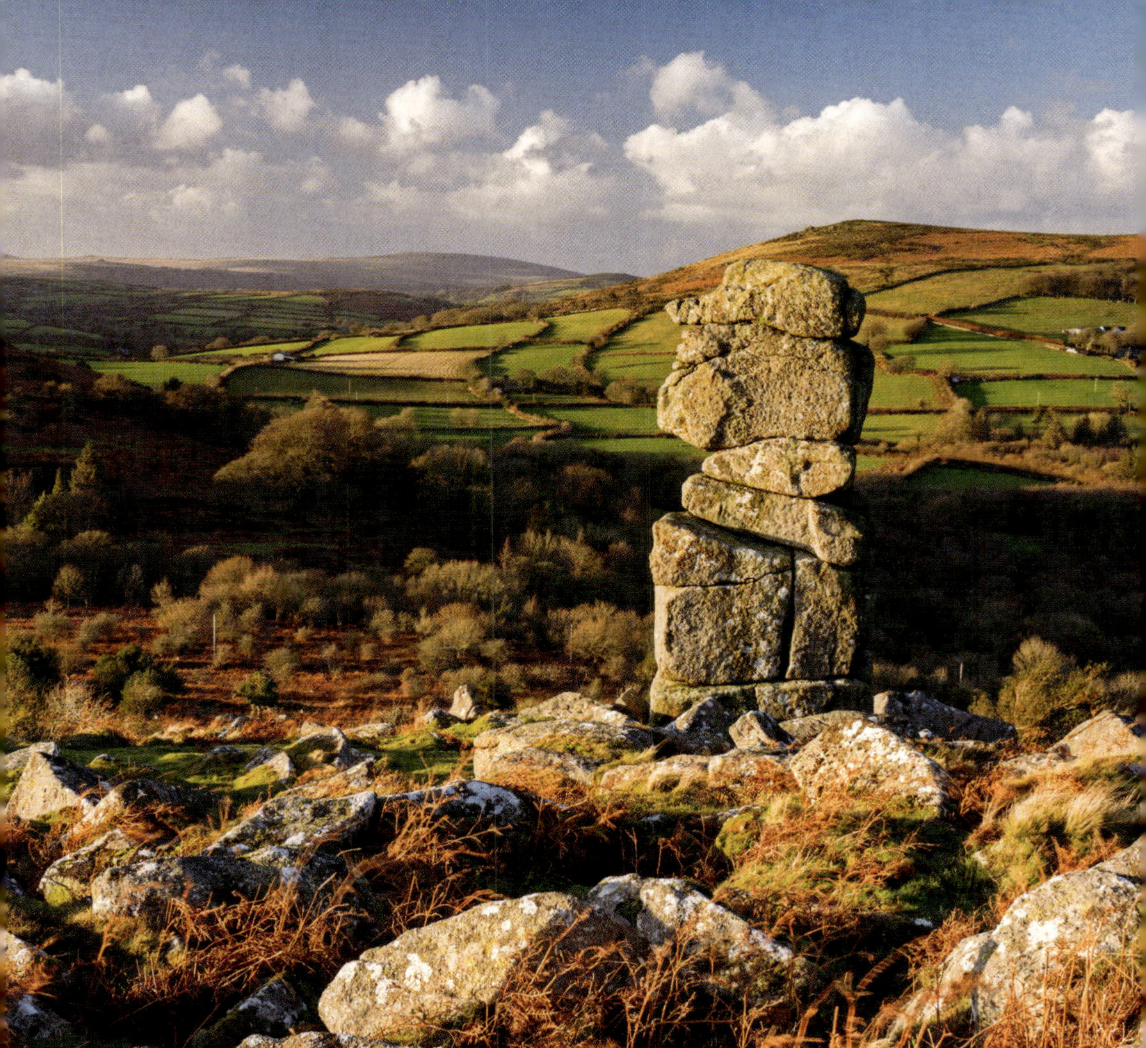

How to Get Here

Although located close to some of Dartmoor's most visited tors, Bowerman's Nose is a world away. From Bovey Tracey, head west on the B3387 towards Haytor Vale. After climbing up onto the moor you will head past Haytor and then cross over a cattle grid. The road now bends to the right, heading in the direction of Widecombe-in-the-Moor. In a few hundred yards take the right hand turning signposted Hound Tor. After a few minutes you will see Hound Tor, and its large car park on the right. Park here, walk back to the road and take the next right hand turning. Follow this road for around half a mile; you will soon notice Hayne Down on your right and Bowerman's Nose will be evident about half way up the hill.

Parking Lat/Long: 50.599028, -3.7822795
Parking Grid Ref: SX 739 792
Location Grid Ref: SX 742 805
Parking Postcode: TQ13 7TT (for nearby Holwell)
Map: OS Explorer Map OL28 (1:25 000) Dartmoor

Accessibility

Although the first part of the walk is along a sealed road, the climb up to Hayne Down is over rough moorland, and is unsuitable for wheelchair users. There is no official footpath to Bowerman's Nose, but several trails do head in the general direction. Good walking boots are recommended.

Best Time of Year/Day

Bowerman's Nose benefits from an afternoon/evening trip in either summer or winter, when late side lighting makes the rocks glow in golden tones. In spring and summer, the sun sets almost directly behind, leaving the stack in shadow. However, don't rule out summer time as the verdant bracken makes ideal foreground for photographs.

It goes without saying that this location looks great in frosty or snowy conditions. If you are fortunate enough to be here during a cold snap, head up at dawn to photograph frost sugar coating the rocks, or virgin snow blanketing the moorland.

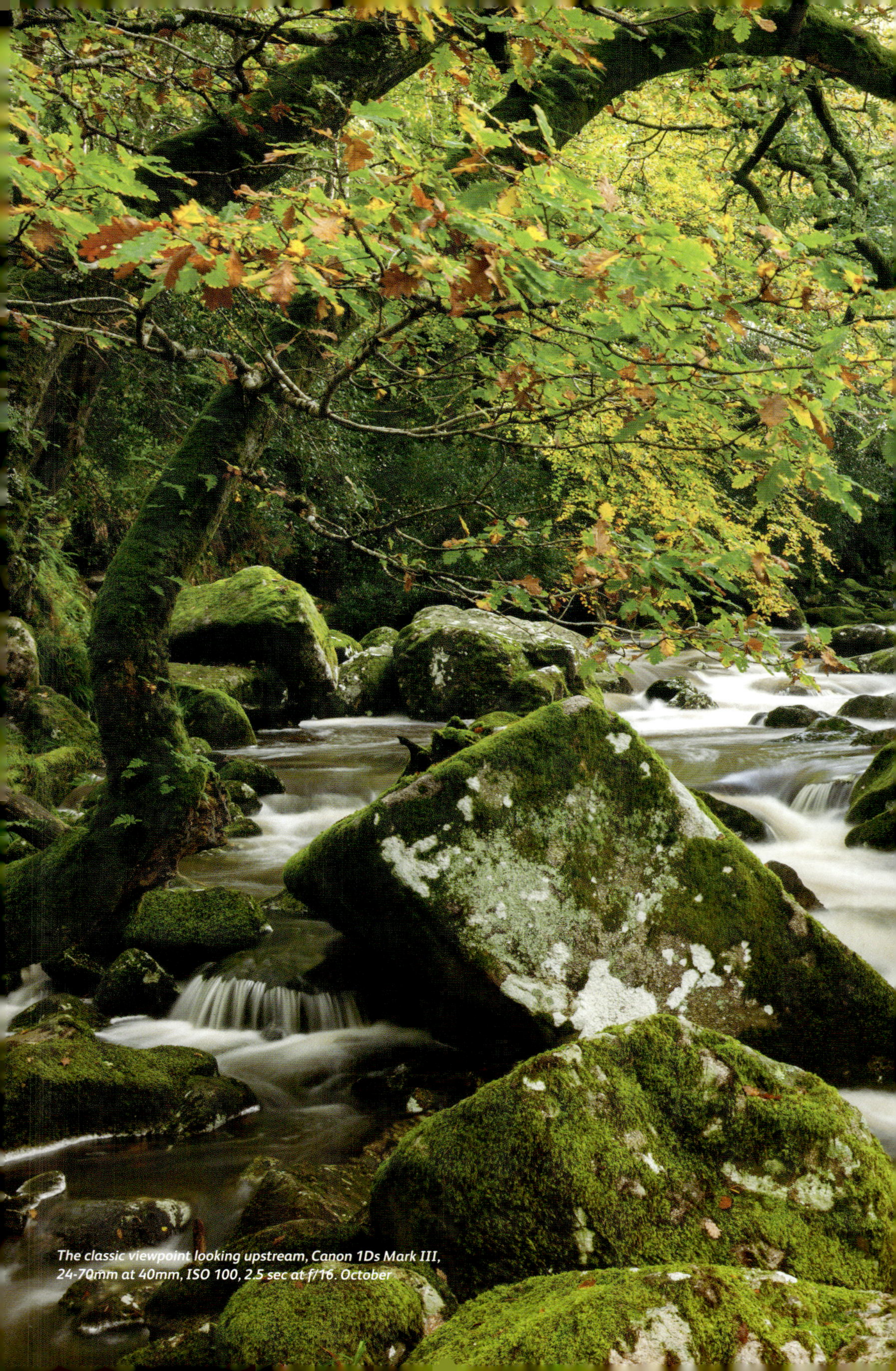

The classic viewpoint looking upstream, Canon 1Ds Mark III,
24-70mm at 40mm, ISO 100, 2.5 sec at f/16. October

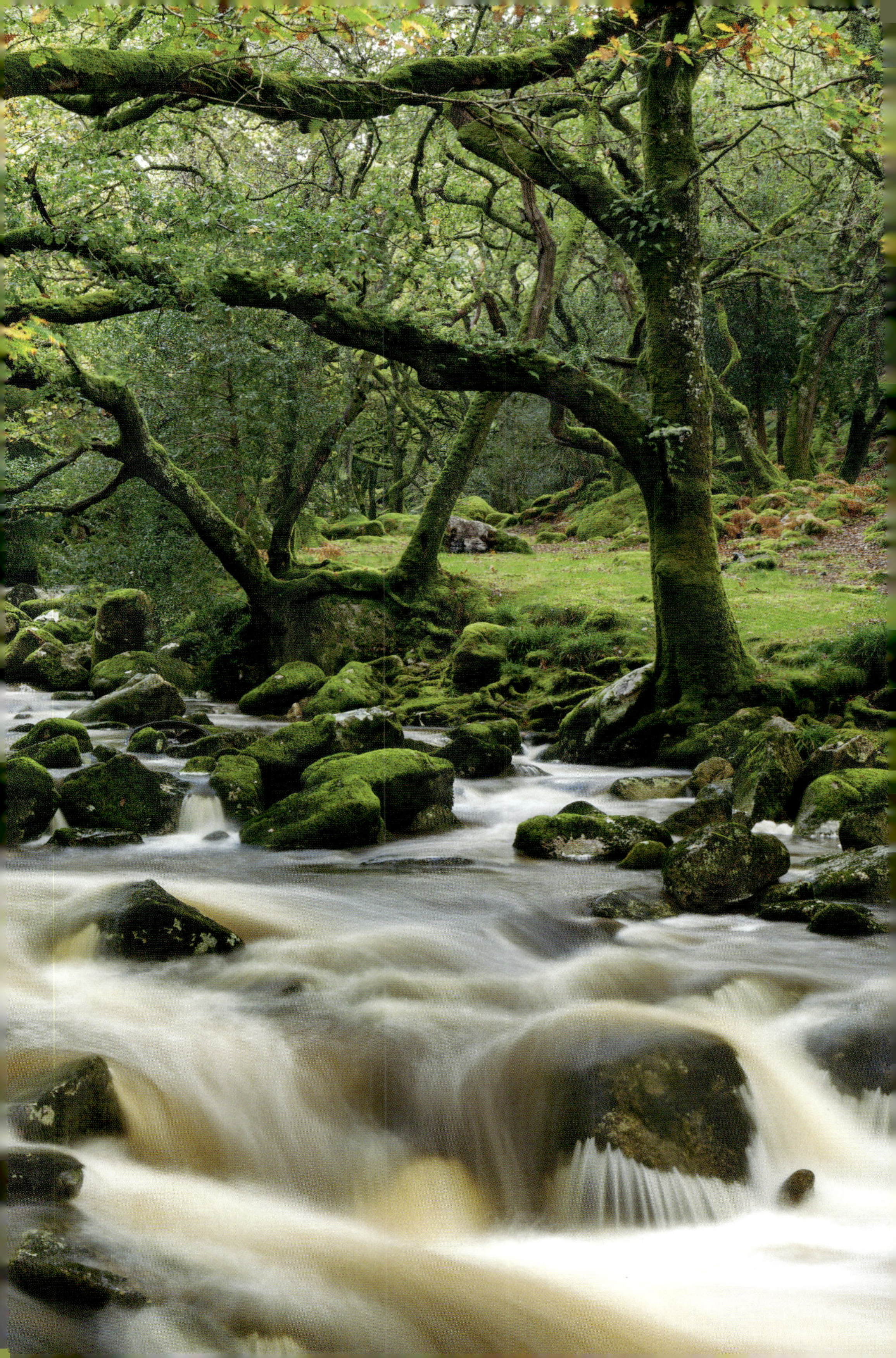

Hidden in wooded valleys below the exposed moorland, Dartmoor has some lovely rocky rivers. Arguably the most photogenic of all is the section of the River Plym near the village of Shaugh Prior. On its meandering journey to reach Plymouth Sound the River Plym passes through the magical Dewerstone Wood. Sharing its name with the towering crags rising vertically above the trees, the woodland has a primeval atmosphere. Ancient trees twist and bend, their moss-covered branches reaching out over the river. This feels like a location from Lord of the Rings, yet it has its own very dark legends that could rival anything from Middle Earth.

The woodland and crags were named after the Wisht Huntsman Dewer, more commonly known as the Devil. Hunting over the moor at night with his pack of phantom hounds, Dewer would chase terrified people up to the top of the crags after which they would fall to their deaths far below.

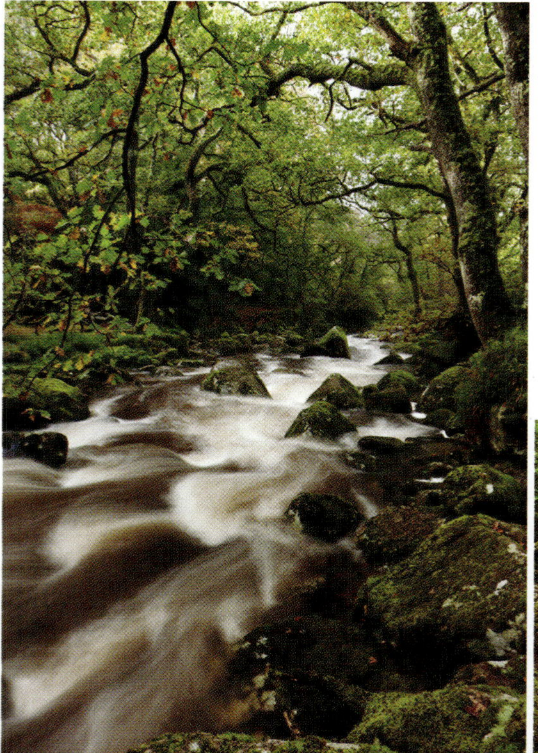

River Plym rushing through beautiful deciduous woodland, Canon 1Ds Mark III, 24-70mm at 25mm, ISO 100, 2 sec at f/16. October

What to Shoot and Viewpoints

Although the woodland is beautiful in its own right, most visitors to Dewerstone Wood are drawn to the river. Within metres of the car park a footbridge gives you the first view over the boulder strewn river and into the woodland. The view from the bridge makes a lovely composition, yet with a little effort the rewards are far better.

Footpaths follow the river on both banks, giving countless opportunities. There is one viewpoint of particular interest; after crossing the bridge, turn right and follow the path upstream for around 100 yards. At this section the footpath looks down to the river about 2 metres below, but set amongst some large boulders a small trail provides safe access down to the water's edge. From this viewpoint you can get low and close to photograph the fast flowing water rushing through narrow channels and plunging over isolated boulders, creating a series of mini cascades.

With a wide angle lens you can include the gorgeous moss covered boulders lining the river bank and shoot the rocky stream set amidst a fantastic frame of gnarled trees above and verdant rocks below.

Most tend to shoot on this side of the bridge, finding viewpoints both upstream and downstream from this spot. However, there are other less visited but equally promising viewpoints on the other side of the river. Retrace your footsteps across the bridge and then follow the small trail to the left. Careful footing is required when venturing this way. The path is narrow at first with a drop on one side, then after crossing a stile it continues over a slippery boulder-covered shoreline. Once past this hazard the route is easy and follows close to the river bank. From this side you can photograph the beautiful moss-covered trees with spidery limbs reaching out over the river.

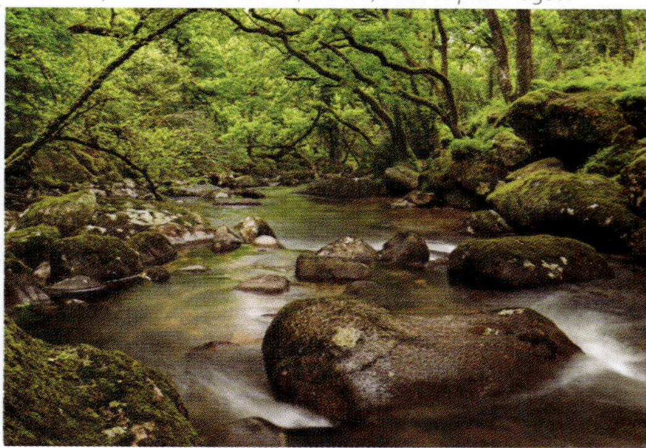

Viewpoint on the opposite bank further upstream, Canon 1Ds Mark III, 17-40mm at 40mm, ISO 50, 8 sec at f/22. August

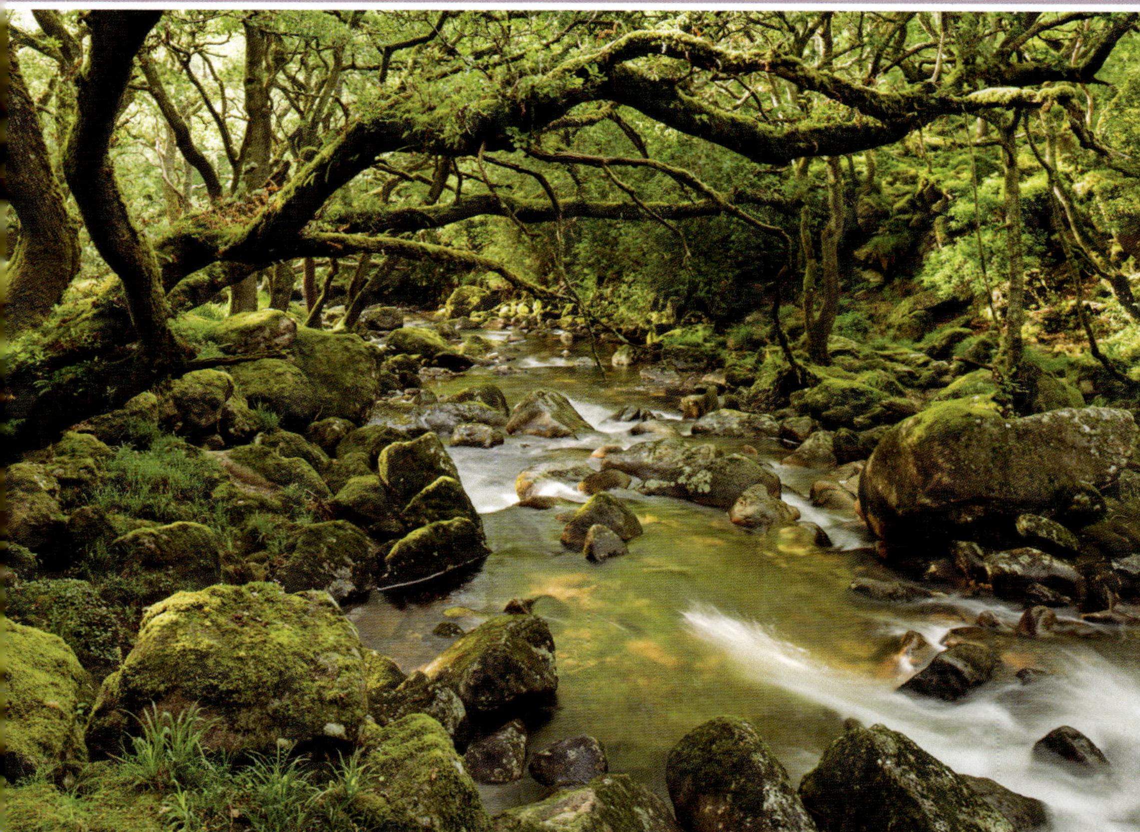

Looking downstream from the eastern bank, Nikon D800E, 17-35mm at 30mm, ISO 100, 1.6 sec at f/11. June

How to Get Here

From Plymouth head north on the A386 Tavistock Road. Upon reaching Roborough turn right and drive through Bickleigh, taking the first left on a country lane after passing through the village, signed for Shaugh Prior. The small lane winds through countryside for a couple of miles before crossing a large bridge surrounded by woodland. Immediately after crossing the bridge, look out for a car park on the left

Parking Lat/Long: 50.454075, -4.0672106
Parking Grid Ref: SX 533 636
Parking Postcode: PL7 5HD
Map: OS Explorer Map OL28 (1:25 000) Dartmoor

Accessibility

The car park offers parking for around 10 vehicles, but there are no facilities. The footpaths are well used and generally level with some uphill sections. As mentioned above some boulders can be slippery so it is advisable to wear walking boots with good grip.

Best Time of Year/Day

As the river is surrounded by deciduous woodland, in the winter and early spring when the branches are bare so less appealing. Late Spring and summer is better although low water levels can mean the river isn't flowing well. The best season to visit is autumn, when higher water levels combine with autumnal foliage.

Whichever season you decide on, plan your visit on an overcast day with flat lighting. Sunny clear days can make photographs very difficult in woodlands, when a camera struggles to capture both sunlit and shadowy areas

With over 200 tors spread over the vast moor, visitors to Dartmoor have an almost endless supply of fantastic locations to explore and photograph. Some can be reached in just a few steps from the nearest car park, while others require somewhat more effort (plus a map and compass) to find. The list and the map on the next pages provides key information to help you visit and photograph some of the more accessible and photogenic Dartmoor tors.

What is a Tor?

Tors on Dartmoor are formed from a rock called granite. 280 million years ago this granite was liquid that welled up from the earth's mantle and cooled slowly allowing the growth of the characteristic crystals of quartz and feldspar. As the rock cooled it contracted and cracked into vertical and horizontal fractures.

Over time the covering rocks were eroded away exposing the granite to weathering processes. A combination of chemical and physical processes, especially during the glacial and periglacial periods of the last ice age, have combined to enlarge those cracks. Frost, wind and rain have removed the softer sediments leaving the protruding rock sculptures called tors we see today. Individual blocks can be finely balanced so they rock, these are called logan stones.

Opposite top: Arm's Tor (no.1), Nikon D800E, 17-35mm at 24mm, ISO 100, 2.5 sec at f/11. August

Opposite lower photos. Top left: Sheep's Tor (no.22), top right: Bell Tor (no.6), bottom left: Sharpitor (no.21), bottom right: Rippon Tor (no.19)

Photos this page. top left: Great Mis Tor (no.10), top right: Pew Tor (no.18), bottom left: Sourton Tor (no.23), bottom right: Cox Tor (no.8)

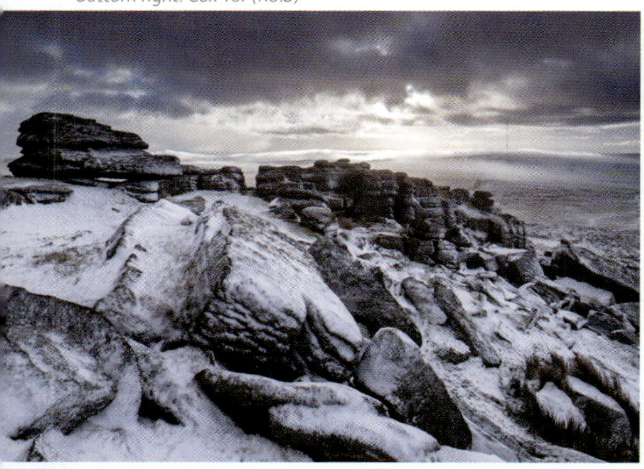

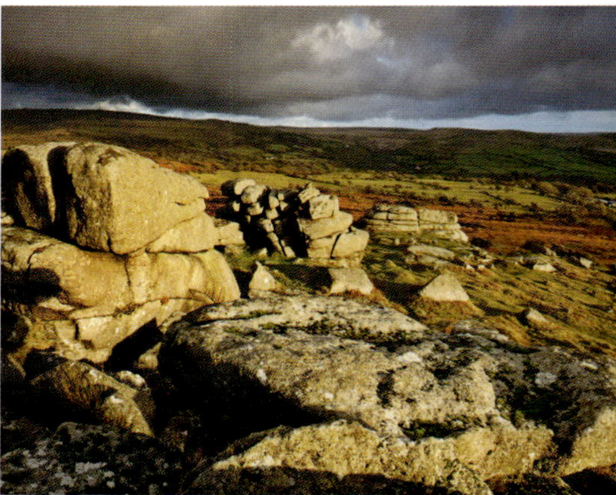

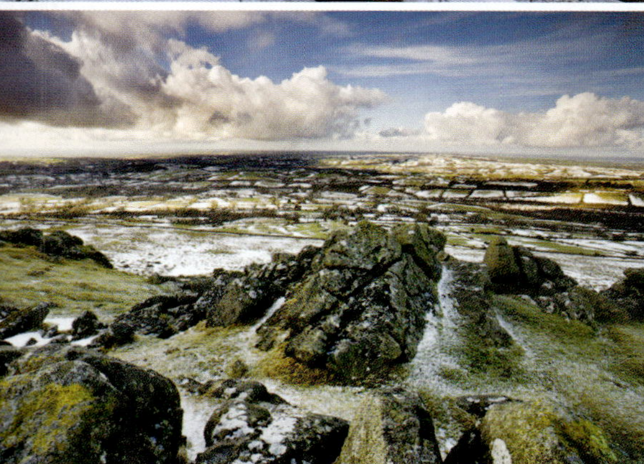

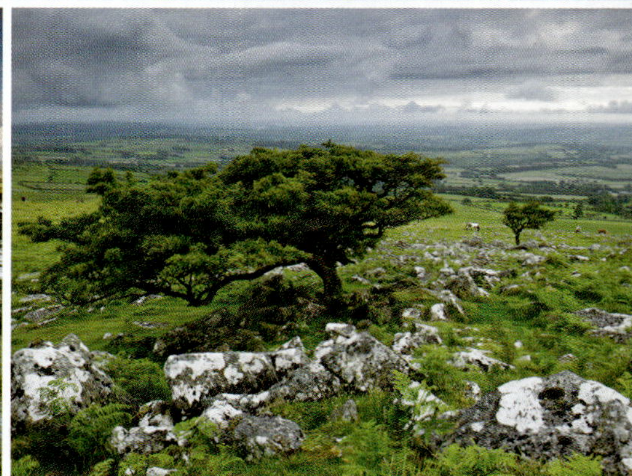

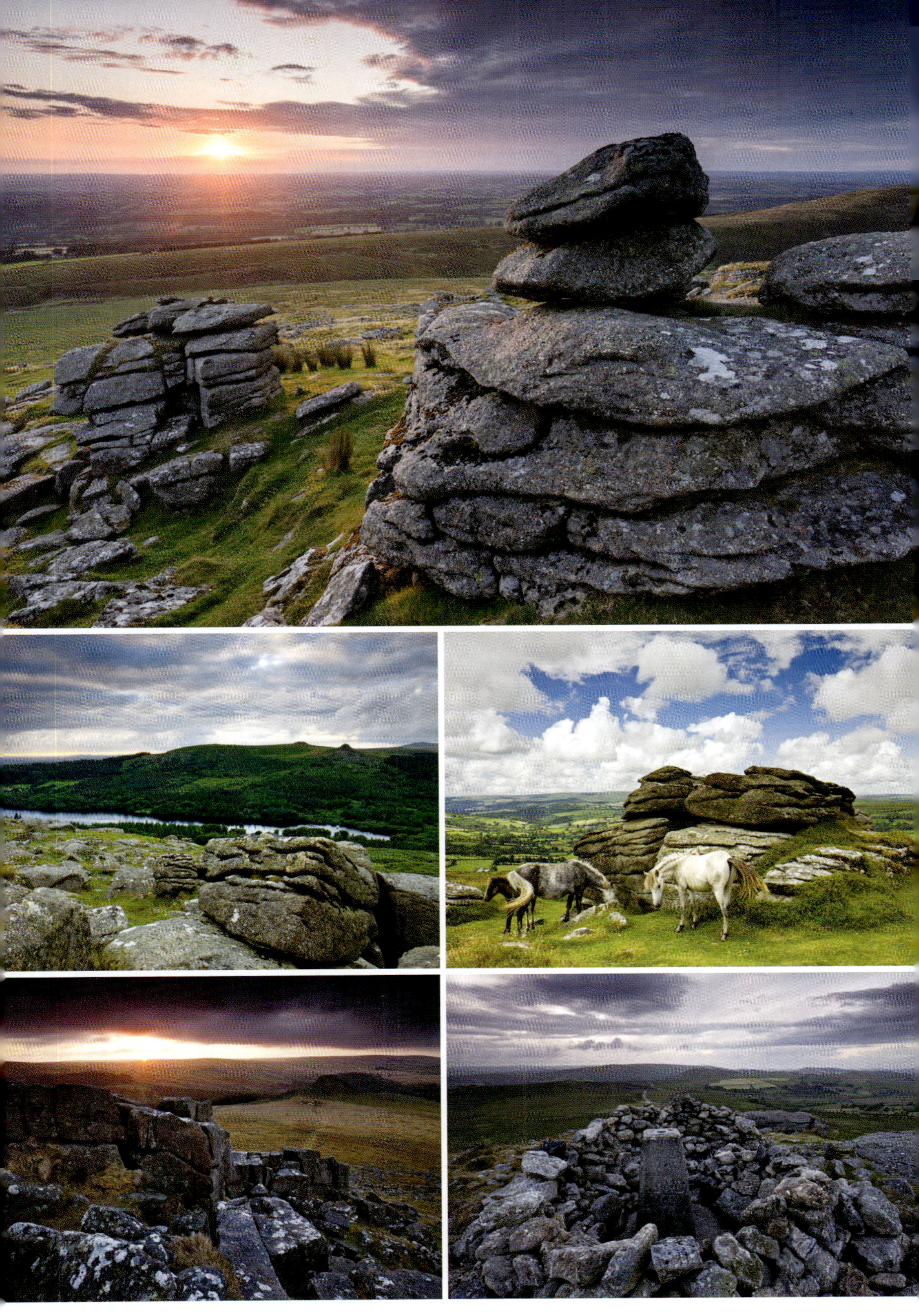

25 Accessible Dartmoor Tors to Visit

Tor Name	Average walking time (mins)	Elevation gain	Height	Grid co-ordinates
1. Arms Tor	45	180m	457m	SX 541 863
2. Beardown Tors	45	170m	513m	SX 604 774
3. Bellever Tor	30	80m	443m	SX 644 764
4. Bench Tor	20	10m	312m	SX 691 716
5. Brat Tor	30	170m	452m	SX 539 855
6. Bell Tor	10	30m	400m	SX 730 778
7. Combestone Tor	1	10m	356m	SX 670 718
8. Cox Tor	30	120m	442m	SX 531 762
9. Easdon Tor	30	220m	439m	SX 729 823
10. Great Mis Tor	45	170m	538m	SX 562 769
11. Greator Rocks	20	30m	371m	SX 746 785
12. Honeybag Tor	20	80m	445m	SX 729 787
13. King Tor	30	90m	488m	SX 709 816
14. Kings Tor	30	60m	380m	SX 556 739
15. Leather Tor	20	20m	370m	SX 563 700
16. Longaford Tor	45	160m	507m	SX 616 779
17. Oke Tor	60	140m	466m	SX 612 900
18. Pew Tor	15	90m	317m	SX 533 735
19. Rippon Tor	20	80m	473m	SX 747 756
20. Saddle Tor	5	30m	428m	SX 751 763
21. Sharpitor	10	30m	402m	SX 559 704
22. Sheeps Tor	30	140m	369m	SX 566 682
23. Sourton Tor	30	190m	440m	SX 542 899
24. Top Tor	10	30m	432m	SX 736 762
25. Yar Tor	20	60m	416m	SX 678 740

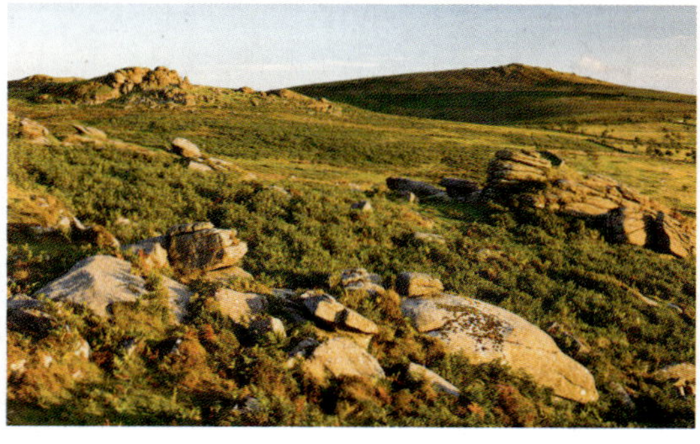
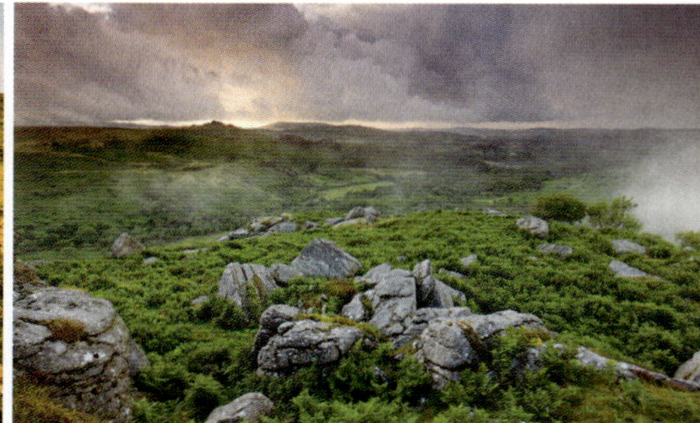

Left: Saddle Tor (no.20), right: Holwell Tor

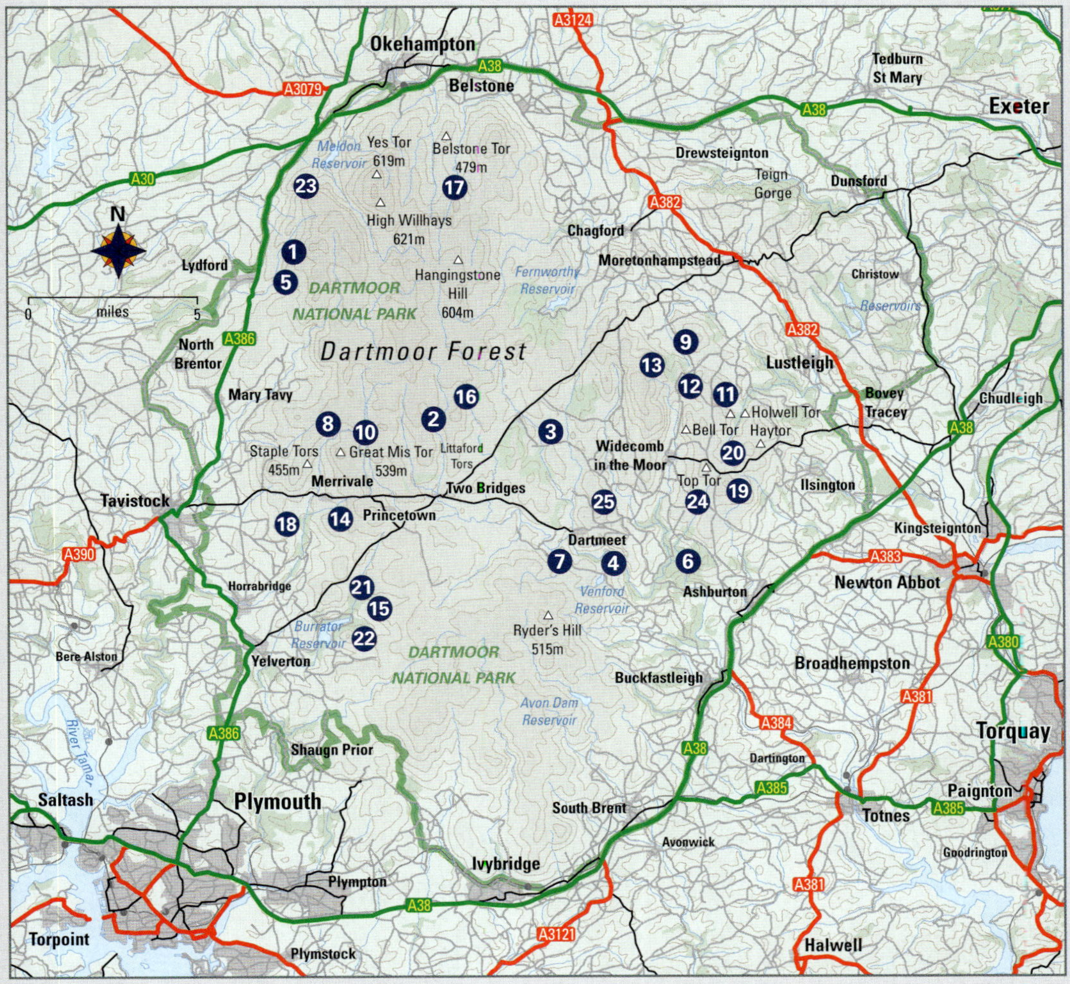

Contains Ordnance Survey data © Crown Copyright and database right (2016), map location overlay © fotoVUE 2016

Left: Littaford Tor, right: Haytor

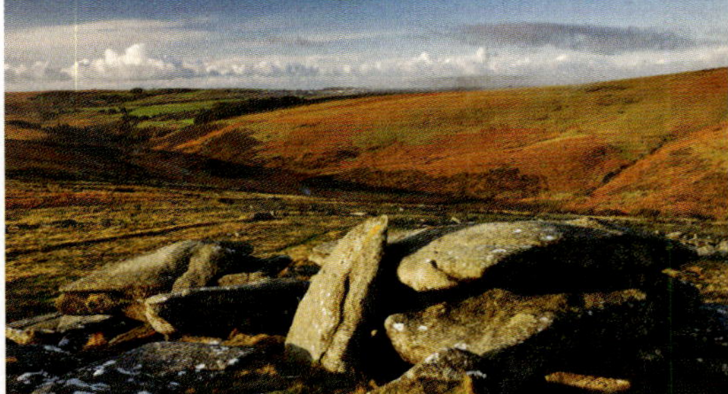

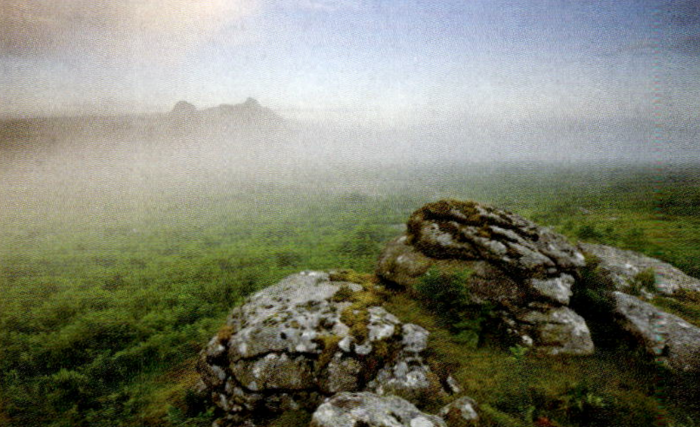

As with Cornwall, the south Devon coast is in large part much more gentle than its northern counterpart, and holds considerably more variety. From Plymouth on the Cornish border down to Start Point in the South Hams, the coastline is a strange mixture of both gentle estuaries and dramatic cliffs.

After rounding Start Point, the long shingle beach at Slapton Sands signals a change in both the nature and direction of the coastline. From here until reaching Exmouth, the coastline heads northwards taking in the hugely popular seaside towns of Paignton and Torquay then the lesser known Teignmouth and Dawlish. Orcombe Point in Exmouth marks the western end of the spectacular Jurassic Coast, Britain's second natural World Heritage Site. The bright red cliffs found in this area such as at Sidmouth and Ladram Bay are characteristic of this coastline and date back to the Triassic period. Further along the coast, at Beer the cliffs change again both in colour and consistency, this time to white chalk, dating from the more recent Cretaceous period.

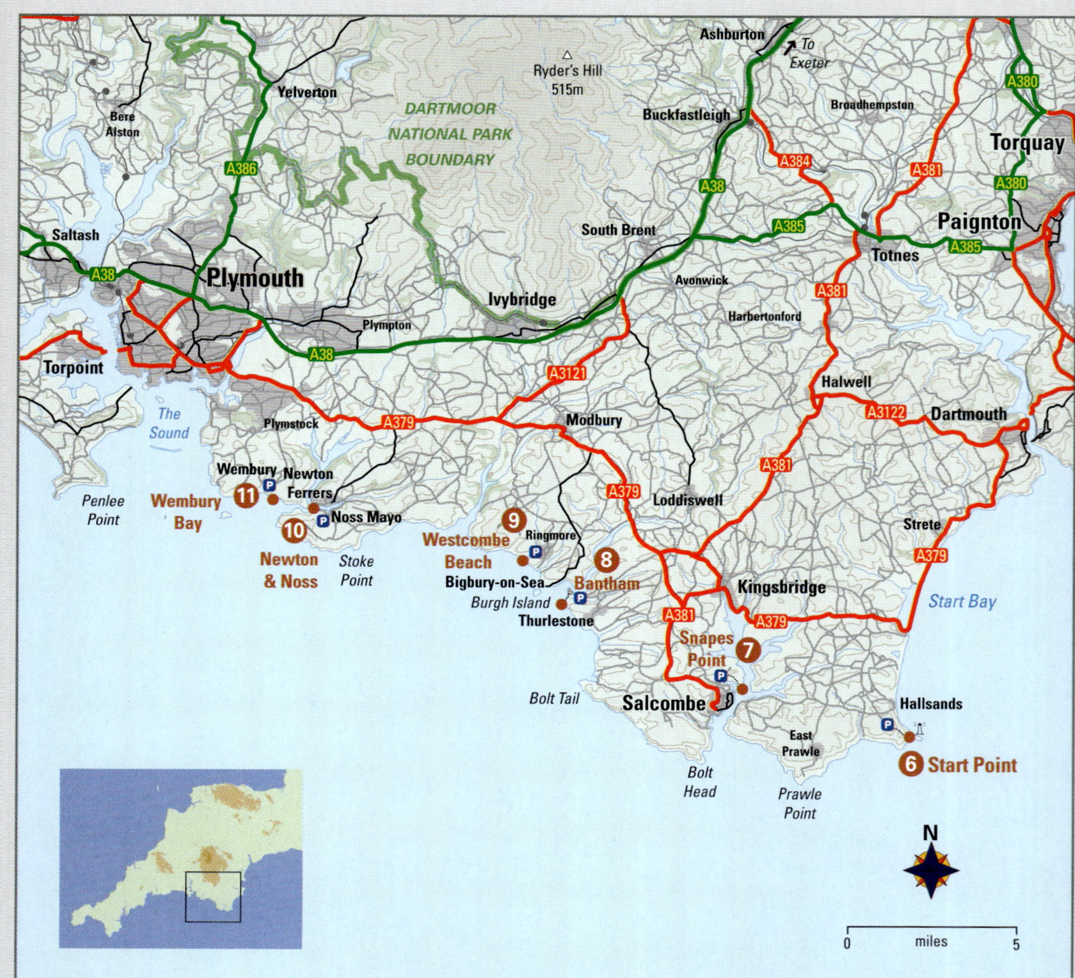

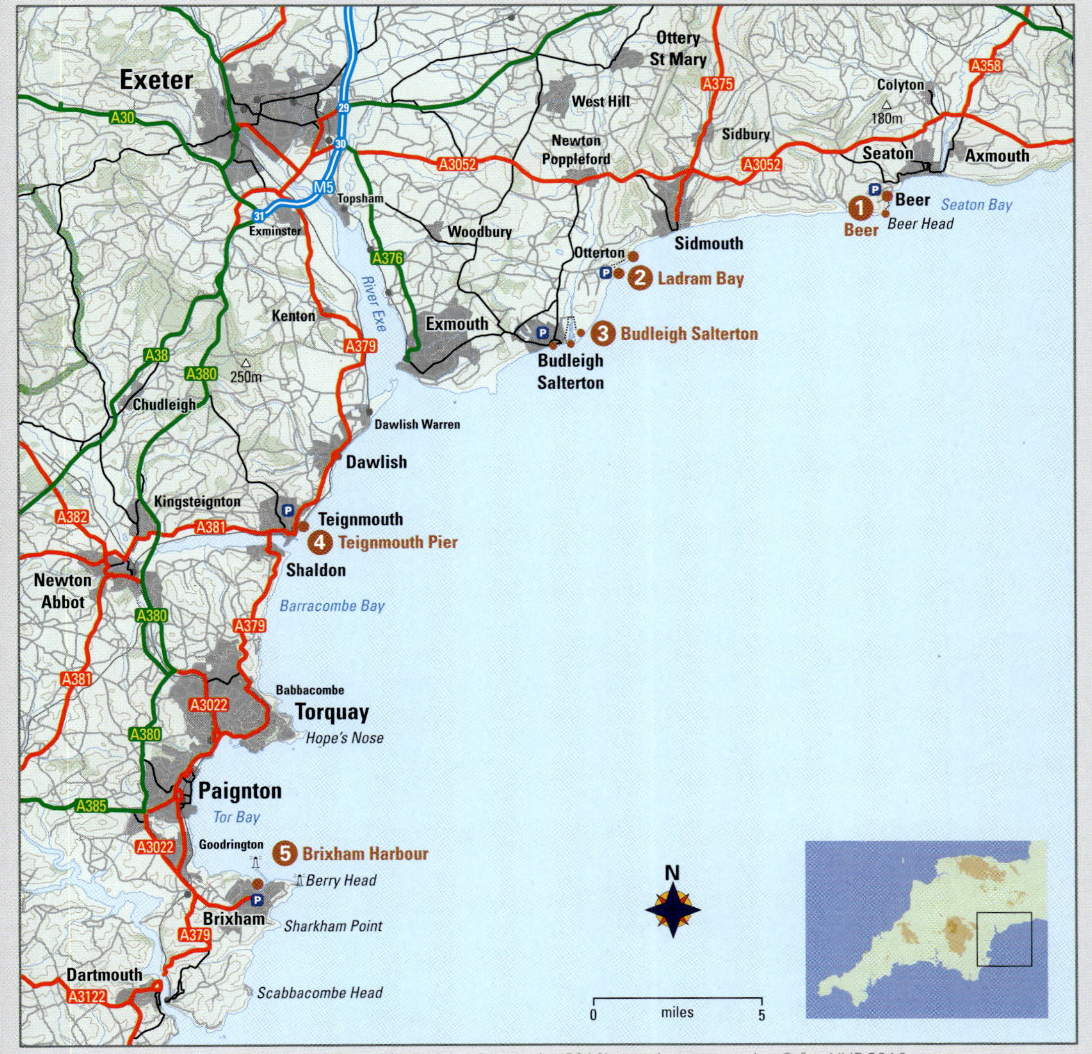

Contains Ordnance Survey data © Crown Copyright and database right (2016), map location overlay © fotoVUE 2016

Beer

Close to Devon's border with Dorset, the pretty fishing village of Beer is one of the highlights of the Devon stretch of the Jurassic Coast World Heritage Site. Distinctive white chalk cliffs overlook a small shingle cove, sheltered from the prevailing winds and secluded enough to once make this an infamous location for smuggling.

The village has for long been associated with fishing; however the absence of any harbour has resulted in the fishing boats being winched high up on the shingle beach. Historically a manual capstan would have been operated by 20 men to winch the boats high enough to escape the tide. Nowadays, electric winches and tractors are used to perform the same task, making the beach an active working area, busy with fishing equipment.

What to Shoot and Viewpoints

Viewpoint 1 – Haytor Rocks

Upon first arrival at Beer, the fishing boats pulled high up the beach seem an obvious place to photograph. The colourful boats can make wonderful subjects, especially on bright sunny mornings with a blue sky for a backdrop. These boats however aren't as easy to photograph as you may at first think. Being a busy working environment the boats are often surrounded by lots of fishing paraphernalia, lobster pots, nets and buoys. While these objects can give the beach a cluttered appearance they are to be expected around fishing boats and can make great photographic interest. There are many less photogenic objects that can prove more challenging; winches, rubber matting and black plastic boxes can spoil pictures and cannot always be excluded.

If the clutter surrounding the boats proves problematic at close quarters, try photographing from a higher vantage point up on the cliffs. The coast path climbs high above the beach and gives great views down into the cove and so minimises the impact of any distracting fishing objects.

Personally, I find the clutter makes the boats unappealing and so try to create compositions that avoid them entirely. This can be easily achieved by walking down to the shore, but the lack of foreground interest can make this area every bit as challenging to photograph. As a solution, venture to either end of the beach and you will usually find objects to break up the mass of shingle. On the eastern end of the beach, a rocky ledge (East Ebb) becomes visible during low tide. This platform offers both foreground interest and the means to position yourself further out to sea if you wish to compose looking back towards the beach and village.

The west side of the beach offers even more potential. At the base of the steep cliffs a jumble of large boulders provides the perfect subject matter to break up the large expanse of shingle in wide angle compositions. The shooting position is better also, giving you a more pleasing vista of the cliffs beyond the beach. The boulders will be covered at high tide so plan a visit to this area from a low to middle tide, ideally at dawn or early morning when the beach will be illuminated warmly but the sun won't be so strong that the white cliffs will overexpose.

Viewpoint 2 – Beer Head

About a mile south of the village, Beer Head marks the point where the east-west coastline abruptly shifts direction to the north. You can follow the coast path directly from the village, or park a little closer on the cliffs but either way will involve at least a twenty minute walk to reach the location.

The viewpoint at Beer Head affords a far reaching vista along Devon's south coast and a glimpse into why this area of the south coast is so remarkable. The distinctive chalk cliffs on the headland below date from the Cretaceous period then suddenly give way to the far older Triassic red cliffs at Branscombe. This gives an insight into the enormous geological forces at work which have folded and shaped this landscape.

As the viewpoint points westerly Beer Head can make a wonderful location to shoot towards a colourful sunset sky. The exposed, high up position can make it a difficult place to shoot on a windy day, so be sure to check the forecast before venturing to this spot.

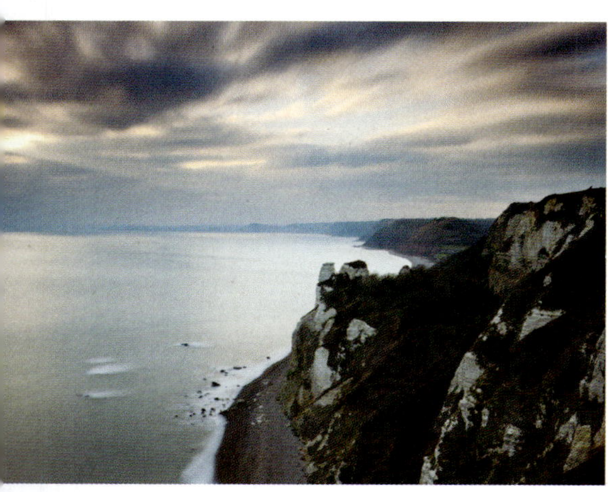

View west from Beer Head, taking in the Hooken landslip, Canon 1Ds Mark III, 24-70mm at 35mm, ISO 100, 45 sec at f/10. January

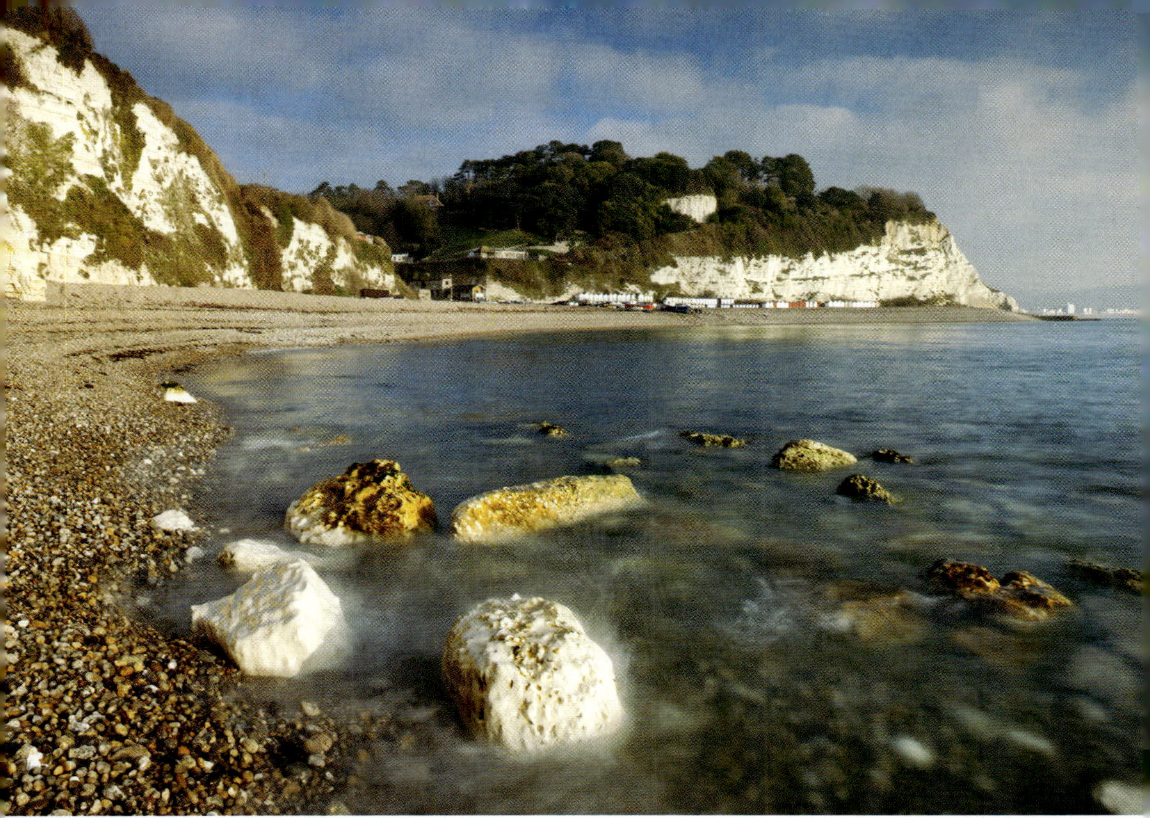

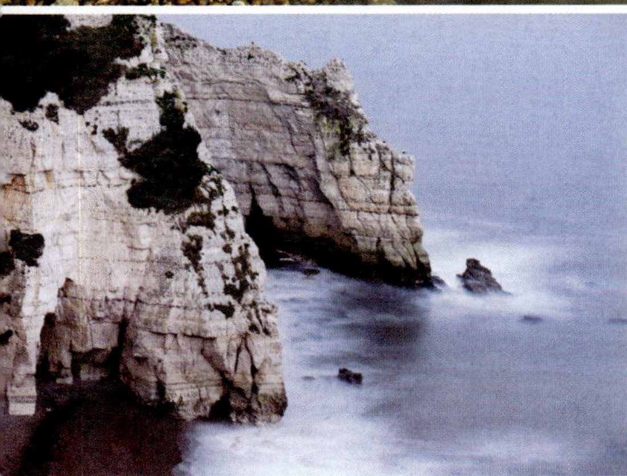

Heavily eroded chalk cliffs near Beer Head, Canon 1Ds Mark III, 70-200mm at 140mm, ISO 100, 30 sec at f/10. January

How to Get Here

Beer is situated on the south coast in East Devon, close to the Dorset border. From the A30 at Honiton head south on the A375 for 3 miles, then turn left onto the Seaton Road. Follow the road for approximately 5 miles, then turn right when you see the road sign for Beer. The road will take you into the centre of the village, where you will find roadside parking close to the beach.

Parking Lat/Long: 50.696821, -3.0919151
Parking Grid Ref: SY 229 891
Parking Postcode: EX12 3ET
Map: OS Explorer Map 116 (1:25 000) Lyme Regis & Bridport

Accessibility

The beach is a minute's walk from the village centre, while Beer Head is approximately 30 minutes walk. A closer car park on the cliff tops reduces the walk to Beer Head to about 20 minutes. Although both the beach and Beer Head are unsuitable for wheelchairs, there is an area on the cliffs overlooking the beach that is accessible.

Best Time of Year/Day

Beer and Beer Head are best photographed in the winter when the sun rises and sets out to sea. The beach works best during sunrise and early morning, while Beer Head is better positioned for sunset.

Top: the seashore and distinctive white cliffs at Beer, Canon 1Ds Mark III, 24-70mm at 24mm, ISO 50, 2 sec at f/16. December

With its distinctive red coloured cliffs and sea stacks Ladram Bay is one of the most impressive bays on the Devon stretch of the Jurassic Coast. The sandstone cliffs date back to the Triassic Period some 220 million years ago making this area the oldest part of the World Heritage Site. The red colouring in the cliffs and stacks is caused by the oxidation of iron, an indication that this area was once a sandy desert.

It is hard to imagine those distant origins now. Ladram Bay is now home to one of the largest holiday parks in the UK, with static caravans, bars and entertainment venues creeping almost up to the cliff edges. Sadly, the caravan park does tend to spoil the ambience of what would otherwise be some of the finest natural coastal scenery to be found anywhere in England.

What to Shoot and Viewpoints

Viewpoint 1 – The Beach

A short 2 minute walk from the car park brings you down to a sheltered wide cove with a narrow pebble beach backed by vertical cliffs. The first thing that will grab your attention is the sizeable sea stack directly in front of you. A second, more impressive, stack is located at the far end of the beach. Both stacks are close to the shore, making a wide-angle lens necessary to fit them in the frame. While the far stack is probably the more photogenic, the first benefits from some small boats often found pulled high onto the beach providing welcome foreground.

A walk to the far end of the beach will reward you with an excellent viewpoint from which to shoot the second stack. From the nearby shore the stack appears as a tall thin tower. As impressive as the sea stack looks from this position the plain pebble beach presents the same compositional issues as before. With a lack of any other objects to include in the foreground of your frame, thoughts turn to the sea. When photographed with a slow shutter speed of 1-3 seconds, waves rushing over the pebbly shore will add drama to the foreground. Perfecting this technique may take several attempts, and with a risk of getting wet feet, but the end results will be worth it.

Early morning sunshine completely transforms the sandstone, making it glow in rich orange tones. Aim to visit around dawn and photograph this view after the sun has risen but before the light becomes harsh. A clear sky further compliments the picture, the blue and orange complimenting each other.

When the tide is low several weathered ledges are exposed just past the sea stack near to Smallstones Point. These ledges, complete with rock pools and channels of water, offer a wonderful alternative to the pebble beach. However, the view of the stack from here is nowhere near as good as before. Not only does the stack appear less elegant but it also merges somewhat with the cliffs beyond. This viewpoint does offer a different and less photographed view of Ladram Bay however.

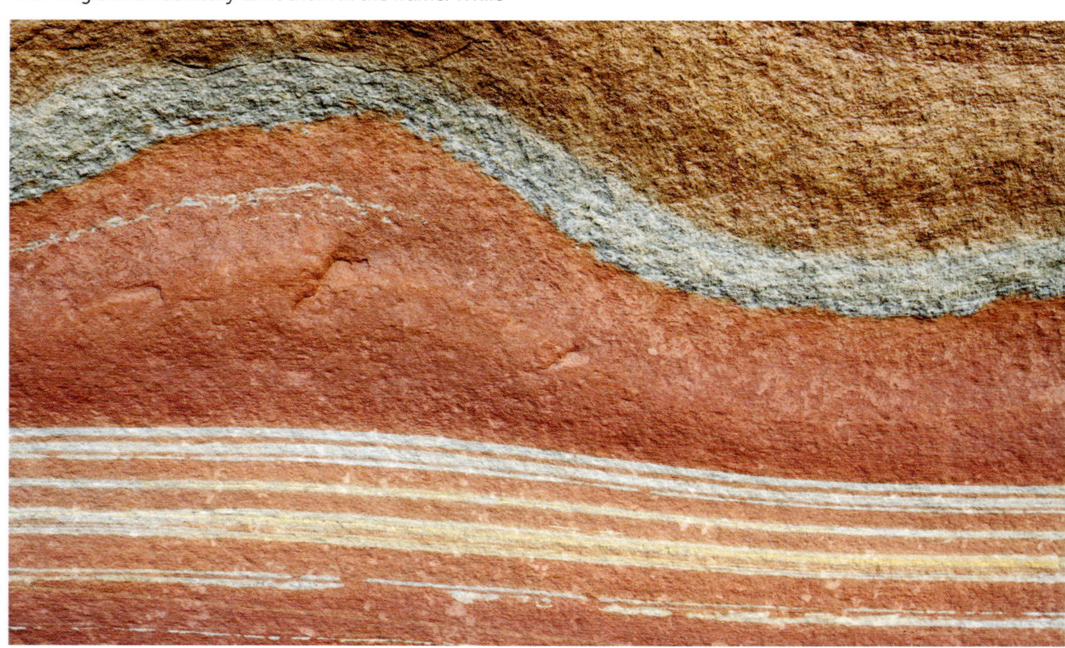

Layers in the distinctive Otterton sandstone cliffs, Canon 5D, 17-40mm at 40mm, ISO 400, 1/20 sec at f/14. April

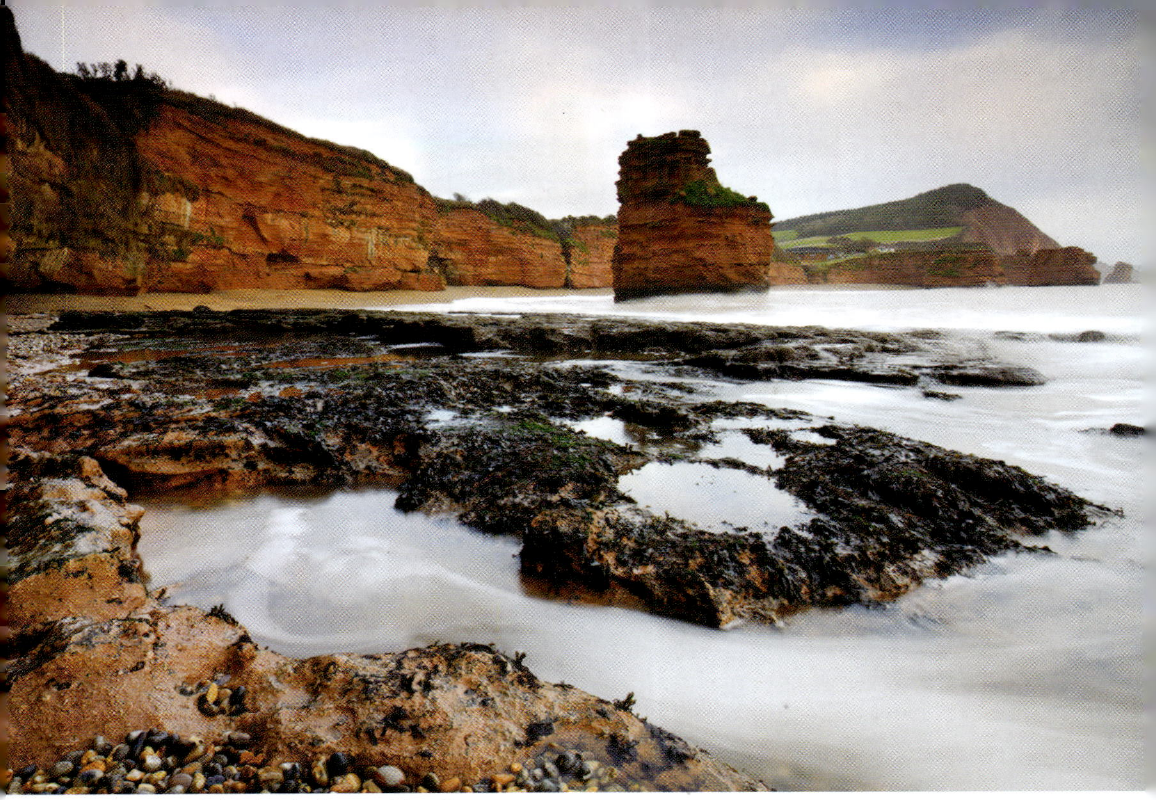

*Ledges at the west end of the beach offer some interesting
foreground, Canon 1Ds Mark III, 17-40mm at 20mm,
ISO 50, 3 sec at f/19. January*

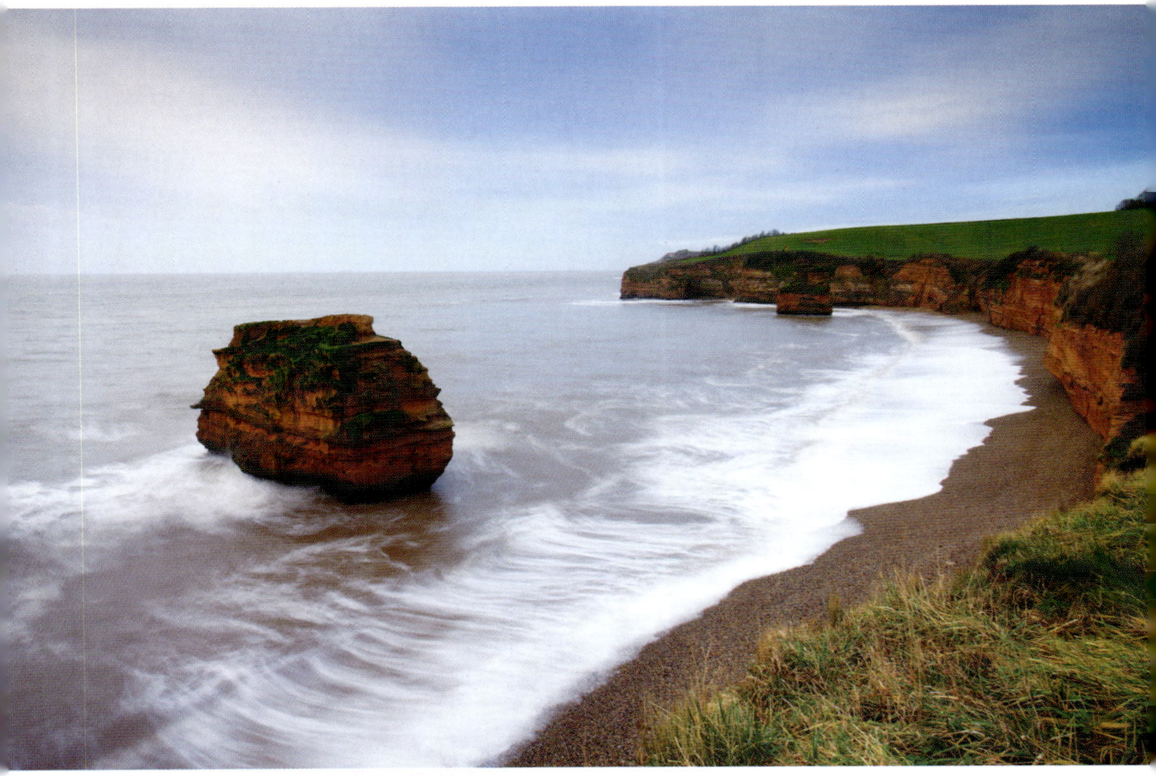

*Overlooking Ladram beach from the cliffs, Canon 1Ds Mark
III, 17-40mm at 21mm, ISO 50, 3 sec at f/16. January*

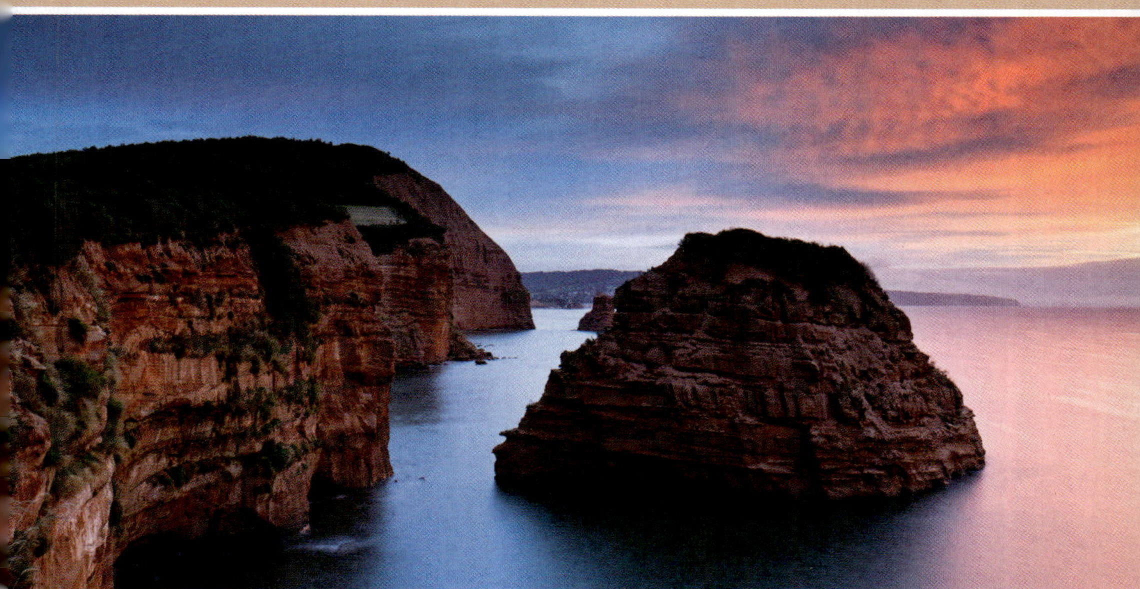

Cliff top viewpoint east at dawn, Nikon D800E, 17-35mm at 28mm, ISO 100, 10 sec at f/11. September

Viewpoint 2 – The Cliffs

Some of the finest and best known views of Ladram Bay can be found from the surrounding cliffs. As well as enabling elevated views over the beach, several viewpoints offer exceptional vistas northwards along the coast.

The cove just around the headland to the north boasts four huge sea stacks, with another a little further along the coast. Such rich coastal scenery should merit Ladram Bay a similar status to Australia's much acclaimed Twelve Apostles. However, the close proximity of these stacks to the cliffs makes photographing them all but impossible from every position but an aerial view.

Thanks to trimming of the bushes growing along the coast path, views of the stacks are more open than previously. But without crossing safety barriers and standing in a dangerous position on the cliff edge, it is impossible to photograph the nearest stacks in their entirety. Rather than risking such a dangerous viewpoint, please stay on the safety of the footpath. From the path several stacks are still visible, including the largest and most impressive, and you can also get a great viewpoint of the red cliffs stretching eastwards.

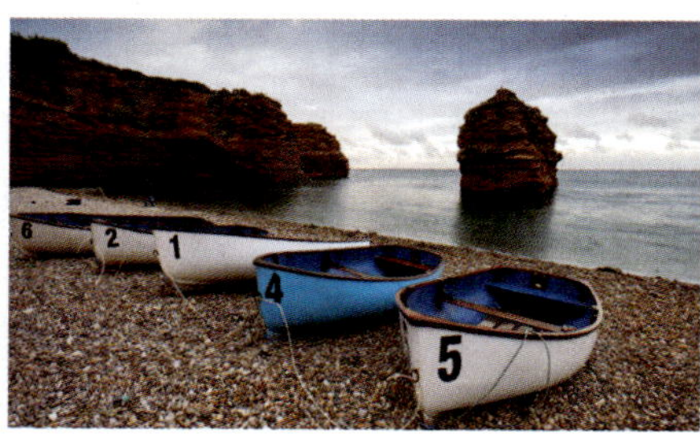

How to Get Here

From Exeter head toward Exmouth on the A376. At Clyst St George take the first exit off the roundabout onto the B3179 heading towards Budleigh Salterton. Stay on this road for 7 miles, ignoring the turn off to Budleigh Salterton. Continue through the village of Otterton; after half a mile you will see a right turn into Ladram Bay Holiday Park. There is a pay and display car park in the holiday park.

Parking Lat/Long: 50.660531, -3.2804516
Parking Grid Ref: SY 095 853
Parking Postcode: EX9 7BX
Map: OS Explorer Map OL28 (1:25 000) Dartmoor

Accessibility

Both the beach and best cliff top viewpoints are only several minutes walk from the car park. The pebble beach is unsuitable for wheelchair access. Holiday park sealed roads and paths have made the cliffs accessible to wheelchairs in several places, however the best views are to be found just off these paths.

Best Time of Year/Day

Ladram Bay works year round as a dawn location; once the sun rises over the sea it glows against the beautiful red cliffs. For the tall sea stack at the far end of the beach, time your visit for high summer when the rising sun will side light the stack.

Left: Boats on the pebble beach, Nikon D800E, 17-35mm at 17mm, ISO 100, 2 sec at f/13. September

Photogenic stack at the western edge of the beach, Canon 5D, 17-40mm at 25mm, ISO 100, 1.6 sec at f/22. April

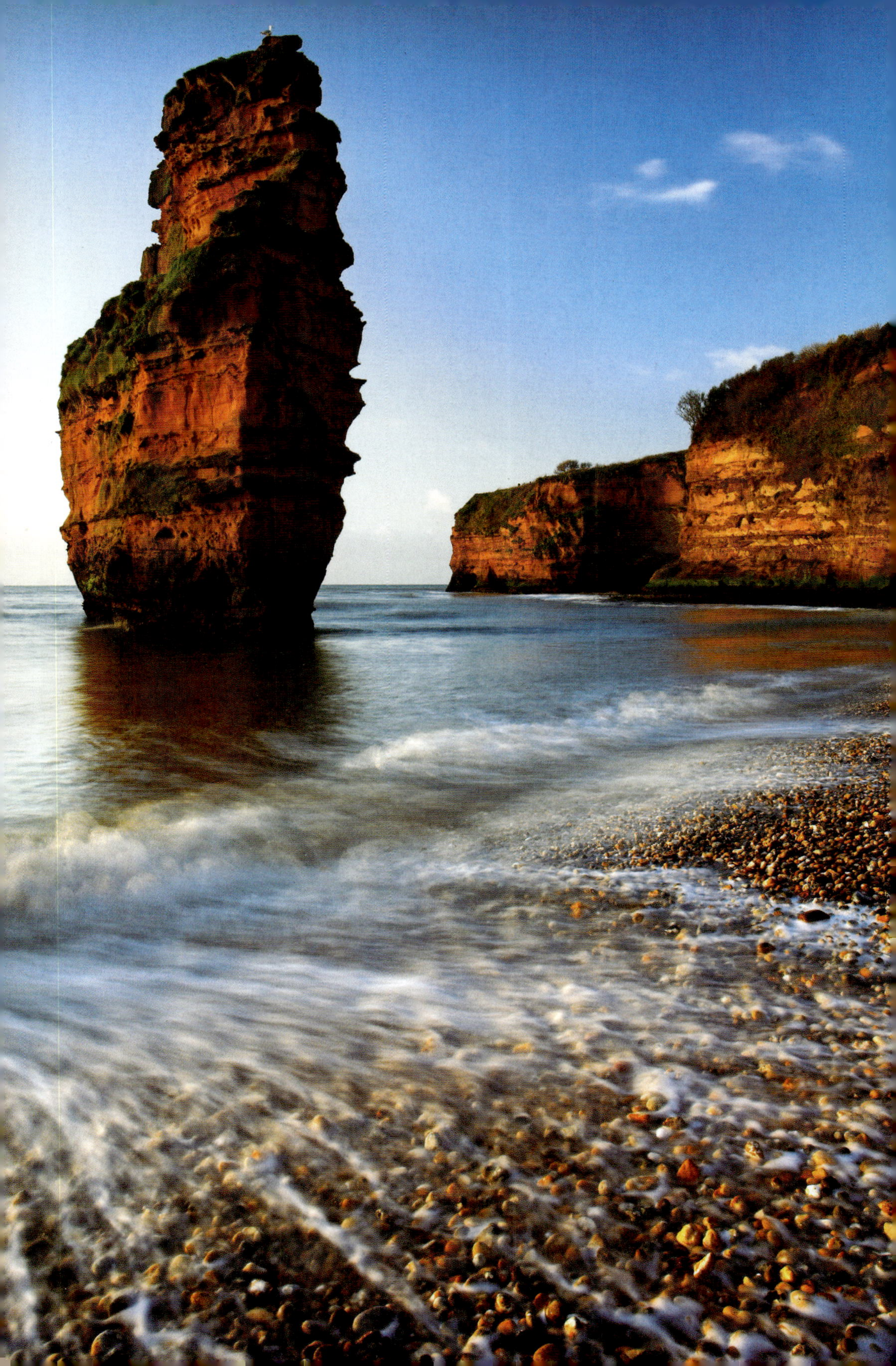

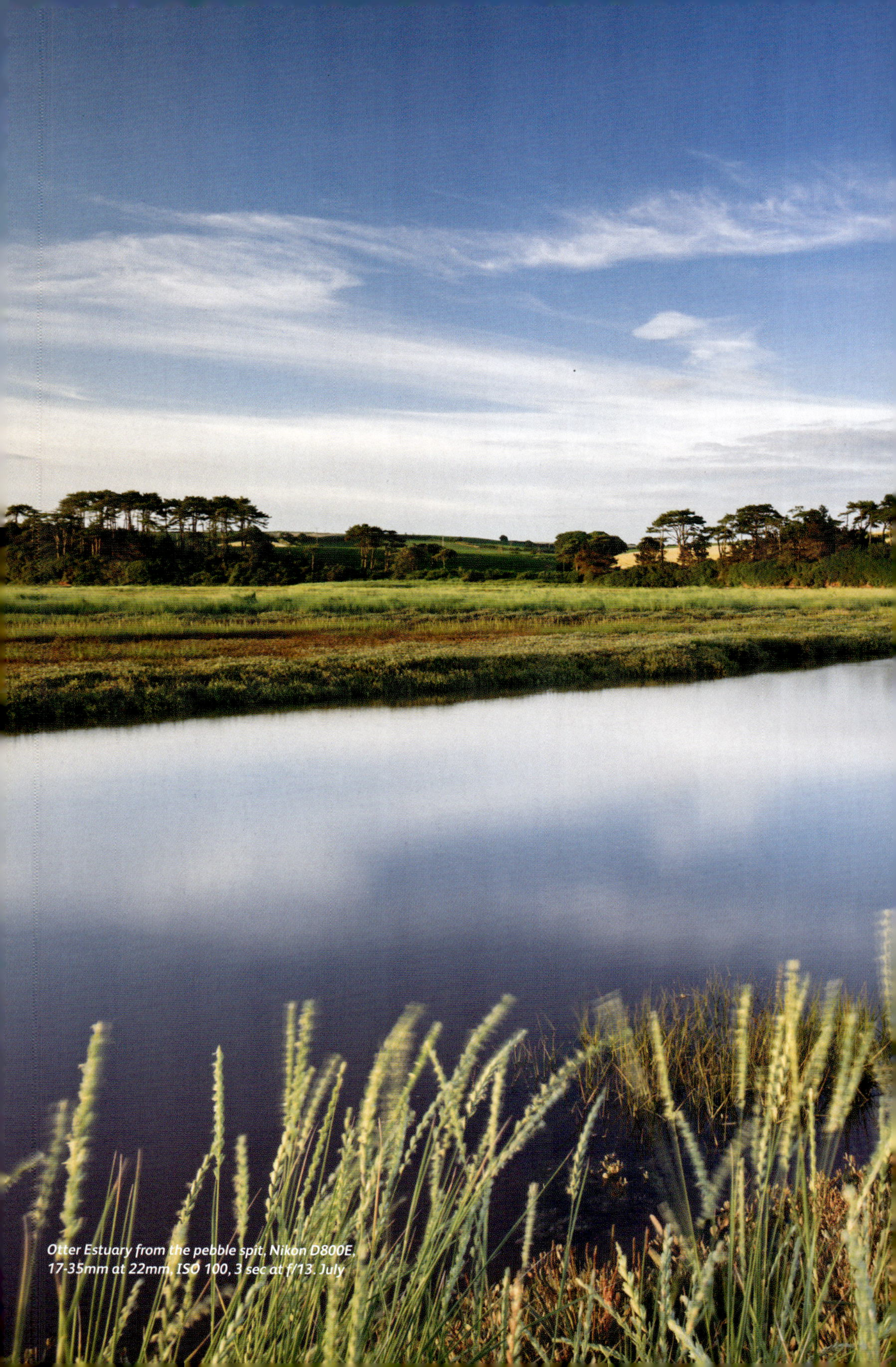

Otter Estuary from the pebble spit, Nikon D800E,
17-35mm at 22mm, ISO 100, 3 sec at f/13. July

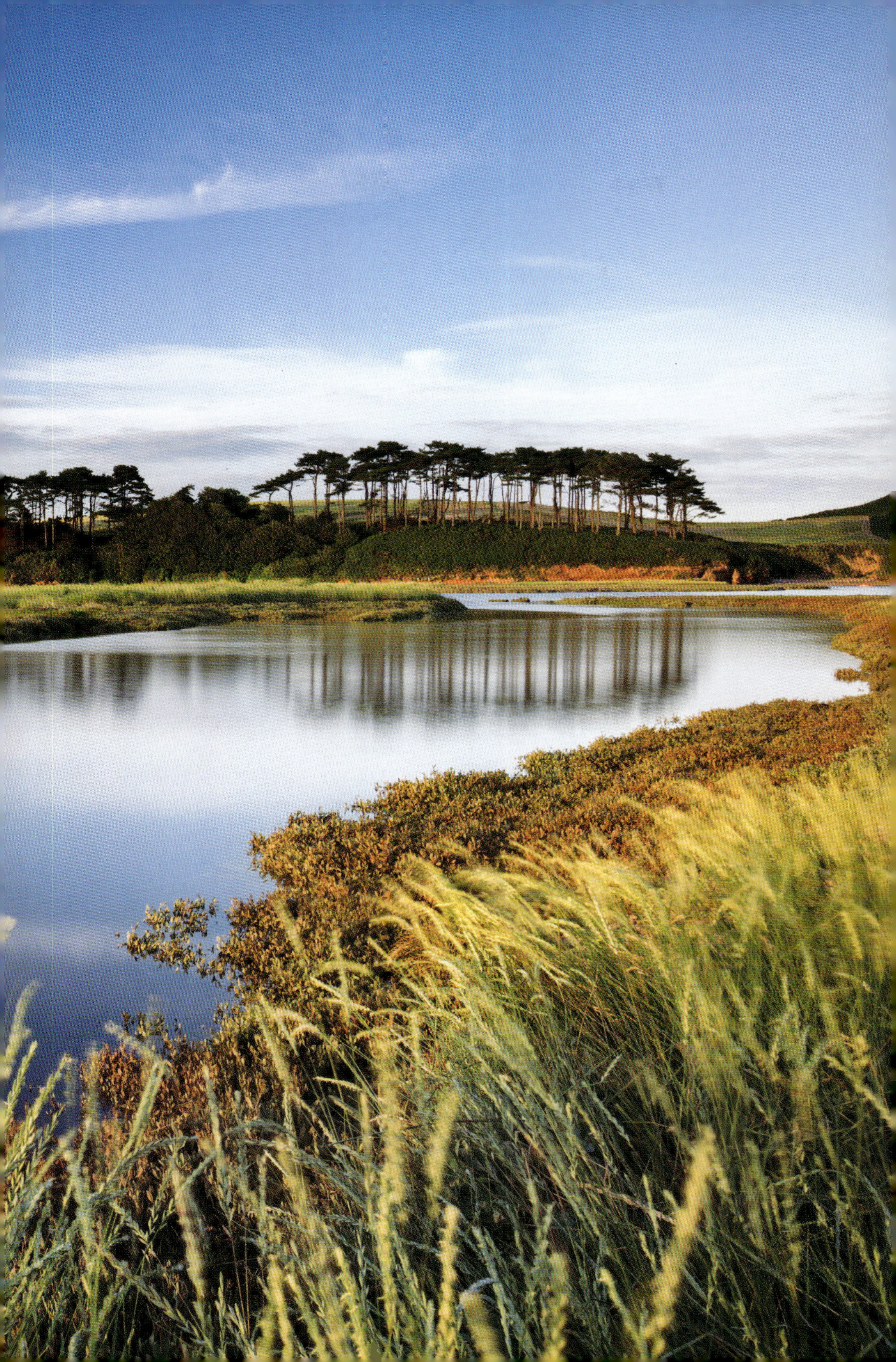

Budleigh Salterton

Located in the East Devon Area of Outstanding Natural Beauty, Budleigh Salterton is a charming little seaside town about fifteen miles south east of Exeter. Like much of East Devon the coastline here is quite different to the dramatic north coast, its calm waters making the town a popular location for holidaymakers.

From a photographer's perspective Budleigh Salterton's appeal may be less apparent than other coastal areas around the South West. With the absence of crashing waves and rugged rocky ledges, you may find yourself contemplating passing over this stretch of the Jurassic Coast in favour of the better known photographic locations in Dorset. Before you do so, spend some time exploring and the character of the town will reveal itself, as always perseverance pays dividends.

What to Shoot and Viewpoints

Viewpoint 1 – The Beach

The main attraction of Budleigh Salterton is its long wide beach which stretches along the length of the town. At its western end huge red cliffs back the beach, characteristic of this stretch of coastline, while a small headland at the opposite end indicates the mouth of the River Otter. In between, the beach consists almost entirely of small round pebbles and, without obvious larger natural features, can make a challenging photographic subject.

Fortunately, a collection of small boats pulled high up onto the beach makes this area an ideal place to head to with your camera. Although the jumble of boats and associated objects can look a little cluttered and messy in places, the bright colours and shapes make very welcome subjects. The boats can be photographed either looking east or west along the beach, the choice will be determined by the timing of your visit as well as the position of the most photogenic boats. Spend time wandering around to identify the best boats; pay particular attention to the condition of the boats and look for bright colours, interesting shapes and arrangements.

Close to the boats a series of wooden beach huts can be found lined up at the top of the beach. These traditional seaside buildings always make colourful and compelling photographic subjects.

Viewpoint 2 – Otter Estuary

At the eastern end of the beach a small pebble spit extends almost to the cliffs, bordered on one side by the sea and on the other by the Otter Estuary Nature Reserve. At high tide saltwater floods the estuary, creating a large expanse of sheltered water protected from the sea by the spit. Although close to the beach, the estuary offers potential for some very different photographs. Looking over the water, the natural backdrop is the sandstone ridge on the opposite side of the River Otter, crested by a clump of very photogenic pine trees. As the estuary here is very sheltered you can often capture perfect reflections of the pine trees in the still water by positioning yourself on the northern edge of the pebble spit, close to the shore. Alternatively, photograph from near the car park to include channels of water leading towards the pines. Sometimes during really high spring tides when the water levels flood the estuary completely, you can stand at the edge of the car park and shoot simple reflective wide angle compositions. This can work especially well at sunrise, when huge colourful skies can be captured both above and reflected below the silhouetted pine trees.

Beach huts on the pebble shore, Nikon D800E, 17-35mm at 35mm, ISO 100, 1/8 sec at f/13. July

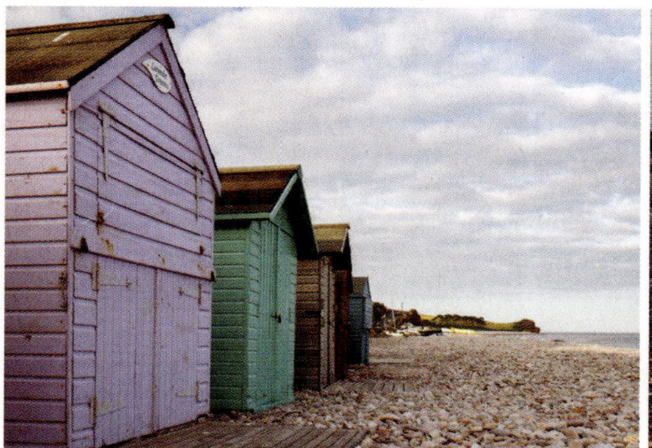

Boats pulled high onto the pebble beach, Nikon D800E, 17-35mm at 20mm, ISO 100, 1/15 sec at f/11. July

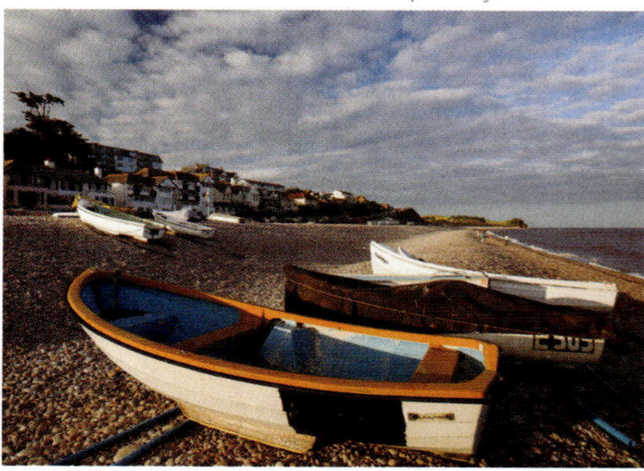

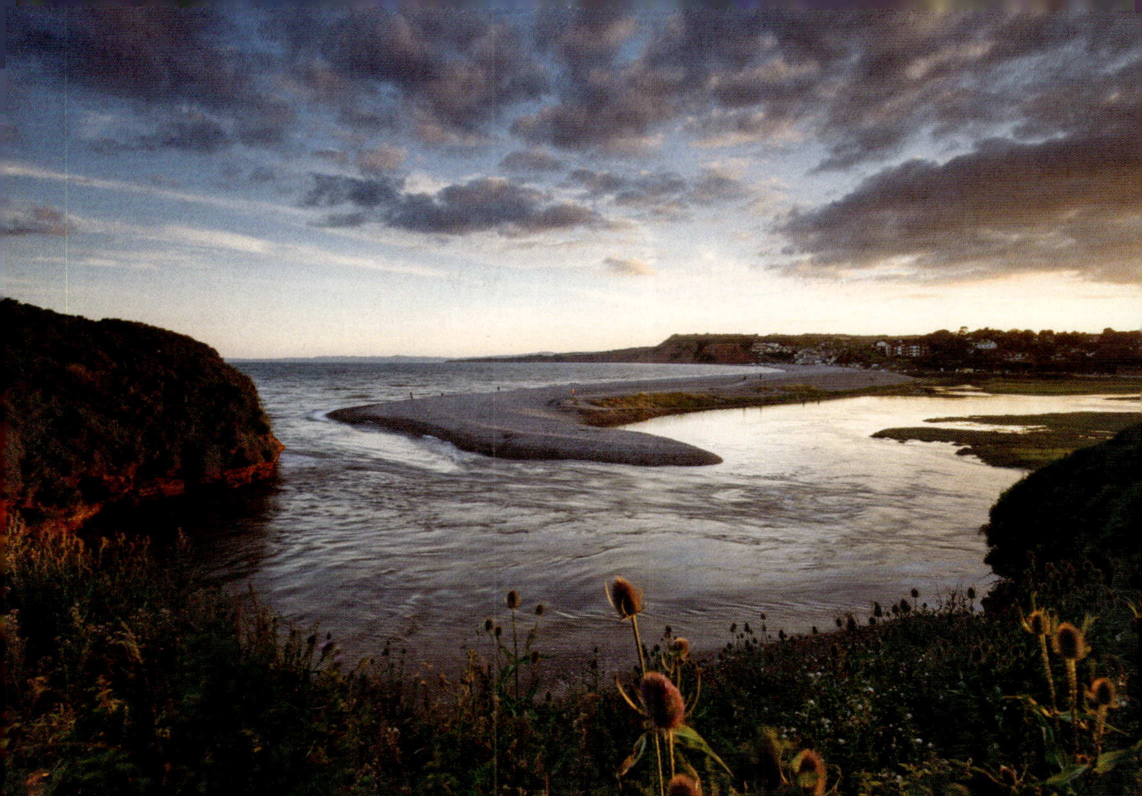

Sunset over Budleigh Salterton from Otter Mouth, Nikon D800E, 17-35mm at 20mm, ISO 100, 0.6 sec at f/14. July

How to Get Here

Budleigh Salterton is in East Devon, approximately fifteen miles from Exeter. Exit the M5 at Junction 30 near Exeter and follow the signs initially for Exmouth. At the second roundabout, head left onto the B3179 and follow the signs to Budleigh Salterton. There is parking on the seafront.

Parking Lat/Long: 50.629218, -3.3204541
Parking Grid Ref: SY 067 818
Parking Postcode: EX9 6NP
Map: OS Explorer Map 115 (1:25 000) Exmouth & Sidmouth

Accessibility

All the viewpoints described are fairly easily reached, but the beach and Otter Mouth do require walking over uneven ground. The Otter Estuary makes an ideal location for wheelchair users as some of the best photographs can be captured from the car park itself.

Best Time of Year/Day

Budleigh Salterton can make a great photographic destination throughout the year and at any time of the day. As always for landscape photography the best light usually occurs near dawn and dusk; for sunrise colours position yourself looking east of the Otter Estuary towards sunrise, while at sunset it's best to position yourself on the headland looking west.

Viewpoint 3 – Otter Mouth

For a very different photograph, follow the well defined footpath north from the estuary car park for approximately 750 metres, then cross over the bridge and head south and equal distance on the opposite side of the river. This follows the route of the South West Coast Path, and brings you back to the coast, this time on top of the headland near the pine trees overlooking the mouth of the River Otter. From this elevated viewpoint a fresh perspective of Budleigh Salterton and its pebble spit can be achieved in a very effective composition. As the viewpoint stretches west, you can shoot here at sunset to capture a colourful sky reflected in the estuary below. For some added interest, shoot with an extreme wide angle to include some of the pine trees in the composition.

Situated on the Teign Estuary on the south coast of Devon, Teignmouth became popular as a seaside resort in Georgian times. The Grand Pier followed a little later, construction being completed in 1867. During the Victorian heydey piers were synonymous with seaside resorts, their long promenade decks offering perfect locations for 'taking the air'. The elegant structure at Teignmouth was positioned in the centre of the beach, thereby separating the Gentlemen's and Ladies bathing machines.

Teignmouth's pier was almost a very short-lived affair. Just a few years after its opening the pier was purchased by Mr Arthur Ryde Denby with the intention of moving the whole structure to nearby Paignton. The project proved impractical and was eventually abandoned in favour of a new pier at Paignton. Both the Grand Pier at Teignmouth and Paignton's are now the only surviving seaside piers in the south west of England.

What to Shoot and Viewpoints

Despite its impressive name, when compared with many elaborate piers at higher profile UK seaside resorts the Grand Pier is quite a modest structure. Thin cast iron columns support a conventional timber-decked promenade, which, apart from several large buildings near the entrance is relatively open. A series of smaller structures housing traditional fairground attractions can be found stretching towards the end of the pier.

The best place to photograph the Grand Pier is from the beach on either side. From the beach the small fairground structures running the length of the pier are unobtrusive, complementing rather than overwhelming its elongated shape. Although the pier is the main interest on the beach and therefore the primary focal point of any picture, it usually looks more effective when included as part of a wider composition. This often results in the structure becoming quite a small element of a picture, but size isn't everything. Placing the subject into context with its wider surroundings is an effective tool.

Sandy beaches can lack the interest required to shoot a wide angle composition, but Teignmouth has a series of wooden groynes stretching into the sea. Groynes make excellent subjects for wide angle coastal photographs, their strong static shapes contrasting magnificently with

Moody dawn sky above Teignmouth Pier, Nikon D800E, 17-35mm at 24mm, ISO 200, 4 sec at f/8. January

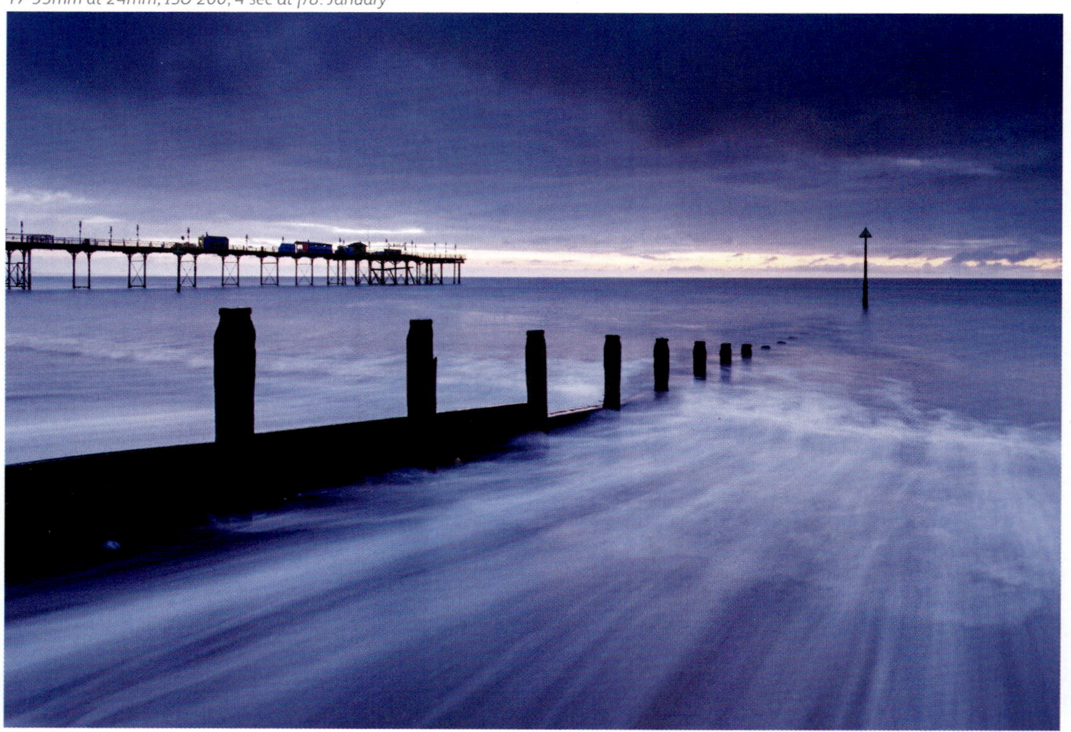

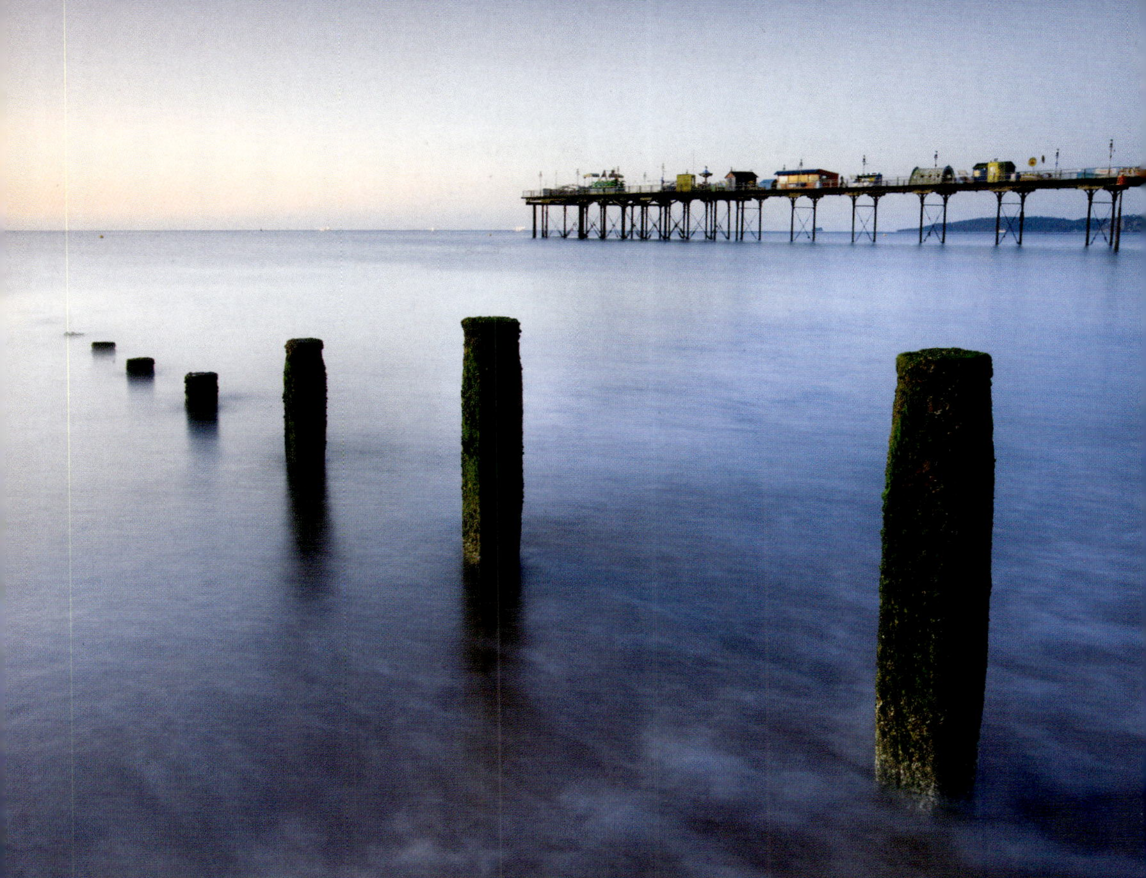

Posts on the northern side of the pier, Canon 1Ds Mark III, 16-35mm at 25mm, ISO 100, 13 sec at f/16. September

flowing water patterns created from rushing waves, while offering repetition and lead in lines. The groynes at Teignmouth would make a great picture in their own right, but look even better when included with the pier.

The pier works equally well whether photographed from the groynes to the east or west, the deciding factor will usually be the position of the sun for the time of your visit. When composing pay particular attention to the vertical groyne posts; ideally keeping some space between the top of these posts and the pier.

Like many wide angle coastal photographs, timing is everything when attempting this kind of shot. Although an incoming wave is powerful and dramatic, it often looks very chaotic and unappealing in a photograph. I prefer to wait for a wave to crash to its highest point, and then fire the shutter when the wave drags back towards the sea. With the right timing, beautiful white patterns can be recorded as the waves pull back towards the sea.

How to Get Here

Teignmouth is on the south coast of Devon, fifteen miles south of Exeter. From Exeter, head south on the A38 heading for Plymouth. When the A38 splits, take the A380 south towards Torquay. After four miles take the left turning signposted Teignmouth, and follow this road for another six miles until you reach Teignmouth. In Teignmouth, follow the road signs for the sea front.

Parking Lat/Long: 50.544585, -3.4947708
Parking Grid Ref: SX 941 727
Parking Postcode: TQ14 8BB
Map: OS Explorer Map 110 (1:25 000) Torquay and Dawlish

Accessibility

There are several car parks close by providing easy access to the beach. Although the sandy beach will be restrictive for wheelchair users, the accessible promenade above provides good views down onto the beach and pier.

Best Time of Year/Day

The pier faces south east making this a good location to shoot at dawn, with the sun rising out to sea. Stand on the western side of the pier during the winter to ensure the building doesn't get in the way of the sunrise. In summer, when the sun rises much further to the north, head to the eastern side. After the sun breaks the horizon the east side of the pier will glow with the first golden rays of morning light.

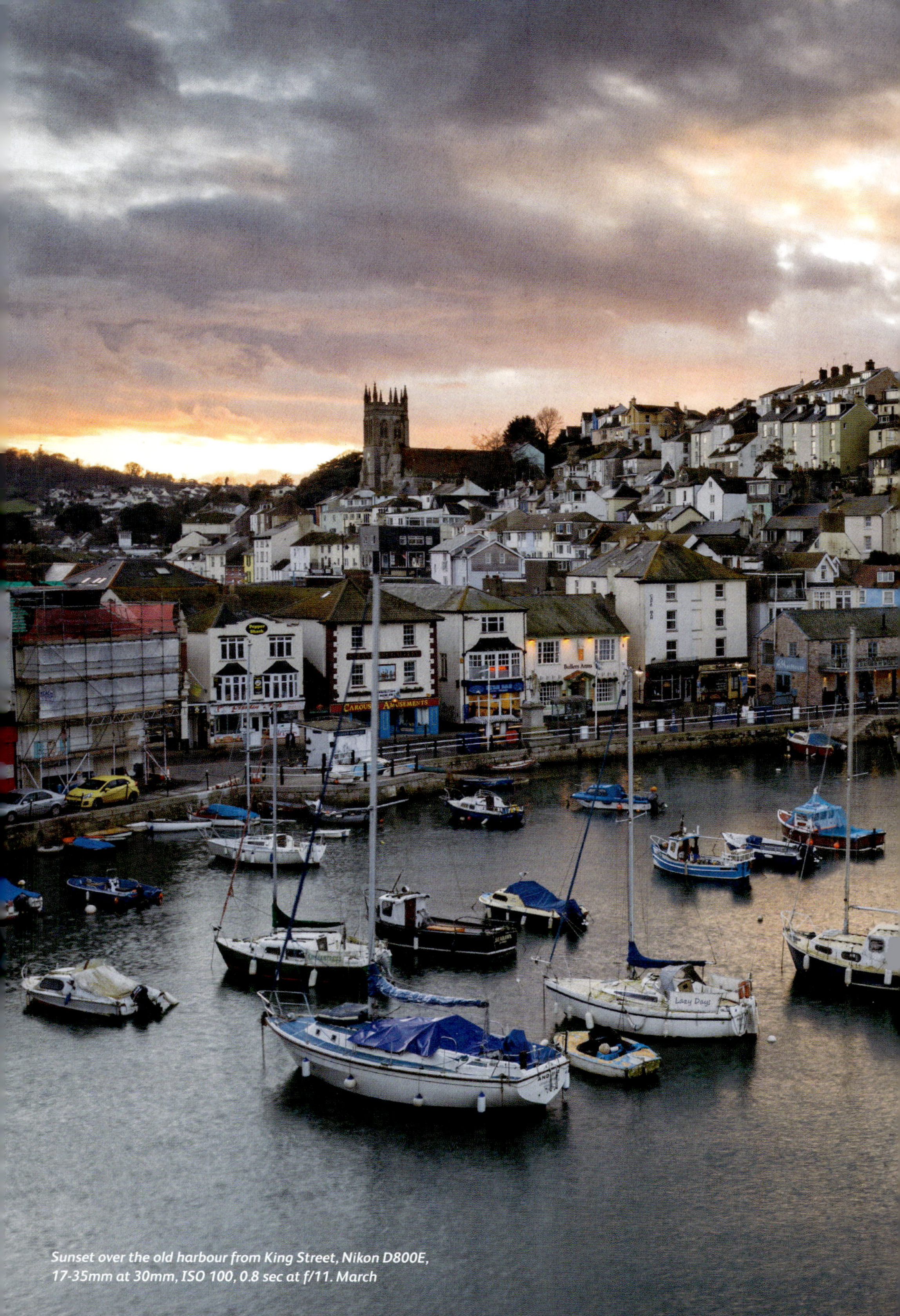

Sunset over the old harbour from King Street, Nikon D800E, 17-35mm at 30mm, ISO 100, 0.8 sec at f/11. March

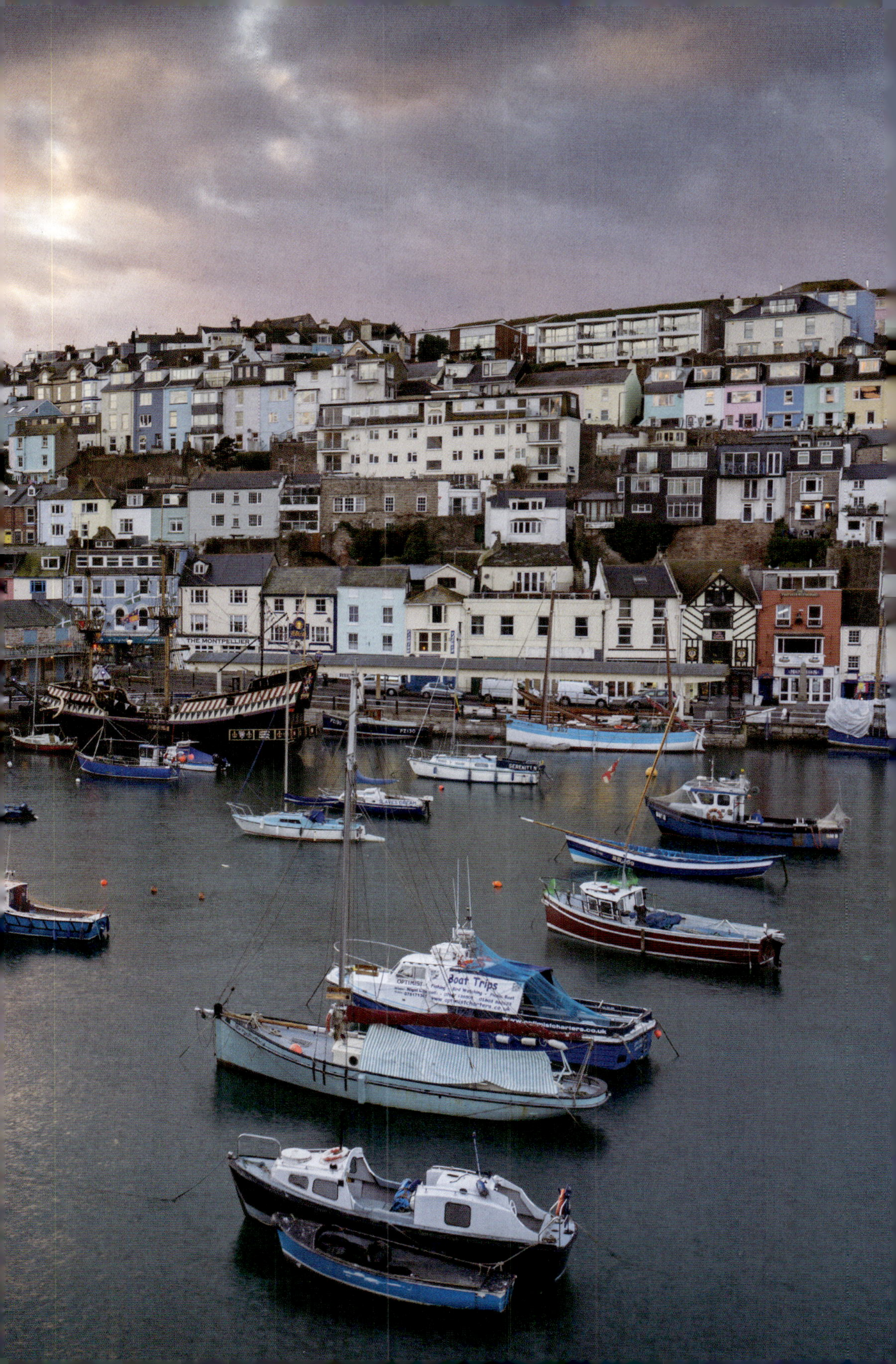

Whereas Torquay, lying at the other end of Tor Bay, has for long been a prominent UK seaside town, Brixham is more closely associated with the fishing industry. In the Middle Ages the town was the largest fishing port in the south west of England, it is still home to one of the largest fishing fleets in the country. It was at Brixham that the sailing trawler was developed in the 18th Century, a new type of fishing boat that revolutionised the fishing industry in Northern Europe and beyond.

Brixham developed around its busy harbour. At its peak in the early 20th Century the inner harbour was crowded with up to 300 sailing vessels. Nowadays modern trawlers unload their catch in the newer harbour close to the plush new fish market building, leaving the picturesque inner harbour for smaller boats and yachts.

What to Shoot and Viewpoints

For visitors looking to photograph Brixham the older Inner Harbour is the star attraction. The steep hilly slopes overlooking the harbour contain row upon row of colourful buildings that typify South West fishing villages, all the houses crowding on top of each other in an endeavour to achieve the best sea view.

Viewpoint 1 – Southern Quay

The most appealing viewpoint from which to shoot the harbour is on or near the Southern Quay. From this side, the shops and houses beyond the harbour are huddled together so tightly to make a feast of interest for any photograph. Additionally, this view enables you to incorporate the full size replica of Sir Francis Drakes famous ship, the Golden Hind, into a composition. This ship has been docked in Brixham's harbour for over 50 years, adding extra interest and a touch of history.

To best appreciate the view from this side you need to climb above Southern Quay; head up King Street and position yourself close to the appropriately named Harbour View Hotel. The elevation this viewpoint offers helps to prevent the boats in the harbour below from overlapping each other too much. From this perspective the rows of houses are more prominent in the frame, emphasising their stacked appearance. The other notable advantage of shooting from the south side of the harbour is that you can include Brixham's lovely All Saints Church tower rising above the houses.

If you wish to include more foreground than this viewpoint permits, head down some steps nearby to the quayside below. From this position you can choose a boat close to the quay to feature more prominently in a foreground with the houses forming an appealing backdrop. This lower view is not as effective as shooting from Kings Street due to the boats overlapping each other but it does offer a different perspective and is just a couple of minutes walk from the higher viewpoint.

View over the old harbour from Southern Quay, Canon 1Ds Mark III, 24-70mm at 60mm, ISO 100, 0.3 sec at f/10. January

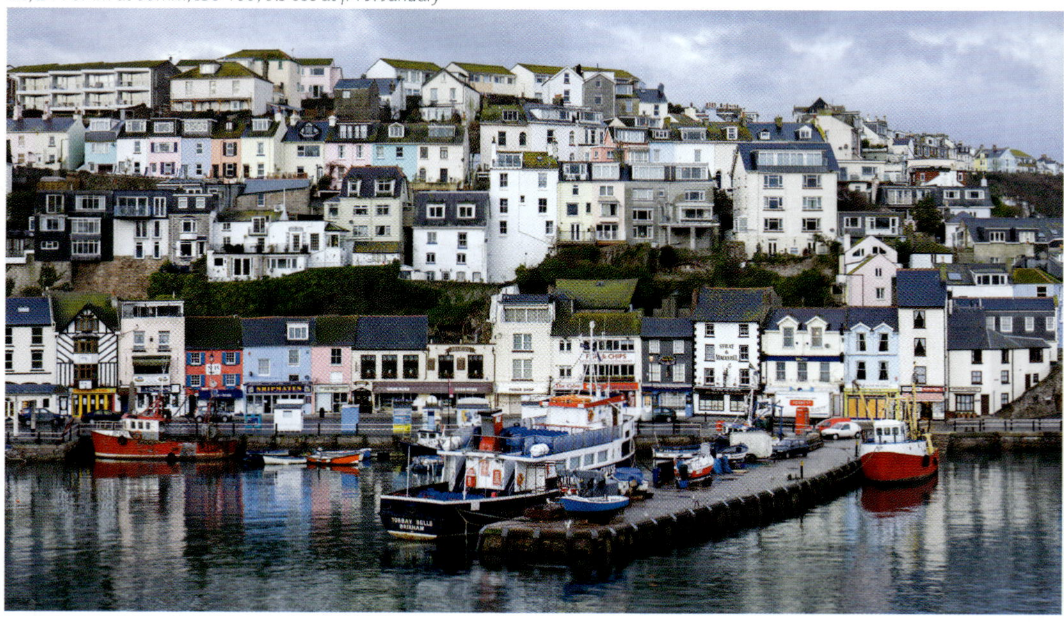

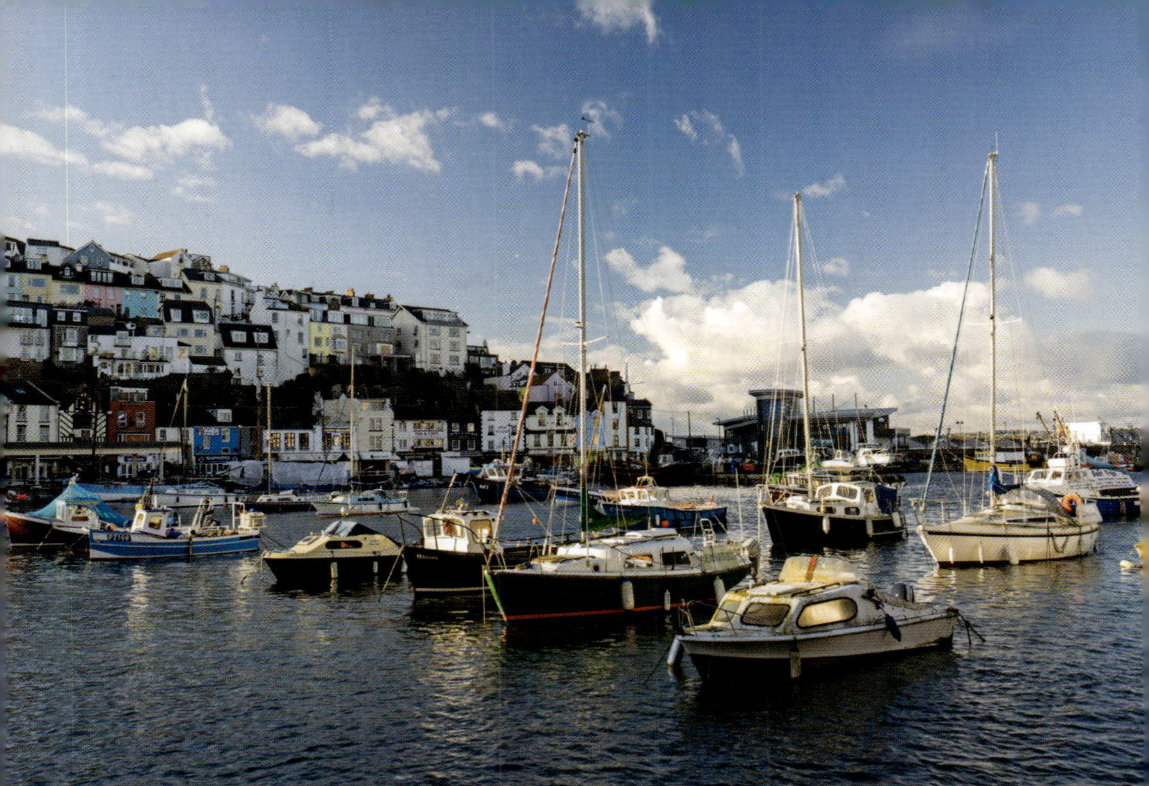

Boats moored in the old harbour near The Strand. Nikon D800E, 17-35mm at 35mm. ISO 100, 1/13 sec at f/11. March

Viewpoint 2 – The Strand

From the Southern Quay walk around towards the Strand to shoot in the direction of the new harbour. On this side a cobbled slipway allows you to get close and low to photograph a collection of little boats bobbing around below the quay. Often some of the small wooden boats are pulled up onto the slipway, making excellent foreground subjects when photographed with an extreme wide angle lens.

It is worth bringing a telephoto lens to capture some more selective compositions. With a focal length of around 150mm, you can isolate a smaller section of the harbour and houses above. A tighter composition helps emphasise the stacked effect of the houses giving them the appearance of being built on top of one another.

As with other harbours, the best photographs are usually captured when the tide is in, and the water is still and reflective. Plan your visit to avoid low tide, at this time the water drains out of parts of the harbour completely and leaves the boats stranded in unsightly mud. Check the weather forecast and visit on days when wind speeds are very low. As well as raising the likelihood of capturing reflections, low wind speeds will give you a better chance of keeping the boats from bobbing around too much and blurring on long exposure photographs.

How to Get Here

Brixham is on the south coast of Devon, approximately thirty miles south of Exeter. From Exeter head south on the A38, soon turning onto the A380 heading for Newton Abbot. Pass by Newton Abbot and continue south on the A380 which soon turns into the A3022; this road will take you into the centre of Brixham.

Parking Lat/Long: 50.395630, -3.5141364
Parking Grid Ref: SX 925 562
Parking Postcode: TQ5 8DY
Map: OS Explorer Map OL20 (1:25 000) South Devon

Accessibility

With roads and pedestrian areas all around the Inner Harbour access is simple for all, and there are plenty of alternative routes for those unable to use the steps described above.

Best Time of Year/Day

With the right tide levels the harbour is photogenic throughout the day and in any season. Many of the brightly painted houses will overexpose during sunny days; in order to avoid this plan to shoot early morning when the rising sun will gently illuminate the buildings. Alternatively, if you are shooting from the south side of the harbour plan to visit at sunset to capture a glowing sky above the houses, hopefully also reflected in the water.

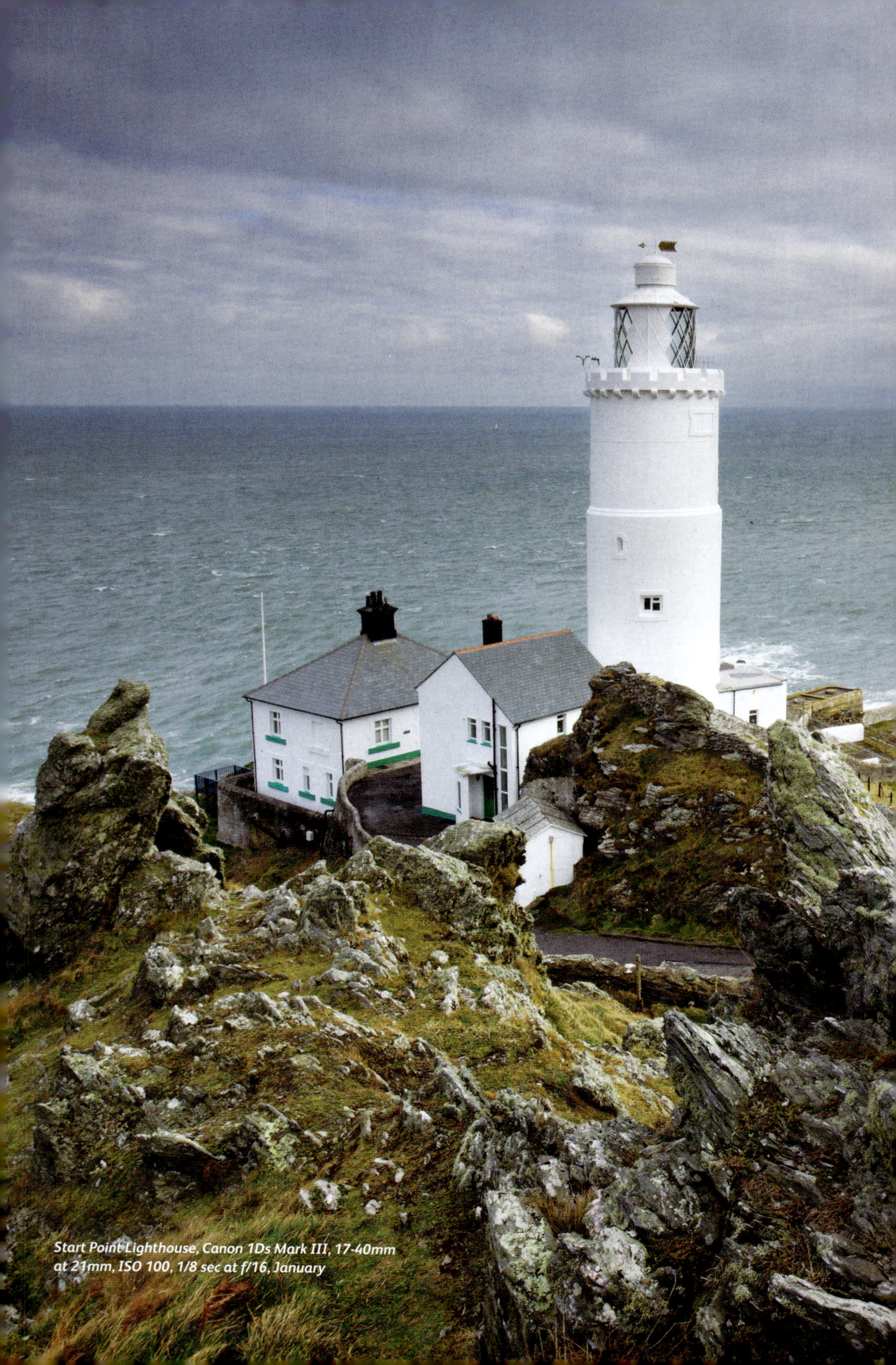

Start Point Lighthouse, Canon 1Ds Mark III, 17-40mm at 21mm, ISO 100, 1/8 sec at f/16, January

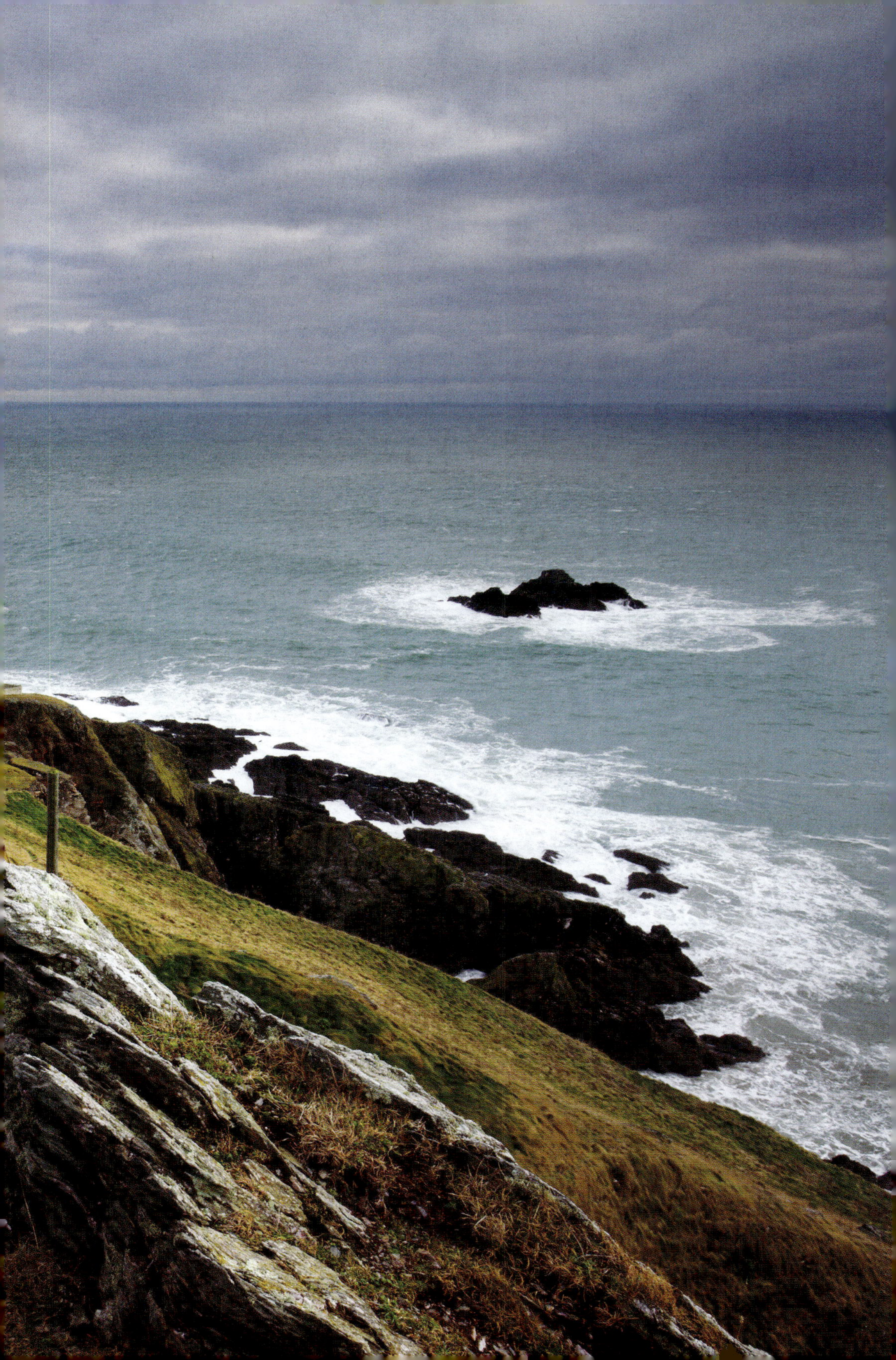

The south coast of Devon and Cornwall is gentler than the battered rugged Atlantic north coast. But every now and again this coastline offers up a dramatic surprise, with Start Point in the South Hams being a prime example. This elongated rocky promontory in the very south of Devon boasts towering cliffs crested with jagged rocky outcrops overlooking vertical drops to ledges and tiny islets far below.

To emphasise the drama, and danger, of the location a lighthouse perches on the cliffs at the end of the headland, a beacon to passing ships warning of the perils of passing too close to the Point. Together with the wonderful coastal views, the lighthouse helps to make Start Point one of the photographic highlights of South Devon.

What to Shoot and Viewpoints

Viewpoint 1 – Above the lighthouse

Lighthouses positioned on rugged cliffs are often difficult to shoot creatively from close up being in inaccessible locations. Fortunately the lighthouse at Start Point is an exception to this. From the car park an easy 15 minute stroll down a sealed private road brings you to the lighthouse. Just before you reach the lighthouse gates, turn to the right of the path and climb up towards the ridge. There is no footpath as such, but usually a track is evident leading up to the top. From the summit, a glorious view of the lighthouse and its accompanying buildings opens up before your eyes, with the sea beyond.

The geology all around this area is fascinating and very photogenic. Angular rocks protrude sharply upwards from the ground and stretch towards the lighthouse, making fantastic foreground interest. Shooting vertically allows you to fit all this geology in together with the lighthouse in the background. Even so, make sure your wide angle lens is packed in your camera bag, as you will need it to make the most of these rocks.

As well as making strong focal points in their own right, with careful attention to composition these protruding rocks can also be utilised to hide any unsightly objects in the vicinity of the lighthouse (cars, bins etc).

Viewpoint 2 – Coast Path views

With the close up view bagged, head back up the road towards the car park. About half way back you will notice a footpath on the left heading up and over the ridge. Follow this narrow track, the South West Coast Path, as it heads southwards sometimes clinging precariously close to the edge of the cliffs.

Very shortly the lighthouse will come into view again, this time appearing small yet prominent in its dramatic headland setting. It is worth spending time exploring the vistas from this stretch of the coast path; from all along the track the views towards the lighthouse are wonderful and quite different.

Look for viewpoints offering elements to bring extra interest to your photographs. From the north end of this path the lighthouse is closer and therefore larger in the frame, also you are able to shoot right along the edge of the headland taking advantage of any rocky islets.

The further you head south on the path the less prominence the lighthouse will have in your picture. Don't let that dissuade you; the view back to the lighthouse from high up on the jagged cliff top path is glorious. Although smaller in the frame the lighthouse is clearly still an important feature of any photograph captured from here, and the shape of the promontory on which is sits is also more evident. In addition, coming into view below are several cliffs jutting into the sea, revealing the twisted geology of this rugged coast. Partially submerged ledges and islets just offshore complete the ingredients for a stunning seascape

Sunrise off Start Point from the coast path, Canon 1Ds Mark III, 16-35mm at 35mm, ISO 50, 0.8 sec at f/16. September

How to Get Here

From Kingsbridge head east on the A379 for approximately 6 miles. When you reach the mini roundabout at Stokenham take a right turn following the brown signs for Start Point. The lanes get very small and rural from this point, but keep looking out for the brown signs and after approximately 4 miles you will reach the car park at Start Point.

Parking Lat/Long: 50.225918, -3.6547941
Parking Grid Ref: SX 820 375
Parking Postcode: TQ7 2ET
Map: OS Explorer Map OL20 (1:25 000) South Devon

Accessibility

From the car park the road down to the lighthouse is tarmac and in good condition, and so suitable for wheelchairs. The coast paths are narrow, uneven underfoot and can be muddy after rain, therefore good walking boots are recommended. When venturing to the cliff top view above the lighthouse, please use caution. This area has some dangerous drop offs and can be very exposed on windy days.

Best Time of Year/Day

Both viewpoints work very well year round at dawn and early morning. Just before and during sunrise colourful cloudy skies can make beautiful back drops to the lighthouse. In winter when the sun sets much further to the south, late afternoon will provide warm sunlight to illuminate the promontory and lighthouse.

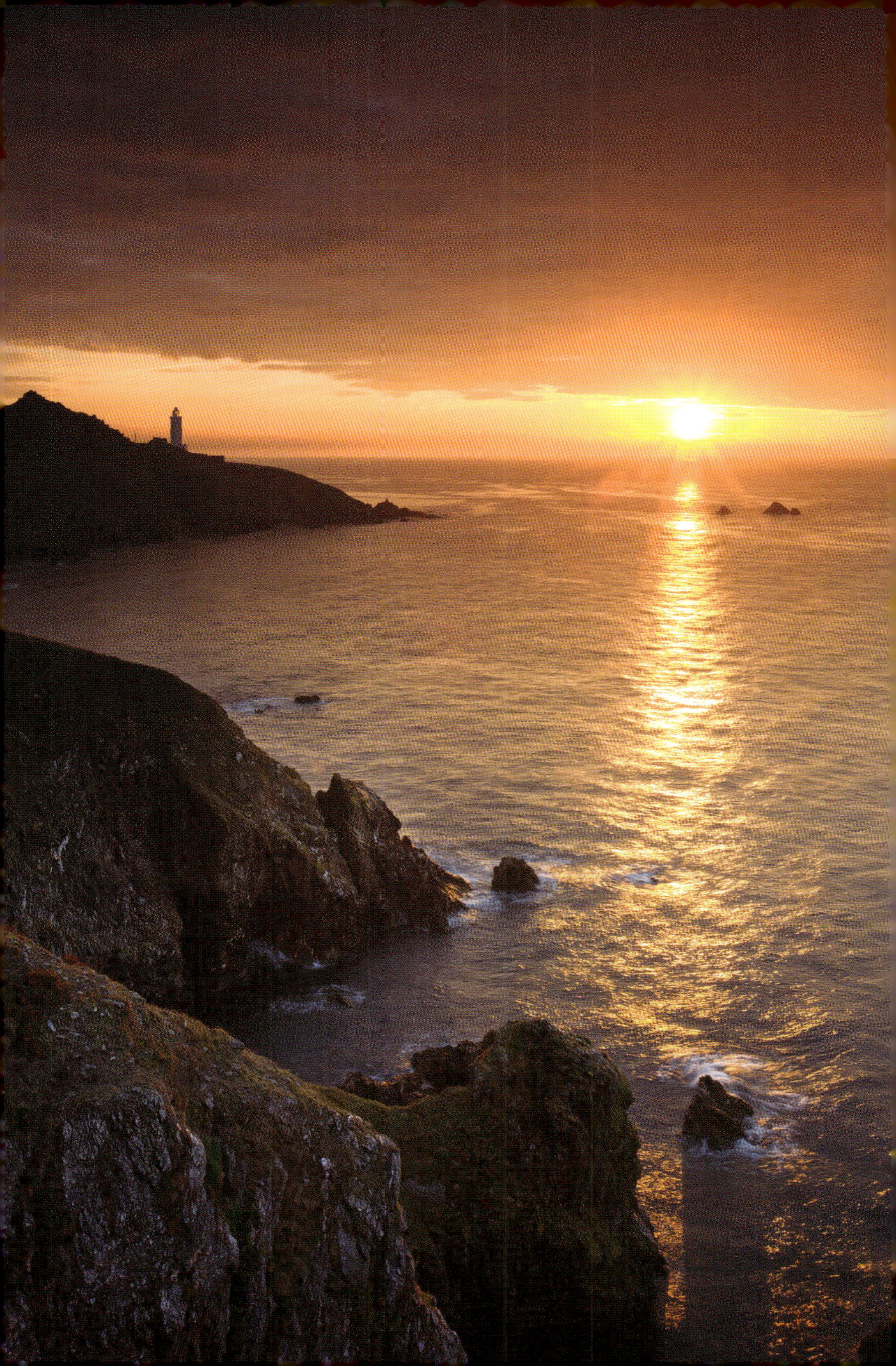

Beautiful Salcombe is one of the jewels of the South Hams in south Devon. This lovely town built into the steep hills overlooking the Kingsbridge Estuary is very photogenic, its pretty houses overlooking a sheltered natural harbour bustling with boats.

The town has a long and important connection with the sea, developed historically through boat and shipbuilding as well as being a major port for shipping fruit. Nowadays, Salcombe is most famous for tourism, and is a very popular location for pleasure sailing and yachting.

What to Shoot and Viewpoints

Although there are many locations from which to shoot Salcombe, one of the best known and finest viewpoints is from Snapes Point. Named after the nearby Snapes Manor, Snapes Point is a headland in the care of the National Trust. A well maintained circular footpath follows the shape of the promontory, ending with the viewpoint at its southern tip. Although fine views can be achieved along the footpath, the extra elevation gained at the final viewpoint offers the best potential for photographs.

The vista towards the south west offers probably the finest view of Salcombe. Across the estuary the picturesque town stretches out in a wide arc, with row upon row of whitewashed buildings overlooking the harbour. Beyond the town, the mighty Bolt Head cliff dominates the distant horizon, while in front of the buildings a flotilla of yachts and small boats spread across the estuary.

The scene is majestic, yet requires good planning and a considered approach to achieve good photographs. While putting together a composition from Snapes Point is fairly straightforward, the format needs consideration. As the town stretches fairly wide, and the estuary further still the ideal picture format is panoramic. You can certainly fit in the whole scene with a standard 3:2 ratio when shooting with a wide angle lens, but this will probably leave you with more sky and ground than your composition requires, especially if the sky is cloudless. One solution is to

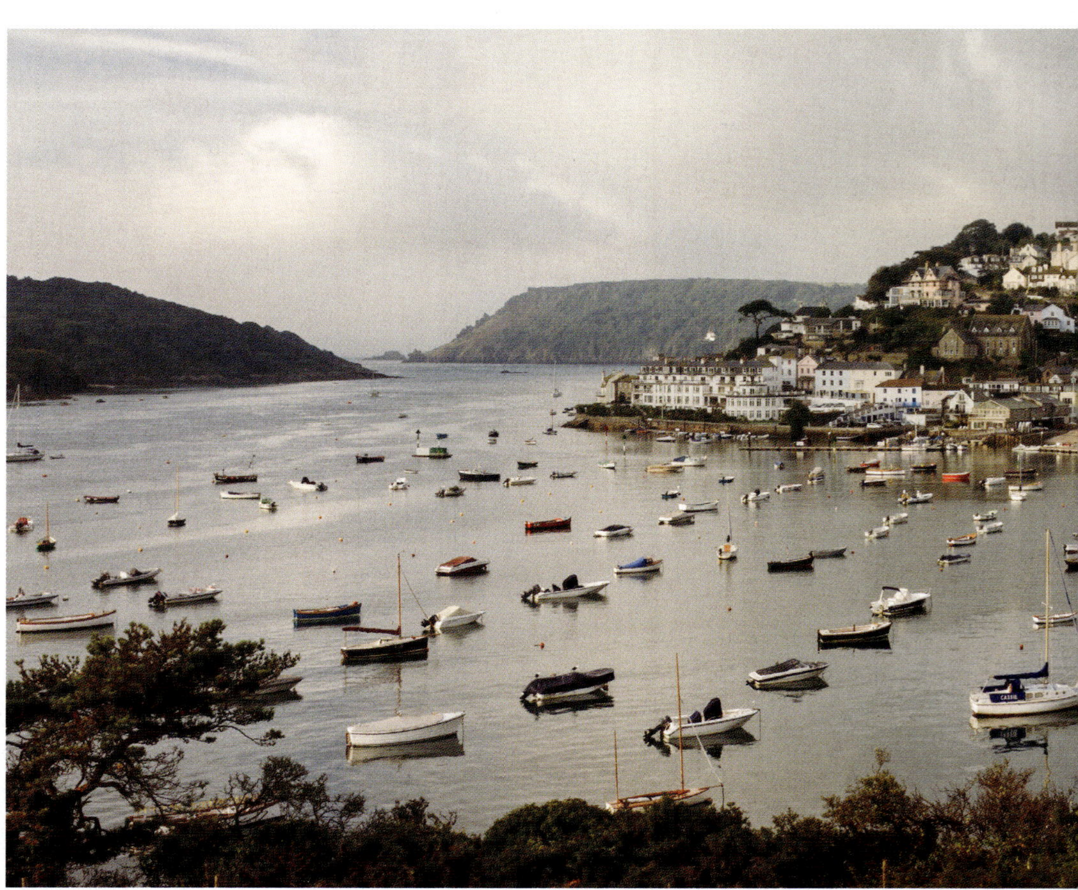

compose a tighter crop around a smaller section of the view, but ideally the best option is to shoot either a series of pictures to stitch to panoramic, or alternatively simply crop off the top and bottom to make the format.

With so many bright buildings, not to mention white boats, photographing this view during a sunny day will result in lots of overexposure as all the bright areas bleach out. The ideal time to shoot is just after dawn, when the first light of a new day glows warmly across the estuary onto the boats and houses. In terms of weather the most important consideration is wind; with a still day the estuary becomes a mirror reflecting both the myriad yachts and houses as well as any colourful clouds above. Although the view from Snapes Point is still impressive on a windy day, the magic evaporates in the rippled water.

After shooting the classic view towards Salcombe from Snapes Point continue around the footpath for a few minutes until you reach Scoble Point. From here you can shoot across to Southpool Creek or further inland up the Kingsbridge Estuary. You will find yachts moored all along these waterways, all making wonderful photographic subjects. Yachts look particularly appealing when photographed emerging from morning mist and fog, so keep a keen eye on the conditions the night before.

How to Get Here

Salcombe is located on the south coast of Devon, approximately six miles from Kingsbridge. From Kingsbridge, head west and then south on the A381, following the signs for Salcombe. Approximately one mile after passing through the village of Malborough, turn left following the signs for Lincombe. Continue down this tiny lane for one mile to a National Trust car park.

Parking Lat/Long: 50.247951, -3.7697851
Parking Grid Ref: SX 739 401
Parking Postcode: TQ8 8NQ
Map: OS Explorer Map OL20 (1:25 000) South Devon

Accessibility

From the car park, an easy one mile walk along a well defined track will lead you towards Snapes Point. Towards the end of the headland a stone flight of steps leads you up to the viewpoint. While the going is relatively easy, the uneven track and steps makes this viewpoint inaccessible for wheelchair users.

Best Time of Year/Day

The view from Snapes Point is best photographed in early morning light. This view can be photographed throughout the year but is less appealing in late Spring and Summer when the sun rises further to the north, behind your shooting position.

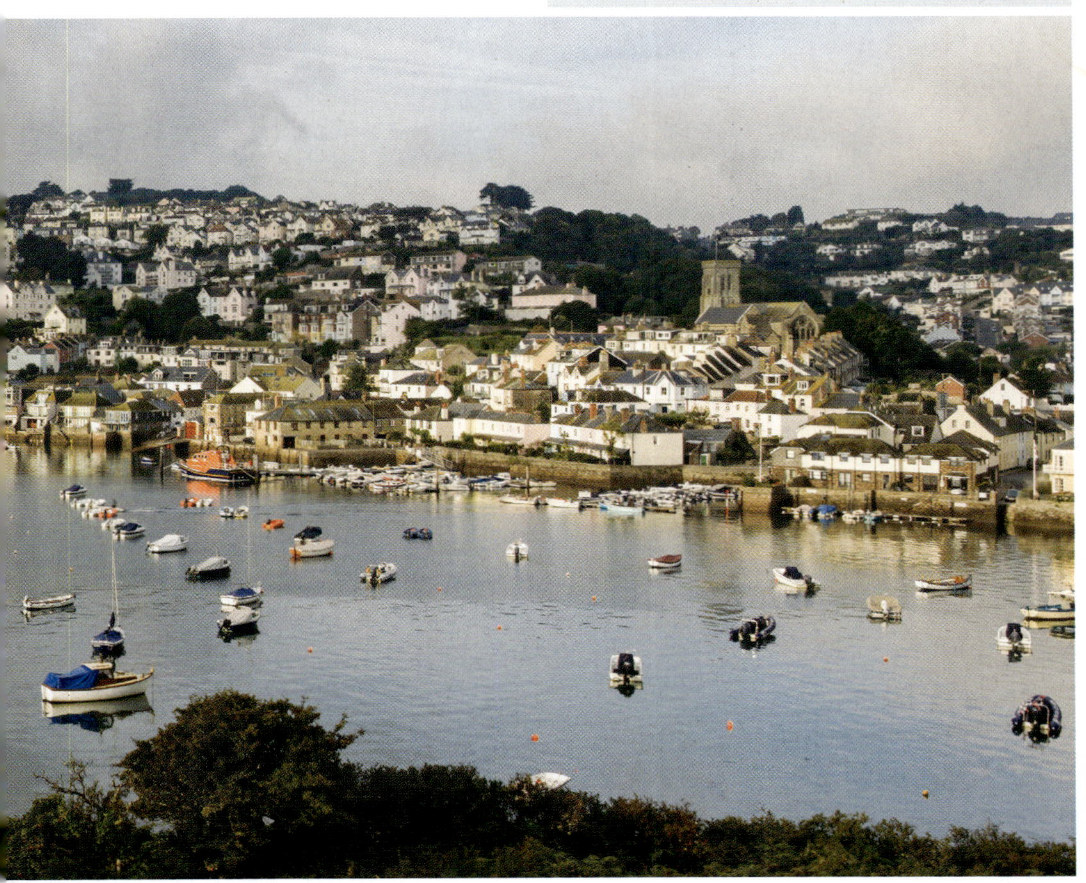

Salcombe photographed from Snapes Point, Canon 1Ds Mark III, 24-70mm at 27mm, ISO 100, 1/8 sec at f/16. September

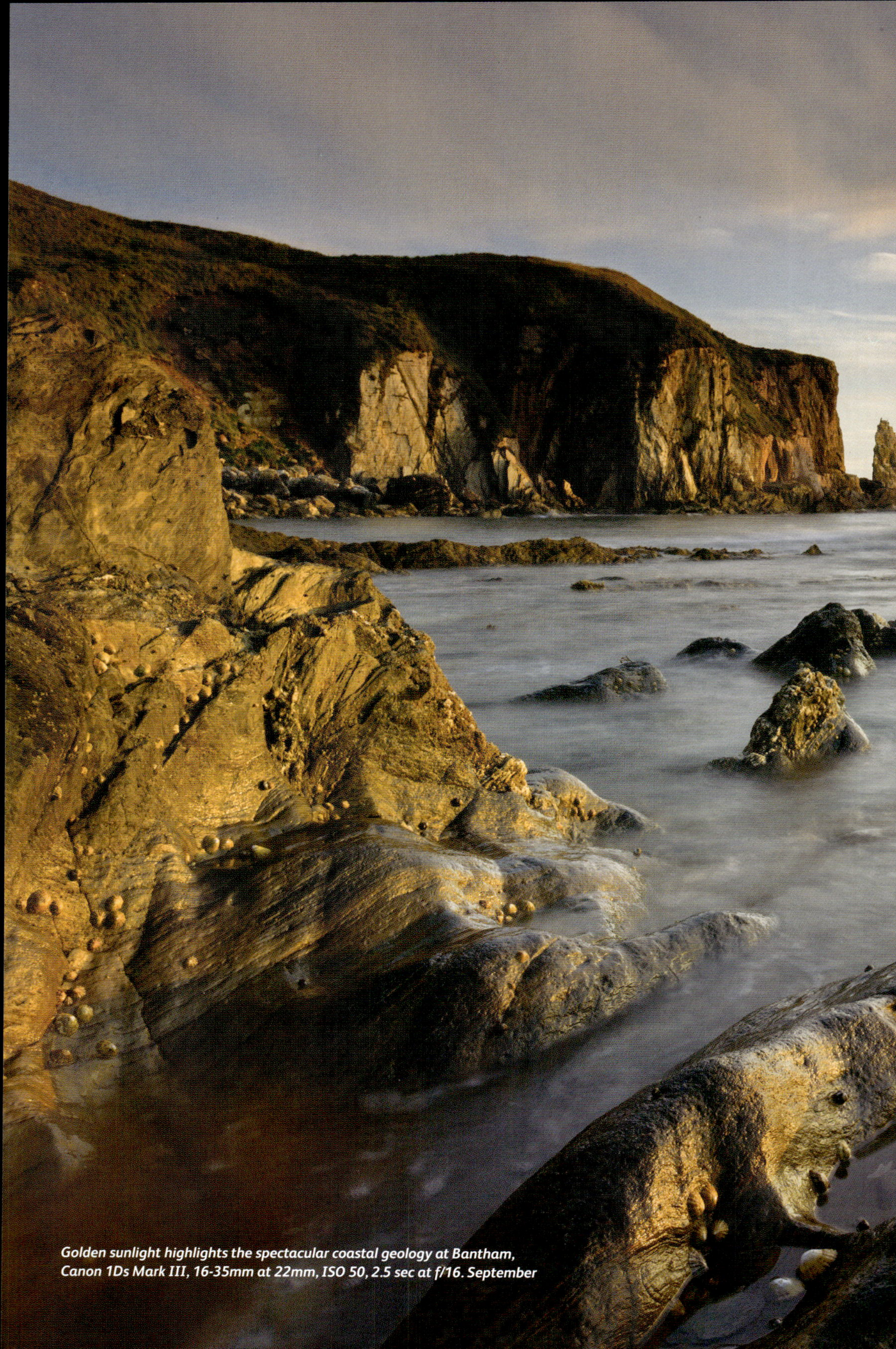

*Golden sunlight highlights the spectacular coastal geology at Bantham,
Canon 1Ds Mark III, 16-35mm at 22mm, ISO 50, 2.5 sec at f/16. September*

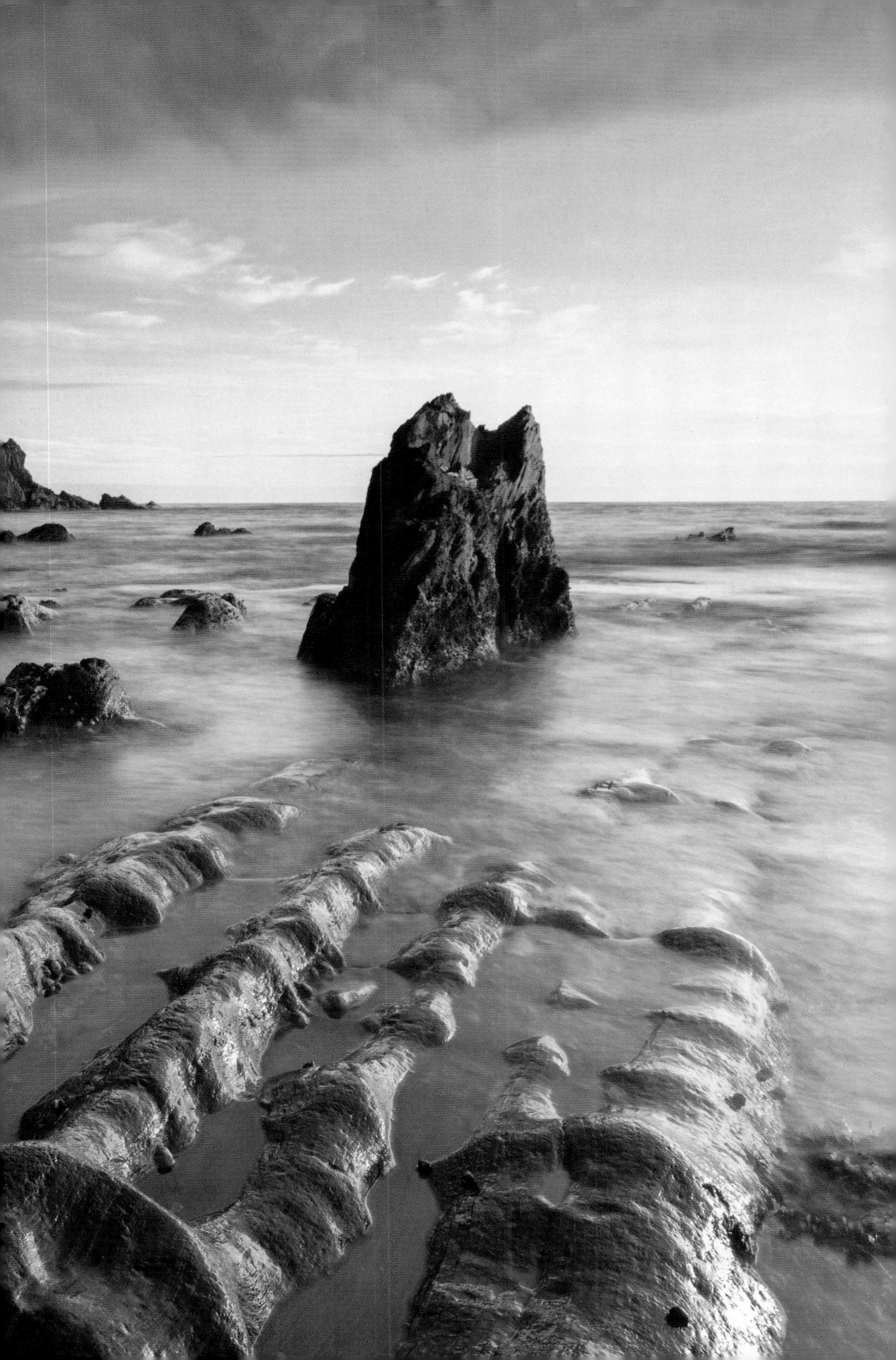

Located near to Burgh Island, Bantham is one of Devon's most popular beaches. Its popularity actually extends much further than Devon; in 2015 it was ranked sixth in the Lonely Planet's guide to the ten best beaches in Europe, the only English beach to make the list.

The beach and nearby village form part of a private estate, compassionately managed and preserved for nearly a century by the same family. In 2014 the estate was sold to another private family who have pledged to continue managing it in the same manner, ensuring the beach will stay open to visitors for the future.

The sandy beach backed by dunes is popular with visitors and is one of Devon's key surfing locations. Whilst the beach is photogenic offering lovely views over to Burgh Island, for photographers the real interest lies just around the headland.

What to Shoot and Viewpoints

On the southern side of the beach, the sand gives way to rocks and ledges. When the tide is low, you can walk out over these ledges and around the base of the cliffs to a secluded little cove. With barely any sand, it's not the kind of beach that appeals to most visitors but for photographers it is a treasure trove.

The appeal of this little cove comes with the fascinating geology. Stretching out to sea like giant skeletal hands, rounded worn ledges make fantastic photographic subjects, especially when water is lapping through the channels between. All around the shore beautiful white and red quartz boulders can be found, sometimes resting on ledges, others trapped in rock pools. The boulders stand out beautifully against the darker ledges, and make delightful foreground subjects.

Every so often shark fin shaped rocks several metres high protrude from the ledges, each one crying out to be photographed. Just to the south, at the base of the cliffs a huge spearheaded sea stack, appropriately named Long Rock, completes the dramatic feel of this cove.

All this geology comes together perfectly to provide a feast of interest making Bantham one of the photographic highlights of the South Devon coast.

Careful planning is required as this small cove can become cut off at high tide. While low tide makes for safe access it is also less than ideal as the water is too far out. At these times, the cove becomes a mass of rock, too chaotic to make a clean composition. The best option is to head around the cliffs on a mid tide, ensuring the tide is going out to prevent chances of being cut off.

As Long Rock provides such a strong appeal most photographs will be taken looking towards it. However, don't forget that from this cove you can also gain excellent views westwards looking diagonally across the ledges towards Burgh Island.

Right: Quartz boulders are plentiful in this area of Bantham, Canon 1Ds Mark III, 17-40mm at 25mm, ISO 100, 3 sec at f/16. March

How to Get Here

From Kingsbridge in the South Hams, head west for 1 mile, taking the sharp right turning onto the A381. Follow this road north for nearly 2 miles, when you reach the roundabout take the first left towards Bantham. After 3 miles you will reach Bantham village, drive through the village and you will come to the beach car park.

Parking Lat/Long: 50.277949, -3.8757907
Parking Grid Ref: SX 666 437
Parking Postcode: TQ7 3AJ
Map: OS Explorer Map OL20 (1:25 000) South Devon

Accessibility

From the car park, walk through the dunes and down onto the beach. The rocky cove can be found just around the base of the cliffs to your left. It is only a 10 minute walk from the car park. Depending on the tide levels some clambering over rocks may be required; caution is advised as the rocks and ledges can be very slippery. As you will typically be shooting close to the water's edge it is advisable to wear welly boots.

Best Time of Year/Day

As the coast faces west evening is always the best time to shoot at Bantham. For the rocky cove, the sun is setting in the best positions during autumn and winter. During these seasons you will benefit from late side lighting on the rocks and cliffs, and raise your chances of capturing a colourful sky around sunset.

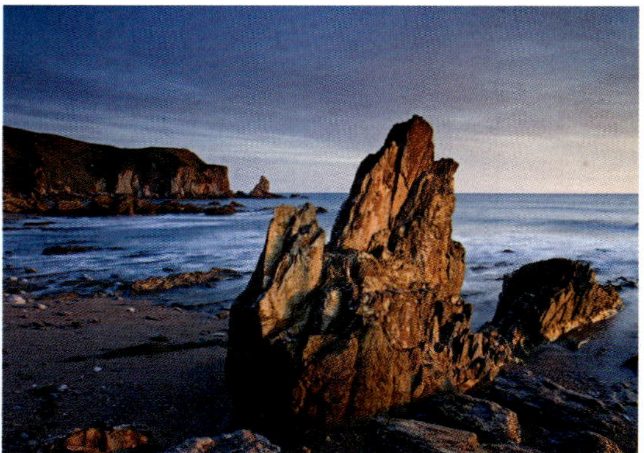

Jagged upright rock on the beach, Canon 1Ds Mark III, 17-40mm at 23mm, ISO 100, 4 sec at f/16. March

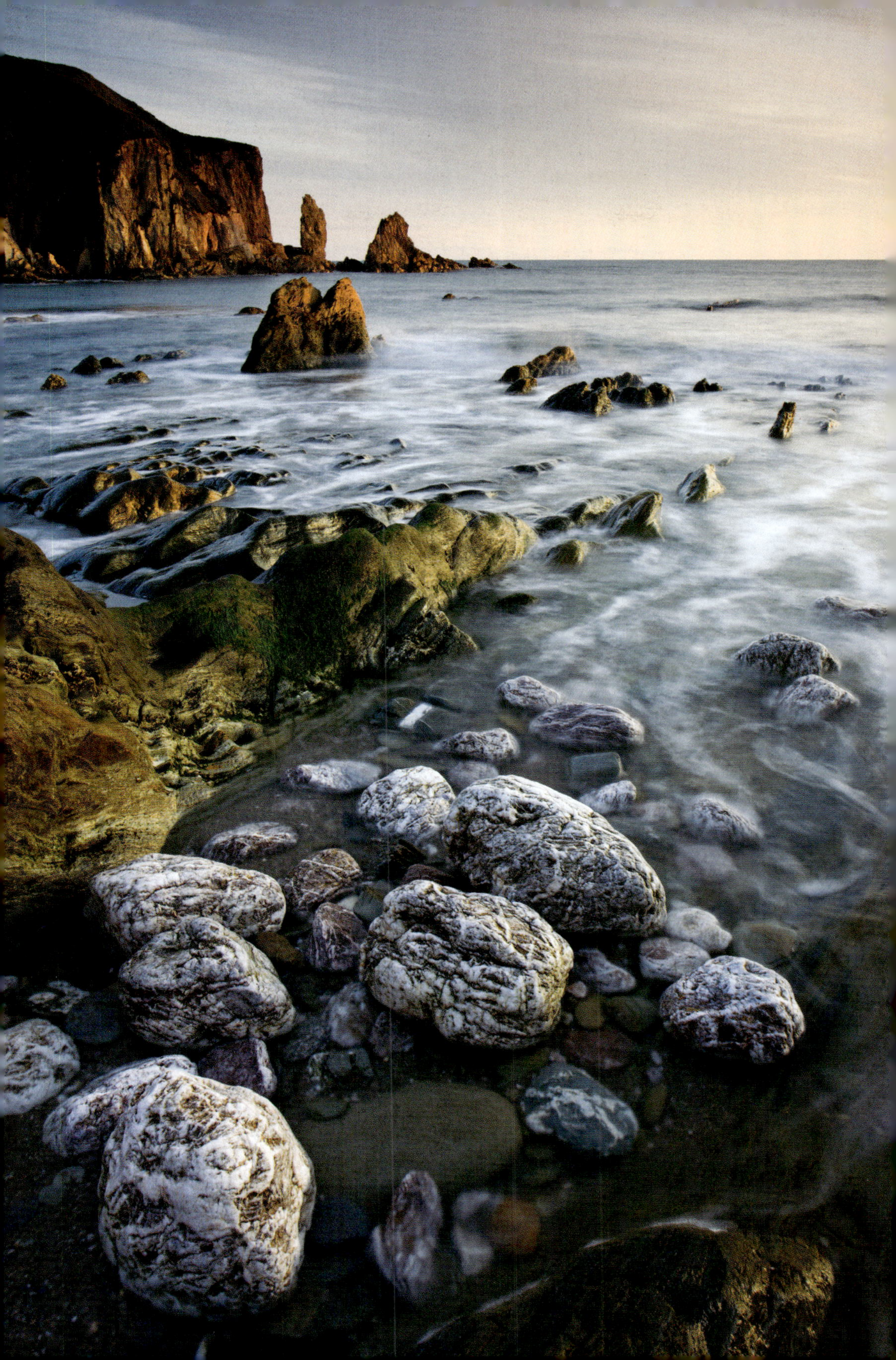

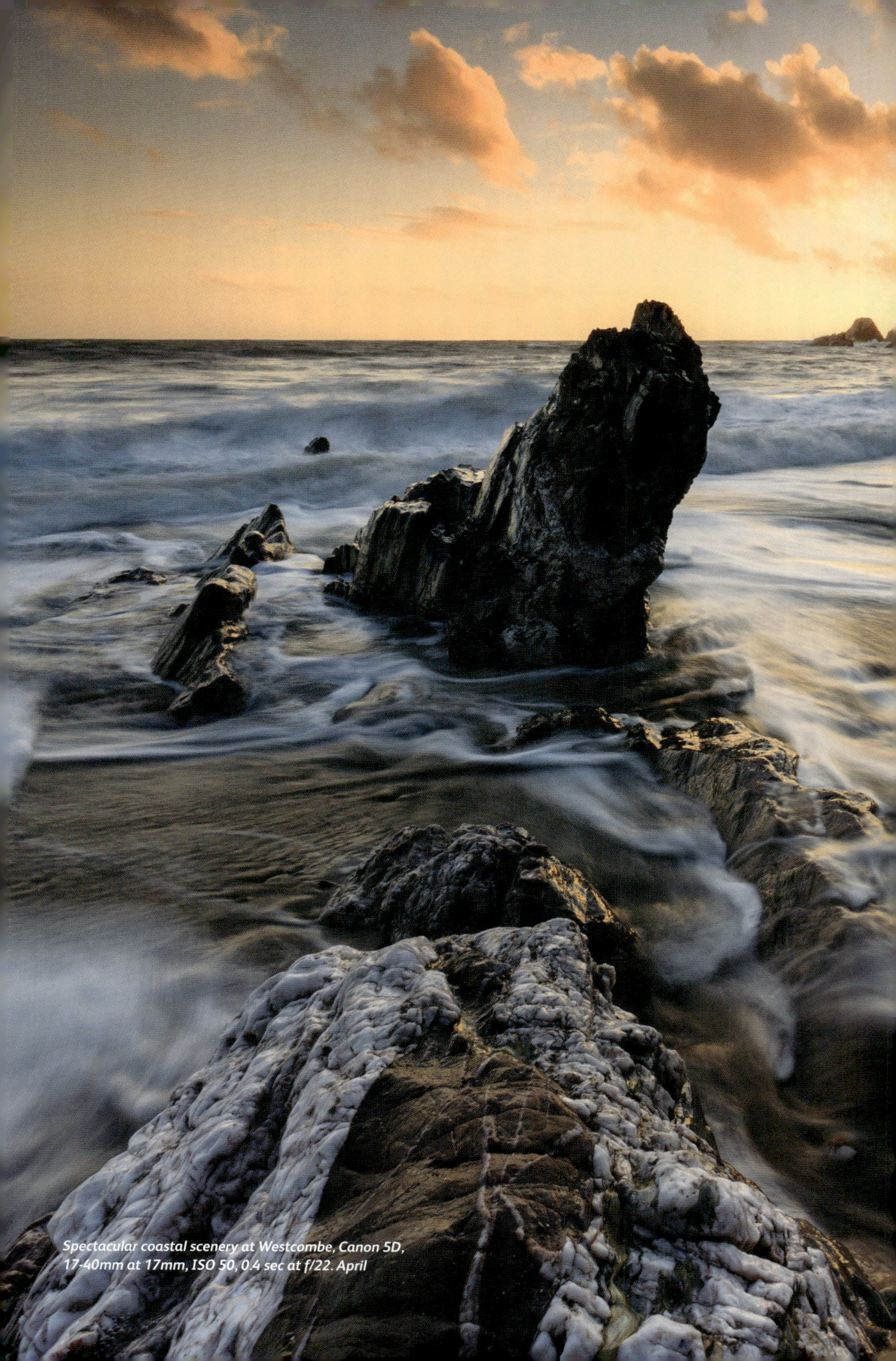

*Spectacular coastal scenery at Westcombe, Canon 5D,
17-40mm at 17mm, ISO 50, 0.4 sec at f/22. April*

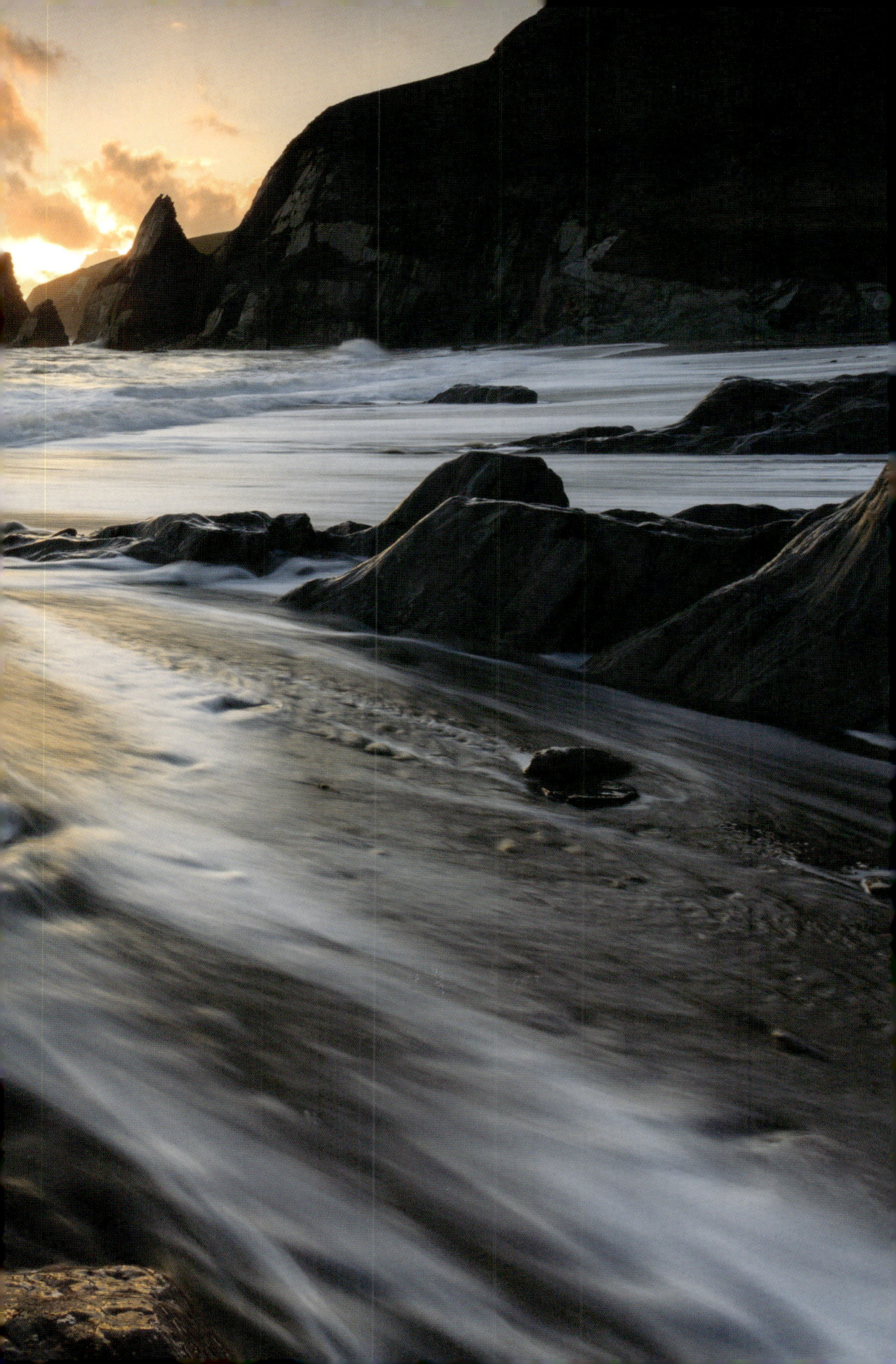

Located close to Burgh Island on the South Devon coast, Westcombe is a remote cove consisting of a grey sandy beach backed by vertical slate cliffs. The absence of a nearby car park or even road ensures this beach remains quiet throughout the seasons. For regular visitors far less effort is involved to reach prettier beaches just along the coast, but for photographers Westcombe contains all the necessary ingredients to make atmospheric and dramatic seascapes.

The cliffs on the western edge of the beach descend into a line of triangular slate sea stacks, resembling huge sharp teeth. These jagged pinnacles form a wonderful backdrop to pictures captured from both the beach and cliffs.

Waves surge around a protruding jagged rock on the shore, Canon 1Ds Mark III, 17-40mm at 20mm, ISO 50, 1 sec at f/16. February

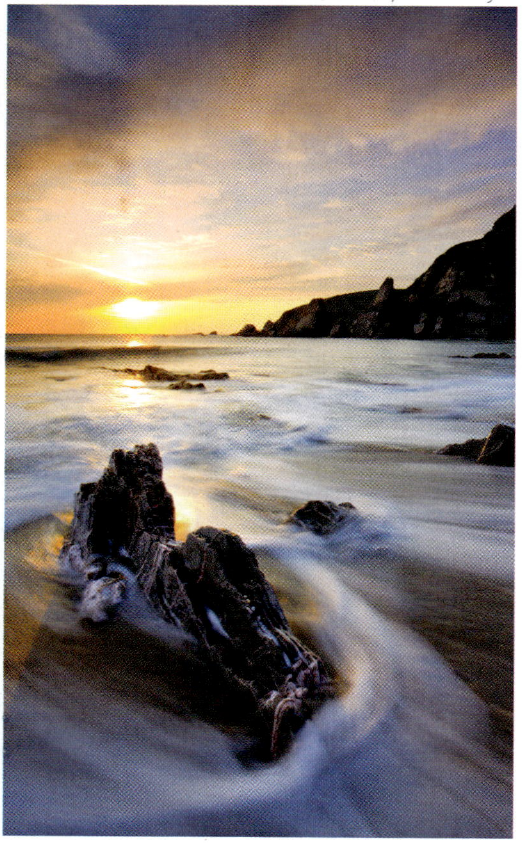

What to Shoot and Viewpoints

Viewpoint 1 – Cliffs

Approaching from the nearest car park in the village of Ringmore, your first view of Westcombe Beach will be from the cliff tops. With the beach finally in sight after a long walk the temptation is to rush past this view in order to reach the shore. Yet this cliff-top vista reveals more of the rugged coastline that can be seen from sea level; a few minutes spent here will reward you with some very different but no less dramatic pictures to those you will go on to capture from the shoreline.

From this elevated position the sandy beach looks quite ordinary. Of far more appeal are the jumble of broken cliffs and stacks on the western fringe of the beach, a longer focal length is good to enable these fantastic subjects to dominate your composition.

Like many cliff-top seascape, this view is enhanced when shooting in low light with longer exposures. With smooth slate rock faces reflecting the light, these cliffs stand out particularly well at twilight. Although you will probably want to be positioned on the beach at sunset, once the sun has dropped below the horizon, a quick dash up the steep cliff may give you the chance to photograph this view before all colour fades and it gets too dark.

Viewpoint 2 – Beach

Depending on tide and sand levels, upon first arrival the beach will either instantly appeal or disappoint. At low tide, with depleted sand levels the potential of the beach is immediately clear. Flat wave-smoothed ledges stretch across the whole shoreline, occasionally protruding in long sharp ridges. Armed with a wide angle lens, the rocks provide a wealth of foreground material, while the jagged sea stacks make an incredible background. The best shots usually involve water from incoming/retreating waves rushing over and around the ledges.

At high tide, the ledges are submerged leaving just a sandy beach somewhat lacking in interest. When compared to the feast of riches that the cliffs offer to the background, the beach is a little plain and ordinary leaving your composition feeling awkward and unbalanced. Even a stream meandering through the sand does little to redress this imbalance.

Fortunately, there is no need to despair at high tide. As luck would have it, the eastern edge of the beach works well on higher tides. Even when the sand levels are higher than normal, several intriguing rocks protrude vertically from the sand in this area making fascinating subjects. Mini ridges streaked with quartz veins, these angular rocks compliment the jagged background stacks magnificently and look especially pleasing when photographed with waves surging around them.

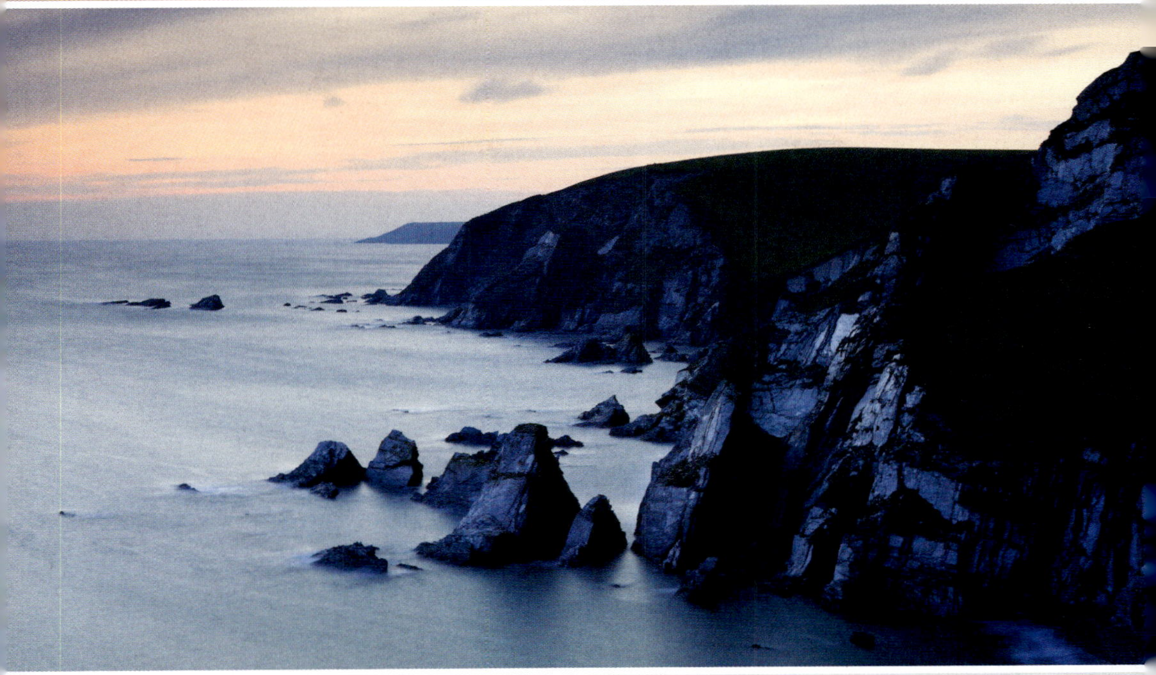

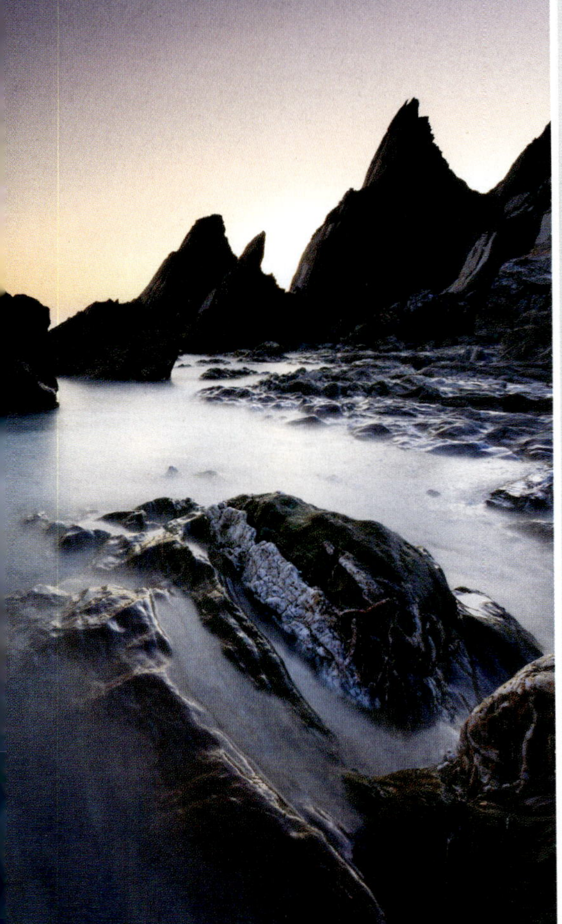

How to Get Here

Exit the A38 at Ivybridge and head south for approximately
5 miles towards the village of Modbury. From Modbury head
south for another 5 miles following signs to Ringmore.
Drive through the village to find a National Trust car park.

Parking Lat/Long: 50.295056, -3.8969010
Parking Grid Ref: SX 649 456
Parking Postcode: TQ7 4HP (Ringmore)
Map: OS Explorer Map OL20 (1:25 000) South Devon

Accessibility

From the car park, a footpath leads downhill to the coast, passing
Ayrmer cove before reaching Westcombe Beach. The footpath is
around 1.5 miles and involves some steep ascents/descents on the
cliffs near Westcombe. If you are planning to shoot from the beach,
wellington boots are recommended to avoid getting wet feet from
incoming waves.

Best Time of Year/Day

Due to the orientation of the coast, Westcombe Beach is best
photographed at sunset during the winter months when the sun
descends over the sea to the southwest. This means you will not
be shooting difficult exposures directly towards the setting sun.
On stormy overcast days, when sunset is not a factor the beach
can be photographed at any time of year.

*Westcombe's rugged coast from the cliff tops, Canon 1Ds Mark
III, 24-70mm at 52mm, ISO 100, 15 sec at f/16. February*

*Up close to the huge triangular sea stacks, Canon 1Ds Mark
III, 17-40mm at 20mm, ISO 100, 20 sec at f/16. March*

The neighbouring villages of Newton Ferrers and Noss Mayo are two of Devon's hidden gems. Situated near the south coast these pretty villages are about a mile inland along the winding River Yealm estuary, facing each other either side of the Newton Creek. Despite their picturesque location both Newton Ferrers and the smaller Noss Mayo seem to have slipped through the net for the majority of summer holidaymakers, each village retaining an innocent charm quite untainted by tourism.

What to Shoot and Viewpoints

As each village offers very similar views this location does not require specific guidance on actual viewpoints. All around Newton Creek similar views present themselves; pretty river scenes with whitewashed cottages forming a charming rural backdrop. Being the larger village Newton Ferrers potentially offers the more interesting background, making Noss Mayo the obvious viewpoint to shoot from. But then shooting from Newton Ferrers on the other side of the water ensures you can include Noss Mayo's prominent church as an interesting background focal point. You can easily spend several hours exploring viewpoints all around the Newton Creek.

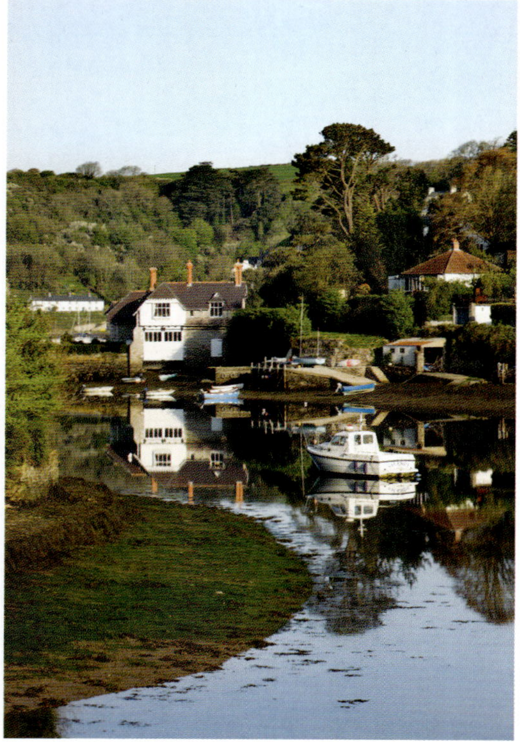

As both villages feature narrow lanes and limited parking, you will most probably find yourself shooting initially from Noss Mayo, where the main car park is located. From the car park it is a fair walk around the creek to Newton Ferrers. At low tide this journey can be shortened considerably by walking over the Newton Voss, a stone walkway connecting the villages. However, low water leaves the shores very muddy and less photogenic, so if you are planning to shoot from Newton Ferrers, it is best to arrive early on a higher tide and allow plenty of time to walk around the creek.

Your choice of shooting position will be restricted to the places where you can get down to the shore; fortunately there are plenty of areas where access has been maintained to launch boats. Whenever you reach the shore, there is usually an abundance of small boats to make excellent foreground subjects for wide angle photographs. At the same time, don't rule out using your telephoto lens. With a telephoto lens compositions are plentiful and really only restricted by your creativity. Look for houses to isolate in a tight composition featuring just a few boats in the foreground.

If you prefer to photograph a more rural scene with fewer buildings, with tide permitting, position yourself on the shore of Noss Mayo near the Newton Voss walkway, and look westwards along the creek. By shooting in this direction, the houses are replaced by thick wooded hills bordering the estuary. For those wishing even less human influence, a footpath from Noss Mayo winds westwards following the River Yealm out towards the sea. The woodland and river scenery is delightful, and eventually opens out at Cellar Beach, a secluded cove popular with local people.

Regardless of your shooting position, photographs from Newton and Noss always look their best when wind levels are low and the creek is reflective. The steep surrounding hills help to shelter the water, but to help matters it is best to plan your trip on a calm day.

Opposite top: Perfect reflections at low tide in Newton Creek, Canon 1Ds Mark III, 16-35mm at 32mm, ISO 200, 240 sec at f/11. May

View west along the creek, Canon 1Ds Mark III, 70-200mm at 126mm, ISO 100, 1/15 sec at f/14. May

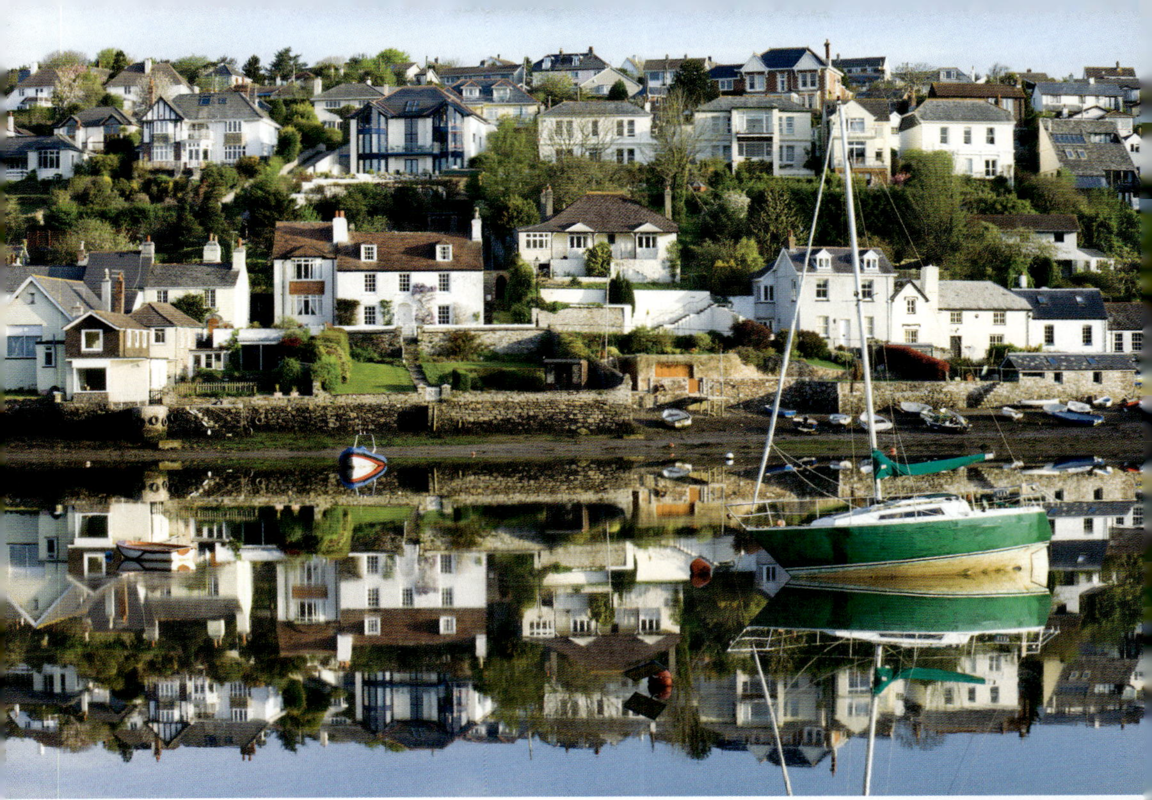

How to Get Here

Newton and Noss are in the South Hams district of South Devon, approximately ten miles from Plymouth. From Plymouth head east on the A379 towards Yealmpton. When you reach Yealmpton turn right onto the B3186 and follow this road all the way to Newton Ferrers. Drive around the creek to Noss Mayo to find the car park.

Parking Lat/Long: 50.310336, -4.0405910
Parking Grid Ref: SX 547 475
Parking Postcode: PL8 1EB
Map: OS Explorer Map OL20 (1:25 000) South Devon

Accessibility

Narrow roads wind through both villages close to the creek, making various viewpoints along the way accessible for wheelchair users.

Best Time of Year/Day

Like many estuaries along the south coast, the tide level is an important consideration for any visit. At low tide the creeks are muddy and less photogenic, while a high tide can restrict shooting positions. Ideally spend a few hours and capture the changing tide, but if time is limited plan to shoot on a mid tide.

You can shoot this area well year round, but the steep wooded hills surrounding the estuary always look better with foliage so ideally plan your visit from spring to autumn. In late spring and summer, early morning offers the best light when shooting across the creek from Noss Mayo, while late evening works for photos captured from Newton Ferrers.

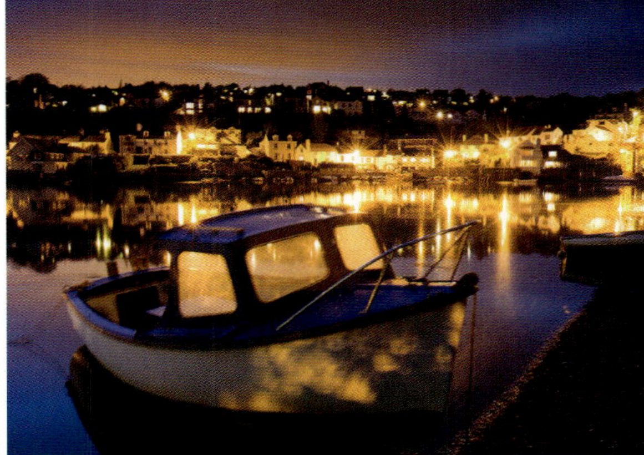

The lights of Newton Ferrer's reflect in the still creek, Canon 1Ds Mark III, 70-200mm at 73mm, ISO 100, 1/8 sec at f/14, May

A lone swan ripples the reflections, Canon 1Ds Mark III, 70-200mm at 200mm, ISO 100, 1/10 sec at f/14. May

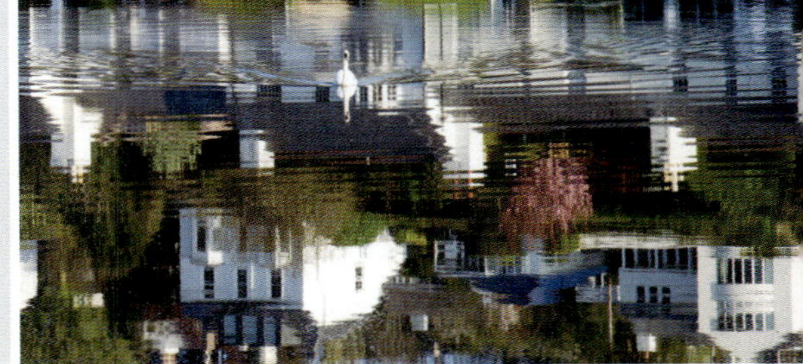

Situated close to Plymouth Sound on the south coast of Devon, Wembury Bay is a delightfully picturesque beach in the care of the National Trust. Although it is sandy in places the beach is perhaps best known for the rock pools found in its wide rocky ledges, making it a popular location for family day trips. Those ledges are also one of the factors that make Wembury such an ideal location for landscape photography, the other being the triangular offshore island, named the Great Mewstone.

The distinctive Mewstone makes a perfect backdrop to seascapes captured from Wembury Bay. Although now uninhabited this island has a long history of occupation; over the years it has played host to both a private home and a prison as well as a hiding place for smugglers. It's most notable resident was a local prisoner named Sam Wakeman, who was interned on the island for seven years as a cheaper alternative than transportation to Australia.

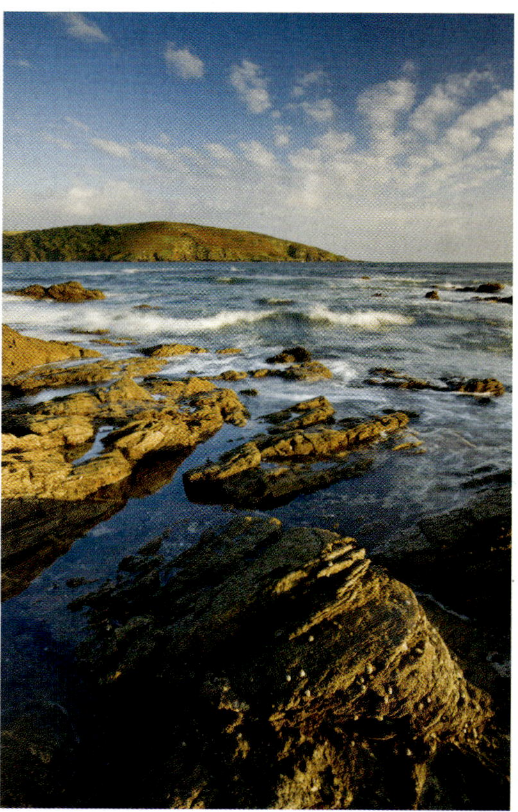

What to Shoot and Viewpoints

When you first pull into the cliff top car park, your initial impressions of Wembury may be somewhat underwhelming. Dependent on tide levels, the beach is small and by South West standards not especially pretty. Were it not for the striking Mewstone island, photographers may pass over the location entirely in search of the South Hams other picturesque locations. But the Mewstone makes Wembury hard to resist; islands always make great subject for seascapes and this one is among the most impressive in the South West.

With the Mewstone providing an obvious and compelling background subject, it's good to explore the shoreline to find the best viewpoint. From the car park some steps lead down to the small sandy beach; given the right conditions this area could provide some great photographs but is often rather messy not to mention busy with visitors. A much better bet is to aim for the rocky ledges on either side of the beach.

East side of beach – Blackstone Rocks

On the eastern edge of the beach a wide flat area, named Blackstone Rocks, makes an ideal platform from which to shoot the bay. Although largely underwater at high tide and difficult to access during these times, the high water does give the rock pools found in this area a daily top up of water. Once the tide retreats and the ledges can be reached, the many rockpools found amongst the jagged rocks make for wonderful photographic subjects.

While shooting south west in the direction of the Mewstone may be the obvious choice, the ledges at Blackstone Rocks also make an excellent vantage point to shoot south towards the headland at Gara Point. This works particularly well during late afternoon on clear days, when the rocky ledges and headland can be beautifully side lit by low sunshine.

West side of beach

Probably the most appealing area for photographers are the expansive ledges that stretch out from the western side of the beach all the way over to Wembury Point. If the tide is low you can access these ledges from the beach itself. Alternatively on a higher tide follow the cliff top coast path, where you will soon find several areas where you can easily get down to the ledges.

With so many dark rocks all around compositions may at first prove challenging. Providing it is safe to do so, head over the jagged ledges so you can position your camera closer to the sea. The water helps to simplify compositions by breaking up the dark rocks while the rushing waves add a sense of drama to pictures.

Towards Gara Point from the ledges at Blackstone Rocks, Canon 1Ds Mark III, 17-40mm at 21mm, ISO 100, 1 sec at f/22. September

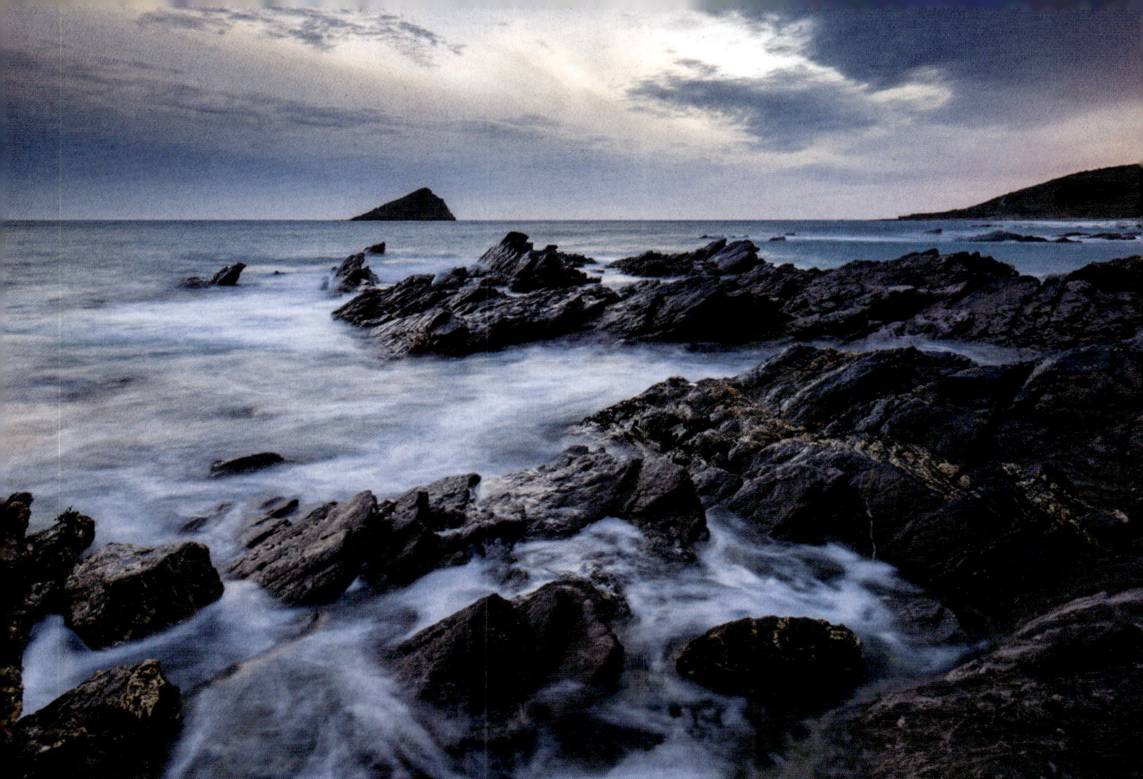

The Great Mewstone from Wembury's rocky shore, Nikon D800E, 17-35mm at 24mm, ISO 100, 4 sec at f/11. April

The rocks along this stretch of coast are very jagged, with many protruding upwards at acute angles. While they can be difficult to walk over, they also make excellent subjects, especially during higher tides when the larger rocks rise out of the sea like shark fins.

If you prefer not to or are unable to venture out to the waters edge, look for one of the many rock pools to use as foreground. Trapped far from the crashing waves rock pools are often perfectly still, which make them ideal for capturing reflections of colourful skies at sunset.

Due to the geology of the coastline the mass of ledges in this area do tend to dominate the right side of pictures, which can lead to compositions appearing unbalanced. To further complicate matters the Mewstone tends to appear on the right side also. With careful attention to your choice of viewpoint and composition you can usually redress any imbalance by positioning the Mewstone on the left side of the horizon to act as a counter balance.

Saint Werburgh's Church

The delightfully positioned Saint Werburgh's Church makes a wonderful subject. Located above the car park, the church enjoys unrestricted views over the coastline below. Follow the steps up through the graveyard, which provide enough elevation to enable you to photograph the church, coastline and island all in one composition.

How to Get Here

Wembury Bay is only 7 miles from Plymouth, in the beautiful South Hams district on Devon's south coast. From Plymouth head east on the A379 and then turn right at Elburton following the road signs to Wembury. Drive through the village and park in the National Trust car park just above the beach.

Parking Lat/Long: 50.317132, -4.0828291
Parking Grid Ref: SX 518 484
Parking Postcode: PL9 0HN
Map: OS Explorer Map OL20 (1:25 000) South Devon

Accessibility

The beach is close to the car park, accessed by a series of steps. The ledges are best accessed by following the cliff top coast path, which passes through the car park. This beach and ledges are not wheelchair friendly, but the car park itself does afford good views over the beach towards the Mewstone.

Best Time of Year/Day

Wembury can be photographed year round at both dawn and dusk. However, with the sun setting out to sea during winter, a late afternoon trip at this time of year offers the best chances of photographing colourful skies beyond the Mewstone

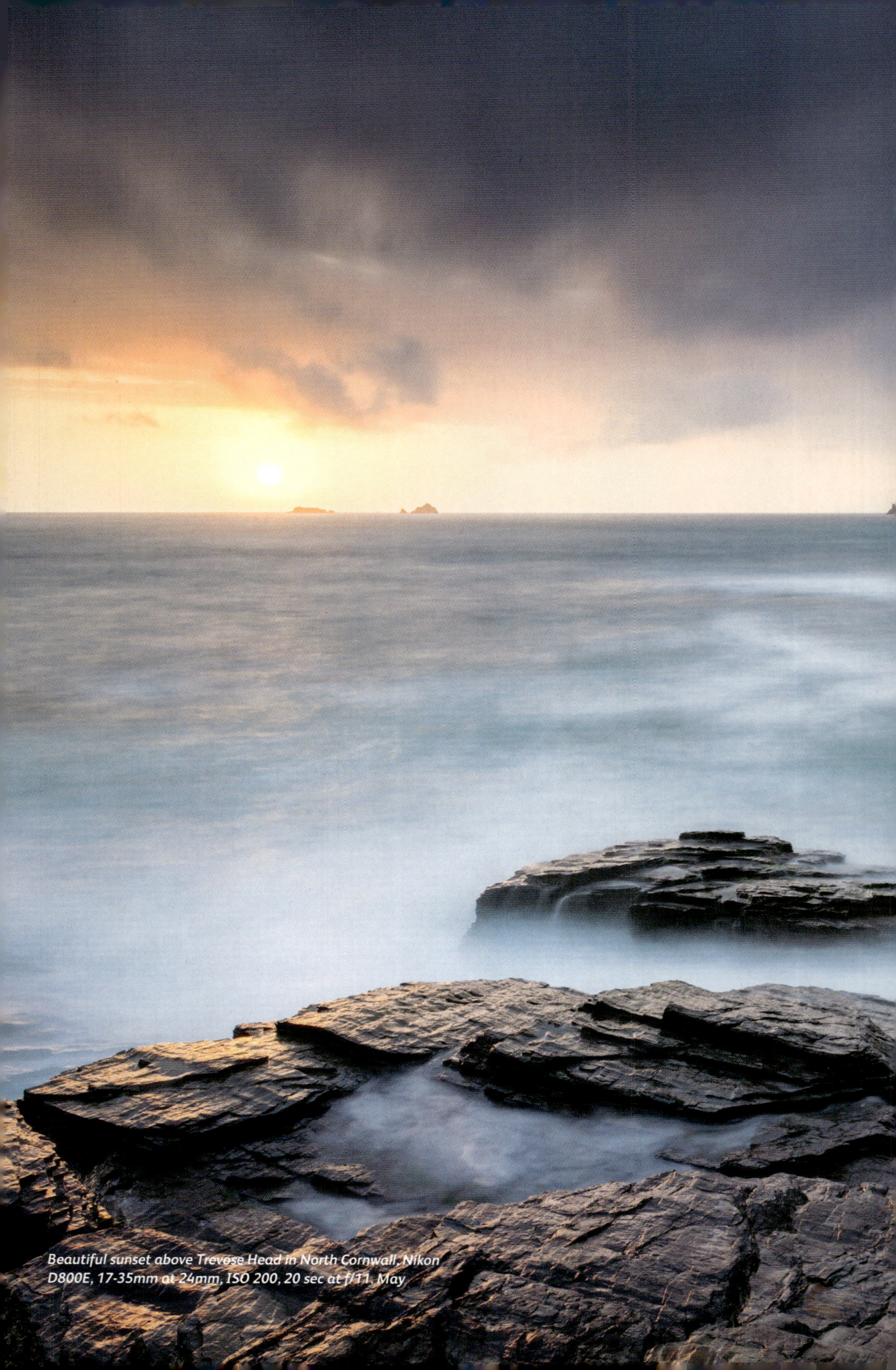

Beautiful sunset above Trevose Head in North Cornwall. Nikon
D800E, 17-35mm at 24mm, ISO 200, 20 sec at f/11. May

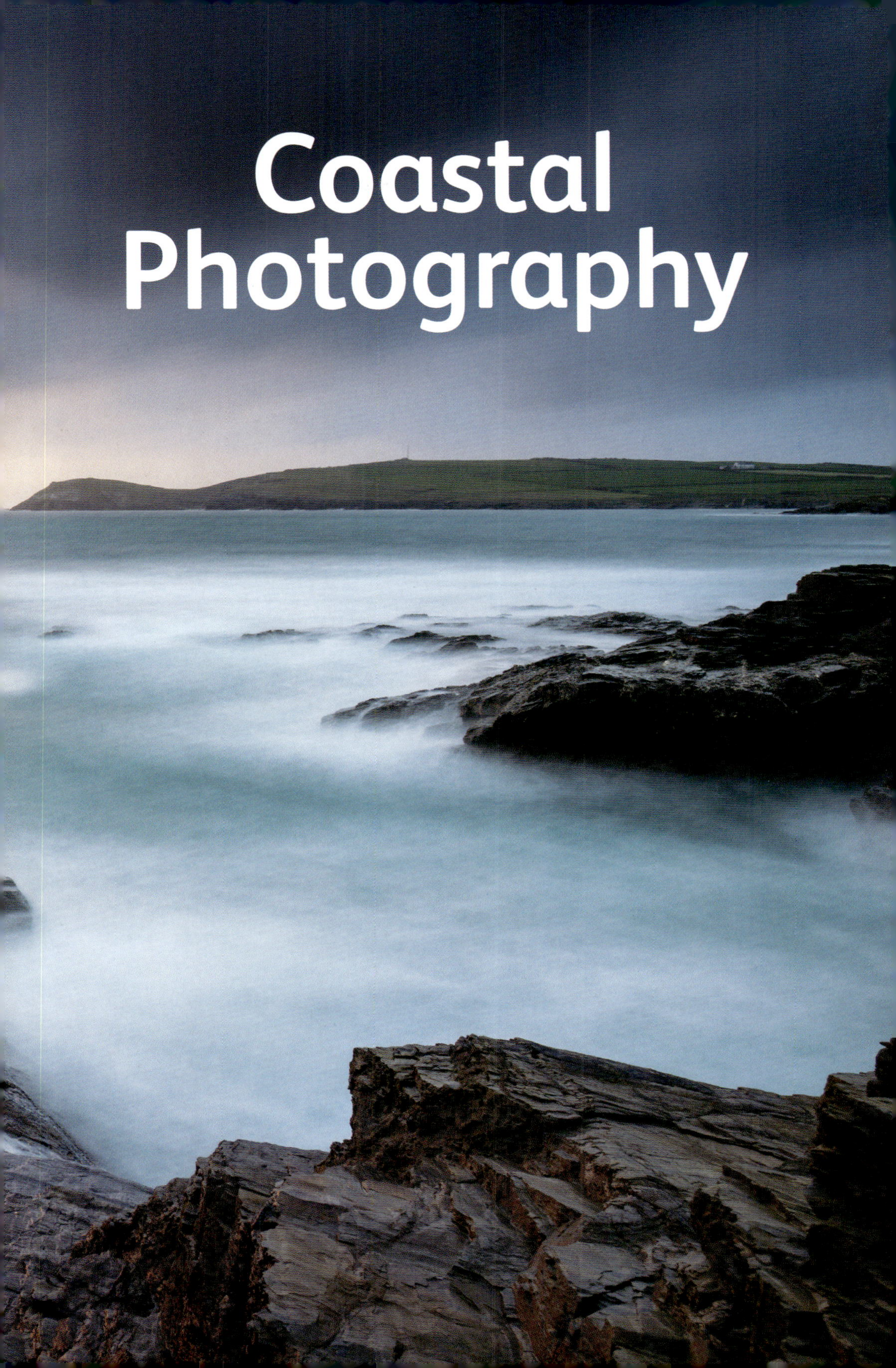

Coastal Photography

Coastal Photography

There are few more exhilarating places to take photographs than on Cornwall and Devon's extensive coast. With serene or raging seas, vast expanses of windswept sand, villages and harbours, and an endless variety of cliffs, sea stacks, arches, rocky platforms, skerries and boulders as subjects, you will be enthralled.

The guide below describes the most popular coastal terrains and provides some essential techniques for photographing them.

On the Beach

The great strength of a beach photograph is often its simplicity – the old adage that less is more. Whether comprised of sand or pebbles, beaches are usually uncluttered enabling simple, tranquil images to be captured. But before grabbing your camera and heading to the nearest beach there are several things to consider.

Timing: Tides and the Sun

The best time for beach photography is when the tide is on its way out. In the UK there are two high tides and two low tides within any 24-hour period, with roughly 12 hours between high tides. Various websites show tide times and recommended is the Met Office website:

www.metoffice.gov.uk

You can also check the weather forecast at the same time. Better still, mobile apps such as Ayetides will show you the anticipated tide levels for your trip.

A receding tide leaves a clean sandy beach free of footsteps and sand castles. A low tide will also provide you with the flexibility to move around and identify viewpoints to photograph without getting your feet too wet.

The ideal is to time your visit to coincide with a falling tide and a sunset to increase the chances of capturing a special image. At the end of day when the sky is painted with heavenly colours, the retreating tide will leave a sandy or pebble beach wet and fantastically reflective.

Due to the geography of the coastline most beaches in the South West are suited to sunset photography, with the sun setting out to sea. Dawn is a little more challenging, although there still are many beaches along the south coast facing east, making them ideal sunrise locations.

The Sun Compass and set off early

For sunrise and sunset times and the position of the sun throughout the year check the Sun Compass on the front flap of this book. It's good to get to your location at least two hours before sunset to take advantage of the often glorious low light of the 'golden hour' before the sun sets.

Beach Composition

While simple, uncluttered images are both ideal and achievable for beach photography, it is still beneficial to scout a location to look for a main focal point for your images. Often at low tide simple tidal pools are revealed in the sand, making ideal foreground subjects for wide-angle compositions. Alternatively set up to use a small beach stream, or a group of boulders, as both foreground and a natural lead-in line towards the sea.

Man-made objects such as wooden groynes can make excellent focal points. Groynes are wooden sea defences and can be found at many locations on the coast and offer huge potential, especially when photographed with waves washing past them or with long exposures.

TOP FIVE BEACHES

Equipment for Shooting Seascapes

The following equipment is recommended.

- **Lenses:** A wide-angle (e.g. 16-35mm) and a telephoto lens (e.g. 70-200mm).
- **Tripod:** The sturdier the better.
- **Filters:** A set of Neutral Density graduated filters (ND Grads), (bracketing shots and exposure blending is the alternative), and one or more straight Neutral Density filters (NDs) for long exposures.
- **Remote Cable:** Allows you to shoot long exposures with shutter into the minutes via the camera's BULB setting.
- **Cleaning Cloth:** Keep a couple of these in your bag and pocket to wipe away any water/spray splashes on lenses.
- **Clean your gear:** Salt water will corrode your camera gear. After returning home from every coastal trip be sure to clean your camera, lenses, filters and tripod.
- **Batteries:** Several fully-charged batteries

Breaking waves on Shippen Beach, South Hams at sunset, Canon 1Ds Mark III, 17-40mm at 24mm, ISO 100, 1 sec at f/16. January

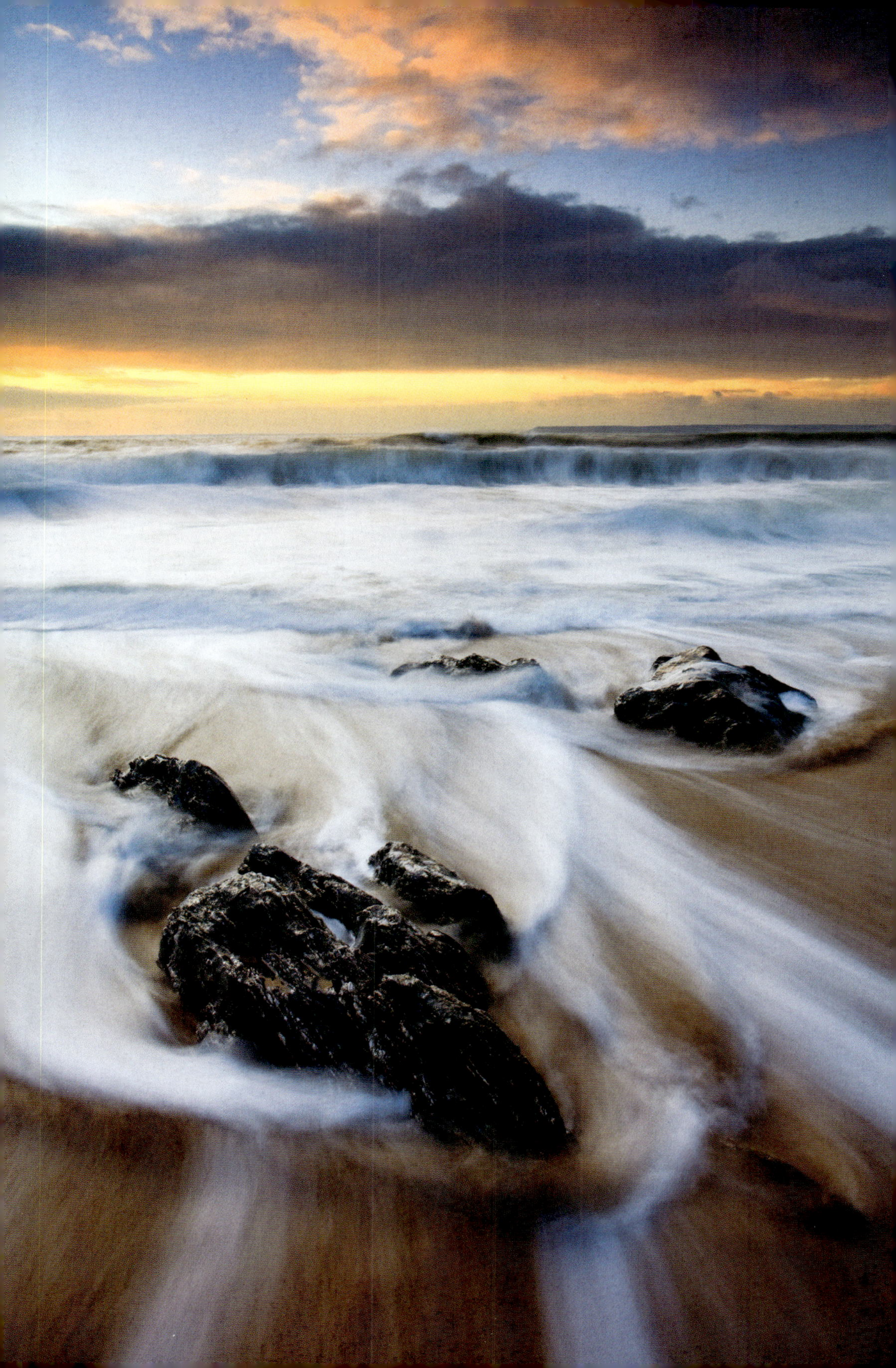

Coastal Photography

On The Rocks

While compositions from beaches can provide simplicity and tranquillity, rocky coves and ledges are the opposite. Rocky scenery offers dramatic photographs for those with a keen eye, sturdy legs and a great deal of perseverance.

Rocky locations can appear busy and cluttered, and without careful consideration of subject matter and composition the resulting images will be over-complicated and confusing. In such instances it is important to know the area well, so spend some time building up your knowledge of the location before you get the camera out.

When shooting from rocky shores, I like to choose mid to high tides. Low tide can reveal the unwelcome clutter of barnacle and seaweed covered rocks which are difficult to photograph well. A higher tide hides not only seaweed, but also covers much of the rocky shore; the water simplifying the busy landscape and making compositions so much cleaner and easier to find.

For the most dramatic images, try to get as close to the water's edge as you are able, while remaining safe. Look for areas where crashing waves can bring white water channelling between the rocks. The water channels can act as both a lead-in line, and also some light detail to balance out the darker rocky foreground of the image. As the tide rises pay particular attention to rocky outcrops that become isolated by the sea, creating mini-islands that can make striking elements to a composition.

To further simplify your composition, consider shooting a long exposure. An exposure of around a minute will turn a choppy sea into a ghostly mist. Any jagged rocks will protrude upwards like daggers through the water, their solid and glistening wet surfaces contrasting strongly against the soft misty veil.

When

As with beaches sunrise and sunset can offer magical results when photographed from rocky shores, but do not rule out visiting these locations on cloudy, overcast days. Moody weather compliments rugged coves very well, enabling you to capture extremely dramatic photographs that appropriately convey the location, and stand out from the usual dawn and dusk coastal imagery.

TOP ROCKY LOCATIONS

Opposite: The perfectly formed rocky shores of Porth Nanven, Canon 1Ds Mark III, 16-35mm at 29mm, ISO 100, 3.2 sec at f/16. April

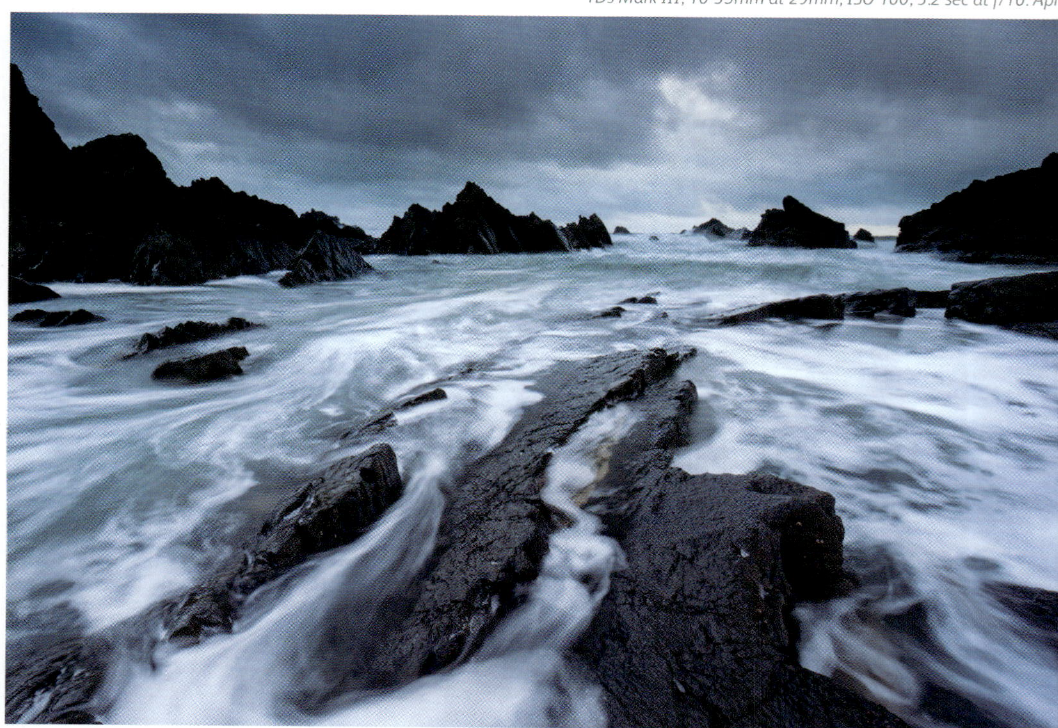

Dramatic coastal scenery at Hartland Quay in North Devon, Nikon D800E, 17-35mm at 19mm, ISO 50, 2 sec at f/11. April

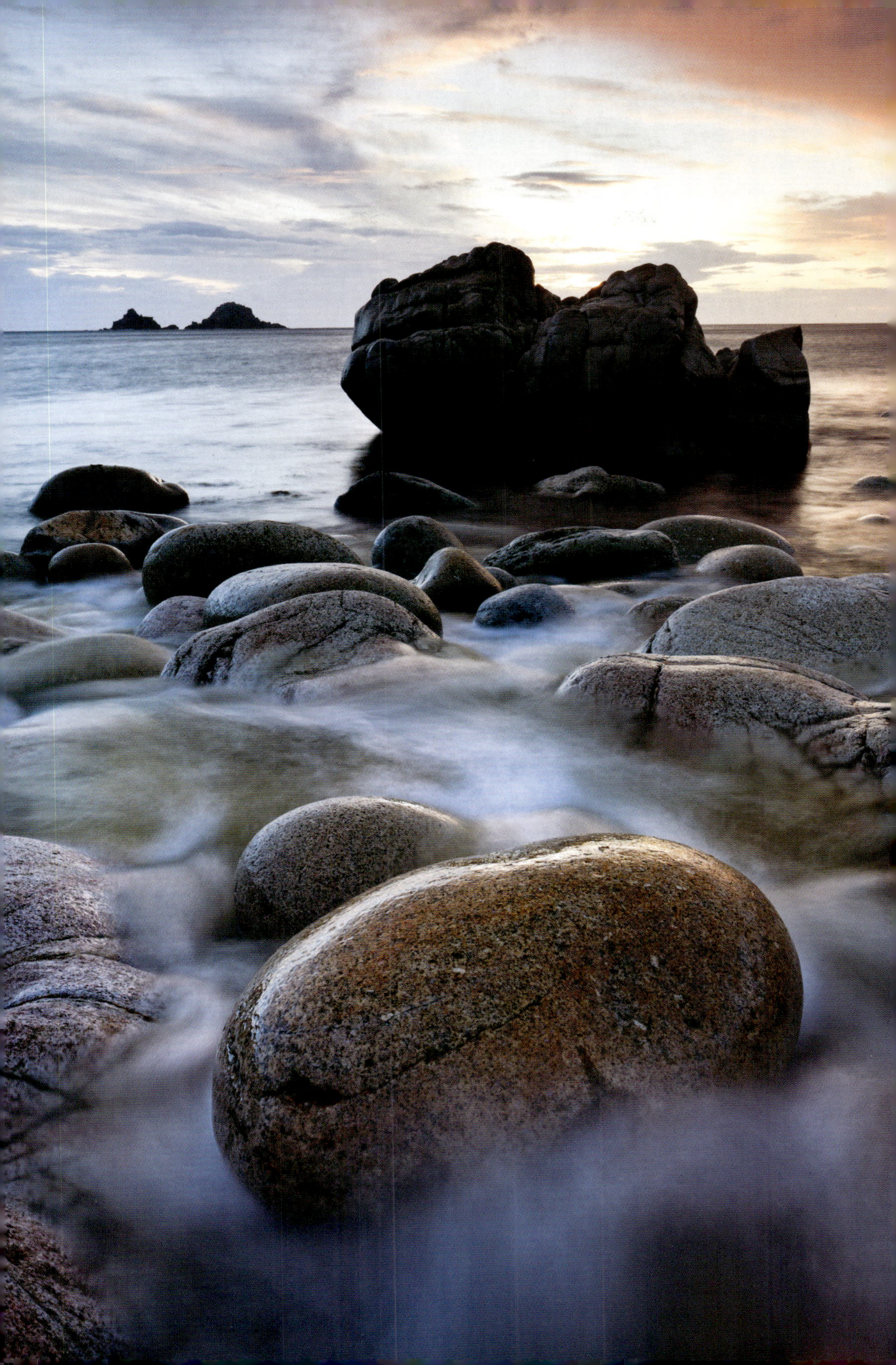

Coastal Photography

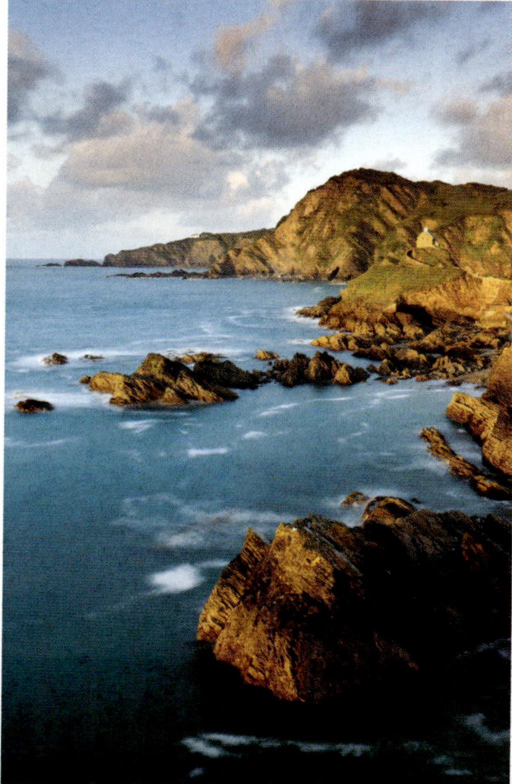

St Nicholas Chapel and Beacon Point on the rocky coast of Ilfracombe, Devon, Canon 1Ds Mark III, 24-70mm at 42mm, ISO 50, 15 sec at f/16. May

Storm over Land's End in Cornwall, Canon 5D, 24-70mm at 63mm, ISO 100, 32 sec at f/19. September

From the Cliff Tops

Cliff top photography offers an exciting perspective for those willing and able to put in the effort walking up steep cliffs where the vistas are often breathtaking. In the South West there are many miles of open cliff tops, with a network of footpaths providing good access.

It's always worth carrying both wide-angle and telephoto lenses in your bag. Wide-angle lenses are useful for when you can position yourself above vertical drops, tilting the camera downwards to capture both the crashing waves on the rocks below and the distant headlands disappearing off into the horizon. Alternatively telephoto lenses ensure cliffs stay big and bold in the frame, compressing coastlines tightly together into a series of dramatic headlands.

Beautiful light on the North Devon coast near Ilfracombe, Nikon D800E, 24-70mm at 48mm, ISO 100, 8 sec at f/11. April

When

The cliffs are at their most beautiful during the months of May and June when the cliff tops burst into vibrant life with the appearance of pretty photogenic wildflowers. Carpets of pink thrift, yellow kidney vetch, and sometimes bluebells paint the cliffs with colour, making ideal foregrounds for wide landscapes. A low and close composition combined with a small aperture of f/16-f/22 will ensure flowers in foregrounds falling away to rocky cliffs and sea beyond all remain in sharp focus.

For the hardy, winter brings stormy weather when fierce seas and waves crash onto the headlands below. To fully capture this drama you will need a shutter speed of around 1/125 sec to freeze motion. Alternatively, go the other way and slow down the action to 15 seconds or more to record swirling and crashing waves as patterns of white trails in a mysterious sea.

TOP CLIFF TOP LOCATIONS

- Land's End page 46
- Bedruthan Steps page 80
- Boscastle page 94
- The Rumps page 88
- Start Point page 236

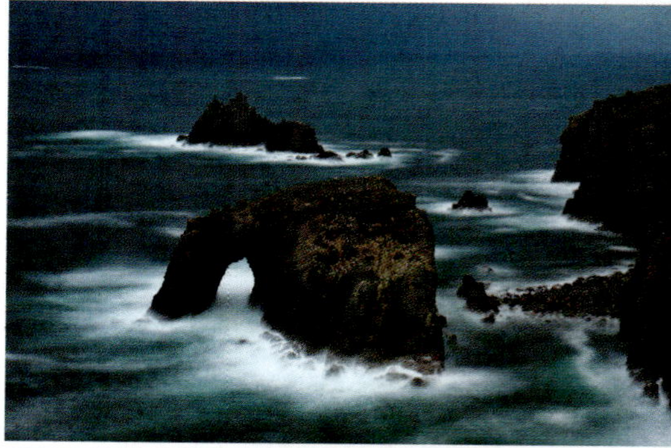

Opposite: Sunrise over cliffs at Pednvounder Beach, Cornwall, Canon 1Ds Mark III, 24-70mm at 25mm, ISO 50, 10 sec at f/16. October

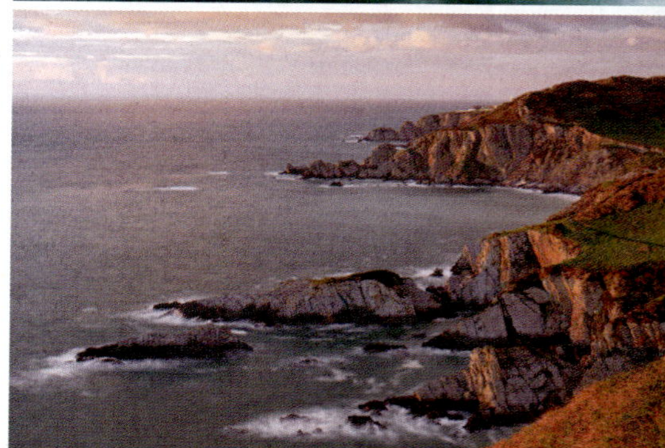

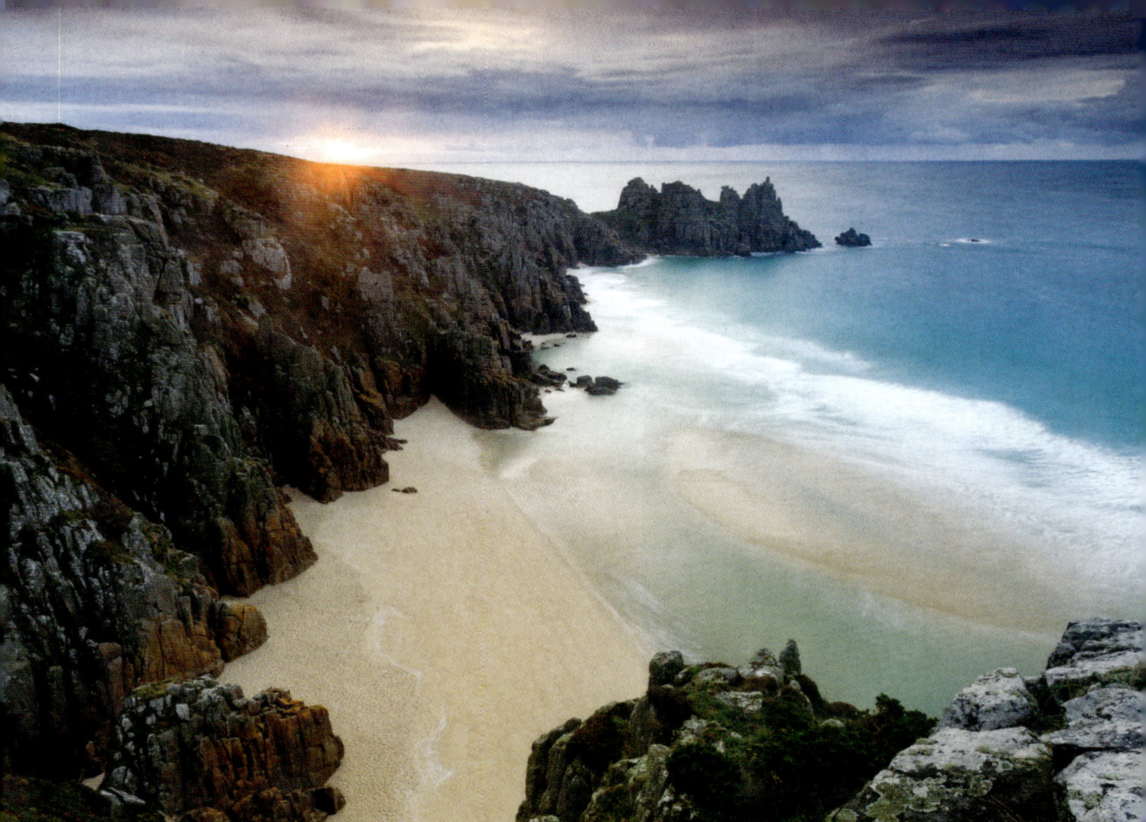

Planning a Shoot

Before visiting a location a little time spent researching
will save you a wasted journey.

- **Know your location.** Ideally scout a location for the
best compositions and to calculate where the light
will fall either by visiting midday or getting there
early. Research on the internet to see what others
have done and at what time of year and day,
try to work out the best times to visit.

- **Tides.** Consult the appropriate tide tables, or use
the Ayetides App to determine the anticipated tide
levels for your trip.

- **Safety.** Coastal photography can be hazardous and
potentially life threatening. By familiarising yourself
with the location you will minimize the risk of placing
yourself in danger. Look for shooting locations which
provide a safe passage away from the beach, even
at high tide. Don't stray too close to the top of cliff
edges, and just as importantly don't stand too near
to the bottom.
**If you do get in trouble call 999 and give them
your exact location.**

- **The Journey.** Get to your location in good time.
Make sure you know where you are going and how
long it will take. Each location chapter includes
directions and location co-ordinates for Sat Navs,
GPS, phones and paper maps.

- **Check the weather forecast.** Use at least
two forecasts – try www.metcheck.co.uk and
www.bbc.co.uk. Don't be put off by overcast
skies – often these can offer ideal conditions for
atmospheric seascapes, especially early or late
in the day when light levels are low.

- **Sun Position.** Check sunrise and sunset times and
the position of the sun using the Sun Compass on
the front flap of this book, websites like www.suncalc.
org or the photographer's ephemeris app.

- **Check the wind direction and strength.** Wind is a
big factor for coastal photography, especially when
shooting wide-angle at sea level. When checking the
weather forecast, pay particular attention to the
wind direction and strength. If the wind direction
is coming directly in off the sea, and the strength is
10mph plus, it is often difficult to avoid your camera
gear becoming coated with sea-spray, and splashes
from waves. Look for forecasts where the wind is
coming from any other direction than directly in off
the sea. Alternatively, stand further up the beach
and use a longer lens to safely capture the breaking
waves with minimal sea-spray.

- **Post Trip: Clean your gear:** Salt water will corrode
your camera gear. After returning home from every
coastal trip be sure to clean your camera, lenses,
filters and tripod.

Coastal Photography

Coastal Villages and Harbours

In stark contrast to seascape photography, where you often have to search out colour and shapes to make interesting photographic subjects, the South West's fishing villages and harbours are literally bursting with photographic potential at almost every turn.

Let's consider subject matter. Fishing boats are often brightly coloured, and can be found bobbing around in harbours, pulled up on a beach, or overturned on a slipway. Wherever they are to be found, they usually make wonderful subject matter for vivid coastal village shots. It is a good idea to spend some time looking for a brightly coloured boat to feature as a prominent foreground in a wide-angle composition.

You will also find other tools of the fishing trade lined up in convenient positions along harbour walls. Coils of rope, lobster pots, nets and buoys are just some of the objects that you may encounter, all of which help to convey the location you are photographing.

To emphasise these foreground objects get in close with your wide-angle lens and fill the lower two thirds of your frame with the colours of details of the harbour. This will enable your viewer to really connect with the image and feel as though they are with you, standing on the harbour wall. To counterbalance such a bold foreground, arrange your composition to include harbour walls, colourful cottages, and pubs in the background.

When

Time of day is an important consideration, not only for light but also to avoid the crowds. By definition, the most picturesque harbour villages attract the most visitors so, unless you are looking to include people in your composition arrive early or late in the day, or time your visit for the winter months. When shooting at dawn keep a keen eye out for delivery vans creeping into your shots. I have lost count of the number of times that I have been preparing to photograph a harbour scene, only to see a huge white lorry pull up on the far side of the harbour.

It can be rewarding to photograph coastal village scenes in the evening when the lights of cottages, pubs, and street lamps are reflected in mirror like harbour waters. Alternatively, a sunny blue sky day will reward you with a bright picture-postcard coastal village scene.

TOP COASTAL VILLAGE

- Mevagissy page 66
- Polperro page 74
- Padstow page 86
- Clovelly page 116
- Porlock Bay page 138

Opposite: Boats pulled high onto the pebbly shore at Clovelly in North Devon, Canon 1Ds Mark III, 17-40mm at 20mm, ISO 100, 0.3 sec at f/16. September

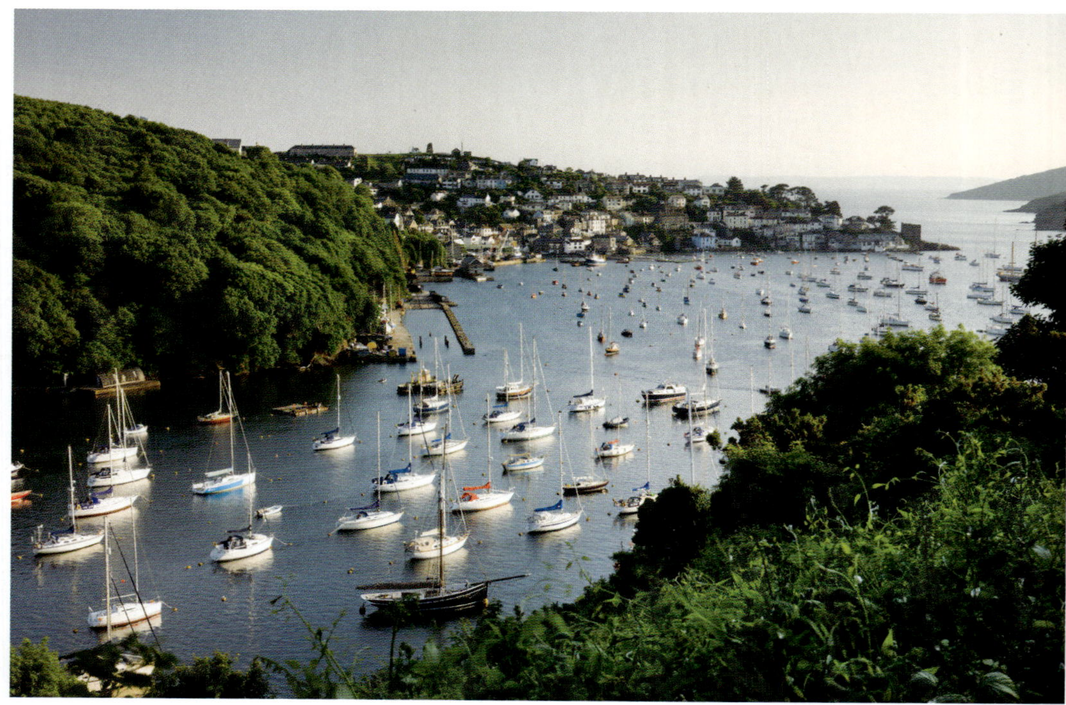

Yachts moored in the sheltered Pont Pill near the Cornish village of Polruan, Canon 1Ds Mark III, 24-70mm at 50mm, ISO 100, 1/6 sec at f/16. June

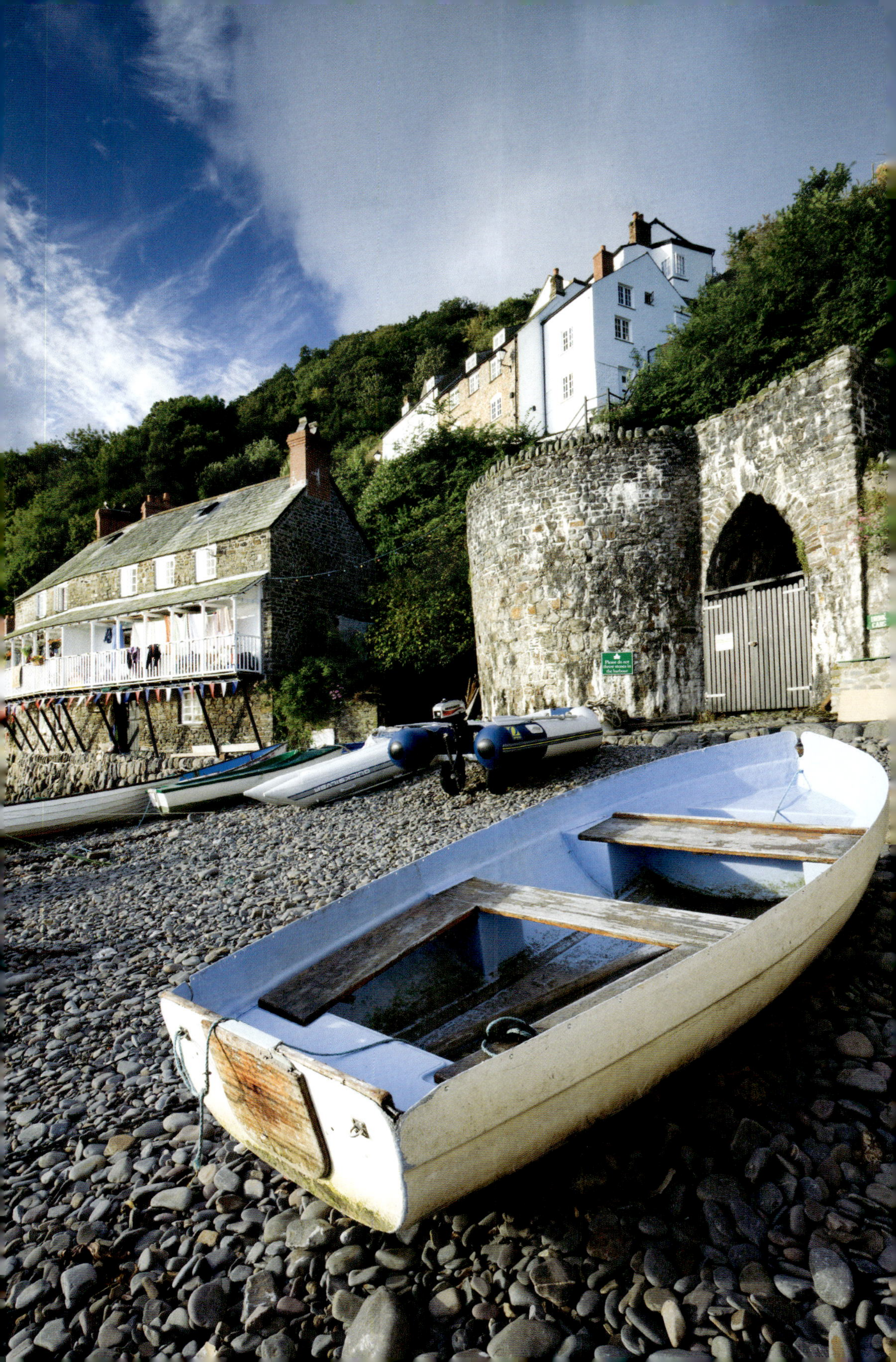

Long Exposures – A Quick Guide

The dynamic coast is a great place to experiment with long exposures. With waves crashing and clouds streaming across the sky some dramatic effects can be achieved.

Long exposures with shutter speeds from one second to several minutes blur the water creating a serene mood. This effect can work on both calm and rougher seas and of course affects moving clouds too.

To achieve a long exposure wait on location until the evening. As twilight approaches light levels will fade quickly, meaning you need to extend your shutter speed to capture a correct exposure. Alternatively, with the benefit of a Neutral Density (ND) filter that blocks the light you can shoot long exposures of a minute and more during the middle of the day.

ND filters are available in a variety of strengths. A single stop ND filter will double the exposure time, a three-stop ND will increase a shutter speed of 1/4 sec to 2 seconds whereas a 10-stop ND such as LEE Filters Big Stopper, will increase a 1/4 sec exposure to four minutes.

Weathered wooden groynes on Porlock Beach in Exmoor, Canon 1Ds Mark III, 16-35mm at 20mm, ISO 100, 30 sec at f/16. February

With longer shutter speeds breaking waves appear 'milky' and waves in deeper water will be smoothed.

The effect works equally well close up on the shore or from a cliff top vantage point.

On a beach the best compositions are where the waves flow back and forth over rocks or around wooden groynes. Get close to these foreground subject so the effect is prominent in the frame.

From cliff tops breaking waves create a white blurry fringe along the coast. Sea stacks, skerries and offshore rock platforms add interest.

Technique

- Use manual mode for shorter exposures of a few seconds or bulb mode with a remote shutter release for longer exposures of more than 30 seconds.

- Set the ISO to its lowest value, (typically 100).

- Use the smallest aperture (highest number) to achieve the slowest shutter speeds, depending on the effect you are trying to achieve.

- Attach your camera to your tripod and compose focussing on a point a third of way up the frame then switch auto-focus and any image stabilisation/vibration reduction off.

- Attach the ND filter to your lens only after you have focussed. A sturdy tripod is essential as small gusts of wind can ruin a long exposure.

- Use the self-timer or for very long exposures use the bulb setting and a shutter release to take your photograph. Some experimentation may be needed to get the required effect, and your image in focus. This technique works for both close-ups near breaking waves and also from a distance on a cliff top looking down to the sea.

Right: Long exposure blurs Atlantic waves at Botallack in Cornwall, Nikon D800E, 24-70mm at 55mm, ISO 100, 89 sec at f/8. October

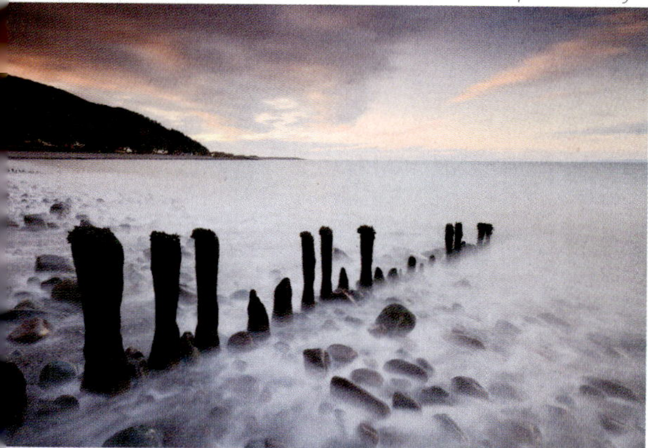

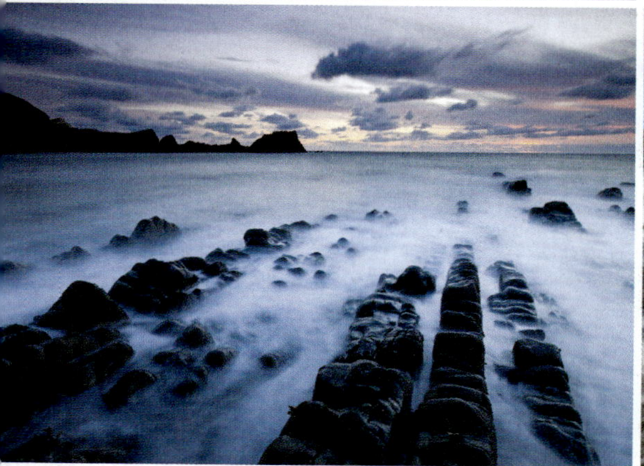

Hartland Quay at dusk from the rocky beach, Canon 1Ds Mark III, 16-35mm at 19mm, ISO 100, 20 sec at f/16. September

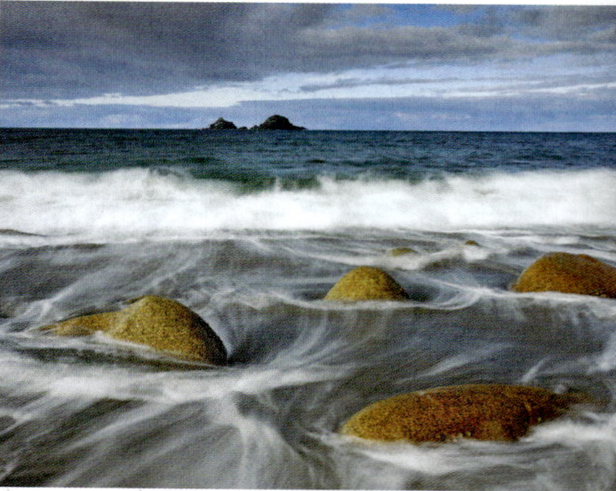

Waves swirl around the granite boulders on Porth Nanven Beach, Canon 1Ds Mark III, 16-35mm at 33mm, ISO 50, 0.8 sec at f/16.

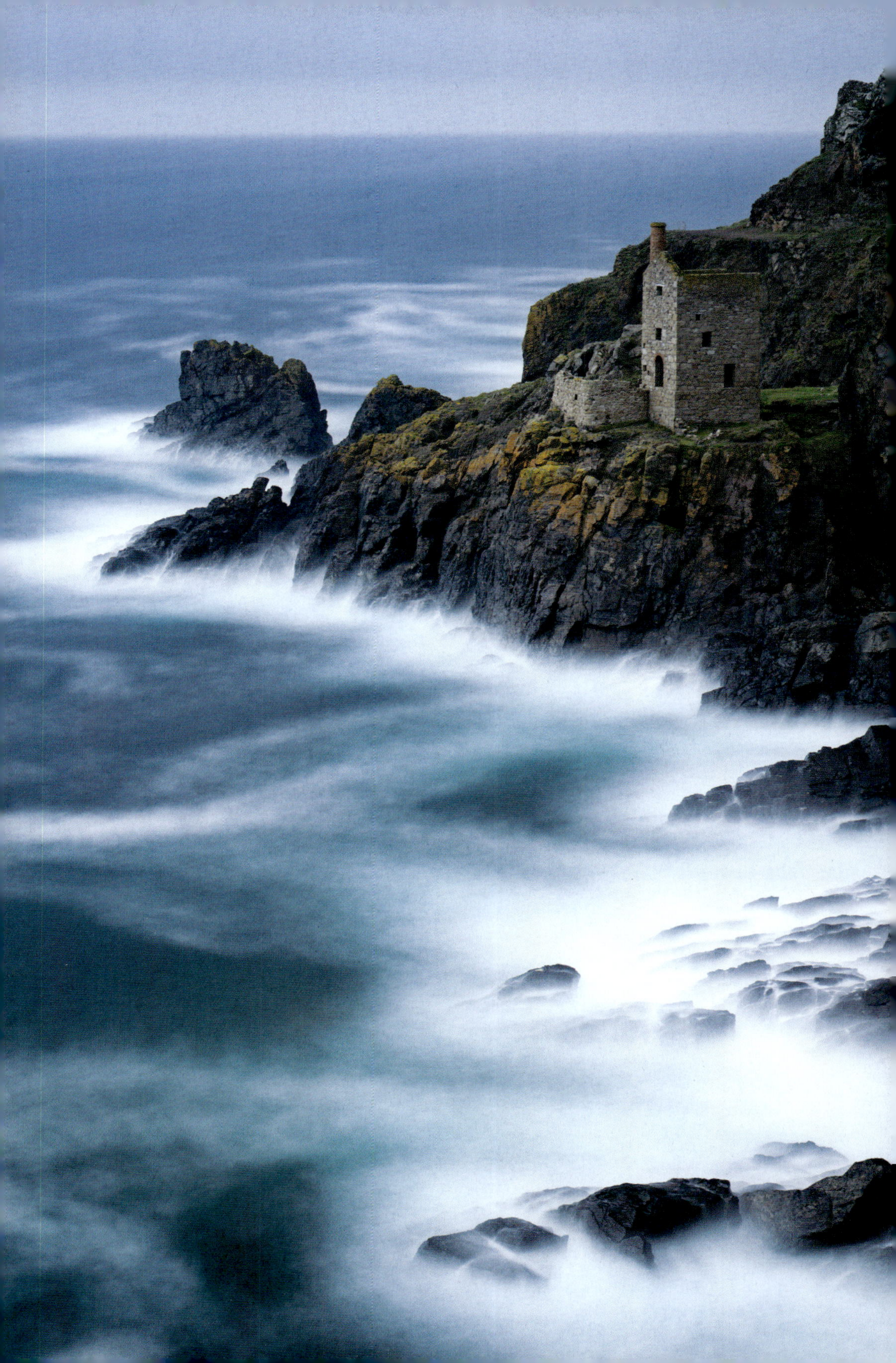

The South West Coast Path Association

Go to the beach anywhere in the South West of England, turn left or right and you'll be on the South West Coast Path and on the edge of an amazing experience.

The South West Coast Path was originally a route for coastguards to walk from lighthouse to lighthouse when patrolling for smugglers. In 1978 this National Trail opened in its entirety from Minehead in Somerset following the coasts of Devon and Cornwall to Poole in Dorset. At 630 miles long it is England's longest way-marked long distance footpath. Due to its undulating nature the total height climbed along the entire route has been calculated as 35,031m, almost four times the height of Everest.

The path is perfect for an afternoon stroll to take you to a beautiful location with your camera, many of the viewpoints described in this guidebook are on the path, or tackle its full length as major expedition.

Most people walk the path in sections or take several weeks to complete the whole thing. The fastest known time was set as we go to press (June 2016) by Damian Hall who ran it in 10 days, 15 hours and 18 minutes, beating Mark Berry's previous time by more than 17 hours. That's around 60 miles a day! Fancy a go?

The coast's heritage, wildlife, geology and scenery are inspirational; with every turn a new experience.

The Path leaves Minehead and travels along the Exmoor coastline passing the iconic Valley of Rocks. It continues along the north Devon coast that is synonymous with surfers looking for the perfect wave.

In between some of the high cliffs and rocky coombes are miles of golden beaches where you can kick off your boots and leave footprints in the sand at the end of a good day's hike.

At Bude, the 300 miles of coastline in Cornwall awaits as it travels around the South West peninsula, through south and east Devon and along the Jurassic Coast in Dorset before it reaches the end at South Haven Point.

A charity, the South West Coast Path Association provides a wealth of information for anyone planning to walk the Coast Path, and also plays a vital role in fund raising to help repair and improve the path.

For more information about the South West Coast Path, how you can help care for it by joining the Association and to pick up a copy of their 'Complete Guide to the South West Coast Path' please visit:

www.southwestcoastpath.org.uk

The Rumps in North Cornwall from the coast path, Canon 1Ds Mk III, 17-40mm at 21mm, ISO 100, 15 sec at f/16. May

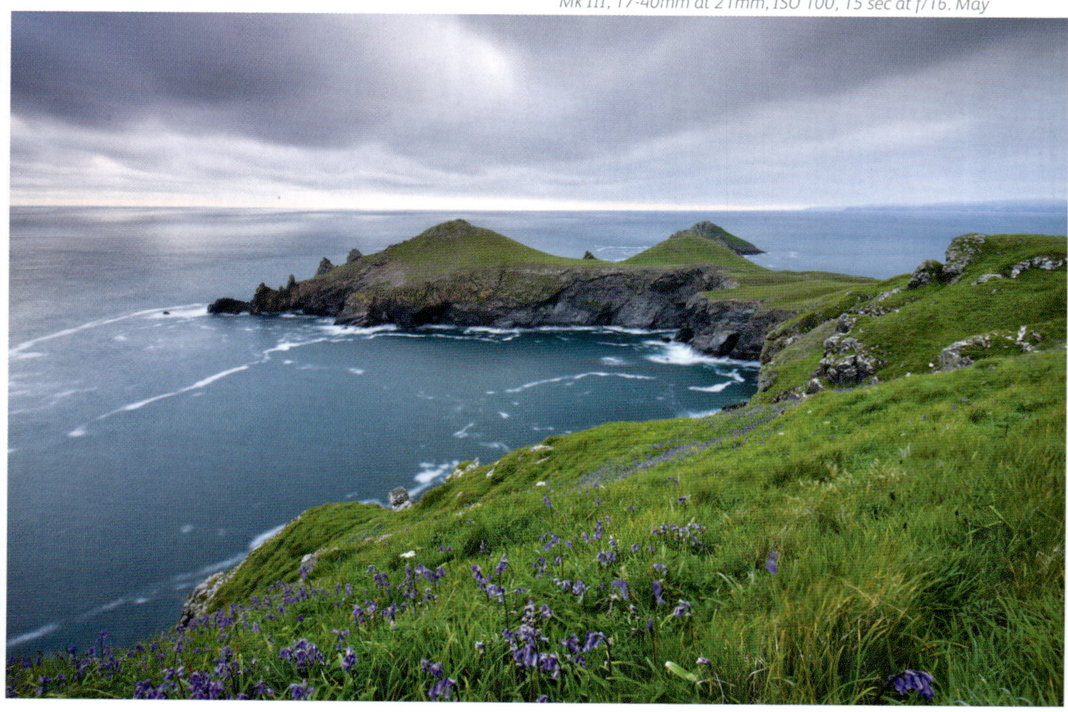

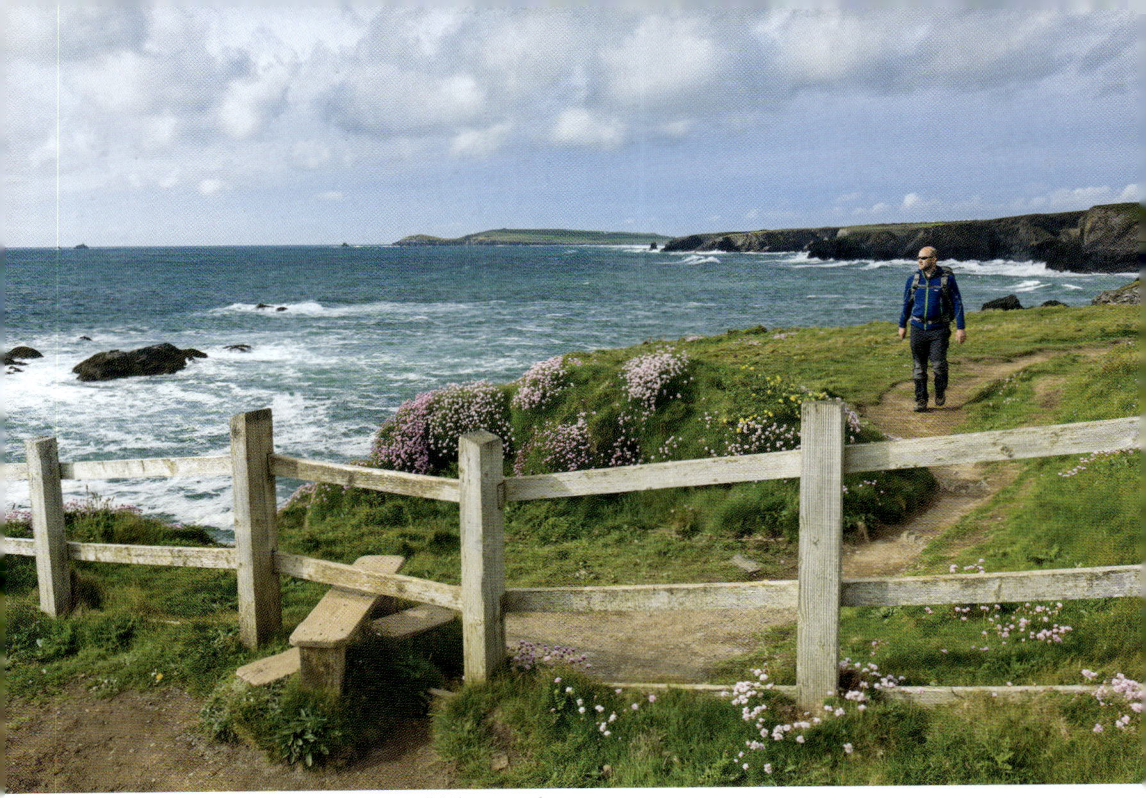

Adam walking along the coast path in North Cornwall, Nikon D800E, 24-70mm at 29mm, ISO 100, 1/30 sec at f/13. May

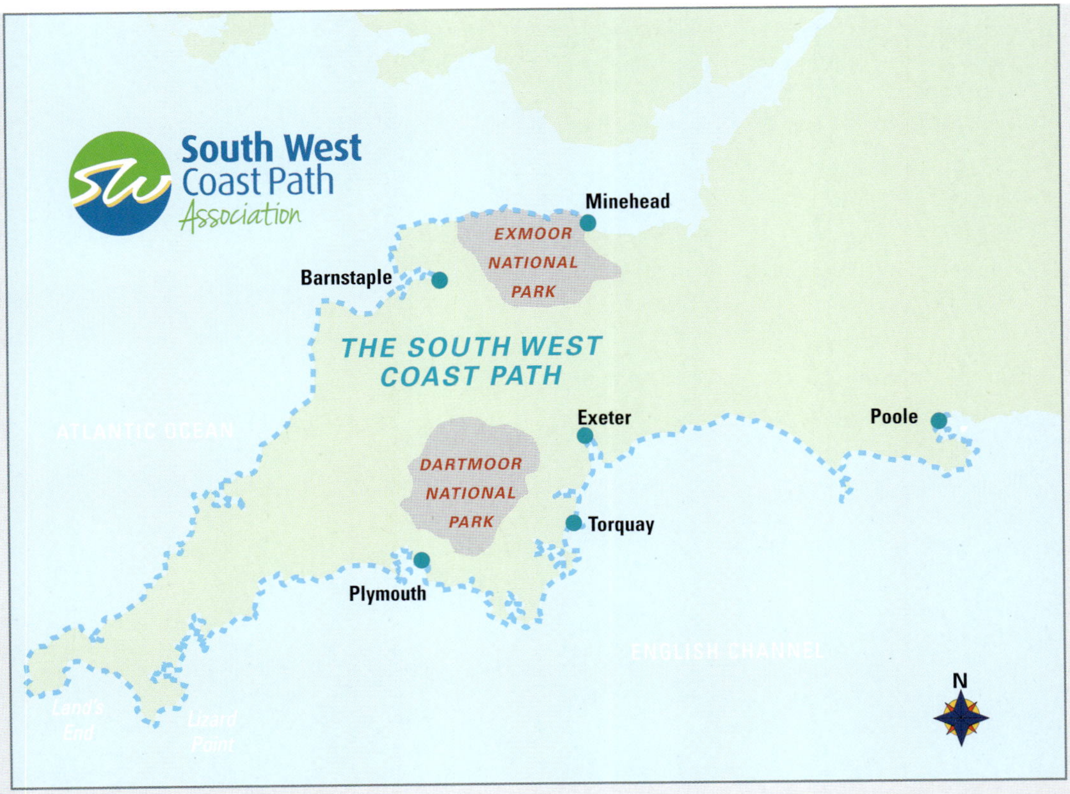

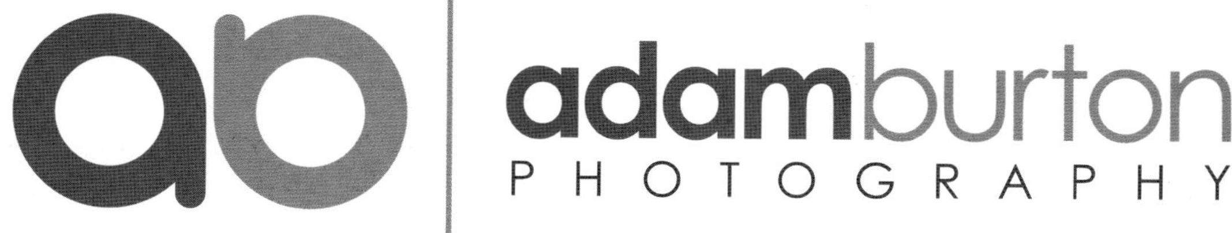

Biography

Adam first began teaching himself photography in 2001, mainly from reading magazines and then putting into practice techniques while on location in the New Forest and along the Dorset coastline.

He is now one of the UK's leading landscape photographers and author of six books. Since 2008 he has been working as a full time professional landscape photographer, supplying imagery and undertaking commissions for a wide range of clients. Although Adam has a broad ranging portfolio from the UK and beyond, he specialises in the landscapes of south west England.

Since 2004 his images have been regularly published in various publications and featured on the covers of hundreds of magazines, books and calendars. Over this time he has worked for many large and prestigious organisations, supplying imagery and undertaking commissions for companies including British Petroleum, The AA, The Times and National Geographic.

Adam's portfolio is represented by various leading photographic libraries, including Robert Harding Picture Library, AWL Images and Getty Images.

Adam lives on the edge of Dartmoor in the beautiful rolling countryside of rural Devon with his wife Beth and children Tom, Ellen and Ted.

He uses the following photographic equipment:

Nikon D800/D800E 36mp DSLRs
Nikon 17-35 f/2.8D
Nikon 24-70 f/2.8G
Nikon 70-200 f/2.8G VRII
Gitzo Systematic 3542LS tripod
Really Right Stuff BH-55 LR Ball Head
Lee Filters
F/Stop Satori Backpack

Workshops and Tuition

Adam leads photographic workshops in the UK and to destinations around the world. With an extensive background in leading workshops over the past eight years, as well as various teaching roles prior to becoming a professional photographer, Adam is an experienced and confident tutor.

In addition to group workshops Adam is available for one-to-one tuition in the South West. Typically a tuition day will take place entirely on location on Dartmoor, but with Adam's extensive knowledge of the South West a day can be arranged anywhere in Devon, Cornwall or further afield.

Visit Adam's website for more information on group workshops and tuition:

www.adamburtonphotography.com

Spring greens beside the River in Yosemite Valley, California, Nikon D800E, 17-35mm at 32mm, ISO 100, 0.3 sec at f/11. June
© Adam Burton

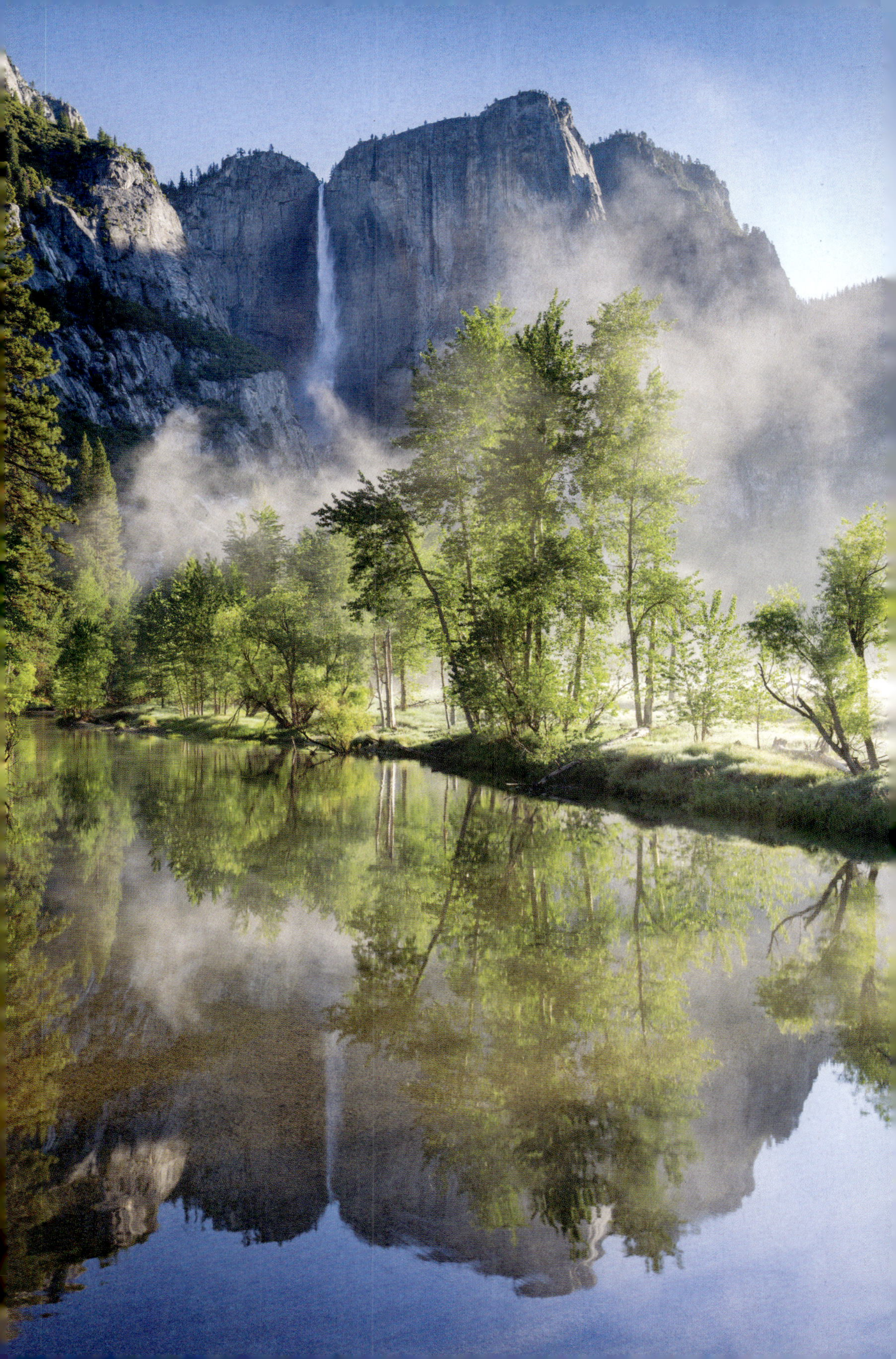

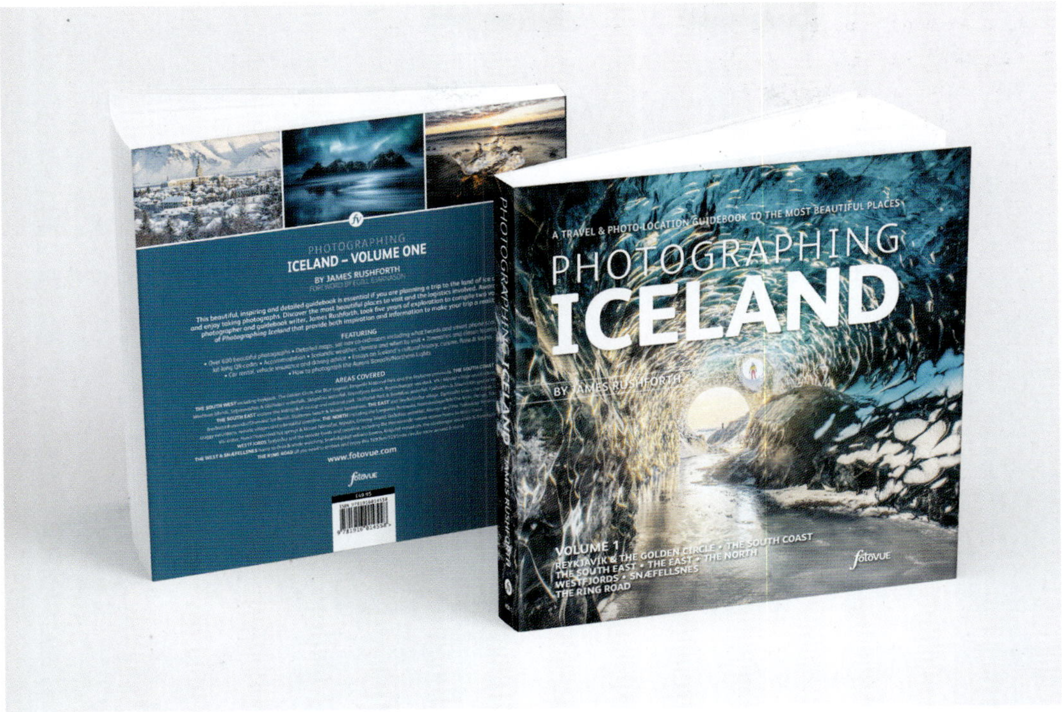

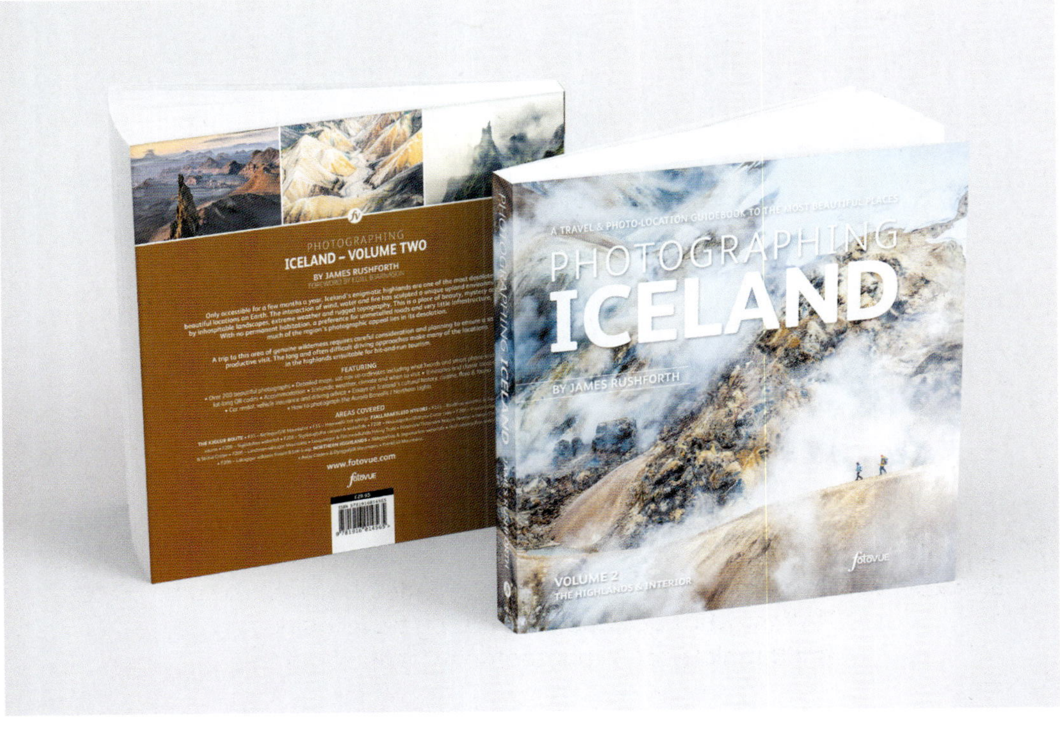

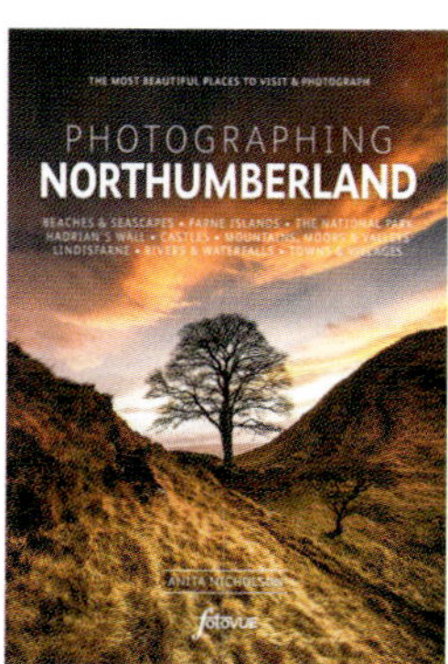

THE MOST BEAUTIFUL PLACES TO VISIT & PHOTOGRAPH
PHOTOGRAPHING
NORTHUMBERLAND
ANITA NICHOLSON
fotovue

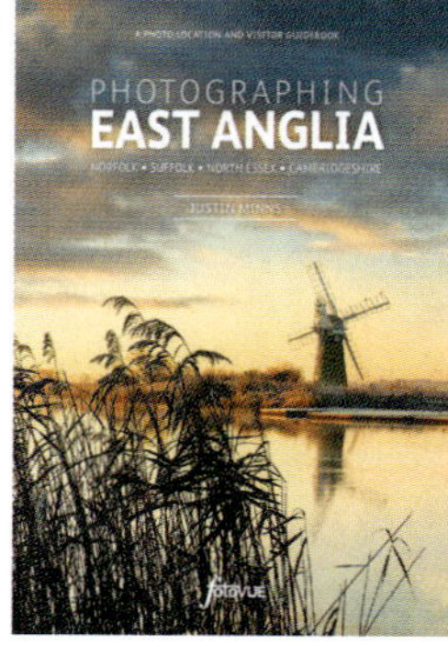

A PHOTO-LOCATION AND VISITOR GUIDEBOOK
PHOTOGRAPHING
EAST ANGLIA
JUSTIN MINNS
fotovue

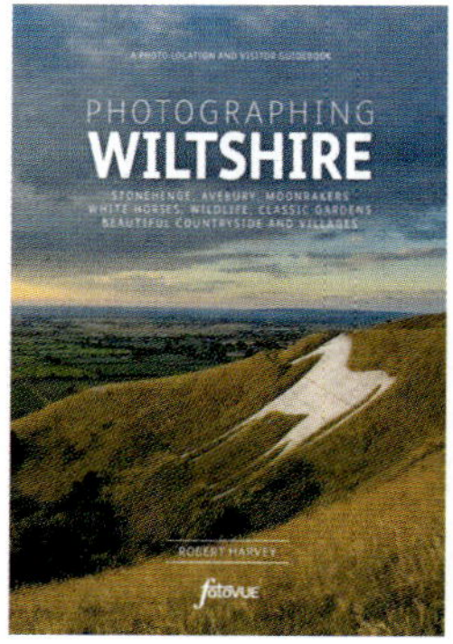

A PHOTO-LOCATION AND VISITOR GUIDEBOOK
PHOTOGRAPHING
WILTSHIRE
STONEHENGE · AVEBURY · MOONRAKERS
WHITE HORSES · WILDLIFE · CLASSIC GARDENS
BEAUTIFUL COUNTRYSIDE AND VILLAGES
ROBERT HARVEY
fotovue

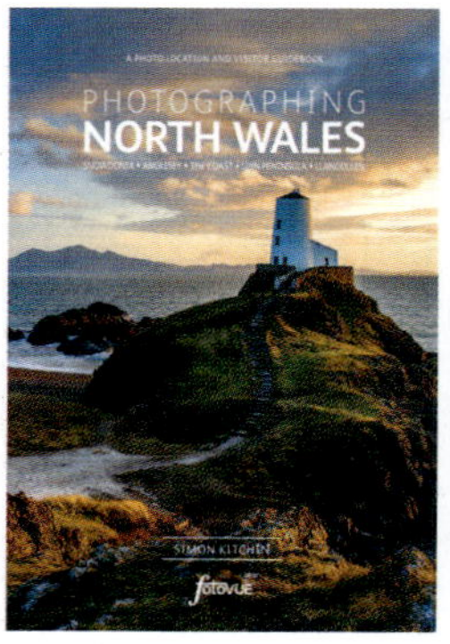

A PHOTO-LOCATION AND VISITOR GUIDEBOOK
PHOTOGRAPHING
NORTH WALES
SIMON KITCHIN

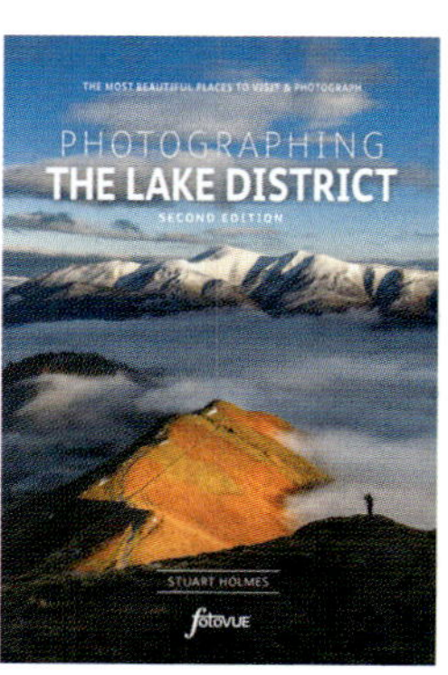

THE MOST BEAUTIFUL PLACES TO VISIT & PHOTOGRAPH
PHOTOGRAPHING
THE LAKE DISTRICT
SECOND EDITION
STUART HOLMES
fotovue

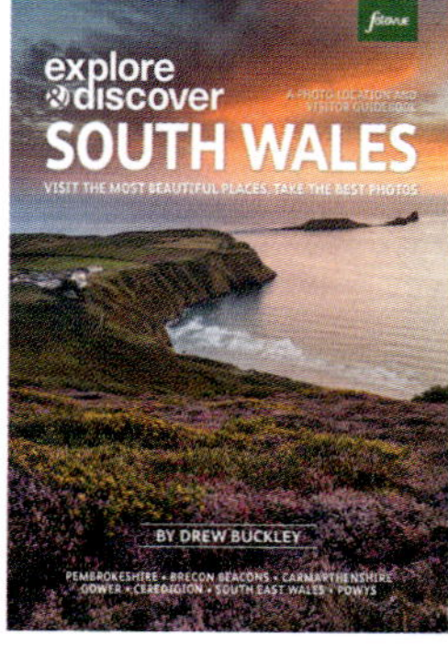

explore
& discover
SOUTH WALES
A PHOTO-LOCATION AND
VISITOR GUIDEBOOK
VISIT THE MOST BEAUTIFUL PLACES, TAKE THE BEST PHOTOS
BY DREW BUCKLEY
PEMBROKESHIRE · BRECON BEACONS · CARMARTHENSHIRE
GOWER · CEREDIGION · SOUTH EAST WALES · POWYS

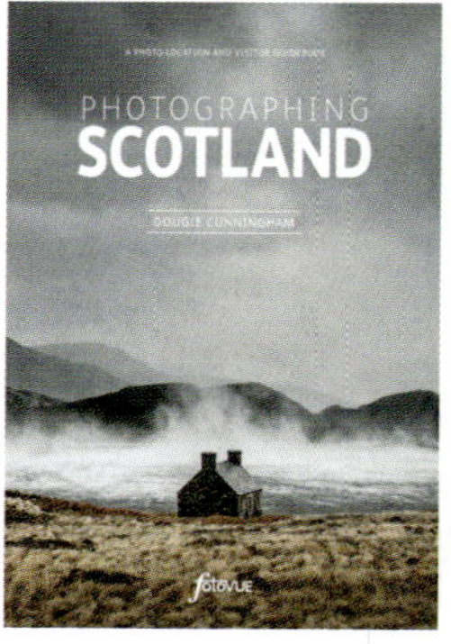

A PHOTO-LOCATION AND VISITOR GUIDEBOOK
PHOTOGRAPHING
SCOTLAND
DOUGIE CUNNINGHAM
fotovue

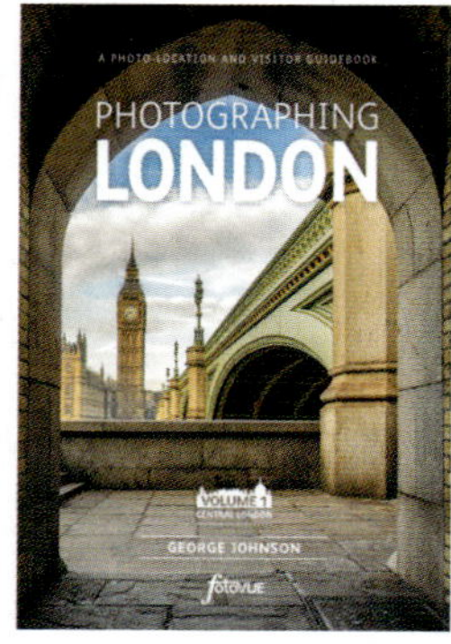

A PHOTO-LOCATION AND VISITOR GUIDEBOOK
PHOTOGRAPHING
LONDON
VOLUME 1
CENTRAL LONDON
GEORGE JOHNSON
fotovue

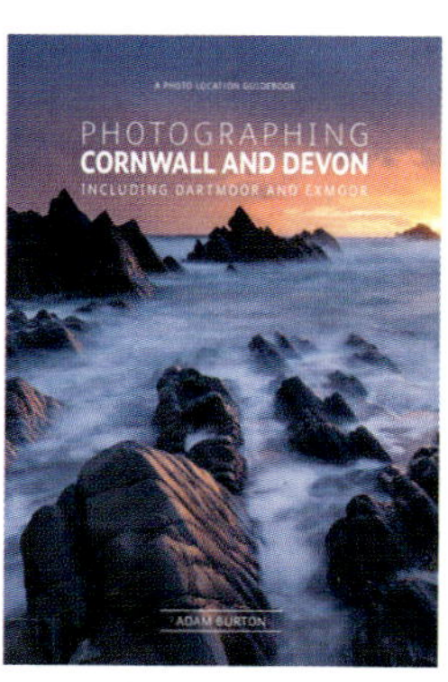

A PHOTO-LOCATION GUIDEBOOK
PHOTOGRAPHING
CORNWALL AND DEVON
INCLUDING DARTMOOR AND EXMOOR
ADAM BURTON

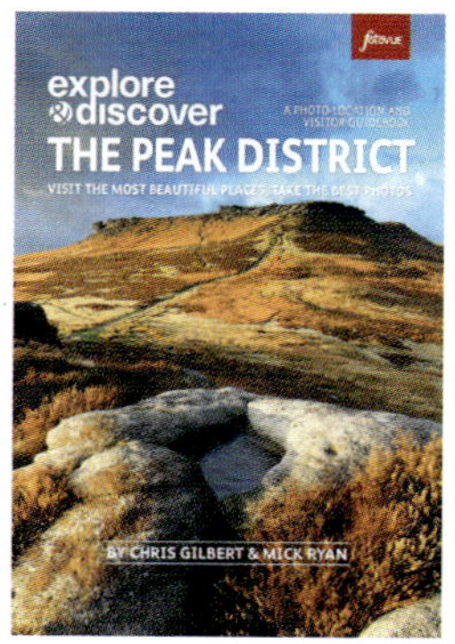

explore
& discover
THE PEAK DISTRICT
A PHOTO-LOCATION AND
VISITOR GUIDEBOOK
VISIT THE MOST BEAUTIFUL PLACES, TAKE THE BEST PHOTOS
BY CHRIS GILBERT & MICK RYAN

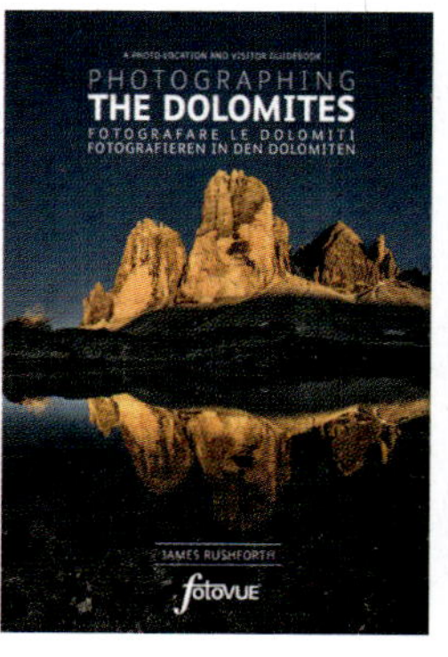

A PHOTO-LOCATION AND VISITOR GUIDEBOOK
PHOTOGRAPHING
THE DOLOMITES
FOTOGRAFARE LE DOLOMITI
FOTOGRAFIEREN IN DEN DOLOMITEN
JAMES RUSHFORTH
fotovue

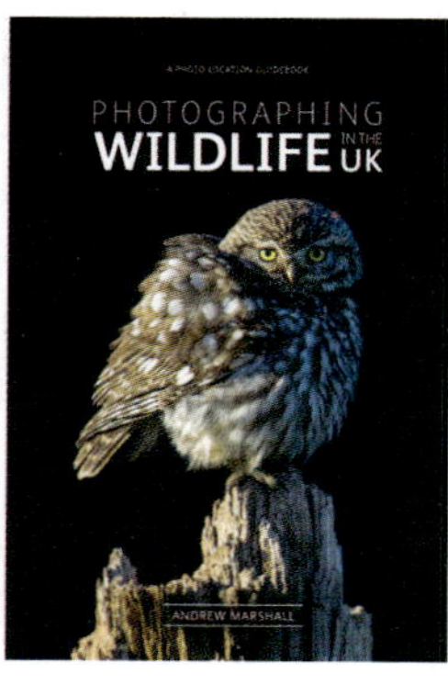

A PHOTO-LOCATION GUIDEBOOK
PHOTOGRAPHING
WILDLIFE IN THE UK
ANDREW MARSHALL

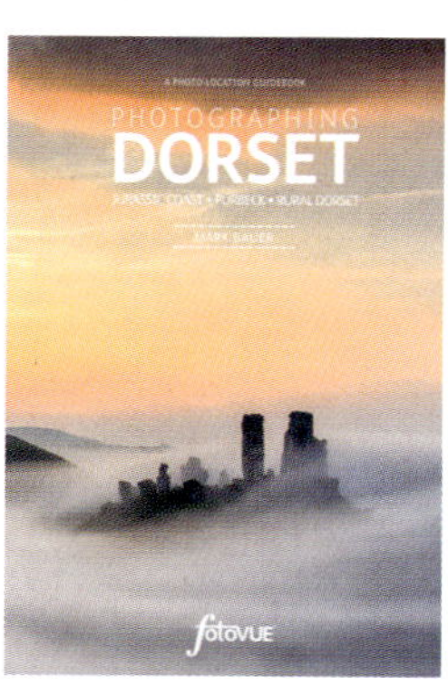

A PHOTO-LOCATION GUIDEBOOK
PHOTOGRAPHING
DORSET
JURASSIC COAST · PURBECK · RURAL DORSET
MARK BAUER
fotovue

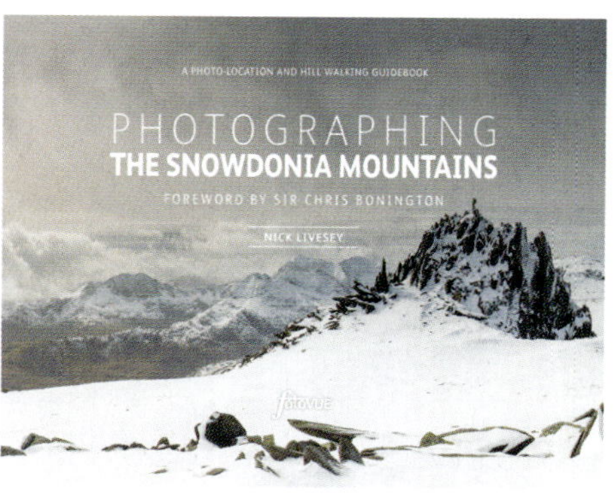

A PHOTO-LOCATION AND HILL WALKING GUIDEBOOK
PHOTOGRAPHING
THE SNOWDONIA MOUNTAINS
FOREWORD BY SIR CHRIS BONINGTON
NICK LIVESEY
fotovue

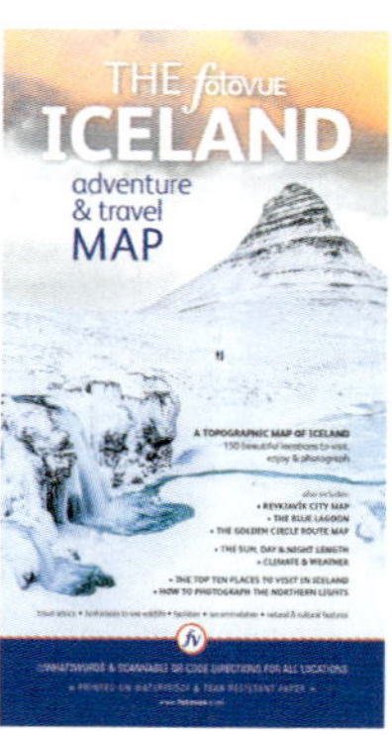

THE fotovue
ICELAND
adventure
& travel
MAP
A TOPOGRAPHIC MAP OF ICELAND
150 beautiful locations to visit,
enjoy & photograph
REYKJAVIK CITY MAP
THE BLUE LAGOON
THE GOLDEN CIRCLE ROUTE MAP
THE SUN, DAY & NIGHT LENGTH
CLIMATE & WEATHER
THE TOP TEN PLACES TO VISIT IN ICELAND
HOW TO PHOTOGRAPH THE NORTHERN LIGHTS
PRINTED ON WATERPROOF & TEAR RESISTANT PAPER